Designing Cities

Critical Readings in Urban Design

Edited by

Alexander R. Cuthbert

Blackwell
Publishing

350 Main Street, Malden, MA 02148–5018, USA
108 Cowley Road, Oxford OX4 1JF, UK
550 Swanston Street, Carlton South, Melbourne, Victoria 3053, Australia
Kurfürstendamm 57, 10707 Berlin, Germany

First published 2003 by Blackwell Publishers Ltd

Library of Congress Cataloging-in-Publication Data

Designing cities: critical readings in urban design / edited by Alexander R. Cuthbert.
   p. cm.
  Includes bibliographical references and index.
  ISBN 0-631-23503-5 (alk. paper) – ISBN 0-631-23504-3 (pbk.: alk. paper)
  1. City planning. I. Cuthbert, Alexander R.
  HT166 .D3867 2003
  307.1′216–dc21

                                              2002066634

ISBN 0-631-23503-5 (hardback); ISBN 0-631–23504-3 (paperback)

A catalogue record for this title is available from the British Library.

Set in 9.5 on 11 pt Sabon
by Kolam Information Services Pvt. Ltd., Pondicherry, India
Printed and bound in the United Kingdom
by MPG Books Ltd, Bodmin, Cornwall

For further information on
Blackwell Publishing, visit our website:
http://www.blackwellpublishing.com

Designing Cities

For Ailsa and Sarah

Contents

Preface   viii

Acknowledgments   x

Introduction   1

Part I   Theory

1   The Process of Urban Social Change   23
     Manuel Castells

2   The Economic Currency of Architectural Aesthetics   28
     Paul Walter Clarke

3   The Postmodern Debate over Urban Form   45
     Sharon Zukin

Part II   History

4   The New Historical Relationship between Space and Society   59
     Manuel Castells

5   Urban Landscapes as Public History   69
     Dolores Hayden

6   Harmonies of Urban Design and Discords of City Form   76
     Abraham Akkerman

Part III   Philosophy

7   Social Justice, Postmodernism and the City   101
     David Harvey

8   The Phenomenon of Place   116
     Christian Norberg-Schulz

9   Recapturing the Center: A Semiotic Analysis of Shopping Malls   128
     Mark Gottdiener

Part IV   Politics

10   Why are the Design and Development of Public Spaces
      Significant for Cities?   139
      A. Madanipour

11   Reflections on Berlin: The Meaning of Construction
      and the Construction of Meaning   152
      Peter Marcuse

12   *Tilted Arc* and the Uses of Democracy   160
      Rosalyn Deutsche

Part V   Culture

13   Urban Spaces as Cultural Settings   171
      Gwendolyn Wright

14   The Urban Landscape   177
      Sharon Zukin

Part VI   Gender

15   Sexuality and Urban Space: A Framework for Analysis   193
      Lawrence Knopp

16   Gender Symbols and Urban Landscapes   204
      Liz Bondi

17   What Would a Nonsexist City Be Like? Speculations on Housing,
      Urban Design and Human Work   218
      Dolores Hayden

Part VII   Environment

18   Sustainability and Cities: Summary and Conclusions   235
      Peter Newman and John Kenworthy

19   Conservation as Preservation or as Heritage:
      Two Paradigms and Two Answers   243
      G. J. Ashworth

20   Zoöpolis   254
      Jennifer Wolch

Part VIII   Aesthetics

21   Aesthetic Theory   275
      Jon Lang

22   The Urban Artifact as a Work of Art   285
      Aldo Rossi

23   Aesthetic Ideology and Urban Design   290
      Barbara Rubin

Part IX Typologies

24 The Third Typology   317
    Anthony Vidler

25 Typological and Morphological Elements of the
    Concept of Urban Space   323
    Rob Krier

26 Heterotopia Deserta: Las Vegas and Other Spaces   340
    Sarah Chaplin

Part X Pragmatics

27 The Design Professions and the Built Environment
    in a Postmodern Epoch   357
    Paul L. Knox

28 A Catholic Approach to Organizing what Urban
    Designers Should Know   362
    Anne Vernez Moudon

Additional Reading by Category   387

Index   394

Preface

In the life experience of most individuals, it is clear that one of the most valued events is to visit beautiful cities and to marvel at the astonishing richness of human invention that they contain. Only here can one experience the entire panoply of magnificent architecture, beautiful sculptures and monuments, waterways and canals, plazas, embarcaderos, boulevards, gallerias, street markets, all assembled into countless fascinating towns and cities. Sienna, Paris, Venice, Prague, Florence, Edinburgh, Dubrovnik: the list is endless. Others may not be so glorious but are nonetheless astounding in their complexity. Los Angeles is a key example of one such place, one hundred miles of mind-bending experiences from east to west, although some of us might disagree with Ed Soja (1989, p. 190) that "it all comes together in Los Angeles." Even cities such as Chicago, Glasgow, and Hamburg, which have apocalyptic industrial inheritances, have managed to craft themselves as significant tourist destinations. The design of cities has always been an absorbing and fascinating subject, of clear and unambiguous significance to emperors, kings, dictators, and presidents, as well as to the ordinary citizen in the street.

Not so clear, however, is the concept of urban design, what we mean by the term, what constitutes "design," and what kind of knowledge is required to participate in designing cities. Great urban spaces attest to the passage of history, the wielding of power and the conflicts that result, the transformation of human consciousness over millennia, and the celebration of collective memory embodied within the fabric of our environment. This reader is an attempt to both clarify and deepen the overall problematic of urban design. It is informed by a lifetime's experience in studying the design of cities, teaching and practicing on four continents, and holding an endless personal debate as to what constitutes an appropriate understanding of urban design. During this time, I have personally assembled around a dozen readers in the subject from various aspects, and the task of assembling only one reader which would convey an appropriate knowledge of the subject constituted an immense project. Given the huge theoretical, empirical, and technological problems which constitute urban design, a theoretical reader seemed the obvious place to begin. Even with this limitation, the problems of choice, exclusion, and continuity were legion. It was also apparent to me that one possible reason for the lack of an integrated viewpoint was due to the fact that Urban Design as a discipline has been unable to develop any substantial theory which it could call its own. It is riddled with historicism, eclecticism, and empiricism, three positions which collectively resist the development of significant theory. To date, Urban Design remains bereft of any complex and integrated perspective on the discipline that seeks to explain its origins within the material development of society as whole, rather than as acts of individual genius, historical accidents, or the random outcome of technological change. *Designing Cities* is a first pass at accomplishing this task.

The present volume is therefore a book on theory. It does not suggest a method of training urban designers, nor what would constitute an appropriate educational experience. The tricky question of "how to do it" I have approached elsewhere (Cuthbert, 1994a, b, 1997, 2001). The 28 articles contained here are therefore limited to perspectives, paradigms, and visions, and do not address the various technologies of development and design control, structure planning, "pattern languages," design methods, sieve mapping, or the impact of the various technologies now available to model building forms and spaces. Separate volumes could easily be assembled on each of these subjects. Also important is that this reader precedes a textbook on Urban Design which I am now writing. My intention is to use the current volume as a base for the second volume. In this text, I have adopted the same basic format, but will extend in significantly greater depth the arguments and propositions which may be somewhat truncated in the brief introduction that follows.

In organizing the present volume I have had the support of many colleagues too numerous to mention, but I would like to recognize the enduring support of three very special people: first, my friend Prem, who has had to deal with both the highs and lows of my somewhat erratic creativity; second, my great friend and colleague Jon Lang, whose adoption of my administrative duties for an entire year made this project possible; third, enduring thanks to my research assistant Catherine Gates for her care, attention to important details, technical skills, and good humor. Finally, I would like to thank those persons who made direct contributions to the book's production. I am grateful to the Faculty of the Built Environment at the University of New South Wales in Sydney for its support in providing me with eight months study leave and the funds necessary to finance aspects of this project, and to two of my colleagues, Michael Bounds and Kevin Dunn, for their penetrating comments on my introduction. I also wish to thank the staff at Blackwell, namely Sarah Falkus, Angela Cohen, Rosie Hayden, Brian Johnson, and John Taylor, whose professionalism kept me on track every step of the way. I sincerely hope that the product is worthy of the investments of time, energy, and finance that have been made by various individuals and institutions. Nonetheless, any errors made in this project are of course my own.

Acknowledgments

The authors and publishers gratefully acknowledge the following for permission to reproduce copyright material:

Chapter 1: Manuel Castells (1983) "The process of urban social change." In *The City and the Grassroots: A Cross-Cultural Theory of Urban Social Movements*. Edward Arnold, London, pp. 301–305, 418. Reprinted by permission of the author.

Chapter 2: Paul Walter Clarke (1989) "The economic currency of architectural aesthetics." In *Restructuring Architectural Theory* (eds M. Diani and C. Ingraham). Northwestern University Press, Evanston, IL: pp. 48–59. Reprinted by permission.

Chapter 3: Sharon Zukin (1988) "The postmodern debate over urban form." *Theory, Culture and Society*, 5(2–3), pp. 431–446. © Theory, Culture and Society 1988. Reprinted by permission of Sage Publications Ltd.

Chapter 4: Manuel Castells (1983) "The new historical relationship between space and society." In *The City and the Grassroots: A Cross-Cultural Theory of Urban Social Movements*. Edward Arnold, London, pp. 311–318, 419–421. Reprinted by permission of the author.

Chapter 5: Dolores Hayden (1996) "Urban landscapes as public history." In *The Power of Place: Urban Landscapes as Public History*. MIT Press, Cambridge, MA, pp. 2–13, 248–250. Reprinted by permission.

Chapter 6: Abraham Akkerman (2000) "Harmonies of urban design and discords of city-form: urban aesthetics in the rise of western civilization." *Journal of Urban Design* (http://www.tandf.co.uk/journals), 5(3), pp. 267–90. Reprinted by permission of Taylor & Francis Ltd and the author.

Chapter 7: David Harvey (1992) "Social justice, postmodernism and the city." *International Journal of Urban and Regional Research*, 16(4), pp. 588–601. Reprinted by permission of Blackwell Publishing.

Chapter 8: Christian Norberg-Schulz (1976) "The phenomenon of place." *Architectural Association Quarterly*, 8(4), pp. 3–10. Reprinted by permission of the Architectural Association, London.

Chapter 9: Mark Gottdiener (1986) "Recapturing the center: a semiotic analysis of shopping malls." In *The City and the Sign: An Introduction to Urban Semiotics* (eds M. Gottdiener and A. Lagopoulos). Columbia University Press, New York, pp. 288–302. Reprinted by permission.

Chapter 10: A. Madanipour (1999) "Why are the design and development of public spaces significant for cities?" *Environment and Planning B: Planning and Design*, 26(6), pp. 879–891. Reprinted by permission of Pion Ltd, London.

Chapter 11: Peter Marcuse (1998) "Reflections on Berlin: the meaning of construction and the construction of meaning." *International Journal of Urban and Regional Research*, 22(2), pp. 331–338. Reprinted by permission of Blackwell Publishing.

Chapter 12: Rosalyn Deutsche (1996) "Tilted Arc and the uses of democracy." In *Evictions: Art and Spatial Politics* (ed. R. Deutsche). MIT Press, Cambridge,

MA, pp. 257–268, 362. Reprinted by permission.

Chapter 13: Gwendolyn Wright (1988) "Urban spaces and cultural settings." *The Journal of Architectural Education*, 41(3), pp. 10–14. Reprinted by permission of MIT Press, Cambridge, MA.

Chapter 14: Sharon Zukin (1991) "The urban landscape." In *Landscapes of Power: From Detroit to Disney World*. University of California Press, Berkeley, pp. 39–54, 285–290. Copyright © 1991 The Regents of the University of California.

Chapter 15: Lawrence Knopp (1995) "Sexuality and urban space: a framework for analysis." In *Mapping Desire: Geographies of Sexualities* (eds D. Bell and G. Valentine). Routledge, London, pp. 149–161. Reprinted by permission.

Chapter 16: Liz Bondi (1992) "Gender symbols and urban landscapes." *Progress in Human Geography*, 16(2), pp. 157–70. Reprinted by permission.

Chapter 17: Dolores Hayden (1985) "What would a non-sexist city be like? Speculations on housing, urban design and human work." *Ekistics*, 52(310), pp. 99–107. Reprinted by permission.

Chapter 18: Peter Newman and John Kenworthy (1999) "Summary and conclusions." In *Sustainability and Cities*. Island Press, Washington, DC, and Alexander C. Hoyt Associates, New York, pp. 333–342. Reprinted by permission.

Chapter 19: G. J. Ashworth (1997) "Conservation as preservation or as heritage: two paradigms and two answers." *Built Environment*, 23(2), pp. 92–102. Reprinted by permission of Alexandrine Press, Oxford.

Chapter 20: Jennifer Wolch (1996) "Zoöpolis." *Capitalism, Nature, Socialism: A Journal of Socialist Ecology*, 7(2), pp. 21–47. Reprinted by permission.

Chapter 21: Jon Lang, "Aesthetic theory." In Creating Architectural Theory: The Role of the Behavioral Sciences in Environmental Design." Van Nostrand Reinhold, New York, pp. 181–187. Reprinted by permission of John Wiley Inc.

Chapter 22: Aldo Rossi (1993) "The urban artifact as a work of art." In *Architecture*

Culture 1943–1968: A Documentary Anthology* (ed. J. Ockman). Rizzoli, New York, pp. 393–395. Reprinted by permission.

Chapter 23: Barbara Rubin (1979) "Aesthetic ideology and urban design." *Annals of the Association of American Geographers*, 69(3), pp. 339–361. Reprinted by permission of the Association of American Geographers and Blackwell Publishing.

Chapter 24: Anthony Vidler (1978) "The third typology." In *Rational Architecture Rationelle: The Reconstruction of the European City*, pp. 28–32. Editions Archives d'Architecture, Brussels. Reprinted by permission.

Chapter 25: Rob Krier (1979) "Typological and morphological elements of the concepts of urban space." In *Urban Space*. Rizzoli, New York, pp. 15–29, 173, 174. Reprinted by permission.

Chapter 26: Sarah Chaplin (2000) "Heterotopia Deserta: Las Vegas and other spaces." In *Intersections: Architectural Histories and Critical Theories* (eds I. Borden and J. Redell). Routledge, London, pp. 203–19. Reprinted by permission of Taylor & Francis Ltd.

Chapter 27: Paul L. Knox (1988) "The design professions and the built environment in a postmodern epoch." In *The Design Professions and the Built Environment* (ed. P. Knox). Nichols Publishing, New York, pp. 1–11. Reprinted by permission.

Chapter 28: Anne Vernez Moudon (1992) "A Catholic approach to organizing what urban designers should know." *Journal of Planning Literature* vol. 6 (4), pp. 331–49. Reprinted by permission of Sage Publications Inc.

Figure 6.2: E. J. Owens (1991) *The City in the Greek and Roman World*. Routledge, London. Reprinted by permission of Taylor & Francis Ltd.

Figure 6.3: R. Chartier, G. Chaussinand-Nogaret, H. Neveux and E. L. Ladurie (1981) *Le Ville Classique de la Renaissance aux Revolutions*. Editions du Seuil, Paris.

Figure 6.5: R. Rosenau (1983). *The Ideal City: Its Architectural Evolution in Europe.* Methuen, London.

Figure 6.12: Tony Garnier (1917) *Une cité industrielle.* Estate of Tony Garnier/Musée des Beaux- Arts de Lyon.

Figure 12.1: Richard Serra's Tilted Arc, Federal Office Plaza, New York 1979 (later removed). Reproduced courtesy of the artist. © DACS 2002.

Figure 23.1: Advertisment for Atlantic Richfield Oil, 1970s.

Figure 23.2: Advertisement for Volvo, 1973.

Figure 23.11: Golden Buddha, Pan-Pacific Exposition, San Francisco, 1915. University Research Library, UCLA.

Figure 23.12: Tin Soldiers, Pan-Pacific Exposition, San Francisco, 1915. University Research Library, UCLA.

The publishers apologize for any errors or omissions in the above list and would be grateful to be notified of any corrections that should be incorporated in the next edition or reprint of this book.

Introduction

Context

With the advent of the information age and the enduring crises of urbanization, the physical organization and design of cities has taken on an inflated role in the world economy. The key reason for this would appear to be fundamentally political, since a major benchmark for successful cities is their capacity to generate a promotional image that can be broadcast internationally. This in turn can be viewed as a reflection of the globalization of economic processes, and a mass of interrelated phenomena which are rapidly altering the socio-spatial structure of the earth. Some of these are reflected in the general progress of *informational* capitalism, a new international division of labor, symbolic economies, and virtual space–time, all of which have influenced a changing aesthetic consciousness toward the built environment. At the center of this whole situation lies the concept of *globalization*, now debated for over a quarter a century since it was first brought to prominence by Immanuel Wallerstein (1974). While globalization is now the buzzword on everybody's lips, with many regions of human knowledge adopting it as the dominant paradigm in contrast to "postmodernity," there is neither the space nor the need to debate this issue in great depth here, and readers would do well to refer to some of the mandatory reading on the subject by scholars such as Castells (1989), Featherstone (1990), Sassen (1991), Robertson (1992), Appadurai (1996), and Scott (1997). Nonetheless, it is necessary to give some indication as to how the form of cities fits into this equation, concentrating on the major factors affecting the built form of cities, since urban design is the focus of this volume. To this extent, several of the branches of geography – economic, human, cultural, and urban – are of paramount importance, and I am in debt to many of the prominent writers in this general area, such as Harvey (1989), Davis (1990), Garreau (1991), Sklair (1991), Featherstone et al. (1995), Biel (2000), Soja (2000, Minca (2001), and many others.

In *The Rise of The Network Society*, Castells makes the important distinction between a *world economy* and a *global economy*. The difference is that in the prior world economy, capitalism had developed since the sixteenth century, based upon a multitude of different centers although acting in accordance with the same basic ideology, when Amsterdam, Hamburg, and Florence were major instigators of a new economic form called *mercantilism*. In today's world,

> a global economy is something different: it is an economy with the capacity to work as a unit in real time on a planetary scale. While the capitalist mode of production is characterized by relentless expansion, always trying to overcome the limits of time and space, it is only in the late twentieth century that the world economy was able to become truly global on the basis of the new infrastructure provided by information and communication technologies. (Castells, 1996, p. 93)

Castells uses the term *informational capitalism*, since the new economy is in a very *real* sense both virtual and symbolic, with the exchange value of information now challenging that of commodity production. Given the massive fluidity of capital that results from the network society, control mechanisms are frequently beyond the reach of national governments, and the traditional levers of economic policy have become seriously weakened. Consequently this new economic paradigm is highly politicized, with enormous impacts on socio-spatial structures. As part of this general process, Castells goes on to suggest that technology and productivity are not undertaken for the overall betterment of society, but are solely driven by profitability and competitiveness. On this basis, political institutions at supranational, national, regional, and local levels are correspondingly reshaped to maximize the performance of their corresponding economies. In searching for some fundamental political cause or overarching rationality for globalization, it would be easy to assume that globalization simply stood for a new phase of American interventionism in the world economy, given the dominance of American imperialism since the Second World War. But as Scott (1997, p. 4) points out, "Even those whose analysis has emerged out of development theory and who are therefore sensitised to the exportation of Western models, stress that the relationship of globalisation to Americanisation is by no means a straightforward one."

The implication here is that despite its enormous economic power, the apparent hegemony of the United States can be challenged in a multitude of ways, not only in the political and economic spheres, but also in regard to cultural and media imperialism, where any assumption of American superiority would be "a profoundly mystifying error" (Sklair, 2000, p. 179). In the same vein, other significant scholars, such as Paul Hirst, are of the opinion that "'Globalisation' remains more myth than reality. This is because the world economy is still predominantly determined by competitive pressures and products generated at national level and is dependent on national social and political institutions" (Hirst, 2000, p. 243). Nonetheless, although the USA remains the world's number one superpower, the critical interrogation of capitalism has diminished since the political influence of the United States was challenged both by different economic systems and by alternative forms of social justice, consciousness, and ideology within socialist states. Instead, the new imperialism represented in the US influence over world affairs is increasingly confronted by its own internal ideological structures, such as the judiciary, the green movement, and the reordering of capitalist priorities as in the *natural capitalism* of Amory Lovins, which in theory proposes a revolutionary paradigm for sustainable capitalist development (Hawken et al., 1999). Lovins's basic argument is economic, that there are fortunes to be made from processing waste as there are in creating it, so "dirty capitalism" has been superseded by new, sanitized environmental technologies that simultaneously provide profits and a clean environment. In order to monitor this shifting ground, the private sector in primate economies is becoming increasingly engaged with issues of social provision and the environmental debate over sustainability and conservation, in all sectors of urban development (with no implication that this is necessarily a philanthropic process). Whether this indicates a genuinely expressed concern for increased social responsibility, or a commitment to extended manipulation of basic human values, remains to be seen. In a highly competitive world, it seems more likely that any benefits of natural capitalism in terms of sustainable energy will only be allowed if the premises of the prevailing assumptions of big capital remain unchallenged.

In this new global economy, vast changes in the restructuring of both capital and labor have created corresponding tectonic shifts in a restructured space economy, where the geographically *uneven development* inherent to advanced capitalist societies is reforming in new and frequently unpredictable ways. Implicit to this process are huge population migrations both within and between countries, the poor seeking work and the wealthy seeking leasure in the form of a global tourist economy, linked in no small part to what Theodore Adorno has referred to as 'the culture industry' (restated by Scott, 2000). At the most fundamental level, the deindustrialization of Western economies and a reconfiguration of newly industrializing economies (NICs) precipitated by the informational economy is generating huge spatial change. The old territorial divisions of labor based upon the nation state are giving way to new associations within the network society and its restructured alliances. This has also spawned *a new regionalism* from the joint effects of a reduction in the political authority of national governments combined with the new networking permitted by electronic communications – "the local and regional geopolitical economy of cities is becoming more closely tied to this far-flung global network than to national urban systems" (Soja, 2000, p. 41). In one sense the most superficial manifestation of this *new imperialism* is the increasing size of cities (Biel, 2000), which of itself is not significant. Increased physical size has no necessary relation to increased complexity, in terms of networks, flows or physical spaces, or, in even greater detail, to the functioning, adaptive properties, or forms, of urban space. Part of the rationality for uneven development is rooted in the degree to which globalization is perceived as being uniform in its effects. The general consensus, apart from "thinking global and acting local," appears to be that globalization has little uniformity about it, and that space is being reorganized in ways that are both inherently unpredictable and dramatic. Hence the term *glocal* is now in common use among academics to describe this phenomenon, where communities at all geographic scales will experience the effects of globality on a wholly uneven basis (Robertson, 1995). Even the term *community* which I have just used has little analytical meaning any more, since the physical constraints implied by the term have diminishing coherence. The informational economy, as Castells points out, conjoins the space of places with the space of flows, resulting in conceptions of space–time

such as virtual reality and the Internet, which symbolically relocate every individual. In this increasingly borderless planet, those who are fortunate enough to find themselves in what Ed Soja calls *postmetropolitan* regions such as Los Angeles, New York, London, and Paris can experience the most heterogeneous city spaces that have ever existed, with not only "an influx of global capital and labour [but] fashions, music, cuisines, architectural styles, political attitudes and life sustaining economic strategies from all over the world" (Soja, 2000, p. 196).

Embedded in this general scenario lurks the impression that postmodernity and the postmetropolis carry with them an overall climate of chaos, lawlessness, and the feeling that globalization is so valorized and diffuse that no one can really be held accountable. In other words, the fractured nature of postmodern urbanism tends to generate the false impression that all regulatory regimes have been suspended or otherwise deprived of power. This would indeed be a false assumption. While one could argue that a general feature of modernism was regulation, and that in postmodern urbanism, deregulation appears to have been the adopted ideology so far, it is more correct to say that the emphasis on *what* is regulated has shifted massively to allow specific economic and political change to occur. To understand this process we must return to the passing of modernity and the fiscal crises of states in the mid-1970s (Arrighi, 1994). The decreasing revenue base of national and state governments and the enduring privatization of state institutions since that time has been guided by a new philosophy called *neo-corporatism* within the finance/commercial capitalist sector. While a basic feature of modernist *corporatism* was its reformation of the existing social order by creating intermediate institutions between civil society and the state, postmodernist neo-corporatism uses these same institutions to penetrate, and hence exert greater control over, the organs of government. Indeed, the changing role and nature of the built environment professions illustrates this quite keenly (Marshall, 2000). Similarly, in regions where the private sector cannot exercise total control, or requires state funds in the form of loans, seed money, or other dispensations, public–private sector partnerships become the *modus operandum*. Welfare goods are also becoming recommodified in the areas of social control (policing), health, education, and other services. For example, in education, where corporate strategies had, in the past, considered state-sponsored education merely a training ground for their employees, over which they exerted specific but nonetheless partial control, in today's neo-corporatism, companies see new markets in actually delivering the educational "products" themselves within tertiary education. On this basis they expand the potential surplus value from simply hiring labor into even greater profits derived from deepening the commodification of the entire educational process.

So it appears that "'the postmodern city' proves *not* to be the outcome of some apparently random set of processes, but the precise outcome of concerted, painstakingly made plans: the dismantling of welfare; the retreat from social housing; the reconfiguration of policing so as to reinforce marginalization; the promotion of plans to annihilate those residents deemed to be the human equivalent of blight," where "whole realms of social reproduction have been auctioned off wholesale to private police forces, prison operators, park conservancies, business improvement districts and the like" (Mitchell, 2001, p. 81). Minca refers to this form of the post-metropolis as *the post-justice city*, where "geographers' (and others') utopian fantasies about supposed postmodernization of the city serve to sustain not a progressive urban politics, but rather, regulatory regimes that are increasingly brutal in intent and practice" (Minca, 2001, p. 9). Here, the operational goal is "to establish a program of public space regulation that does not rely on the universalizing tendencies of either law or rights" and where varying communities of interest can establish their own laws of exclusion or inclusion over the spaces they own or inhabit (Mitchell, 2001, p. 73). Part and parcel of the privatization of social goods is the inherent threat to one of the greatest symbols of democracy, namely control over public space and the public realm. A deepening neo-corporate ideology, I suggest, will be wholly unable to resist targeting public space as a private good, with the implied limitation on collective social behavior, freedom of expression, and civil rights, and the overall Panopticon that is implied in this process. Indeed, there is already an emerging body of literature which addresses this topic, the classics being Mike Davis's *City of Quartz* (1990) and *Ecology of Fear* (1998), Nan Ellin's *Architecture of Fear* (1997), and David Harvey's *Spaces of Hope* (2000).

Directly connected to this overall process of *deregulation* is the feeling of uncertainty generated by increasing private control over public space. I have referred to this environment as "ambiguous space" and have explored the general problematic in relation to the design of social space in Hong Kong, although the basic principles apply to the contemporary postmetropolis as a whole (Cuthbert, 1995; Cuthbert and MacKinnell, 1997). Central to this concept is the birth of *surveillance society*. While surveillance occurs at all levels of human activity, it constitutes a particular manifestation of power where the prime site is the administrative bureaucracy of the state. Space is one medium through which such power is exercised. "Power in this sense means the ability to control subject populations through a command over information. As vehicles for state policy, the environmental professions assist in this process, usually unwittingly, by packaging, manipulating, and designing spaces to suit. In this regard, the question of *the right to the city* has become increasingly important to the conscience of urban planning, which actively negotiates the boundary between social relations and spatial structures on behalf of the state. (Cuthbert, 1995, p. 294). Surveillance as a social activity is by no means new, since it can be argued that all societies have had some form of monitoring to support various forms of social control. Electronic communication, however, gives the word an altogether new significance, beyond anything conceived by George Orwell in *Nineteen Eighty-four*. As Giddens notes, surveillance has held a dominant function in the creation of modernity, since "no less than capitalism or industrialism, surveillance is a means of levering the modern social world away from traditional modes of social activity" (Giddens, 1990, p. 20). Without doubt, the design of urban space is increasingly affected by all forms of surveillance and policing, and the systems currently in place in cities are primitive in comparison to what we can anticipate over the next twenty years. Today's electronic systems create an altogether new realm of influence over the general population (Poster, 1990; Lyon, 1994; Bogard, 1996; Parker, 2000). Significantly, today's electronic surveillance systems also have a carry-over into the physical design of buildings and spaces, and a new corporate architecture and urban design, where design strategies have the policing of space rather than its public use as first priorities. This overall phenomenon can, at root, be traced back to the fiscal crisis of states mentioned above, and the reduction in public sector spending which went with it, thus weakening the confidence of the middle classes in the state's ability to provide personal and public security. One singular feature of this general distrust is the massive increase in private policing, gated communities, and restricted access to certain types of shopping center. Another is a new architectural and urban planning paradigm which has been referred to as *neo-traditional* in Britain and the *new urbanism* in the United States, where "a plausible argument can be made that in addition to an aesthetic rejection of suburbia, architectural new urbanism represents a highly localized political reaction against the new urban realities of city life" (Smith, 2001, p. 157).

This new urbanism now has a burgeoning global presence, despite its fundamentally reactionary aesthetics and conservative tendencies (Audirac and Shermyen, 1994; Katz, 1994; McCann, 1994; Till, 1994). At one level, it constitutes a genuine search for a secure and humane community. Others are not so sure, since good intentions at the local level, and in the types of communities being built, simply represent a masking of existing class struggles (Al-Hindi and Staddon, 1997). The point of departure for the new urbanism was a project in Seaside, Florida, by Andreas Duany and Elizabeth Plater-Zybeck, which heralded a born-again nostalgia for a plethora of historical referents. At the same time the movement is deeply subversive of existing urbanization, with a tendency toward isolationism in the form of middle-class values and prices, greenfield sites, and gated communities. Despite its symbolism, ownership of the image is crucial to an increasing number of individuals in a rapidly expanding sphere of global influence. While the ideology of the new urbanism now has a global profile, it is paralleled by developing nations seeking a reinforced or new identity, seminally expressed in Frampton (1983) and more recently in a developing Asian consciousness, where a progressive new aesthetic is being forged by individuals such as Tay Kheng Soong (1989), Malaysian architect Ken Yeang, and others. The difference between the two movements is that whereas the former is basically driven by a fundamentally economic and political agenda, the latter is at least in part a reaction to colonialism. While the new urbanism is reactionary, localized, and historicist in nature, critical regionalism is progressive, has a national agenda, and seeks to reinterpret the historical process. Overall, the concept of a *critical regionalism* seems to have a politically healthier agenda than either *neo-traditionalism* or the *new urbanism*, if for no other reason than that it looks forward rather than backward.

At the same time that residential suburbia is being challenged by the new urbanism, the appearance of cities is also being transformed by the desire of transnational corporations to locate in environments that will attract the best staff, and for corporate imagery in the form of symbolic capital to dominate in many new developments: "such sought after people have become sophisticated consumers of place, be they the high-tech 'nerdistans' such as Raleigh, North

Carolina, elite rural 'Valhallas' or revived metropolitan regions such as Manhattan, Seattle or the inner lakeshore districts of Chicago" (Kotkin, 2000, p. 28). However, on the realization that, despite the informational economy and web-based communication, face-to-face relations remain important, many central city areas are being revitalized rather than degrading, provided that such a strategy coincides with a significant corporate presence and diminished state intervention. Given the burgeoning importance of *branding* everything from corporations to the buildings they inhabit, *ownership of the image* becomes at least as important to corporate involvement in the postmodern city as it is to the new urbanism. In urban design terms this signifies a transition from a prior urban "image bank" based on state power and control to one founded in neo-corporate ideology. The old term *civic design* used until the 1960s to describe the physical restructuring of urban space was used at a time when the state was both manager and builder of its own institutions. This process has now given way to a neo-corporate state where the imagery of traditional social institutions has been swamped by the branding of corporate architectural space and form as the dominant paradigm. This implies not only a shift in the representation of spatial forms reflecting a profound economic and political transition, but also an ethical reorientation from any serious consideration of social welfare to an increasing domination of social life and its institutions – in education, health, welfare, crime, etc. – by private sector interests.

Being a central part of these general urban transformations, urban design has increasingly become a politically charged process as the "society of the spectacle" becomes slowly realized in space (Debord, 1983; Marcuse, 1998; Campbell, 1999). Such increased formalization of aesthetics production as an integral part of standard economic processes reflects a fundamental need of cities to advance their competitiveness in a world market which has come to recognize that economic efficiency and an improved built environment are both synergistic and good

for business. This context also deepens the idea of uneven development mentioned above, since in the process cities are placed in the position of medieval states where city wars over limited commercial opportunities prevail. Today, all cities are in a state of siege. Any city which creates a more aesthetically satisfying environment for its urban elites and whose *urban design* qualities are enhanced automatically has improved prospects on the world stage and hence an improved economy – although it is by no means certain that particular mega-events such as the Olympic Games automatically carry big financial rewards (the final cost to the taxpayer of the Sydney Olympics is AU$1.35 billion). This in turn is to a large degree dependent on financial support in the form of spectacles, successful cities capturing a host of functions that demand accommodation – international conventions, Olympic Games, grand prix, arts festivals, and the rest – all of which generate revenue and increase the complexity of available urban forms. The corollary, however, is that failure to comply with the ruthless benchmarking and performance criteria which are an integral part of postmodern urbanism carries serious economic penalties. In these terms, cities that are successful survive and thrive; the remainder are left to ponder a dearth of symbolic capital, decreasing resources, and a diminished urban prospect. In combination, all of the above situations will underwrite urban form in the developed world into the foreseeable future.

Finally, there is also a dark side to how the form of cities is likely to develop: urban design will continue to be affected throughout the world as cities are rebuilt or recover from man-made or natural disasters; for example, Beirut, Sarajevo, Dilli, and other regions affected by typhoons, earthquakes, and wars of imperialism, ethnicity, and religious difference, frequently in combination. As this book was being assembled, another new and significant influence on urban design came into existence, namely global terrorism, with proposals for the World Trade Center to be rebuilt in four low-rise towers. The destruction of two of the world's largest monuments to the market economy has forced governments in all developed countries to rethink urban design policies which encourage wholly unnecessary high-rise, monumental architecture. This will result in a significant consideration of, and reorientation toward, defensive urban forms and the vexed policing problems associated with surveillance and defensible space mentioned above (Newman, 1972). We will also do well to remember Manuel Castells's prediction that a major factor in the new global system in the twenty-first century will be the global criminal economy, and that even in 1994, the value of the global trade in drugs alone was larger than the global trade in oil. Much of the illegitimate profit from the trade in illegal drugs (and in everything else from body parts to plutonium) will be laundered and invested in the built environment, with a significant if invisible role in the creation of urban form (Castells, 1998, p. 169).

The Question of Theory

Given the complexity of the above phenomena, it is clear that the design of urban space cannot be encompassed by any single theory. Most of the great theorists in economics or social science were, at best, incidentally concerned with space, and wholly unconcerned with urban design. Karl Marx, Max Weber, Emile Durkheim, George Simmel, Adam Smith, John Maynard Keynes, Vilfredo Pareto, and other key thinkers were primarily concerned with the underlying processes that drive urban development. How the city appeared was of little consequence to them. Indeed, space itself was never discussed as having any significance. Abstract social science chose to ignore the fact that "social processes do not occur on the head of a pin" and that "the degree of abstraction from the actual forms in which objects relate, is such that the process by which mechanisms produce their effects is simply obscured" (Sayer, 1984, p. 135). Between the great wars, the development of space as an important concept within materialist social science was advanced by the Marxist

theorist Antonio Gramsci, but it was not until the production of two ground breaking texts – La Revolution Urbaine by Henri Lefebvre (1970), and La Question Urbaine by Manuel Castells (1972) – that the debate on the theory of space became central to the development of social science. The challenge that Castells posed to neo-Marxist theorizing on urban development was not merely that space was important, but, critically, that any analysis of social space and social reproduction would have to concentrate on the importance of consumption processes over those of production, thus standing Marxist orthodoxy on its head. To his credit, Castells broke through the cocoon surrounding traditional aspatial social theory into a new dimension of spatial urban theory. For the first time, and within this new paradigm, he located the problematic of urban form and urban design, first in The Urban Question, where he raised the important issue of "the urban symbolic" within the larger context of a political economy of space, and second in The City and the Grassroots.

From the early 1970s (when coincidentally Charles Jencks announced the birth of postmodernism), the difference that space makes started to become central to social science based disciplines and urban geography alike. The debate that ensued lasted with some intensity for about ten years and made a lasting impression that is still felt today. Some of the classics produced over that period were David Harvey's Social Justice and the City (1973), Allen Scott's The Urban Land Nexus and the State (1980), Anthony Giddens's A Contemporary Critique of Historical Materialism (1981), Enzo Mingione's Social Conflict and the City (1981), Doreen Massey's Spatial Divisions of Labour (1984), and many others. Peter Saunders neatly summed up the debates in Social Theory and the Urban Question (1981). In the intervening twenty years, there has been a paradigm shift in both theory and methodology, induced by parallel changes in society, but predominantly by the transition from industrial capitalism to informational capital, combined with an enduring and deepening fiscal crisis in states across the world. Similarly, the most significant theoretical development has been toward a valorized socio-spatial analysis where there are as many positions as there are authors, and whatever certainty existed until 1980 has since evaporated into a plethora of different "voices" all seeking to be heard. Two key texts exemplify the difficulties experienced by theorists in grappling with new phenomena, while at the same time adapting their theoretical workbench to fit. I refer to David Harvey's *The Condition of Postmodernity* (1989) and Ed Soja's *Postmetropolis* (2000), which represent ten-year markers since the debate on "the urban" started to cool off, but these could be supplanted by a great many others. Harvey bites the bullet and takes a radical step sideways from his commitment to a neo-Marxist analysis and confronts the problematic of culture head-on. The result is a direct reflection of the time, where many of the elements of a new theoretical approach are inherent: payment of tribute to Barthes, Foucault, Lyotard, and the French poststructuralists such as Derrida, Deleuze, and Guattari; the use of art, predominantly painting, sculpture, and photography, to explain important points, not to mention a whole section on postmodern architecture and urban design. Despite the new wave text, which has all the outward appearance of a substantial attempt to accommodate postmodern theory, Harvey remains convinced that much of this is aerosol, and the substance of Marx's original conception of capitalism still retains the correct fundamentals.

Re-reading his account of *Capital* strikes home with a certain jolt of recognition. Even though present conditions are very different in many respects, it is not hard to see how the invariant elements and relations that Marx defined as fundamental to any capitalist mode of production still shine through, and in many instances with an even greater luminosity than before, all the surface froth and evanescence so characteristic of flexible accumulation. (Harvey, 1989, p. 187)

Ed Soja is one theorist who to a large degree represents the next big jump, where original vocabularies are invented to encapsulate new phenomena as well as the enduring need for difference (new, but nonetheless part of an ancient tradition). In his latest book *Postmetropolis*, even the word "theory" is not used as an operational imperative, being replaced by "a defining conceptual framework," which involves "the trialectics of cityspace." While his commitment to the theoretical history of Urban Studies is exposed in detail, he nonetheless feels the need to escape even the limitations of vocabulary, as well as more traditional theoretical constraints. Words such as "synekism" are created, since "another term needs to be introduced to capture in a clearer way one of the most important human dynamics that arise from the very nature of urban life" (Soja, 2000). The same may be said of "cosmopolis," "exopolis," "third space," and the "fractal city," all of which are applied to the same place – contemporary Los Angeles – in order to describe the layering of complex and difficult phenomena.

For disciplines such as architecture and urban design that had already accepted the idea several hundred years prior to 1980 that "space makes a difference" (albeit on a different rationality), the possibility emerged with the growth of spatial political economy that the empirically held beliefs of environmental designers, such as landscape architects, architects, planners, and urban designers, might now have a substantial body of theory to inform them, as indeed systems theory had offered planning in the late 1960s (Von Bertallanfy, 1952; Chadwick, 1966; McLoughlin, 1969). The connections between these professions and spatial political economy would be by no means easy, and although a few insightful theorists would make the effort from within the traditional disciplines of architecture, urban design, and urban planning (Cosgrove, 1984; McLoughlin, 1994), most would come from external sources within the social sciences. One of the more ground-breaking texts had already emerged seven years earlier in Manfredo Tafuri's

Architecture and Utopia – Design and Capitalist Development, first published in Italian in 1973, and then in English in 1976. Several books and articles followed in the general tradition of historical materialism, such as Denis Cosgrove's classic text *Social Formation and Symbolic Landscape* (1984), Diani and Ingraham's book *Restructuring Architectural Theory* (1989), Sharon Zukin's *Landscapes of Power* (1991), and others, but in the past ten years the general trend in postmodern urbanism has been toward more narrative and discursive works. While many scholars still pay homage to major theorists such as Marx, Heidegger, Foucault, Bourdieu, Merleau-Ponty, and others, interpretations of the built form of cities have become much more personal and diffuse. While it is difficult to denote any major paradigm today as it was twenty years ago, there is no doubt that a "cultural turn" is clearly identifiable within geography. Examples of this new eclecticism are explored in Nan Ellin's collection of essays *The Architecture of Fear* (1997), Kim Dovey's fascinating text *Framing Places* (1999), Groth and Bressi's *Understanding Ordinary Landscapes* (1997), and *Gender Space and Architecture* by Rendell, Penner and Borden (2000).

Despite the considerable differences between the above theorists' "readings" of the city, the fact remains that primacy should be given to theories of economic development as formative in the design of cities, and hence to any meaningful understanding of urban design as praxis. Its theoretical roots must in the main be derived from a loose coalition of disciplines, primarily urban geography, sociology, and economics, sometimes lumped under the banner of "spatial political economy," simply because they deal with the bedrock of social life, and are directly derived from the mother lodes of economics and the social and natural sciences. Brian McLoughlin in his posthumously published paper *Centre or Periphery* suggested:

Political economy is an interdisciplinary project aimed at achieving a rounded understanding of the world we live in, encompassing sociological, economic, political and other social-scientific perspectives *without giving priority to any academic disciplines.* Spatial political economy takes us one step further to allow for the insistence of the constitutive role of geography in the constant reshaping of social relations. (McLoughlin, 1994, p. 1114; italics added)

Spatial political economy therefore provides an extremely valuable set of principles which perform a synthesizing role between those disciplines which are concerned with urban space. Through its "non-sectarian" focus, standing clear of any single disciplinary position, it offers an intellectual lens through which the city may be analyzed, debated, and shaped to new purposes. For this very reason, spatial political economy may be perceived as threatening to the environmental professions and academe alike. It suggests that professional monopolies are part and parcel of the ideological relations of capitalism, or, as Bernard Shaw would have it, "all professions are a conspiracy against the public." Their basic orientation is now driven by vested interest and profit, rather than any scientific quest for theory and understanding, particularly beyond the point when professionals were allowed to form limited companies. That process relocated professions firmly within the capitalist economy not only as employers of intellectual labor but as shareholders in capital as well, thus consigning the idea of professional neutrality to history. Similarly, academic institutions have also been tied into this process through professional intervention in education. Being rapidly absorbed by neo-corporatism and its ruthless philosophy of functionalism, microeconomics, performance criteria, user pays, benchmarking, and the rest, universities are increasingly reluctant to recognize that their primary obligation is to civil society, not to private sector interests. Removing the process of environmental education as a whole from programs structured around the ideological interests of the professional-business sector to programs oriented around various aspects of a political economy of space therefore becomes problematic. Thankfully, knowledge is not yet wholly deprived of some inherent authority, and makes its own interventions, primarily through the creation of boundary disciplines which emerge from overlaps between more traditional academic regions. For example, disciplines such as urban design are being valorized at an altogether different level, where an incipient reaction to narrowly defined professional programs is now being made from complex interactions within and between such diverse subjects as mathematics, art history, social anthropology, human ecology, feminism, gender, and cultural studies. Faced with such diversity, the tendency of spatial political economy toward structuralist theorizing is simultaneously forced to confront a variety of discourses inherent within postmodernist thought: "the discourse is multi-faceted and includes (at least) insights which are drawn from critiques of positivist geography and neo-classical economics, as well as Neo-Marxist and Neo-Weberian social theory, feminist geography, the 'green' movement and much else. It is a puzzling and sometimes conflictual set of discourses" (McLoughlin, 1994, p. 1114). While McLoughlin was focused primarily on the statutory planning process, the same commentary applies equally to urban design. While singularly confusing at times, this context nonetheless offers a healthy and dynamic environment for substantial theoretical engagement and new forms of intellectual integration across a multitude of disciplines, all of which touch on the design of cities.

While it would be incorrect to lump all of these diverse perspectives under the banner of "spatial political economy," one shared ingredient is a concern with urban space as the significant baseline for the environmental disciplines, such as architecture, landscape architecture, urban planning, urban design, and urban studies. It is also significant that one of the most insightful definitions of urban design and its relationship to urban planning, a definition which has informed this reader, comes from this source. In *The Urban Question* (1977) Manuel Castells offers a rare analysis of urban spatial forms as products of basic economic processes – production, consumption, exchange, and administration – and the reflection of ideological structures in symbolic configurations, elements, and places. It is therefore unsurprising that his definition of urban design, from *The City and the Grassroots*, contrasts with those which follow, and stands out as a singularly rare attempt to connect the process of designing cities to the overall process of the production of space within capitalism. "We call urban social change the redefinition of urban meaning. We call urban planning the negotiated adaptation of urban functions to a shared urban meaning. *We call urban design the symbolic attempt to express an accepted urban meaning in certain urban forms*" (Castells, 1983, p. 304; italics added).

Defining the Field

It goes without saying that the design of cities appears to have increasing significance within urban development as a whole, and the discipline of *urban design* has a major role to play in delineating the formal outcomes of urban projects across the globe. A definition of "urban design" as both process and product remains problematic. Relatedly, theory in urban design is a wholly vexed subject.

Overall it is fair to say that within the discipline of urban design, there is a tendency toward a somewhat eclectic use of theory, *such that urban design has nothing to lose and much to gain by admitting it is a discipline that is theoretically inconsequential in and of itself*. Its power derives from the fact that, irrefutably, it is a deeply embedded social practice that societies have valued from time immemorial, and therein also lies its value. As such it does not have to justify its existence through reference to a discrete set of home grown theory. The entire vocabulary of urban design in the West remains rooted to its own historical and formal origins, from the fertile valleys of Egypt and Sumeria to Ancient Greece and Rome, and thence to Fin-de-siècle Vienna and the birth of modernism. Serious attempts to advance the idea that urban design has its own inherent theoretical integrity, however, have usually resulted in narrow technocratic answers, practice-based methodological definitions, or vague attempts to define what Michael Dear has called a "pastiche of practices" similar to, or dependent upon, those within urban planning. Paradoxically, gaining credibility for urban design as a "field" is dependent on relinquishing the idea that it somehow has its own inherent integrity and standardized "choreography of routines" (Dear, 1986, p. 379). This does not mean that theory is unimportant to the comprehension of urban design as it fits within the social formation. Quite the opposite. What it *does* suggest is that urban design, like urban planning, is not an independent force in urbanization, and therefore any substantial theory must be *about* urban design, rather than *of* it. This same general position was powerfully phrased by Ross King, in *Urban Design in Capitalist Society*, where he wrote:

Urban Design is concerned with the purposive production of urban meaning, through the coordinating design of conjunctures or relationships between spatial elements. It is argued that, in capitalist society, this production of meaning has typically supported shifts in capital accumulation, social reproduction, and legitimation, in ways crucial to the reinforcing of dominant interests. Its effect has been to help counteract instability, system "degeneration" (from the standpoint of such interests) and any fundamental transformation of the social system. (King, 1987, p. 445)

Or, to paraphrase Scott and Roweis (1977, p. 1011):

we cannot assume that urban design emerges, acquires its observable qualities, and evolves, according to forces that reside solely within itself.... Urban Design is not invented in a vacuum, but is structurally produced out of the basic contradiction between capitalist social and property relations (and their specifically urban manifestations) and the concomitant necessity for collective action.

In contrast to these powerful definitions, which attempt to locate urban design as an overall part of a singularly larger social equation, many academics and practitioners within the field of urban design have chosen to situate the discipline in relation to other professions, to its most dominant functions, or to a specific basket of skills. To many, urban design is either "architecture writ large" or "urban planning writ small," and indeed it is inextricably tied to both. At least part of the problem in locating urban design is due to the fact that it has never been established as an independent profession. Central to this situation are the sectarian politics of its two closest disciplines, namely architecture and urban planning. Traditionally, urban design has been caught in the professional equivalent of no man's land, claimed by both and recognized by neither. For reasons of professional liability, architectural professions worldwide have never given full recognition to urban design programs in universities, unless programs were monopolized by graduate architects. On the other hand, planning professions have also been reluctant to recognize "physical design" largely because of an ideological commitment to social science based disciplines as the foundation for urban planning practice, a situation which has endured since 1970. Not only did this make for a one-dimensional approach to planning from which it has never fully recovered, it has also rendered standard planning practice unfit to deal with the current trend to project-based site planning. Despite the fact that planning systems retain control over the formal and aesthetic production of cities through the overall mechanisms of development control, specifically design briefs, planners are manifestly unfit to cope with the urban design process. For these and other reasons, many definitions of urban design have been given by professionals and academics alike that seek to locate it within the dominant fields of architecture and urban planning. For example, definitions such as the following underwrite most of the literature in urban design: "urban design is the art of three-dimensional city design at a scale greater than that of a single building"; "urban design links planning, architecture, and landscape architecture together to the extent that it fills whatever gaps may exist among them"; "urban design is that part of city planning which deals with aesthetics, and which determines the order and form of the city"; "urban design is the design of the general spatial arrangement of the activities and objects over an extended area, where the client is multiple, the program is indeterminate, control is partial, and there is no state of completion"; "urban design is primarily concerned with the quality of the urban public realm, both social and physical, and the making of places that people can enjoy and respect"; "the art of urban design is the art of making or shaping townscapes"; and so on.

While most of these statements are true, they are nonetheless trivially correct. Or as Karl Popper would say, they are structured for low levels of refutability, the opposite of what is required for any significant theory to emerge. While we can agree with them, we learn little, and as propositions they are useless in establishing a theoretical domain of any real content. Given this context, it is undeniable that Schurch (1999, p. 7) is correct in deciding that "there is neither consensus nor clarity as to what defines urban design." While both Gosling (1984) and Rowley (1994) have written long articles on "the definition of urban design," others have decided, perhaps sensibly, to bypass the issue by locating urban design in relation to a specific problematic; for example, public policy (Barnett, 1982), regulation (Baer, 1997), design control (Carmona, 1996), by project types and their methodological implications (Lang, 1996), to aesthetics (Isaacs, 2000), as part of a typology of urban planning practice (Yiftachel, 1989), or in relation to ideas such as "authenticity" (Salah Ouf, 2001), "townscape" (Taylor, 1999), "private property" (Rowley, 1998) or "cultural regeneration" (Wansborough and Mageean, 2000).

While all of the above positions are valuable in shedding light on specific characteristics of the urban design process and on the basic features of urban design practice, there

are two fundamental issues that are not considered if we wish to arrive at a proposition of high refutability, a satisfying definition, or a significant explanation of urban design as praxis. The first issue is that none of the above definitions or approaches is connected to any fundamental social reality. Overall they seek to define urban design largely in terms of practice first, and social, economic, and political processes not at all. Nor do they even consider urban design in terms of a particular philosophy or paradigm. Second, and consequently, they cannot lead to any significant theoretical explanation of the place of urban design in society. The overarching assumption one must make in order to legitimate the discipline is that knowledge is socially reproduced and it is axiomatic that the most profound theories are those that contribute the greatest insights into the evolution of social life. In addition, theory can be allocated two fundamental tasks, first as *explanation*, second as a guide to *praxis*. While there is no clear and necessary relationship between these two functions, there is a tendency within the environmental professions in general, and urban design in particular, to conflate one with the other. This is not so difficult to do, since arguably the theoretical base is weak across the board, as I have indicated above. Hence what are essentially trivial operational features of urban environments become allocated explanatory powers – "theory." Examples of this would be Christopher Alexander's *Pattern Language* (1977), Gordon Cullen's *Townscape* (1961) (restated in Taylor, 1999), and Kevin Lynch's *Theory of Good City Form* (1981). While each set of ideas is extremely useful in generating insights into the qualities of cities we might wish to emulate, they do not constitute *theory* in any meaningful sense. I do not wish to suggest, however, that theory "from the outside" has been wholly absent, and three regions that continue to contribute interesting models and interpretations are those deriving in the main from environmental psychology (Zube and Moore, 1991), mathematics (Hillier, 1996), and policy studies (Carmona, 1996). Nonetheless, while they are important in themselves, each has had only a marginal impact on the field as a whole.

The Concept of the Book

Given the above context, this reader could have taken a multitude of different directions, and there were a significant number of prototypes in disciplines directly relevant to urban design. In social science many examples exist of edited collections, e.g. Lewis Coser's *Masters of Sociological Thought* (1971), or Eike Gebhardt and Andrew Arato's *The Essential Frankfurt School Reader* (1982). Similarly, urban studies has many edited collections, such as Gregory and Urry's *Social Relations and Spatial Structures* (1985), LeGates and Stout's *The City Reader* (1996), Paddison's *The Handbook of Urban Studies* (2000), and Fainstein and Campbell's *Readings in Urban Theory* (1996b). However, collections within the built environment disciplines are rare. Architecture has some interesting new selections of papers such as Hayes's *Architecture Theory since 1968* (2000), and *Gender Space and Architecture* (Rendell et al., 2000). Three recent volumes somewhat improved a sparse situation in urban planning, namely Jay Stein's *Classic Readings in Urban Planning* (1995), Mandelbaum et al.'s *Explorations in Planning Theory* (1996), and Fainstein and Campbell's *Readings on Planning Theory* (1996b), the companion volume to the text mentioned above – *Readings in Urban Theory*. In contrast to all of these related disciplines, urban design to date has been bereft of any complex and integrated perspective on the discipline as it emerges from a much larger field of politics, geography and social science. *Designing Cities* constitutes an initial foray into a difficult and exciting future for the discipline.

In assembling the edited material, I considered that it was of primary importance to explain the editing process so that the reader could be seen in context, and to reveal the thought process behind the book's structure. In order to complete this task, several basic considerations were paramount in guiding the selection of works to be included from several thousand possibilities, unearthed over the year of research that preceded the book's production. The first principle I adopted was to limit content to urban design in *Western* societies, for the simple reason that the entire process of urbanization has progressed in accordance with rules that are utterly different to those elsewhere, such as in Central and South America, Africa, and other countries. One major dividing line, for example, has been the experience of colonizing and colonized societies, and here we can see a clear divide between, for example, Western and Asian societies. While there are a few gems such as Anthony King's 1984 paper "The social production of building form," attempts to link East and West are few and far between. King's article was a landmark in the effort to remake architecture as typology and social product linked to the march of Imperialism, rather than seeing it as the ineffable product of individual genius. Second, the final text had to be used both as a general theoretical reader for interested lay persons and professionals alike and as a working tool for built environment studies within universities, so a fairly comprehensible structure and organization was required. Third, I have a longstanding commitment to historical materialism and spatial political economy, which I have used as an organizing principle as far as this has been possible, so that there is some uniformity to the material. Finally, I wanted this reader to reflect my conviction that urban design is a wholly contextual process, so that the question of "skilling," which has always been an obsession in the profession, becomes wholly dependent on the context for design. The idea of "skilling" has no meaning outside a particular social environment, and the constraints of economy, culture, technology, and place. The idea that there is a set of practical skills and standard knowledge base that all urban designers should possess must be seriously challenged. This position is best summed up in the simple observation that "our thinking belongs in the same universe that we are thinking about" (Soros, 1998, p. 15). It is therefore of paramount importance that we place our emphasis not on core skills, but on core "*knowledges*" (after Foucault) – stressing the reflexive relationship between actors, processes, concepts, and traditions. This was the dominant consideration in assembling this work where a diverse range of authors was involved. Principles apart, there were several ways the material could have been organized; for example, chronologically in terms of significant contributions, by disciplinary boundaries to illustrate the contributions that have been from various academic or professional disciplines, or according to various theoretical positions such as environmental psychology, mathematics, or policy studies. On balance it seemed more appropriate to use categories related to major elements of content such as history or politics, and so an elemental structure was finally adopted.

The material in the text is therefore assembled in the following categories, which are organized from general/theoretical to specific/practice, with an associated guiding question for each. For example:

1 Theory. How are we to understand urban design as a theoretical endeavor?
2 History. What can we learn from history about the design of cities?
3 Philosophy. What system of meanings informs the urban process?
4 Politics. What value systems and compromises are involved in the design of cities?
5 Culture. How do society and culture give rise to urban form?
6 Gender. What implications does "gender" hold for the design of urban space?
7 Environment. What are the key implications of the natural world for the design process?
8 Aesthetics. How are we to understand the realm of the senses in relation to urban form?
9 Typologies. What organizational forms can be identified in the design of cities?
10 Pragmatics. What do urban designers need to know?

As with any taxonomy, there are many practical problems and there are compromises to be made with every decision, for the simple reason that each defined element is to a large degree artificial. It would have been simpler, for example, to have only four categories, or perhaps to have two more, and economics and ideology stand out as candidates for an expanded version. Overall, it is impossible to gain the accuracy one would like in any event, simply because content spills over from one category to the next. The overlap between theory, history, and philosophy is frequently absolute, since it is often necessary to discuss all three at the same time. Harvey's article *Social Justice, Postmodernism and the City* is one such example. Having ten categories meant that each section would have to be limited to about three articles, which placed some stringent limitations on the choice of material. In many instances there appeared to be some correlation between the quality of a work and its length, and many wonderful articles had to be excluded simply because they were too long. So the current choice of categories represents the best option given the working limitations of the reader and its content.

The choice of the material itself was extremely difficult, and the final selection was refined from an original pool of 300 articles and book chapters. Work which was excluded in many instances was frequently ground breaking, but had to be left out for many reasons unconnected to quality because the article/chapter was too long, contained too many plates, or simply could not fit into the classification of each section, where the material has been carefully chosen to be read sequentially as far as possible. There are countless examples of such exclusions, and a few of these must be mentioned because of their importance to urban design theory. Probably the most significant omission is the second chapter of Schorske's book *Fin De Siecle Vienna*, subtitled *The Ringstrasse, Its Critics and the Birth of Urban Modernism*. In Schorske's own words, "it was against the anvil of the Ringstrasse that two pioneers of modern thought about the city and its architecture, Camillo Sitte and

Otto Wagner, hammered out ideas of urban life and form whose influence is still working among us" (Schorske, 1981, p. 25). The importance of these two figures to urban design cannot be underestimated, and the struggle between rationalism/functionalism and contextualism remains one of the most significant conflicts for both architects and urban designers today. Similarly, if we take only one of the above categories – politics – many wonderful pieces had to be excluded and a volume could be assembled on that subject alone. For example, Bremner's 1994 article "Space and nation – three texts on Aldo Rossi," apart from encapsulating the work of one of the greatest architects of the twentieth century, illuminates the important relationship between urban design and politics which is too frequently ignored, as in fact does Rossi's own article "The urban artefact as a work of art" (1993). Another omitted classic is Kevin Cox's "Capitalism and conflict round the communal living space" (1983), where he focuses on arguably the central issue and defining component of urban design, namely communal living space both as community and commodity. Finally a brilliant article by Charles Jencks and Maggie Valentine (1987) called "The Architecture of democracy" traces the idea of the public realm as a democratic plurality, adding yet another dimension to the work of Cox and Bremner. The same kinds of exclusions apply across the board, and in order to compensate for these omissions, many additional references in each section are suggested in a supporting bibliography as an appendix to this reader.

But for practicing urban designers, some explanation is needed for what will be perceived as *singular* exclusions, namely those writers who are traditionally associated with "urban design theory," only one of whom appears in this volume: Christopher Alexander, Donald Appleyard, Kevin Lynch, Gordon Cullen, and a host of others. There are at least four major reasons for this. The first reflects the statement I made above, that any substantial theory must be *about* urban design, rather than *of* it, and I have already mentioned that most of what passes for theory in urban design orthodoxy is disconnected from any larger social context. It therefore tends to be wholly eclectic, almost anarchic in its lack of focus on some substantial body of knowledge. Second, and in consequence, if this reader were to have any overall coherence, logically it could not come from within the discipline, and the adoption of spatial political economy as the steering mechanism both reinforced this position and allowed a much larger picture of the discipline to emerge. Third, while it is not possible to present a theory of urban design from the chosen selection, my hope is that at least there is the indication of a paradigm reading through the collected work of many authors, few of whom are directly connected to practice. Fourth, the examples given below of urban design "classics" are all texts that are extremely difficult to summarize by removing a single chapter, since continuity is all-important, and they are not user-friendly when it comes to extracting one chapter at the cost of the remainder. Hence, few chapters of these or other works are featured in the final selection. However, as an act of homage, I have assembled a short list of thirty classic texts in urban design, which I would consider among the most influential writing of the past thirty years. Many of the books listed below have been instrumental in my own education as well as that of other professionals. While this short bibliography reflects my personal choice, and could be extended several times, I feel that most academics and practitioners would agree that there is not much missing as a traditional baseline for the discipline. Although there may be minor variations in what should be included in this list, each item has made a major contribution to "mainstream" urban design, and collectively I owe the authors a great debt for encouraging my interest in designing cities:

Alexander, C.: *The Pattern Language*
Alexander, C.: *A New Theory of Urban Design*
Bacon, E.: *The Design of Cities*
Banham, R.: *The Architecture of Four Ecologies*

Barnett, J.: *An Introduction to Urban Design*

Broadbent, J.: *Emerging Concepts in Urban Space Design*

Chermayeff, S.: *Community and Privacy*

Cullen, G.: *Townscape*

Halprin, L.: *Cities*

Halprin, L.: *RSVP Cycles*

Jacobs, J.: *The Death and Life of Great American Cities*

Katz, P.: *The New Urbanism*

Krier, R.: *Urban Space*

Lang, J.: *Urban Design: The American Experience*

Lynch, K.: *Site Planning*

Lynch, K.: *Image of the City*

Lynch, K.: *A Theory of Good City Form*

McHarg, I.: *Design with Nature*

Mumford, L.: *The City in History*

Newman, O.: *Defensible Space*

Norberg-Schultz, C.: *Genius Loci*

Proshansky, H. M. et al.: *Environmental Psychology*

Rappoport, A.: *Human Aspects of Urban Form*

Rowe and Koetter: *Collage City*

Rudofsky, B.: *Streets for People*

Sitte, C.: *The Art of Building Cities*

Sommer, R.: *Personal Space*

Tafuri, M.: *Architecture and Utopia*

Venturi, R.: *Learning from Las Vegas*

Webber, M.: *The Place and Non-place Urban Realm*

Taking into account the standard requirements of the publishers, the choice of material to be included was therefore based primarily on three major factors: the size of the work, its theoretical integrity, and its "fit" with other authors in creating continuity and adding meaning. The overarching consideration was the quality of the work itself, and its ability to penetrate to the heart of issues by being rooted into *some* major theoretical paradigm as far as this was possible. On balance, I considered that it was more important for one article to lead into the next, thus inferring connections and transitional relationships, than it was to pick a piece of writing which stood alone as a classic. So there has been an attempt to work from the general to the specific not only from chapter to chapter, but also within each section. To give a couple of examples, in part I, on theory, the section begins with Castells's piece, where urban design is defined within both the process of urban social change and the new historical relationship to space. Modern urban theory is then discussed and carried into the concrete effects of urban development on the design of cities in Paul Clarke's superb article on "The economic currency of architectural aesthetics." The section concludes with a more detailed debate on urban form, and how the specificity of urban design as an outcome can be defined in context, by Sharon Zukin. Each piece of writing therefore represents a deliberate progressive development from the largest historical dimension to the specificity of urban design as an intervention in the overall trajectory of cities. Similarly, the section on philosophy deals with three interrelated conceptual systems, i.e. Marxism, phenomenology, and semiotics, which address issues of social justice, identity, and signification, or, alternatively, ethics, existence, and meaning or symbolism. As such the entire text suggests one way in a constellation of possible paths toward an improved understanding in the art of designing cities. I hope that "reading the reader" will be an enjoyable and fulfilling process for everyone who takes the journey.

BIBLIOGRAPHY

Adorno, T. (1991) *The Culture Industry*. London: Routledge.

Alexander, C. (1977) *A Pattern Language: Towns, Buildings, Construction*. New York: Oxford University Press.

Alexander, C. (1987) *A New Theory of Urban Design*. New York: Oxford University Press.

Al-Hindi, K. F. and Staddon, C. (1997) The hidden histories and geographies of neotraditional town planning: the case of Seaside, Florida. *Environment and Planning D: Society and Space*, 15(3), 349–72.

Appadurai, A. (1996) *Modernity at Large: Cultural Dimensions of Globalisation*. Minneapolis: University of Minneapolis Press.

Arrighi, G. (1994) *The Long Twentieth Century: Money, Power and the Origins of Our Times*. London: Verso.

Audirac, I. and Shermyen, A. (1994) An evaluation of neotraditional design's social prescription: postmodern placebo or remedy for suburban malaise? *Journal of Planning Education and Research*, 13(3), 161–73.

Bacon, E. (1967) *Design of Cities*. New York: Viking.

Baer, W. C. (1997) Toward design of regulations for the built environment. *Environment and Planning B: Environment and Design*, 24, 35–57.

Banham, R. (1973) *Los Angeles: The Architecture of Four Ecologies*. Harmondsworth: Penguin.

Barnett, L. (1982) *An Introduction to Urban Design*. New York: Harper and Row.

Biel, R. (2000) *The New Imperialism*. London. Zed Books.

Bogard, W. (1996) *The Simulation of Surveillance*. Cambridge: Cambridge University Press.

Bremner, L. (1994) Space and the nation: three texts on Aldo Rossi. *Environment and Planning D: Society and Space*, 12(3), 287–300.

Broadbent, J. (1990) *Emerging Concepts in Urban Space Design*. New York: Van Nostrand.

Campbell, S. (1999) Capital reconstruction and capital accumulation in Berlin: a reply to Peter Marcuse. *International Journal of Urban and Regional Research*, 23(1), 173–9.

Carmona, M. (1996) Controlling urban design. Part 1: a possible renaissance? *Journal of Urban Design*, 1(1), 47–73.

Castells, M. (1977) *The Urban Question: A Marxist Approach*, trans. A. Sheridan. Cambridge, MA: MIT Press (originally published 1972).

Castells, M. (1983) *The City and the Grassroots. A Cross-cultural Theory of Urban Social Movements*. Berkeley: University of California Press.

Castells, M. (1989) *The Informational City*. Oxford: Blackwell.

Castells, M. (1996) *The Rise of the Network Society*. Oxford: Blackwell.

Castells, M. (1998) *End of Millennium*. Oxford: Blackwell.

Chadwick, G. (1966) A systems view of planning. *Journal of the Town Planning Institute*, 52, 184–6.

Chermayeff, S. and Alexander, C. (1963) *Community and Privacy: Toward a New Architecture of Humanism*. New York: Doubleday.

Coser, L. (ed.) (1971) *Masters of Sociological Thought*. New York: Harcourt.

Cosgrove, D. (1984) *Landscape and Social Formation*. London: Croom Helm.

Cox, K. R. (1983) Capitalism and conflict around the communal living space. In M. Dear and A. Scott (eds), *Urbanisation and Urban Planning in Capitalist Society*. London: Methuen, pp. 431–55.

Cullen, G. (1961) *The Concise Townscape*. New York: Reinhold.

Cuthbert, A. (1994a) Flexible production, flexible education? Part 1. *The Australian Planner*, 31(4), 207–13.

Cuthbert, A. (1994b) Flexible production, flexible education? Part 2. *The Australian Planner*, 32(1), 49–55.

Cuthbert, A. (1995) The right to the city: surveillance, private interest and the public domain in Hong Kong. *Cities*, 12(5), 293–310.

Cuthbert, A. (1997) Trial by facts. *The Australian Planner*, 34(4), 213–20.

Cuthbert, A. (2001) Going global: reflexivity and contextualism in urban design education. *Journal of Urban Design*, 6(3), 297–316.

Cuthbert, A. and MacKinnell, K. (1997) Ambiguous space, ambiguous rights: corporate power and social control in Hong Kong, *Cities*, 14(5), 295–311.

Davis, M. (1990) *City of Quartz: Excavating the Future in Los Angeles*. London: Verso.

Davis, M. (1998) *Ecology of Fear: Los Angeles and the Imagination of Disaster*. New York: Metropolitan Books.

Dear, M. (1986) Postmodernism and planning. *Environment and Planning D: Society and Space*, 4(3), 367–84.

Debord, G. (1983) *The Society of the Spectacle*. Detroit: Black and Red Press.

Deutsche, R. (1996) Tilted arc and the uses of democracy. In *Evictions: Art and Spatial Politics*. Cambridge, MA: MIT Press, pp. 257–68, 362.

Diani, M. and Ingraham, C. (eds) (1989) Introduction. In *Restructuring Architectural Theory*. Evanston, IL: Northwestern University, pp. 1–8.

Dovey, K. (1999) *Framing Places*. London: Routledge.

Ellin, N. (1997) *The Architecture of Fear*. New York: Princeton Architectural Press.

Fainstein, D. and Campbell, S. (eds) (1996a) *Readings in Planning Theory*. Oxford: Blackwell.

Fainstein, D. and Campbell, S. (eds) (1996b) *Readings in Urban Theory*. Oxford: Blackwell.

Featherstone, M. (ed.) (1990) *Global Culture: Nationalism, Globalisation and Modernity*. Newbury Park, CA: Sage.

Featherstone, M., Lash, S. and Robertson, R. (eds) (1995) *Global Modernities*. London: Sage.

Frampton, K. (1983) Towards a critical regionalism: six points for an architecture of resistance. In H. Foster (ed.), *Postmodern Culture*. London: Pluto Press, pp. 16–30.

Garreau, J. (1991) *Edge City: Life on the New Frontier*. New York: Doubleday.

Gerbhardt, E. and Arato, A. (eds) (1982) *The Essential Frankfurt School Reader*. New York: Continuum.

Giddens, A. (1981) *A Contemporary Critique of Historical Materialism*. London: Macmillan.

Giddens, A. (1990) Modernity and utopia. *New Statesman and Society*, November 20–22.

Gosling, D. (1984) Definitions of urban design. *Architectural Design*, 54(1/2), 16–25.

Gregory, D. and Urry, J. (eds) (1985) *Social Relations and Spatial Structure*. London: Macmillan.

Groth, P. and Bressi, T. W. (1997) *Understanding Ordinary Landscapes*. New Haven, CT: Yale University Press.

Halprin, L. (1963) *Cities*. New York: Reinhold.

Halprin, L. (1969) *The RSVP Cycles: Creative Processes in the Human Environment*. New York: G. Braziller.

Harvey, D. (1973) *Social Justice and The City*. Baltimore: Johns Hopkins University Press.

Harvey, D. (1989) *The Condition of Postmodernity*. Oxford: Blackwell.

Harvey, D. (2000) *Spaces of Hope*. Edinburgh: Edinburgh University Press.

Hawken, P., Lovins, A., and Lovins, L. (1999) *Natural Capitalism: The Next Industrial Revolution*. London: Earthscan.

Hayes, K. M. (2000) *Architecture Theory Since 1968*. New York: MIT Press.

Hillier, B. (1996) *Space Is the Machine*. Cambridge: Cambridge University Press.

Hirst, P. (2000) Why the nation still matters. In Beynon and Dunkerley, pp. 241–6.

Isaacs, R. (2000) The urban picturesque: an aesthetic experience of urban pedestrian places. *Journal of Urban Design*, 5(2), 145–80.

Jacobs, J. (1961) *The Death and Life of Great American Cities: The Failure of Town Planning*. New York: Vintage.

Jencks, C. and Valentine, M. (1987) The architecture of democracy: the hidden tradition. *Architectural Design*, 57(9/10), 8–25.

Johnson, N. (1995) Cast in stone: monuments, geography, and nationalism. *Environment and Planning D: Society and Space*, 13(1), 51–65.

Katz, P. (1994) *The New Urbanism*. New York: McGraw-Hill.

King, A. D. (1984) The social production of building form: theory and practice. *Environment and Planning D: Society and Space*, 2, 429–46.

King, R. J. (1987) Urban design in capitalist society. *Environment and Planning D: Society and Space*, 6(4), 445–74.

Kotkin, J. (2000) *The New Geography*. New York: Random House.

Krier, R. (1979) *Urban Space*, trans. C. Czehowski and G. Black. New York: Rizzoli.

Lang, J. (1994) *Urban Design: The American Experience*. New York: Van Nostrand.

Lang, J. (1996) Implementing urban design in America: project types and methodological implications. *Journal of Urban Design*, 1(1), 7–22.

Lefebvre, H. (1970) *La Révolution Urbaine*. Paris: Gallimard.

LeGates, R. T. and Stout, F. (eds) (1996) *The City Reader*. London: Routledge.

Lynch, K. (1960) *Image of the City*. Cambridge, MA: MIT Press.

Lynch, K. (1971) *Site Planning*. Cambridge, MA: MIT Press.

Lynch, K. (1981) *A Theory of Good City Form*. Cambridge, MA: MIT Press.

Lyon, D. (1994) *The Electronic Eye*. Cambridge: Polity Press.

McCann, E. (1994) Neotraditional developments: the anatomy of a new urban form. *Urban Geography*, 13, 210–33.

McHarg, I. (1969) *Design with Nature*. Natural History Press.

McLoughlin, J. B. (1969) *Urban and Regional Planning: A Systems Approach*. London: Faber.

McLoughlin, J. B. (1994) Centre or periphery? Town planning and spatial political economy. *Environment and Planning A*, 26(7), 1111–22.

Mandelbaum, S. J., Mazza, L., and Burchell, R. W. (eds) (1996) *Explorations in Planning Theory*. New Brunswick, NJ: Rutgers.

Marcuse, P. (1998) Reflections on Berlin: the meaning of construction and the construction of meaning. *International Journal of Urban and Regional Research*, 22(2), 331–8.

Marshall, N. G. (2000) Into the third millennium: neocorporatism, the state and the urban planning profession. Doctoral thesis, Faculty of the Built Environment, University of New South Wales, Sydney.

Massey, D. (1984) *Spatial Divisions of Labour*. London: Macmillan.

Minca, C. (ed.) (2001) *Postmodern Geography: Theory and Praxis*. Oxford: Blackwell.

Mingione, E. (1981) *Social Conflict and the City*. Oxford: Blackwell.

Mitchell, D. (2001) Postmodern geographical praxis? The postmodern impulse and the war against homeless people in the "post justice city." In C. Minca (ed.), *Postmodern Geography: Theory and Praxis*. Oxford: Blackwell, pp. 57–91.

Mumford, L. (1961) *The City in History*. New York: Harcourt, Brace, Jovanovich.

Newman, O. (1972) *Defensible Space: People and Design in the Violent City*. New York: Macmillan.

Norberg-Schulz, C. (1979) *Genius Loci. Towards a Phenomenology of Architecture*. New York: Rizzoli.

Paddison, R. (ed.) (2000) *The Handbook of Urban Studies*. London: Sage.

Parker, J. (2000) *Total Surveillance*. London: Piatkus.

Poster, M. (1990) *The Mode of Information*. Oxford: Blackwell.

Proshansky, H. M., Ittelson, W. H. and Rivlin, L. G. (1970) *Environmental Psychology: Man and His Physical Setting*. New York: Holt, Rinehart and Winston.

Rappoport, A. (1977) *The Human Aspects of Urban Form*. Oxford: Pergamon.

Rendell, J. Penner, B. and Borden, I. (2000) *Gender, Space and Architecture*. London: Routledge

Robertson, R. (1992) Globalization. *Social Theory and Global Culture*. London: Sage.

Robertson, R. (1995) Glocalisation: time–space and homogeneity–heterogeneity. In M. Featherstone et al. (eds), *Global Modernities*. London: Sage, pp. 25–44.

Rossi, A. (1993) The urban artifact as a work of art. In J. Ockman (ed.), *Architecture Culture 1943–1968: A Documentary Anthology*. New York: Rizzoli, pp. 393–5.

Rowe, C. and Koetter, F. (1978) *Collage City*. Cambridge, MA: MIT Press.

Rowland, K. (1966) *The Shape of Towns*. London: Ginn.

Rowley A. (1994) Definitions of urban design. *Planning Practice and Research*, 9(3), 179–97.

Rowley, A. (1998) Private-property decision makers and the quality of urban design. *Journal of Urban Design*, 3(2), 151–73.

Rowley, A. and Davies, L. (2001) Training for urban design. *Quarterly Journal of the Urban Design Group*, 78 (http://www2.rudi.net/ej/udq/78/research-udq78.html), accessed July 25, 2001.

Rudofsky, B. (1969) *Streets for People*. Garden City, NY: Doubleday.

Salah Ouf, A. M. (2001) Authenticity and the sense of place in urban design. *Journal of Urban Design*, 6(1), 73–86.

Sassen, S. (1991) *The Global City*. Princeton, NJ: Princeton University Press.

Saunders, P. (1981) *Social Theory and the Urban Question*. London: Hutchinson.

Sayer, A. (1984) *Method in Social Science*. London: Hutchinson.

Schorske, C. (1981) *Fin De Siecle Vienna*. New York: Vintage.

Schurch, T. (1999) Reconsidering urban design: thoughts about its status as a field or a profession. *Journal of Urban Design*, 4(1), 5–28.

Scott, A. J. (1980) *The Urban Land Nexus and the State*. London: Pion.

Scott, A. J. (ed.) (1997) *The Limits of Globalisation*. London Routledge.

Scott, A. J. (1998) *Regions and the World Economy*. Oxford: Oxford University Press.

Scott, A. J. (2000) *The Cultural Economy of Cities*. London: Sage.

Scott, A. J. and Roweis, S. T. (1977) Urban planning in theory and practice: a reappraisal. *Environment and Planning A*, 9(10), pp. 1097–119.

Sitte, C. (1965) *City Planning According to Artistic Principles*, trans. G. Collins and C. Collins. New York: Random House (originally published 1889).

Sklair, L. (1991) *The Sociology of the Global System*. Hemel Hempstead: Harvester Wheatsheaf.

Sklair, L. (2000) Media imperialism. In Beynon and Dinkerley, pp. 178–9.

Smith, N. (1984) *Uneven Development: Nature, Capital and the Production of Space*. Oxford: Blackwell.

Smith, N. (2001) *Rescaling Politics: Geography, Globalism, and the New Urbanism*. In C. Minca (ed.), *Postmodern Geography: Theory and Praxis*. Oxford: Blackwell, pp. 147–68.

Soja, E. (2000) *Postmetropolis*. Oxford: Blackwell.

Sommer, R. (1969) *Personal Space: The Behavioral Basis for Design*. Englewood Cliffs, NJ: Prentice Hall.

Soong, T. K. (1989) *Mega Cities in the Tropics*. Singapore: Institute of South East Asian Studies.

Soros, G. (1998) *The Crisis of Global Capitalism*. London: Little Brown and Co.

Stein, J. (ed.) (1995) *Classic Readings in Urban Planning*. New York: McGraw-Hill.

Tafuri, M. (1976) *Architecture and Utopia: Design and Capitalist Development*. Cambridge, MA: MIT Press.

Taylor, N. (1999) The elements of townscape and the art of urban design. *Journal of Urban Design*, 4(2), 195–209.

Till, K. (1994) Neotraditional towns and urban villages: the cultural production of a geography of "otherness." *Environment and Planning D: Society and Space*, 11, 709–32.

Venturi, R., Brown, D. S. and Izenour, S. (1977) *Learning from Las Vegas*. Cambridge, MA: MIT Press.

Von Bertallanfy, L. (1951) An outline of general systems theory. *British Journal of the Philosophy of Science*, 1, 134–65.

Wallerstein I. (1974) *The Modern World System*. New York: Academic Press.

Wansborough, M. and Mageean, A. (2000) The role of urban design in cultural regeneration. *Journal of Urban Design*, 5(2), 181–97.

Webber, M. (1963) The urban place and the non-place urban realm. In *Explorations into Urban Structure*. Philadelphia: University of Pennsylvania.

Yiftachel, O. (1989) Towards a new typology of urban planning theories. *Environment and Planning B: Planning and Design*, 16, 23–39.

Zube, E. H. and Moore, G. (1991) *Advances in Behaviour and Design*. London: Plenum.

Zukin, S. (1991) *Landscapes of Power: From Detroit to Disney World*. Berkeley: University of California Press.

Part I
Theory

1

The Process of Urban Social Change

Manuel Castells

Societies only exist in time and space. The spatial form of a society is, therefore, closely linked to its structure and urban change is interwined with historical evolution. This formula, however, is too general. To understand cities, to unveil their connection to social change, we must determine the mechanisms through which spatial structures are transformed and urban meaning is redefined. To investigate this question based on the observations and analyses presented in this book, we need to introduce some fundamental elements of a general theory of society that underlie our analyses. But for these elements to be considered as the effective tools used in our research, we must first be more precise about our research questions.

Our goal is to explain how and why cities change. But what are cities? Can we be satisfied with a definition like, spatial forms of human society? What kind of spatial forms? And when do we know that they are cities? At which statistical threshold of density or population concentration does a city become a city? And how are we sure that, in different cultures and in diverse historical times, we are referring to the same social reality on the basis of a similarly concentrated, densely settled and socially heterogeneous population? Urban sociologists of course, have repeatedly asked the same questions without ever producing a fully satisfactory answer (Castells, 1968, 1969; Fischer, 1976; Saunders, 1981). After all, it seems a rather academic debate, too far removed from the dramatic issues currently arising from the worldwide reality of urban crisis. And yet it seems intellectually dubious to under-take the explanation of change in a social form whose content we ignore or whose profile could be left to a category that is ill-defined by the Census Bureau. In fact, our basic theoretical perspective supersedes the question by studying the city from the viewpoint of historical change.

Let us begin, at the risk of appearing schematic, with the clearest possible statement. Cities, like all social reality, are historical products, not only in their physical materiality but in their cultural meaning, in the role they play in the social organization, and in people's lives. The basic dimension in urban change is the conflictive debate between social classes and historical actors over the meaning of urban, the significance of spatial forms in the social structure, and the content, hierarchy, and destiny of cities in relationship to the entire social structure. A city (and each type of city) is what a historical society decides the city (and each city) will be. Urban is the social meaning assigned to a particular spatial form by a historically defined society. Two remarks must immediately qualify this formulation:

1 Society, as we will discuss a few pages below, is a structured, conflictive reality in which social classes oppose each other over the basic rules of social organization according to their own social interests. Therefore the definition of urban meaning will be a process of conflict, domination, and resistance to domination, directly linked to the dynamics of social struggle and not to the reproductive spatial expression of a unified culture. Futhermore, cities and space

being fundamental to the organization of social life, the conflict over the assignment of certain goals to certain spatial forms will be one of the fundamental mechanisms of domination and counter-domination in the social structure.[1] For instance, to achieve the establishment of the city as a religious centre dominating the countryside is to obtain the material support for the exploitation of agricultural surplus by exchanging symbolic legitimacy and psychological security for peasant labour. Or, in another instance, declaring the city a free space for common trade and political self-determination is a major victory against feudal order. Thus, the definition of the meaning of 'urban' is not the spatialized xerox copy of a culture, nor the consequence of a social battle fought between undetermined historical actors in some intergallactic vacuum. It is one of the fundamental processes through which historical actors (social classes, for instance) have structured society according to their interests and values.

2   The definition of urban meaning is a social process, in its material sense. It is not a simple cultural category in the vulgar sense of culture as a set of ideas. It is cultural in the anthropological sense, that is, as the expression of a social structure, including economic, religious, political, and technological operations (Godelier, 1973). If the city is defined by the merchants as a market it will mean street fairs and intense socializing, but it will also mean the commodification of economic activity, monetarization of the work process, and the establishment of a transport network to all potential sources of goods and to all markets that maybe expanded. In sum, the historical definition of urban is not a mental representation of a spatial form, but the assignment of a structural task to this form in accordance with the conflictive social dynamics of history.

We define *urban meaning as the structural performance assigned as a goal to cities in general (and to a particular city in the inter-urban division of labour) by the conflictive process between historical actors in a given society.* We will examine below how societies are themselves structured around modes of production. Thus, the definition of urban meaning might vary both with different modes of production and with different outcomes of history within the same mode of production.

The historical process of defining urban meaning determines the characteristics of urban functions. For instance, if cities are defined as colonial centres, the use of military force and territorial control will be their basic function. If they are defined as capitalist machines, they will subdivide their functions (and sometimes specialize them in different cities) between the extraction of surplus value in the factory, the reproduction of labour power, the extraction of profit in urbanization (through real estate), the organization of circulation of capital in the financial institutions, the exchange of commodities in the commercial system, and the management of all other operations in the directional centres of capitalist business. So we define *urban functions as the articulated system of organizational means aimed at performing the goals assigned to each city by its historically defined urban meaning.*

Urban meaning and urban functions jointly determine urban form, that is, the symbolic spatial expression of the processes that materialize as a result of them. For instance, if the city is defined as a religious centre, and if the ideological control by the priests over the peasant population is the function to be accomplished, permanence and stature, mystery, distance, and yet protection and a hint of accessibility will be crucial elements in the buildings and in their spatial patterning in the urban landscape. Few architects believe that the skyscrapers in downtown America only concentrate the paperwork of giant corporations: they symbolize the power of money over the city through technology and self-confidence and are the cathedrals of the period of rising corporate capitalism (see Tafuri, 1973; also 1968). Yet they also perform a number of crucial managerial functions, and are still major real estate investments in a space that has become a commodity in itself. There is naturally, no direct reflection of the urban meaning and function on the symbolic forms, since semiological research has established the complex derivations of the language of formal representation and its relative autonomy in relationship to their functional content (Burlen, 1975; also Raymond et al., 1966; Dunod, 1971). In any event, we are not arguing that the economy determines urban forms but, rather, we are establishing a relationship and hierarchy between historical meaning, urban functions, and spatial forms. This is entirely different as a theoretical perspective. In certain urban forms, such as the early medieval cities for instance, the symbolic element of the cathedral was the major factor structuring urban form and meaning. But this was because the urban meaning was based upon the religious relationship between peasants, lords and God, with the Church as intermediary (Panofsky, 1957).

Furthermore, urban forms are not only combinations of materials, volumes, colours, and heights; they are, as Kevin Lynch has taught us, uses, flows, perceptions, mental associations, systems of representations whose significance changes with time, cultures, and social groups (Lynch, 1960, 1972). For our purpose, the only important question is to emphasize both the distinctiveness of the dimension of urban forms and its relationship to urban meaning and urban functions.

We therefore define as *urban form the symbolic expression of urban meaning and of the historical superimposition of urban meanings (and their forms) always determined by a conflictive process between historical actors.*

In any particular situation, cities are shaped by three different, though interrelated, processes:

1 Conflicts over the definition of urban meaning.
2 Conflicts over the adequate performance of urban functions. These conflicts can arise both from different interests and values, within the same accepted framework, or from different approaches about how to perform a shared goal of urban function.
3 Conflicts over the adequate symbolic expression of urban meaning and (or) functions.

We call urban social change the redefinition of urban meaning. We call urban planning the negotiated adaptation of urban functions to a shared urban meaning. We call urban design the symbolic attempt to express an accepted urban meaning in certain urban forms.

Needless to say, since defining urban meaning is a conflictive process so is urban planning and urban design. But the structural role assigned to a city by and through the social conflict over its meaning, conditions the functions and symbolism through which this role will be performed and expressed.

Urban social change conditions all aspects of the urban praxis. The theory of urban social change therefore lays the ground for any other theories of the city.

Where does such a change come from? And how do we know that there is a change?

The crucial question here is to reject any suggestion that there is a predetermined direction of urban change. History has no direction, it only has life and death. It is a composite of drama, victories, defeats, love and sorrow, joy and pain, creation and destruction. We now have the possibility of enjoying the most profound human experiences as well as the chance to blow ourselves up in a nuclear holocaust. We can make the revolution with the people or trigger the forces of revolutionary terror against the same people. If we therefore agree that the outmoded ideology of natural human progress must be abandoned, we must also proceed similarly with urban social change. Thus by change we refer simply to the assignment of a new meaning to the urban realm or to a particular city. What does new mean? On the one hand, the answer is specific to each historical context and to each city we have observed, but on the other, the answer is related to a more general and theoretical assessment of social transformation. So we must wait a few pages before settling this key question.

A major conclusion can, however, far be drawn from our definition of urban social change: its assessment is value free. We do not imply that change is improvement, and therefore we do not need to define what improvement is. As we have said before, our theory is not normative, but historical. We want to understand how processes happen that the most humanistic urban designers, such as Allan Jacobson and Kevin Lynch, would find positive for the well-being of our own environment. Although we generally agree with their criteria, our purpose is not to define the good city. It is rather to understand how good and evil, heaven and hell are produced by the angels and devils of our historical experience (our own feeling being that the devils are likely to be more creative than the angels).

Urban social change happens when a new urban meaning is produced by one of the four following processes (all of them conflictive and in opposition to one or more historical actors):

1 The dominant class in a given society, having the institutional power to restructure social forms (and thus cities) according to its interests and values, changes the existing meaning. We call this urban renewal (for cities) and regional restructuring (for the territory as a whole). For instance, if the South Bronx is deliberately abandoned, or if the Italian neighbourhoods of Boston are transformed into a headquarters city, or if some industrial cities (like Buffalo, New York) become warehouses for unemployed minorities, then we have instances of urban renewal and regional restructuring.

2 A dominated class accomplishes a partial or total revolution and changes the meaning of the city. For instance, the Cuban revolution deurbanizes La Habana (Eckstein, 1977), or the workers of Glasgow in 1915 impose housing as a social service, not as a commodity (Melling, 1980).

3 A social movement develops its own meaning over a given space in contradiction to the structurally dominant meaning, as in the feminist schemes described by Dolores Hayden (1981).

4 A social mobilization (not necessarily based on a particular social class) imposes a new urban meaning in contradiction to the institutionalized urban meaning and against the interests of the dominant class. It is in this case that we use the concept of urban social movement: a collective conscious action aimed at the transformation of the institutionalized urban meaning against the logic, interest, and values of the dominant class. It is our hypothesis that only urban social movements are urban-orientated mobilizations that influence structural social change and transform the urban meanings. The symmetrical opposite to this hypothesis is not necessarily true. A social change (for instance the domination of a new class) might or might not change the urban meaning; for example, a working class revolution that keeps the role of a city as the site for a centralized non-democratic state apparatus.

At this point of our analysis, it becomes necessary to make explicit some of our assumptions on social change to be able to establish more specific links between the change of cities and the change of societies. This task requires a brief and schematic detour into the hazardous land of the general theory of social change.

NOTE

1 Anthony Giddens insists on the mistaken neglect by the theories of social change of the fundamental time-space dimensions of human experience as the material basis for social activity (see Giddens, 1981, especially pp. 129–56).

REFERENCES

Boudon, P. (1971) *Sur l'Espace Architectural: Essai d'Epistemologie de l'Architecture*. Paris: Dunod.

Burlen, K. (1975) L'image achitecturale. PhD thesis, University of Paris.

Castells, M. (1968) Y a-t-il une sociologie urbaine? *Sociologie du Travail*, 1.

Castells, M. (1969) Theorie et ideologie en sociologie urbaine. *Sociologie et Société*, 2.

Eckstein, S. (1977) The de-bourgeoisement of Cuban Cities. In I. L. Horowitz (ed.), *Cuban Communism*. New Brunswick, NJ: Transaction Books.

Fischer, C. (1976) *The Urban Experience*. New York: Harcourt Brace Jovanovich.

Giddens, A. (1981) *A Contemporary Critique of Historical Materialism*. London: Macmillan Press; Berkeley: University of California Press.

Godelier, M. (1973) *Horizons: Trajets Marxistes en Anthropologie*. Paris: Maspero.

Hayden, D. (1981) *The Grand Domestic Revolution: A History of Feminist Designs for American Homes, Neighborhoods, and Cities*. Cambridge, MA: MIT Press.

Lynch, K. (1960) *The Image of the City*. Cambridge, MA: MIT Press.

Melling, J. (ed.) (1980) *Housing, Social Policy and the State*. London: Croom Helm.

Panofsky, E. (1957) *Gothic Architecture and Scholasticism*. New York: Meridian Books.

Raymond, H. et al. (1966) *Les Pavillonnaires*. Paris: Centre de Recherche d'Urbanisme.

Saunders, P. (1981) *Social Theory and the Urban Question*. London: Hutchinson.

Tafuri, M. (1968) *Teoriae e Storia della Achitettura*. Rome and Bari: Laterza.

Tafuri, M. (1973) *Progetto e Utopia: Architettura e Sviluppo Capitalistico*. Rome and Bari: Laterza.

2

The Economic Currency of Architectural Aesthetics

Paul Walter Clarke

My objective is to argue that the shift in architectural philosophy from modernism to postmodernism reflects a profound transition in advanced capitalism and accordingly in the production and control of space and space relations. It is a simple assertion that architecture costs money and occupies space. It is therefore integral to the production of space and the spatial configurations of the urbanism of our political economy. Not so simple is the assertion that architectural theories and aesthetics themselves possess political and economic significance. In other words, phenomena like modernism and postmodernism are political agendas; each confronts us not simply as a style, but rather as a cultural evocation which promotes and propels a range of very different urban phenomena.

This objective raises immediate questions: How do changes in the economy become manifest in the urban landscape? What was the engine that powered modernism and what now is the engine that propels postmodernism? The response to these questions demands an examination of urban, economic and architectural history. What follow are descriptions, first of the destructive tendencies of capitalism; second, how these tendencies facilitated the change from the industrial city to the corporate city and the role of modernism in this capitalist transition; and third, the further evolution of the corporate city with the requisite, ongoing destruction of its previous self and the role of postmodernism in this urban reorganization.

Before proceeding, certain caveats must be stated. Not all cultural production today is "postmodern"; neither postmodernism nor modernism is a holistic, homogeneous phenomenon. I will not attempt to make absolutely explicit, "stylistically," what is modern and what is postmodern. I do not consider either to be just an architectural "style" but to be cultural dominants that have architectural manifestations. Every era has contained within it the seeds of the subsequent era. I believe that the cultural phenomena of postmodernism was physically expressed in the "modernist" style. Hence I will be confusing what are typically considered distinct architectural styles. The argument I present is tentative, not plenary. My intention is neither to embrace modernism or postmodernism as a capitalist necessity nor to promote any argument for economic determinism. Subtleties and complexities characterize the physical and spatial operations of any society. The practice of architecture may be economically contingent, yet it is also capable of autonomous developments engendered by struggles, conflicts, innovations, contradictions and ambiguities.

Creative Destruction

A common perception is that the architecture of postmodernism arose from the failures of modern architecture. This is, at best, a naive truth; a simplistic formula for a complex reaction. Modernism concerns more than an architectural movement. Indeed, modernism radically changed the urban landscape of twentieth century capitalism. In that regard, modernism was a resounding success. However, this success was the result of its relationship to other parts of society. Success is seldom absolute. The awe inspired by our urban skylines is inhabited by a sense of dread. The forces that wrought these grand constructions are still in motion. As these buildings replaced earlier landscapes, so too will the newest architecture fall. Intentional destruction of the built environment is integral to the accumulation of capital. The emergence of postmodernism does not signal the demise of this "creative destruction."

"Built environment" is a simplistic title, of credible utility, for a complex assemblage of various constructions (roads, buildings, transit systems, utilities); each produced within specific conditions and according to various regulatory and financial strictures. The built environment is long-lived, difficult to alter, space specific, and absorbs large aggregates of capital. Its value must be maintained throughout its life in order to amortize the immense costs it entails. A proportion of this environment is at times used in common by capitalists and consumers. Nevertheless, even those elements privately appropriated (houses, shops, factories) are situated and utilized within an economic context and contribute immensely to the flow of capital. This suggests that the constellation of various elements that comprise the urban landscape must function as an ensemble. This characteristic, plus all the aforementioned characteristics, has implications for capitalist investment (Harvey, 1985, p. 16).

The elements of the built environment serve as a vast investment field for surplus capital. Consequently, through the process of capitalist development, urban form will be more and more affected by the exigencies of capitalist accumulation. If this argument appears tautological, it is presented because typically we have tended to view urban form fatalistically, as an inevitable corollary of advanced industrial (or now, "post-industrial") society. From this perspective, patterns of movement and settlement (from countryside to city, from center city to suburbs, from suburbs to "gentrified" center city) and spatial divisions of work and home, of commercial and residential districts, of upper-class and lower-class neighborhoods, of even week and weekend, appear to be politically neutral, forged outside of the economic system by pragmatic necessities. Such an impression has been an enduring myth until recently. It is being exorcised by a growing popular awareness, wrought by "deindustrialization" and massive loss of employment, that cities will atrophy if not redeveloped to facilitate and reinforce capitalist production and consumption. Otherwise investment will move elsewhere. This is not new and has been integral to the "free market" economy since before the inception of industrialization. Capitalism has a demonic appetite to build and to rebuild. Each new construction adds value to the urban matrix. The built environment both expands and expends capital. Construction in central city areas forces other enterprises and occupancies to the periphery. Construction in outlying areas gives greater worth to the center.

Buildings occupy space. If the location, not the building, becomes more valuable, then the existing building prevents the realization of that value. Under these circumstances, it is only through the destruction of old values in the build environment that new values can be created. With a voracious appetite, capitalism bites its own tail.

Capitalist development has therefore to negotiate a knife-edge path between preserving the exchange values of past capital investments in the built environment and destroying the value of these investments in order to open up fresh room for accumulation. Under capitalism there is, then, a perpetual struggle in which capital builds a physical landscape appropriate to its own condition at a particular moment in time, only to have to destroy it, usually in the course of a crisis, at a subsequent point in time. The temporal and geographic ebb and flow of investment in the built environment can be understood only in terms of such a process. The effects of the internal contradictions of capitalism, when projected into the specific context of fixed and immobile investment in the built environment, are thus write large in the historical geography of the landscape. (Harvey, 1978, p. 124)

Modernism is credited with the destruction of the traditional city and of its older neighborhood culture. But this destruction was inevitable. Haussmann could have died at birth, but Paris would still have had to be changed if capitalism was to be accommodated. If Le Corbusier had remained a watch engraver, corporate capitalism would have found a utopian image other than the *ville radieuse* with which to remodel its cities. Again I do not wish to portray an economically determined manifest destiny, but rather to illustrate that in all epochs, whatever the significance of his or her role, the architect has been subject to the "reason" of those in power (de Carlo, 1972, p. 9).

> The pathos of all monuments is that their material strength and solidity actually count for nothing and carry no weight at all, that they are blown away like frail reeds by the very forces of capitalist development that they celebrate. Even the most beautiful and impressive buildings are disposable and planned to be obsolete, closer in their social functions to tents and encampments than to "Egyptian pyramids, Roman Aqueducts, or Gothic cathedrals." (Berman, 1982, p. 99)

Capitalist cities are cities of constant flux. If the physical world offers a frame of reference for what is "constant," then the latent power of the physical ordering of the world must be contradicted, even destroyed. This was essential for the success of modernism and the legacy of this constant destruction has contributed to the essence of postmodernism: a tenuousness, a new superficiality, a "depthlessness" (Jameson, 1984, pp. 60–2). The critical question for architects is what processes of legitimation arise to mask this violence?

Modernism and the Crucial Value of Image

By mid-nineteenth century, the dominant economic character of cities shifted from centers of commerce to centers of production. What followed was the era of emerging monopoly capitalism, of robber barons, and the extension and refinement of the factory system. The transition from commercial accumulation to industrial accumulation wrought immense urban upheaval. No capitalist city escaped some change and most underwent radical and traumatic alteration. Huge factories were concentrated in downtowns near rail and water heads. Working class housing districts emerged in central locations, segregated in various districts by class. The middle and upper classes fled from the center city as fast and as far as their affluence permitted (Gordon, 1977, p. 99). Many pieces of literature describe the horrific conditions of the land speculation that preyed upon the working class in the industrial city: from Dickens, to Riis, to Engels.[1] Only the most desperate of conditions forced the laboring classes to submit to capitalist exploitation. While the hegemony of industry left a minimum of opportunities for manifestations of independence, there was resistance, urban riots and unionization.

The Industrial Revolution could hardly proceed without Labor. The working class had to be accommodated, at least to the point of their compliance. The subsequent, bourgeois, urban reform movement that followed was to prove more pro-capitalist than pro-labor. Gordon very convincingly argues that the fundamental transformation of our cities from industrial to corporate in character came not so much from the obvious innovations in technology that allowed production to leave the center city, or from the economies of administrative agglomeration that warranted the geographic separation of administration from production; but from the capitalist drive to control labor (Gordon, 1977, pp. 100–3). The co-optation of labor occurred, in part, through the mediations of newly formed professions;

among them, law, medicine, social work, and germane to this discussion, architecture. The requisite urbanism for industrialization gestated modernism, which, in turn, was instrumental in the later urban reorganization that produced the corporate city of the mid-twentieth century. This period also brought the full flowering of the professionalization of architecture. These are not unrelated phenomena.

The architect is, by convention, identified with the ruling powers of society. The ruling power has universally been the only force capable of amassing and supplying capital, materials, land, and the authority to act; typically considered prerequisites for architecture. Prior to the Industrial Revolution, architects, for the most part, came from the ranks of the ruling elite. They designed for their own class. Architectural objects had as their subject the architect's own class. This changed with the rise of industrial accumulation and this change had great significance in the formation of the architectural credos of modernism.

Typical of an avant-garde, the early modernists of the 1920s attempted to divorce themselves from the practices of the dominant regime. Their program called for the elimination of concepts of form in the sense of fixed or traditional types. Formal ordering methods of the Beaux Arts and other historical architecture were scorned as the architectural representation of an exploitive and moribund society. Historical styles were also viewed as having been made obsolete by innovations in techniques and materials. The modernists sought a vernacular of modern technology that would address and satisfy the shelter crisis of the new concentration of urban populations. Furthermore the new architecture was to be *functional*, developing out of the exact determination of needs and "practical demands" (van Does-berg, 1970, p. 78). The struggle was to evolve a language of form premised upon a minimum of costly ornamentation and traditional labor-intensive construction.[2] The geometric play of proportions, new materials and color would give significant richness to the new architecture. The intended economy of means gave credence to the exhaltation of spareness as a style. Having dismissed previous architectural paradigms, the modernists substituted their own: universal space, column grids, moveable wall planes, and an asymmetrical and nonhierarchical orientation; all signifying an architectural intent to create an egalitarian society.

Modern architecture is surely most cogently to be interpreted as a gospel...its impact may be seen as having very little to do with either its technological innovations or its formal vocabulary. Indeed the value of these could never have been so much what they seemed as what they signified...they were didactic illustrations, to be apprehended not so much for themselves but as the indices of a better world, of a world where rational motivation would prevail and where all the more visible institutions of the political order would have been swept into the irrelevant limbo of the superseded and forgotten...its ideal...was to exhibit the virtues of an apostolic poverty, of a quasi-Franciscan *Existenz minimum*...one definition of modern architecture might be that it was an attitude towards building which was divulging in the present that more perfect order which the future was about to disclose. (Rowe and Koetter, 1978, p. 11)

Unfortunately, the new style as an image supplanted the initial social intent. While a new architecture was created, it proved to have a negligible effect on the social order. Housing for the masses became confused as mass housing. The aesthetic of pure geometry – the unadorned cube – was mistaken as a desired end unto itself. The opposition to ornament became a pursuit of new visual patterns and not, as was initially proclaimed, the elimination of visual determinants of design. The agenda of social reform was divested. The concern that a building *employ* rational methods in its design was eclipsed by the concern that a building *appear* rational.

The style of the pure and unadorned object has enigmatic corollaries. It signifies that the object is separate from social meaning.

The object has no history and continues no history. It is ahistorical. Meaning and form are independent; the object has only to refer to itself to be legitimate. The purity of the object is untainted because the object has no subject. All of these are futile assertions, the stuff of myths.

However, if as stated earlier, modern architecture was a resounding success, it was because its mystifications were essential for an economy that was destroying in order to create. It was an economy which appropriated the practice of architecture and which alienated the very act of *dwelling* and called it *housing*. The architect was no longer designing for her or his class. The housing, factories, schools, "public" libraries, warehouses, and other new building types were commissioned by the capitalist class, but not occupied by them, and certainly not occupied by architects. The subject of these objects was not the working classes, although indeed, they inhabited them. The subject was capitalism. The modernist architects were the first to have disenfranchised "clients." Objectified by a mode of production, the laboring masses were further objectified by an architectural philosophy which did not respect history, that rebelled against notions of class and thereby refused to recognize the continued relations of class. It was a philosophy of universal norms, unconcerned with aspects of existing culture since its proposed architecture was the vanguard of a new "emancipating" culture. The major success of the modernists was the creation of a model of utilitarian construction and a rationale for it. This model was then appropriated and debased by the very economic forces from which the model was to be the salvation.

The so-called Modernist architecture ... devoted itself to the cultivation of the fantasy that the *appearance* of lifeless objects could gratify man [or woman] and relieve him [or her] from the anxiety and terror of oppression. By ostracizing the ornament and emphasizing the significance of the surface structural relations as the vessels of contained functions, it was thought that the building could be made a rational product, that the consumer was obtaining indeed a utility, a real one, and not a signifier of value. However, the exposure of the structural skeleton, the articulations of functions, the adoption of elementary geometric forms, did not in the least make the skeleton more effective or improve the contained functions; these were all attempts to build up a new visual vocabulary for a language that now had a new purpose, the temporary abandonment of power to the producer of rapidly obsolescing products. (Tzonis, 1972, p. 87)

Modernists, like any avant-garde, ignored existing material. In fact, they encouraged its destruction on the basis that it was decadent, obsolete, a fetter to real progress and true creativity. The early modernists appropriated the technology of modern capitalism and, in so doing, also embraced the social logic of that technology regardless of how neutral they considered it. The modernist movement was utopian in aim but wasn't, and couldn't be, within capitalism. It was a utopia of objects – a revolution of objects. The failure of modernism was not simply in the architecture, but in the social logic behind it. That logic was that the object is neutral; outside of social relationships.

Ultimately the modernist stance was defensive and insular, a trait still endemic to an architectural culture which prefers "to deduce from its own centre what could have only been found by a complete and unprejudiced analysis of the ways in which the mythical *society* being addressed decodes, distorts, transforms, makes factual use of the messages launched by the *builders of images*" (Tafuri, 1980, p. 103).

The modernist city has yet to be built as the shanty towns of Brasìlia painfully illustrate. Nevertheless, it was under the cosmetic of modernism that the corporate city arose from the contradictions of the industrial city. To be sure, industrial activity continued within the corporate realm which ultimately depended upon the production and realization of value. A new distinction was that these operations and tendencies were guided by the decisions of fewer and much larger economic bodies which sought legitimations in various forms, not the least of which was architecture. Equally crucial was that economic production increasingly included the production of space and long-term investments in land improvements. The "builders of images" were integrally involved as the centers of cities became more and more dominated by central business districts comprised of towering corporate skyscrapers.

While the corporate city and the skyscraper were epiphenomena of the same economy – a roughly tuned engine and its hood ornaments – it is paradoxical that, symbolically, the two were mutually antagonistic. The corporate city was distinguished from the industrial city by several characteristics. Administration and production became geographically separated. Manufacturing moved rapidly away from the center of the city rather than being concentrated at its center. Corporate icons spiked the landscape of the central business districts, the chosen locale for key control and command functions of business and high finance. It was also critical that the city became politically balkanized, fragmented into hundreds of separate urban and suburban jurisdictions. This trait is significant in that manufacturing was able to escape, across legal fences, the conflicts and contradictions brought by the centralization of large masses of labor in the industrial city. What had previously proven efficient had become a liability (Gordon, 1977, p. 102). The city and its hinterland were being reorganized as a single realm for corporate efficiency. This efficiency was not complete; there was some confusion between the dancers and the dance. The skyscraper was emblematic of the paradox that, while each phase of capitalism has engendered a commensurate form of urbanism, certain factors of urbanism operate, at times, in an autonomous fashion. Land speculation and the production of space are prominent examples.

The skyscraper was an "event," as an "anarchic individual" that, by projecting its image into the commercial center of the city, creates an unstable equilibrium between the independence of the single corporation and the organization of collective capital.

The single building operations within the city, as speculative ventures, entered into conflict with the growing need for control over the urban center as a structurally functional whole. In the face of the problem of ensuring the efficiency of the central business district in terms of integrated functions, the exaltation of the "individuality" of the skyscraper in downtown Manhattan, already dramatically congested, was an anachronism. The corporations, still incapable of conceiving the city as a comprehensive service of development, in spite of their power, were also incapable of organizing the physical structures of the business center as a single coordinated entity. (Tafuri, 1979, pp. 390–1)

In a corporate world, architecture is image. The skyscraper is the epitome of the centralization of power. It is also sunk capital which must have credentials in the marketplace. As a building program, the office tower consists of accretions of cellular spaces or open, continuous, modular spaces. It is a building type that has remained stubbornly the same.

Being of recent origin, this building type lacks a well established iconography deriving its legitimacy from precedents, and unlike the town hall, the museum, or the railway station, it is endlessly repeated within our city centers. Paradoxically a lot of its success will rest on its distinctiveness from its surroundings, inasmuch as it is meant to represent and advertise the power of corporations or of commercial organizations. Therefore, the office building as a semantically neutral type is yet most likely to be dressed in a seductive image. (Pertuiset, 1986, p. 87)

The Tribune Tower competition of 1922 documented the inventory of architectural skins and the construction almost proved the inelasticity of neoclassicism as regards height. A more pliable skin for this urban metamorphosis was Art Deco; an aesthetic of industrialized art nouveau (to turn the eye of the elder avant garde while the younger still struggled for legitimacy), a machined "Arts and Craft" (labor, if not accommodated, must at least be heralded), the last aesthetic gasp of the Beaux Arts that recognized much of the modernists' formal agenda despite the chiseled surfaces.

The shift in seductive images, from Deco to the pure modernist skin of taut, Miesian, graph-paper facades enveloping Platonic volumes, bridges a chasm of infinite tears: the Depression and the second World War.[3] The trauma of these years further deteriorated urban conditions and fostered, within popular consciousness, the rejection of the traditional city. The Great Depression was considerably more than a crisis of underconsumption. However, it appeared as such and the capitalist class responded to it as such. Despite the New Deal, the Depression was ended by the defense spending of World War II. Fear of the Depression (among other fears) has since maintained defense spending in the subsequent Cold War. Thus appeared a corollary of the corporate city; the Keynesian city (Harvey, 1985, pp. 202–11). This response was another transformation of the urban process, one in which corporate accumulation forged a new spatial dynamic. Shaped as consumption artifacts, the social, economic, political and physical attributes of capitalist cities depended upon state-backed, debt-financed consumption. Several features warrant discussion since they contributed to the increasing dependency upon image.

The Keynesian City

First, federal policies, the zoning practices of the politically fragmented, metropolitan regions, the uneven, geographic investment patterns of banking institutions, the real estate developers and the construction industry all contributed to the creation of sprawling, extensive, single-family housing developments in the 50s and 60s. The massive increase of single-family homes intensified the isolation and separation of individual families from their communities and class. The consequence of this was that the search for identity was collapsed into innumerable consumer choices ranging from the prestige value of house and neighborhood to "better schools for the children." Architectural images were just one mode of these distinctions. New enclaves of class exclusion and racial segregation underwrote the suburban dream.

Second, the sprawling, circumferential development of the Keynesian city was reinforced by the energy, auto and highway construction industries. Auto and highway development accentuated the disadvantanges of the older central cities and further reinforced people's isolation within the metropolis.

Third, when manufacturing employment moved outside of the center city, financial and real estate interests and city governments ("coalitions for growth"), intent upon maintaining the value of municipal investments in infrastructure, realized that their mutual interests could be advanced only if more and more corporate headquarters located in their central business districts. The modernist program became bureaucratically operational in "urban renewal." "Decaying," "blighted," "slum" districts were "cleared" for "redevelopment." Demolition and renewal occurred to an extent previously unknown. These programs of renewal had the effect of pushing the poor into more crowded quarters and, in many cases, vacating vast downtown tracts of land for long ghostly periods of "incubation" (Gordon, 1977, p. 107).

These three traits illustrate how powerful growth coalitions promoted their own interests through urban renewal and suburbanization. Creative destruction became geographically disparate. The suburbs were created as the neighborhoods of the center city were destroyed. New instrumentalities were forged in the practices of finance capital and federal, state and local government. The consequence was ideological control "to ensure that consumer sovereignty was sovereign in the right way, that it produce rational consumption in relation to accumulation through the expansion of certain key industrial sectors (autos, household equipment, oil and so forth)" (Harvey, 1985, p. 211). By the sixties, America had very different-looking cities of low-density sprawl, with distinctive spaces of consumption (rural to suburban to center-city) premised on "strange significations of life-style and social status etched into a landscape of unrelieved consumerism" (ibid.). Many of these traits of "demandside" urbanization would prove even more invidious in the next phase of capitalism.

The Spread of Modernism

What of modernism? Why did this imagery, fashioned and championed in the twenties and thirties, become so widely subscribed to by corporations in the fifties and sixties? The skyscrapers of the fifties were exemplary in that, while still emblematic of corporate values, they appealed to ideals higher and more widely respected than those of business. In that decade, modernism was not the credo of an avant garde but was the anthem of a rebuilding society and an expanding economy. For two decades, during the Depression and World War II, construction of all types was thwarted; initially for lack of capital and then, during the war, there was a surplus of capital frustrated by a lack of materials. The fifties were the postponed gratification of twenty years of austerity. Madison Avenue was not lax in helping to establish the anthem: "There is a Ford in your future!" That future became the present in the Eisenhower years. American cities had changed during the war; rural exodus from agricultural reorganization, combined with urban employment, brought American cities to their greatest and densest populations ever. Popular, middle-class sentiment was that the cities, changed, had to be rechanged. The modernist cry of sunlight and air and open green spaces gave credence to the suburbs and an image to the urban renaissance. Architecture was the visible evidence that governments and corporations were involved in building the future. The open space of Seagram's Plaza was a "gift" to Manhattan. It did not matter that it was a *quid pro quo* for a zoning variance of greater height for the Seagram's Tower. Ignored in this era of middle-class and corporate affluence, of

urban demolition and frenzied construction, was the popular anti-business sentiment created by the Depression. This sentiment still had credence with the poorer classes who resided within the urban renewal zones and within the highway easements. Now, however, it was the state as the instrument of urban renewal that bore the backlash.

Postmodernism, Commodity Reification and Symbolic Capital

The prosperity of the Keynesian city had considerable costs which reached crisis proportions in the late sixties and early seventies. This period defies a short description. The Civil Rights Movement, the Vietnam War, urban riots, the anti-war movement and the student revolts, all had complex and subtle consequences in urban politics. Notions of neighborhood and community became central in the formation of resistance to continued urban transformation. Resistance was not limited to the neighborhood conservation struggles of the besieged urban poor. Suburbanites pushed for "limits to growth." The production of space became impeded by a sensitivity to *place*. The final ravages of urban renewal is not so distant that it needs to be recounted here. In short, the future that was promised proved unacceptable. Much of the modernist vision that had been constructed was experienced as barren and fragmented landscapes; one more form of alienation in a society and time almost awash in strife and angst. Modernism seemed exhausted at the same time as the economic engine faltered. The postwar strategies of the Keynesian program eroded as revived world trade increased foreign competition in durable and consumer goods. Inflationary financing temporarily assuaged the falling capacity of the economy to absorb further investments. In the search for the highest rate of return, a wave of international lending that culminated in the weakening of the dollar and the international debt crisis of the eighties.

It bears repeating that the inherent and ineluctable character of capitalist urbanization is flux and that crisis is a significant mode of transition for capitalism. The recession of 1973, the "stagflation" of the late 1970s, and the "Reagan" recession of 1981–82 have produced subsequent phenomena of shrinking commercial markets, vast unemployment, rapid shifts in the global division of labor (indicated by plant closings, "deindustrialization,"[4] capital flight, and technological and financial reorganization). Harvey is an excellent observer and commentator on the effects of this crisis on urbanism and the built environment:

> When monetary policy was tightened in response to spiraling inflation in 1973, the boom of fictitious capital formation [e.g.: land speculation] came to an abrupt end, the cost of borrowing rose, property markets collapsed..., and local governments found themselves on the brink of...the traumas of fiscal crisis. Capital flows into the creation of physical and social infrastructures...slowed at the same time as recession and fiercer competition put the efficiency and productivity of such investments firmly on the agenda.... The problem was to try to rescue or trim as much of that investment as possible without massive devaluations of physical assets and destruction of services offered. The pressure to rationalize the urban process and render it more efficient and cost-effective was immense.
>
> And to the degree that urbanization had become part of the problem, so it had to be part of the solution. The result was a fundamental transformation of the urban process after 1973. It was, of course, a shift in emphasis rather than a total revolution.... It had to transform the urban legacy of preceding eras and was strictly limited by the quantities, qualities, and configurations of those raw materials.
>
> The question of the proper organization of production came back center stage after a generation or more of building an urban process around the theme of demandled growth. (Harvey, 1985, pp. 212–13)

Harvey addresses the question: In the 1980s, how can urban regions, blessed largely with a demand-side heritage, adapt to a new supply-side world? He lists four current practices, none of them mutually exclusive, none without serious political ramifications and economic risks and none without some requisite form of destruction and re-creation. The following is a synopsis of Harvey's descriptions (ibid., pp. 215–18).

First, cities can aggressively compete within the spatial division of labor to improve their productive capacity. Efforts in this regard are to attract new industry to an area. Typical of this competition are the recent lobbying of state governments vying for the location of domestic production plants of foreign automobile manufacturers. The overall, long term effect of this type of competition is seldom beneficial. Typically, the concessions granted to entice an industry to relocate are considerable, with short-fall gains and long-term liabilities.[5] A vast repertoire of resources is necessary for successful enticement of industry: infrastructure ranging from highway and transit systems to quality academic institutions, capital resources and finance opportunities, and finally, a surplus of skilled labor power. Labor often has not benefited from this competition since union contracts and innovative, labor-saving technologies are often included in the negotiations of concessions.

Second, urban regions can seek to improve their competitive position with respect to the spatial division of consumption. This entails more than expenditures made by tourism, considerable as they may be. Demand-side urbanization has, since the end of World War II, focused energy and investment upon significance of life-style, the construction of "community," and the organization of space in terms of the signs and symbols of prestige, status and power. This urbanization has constantly expanded the opportunities for participation in such consumerism while concurrently distinguishing its class exclusivity, since recession, unemployment, and the high cost of credit forecloses participation by significant numbers of the population. This form of interurban competition is incredibly risky as investments that establish a prestigious living environment, and that seek to enhance "quality of life," are anything but cheap. In this endeavor, image is paramount.

Examples abound: Ghiradelli Square in San Francisco, Faneuil Hall in Boston, Harbor Place in Baltimore, Union Station in St Louis, Renaissance Center in Detroit. Even recent corporate headquarters, the Humana Tower of Louisville or the Proctor and Gamble Expansion contribute to this urban competition of status and consumer attraction. An example, as yet unresolved, is that of Oakland, Phoenix, Memphis, Jacksonville and Baltimore, who are all petitioning the National Football League for franchises. Baltimore, in efforts to retain its baseball team and to obtain a NFL team, has proposed a $200 million, two stadium, 85-acre development near its downtown inner harbor (Schmidt and Barnes, 1987). It should be clear that this urban clamor for prestige and life-style is not a new trend (consider the Sydney Opera House, or even the Paris Opera House). However, particularly telling is the linkage to overall, urban economic health and the competitive anxiety that has fostered these recent constructions. The result is an inner urban dichotomy of the construction of locales of conspicuous consumption within a sea of insidious austerity. Indeed, the Paris Opera House is the true precursor of this malaise.

Third, metropolitan areas can compete for those key control and command functions of conglomerates, high finance and government that embody immense power over all manner of activities and spaces. This competition fosters and protects centers of finance capital, of information gathering and control, and of government decision-making. Competition of this sort demands a careful strategy of infrastructure provision. Within a worldwide network of transport and communication, centrality and efficiency are paramount. This necessitates immense expenditures in airports, rapid transit, communication systems. Adequate office space is a requisite for this competition and it depends upon a public-private coalition of property developers, banking financiers, and public interest groups capable of anticipating and responding to possible needs. Here, also, architectural image is significant. The consolidated locations of the electronics indus-

try are exemplary: Silicon Valley in California and the redevelopment of Route 128 outside Boston. This bicoastal domination was recently challenged by the efforts of the state of Texas to establish Austin and the University of Texas as the major American research and development center of electronics.

Fourth, the Keynesian program is not entirely gone. Huge expenditures on redistribution, the defense budget chief among them, present opportunities for regional and urban competition. The federally-financed, multibillion, super cyclotron is one current example of the awards possible from this type of competition.

The Postmodern City

Cities are following the path of these four trends. The resulting shifts – some radical, some subtle – in spatial constraints and in the production of urban space have allowed geographical redispersion of production, consumption, and speculative investment on a very large, national and, at times, international scale. The net effect is an exacerbated state of intra-city, inter-city, inter-state, inter-regional and inter-national competition. Such fragmentation is realized within a skin of desperate utopian imagery. All these traits were present before the 1970s and 1980s However, the speed, appearance and general character are newly distinctive. The flexibility and alacrity of corporate and state bureaucratic institutions and small enterpreneurs to adapt and respond to, and even promote, the rate of change is unique to the present. Harvey has called this current period of late capitalism the era of *flexible accumulation* (Harvey, 1987).

Concurrent with flexible accumulation, aesthetic production has become more integrated into commodity production. As Fredric Jameson argues, there is a frantic economic urgency to produce more environments with the appearance of novelty at greater rates of turnover (Jameson, 1984, p. 56). This is the structural role of postmodernism: aesthetic innovation and experimentation to support flexible accumulation.

Flexible accumulation is subsumed in postmodernism and this reflects the demise of the welfare state and of the architectural credos of modernism. The naiveté of universal norms and of ideal environments for living and working is lost. There is little security in this process because flexible accumulation makes long-range planning horizons unrealistic. "Creative destruction" no longer advances under the single umbrella of a grand, unified ideological system. Postmodernism is a cultural equivocation that allows for divergence and heterogeneity. The term signifies a directionality, but no destination. Its architectural agenda suggests an antithesis. Modernism denied history, postmodernism embraces it. Modernism ravaged the landscape of the city, postmodernism respects the existing context and culture of urban life. Modernism disdained existing culture, postmodernism endorses it in all its "popular" forms. Modernism ignored vernacular prototypes, postmodernism elaborates typologies of all origins. It is difficult to give a comprehensive survey of postmodernism since its boundaries and strictures are so amorphous. However, postmodernism has a legacy from modernism it has yet to contradict. The current fabrications of architects are solitary objects divorced from their subjects. We may no longer be talking of the unadorned cube as the aesthetic model, but still remaining are fragmented social relationships, different and yet similar to those of modernism. "The alienation of the subject has been displaced by the fragmentation of the subject" (ibid., p. 63).

The field is now one of stylistic and discursive heterogeneity that lacks any great collective project in an epoch of great collective need. Exchange-value has been exalted by such religious zeal that the very memory of use-value is tantamount to sacrilege (ibid., p. 66). The capture of exchange value (value realized only through the market system – speculation is one form) is preeminently the creation of image.

In the business of renting commercial space . . . developers must concentrate on at-

tracting tenants from other buildings by providing a superior situation both physically and financially. The nature of their business tempts them to focus on short term benefits rather than long-term stability. Their buildings must be seductive, trendy, and as inexpensive as possible to build. (Drummond, 1986, p. 74)

With few exceptions, newer buildings age faster, but their tenuousness is due to more than insubstantial construction. It is also due to the vacuousness of image. Jameson uses the word "depthlessness," the virtual deconstruction of the very aesthetic of expression itself, to describe this condition. The "depth" models of modernism have generally been repudiated: essence and appearance, latent and manifest, authenticity and inauthenticity, and the opposition between signifier and signified. "Depth is replaced by surface or by multiple surfaces." The medium decries the lack of a message. As Debord comments: "The image has become the final form of commodity reification" (quoted in Jameson, 1984, p. 66).

Symbolic Capital

What *commodity reification* is to Debord is *symbolic capital* to Harvey (Harvey, 1987). Symbolic capital is the collection of luxury goods attesting to the taste and distinction of the owner. Symbolic capital describes little that is new. Yet, coupled with flexible accumulation, the term greatly enhances descriptions of gentrification (the usurpation of the place and history of "others"), the recuperation of "history" (real, fantasies, re-created, usurped, or assembled as pastiche), the idealization of "community" (real or as consumable commodity), and the role of ornament and "style" with which to establish codes and symbols of distinction. Creative destruction is integral to the pursuit of symbolic capital. This is true even with current projects of architectural rehabilitation and preservation where a structure is reconstituted but destroyed as a cultural and historic symbol.

Money capital itself became unstable in the 1970s due to inflation. Economic recessions forced the exploration of product differentiation, hence the desire to seek symbolic capital surged in the production of the built environment. The ability to convert symbolic capital into money capital is inherent in the cultural politics of the contemporary urban process.[6] Flexible accumulation has become the mobilization of image – the employment of spectacle within the urban arena. Disneyland becomes an urban strategy.

Despite the seductive images, and deference to the context in which they are placed, these Disneylands seem alien. They seem alien because they are components of an urban scheme that appears familiar, yet remains stubbornly vague; that appears vibrant in spirit, but aloof in engagement; and alien because our cities are becoming more and more fragmented with these postmodern visions. This fragmentation occurs because symbolic capital must distinguish itself. It must define its edges to protect itself as a symbol and to protect itself as investment. As such, it cannot be "infill" within the urban continuum. It has to be a separate event. The fragmentation of our cities is a result of multiple attempts to impose order, the success of which depends entirely on how geographically discrete the imposition is made.

This fragmentation of the landscape of daily life can have banal manifestations. Recently constructed shopping malls reveal the endorsement of, for lack of a better term, *one-way portals*. The entrances from the malls into the major anchors of the development, the department stores, are highly visible on the mall side. The doors typically are framed with heavy mouldings, are centered in a dramatically modulated wall and are usually axially located with the concourse, which itself expands in width in proximity to the entry. Few architectural tactics are ignored in celebrating the promise of the domain beyond the door. Once inside the door, the circulation of the department store tends to be a circular path that leads both right and left; the means of vertical circulation is usually not directly visible from this entry. Exploration is mandatory.

Whereas the path of the mall is explicit and informing; now, within the store, the path is ambiguous. The circular track defies orientation. It occasionally jogs or splits around distracting display obstacles. Indeed, the entire path and environment is beguiling. To return takes effort. Not remembering having entered past the perfume counters (or whatever), the search for re-entry back into the mall is difficult. The door you thought was the one you first entered leads to the parking lot. The exit doors are all remarkably similar. The architecture obnoxiously asserts that the department store is a shopping mall unto itself. Your return to the mall is obviated. The store's entry into the mall is judged not as important as the mall entry into the store. The portal to the mall which, on the mall side, has a high ceiling, has a low ceiling within the store. The wall it pierces is like many of the interior walls of the store, ladened with racks or shelves. On first encounter, the irritation is subliminal. The second time, the irritation is conscious and you learn the appropriate clues so as not to repeat the mistake. Our cities likewise render us lost. We travel their landscape awkwardly, our bodies invent and rely upon stutter-steps as we navigate the terrain.[7]

Postmodernist spaces, like modernist spaces, refuse to speak of what is "outside." They are secular spaces that depend upon the city, yet deny the inherent interconnectiveness of daily life within the city. One can walk to Faneuil Hall from the Boston Government Center or from the Financial District. As you cross the street into the commercial zone, the compression is almost palpable. Faneuil Hall is vibrant with crowds, the pace is immediately fatiguing. The human frame reacts with anxiety – to shopping, eating, working, or the throngs of tourists one has to negotiate. Does this anxiety stem from the fact that if you wish to participate in this place, or even linger here, you must spend money?[8]

Similarly, enter any of Portman's Hyatt Regency's. Follow the structure's perverted *marche* across the celebrated atrium that has all the charm and grace of a missile silo, enter the glass elevator capsules that beckon you upward for the view inward and outward. Upon your arrival you will be greeted by a host or hostess inquiring whether it will be drinks or dinner. Some may argue that you are being "served," but you are an object in this enterprise.

When Haussmann cut the boulevards through Paris, Baudelaire observed one interesting and vital aspect of the café culture that ensued: one could participate in the public realm and still maintain one's anonymity. With the privatization of the public realm that is occurring today, this is jeopardized. You are not anonymous when using your credit card. Nor are you anonymous if your social status is revealed by your inability to participate in the spending.

The Piazza d'Italia, with its St Joseph's Fountain, has become an integral part of the identity of New Orleans, especially if you view recent cinema. Completed in 1978, designed by Perez and Associates and Charles Moore, the Piazza was heralded, for a while, as one of the major events of postmodernism (Filler, 1978). The Piazza, a monument to the contribution of the Italian community to the cultural vitality of New Orleans, is an architectural Mardi Gras, seemingly a "Fat Tuesday" float permanently moored in a warehouse district near the central business district. Classicizing details run amok in this vibrant, dizzying, tumultuous construction. Historic elements that allude to the permanence of architecture are sliced and chopped and then reassembled into an ethereal, "depthless" pastiche of the Fontana di Trevi of Rome and possibly the Palace of Fine Arts of San Francisco. Pseudo-Corinthian columns have neon necking while adjacent columns with stainless-steel Composite capitals have water-jet "socks." The shafts of other columns are omitted and replaced by a cylinder of water flowing from the bottom of suspended Doric capitals. The space is animated with the dancing pet of the Piazza: water. Water spraying, spritzing, flowing, exploding, coursing, churning, the centerpiece of which is a eighty-foot long, three-dimensional map of the Italian peninsula with the island of Sicily

at the focal center of the Piazza. The contours shimmer with the water of three fountains emanating from the locations of the Po, Arno and Tiber Rivers cascading down to two basins representing the Tyrrhenian and Adriatic Seas.

By 1985, when I visited it, the Piazza seemed aged well beyond its few years. Vandalism and grafiffiti testified that this was not the "people-place" it was intended to be. The stucco surfaces had weathered poorly and other elements were being eroded by the coursing waters of the fountains. The Piazza, with its fountains, was to be the initial investment of an urban renewal scheme to revitalize an "underused" area near the central business district. The revitalization has not occurred and therein lies the fate of the Piazza. To its developers, it remains a rhinestone in the mud. As architecture, the Piazza is a fiction. Its choreography is without people. It has no resident neighborhood to occupy and nurture it and it has, as yet, no infrastructure to sustain it. Its proximity to the central business district is labored and it has fallen victim to the very context it was intended to change. The Piazza stands as the frustrated prophet of a redevelopment which it may not survive. Recently the Piazza has been a locale for two different movies, *Tightrope* and *The Big Easy*. Incredibly, in each movie a dead body is discovered deposited in St Joseph's Fountain. Paradoxically, both of these police-detective stories – fiction – treat the Piazza more realistically, that is, as an empty place, than the architecture itself. It is more a potential space than a real place.

The fiction and mythology of postmodernism is not lost on its practitioners, some of whom are candid, yet unapologetic:

The people who live in these buildings are of course like everyone else running around earning the money to live in such places and they never really sit on the chair on the porch, gazing at the sea, anymore than you sit in the Piazza and look leisurely at the Duomo. You rush around and take two seconds for a cup of coffee, but those moments imagined, are the anchors which make it possible to survive. That is the price of our modern condition. We must have that memory and tradition, even if it has to become its own myth, if we are to survive in the present. (Stern, 1987)

To repeat, American cities are becoming more dominated by these potential spaces that will forever be denied the authenticity of *place*. The peristyle court of Kohn, Pedersen and Fox's Proctor and Gamble Headquarters expansion was celebrated as a wonderful addition of green space to the city of Cincinnati, whose overburdened Fountain Square was the only downtown, public outdoor space. The court, bifurcated by a busy city street, is separated from the Headquarters by a wide ceremonial drive and is, at its outer edges, divorced from the city by broad, heavy traffic avenues. This green apron serves neither as a physical extension of the headquarters nor as an oasis for the city, although both uses were promised by its promotion. It is an Arcadian view from corporate windows. The ambulatory of the trellised colonnades is raised several feet above the sidewalk and above the interior green. This grass surface, consequently, is not visible to a distant pedestrian. From outside, the effect is more wall than space. This is no accident of design. The court is a space of power, nothing else. This space is not for habitation; it is not for the city. The embroidered void is an appropriate symbol and, as symbolic capital, it is more symbol than capital. And, in case the message is not clear from across the avenues, the entries are frequently draped with stainless-steel chains barring passage. In a design that is adamantly aloof, the chain is not redundant. The spaces of power require defense.

Union Station, St Louis, is the latest progeny of the Ghiradelli Square, "bread and festival," interurban, shopping emporiums. The station and its hotel have been lavishly restored and the train shed, reputed to be the largest in the world, now covers several concourses of shops and an additional hotel. The scrupulous restoration of the original station and hotel establishes the rich character of the redevelopment. However, as one ventures

through the shops, towards the rear, the design loses the clarity that the original buildings establish. The lagoon and the stages are the awkward transition from the enclosed shops to the parking lot which occupies the majority of the sheltered area of the shed. The ethos of the grandiloquent station was as an entry to St Louis. Despite its grandeur, it had a calculated deference to the city. It was a processional threshold to the city. It was part of the city. Now, the spirit of its redevelopment is the introverted specter of the suburban shopping mall. The outcome is confusion; one is always *behind* the station, not *at* the station. The parking lot, given prominent space under the shed, confirms that this mall has no center. The original station and hotel are reduced to a stage front, yet this architecture is so dense and majestic that it eclipses its own redevelopment. Here, as in other urban renovations of existing monuments, the rehabilitation of a significant building has stripped them of symbolism. The building remains, pristinely reclaimed, but its cultural identity is destroyed. It is history appropriated.

Surely at some time during the preliminary phase of the Union Station design, someone must have suggested that passenger train service be restored to the rear of the train shed, however diminished that service may now be. Then the ethos of the original design could be reclaimed and expanded to the full length of the train shed. It would be a station, an entry to the city, a part of the city, not the fragmented island that redevelopment has made of it.[9] Just as surely, that idea must have been dismissed because those that now ride the trains are not the shoppers that the developers cared to entertain. The station, a monument to the industrial city and its ruling class, long vacant and devalued, has been reclaimed as symbolic capital for a new city and a new ruling elite, apparently less tolerant than the age of the robber barons.

A change in taste can devalue symbolic capital. One can tire of Disneyland. And what of "bread and festivals" when there is little bread to be shared? More festivals?

The Critical Value of Image: The Return of the Subject

We need more festivals, but not the urban placebos that are currently being produced. We need an architecture that initiates a movement toward human fulfillment, not an architecture that accommodates human existence in a less than humane world. Creative destruction must be harnessed to a vision in which harmful mystifications and legitimations are destroyed and potentialities for human growth are created.

Postmodernism, as an ideology, purports to embrace history, respect context, endorse "popular" forms of culture, and elaborate vernacular typologies. Certain questions are troubling: Whose history? Whose notion of context? Whose vernacular? Whose "popular" culture? A result of genuine tradition or another product of a consumer economy? These questions, and others, have not been asked, and, having not been asked, the drafted line will never negotiate the potent issues they address. The quality of architecture must be premised upon a critical and attentive exploration of the instances of creative participation that are typically labeled "disorder" (de Carlo, 1972, p. 19). "Any theory of the city must be, at its starting point, a theory of social conflict" (Castells, 1983, p. 318). We need to reestablish the pure terms of the class struggle, an often maligned and misunderstood Marxist term, yet a powerful and potentially joyous term. This struggle must recognize the truth of the present moment, that is, the truth of postmodernism – i.e., that ours is a world of multinational corporations and flexible accumulation. We cannot retrieve aesthetic practices that were responses to historical moments that no longer exist. With struggle and participation, architectural objects can have an authentic subject. The image can be liberative, it can have critical content and allow for pluralist interpretation. And the operations that govern architectural production are open to productive questioning.

These are easy truths to some, heresy to others, and bombastic irrelevance to many. In a world needing radical change, perhaps not everyone needs to be a radical (although I would certainly welcome more radicals). Nevertheless, even the conservative position can acknowledge the interconnections of architectural and economic history. Quite often, architects are the vocal critics of the current condition, within the very creation of which they are tremendously instrumental. The profession must become an arena of discourse that engages with, and beyond, itself. This can begin in our schools, in our studios. But it cannot end there; the discourse must become architecture.

Criticism of our current condition must be expressed in architectural forms, rather than words. What is necessary is to establish a new conception of architectural quality. If an elegant design collapses the liberating potentialities of human and social behavior, if a formal or technical discovery does not improve the material conditions of human society, if an architectural event, though technically pristine and artistically emotional, fails to contradict the fragmentation of daily life . . . it is not architecture.

NOTES

1 See Engels (1973), Gauldie (1974), and Cole and Postgate (1971, pp. 129–42). For a vision of the social costs borne by the middle class in Chicago of the same period, see Sennett (1974).
2 "The idea of 'economic efficiency' does not imply production furnishing maximum commercial profit, but production demanding a minimum working effort" (CIAM, 1970, p. 109). "The new architecture is *economic*; that is to say, it employs its elemental means as effectively and thriftily as possible and squanders neither these means nor the material" (van Doesberg, 1970, p. 78).
3 For a detailed history of the political and aesthetic evolution of the American skyscraper, see Tafuri (1979).

4   For an extensive description of the phenom-
    enon see Bluestone and Harrison (1982).
5   How Volkswagen came to western Pennsyl-
    vania is representative of the costs
    expended in these competitions. See Cher-
    now (1978, pp. 18–24) and Goodman
    (1979, pp. 1–31).
6   That symbolic capital can indeed be liquid-
    ated is best illustrated by the sale by US Steel
    (now USX) of its Pittsburgh headquarters
    for $250 million in 1982. The corporation
    now rents its office space (Nader and Taylor,
    1986, p. 30). Another example is the sale of
    $1 billion in assets, including its 611 acre
    headquarters site in Danbury, Connecticut,
    by Union Carbide Corporation, after it was
    "heavily pummeled by industrial accidents
    and a hostile takeover offer" (Cuff, 1986).

7   For a detailed discussion of architecture and
    human response and body sensibilities, see
    Knesl (1978).
8   In the movie *Charly*, of the early 60s,
    there is the briefest of scenes in which Claire
    Bloom and Cliff Robertson shop – without
    anxiety – for groceries in the open-air stalls
    of Faneuil Hall obviously some time
    before its redevelopment. The scene shows
    the grit and the casualness of the urban
    market which is an undeniable part of
    the city. The scene foretells the redevelop-
    ment. In the background rises the
    nascent form of the Boston City Hall
    construction.
9   I would like to thank Frank Ferrario of St
    Louis for this critique of the Union Station
    redevelopment.

REFERENCES

Berman, M. (1982) *All that Is Solid Melts into Air*. New York: Simon and Schuster.
Bluestone, B. and Harrison, B. (1982) *The Deindustrialization of America*. New York: Basic Books.
Castells, M. *The City and the Grassroots*. Berkeley: University of California Press.
Chernow, R. (1978) The rabbit that ate Pennsylvania. *Mother Jones*, January, 18–24.
CIAM (1970) La Sarraz Declaration [1928]. In U. Conrads (ed.), *Programs and Manifestoes on 20th-century Architecture*. Cambridge, MA: MIT Press.
Cole, G. D. H. and Postgate, R. (1971) *The Common People 1746–1946*. London: Methuen.
Cuff, D. F. (1986) $1 billion asset sale by Carbide. *New York Times*, 8 April.
deCarlo, G. (1972) Legitimizing architecture. *Forum*, April.
Drummond, D. (1986) Identifying risks in corporate headquarters. In T. A. Dutton (ed.), *Icons of Late Capitalism: Corporations and Their Architecture*. Oxford, OH: Department of Architecture, University of Miami.
Engels, F. (1973) *The Condition of the Working Class in England*. Moscow: Progress Publishers.
Filler, M. (1978) The magic fountain. *Progressive Architecture*, November.
Gauldie, E. (1974) *Cruel Habitations*. London: Allen and Unwin.
Goodman, R. (1979) *The Last Entrepreneurs*. Boston: Simon and Schuster.
Gordon, D. M. (1977) Capitalism and the roots of urban crisis. In R. E. Alcaly and D. Mermelstein (eds), *The Fiscal Crisis of American Cities*. New York: Vintage Books.
Harvey, D. (1978) The urban process under capitalism: a framework for analysis. *International Journal of Urban and Regional Research*, 124.
Harvey, D. (1985) *The Urbanization of Capital: Studies in the History and Theory of Capitalist Urbanization*. Baltimore: Johns Hopkins University Press.
Harvey, D. (1987) Lecture given at the symposium Developing the American City: Society and Architecture in the Regional City, Yale School of Architecture, 6 February.
Jameson, F. (1984) Postmodernism, or the cultural logic of late capitalism. *New Left Review*, July/August.
Knesl, J. (1978) Foundations for liberative projectuation. *Antipode*, 10(1).
Nader, R. and Taylor, W. (1986) *The Big Boys*. New York: Pantheon Books.

Pertuiset, N. (1986) The Lloyds Headquarters: imagery takes command. In T. A. Dutton (ed.), *Icons of Late Capitalism: Corporations and Their Architecture*. Oxford, OH: Department of Architecture, University of Miami.

Rowe, C. and Koetter, F. (1978) *Collage City*. Cambridge, MA: MIT Press.

Schmidt, S. and Barnes, R. (1987) Maryland stadium foes lose in court. *Washington Post*, 9 September.

Sennett, R. (1974) *Families Against the City*. New York: Vintage Books.

Stern, R. (1987) Lecture in Verona. *Art and Design*, April.

Tafuri, M. (1979) The disenchanted mountain. In G. Ciucci, F. Dal Co, M. Manieri-Elia and M. Tafuri, *The American City from the Civil War to the New Deal*. Cambridge, MA: MIT Press.

Tafuri, M. (1980) *Theories and History of Architecture*. New York: Harper and Row.

Tzonis, A. (1972) *Towards a Non-oppressive Environment*. Boston: Simon and Schuster.

van Doesberg, T. (1970) Towards a plastic architecture. In U. Conrads (ed.), *Programs and Manifestoes on 20th-century Architecture*. Cambridge, MA: MIT Press.

3

The Postmodern Debate over Urban Form

Sharon Zukin

During the 1980s scholarship in a number of fields has been permeated by the terms of "postmodern" debate. To some extent this reflects a broadening of intellectual horizons, with a transdisciplinary migration of concepts infusing new life into inquiries and arguments that had become predictable. The postmodern influence also reflects a long-term disintegration of hegemonic discipline in most of the social sciences and the seductiveness – in the twilight of marxist political parties – of literary, as opposed to political, models. But the shared attraction to postmodernism responds at a deeper level to something "out there" in the world beyond academic crisis. Many social scientists identify with the multiplicity and pervasiveness of new cultural forms, and they yearn to explain, though so far inconclusively, the "fragmented" social structure from which these forms derive.

There is no coherent definition of postmodernism to guide its appropriation by those social scientists who are so inclined. Fredric Jameson (1984) distinguishes between postmodernism as a cultural product and a cultural period; in either case it arises in the late twentieth century from the ashes of a discredited modern movement. While in architectural theory postmodernism refers to a style, in literary theory it refers to a method; both buildings and books are "read" for the primacy of an internally consistent "language" (cf. Jencks, 1984) or "text" (cf. Hassan, 1987). It could be argued, further, from the many references to music

videos, ornamentation, and pastiche that postmodernism in general is inherently a visual – as opposed to verbal – apprehension of the world; yet there is no consensus that films and paintings are more postmodern than other cultural forms. Even as a rallying point for a political agenda, there is both "a postmodernism of resistance and a postmodernism of reaction" (Foster, 1983, p. xii). When aesthetic and political agenda meet, moreover, as in the state-run art museum, postmodernism becomes a programme for reviewing the history of art in both more populist and more elitist ways (cf. Mainardi, 1987).

The fungibility of the concept may account for some of its appeal. Yet it also speaks to the zeitgeist in which those who merely study society play a part: postmodernism is "the sum of self-awareness, of a shared culture, of a niche in time [and] space" (Dear, 1986, p. 373).

When Jameson's article "Postmodernism, or the Cultural Logic of Late Capitalism" was published in *New Left Review* (1984), it was widely read by sociologists and political economists in the United States. People who had barely marked the passage of authority from Althusser to Foucault and Derrida, who couldn't tell "complexity" from "contradiction" in architecture, who still thought of Philip Marlowe as the direct descendant of Sherlock Holmes (Poster, 1984; Venturi, 1977 [1966]; Tani, 1984) – these people were both stimulated and provoked by Jameson's approach.

Many criticized Jameson for his facile elision of capital and culture and the superficial sense in which he called for a postmodern "mapping" of the cognitive world. Some objected to the polymorphous postmodernism that Jameson found in equal measure in art and architecture, cinema and writing. Still others rebuked him (Davis, 1985) on the problematic identification of postmodernism with an expanding rather than a crisis-ridden capitalism. Yet largely by means of Jameson's essay, the issues he identified and the examples he described gained currency in social analysis.

In urban research the postmodern debate struck a common chord. First, the rhetoric of Jameson's statement – especially the call for mapping and the impressive though flawed example of John Portman's atrium-hotels – spoke to geographers, sociologists and political economists who studied urban space. Second, urban researchers were already attuned to an interdisciplinary reading of the "built environment"; by necessity, they had to take into account architecture, art markets, urban planning, and capital investment in order to make sense of contemporary urban developments (Zukin, 1982). Marxist urban studies, moreover, had recently undergone a traumatic self-examination, in which economic determinism receded before a more open materialist analysis that embraced culture and politics as well as economic structures (Berman, 1982; Castells, 1983; Harvey, 1985; Gottdiener, 1985).

Jameson's linking postmodernism to a current stage of capitalism complemented the tendency to connect urban and regional developments to the global reorganization of capital (cf. Massey, 1984). Often the analysis of local "restructuring" was accompanied by an effort to visualize the changing power relations between capitalists, or between capitalists and other social groups, in spatial terms (see the vastly different approaches of Fainstein and Fainstein, 1982; Smith, 1984; and Soja, 1986). Perhaps the postmodern debate has had its greatest impact on urban studies by framing issues of uneven economic development in terms of the mutual relation between a more socially conceptualized space and a more spatially conceived society (Soja, 1987).

While this contribution has been called "the postmodernization of geography" (Soja, 1987), the acknowledgment seems to outweigh the actual intellectual debt. Urban researchers have had a great deal of trouble in moving postmodernism from an aesthetic category into the debate over urban forms.

Certainly the postmodern notion of pluralism in the visual arts has influenced an appreciation of plural or "flexible" strategies of capital accumulation, especially in cities (Harvey, 1987; Cooke, 1988). Further, the postmodern concept of narrative fragmentation seems relevant to the fracturing of social relations based on geographical or other traditional ties, a process that is evident in older industrial cities and regions (Friedmann, 1983; Scott and Storper, 1986). Finally, the language of postmodern architecture and poststructuralist criticism is apt for describing a material environment that "decontextualizes" and recreates historical forms of city building for purposes of distraction, entertainment and "spectacle" (Debord, 1983 [1967]). These urban spaces include the atrium-hotel as Jameson describes it, Disneyland and various reconstructed downtown shopping centres (Faneuil Hall, South Street Seaport, Inner Harbor) and more generally, the "nonplace" spaces that standardize or ignore regional traditions (cf. Relph, 1976; Frampton, 1983).

Using the term postmodernism in the debate over urban form offers certain advantages. Intuitively it "sounds right" because it resonates with the fragmentation of geographic loyalties in contemporary economic restructuring and its expression in new urban polarities. It also solidifies a commitment among urban political economists and geographers to bring culture out of the superstructure and study it, along with politics and economics, as a basic determinant of material forms. And using postmodernism aligns urbanists in an interdisciplinary enterprise with a more or less common vocabulary and a common subject, the city.

Yet if social scientists don't move beyond the sensual evocation of the city that postmodernism now represents, they risk being overwhelmed by another of the "chaotic concepts" that have plagued recent urban studies (Sayer, 1982; Zukin, 1987). To use postmodernism reasonably, we must conceptualize it as a social process and periodize it in terms of production as well as consumption of urban space. The historical continuities that come to light challenge the identification of postmodernism with a new stage in the social organization of capital (cf. Fainstein and Fainstein, 1989).

"Postmodernization" as a Social Process

The awkward term postmodernization signals our interest in a dynamic process whose scale and complexity are comparable to the great structuring forces of modernization. Like modernization, postmodernization presents the problem of analysing discontinuous or dissonant social processes on different geographic scales. On the global level postmodernization refers to the restructuring of socio-spatial relations by new patterns of investment and production in industry and services, labour migration and telecommunications (cf. Portes and Walton, 1981; Urry, 1987). On the level of the metropolitan region, postmodernization refers to socio-spatial relocation based on opposing claims of affordability and legitimacy (cf. Smith and Williams, 1986; Smith, 1987). Both global and metropolitan processes are represented by some degree of decentralization. On the urban level, however, postmodernization is represented by some sort of recentralization in core cities of global markets (e.g. Soja, 1986).

If aesthetically postmodernism suggests new neo-classical buildings and historical recreations, it covers only part of the changes in major US and European cities since the early 1970s. This description works best when it is limited to the high-class rebuilding of downtowns and waterfronts for highly competitive business services, high-rent residences, and high-volume or high-style cultural consumption. The conjunction of historic preservation and the arts as a method of real estate investment and a means of perception does reflect real changes in culture and society (Zukin, 1982, 1988; Wright, 1985; Hewison, 1987). Yet limiting postmodernism to this usage doesn't deal with the relation between visualization and social reconstruction, a dual effort "to map one form of social control upon another" (Clark, 1985: 49; cf. Harvey, 1985; Boyer, 1987).

In looking at postmodernism we should be guided by older notions of polarities in architectural patronage and perception (Sarfatti Larson, 1982, following Walter Benjamin). Adapting these categories, on the one hand, postmodernization refers to the structural polarity between markets and places, between the forces that detach people from or anchor them to specific spaces. On the other hand, postmodernization refers to the institutional polarity between the public and private use of urban space. The analysis of postmodern urban forms emphasizes markets over places and denies the separation of private and public space. It therefore requires attention to both *structural* forces and political, economic, and cultural *institutions*.[1]

Architectural Production

The constant rebuilding of cities in core capitalist societies suggests that the major condition of architectural production is to create shifting material landscapes. These landscapes bridge space and time; they also directly mediate economic power by both conforming to and structuring norms of market-driven investment, production and consumption.

While architects today work mainly under corporate patronage, they also work – along with urban planners, real estate developers, and city officials – in a matrix of state institutions and local preferences. They are neither free nor unfree from market forces and the attachments of place. Although architects usually work to specifications set by individual clients, their largest commissions come from businesses and real estate developers who build "on speculation", that is, with the intention of selling or renting space after construction has begun. These clients impose market criteria on architects by demanding more rentable or saleable space in less construction time. More and more, such clients are national and international investors rather than local developers. For this reason, Jameson and others see urban architecture as a direct expression of "multinational capitalism" (Jameson, 1984; Davis, 1985; Logan and Molotch, 1987).

Architects, moreover, pursue these clients under conditions of increasing competition. Major architectural firms have recently experienced the same kind of growth and international expansion of activity as corporate law, accounting and advertising firms – although professional corporations are legally prohibited from selling ownership shares to the public and typically grow by opening branches rather than making mergers and acquisitions. Consequently, new architecture and urban forms are produced under nearly the same social organization as consumer products and business services.

We see, therefore, in urban forms market-driven patterns of standardization and differentiation. Despite local variations, as well as variations that are imposed for aesthetic, ideological or "sentimental" reasons (Jager, 1986; Logan and Molotch, 1987, chapter 4; Harvey, 1987), the major influence on urban form derives from the internationalization of investment, production and consumption. In socio-spatial terms, however, internationalization is associated with the concentration of investment, the decentralization of production, and the standardization of consumption.

After 1945, the process of suburbanization in the United States demanded centralized control over finance and construction even while it rapidly decentralized housing and shopping malls, with their anchor stores, controlled environment, and inner streets of shops, and destroyed the commercial viability of many central business districts (Checkoway, 1986; Kowinski, 1985; Mintz and Schwartz, 1985, p. 43). From the early 1970s, however, centralized, multinational investment supported both continued decentralization and a reconcentration, with greater stratification, of urban shopping districts. The same products and ambiance came from multinational corporations in New York, France, Japan and Italy. Increasingly, they could just as well be found in shops on upper Madison Avenue as on Rodeo Drive, the Rue du Faubourg St Honoré, or the via Montenapoleone. When local merchants were displaced by the higher rents these tenants paid, they correctly blamed showplace boutiques whose rents were subsidized by their parent multinational corporations. In a subtle recapitulation of earlier transformations, more international investment shifted shopping districts from craft (quiche) to mass (McDonald's or Benetton) production and consumption (Giovannini, 1986; Meislin, 1987).

McDonald's and Benetton epitomize the connections between international urban form and internationalized production and consumption. Their shops are ubiquitous in cities around the world, giving strength to the parent firms' strategy of international expansion (Lee, 1986; *Business Week*, October 13, 1986). The two companies differ in the way they run their worldwide operations: while McDonald's sells traditional franchises to local operators, Benetton neither invests in nor collects franchise fees from Benetton stores. McDonald's managers, moreover, buy their food supplies locally, but Benetton managers buy all their inventory from Benetton. The uniform standards of both chains are maintained by other corporate policies: rigorous training of store managers; adherence to company standards for quality, service, and at Benetton, decor and window display; and frequent on-site inspections by visitors from company headquarters.

Despite differences in the types of products that they sell, both Benetton and McDonald's owe their growth in part to organizational innovation. Much of this advance centres on production and distribution. McDonald's honed to a fine point the "robotized" operations of fast-food cuisine; Benetton developed cheaper methods for softening wool and dying coloured garments as well as investing in computerized manufacturing and design and real robots for warehouse operations. In the process, both chains developed a total "look" that merges product, production methods, a specialized consumption experience, and an advertising style. Just as their "classic" mass-produced sweaters and burgers link consumers around the world, so do these multinational corporations become more significant players in each domestic economy. McDonald's voracious demand for beef inflicts potential damage up and down the food chain in cattle-raising countries of Latin America (Skinner, 1985); by contrast, Benetton's new US factory in North Carolina provides (automated) employment to textile workers.

Unlike mass-produced consumer goods, architecture maintains a high profile. While individual buildings become more standardized, their designers claim more distinction for their clients. Professional architects continue to theorize an underlying aesthetic or social programme, especially the faux populism that adheres to many postmodern styles. The demotic urge facilitates architects' acceptability to corporate patrons, who want to gain public acceptance as well as to distinguish their companies from those that inhabit the glass boxes commercially adapted from modernism from the 1950s through the 1970s (see Venturi, 1977 [1966]; Venturi et al., 1977; cf. Kieran, 1987).

Developers are less constrained in talking about the conditions of architectural production. "My buildings are a product," a developer says (*Architectural Record*, June 1987, p. 9). "They are products like Scotch Tape is a product, or Saran Wrap. The packaging of that product is the first thing that people see. I am selling space and renting space and it has to be in a package that is attractive enough to be financially successful." He emphasizes, "I can't afford to build monuments because I am not an institution."

The distinguished architectural critic Ada Louise Huxtable (1987) turns this comment around in her criticism of the monumentally sized, egregiously individualized new skyscrapers that are especially common in New York City. "In the last five years," she says, "a

new kind of developer has been remaking the city with something called 'the signature building', a postmodernist phenomenon that combines marketing and consumerism in a way that would have baffled Bernini but is thoroughly understood by the modern entrepreneur."

An emphasis on individualized products that can be identified with individual cultural producers is inseparable from intensified market competition in an age of mass consumption (Forty, 1987). The "Egyptoid" character of postmodern skyscraper design was paralleled, in the 1920s, by the "Mayan" pyramids of speculative office buildings competing in a real estate boom (Stern et al., 1987, pp. 511–13). Similar competition among Hollywood film studios from the 1930s through the 1950s for audience loyalty to their products encouraged individual directors to make the "signature film". In architecture, as labour costs have increased and craft skills have atrophied, the burden of social differentiation has passed to the use of expensive materials and the ingenuity of the design itself. Not surprisingly, like Hollywood directors, architects assume and even become commercial properties.

To some extent, the commercialization of architects reflects the market competition of architectural products. But it also reflects the increasing commercialization of the social category of design. This occurs both under market and nonmarket competition. Indeed, it occurs so typically in a fluid social space that joins market and nonmarket institutions (and their patrons) that it draws our attention to a public-private "liminal space" in new urban forms.

Liminal Spaces

The liminal space of postmodern urban forms is socially constructed in the erosion of autonomy of cultural producers from cultural consumers. Autonomy from patrons has always been especially problematic for architects and designers because of the material resources required to realize their designs. In theory, professionalization, with its special educational requirements and licensing

procedures, should enhance the distance between architectural producers and their
patrons. In practice, however, the activities
of these producers and "cultivated" cultural
consumers increasingly converge.[2]

Convergence is structured by new and revived institutional forms, such as trade fairs,
department store promotions, and museum
events, that have become major urban attractions. While New York City and Los Angeles
can no longer claim to be world centres of
garment and furniture production, for
example, they do expand their design and
cultural centres and merchandise marts for
the concentration of business activities connected with conception, display and sales. It
is important for these cities to claim to be
world centres of design. That role both symbolizes and provides material resources for
the specialization in high-level business services to which core cities aspire. And it at-
tracts the heterogeneous new elites of
business, politics and fashion that comprise
a visible part of an international upper class
(cf. Silverman, 1986).

The common socio-spatial element shared
by department stores and museums is that
they create a new linkage between designers,
mass consumers and wealthy patrons of high
culture. Regional genres and individual
artists' *oeuvres* provide motifs that are invoked as a consumption package for both
cultural and mass consumption. Annual
sales promotions at Bloomingdale's parallel
new exhibitions at the costume wing of the
Metropolitan Museum of Art, and both are
used to enhance the competitive status of their
respective institutions (Silverman, 1986).

Much as it did in the late nineteenth century, the department store frames "the dem-
ocratization of luxury" (Williams, 1982,
p. 11) so that it encourages consumption by
both affluent and lower classes. Similarly, the
heightened competition among museums for
such nonmarket resources as government
patronage encourages them to frame a dem-
ocratized connoisseurship that appeals to
segments of a cultivated upper and middle
class.

Department stores and museums thus
form liminal spaces that frame the percep-

tion of cultural products as straddling pure
art and art for markets. In both institutions
public gatherings for display and sales
merge with private functions (market and
nonmarket competition for resources, charity "events").

While postmodern art critics have noted
the outcome of these social processes, they
generally limit themselves to observing that
cultural producers no longer preserve a critical distance from the market (Jameson,
1984; Solomon-Godeau, 1989). On the contrary, it is the very essence of postmodern
cultural institutions to blur distinctions between high and low culture, especially by
plying cultural meanings to an enlarged
public of "connoisseurs". Similarly, it is the
very essence of postmodern urban forms to
provide the liminal spaces for such meanings
to be played out, blurring distinctions between privacy and publicity and market and
nonmarket norms.

Periodizing Postmodern Urban Form

The institutional symbiosis between department stores and museums dates back to
the 1920s (DiMaggio, 1986; Stern et al.,
1987, pp. 336–8). Similarly, the production
of highly individualized buildings and
public–private liminal spaces derives from
the speculative building booms of modern
architecture between 1870 and 1930. History thus complicates an attempt to define
postmodernism as a distinct period in
architectural production. On the contrary,
in modernism begins the marketing of
design as both a spatial and a cultural
commodity.

"Superstar architecture" is taken to be a
hallmark of postmodern urban form. Like
superstars in rock music or on Wall Street,
production of superstar architects reflects
the desire by major corporations in the services to recoup value from long-term, large-
scale investments in product development.
Investments on this scale in urban redevelopment generate market demand for highly individualized yet increasingly standardized
architectural designs. Many of the important
commissions that are involved are awarded

to internationally active architects with superstar reputations.

Just as these projects are often out of scale with the histories of specific places, so the architects who are recruited to design them have reputations that are out of scale with those of local cultural producers. "Suddenly," a local architect complains about Fan Pier, a major new project on the Boston waterfront, "the demand for the 'name' architect, often overcommitted elsewhere, has placed these architects and their products side by side." This threatens "the identity of Boston, Back Bay, and Newbury Street" with being submerged in that of any other place (*Architectural Record*, May 1987, p. 4).[3]

Yet the production of superstar architecture derives from the same speculative building activity that generated high modernism. As early as the 1870s in Chicago, constant cycles of rebuilding initiated by business cycles and fires resulted in an aggressive construction industry and a commercially-oriented architecture. "Chicago architects", said a French observer undoubtedly immured by Haussmann and the Napoleonic *corps*, "brazenly accepted the conditions imposed by the speculator" (Saint, 1983, p. 84).

When Henry James returned to New York in 1905 after 20 years of living in Europe, he found the mid-nineteenth-century Trinity Church threatened with sale by its own wardens and imminent demise (James, 1968 [1907], pp. 83–4). The architectural monotony with which it would be replaced confirmed, for James, "the universal will to move – to move, move, move, as an end in itself, an appetite at any price".

For the next generation in the two American capitals of big business and modern architecture – New York and Chicago – rising land values, growing corporations and real estate speculation made a constantly changing landscape. The average longevity of an office building in New York shrank to only 20 years. Modern replacement buildings, moreover, as James had suspected, were less distinguished – and cheaper to build or maintain – than their classical predecessors. By the 1920s, production of com-

mercial buildings depended on a nexus of speculators whose financing got a project underway, architects who could "draw... an imposing picture of a skyscraper; if it is several stories higher than the Woolworth Tower, so much the better," and newspapers that eagerly published "pictures of high buildings, real or imagined, because... readers have a weakness for them" (builder William A. Starrett [1928] quoted in Stern et al., 1987, pp. 513–14).

The historic nexus of superstar architecture, commercialization and speculation is paralleled by a hybrid public–private mode in the appropriation and production of urban forms.

Current observers tend to suggest that this institutional hybrid is historically new. Consequently, the postmodern period of urban redevelopment refers to the public–private partnerships which thrive even under "progressive" municipal administrations (Hartman, 1984; Bennett, 1986; Judd, 1986) as well as to the "privatization" that occurs with the transformation of public spaces along the waterfront into emporia of mass consumption and the encroachment of private institutions into public space (e.g. the expansion of the Metropolitan Museum into Central Park).

But again the postmodern perception derives from processes inherent in high modernism. From the 1880s, increasing use of new mechanical inventions for transportation and telecommunications forged hybrid public-private cultural forms (Kern, 1983, pp. 187–91). Telephones provided men and women with both accessibility and distraction. Newspapers achieved mass circulation as means of both intimacy and information. Railroads, moreover, bridged the private scale of the journey and public arrival in the city with the liminal transparent tunnel of the great railroad station, built of iron and glass (Schievelbusch, 1979, pp. 161–9). Similarly, social life in modern cities has often been generated by new means of market consumption – coffee houses, tearooms, restaurants, department stores – that are diffused from an essentially private group to a broader public (Thorne, 1980; Barth,

1980; Williams, 1982; Benson, 1986; cf. Wolff, 1985).

In contrast, moreover, to the "postmodern" Portman-built hotel that Fredric Jameson describes, the private use of public space was first noted by that earlier intrepid consumer, Henry James, when he visited New York's Waldorf-Astoria Hotel (1968 [1907], pp. 104–5; cf. Agnew, 1983).

For James, the tearooms and shops of the American grand hotel created "a world whose relation to its form and medium was practically imperturbable;...a conception of publicity *as* the vital medium organized with the authority with which the American genius for organization, put on its mettle, alone could organize it". In the cavernous lobby of "the universal Waldorf-Astoria" James saw entrapped "the great collective, plastic public" by "the great glittering, costly caravansery". No less than Jameson in the atrium does James in the Waldorf see "the whole housed populace move as in mild and consenting suspicion of its captured and governed state, its having to consent in inordinate fusion as the price of what it seemed pleased to regard as inordinate luxury" (James, 1968 [1907], pp. 440–1).

Conclusion

The postmodern debate over urban form suggests a more subtle "cultural logic of capitalism" (Jameson, 1984) than has so far been entertained. Conveying a sense of rupture and discontinuity, and taking for granted that progress is fragile, the postmodern landscape represents the same destruction of longevity, of cultural layers, and of vested interests that opposes markets to place. For this reason there is both similarity and continuity with the modernism that represents (and opposes) the "high" capitalism of an advancing industrial age.

By contrast, postmodernization occurs in a social context when markets are more volatile and places – even the occupational category of cultural producers – less autonomous. The part played by postmodern urban form is to appropriate or restore designated meaning through processes of social and spatial redifferentiation. Just as economic internationalization has very different spatial and social consequences in the spheres of investment, production and consumption, so postmodernization should be carefully analysed for the social production of its aesthetic effects.

NOTES

1 The following material is drawn from chapter 2 of my book-in-progress, *American Market/Place* (Berkeley and Los Angeles: University of California Press), and represents a greatly condensed version of the argument.

2 These terms bring up the usual modern distinctions between clients who directly commission architectural products and patrons who by their connoisseurship and command of institutionalized cultural resources support the general process of architectural production. As we shall see, the marketing of connoisseurship calls in turn for new terms of distinction.

3 The same submersion of locality (and local capital) by superstar architecture is illustrated by 1 Liberty Place, Helmut Jahn's new office building in Philadelphia. The design by Jahn, a well-known postmodern architect based in Chicago, had to receive special authorization from the city government because it rose above the symbolic limit set by the statue of William Penn atop City Hall. Penn, founder of the commonwealth of Pennsylvania, laid out Philadelphia's initial city plan in the seventeenth century.

REFERENCES

Agnew, Jean-Christophe (1983) The consuming vision of Henry James. In Richard Wightman Fox and T. J. Jackson Lears (eds), *The Culture of Consumption*. New York: Pantheon.

Barth, Gunther (1980) *City People: The Rise of Modern Culture in Nineteenth-century America*. New York: Oxford University Press.

Bennett, Larry (1986) Beyond urban renewal: Chicago's North Loop redevelopment project. *Urban Affairs Quarterly*, 22, 242–60.

Benson, Susan Porter (1986) *Counter Culture: Saleswomen, Managers and Customers in American Department Stores, 1890–1940*. Urbana: University of Illinois Press.

Berman, Marshall (1982) *All that Is Solid Melts into Air*. New York: Simon and Schuster.

Boyer, M. Christine (1987) The city of collective memory. Unpublished paper.

Castells, Manuel (1983) *The City and the Grassroots*. Berkeley and Los Angeles: University of California Press.

Checkoway, Barry (1986) Large builders, federal housing programs, and postwar suburbanization. In Rachel G. Bratt et al. (eds), *Critical Perspectives on Housing*. Philadelphia: Temple University Press.

Clark, Timothy (1985) *The Painting of Modern Life*. New York: Viking.

Cooke, Philip (1988) The postmodern condition and the city. *Comparative Urban and Community Research*.

Davis, Mike (1985) Urban renaissance and the spirit of postmodernism. *New Left Review*, 151 (May–June), 106–13.

Dear, M. J. (1986) Postmodernism and planning. *Environment and Planning D: Society and Space*, 4, 367–84.

Debord, Guy (1967, 1983) *Society of the Spectacle*. Detroit: Black and Red.

DiMaggio, Paul J. (1986) Why are art museums not decentralized after the fashion of public libraries. Paper presented to Workshop on Law, Economy and Organizations, Yale Law School (December).

Fainstein, Norman I. and Fainstein, Susan S. (1982) Restructuring the American city: a comparative perspective. In Fainstein and Fainstein (eds), *Urban Policy Under Capitalism, Urban Affairs Annual Review*, 22.

Fainstein, Susan S. and Fainstein, Norman I. (1989) Technology, the new international division of labor, and location: continuities and disjunctures. In Robert Beauregard (ed.), *Industrial Restructuring and Spatial Variation, Urban Affairs Annual Review*, 29.

Forty, Adrian (1987) *Objects of Desire: Design and Society From Wedgwood to IBM*. New York: Pantheon.

Foster, Hal (ed.) (1983) *The Anti-Aesthetic: Essays on Postmodern Culture*. Port Townsend, WA: Bay Press.

Frampton, Kenneth (1983) Towards a critical regionalism: six points for an architecture of resistance. In Hal Foster (ed.), *The Anti-Aesthetic*. Port Townsend, WA: Bay Press.

Friedmann, John (1983) Life space and economic space: contradictions in regional development. In Dudley Seers and Kjell Ostrom (eds), *The Crises of the European Regions*. London: Macmillan.

Giovannini, Joseph (1986) The "new" Madison Avenue: a European street of fashion. *New York Times*, 26 June.

Gottdiener, Mark (1985) *The Social Production of Urban Space*. Austin: University of Texas Press.

Hartman, Chester (1984) *The Transformation of San Francisco*. Totowa, NJ: Rowman and Allenheld.

Harvey, David (1985) Paris, 1850–1870. In *Consciousness and the Urban Experience*. Baltimore: Johns Hopkins University Press.

Harvey, David (1987) Flexible accumulation through urbanization: reflections on "postmodernism" in the American city. Paper presented to Symposium on Developing the American City: Society and Architecture in the Regional City, Yale School of Architecture (February).

Hassan, Ihab (1987) *The Postmodern Turn: Essays in Postmodern Theory and Culture*. Columbus: Ohio State University Press.

Hewison, Robert (1987) *The Heritage Industry*. London.

Huxtable, Ada Louise (1987) Creeping Gigantism in Manhattan. *New York Times*, 22 March.

Jager, Michael (1986) Class definition and the aesthetics of gentrification: Victoriana in Melbourne. In Neil Smith and Peter Williams (eds), *Gentrification of the City*, Winchester, MA: Allen and Unwin.

James, Henry (1907, 1968) *The American Scene*. Bloomington: Indiana University Press.

Jameson, Fredric (1984) Postmodernism, or the cultural logic of late capitalism. *New Left Review*, 146 (July/August), 53–93.

Jencks, Charles (1984) *The Language of Postmodern Architecture*, 4th edn. New York: Rizzoli.

Judd, Dennis R. (1986) Electoral coalitions, minority mayors, and the contradictions in the municipal policy agenda. In M. Gottdiener (ed.), *Cities in Stress, Urban Affairs Annual Review*, 30.

Kern, Stephen (1983) *The Culture of Time and Space, 1880–1918*. Cambridge, MA: Harvard University Press.

Kieran, Stephen (1987) The architecture of plenty: theory and design in the marketing age. *Harvard Architecture Review*, 6, 103–13.

Kowinski, William Severini (1985) *The Malling of America*. New York: William Morrow.

Lee, Andrea (1986) Profiles: being everywhere (Luciano Benetton). *The New Yorker*, 10 November.

Logan, John and Molotch, Harvey (1987) *Urban Fortunes*. Berkeley and Los Angeles: University of California Press.

Mainardi, Patricia (1987) Postmodern history at the Musée D'Orsay. *October*, 41 (Summer), 30–52.

Massey, Doreen (1984) *Spatial Divisions of Labor*. New York: Methuen.

Meislin, Richard J. (1987) Quiche gets the boot on Columbus Avenue. *New York Times*, 25 July.

Mintz, Beth and Schwartz, Michael (1985) *The Power Structure of American Business*. Chicago: University of Chicago Press.

Portes, Alejandro and Walton, John (1981) *Labor, Class and the International System*. New York: Academic.

Poster, Mark (1984) *Foucault, Marxism and History*. Cambridge: Polity Press.

Relph, E. (1976) *Place and Placelessness*. London: Plon.

Saint, Andrew (1983) *The Image of the Architect*. New Haven, CT: Yale University Press.

Sarfatti Larson, Magali (1982) An ideological response to industrialism: European architectural modernism. Unpublished paper.

Sayer, Andrew (1982) Explanation in economic geography: abstraction versus generalization. *Progress in Human Geography*, 6 (March), 68–88.

Schievelbusch, Wolfgang (1979) *The Railway Journey*, trans. Anselm Hollo. New York: Urizen.

Scott, A. J. and Storper, M. (eds) (1986) *Production, Work, Territory*. Winchester, MA: Allen and Unwin.

Silverman, Debora (1986) *Selling Culture: Bloomingdale's, Diana Vreeland, and the New Aristocracy of Taste in Reagan's America*. New York: Pantheon.

Skinner, Joseph K. (1985) Big Mac and the tropical forests. *Monthly Review*, (December), 25–32.

Smith, Neil (1984) *Uneven Development*. Oxford: Basil Blackwell.

Smith, Neil (1987) Of yuppies and housing: gentrification, social restructuring, and the urban dream. *Environment and Planning D: Society and Space*, 5, 151–72.

Smith, Neil and Williams, Peter (eds) (1986) *Gentrification of the City*. Winchester, MA: Allen and Unwin.

Soja, E. W. (1986) Taking Los Angeles apart: some fragments of a critical human geography. *Environment and Planning D: Society and Space*, 4, 255–72.

Soja, E. W. (1987) The postmodernization of geography: a review. *Annals of the Association of American Geographers*, 77(2), 289–323.

Solomon-Godeau, Abigail (1989) Living with contradictions: critical practices in the age of supply-side aesthetics. In Andrew Ross (ed.), *The Politics of Postmodernism*. Minneapolis: University of Minnesota Press.

Stern, Robert A. M. et al. (1987) *New York 1930: Architecture and Urbanism Between the Two World Wars*. New York: Rizzoli.

Tani, Stefano (1984) *The Doomed Detective: The Contribution of the Detective Novel to Postmodern American and Italian Fiction*. Carbondale, IL: Southern Illinois University Press.

Thorne, Robert (1980) Places of refreshment in the nineteenth-century city. In Anthony D. King (ed.) *Buildings and Society*. London: Routledge and Kegan Paul.

Urry, John (1987) Some social and spatial aspects of services. *Environment and Planning: Society and Space*, 5, 5–26.

Venturi, Robert (1966, 1977) *Complexity and Contradiction in Architecture*, rev. edn. New York: Museum of Modern Art.

Venturi, Robert et al. (1977) *Learning From Las Vegas*, rev. edn. Cambridge, MA: MIT Press.

Williams, Rosalind H. (1982) *Dream Worlds: Mass Consumption in Late Nineteenth-century France*. Berkeley and Los Angeles: University of California Press.

Wolff, Janet (1985) The invisible flâneuse: women and the literature of modernity. *Theory, Culture and Society*, 2 (3), 37–48.

Wright, Patrick (1985) *On Living in an Old Country*. London: Verso.

Zukin, Sharon (1982) *Loft Living: Culture and Capital in Urban Change*. Baltimore: Johns Hopkins University Press.

Zukin, Sharon (1987) Gentrification: culture and capital in the urban core. *Annual Review of Sociology*, 13, 129–47.

Zukin, Sharon (1988) Postscript: more market forces. In *Loft Living*, 2nd edn. London: Radius/Hutchinson.

Part II
History

4

The New Historical Relationship between Space and Society

Manuel Castells

On the basis of our understanding of the process of historical change, we can now undertake the exploration of its relationship to spatial functions and forms, and therefore to the production of urban meaning. It has been a custom in the recent literature of urban studies to use the formula according to which space is the expression of society. While such a perspective is a healthy reaction against the technological determinism and short-sighted empiricism too frequently predominant in the space-related academic disciplines, it is clearly an insufficient formulation of the problem, besides being too vague a statement.

Space is not, contrary to what others may say, a reflection of society but one of society's fundamental material dimensions and to consider it independently from social relationships, even with the intention of studying their interaction, is to separate nature from culture, and thus to destroy the first principle of any social science: that matter and consciousness are interrelated, and that this fusion is the essence of history and science. Therefore spatial forms, at least on our planet, will be produced by human action, as are all other objects, and will express and perform the interests of the dominant class according to a given mode of production and to a specific mode of development. They will express and implement the power relationships of the state in a historically defined society. They will be realized and shaped by gender domination and by state-enforced family life. At the same time, spatial

forms will also be marked by resistance from exploited classes, oppressed subjects, and abused women. And the work of this contradictory historical process on space will be accomplished on an already inherited spatial form, the product of history and support of new interests, projects, protests, and dreams. Finally, from time to time social movements will arise, challenging the meaning of a spatial structure and therefore attempting new functions and new forms. Such are the urban social movements, the agents of urban-spatial transformation, the highest level of urban social change.

We cannot here use the proposed analytical model to explore the production of spatial forms and urban meaning across time and cultures. But we can introduce into the discussion some recent trends of the transformation of spatial forms that underlie the production of new urban meaning by urban social movements.

We know that the dominant interests of the capitalist mode of production, during its industrial model of development, led to a dramatic restructuring of the territory and to the assignment of new social meaning to the city. Four socio-spatial processes account for this transformation:

1 The concentration and centralization of the means of production, units of management, labour power, markets, and means of consumption in a new form of the gigantic and complex spatial unit known as the metropolitan area

(see Hall, 1966; Duncan et al., 1964; Harvey, 1978).

2 The specialization of spatial location according to the interests of capital and to the efficiency of industrial production, transportation, and distribution (see Pred, 1997; Cohen, 1981).

3 The commodification of the city itself, both through the real estate market (including land speculation) and in its residential areas triggering, for instance, suburban sprawl as a way of opening up construction and transportation markets, and of creating a form of household designed to stimulate individualized consumption (see Harvey, 1975).

4 The basic assumption that the accomplishment of this model of metropolitan development necessitated the mobility of the population and resources, shifting to where they were required for profit maximizing. This assumption followed massive migration, disruption of communities and regional cultures, unbalanced regional growth, spatial mismatching between existing physical stock and need for housing and facilities, and a self-spiralling urban growth beyond the limits of collective efficiency and short of the minimum space-time requirements for the maintenance of patterns of human communication (see Sawyers and Tabb, 1977; Bluestone and Harrison, 1980).

This model led to a generalized urban crisis in housing, services, and social control, as we have shown and analysed elsewhere (Castells, 1981). The action of the state to cope with the urban crisis led to the increasing politicization of the early type of urban movements.

The response of the dominant interests of a given system to a structural crisis has always been two-fold: on the one hand, political – repression and integration (this was the experience in all capitalist countries between 1960 and 1980, with different results depending upon the social situations); and on the other, technological – shifting gears towards new systems of management and new techniques of production. Thus, the in-formational mode of development created the conditions for a new restructuring of a spatial form in crisis, and at the same time it needed new spatial conditions for its full expansion (see Mollenkopf, 1981). The main spatial impact of the new technology, based upon the twin revolution in communication systems and microelectronics, is the transformation of spatial places into flows and channels – what amounts to production and consumption without any localized form.[1] Not only can information be transmitted from individual sender to individual receiver across distance, but consumption can also be individualized and transformed into the exchange of a cable television image against a credit card number communicated by telephone. Technically speaking, shopping centres are already obsolete. To be sure, shopping is more than buying, but the dissociation of the economic and symbolic functions leads to the differentiation of their spatial form and, potentially, to the transformation of both functions into non-spatial flows (entertainment through images and drugs at home; buying through advertising and home computers connected to the telephone).[2] There are four limits, from the point of view of the dominant class, to this tendency towards the de-localization of production and consumption.

1 An enormous amount of capital stock is in fixed assets in the gigantic concentrations created by them during the preceding phase. Manhattan or the City of London cannot be written off as easily as the South Bronx or Brixton.[3]

2 Some cultural institutions, historical traditions, and interpersonal networks in the upper echelons of the ruling elites must be preserved and improved, since capital means capitalists, managers, and technocrats; that is, people are culturally defined and orientated, and are certainly not ready to become flows themselves.[4]

The spatial process that the dominant class has designed to deal with these two problems is a well-known device: urban renewal. This is the rehabilitation, revitalization, improvement, and protection of a limited, exclusive space of residence, work and leisure, insulated from its immediate surroundings by a computerized army of bodyguards, and related to the other islands of the elite (including resorts) by increasingly protected air communication (private jets and airport VIP rooms) and tele-conference systems.

3   Yet the informational mode of development requires some centres where knowledge is produced and information stored, as well as centres from which images and information are emitted. So universities, laboratories, scientific design units, news centres, information agencies, public service financial centres, managerial units, with all their corresponding technicians, workers, and employees, must still be spatially concentrated.

4   Furthermore, the informational mode of development is inextricably intertwined with the industrial mode of development, including industrialized agriculture, mining, and crop-collection around the world. Thus factories, fields, housing, and services for workers and peasants must have some spatial organization.

The spatial process designed from the point of view of the dominant class to cope with these third and fourth obstacles to the dismantling of the structure of space places the emphasis on increasing hierarchy and specialization of spatial functions and forms, according to their location (see Idris-Soven et al., 1978). What the informational mode of development allows is the separation of work and management, so that different tasks can be performed in different places and assembled through signals (in the case of information) or through advanced transportation technology (standardized pieces shipped from very remote points of production). Work at home or in community centres, regional differentiation of production, and concentration of the units of management and production of information in privileged spaces could be the new spatial model of the capitalist-technocratic elite.

Furthermore, the expansion and integration of the capitalist mode of production at the world level accelerates the international division of labour and hierarchically organizes production in a world assembly line, opens up a world market, imports and exports labour where it is convenient, and transforms the flows of capital in multinational corporations into the final, most powerful immaterial property of the capitalist system: money. The spatial project of the new dominant class tends towards the disconnection between people and spatial form, and therefore between people's lives and urban meaning. Not that people will not be in places or that cities will disappear; on the contrary, urbanization will accelerate in most countries and the search for housing and services will become the most dramatic problem facing people.

Yet, what tends to disappear is the meaning of places for people. Each place, each city, will receive its social meaning from its location in the hierarchy of a network whose control and rhythm will escape from each place and, even more, from the people in each place. Furthermore, people will be shifted according to the continuous restructuring of an increasingly specialized space. Unemployed blacks in Detroit are already invited to go back to their now-booming industrial cities in the deep South. Mexicans will be brought into America and Turks will remain in Germany until General Motors develops its production in Mexico, and Japan takes over the European market, once controlled by the German cars, by adopting such measures as acquiring ailing Spanish car factories. The new space of a world capitalist system, combining the informational and the industrial modes of development, is a space of variable geometry, formed by locations hierarchically ordered in a continuously changing network of flows: flows of capital, labour, elements of production, commodities, information, decisions, and signals. The new urban meaning of the dominant class is the absence of any meaning based on experience. The abstraction of production tends to become total. The new source of power relies on the control of the entire network of information. Space is dissolved into flows: cities become shadows that explode or disappear according to decisions that their dwellers will always ignore. The outer experience is cut off from the inner experience. The new tendential urban meaning is the spatial and cultural separation of people from their product and from their history. It is the space of collective alienation and individual violence, transformed by undifferentiated feedbacks into a flow that never stops and never starts. Life is transformed into abstraction, cities into shadows.

Yet this is not the spatial form to emerge or the urban meaning to be imposed without resistance by the new dominant class, because space and cities, as well as history, are not the products of the will and interests of the dominant classes, genders, and apparatuses, but, the result of a process in which they are resisted by dominated classes, genders, and subjects, and in which they are met by alternative projects of new, emerging social actors. So the spatial blueprint of capitalist technocracy is historically being challenged by the alternative urban meaning projected by labour, women, cultures, citizens, urban social movements, along a series of dimensions that we must point out before introducing the connection between the drama we are describing and the social processes observed in our research on urban movements.

Each spatial restructuring attempted by the new, dominant class, each urban meaning being defined by the capitalists, managers, and technocrats is being met by conflicting projects of urban meaning, functions, and forms, coming from a variety of social actors. To use the terms of Charles Tilly (1977), some movements are reactive to the disruptions operated in their space by the dominant class, while others are proactive by proposing new relationships between space and society. Let us outline the basic tendencies of this new struggle over the definition of urban meaning before entering into the analysis of the urban social movements we have observed and how they relate to historical change.

For the sake of clarity, we will enumerate the different contradictory relationships established between the spatial project of the dominant class and the alternative meaning proposed by popular classes and (or) social movements:

(1) The adaptation of old spaces to new dominant functions through urban renewal, and the regional restructuring on the basis of a new specialization of the territory are resisted by neighbourhoods that do not want to disappear, by regional cultures that want to cluster together, and by people who, previously uprooted, want to create new roots. At the time of writing, the most lucid publication of the American corporate establishment, *Business Week*, realized the problem. Its issue of 27 July 1981 is titled "America's New Immobile Society", reporting that:

America's celebrated "mobile society" is putting down roots. After a quarter-century in which 20% of the population changed addresses each year, the percentage is dropping. It fell to 17.7% in the last Census Bureau study in 1976 and is continuing to decline, according to census officials ... Larry H. Long, the bureau's chief migration specialist, says the US is very unlikely to return to the mobility of the 1950s and 1960s. That easy *mobility* – which had been both evidence and a cause of the nation's freewheeling ways and innovative economy – has ended. Dealing with the effects of this change will be one of the top challenges of the 1980s for US industry.... Evidence that Americans are staying put is as close as the next house or office. Tied down by dual-career marriages, housing costs, inflation, and a growing emphasis on leisure and community activities – the "quality of life" – workers are resisting relocation. (p. 58)

Business Week dixit. Mobility, a major spatial prerequisite of the industrial mode of development and, to some extent, of the informational mode, is being challenged by the defense of neighbourhoods and the search for a quality of life.

(2) A somewhat more complex pattern appears to be happening at the level of the new international division of labour. On the one hand, the penetration of the national economies by the multinational corporations, the green revolution, and the international financial networks, entirely disrupts the existing productive structure and triggers the accelerated rural–urban and urban–metropolitan migrations (see Santos, 1975). On the other hand, once in the big city, the newcomers try to settle in stable communities, build up neighbourhoods, and rely on local networks (e.g. Portes, 1981). The world's rootless economy and the local co-operative community are two faces of the same process, heading towards a potentially decisive confrontation

(3) The third major debate over the city concerns the spatial consequences of information and knowledge as a major source of productivity, founding a new model of development (see Stanback, 1979). The major social problem with the reliance on information is that because of the power and class relationships that dominate the framework within which information develops, their monopoly becomes a major source of domination and control. Therefore in the context of a class and statist society, the more that information develops, the more the communication channels must be controlled. In other words, for information to become a source of control, information and communication must be disjointed, the monopoly of the messages must be ensured, and the sending of images must be programmed, as well as their feed-back. Here again, the source of the new form of domination is neither the computer, video, nor mass media. Interactive systems of communication and computerized dissemination of knowledge have developed enough to dramatically improve, instead of reduce, the communication and information among people, as well as the cultural diversity of their messages.[5] Yet the monopoly held by capital-controlled or state-controlled mass media, as well as the monopoly of information by the technocracy, has generated a reaction by local communities emphasizing the construction of alternative cultures and patterns of communication through face-to-face interaction and the revival of the oral tradition. The tendency towards communication and culture without any spatial form as a result of centralized one-way information flows is being met by the localization of communication networks on the basis of territorially rooted cultural communities and social networks. The cultural uniformity of mass media is met by the cultural specificity of spatially based inter-personal networks. The informational technocrats dissolve the space in their flows. Distrustful people increasingly tend to rely on experience as their basic source of information. The potential breaking of two-way communication would create a dramatic gap in the legitimacy of our informational society.

(4) The popular movements, triggered by the acceleration of the restructuring of space by the informational mode of development and the new international division of labour have come to rejoin urban protests stemming from other structural contradictions of the capitalist city. Foremost among these urban movements is what we have named collective consumption trade unionism. The economic and spatial concentration of production led to the socialization of consumption under conditions such that most of these collective means of consumption (like housing, schools, health centres, and cultural amenities) were insufficiently profitable for private capital investment unless the state provided the conditions for a risk-free market or took direct responsibility for the delivery and management of urban services. The conditions of living in the city became a crucial part of the social wage, itself a component of the welfare state. While these developments released pressure on demands over direct wages and created a framework of relative social peace between capital and labour, they also led to the formation of a new type of demand movement dealing with the standards, prices, and ways of living as conditioned by urban services. When the economic crisis of the 1970s expressed

the structural limits of the contradiction of a capitalist economy relying increasingly on an ever-expanding state sector of service distribution, the urban fiscal crisis in America Alcaly and Mermelstein (1977) and the austerity policies in Europe (see, for instance, Conference of Socialist Economists' State Group, 1979) had to meet the popular demands for collective means of consumption that had become the material basis for everyday life. The recommodification of the city had to challenge the collective demand for a good city as a social service to which all citizens were entitled (see Harloe and Paris, 1982).

(5) Another major tendency of the capitalist mode of production in its new industrial development at the world level was to incorporate workers from different ethnic and cultural origins in such a way that they would be much more vulnerable, socially and politically, to capital's requirements than the native citizen workers of core countries.[6] Furthermore, the split introduced within the ranks of labour could lead towards the ethnic fragmentation of the working class that had been so successful in the formation of American capitalism, paving the ground for the complete victory of business over labour (see Aronowitz, 1973). In fact experience has shown that immigrant workers were less submissive than anticipated and in some countries, like Switzerland and Germany, have been at the forefront of a new wave of social struggle (see Castles and Kosack, 1973). Yet the economic mechanism of overexploitation of immigrants still works, both in America and Western Europe, in spite of widespread unemployment and the increasing militancy of immigrant labour. As a consequence the ethnic structure of major capitalist cities has undertaken another major transformation in the last two decades, and the process is expanding. Combined with the classical process of spatial segregation, racial discrimination, and segmented housing markets, territorially-based ethnic communities are increasingly in evidence. The recent development of an informal economy in the metro-

politan area, based on cheap labour and illegal conditions of work and living, is self-perpetuating and adding to the harshness of the newcomers' existence. The basis of their usefulness for the new economy is their defenseless situation, which requires the maintenance of a situation of dependency and disorganization in relationship to the labour market, to state institutions, and to the city's mainstream life.

On the other hand, for the new city dwellers to survive, they need, more than ever, to reconstruct a social universe, a local turf, a space of freedom, a community. Sometimes the community is built on the basis of the reconstruction of the social hierarchy and economic exploitation of the society they left behind, as in San Francisco's Chinatown dominated by the six companies, or in Miami's Cuban community dominated by the exiled Cuban bourgeoisie. In other cases, ethnically-based community organizations have mobilized a neighbourhood, both for their urban needs and against institutionalized prejudice; Latinos in Los Angeles for example, Puerto Ricans in New York, or West Indians in London. Most often, the self-organization, particularly among the youth, takes the form of clubs, gangs, or groups, where in-group identity is tied to collective survival, where the drug economy and the underworld find their manpower, and where the territorial boundaries of a gang's turf become at the same time the material proof of their power and their shop-floor – the source of their income. Sometimes all these elements combine into major outbursts. The inner city communities combat the segregated space of ethnic fragmentation, cultural strangeness, and economic over-exploitation of the new post-industrial city with the defense of their identity, the preservation of their culture, the search for their roots, and the marking out of their newly acquired territory. Sometimes, also, they display their rage, and attempt to devastate the institutions that they believe devastate their daily lives.

(6) Space has always been connected to the state. This is even more evident in the new

urban forms and functions of the capitalist system. The management of urban services by state institutions, while demanded by the labour movement as a part of the social contract reached through class stuggle, has been one of the most powerful and subtle mechanisms of social control and institutional power over everyday life in our societies, as the researchers of the CERFI, a Paris-based research centre directed by Michel Foucault, have established both theoretically and empirically.[7] Furthermore, the centralization of the state, the increasing role of the executive branch, the shrinkage and bureaucratization of the political system, and the reduction of fiscal resources and legal power for local governments have led to a situation where the exercise of democracy is limited to some isolated, although crucial, votes, choosing between a limited number of alternatives the origin of which has been largely removed from public information, consciousness, opinion, and decision.

The gap between civil society and the political system is widening because of the rigidity of the political parties and the difficulty they find in being receptive to the values and demands expressed by the new social movements (for instance, feminists, ecologists, anti-establishment youths). The crisis of legitimacy for the democratic state (Habermas, 1973). has convinced the experts of the Trilateral Commission that democracy should be restricted and limited, so that people will not take excessive liberties (Crozier et al., 1975). On the other hand, there is a growing tendency towards political tribalism, calling for the abandonment of democratic life and the withdrawal into the wilderness of squatter houses, free communes, and alternative institutions.[8] A fundamental debate over the state is going on at the core of our civilization and, surprisingly enough, it tends to use a territorial language. The new capitalist, technocratic elite calls for a state without boundaries, territories, limits: again, for a state that governs overflows. Its blueprint includes informational control over the entire population by electronic means and storage of files in interconnected memories; blurring national boundaries; state-centralization of energy in the form of nuclear power; concentration of decisions in small cabinets and *ad hoc* groups relying on powerful bureaucratic machineries, with local governments considered as parochial and incompetent to view the overall picture, and therefore undeserving of their responsibilities. This new form of enlightened despotism calls for a non-localized world order where the representation of citizens on the basis of the membership of their cities must be replaced by the controllers of know-how who take a broader look at the problems of this planet from the carpeted meeting room of a space shuttle.[9]

People of all *classes* have proposed views of the relationship between the city and the state that are opposite to this urban system, increasingly penetrated and controlled by a centralized state via insulated bureaucracies. On the one hand, when the German squatters asked for an urban reservation in which to live and a modest state allowance to survive in it, they were taking the ultimate step in the disintegration of the relationship between state and civil society (see Mayer, n.d.). The Christiania commune in Copenhagen, the Indiani Metropolitani in Italy during the 1970s, some of the Dutch squatters, parts of the Californian gay community, and certainly the youth of Zurich, all share a similar attitude: if the city cannot get rid of the state, let us seek the state's agreement to siphon off a small part of the city, on the condition that it should be a real neighbourhood, with an intense urban life and historical tradition, as opposed to a piece of land in some anonymous suburban apartment complex.

Yet the tendency towards state centralism and domination by the state over the city is being opposed all over the world by a massive popular appeal for local autonomy and urban self-management. The revival of democracy depends upon the capacity of connecting the new demands, values, and projects to the institutions that manage society (that is, the state) on the basis of its increasing penetration by civil society, starting where people can most actively participate in decision-making: the communal institutions of local government (Castells, 1981), as decentralized as possible in neighbourhood councils a system begun 20 years ago in Bologna (Nanetti, 1977). Between the state and its undifferentiated hinterland, on the one hand, and the demand for urban reservation, on the other, a new project of self-management appears able to reconstruct the relationship between the state and the city on the basis of their mutual grassroots.

This is, then, the historical framework in which our observation of emerging urban movements took place. Let us now turn to the integration of this general framework and our research findings, so that historical trends can be fleshed out, and the results of our observations fully understood.

NOTES

1   An evolution that was foreseen, many years ago, by Richard Meier (1962).

2   Alvin Toffler, in a somewhat superficial but perceptive manner, has popularized these themes in his best seller *The Third Wave*. A good simple description of the new technologies under way can be found in Osborne (1979); also see Martin (1981). For a preliminary assessment of the spatial impact of this development see Stanback (1979). We also benefited for the analysis of the relationship between the new technologies and spatial restructuring from talks given by Ann Markusen as she progressed towards the completion of a major book on regional political economy.

3   As Roger Friedland (1982) explains in his analysis of American central cities.

4   A trend made abundantly clear by the remarkable research monograph by Anna Lee Saxenian (1980) on the formation of the

Silicon Valeey, the largest concentration of microelectronics industry in the world, around Santa Clara (California) and Stanford University. In relationship to the more urban-orientated managerial and professional elite, this cultural pattern seems to underlie the so-called back to the city movement that, in America, sees a tendency of middle class professionals living in places of active urban life. See Laska and Spain (1980).

5   We are indebted for information and ideas on this subject to Françoise Sabbah, from the Department of Broadcasting and Communication Arts, San Francisco State University.

6   See Castells (1975). The analysis appears, overall, to be verified for America by the statistical and historical research on immigration currently being undertaken by Alejandro Portes, Professor of Sociology at Johns Hopkins University.

7   See, for instance, Fourquet and Murard (1977), or Murard and Zylbermann (1976). The main theoretical inspiration for all this work comes from Michel Foucault, as expressed, for example, in his book *Surveiller et Punir* (1975).

8   Observed, for instance, in the Christiana commune, located in the core of Copenhagen in the buildings that were formerly occupied by the army; or again in the powerful squatter movements in Holland. See, for instance, Anderiesen (1981).

9   To be sure, we are not referring to specific societies but pointing out tendencies of the new dominant class. For instance, the Reagan administration emphasizes the role of local governments, both to dismantle the welfare state and in confidence of conservative support in most segregated communities of suburban America. But when local governments pass rent control laws, the Republican Urban Task Force Threatens them with the withdrawal of Federal funds.

REFERENCES

Alcaly, R. and Mermelstein, D. (eds) (1977) *The Fiscal Crisis of American Cities*. New York: Vintage Books.

Anderiesen, G. (1981) Tanks in the streets: the growing conflict over housing in Amsterdam. *International Journal of Urban and Regional Research*, 5(1).

Aronwitz, S. (1973) *False Promises: The Shaping of the American Working Class Consciousness*. New York: McGraw-Hill.

Bluestone, B. and Harrison, B. (1980) *Capital and Communities*. Washington, DC: The Progressive Alliance.

Castells, M. (1975) Immigrant workers and class struggle. *Politics and Society*, 5(1).

Castells, M. (1981a) *Crisis Urbana y Cambio Social*. Madrid and Mexico: Siglo XXI.

Castells, M. (1981b) Local government, urban crisis and political change. In *Political Power and Social Theory: A Research Annual, volume 2*. Greenwich, CT: JAI Press.

Castles, S. and Kosack, G. (1973) *Immigrant Workers and Class Structure in Western Europe*. Oxford: Oxford University Press.

Cohen, R. B. (1981) The new international division of labor: multinational corporations and urban hierarchy. In M. Dear and A Scott (eds), *Ubanization and Urban Planning*. London: Methuen, pp. 287–315.

Conference of Socialist Economists' State Group (1979) *Struggles over the State: Cuts and Restructuring in Contemporary Britain*. London: CSE Books.

Crozier, M., Huntington, S. and Watanuk, J. (1975) *The Crisis of Democracies: Report on the Governability of Democracies*. New York: Columbia University Press.

Duncan, O. D. et al. (1964) *Metropolis and Region*. Baltimore: Johns Hopkins University Press.

Foucault, M. (1975) *Surveiller et Punir*. Paris: Gallimard.

Fourquet, F. and Murard, L. (1977) *Les Equipments du Pouvoir*. Paris: Christian Bourgeois.

Friedland, R. (1982) *Power and Crisis in the City*. London: Macmillan.

Habermas, J. (1973) *Legitimation*. Boston: Beacon Hill.

Hall, P. (1966) *The World Cities*. (London: Weidenfeld and Nicolson, 1966).

Harloe, M. and Paris, C. (1982) The decollectivization of consumption. Paper delivered at the Tenth World Congress of Sociology, Mexico.

Harvey, D. (1975) The political economy of urbanization in advanced capitalist countries: the case of the US. In *Urban Affairs Annual Review*. Beverly Hills, CA: Sage.

Harvey, D. (1978) The urban process under capitalism. *International Journal of Urban and Regional Research*, 2(1), 101–32.

Idris-Soven, A. et al. (eds) (1978) *The World as a Company Town: Multinational Corporations and Social Change*. The Hague: Mouton.

Laska, S. and Spain, D. (1980) *Back to the City*.

Martin, J. (1981) *Telematic Society*. Englewood Cliffs, NJ: Prentice Hall.

Mayer, M. (n.d.) Urban squatters in Germany. *International Journal of Urban and Regional Research*.

Meier, R. (1962) *A Communication Theory of Urban Growth*. Cambridge, MA: MIT Press.

Mollenkopf, J. (1981) The north-east and the south-west: paths toward the post-industrial city. In G. Burchell and David Listokin (eds), *Cities under Stress*. Piscataway, NJ: Rutgers University Center of Urban Policy Research.

Murard, L. and Zylbermann, P. (1976) *Ville, Habitat et Intimité*. Paris: Recherches.

Nanetti, R. (1977) Citizen participation and neighborhood councils in Bologna. Unpublished PhD thesis, Department of Political Science, University of Michigan, Ann Arbor.

Osborne, A. (1979) *Running Wild: The Next Industrial Revolution*. Berkeley, CA: Osborne/McGraw-Hill.

Portes, A. (1981) Immigracion, etnicidad y el caso Cubano. Unpublished research report, Johns Hopkins University, May.

Pred, A. (1977) *City-systems in Advanced Economies: Past Growth, Present Processes and Future Development Options*. New York: John Wiley.

Santos, M. (1975) *The Shared Space: The Two Circuits of Urban Economy in the Underdeveloped Countries and Their Spatial Repercussions*. London: Methuen.

Sawyers, L. and Tabb, W. (eds) (1977) *Marxism and the Metropolis*. New York: Open University Press.

Saxenian, A. L. (1980) Silicon chips and spatial structure: the industrial basis of urbanization in Santa Clara County, California. Unpublished master's thesis, Department of City Planning, University of California at Berkeley.

Stanback, T. M. (1979) *Understanding the Service Economy: Employment, Productivity, Location*. Baltimore: Johns Hopkins University Press.

Tilly, C. (1977) *From Mobilization to Revolution*. Reading, MA: Addison Wesley.

Toffler, A. (1980) *The Third Wave*. New York: William Morrow and Co.

5

Urban Landscapes as Public History

Dolores Hayden

In January and February of 1975, Herbert J. Gans and Ada Louise Huxtable debated the public meaning of the built past on the op-ed pages of the *New York Times*. Gans, an urban sociologist, opened the controversy by attacking New York's Landmarks Preservation Commission for what he called rewriting New York's architectural history: "Since it tends to designate the stately mansions of the rich and buildings designed by famous architects, the commission mainly preserves the elite portion of the architectural past. It allows popular architecture to disappear.... This landmark policy distorts the real past, exaggerates affluence and grandeur, and denigrates the present" (Gans, 1975a).

Ada Louise Huxtable, architectural critic, member of the editorial board of the *Times*, and a supporter of preservation, defended the commission's record. She warned: "to stigmatize major architectural monuments as products of the rich, and attention to them as elitist cultural policy, is a perverse and unserviceable distortion of history.... These buildings are a primary and irreplaceable part of civilization. Esthetic singularity is as important as vernacular expression. Money frequently made superb examples of the art of architecture possible, and there were, fortunately, great architects to design and build great buildings" (Huxtable, 1975). She also argued that, in addition to monumental buildings she judged essential to public culture, the Landmarks Preservation Commission had designated twenty-six historic districts including 11,000 buildings, most of them what she called "vernacular."

Gans countered Huxtable's plea for "great buildings" by great architects in a second article, where he made the case for a broader approach to ordinary buildings as part of public history: "Private citizens are of course entitled to save their own past, but when preservation becomes a public act, supported with public funds, it must attend to everyone's past" (Gans, 1975b).[1] He went on to analyze New York's designations in quantitative terms, looking at landmark designations among buildings erected after 1875: 105 of 113 were by major architects, 25 by one firm, McKim, Mead and White. Most of these were not accessible to the public. 91 were located in Manhattan, which left the other boroughs with very few or no historical landmarks. 17 of the 26 historic districts were built as neighborhoods of the affluent. Although these numbers might have won the day, Huxtable nevertheless had the last word. Gans's second article was not published on the op-ed page, but appeared in abbreviated form as a letter to the editor. His arguments about the equitable use of public funds and the neglect of boroughs other than Manhattan never reached a metropolitan audience.

In this exchange from two decades ago, a leading urban sociologist and a distinguished architectural critic were unable (or unwilling) to understand each other's language. When he said "architecture," he meant all urban buildings, or the built environment. When she said "architecture," she meant buildings designed by professionally trained architects operating with aesthetic intent, or perhaps one percent of the built environment. When he said "vernacular" he was classifying buildings by social use, referring to definitions of social class and accessibility, and implying tenements, sweatshops, saloons, and public bathhouses. When she said "vernacular," she meant that the architect was unknown, and the classification was by architectural style and/or typology, such as Greek Revival side-hall row house, so that, in her terms, there would be many "vernacular" town houses on the wealthy Upper East Side, as well as in more modest areas. When he said "neighborhood" he meant a complex network of social as well as spatial ties, and implied a working-class population, giving examples like Williamsburg and Bushwick. She said "neighborhood" and meant the physical line bounding a historic district such as the Upper East Side or Greenwich Village.

As they argued, their underlying values made the debate more heated. He wanted more social history, she wanted more culture. He wanted taxpayers' money spent equitably in all neighborhoods. She believed aesthetic resources should be ranked in order to buy the best in terms of connoisseurship. She wasn't against designating the occasional public bathhouse or tavern or tenement or philanthropic housing project as a landmark, but her passion was for preserving the aesthetic qualities of great buildings: "Because their restoration and re-use are formidably difficult and costly and their land values usually high, these are the hardest buildings to preserve." She scolded Gans, "So 'elite' them not; they need all the help they can get" (Huxtable, 1975).

They exasperated each other, because he wasn't interested in aesthetic quality and she didn't want to spend a lot of money on social issues. He believed the past had different meanings for different people, all equally valid in social terms, but he had little interest in design: "whether buildings are beautiful or ugly is a personal judgment that should not be left solely to professional estheticians." She argued that history, expressed in designated landmarks, was socially "inclusive," yet she didn't agree that there could be more than one standard of what was important when it came to aesthetics.

Neither delved into the downside of what they promoted. He did not explore the problems of preserving and interpreting ghetto locations or bitter memories. She did not ask how to justify spending taxpayers' money without giving public access or interpretation. And neither of them tried to identify opportunities to realize both his ideal of urban preservation and her ideal of architectural preservation. For instance, more warehouses, shops, and boardinghouses, the kind of urban vernacular buildings he defended, might have been saved to supply the social and economic context for the row houses she defended. Or the private clubs and mansions she defended could have been interpreted in terms of the masons' and carpenters' skills in constructing them, and the maids' and gardeners' skills in maintaining them, to supply the urban working-class history he desired.

The debate appeared to be a dead end at the time. But from today's perspective, both Gans and Huxtable seem to have shared a common concern that Americans were losing significant public memories when neighborhoods like Boston's Italian American West End were bulldozed or monuments like New York's Penn Station met the wrecking ball. And they shared an inability to predict either the changed social composition of the city's population two decades after their debate, or the worsening economic condition of the American city. As an eminent sociologist, Gans was an outsider to preservation, raising some polemical questions. He thought this debate was primarily about social class in the city. As a distinguished architectural critic, Huxtable emphasized buildings. Neither anticipated that the 1990s would involve major controversies about the definitions of public history and public culture in a democratic society.[2]

Today, debates about the built environment, history, and culture take place in much more contested terrain of race, gender, and class, set against long-term economic and environmental problems, especially in the large cities of the United States. The citizens of New York were still over 75 percent white in the 1970 Census. By 1990, New

York had a white population of only 38 percent, outnumbered by African Americans, Latinos, and Asian Americans who comprised 61 percent of the city, including both long-term residents and new immigrants.[3] (Across the nation, the top ten cities show similar changes, from about 70 percent white in 1970 to less than 40 percent in 1990 (Davis, 1993).) Federal support for cities has declined over the past twenty years, while extreme poverty and homelessness have become increasingly concentrated in the inner city. Environmental problems are concentrated there as well – unhealthy air, polluted harbors, abandoned housing units, rusting bridges, broken water mains.

While the urban landscape may be less attractive, there are far more claims being made upon it to furnish resources for public history and public culture. Today, James Baldwin's question "And why isn't it for you?" echoes across the city streets where he felt excluded as a young boy. An African American group seeks support for the protection of the remaining traces of the African Burial Ground near the present City Hall in Manhattan, and its sympathetic interpretation as a site where people of color were buried in the colonial period. "The city has been commemorating other aspects of its history for three hundred years," notes Howard Dobson, head of the Schomburg Center for Research on Black Culture in New York (Myers, 1993; Fabre and O'Meally, 1994). His indignation is echoed by many other groups across the city and across the country. Centuries of neglect of ethnic history have generated a tide of protest – where are the Native American, African American, Latino, and Asian American landmarks?

Gender involves similar, interconnected questions. Why are so few moments in women's history remembered as part of preservation? Why are so few women represented in commemorative public art? And why are the few women honored almost never women of color? Issues about working-class and poor neighborhoods remain – what, if anything, can public history or preservation projects add to their identity

and economic development? How do these issues intersect with the claims for ethnic history and women's history? And what kind of public processes and techniques best represent commitment to social history in public places?

Private nonprofit institutions (such as museums and preservation groups), as well as public agencies (city landmarks commissions and arts councils), are challenged daily to become accountable to the diverse urban public, whose members are both taxpayers and potential audiences. Current census statistics suggest that it is indeed appropriate to find new ways to deploy tax dollars in cultural programs that may range from exhibits to the preservation of historic buildings and landscapes, or the creation of permanent works of public art. While some private institutions and public agencies struggle to address their ways of working, and sponsor various kinds of "cultural planning" in order to become more accountable, many impatient citizens' groups are putting forward their own projects to represent their communities' history and tell their own stories in public space (see Karp et al., 1992, for examples). The politics of identity – however they may be defined around gender or race or neighborhood – are an inescapable and important aspect of dealing with the urban built environment, from the perspectives of public history, urban preservation, and urban design.

Indeed, interest in themes of identity is not limited to the city. Women's history and ethnic history drive many preservation controversies across the country. Recently, the National Trust for Historic Preservation established goals for cultural diversity in preservation (Anon., 1993).[4] There have been successful efforts in Tennessee, Alabama, and Georgia to preserve buildings associated with the civil rights movement and Martin Luther King. *Historic Preservation News* recently announced the start of an effort to preserve the Woolworth's store in Greensboro, North Carolina, "where four black students staged a historic sit-in at the whites-only lunch counter in 1960" (Anon., 1994). At the same time, the first national conference on Preserving Women's History was held at Bryn Mawr in 1994, coinciding with the publication of a guide to landmarks of women's history across the nation, *Susan B. Anthony Slept Here* (Kazickas and Scherr, 1994). Dozens of other guides to landmarks of ethnic and women's history are becoming available from states and cities around the country, as well as scholarly accounts (Wade, 1994). Yet both the ethnic and women's landmarks are proposed at a time when some of the large questions Gans and Huxtable debated are still unresolved. Architecture, as a discipline, has not seriously considered social and political issues, while social history has developed without much consideration of space or design. Yet it is the volatile combination of social issues with spatial design, intertwined in these controversies, that makes them so critical to the future of American cities.

Change is not simply a matter of acknowledging diversity or correcting a traditional bias toward the architectural legacy of wealth and power. It is not enough to add on a few African American or Native American projects, or a few women's projects, and assume that preserving urban history is handled well in the United States in the 1990s. Nor is it enough to have a dozen different organizations advocating separate projects. Instead, a larger conceptual framework is required to support urban residents' demands for a far more inclusive "cultural citizenship," as Rina Benmayor and John Kuo Wei Tchen have defined it, "an identity that is formed not out of legal membership but out of a sense of cultural belonging" (Inter-University Project for Latino Research, Hunter College, 1988, quoted in Tchen, 1990). Benmayor and Tchen argue that public culture needs to acknowledge and respect diversity, while reaching beyond multiple and sometimes conflicting national, ethnic, gender, race, and class identities to encompass larger common themes, such as the migration experience, the breakdown and reformulation of families, or the search for a new sense of identity in an urban setting. They are asking for an extremely subtle evocation of American diversity, which at the same time reinforces our sense of common membership in an American, urban society.

Public space can help to nurture this more profound, subtle, and inclusive sense of what it means to be an American. Identity is intimately tied to memory: both our personal memories (where we have come from and where we have dwelt) and the collective or social memories interconnected with the histories of our families, neighbors, fellow workers, and ethnic communities. Urban landscapes are storehouses for these social memories, because natural features such as hills or harbors, as well as streets, buildings, and patterns of settlement, frame the lives of many people and often outlast many lifetimes. Decades of "urban renewal" and "redevelopment" of a savage kind have taught many communities that when the urban landscape is battered, important collective memories are obliterated. Yet even totally bulldozed places can be marked to restore some shared public meaning, a recognition of the experience of spatial conflict, or bitterness, or despair. At the same time, in ordinary neighborhoods that have escaped the bulldozer but have never been the object of lavish municipal spending, it is possible to enhance social meaning in public places with modest expenditures for projects that are sensitive to all citizens and their diverse heritage, and developed with public processes that recognize both the cultural and the political importance of place.

The power of place – the power of ordinary urban landscapes to nurture citizens' public memory, to encompass shared time in the form of shared territory – remains untapped for most working people's neighborhoods in most American cities, and for most ethnic history and most women's history. The sense of civic identity that shared history can convey is missing. And even bitter experiences and fights communities have lost need to be remembered – so as not to diminish their importance.

To reverse the neglect of physical resources important to women's history and ethnic history is not a simple process, especially if preservationists are to be true to the insights of a broad, inclusive social history encompassing gender, race, and class. Restoring significant shared meanings for many neglected urban places first involves claiming the entire urban cultural landscape as an important part of American history, not just its architectural monuments. This means emphasizing the building types – such as tenement, factory, union hall, or church – that have housed working people's everyday lives. Second, it involves finding creative ways to interpret modest buildings as part of the flow of contemporary city life. A politically conscious approach to urban preservation must go beyond the techniques of traditional architectural preservation (making preserved structures into museums or attractive commercial real estate) to reach broader audiences. It must emphasize public processes and public memory. This will involve reconsidering strategies for the representation of women's history and ethnic history in public places, as well as for the preservation of places themselves.

Despite the eloquent pleas of a few architects in favor of building and city as "theatres of memory" as much as futuristic "theatres of prophecy" (Rowe and Koetter, 1978),[5] most consideration of the built past in the United States has dealt with European architectural fashions and their application to American monumental buildings. For many years American cultural landscapes and urban vernacular buildings were ignored. Today the vernacular is subjected to more thoughtful scholarly and professional analysis, but often this is still based on physical form rather than social and political meaning. The same kind of creative work writers and artists have undertaken in claiming American places is yet to be accomplished by American architects, landscape architects, and urban planners, locating ourselves in the cities of the United States in a serious way, coming to terms with the urban landscape as it exists and has existed, connecting the history of struggle over urban space with the poetics of occupying particular places.[6]

This implies a stronger connection between scholarship in urban landscape history and work on cultural identity, as well as firmer links between theory and practice in

urban design. In the last decade there has been an explosion of scholarly work on cultural identity. Cultural and political geographers have mapped the tensions as urban communities struggle for terrain; social historians have looked at women's, workers', and ethnic history. Scholars in cultural studies have forged new syntheses of work on feminist, class, and ethnic issues, and emphasized new ways of looking at popular culture. At the same time there has been new interest in studying space as a cultural product. Environmental psychologists and anthropologists have examined people's responses to places. Environmental historians have applied new agendas to urban history. Geographers have put forth "postmodern geographies" with some connection to architecture and literary studies. But all this work is fragmented in separate disciplines, disciplines that are constantly attempting to reconnect aspects of knowledge within themselves, whether social, economic, environmental, or cultural. Also, scholars' fresh insights about urban space are not always available to professionals and community activists struggling to create new kinds of projects. And the activists' or artists' experience does not always reach either professionals or scholars.

A socially inclusive urban landscape history can become the basis for new approaches to public history and urban preservation. This will be different from, but complementary to, the art-historical approach to architecture that has provided a basis for architectural preservation. A more inclusive urban landscape history can also stimulate new approaches to urban design, encouraging designers, artists, and writers, as well as citizens, to contribute to an urban art of creating a heightened sense of place in the city. This would be urban design that recognizes the social diversity of the city as well as the communal uses of space, very different from urban design as monumental architecture governed by form or driven by real estate speculation.

As the debate between Gans and Huxtable demonstrated, saving a public past for any city or town is a political as well as historical and cultural process. Decisions about what to remember and protect involve the grounding of historical scholarship as well as the possibilities of public history, architectural preservation, environmental protection, and commemorative public art. Yet all of these approaches to conserving the past operate in partial and sometimes contradictory ways. The traces of time embedded in the urban landscape of every city offer opportunities for reconnecting fragments of the American urban story. (Lynch, 1972). But until historians have more understanding of the intricate relationship between cultural landscape history and place-specific memory, making the whole more than the sum of the parts will be difficult.

George Kubler once described the historian's craft as delineating the "shape of time." The art of the historian, he wrote, resembles that of the painter, "to discover a patterned set of properties that will elicit recognition all while conveying a new perception of the subject" (Kubler, 1962). The historian who confronts urban landscapes in the 1990s needs to explore their physical shapes along with their social and political meanings. Learning the social meanings of historic places by discussing them with urban audiences involves the historian in collaboration with the residents themselves as well as with planners and preservationists, designers and artists. It engages social, historical, and aesthetic imagination to locate where narratives of cultural identity, embedded in the historic urban landscape, can be interpreted to project their largest and most enduring meanings for the city as a whole.

NOTES

1 Gans supplied me with the complete text of his article, which appeared in very abbreviated form.
2 Gans wrote *Popular Culture and High Culture* (1975c) but didn't anticipate ethnic diversity as a focus. The Organization of American Historians [held] its 1995 meeting on "Public Pasts and Public Processes." An overview of some current museum efforts is Karp et al. (1992). Also see Karp and Lavine (1991), Leon and Rosenzweig (1989).
3 Cisneros (1993) provides a good summary of changing demographics. Also see Davis (1993).
4 Also see Anon. (1992) for an extensive list of ongoing projects.
5 They are quoting Frances Yates's term from *The Art of Memory.*
6 Turner (1989) is an admirable account of several American writers coming to terms with American places. Simonson and Walker (1988) is a good introduction to current writing. Lippard (1990) is an excellent analysis of how American artists are dealing with ethnic heritage.

REFERENCES

Anon. (1992) *Cultural and Ethnic Diversity in Historical Preservation.* Information series no. 65. Washington, DC: National Trust for Historic Preservation.
Anon. (1993) Focus on cultural diversity II. *Historical Preservation Forum,* 7 (January/February), 4–5.
Anon. (1994) Historic store slated to become Civil-Rights museum. *Historical Preservation News,* 34 (February/March), 2–3.
Cisneros, H. G. (ed.) (1993) *Interwoven Destinies: Cities and the Nation.* New York: W. W. Norton.
Davis, M. (1993) Who killed LA? The war against the cities. *Crossroad,* 32 (June), 9–10.
Fabre, G. and O'Meally, R. (1994) *History and Memory in African-American Culture.* New York: Oxford University Press.
Gans, H. J. (1975a) Preserving everyone's Noo Yawk. *New York Times,* January 28, op-ed. page.
Gans, H. J. (1975b) Elite architecture and the Landmarks Preservation Commission: a response to Ada Louise Huxtable. *New York Times,* February 25, editorial page, letters column.

Gans, H. J. (1975c) *Popular Culture and High Culture*. New York: Basic Books.

Huxtable, A. L. (1975) Preserving Noo Yawk landmarks. *New York Times*, February 4, op. ed. page.

Karp, I. and Lavine, S. D. (1991) *Exhibiting Cultures: The Poetics and Politics of Museum Display*. Washington, DC: Smithsonian Institution Press.

Karp, I., Mullen, C., and Lavine, S. D. (1992) *Museums and Communities: The Politics of Public Culture*. Washington, DC: Smithsonian Institution Press.

Kazickas, J. and Scherr, L. (1994) *Susan B. Anthony Slept Here*. New York: Times Books.

Kubler, G. (1962) *The Shape of Time: Remarks on the History of Things*. New Haven, CT: Yale University Press.

Leon, W. and Rozenzweig, R. (eds) (1989) *History Museums in the United States*. Urbana: University of Illinois Press.

Lippard, L. (1990) *Mixed Blessings: New Art in a Multicultural America*. New York: Pantheon.

Lynch, K. (1972) *What Time Is This Place?* Cambridge, MA: MIT Press.

Myers, S. L. (1993) Politics of present snags remembrance of past. *New York Times*, July 20, B1, 2.

Rowe, C. and Koetter, F. (1978) *Collage City*. Cambridge, MA: MIT Press.

Simonson, R. and Walker, S. (eds) (1988) *Multi-cultural Literacy: opening the American Mind*. St Paul, MN: Greywolf Press.

Tchen, J. K. W. (1990) The Chinatown–Harlem initiative: building a multicultural understanding in New York City. In J. Brecher and T. Costello (eds), *Building Bridges: The Emerging Grassroots Coalition of Labor and Community*. New York: Monthly Review Press.

Turner, F. (1989) *Spirit of Place: The Making of an American Literary Landscape*. San Francisco: Sierra Club Books.

Wade, B. (1994) New guides to landmarks of black history. *New York Times*, February 13, section 5, 4.

6

Harmonies of Urban Design and Discords of City Form

Abraham Akkerman

Introduction

Between antiquity and the early Renaissance, urban design often reflected images of current religious beliefs in cosmic harmony. Throughout antiquity and the Middle Ages these beliefs were reflected in notions of the Ideal City, conveying symmetry of city-form typified, for example, by the perimeters of new towns or newly founded colonies, often fashioned after the square or the circle. During the Renaissance, Mannerism and the Baroque, the notion of universal harmony continued to play a major role in ideal city plans and in planned cities, frequently corresponding to configurations geared for military defence (Rosenau, 1983, pp. 14–15). Urban design during the industrial revolution and through to the 20th century, inspired by the image of success in science, was guided by a conceited notion of planned coherence into sociospatial renditions of balance and coordination (see, for example, Wilson, 1983). In the guise of accord, order or optimization, mechanistic equilibria became the standard in conscious urban design through much of the 20th century (e.g. Friedman, 1962). As a central concept in mathematics and mechanics, the equilibrium has also come to epitomize rationality in urban planning, in the configuration of urban spaces, transportation arteries and complementary land uses. The planned town of the 20th century, an outcome of urban design since early modernity, thus recapitulated ancient notions of cosmic harmony as an archetype of the Ideal

City (cf. Benjamin, 1972, in Buck-Morss, 1990, p. 114).

Yet, while the adherence to geometrical symmetry, for example, has often been quite useful in the planning of new Greek or Roman colonies, where ownership of land had to be clearly delineated, or in the construction of fortress towns prior to the advent of gunpowder, the contrived equilibrium in the newfangled planned city has yielded results that are at considerable variance from its avowed design objectives. Whether it be an industrial metropolis or a suburban neighbourhood, a postindustrial town or a new subdivision, a genuine perception of urban development has led to a recognition of the city that is inimical to the city's planned image. It is the discernment of disequilibrium in the factual city, rather than the stability and composure planned for the city, that has become the city's earmark. To fervent observers the singularity of the authentic metropolis has been in its imbalance, absurdity and meaninglessness. These derisive qualities themselves, furthermore, have often resulted from the very same equilibria prevailing, or sought after, in the planned city. The tension between the authenticity of disequilibrium within the factual metropolis and the remoteness of the humanly alienating, mechanistic equilibrium emerging from a city plan led to striking reflections by leading writers of the 20th century. No commensurate deliberations, however, emerged in urban design.

In *The Castle*, an incomplete novel for which Franz Kafka has been recognized as one of the greatest of 20th-century writers, the alienation of the individual is firmly entrenched in the built form:

At every turn K. expected the road to double back to the Castle, and only because of the expectation did he go on; he was flatly unwilling, tired as he was, to leave the street, and he was also amazed at the length of the village, which seemed to have no end; again and again the same little houses, and frostbound window-panes and snow and the entire absence of human beings. (Kafka, 1992, p. 17 [1919])

Writing at the turn of the century, Kafka might well have prophesied a North American subdivision at the century's end. K., the novel's hero, is a land surveyor who never attains his goal of reaching the Castle where the chief bureaucrat resides, just as Kafka himself never completes his novel. The town, with its streets leading to nowhere, and the Castle, with its bureaucrats accessible to none, thus appear as a forgery, and the only pure realization is alienation itself. For indeed, the land surveyor, the foremost professional who since antiquity has measured property lots and laid new towns, has no reason to stay in this town once all has been measured and once the town's layout has been completed. He forever leaves the towns of his residence behind, perpetually having to move from one territory to another to practice his profession of perfection. Towns laid out already will have no need for land surveyors:

"You've been taken as Land Surveyor, as you say, but, unfortunately, we have no need for a Land Surveyor. There wouldn't be the least use for one here. The frontiers of our little state are marked out and all officially recorded. So what should we do with a Land Surveyor?" (Kafka, 1992, p. 61 [1919])

More than any other realm merging art and technology, urban design carries with it the most commonplace impact. The tragic distortion of modernity is embodied by this merger, competent in the demolition of destitute neighbourhoods, yet seldom able to replace them by anything but desolate perfection. Kafka calls on his reader to recognize that perfection is humanly meaningless; that an ideal is repugnant.

Interpreting such a call as a challenge to contemporary urban design broaches the question as to whether incompleteness and imperfection in city-form carry a virtue. This study suggests that this, indeed, may be the case. Moreover, the historical review offered here suggests that the 20th century posed a milestone in the history of city-form. While urban design has been guided by the various notions of harmony throughout the ages, the alienating city of the 20th century brought forward the longing for human authenticity, precisely through the humanistically irrelevant attempts to keep the city's organization and infrastructure in balance. The contradiction between urban efficiency and human authenticity perhaps has no solution. However, if urban design recognizes this dilemma, Kafka's challenge will have been addressed: lest the frontiers of our cities "are marked out and all officially recorded".

Cosmic Harmony and Urban Planning in Classical Greece

The belief in cosmic harmony had been inborn in the conscious layout of cities since antiquity. The first sign of systematic city planning in the history of civilization, an orthogonal grid plan of straight streets, had appeared in Indus cities as early as *c.*2400 BCE. At Mohenjo-Daro 12 orthogonal city blocks measuring 1200 × 800 feet were formed by three 30-foot-wide avenues and two streets crossing them at right angles. These very large blocks were subdivided by alleys up to 10 feet wide, onto which many of the houses opened. The three avenues were identified to run north and south, with corresponding positioning in the subdivision of street blocks. It is the orienting of Mohenjo-Daro to the points of the compass, and the 12

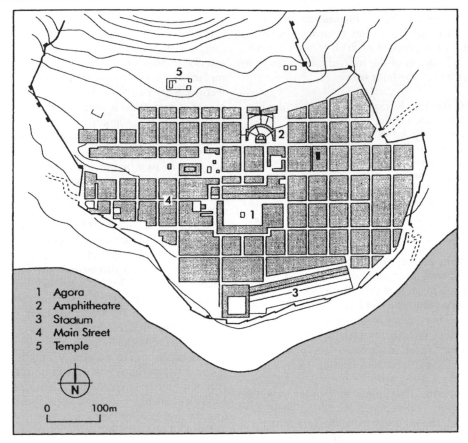

Figure 6.1   Plan of Priene, c.450 BCE.

blocks, apparently corresponding to the 12 lunar months, that suggest adherence to a perceived cosmic order in early cities of India (cf. Hawkes, 1973). Indian urban culture had an impact upon the deliberate design of cities in ancient Greece, by way of Mesopotamia and Egypt, already in the 7th century BCE (Roth, 1993, p. 183). Land in both town and country throughout much of Classical Greece was being subdivided into uniform rectangles, to ensure equitable land division (Jameson, 1991). Insofar as landscape permitted, the orthogonal layout of new settlements or rebuilt old settlements (figure 6.1) was therefore the norm in much of Classical Greece (Roth, 1993, p. 191–193).

In Greece too, however, the adherence to an orthogonal street pattern is significant due to its intriguing consistency with the Greek idea of the universe. Stemming from the practical need for the measurement of right angles to parcel out land, consistent development of orthogonal geometry is attributed to the philosophical school that commenced with Pythagoras in southern Italy in 525 BCE, and lasted for almost 1000 years carrying his name. It was the fortuitous unanimity of this pragmatic origin with Pythagorean geometry, and its fixation with musical form, that led to the school's canon of cosmic harmony.

This consistency can be observed also in the preoccupation of the Pythagorean School with the number 4 (the very first integer which is the second power of any other integer), with the geometry of the square and with the hypotenuse (see Burnet, 1964, pp.

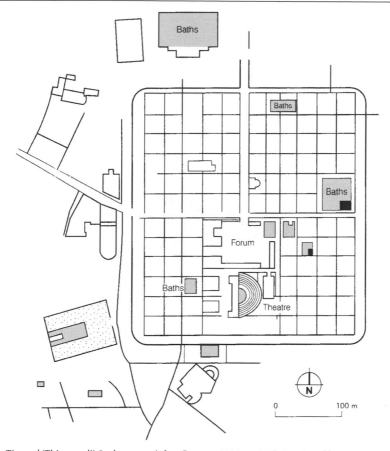

Figure 6.2 Timgad (Thimugadi) 2nd century (after Owens, 1991, p. 135). Reprinted by permission of Taylor & Francis Ltd.

105–106). Influenced by the Pythagoreans, the 5th-century BCE poet and philosopher Empedocles introduced the concept of *Kosmos*, as composed of four primeval elements (earth, fire, water and air). The doctrine of the four elements was adopted by Aristotle (384–322 BCE) a century later, was fully embraced by scholasticism throughout the Middle Ages and further sustained during the Renaissance.

In the history of urban design, the adoption of the number 4 as a paradigm of balance is also exemplified by the square, a significant element in the planning of fortified towns from the time of 2nd-century Roman colonies, such as Timgad (figure 6.2), through to Baroque urban places and towns such as the 17th-century Richelieu (figure 6.3).

The Pythagorean legacy of an orderly universe reveals itself in the reconstruction plan of Miletus (*c.*479 BCE, figure 6.4), where rigid geometrical layout is imposed upon topography, rather than following it. The rebuilding of Miletus is described by Aristotle with reference to a tripartite division of the city into distinct zones:

Hippodamus [*c.*500–440 BCE], the son of Euryphon, of Miletus, who invented the division of cities and laid out Piraeus . . . wanted to institute a city of ten thousand men, divided into three parts, and to make one part artisans, one farmers, and the third the military part and that possessing arms. He also divided the territory into three parts, one sacred, one public and one private. (*Politics* II, 8, in Apostle and Gerson, 1986, p. 55)

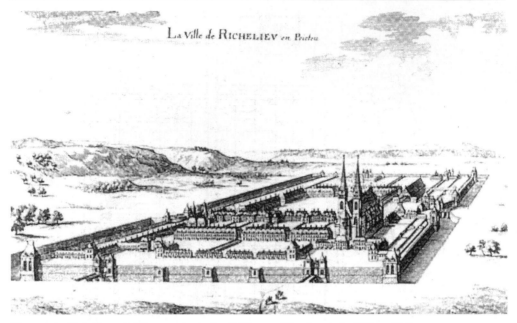

Figure 6.3   Richelieu *c.*1638, engraving by Israël Silvestre (Chartier et al., 1981, p. 114).

Based on Aristotle's figures, Miletus may have had perhaps 30 000 inhabitants, whereas the typical Greek city, the *polis*, had population much smaller than that: Aristotle's teacher, Plato (427–347 BCE), described the ideal *polis* as having 5040 citizens. In fact, only Athens, Syracuse and Akragas had recorded population over 20 000.

Plato's own most significant work, the *Republic* (Adams, 1963), completed *c.*380 BCE, refers to the ideal *polis* as composed also of three classes of citizens, a fact that led to speculations as to the impact the plan of Miletus may have had upon Plato (Von Gerkan, 1924, p. 62; Lang, 1952). The social structure of Plato's Ideal City is austere and, to the extent that Plato elaborates on the city's physical layout, it corresponds in rigidity to his view of the city's social structure:

> The conditions suppose a population with no disrelish for... social regulations, who will tolerate life-long limitations of property, restrictions such as those we have proposed on procreation, and deprivation of gold and other things which it is certain, from what has been said already, that the legislator will prohibit; they presuppose further the central position of the capital, and the distribution of the dwelling-houses over the territory, as [the legislator] has prescribed, almost as though he were telling his dreams or fashioning a city and its inhabitants out of waxwork. (*Laws* V, 746, in Saunders, 1970, p. 217)

To Plato, orderliness in the tripartite division of the city-state arises from the depths of the human soul (*Republic* II). In Plato's mind, there is a fastidious mutuality, mirrored by the human soul onto the Ideal City (*Republic* II), and thus the Ideal City is a universal archetype, common to all.

The Ideal City of Stoicism and Early Christianity

The notion of the harmonious city as a universalist imprint was further advanced by the Stoics, about 300 BCE, most evidently in their concept of *Kosmopolis*, the universe "as it were, the common home of gods and man, or a city that belongs to both" (Dio Chrysostom [1st-century CE], 36th logos, para. 21, translated in Schofield, 1991,

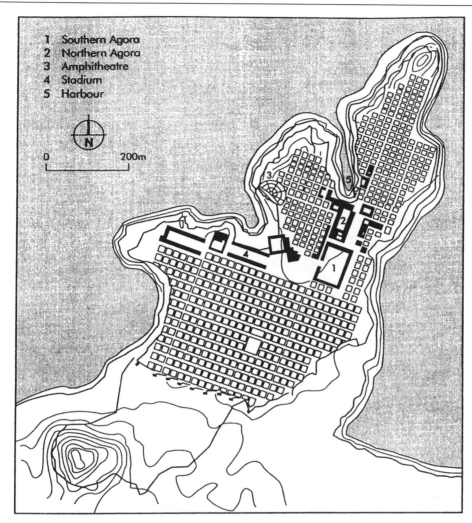

Figure 6.4 Plan of Miletus, c.479 BCE.

p. 62). The universe, in this view, is the only true city, "for no one knows of a good city, made up entirely of good elements – neither a mortal one that came to be in the past, nor one that is to be one day in the future worth conceiving of – unless it be a city of the blessed gods in heaven" (Dio Chrysostom, translated in Schofield, 1991, p. 62).

Harmony, and the allied concepts of order and symmetry, as guiding principles in the arts and the sciences since ancient Greece also became pivotal in the history of later urban thought. The most important link between the morphology of the Classical Greek city and urban perception of the Middle Ages and the Renaissance is the notion of the planned town, expounded in *De architectura* of the Roman military architect and engineer Marcus Vitruvius Pollio (active 46–30 BCE). Based upon concepts Vitruvius put forward in his own ideal city plans (figure 6.5), the suggestion was made that his main concern, too, was to satisfy the premises of harmony, only using circular (rather than square) forms for compliance with regularity, enclosure and wind protection (Rosenau, 1983).

In the 5th century, the Stoic ideal of *Kosmopolis* had received a magnificent

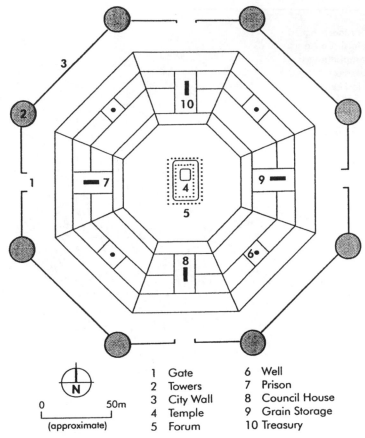

1	Gate	6	Well
2	Towers	7	Prison
3	City Wall	8	Council House
4	Temple	9	Grain Storage
5	Forum	10	Treasury

0   50m
(approximate)

N

Figure 6.5   Vitruvius's plan of an ideal city (after 18th-century edition of Vitruvius by Galiani (Rosenau, 1983, p. 70)).

amplification in St Augustine's 18 books of *The City of God* (Tasker, 1945). It is perhaps no coincidence that Aurelius Augustinus (354–430), as the bishop of Hippo, found it significant enough to address the base nature of the *real* city of his time, when deliberating on a heavenly community in *The City of God*. Borrowing from the Stoics to contrast the terrestrial city of sin, the underlying tenets of St Augustine's treatise are the concepts of justice and accord as theological principles in an ideal community. Significant in St Augustine's social ideal, it has been pointed out, was, yet again, the notion of harmony and balance, or *Ordo*, allied to a cosmic system of flawless relations, *Ordo creaturum* (Barker, 1962, p. xii). St Augustine's juxtaposition of the two cities, too, points to a universal parity:

Two cities were formed by two loves: the earthly by the love of self, even to the contempt of God; the heavenly by the love of God, even to the contempt of self. The former, in a word, glories in itself, the latter in the Lord. (*City of God* XIV, 28, in Tasker, 1945)

The notion of the Ideal City in St Augustine emerges thus as an ontological component of cosmic balance, not a mere religious and social attempt at rectifying conditions in the existing society.

The "love of self", by which the terrestrial city is characterized by St Augustine, has a factual expression in the prevailing irregular plans of most medieval cities. The orientation of houses in relation to streets as well as to adjacent dwellings often mirrored the desire of property owners for access to market places or main thoroughfares rather than pointing to a prearranged, centralized scheme (Dickinson, 1963, p. 315). On the other hand, the coveting of geometrical symmetry in a plan continued to characterize medieval new towns, outposts of dominant city-states such as Florence or Siena in the late Middle Ages. Florence's own original street plan, dating back perhaps to 90–80 BCE, was possibly laid out in a chess-board fashion (Haverfield, 1913, p. 92), a fact that may have reinforced the fancy for orthogonal, symmetric plans in the new towns as well.

Particularly striking examples are the two Florentine new towns, San Giovani and Terranuova. In both towns the deepest lots face onto the main street in the centre of town, perceived as the first or the central city block. Retreating towards the city wall, there are several rows of blocks that succeed the first block. As they near the town wall, the blocks within each row, and their respective lots, become progressively shallower. While lots in different rows retain the same width, they differ from one another in their depths, determined by the distance of their respective row from the central block. In San Giovani (founded 1299) the lot depth is determined by the shorter and the longer side of right-angled triangles opposite the angles of 30° and 60°, respectively. In Terranuova (founded 1377) the depths are determined by the sides of right-angled triangles, opposite the corresponding angles of 15°, 30°, 45°, 60° and 75° (Friedman, 1988). Other medieval examples of orderly plans, often intimating aspects of property development and speculation but also of trade and commerce, can be found as far as the British Isles (Slater, 1990).

Equilibria in Ideal Cities of the Renaissance and Mannerism

The Pythagorean concept of harmony appears to have culminated in the aesthetic and scientific advances of the Renaissance and Mannerism. As a methodological tool

emerging prior to and during the Renaissance, geometrical symmetry had continued to be an essential tenet in both the art and the natural sciences of early modernity. Given their great emphasis on defensive fortifications, Renaissance plans for ideal cities can rightfully be viewed as a creative union of art and technology within a single project. Perhaps more than any other such union, Renaissance town planning had further recast the concept of harmony into a more generalized and articulate notion of equilibrium, thus encompassing a transformation of the Greek heritage into early modern art and science.

The Renaissance recognition of balance as an aesthetic feature in a physical object had been brought forward first by Leone Battista Alberti (1404–1472) who, in his 10-book treatise, *Libri de re aedificatoria decem*, defined beauty "as that reasoned harmony of all the parts within a body, so that nothing can be added, taken away, or altered, but for the worse" (Alberti, [1485], VI, 2, in Rykwert et al., 1988, p. 156). Almost 100 years prior to Alberti, rendition of the perspective was introduced in painting by Duccio di Buoninsegna in Siena and Giotto di Bondone in Florence. Alberti's adherence to aesthetic balance through the introduction of the perspective into urban design became evident shortly after 1447, when he became the architectural advisor to Pope Nicholas V. Commissioned by the Pope to prepare a plan for Rome, Alberti never saw the full implementation of his proposal (due to the Pope's death in 1455), but the plan itself discloses Alberti's proclivity:

> From [a large] square three straight and broad avenues were to start, and terminate in another open space at the foot of the Vatican Hill; the central avenue was to lead to the Basilica, the one to the right to the Vatican Palace, that on the left to the building facing it. (Pastor, 1899, pp. 171–176)

Alberti articulated the notion of the perspective and the vanishing point in *De re aedificatoria*, and through it wielded influence on many of his contemporaries. Among the

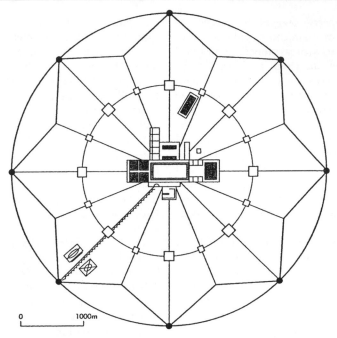

Figure 6.6   Filarete's plan of Sforzinda (after his *Trattato d'architettura, c.* 1464).

theoreticians, Antonio Averlino Filarete (*c.*1400–1469) marked Renaissance urban design with lasting profundity. His treatise, *Trattato d'architettura*, is an impassioned persuasion of the Milan count Francesco Sforza to commission Filarete with the construction of a new town, Sforzinda. Filarete describes the plan of his Ideal City as a perfect octagon, created by two superimposed squares, with details on fortifications and gates (figure 6.6). There are 16 evenly distributed main avenues, each 24m wide, leading from the gates to the centre of the city (Filarete, 1457, Book VI, 43v, in Spencer, 1965).

Filarete's Ideal City echoed some existing practices in the layout of streets, but primarily it portended urban design principles that came to be adopted in the construction of Renaissance new towns in Italy, France and Germany: the introduction of secondary *piazze*; the configuration of streets; and the placement of monumental buildings (Rosenau, 1983).

Akin to existing monasteries and to ideal physical layouts of new towns, ideal harmonious communities were envisaged by social and religious thinkers of the Renaissance. Perhaps intended primarily as a satire on contemporaneous English society, Sir Thomas More's *Utopia*, first published in 1516, became epithetic to all notions of ideal communities. Although the extent to which More was aware of the works on ideal cities of his European contemporaries remains unclear, their overall cultural context was not lost on him. On his imaginary island there were 54 cities designed almost identically after Amaurot, the capital. Amaurot itself

> lies up against a gently sloping hill; the town is almost square in shape.... The streets are conveniently laid out for use by vehicles and for protection from the wind. Their buildings are by no means paltry; the unbroken rows of houses facing one another across the streets through each ward make a fine sight. The streets are twenty feet wide. (More, 1516, in Logan and Adams, 1989, pp. 43–47)

Harmony also guided the civic programme of *Utopia*, where More touched upon such modern concepts as optimal city size and transportation within the context of agricultural production and labour.

The results of continuing explorations into the perspective in painting became a guiding principle entrenched in Renaissance town planning. This is perhaps best exemplified by some of the notes of Andrea Palladio (1508–1581) in his *Four Books on Architecture*:

> The principal streets . . . ought to be so comparted, that they may be straight, and lead from the gates of the city in a direct line to the greatest and principal piazza; and sometimes also, the site permitting it, lead in the same manner directly to the opposite gate . . . by the same line. (Palladio, 1570, in Placzek, 1965)

Palladio's contemporaries and compatriots used Filarete's work as a reference to further develop ideal city plans as projects on circular defensive systems and fortifications, e.g. Pietro Cataneo in his *L'Architettura* (1554) and Girolamo Maggi in *Della Fortificatione delle Città* (1564), or in the actual design of new towns such as Palmanuova (1593), near Venice, attributed to Vicenzo Scamozzi.

The appeal to confer a geometrically symmetrical perimeter upon a city was directly related to the delineation of a city's boundaries by its fortification walls. As people were driven from surrounding rural areas, the walled perimeter of cities also provided safety and relative tranquillity. Cities thus filled up quickly, and whereas within city walls one could still find relative placidity, the suburbs outside walls became hubs of crime and destitution (Blake, 1939).

The political ideal of More's *Utopia*, combined with a cosmic vision of harmonious relations, led Tommaso Campanella in the late 16th century to write *The City of the Sun* (Donno, 1981) (first published 1602). Campanella wrote his book upon a brief respite from a Rome prison in 1595, just at a time when Domenico Fontana, under Pope Sixtus V (during 1585–1590), significantly redesigned the city. Whereas Fontana placed four avenues radiating from the Santa Maria Maggiore Church, Campanella's vision of *The City of the Sun*, perhaps also referring to Rome's seven hills, was of

> a hill upon which the greater part of the city is situated. . . . The city is divided into seven large circuits, named after the seven planets. Passage from one to the other is provided by four avenues and four gates facing the four points of the compass . . . the entire city is two miles and more in diameter and has a circumference of seven miles. (Donno, 1981, pp. 7–27)

Equilibria as Seeds of Modernity in Baroque City Planning

In many respects, Sixtus's design was ingrained in the plan launched in the 1450s under Nicholas V. The papal design principle was characterized by two features: first, to have a wedge of three streets meeting at a single point and axially aligned with a fourth street; and second, to have the street complex itself aligned with hoisted obelisks as place makers and orientation guides. However, the overriding concern of Rome's early Baroque urban renewal was, possibly for the first time in the history of urban design, a conscious focus on harmonizing transportation and the movement of people, pilgrims in particular, with the configuration of monuments, streets and open spaces (Burroughs, 1994).

Changes in the layout of Roman streets, following Nicholas's initiative, had occurred already under the Popes Julius II (pontificate 1503–1513) and Leo X (pontificate 1513–1521), and Sixtus's redesign was the pinnacle of efforts over the century preceding him. Major among these early changes in the redesign of Rome was a new configuration of open spaces proposed or made by Donato Bramante (1444–1514), under Julius II, and later by Michelangelo (1475–1564). In 1505 construction began on Bramante's plan for the immense church of St Peter (replacing an ancient basilica built by Constantine in 333), with the intention of building a large open space around the stupendous temple. Michelangelo's revised design of St Peter's (c.1536) focused on centralizing the church within its

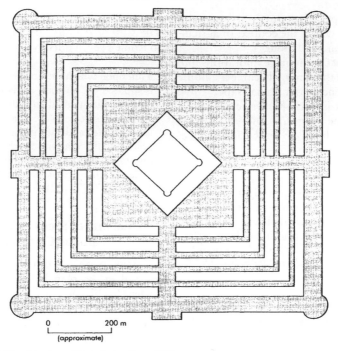

Figure 6.7   Schickhardt's plan of Freudenstadt, *c.* 1599.

context of open space and access. A similar attempt at visual balance was made by Michelangelo in the redesign of the Campidoglio, the Capitoline Hill in Rome, where a measure of order was introduced into the initially irregular landscape geometry (Roth, 1993, pp. 375–376).

Sixtus's vast spatial reorganization of Rome linked the major religious sites through a vast network of new roads supported by fountains to which water was piped, for the first time since Roman times, through a rebuilt ancient aqueduct. The lofty attempt of Sixtus V was to physically link the great basilicas of San Lorenzo, Santa Croce, San Giovanni and the church of St Peter. Thus the great basilicas became nodes of a new, monumental street network in which ancient obelisks were raised and consecrated as beacons of pilgrims' final destination points. Here the notion of equilibrium evolved into a new dynamic form heralding a modern concern for the balancing of utilitarian needs, movement in particular, within the context of urban development opportunities.

However, classical symmetry in urban design retained its appeal well into the 18th century. In the early 17th century, the Bavarian town of Freudenstadt (figure 6.7) was built by Heinrich Schickhardt (1558–1635), following an ideal town plan (figure 6.8) by Albrecht Dürer in his treatise *Etliche Underricht zu Befestigung der Stett, Schloss und Flecken* (1527). Along with Campanella's *The City of the Sun*, the unfolding of Dürer's plan at Freudenstadt inspired the German theologian Johann Valentin Andreae in his vision of the utopian community *Christianopolis* (Andreae, *c.*1619, in Held, 1914, p. 140):

> Its shape is a square, whose side is seven hundred feet, well fortified with four towers and a wall. It looks, therefore, toward the four quarters of the earth. Eight other very strong towers [are] distributed throughout the city. (*Christianopolis*, Chapter VII, in Held, 1914, p. 140)

The conformity to geometric balance that appears in the imaginary blueprints of

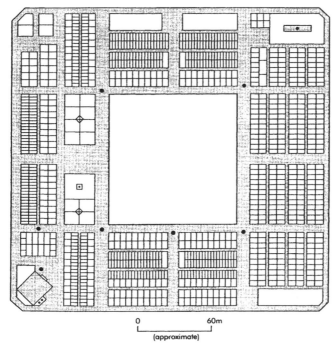

0   60m
(approximate)

Figure 6.8   Albrecht Dürer's plan of an ideal city (after his *Etliche Underricht zu Befestigung der Stett, Schloss und Flecken*, 1527).

Christianopolis (figure 6.9) or *The City of the Sun* runs in parallel to actual physical layouts such as those of Freudenstadt and of other Mannerist or Baroque planned cities or city-forms. Geometric balance is the signature of Parisian urban places built by Henri IV, and of the new towns of Henri-chemont, Charleville, Richelieu and others, all examples of Mannerist and early Baroque town planning in the early 17th century. The social awareness of More's *Utopia* or Francis Bacon's *New Atlantis* (1627), however, is often absent in Mannerist plans, as they seldom pay attention to detailed physical configurations within their cities.

The ideal city plans of the Frenchman Iaques Perret (figure 6.10) and, later, the plan of Versailles by André le Nôtre and Louis Le Vau, as well as the layout of Mannerist planned cities such as Naarden in Holland (late 17th century), all show affinity with axial, symmetrical design. Idealized geometric forms, which had flourished in Renaissance city planning, however, gradually became more conservative, keeping a

nominal balance instead of the unequivocal symmetry of detail (Rosenau, 1983, p. 58).

Much as the planned city of the Renaissance and Mannerism appears to have addressed the notion of equilibrium through the works of Alberti and Filarete, so the early modern notions of equilibrium in the city are indebted to Sir Christopher Wren (1632–1723). Wren's proposed plan for London following the Great Fire of 1666 balanced pedestrian traffic with emerging modes of vehicular transportation, adhering, at the same time, to the Vitruvian ideal plan (figures 6.5 and 6.11).

Wren's was one of numerous other plans that followed the Great Fire. It is noteworthy that among these was a plan for London by the physicist Robert Hooke, the discoverer in 1678 of the elasticity law in which the notion of equilibrium is fundamental. It is a matter of historical record that, four years prior to Wren's 1666 proposal, another distinguished physicist, Robert Boyle, had already shown an equilibrium in the elasticity of solid bodies. Wren himself presented

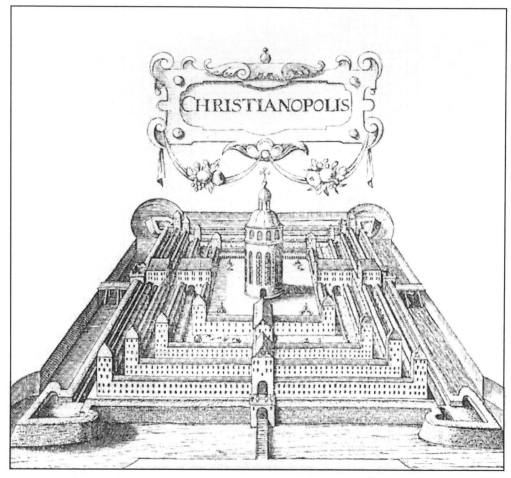

Figure 6.9   Andreae's *Christianopolis*, in a late 17th-century edition of his *Rei publicae Christianopolitanae descriptio.*

in 1661 a theory of elastic impact, in which he equalled the force of collision to balance in a mechanical system (Bennett, 1972, p. 72).

Harmony and Discord in Early Modern Urban Design

Although Wren's plan for London was never executed, it foreshadowed the dawn of the ideal industrial city that became the motif of much of urban design during and after the 18th-century Enlightenment. It is fair to say that urban design of the Enlightenment was affected by two antithetic developments: on the one hand, the archaeological discovery of

Pompeii and Herculaneum in the mid-18th century; and on the other hand, the emergence of Romanticism as the longing for naturalness in reaction to the mathematically ideal paradigms of early modern science.

The streets of the two Roman cities destroyed in the sudden eruption of Vesuvius in 79 CE, showed impressive adherence to geometry, thus reinforcing the universalist notion of mathematics and rationality as perpetual standards in urban design. The rationalist standard became most apparent in the 1755 plan of Claude-Nicolas Ledoux for Chaux, an ideal industrial town that was to be located in eastern France. The town was to be set on an oval plan in the centre of

Figure 6.10 Perret's town plan (after his *Des fortifications et artifices architecture et perspective*, 1601; the plan led to the actual design of Henrichemont).

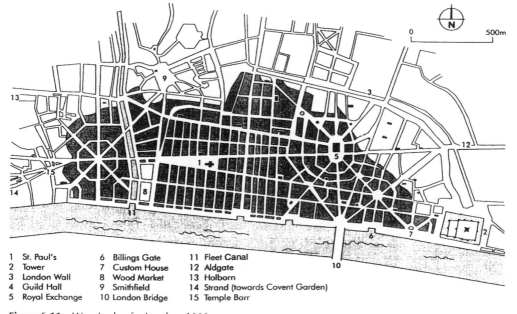

1	St. Paul's	6	Billings Gate	11	Fleet Canal
2	Tower	7	Custom House	12	Aldgate
3	London Wall	8	Wood Market	13	Holborn
4	Guild Hall	9	Smithfield	14	Strand (towards Covent Garden)
5	Royal Exchange	10	London Bridge	15	Temple Barr

Figure 6.11 Wren's plan for London, 1666.

which the house of the town's administrator would be located, adjoined by industrial buildings in which the processing of brine, dug in the nearby salt mines, was to take place. In the oval ring around the industrial centre, workers' apartments would be placed, the whole town complex being surrounded by a green belt in which public facilities, gardens and parks would be located.

This geometric precision found many adherents on the Continent, but it was also countered, in the British Isles, by rustic garden designs such as Stourhead and Blenheim, and by fake medieval ruins such as Hagley Park (Roth, 1993). The disillusion with the emerging industrial city was ultimately articulated by Jean-Jacques Rousseau (1712–1778). The Swiss thinker made a persuasive argument for the rejection of conventions exposed as hiding corrupt practices in urban society, and for the celebration of the natural man. A suburban park, picturesque yet unkempt, was established just outside Paris by one of Rousseau's patrons, to challenge the rationalism of the Englightenment using the precepts of Rousseau's philosophy.

The 19th- and 20th-century visionary plans, such as the Garden City (1898) of Ebenezer Howard or *La ville radieuse* (1933) of Le Corbusier, as well as the modern redesign of cities such as Karlsruhe (1804–1824) by Friedrich Weinbrenner or Paris (1853–1870) by Baron Georges-Eugène Haussmann, attempted to introduce urban equilibrium in a yet further blend of art and technology. To what extent these modern attempts were successful as city planning notions is still open to debate (Roth, 1993, p. 442).

Haussmann's project, the more pragmatic among those mentioned, is a case in point. The narrow, dark and vermin-infested streets and alleys of Paris, much as in other European cities, were often the outcome of unwitting building schemes from the Middle Ages. Void of sunlight or adequate air circulation, as well as being frequent focal points of simmering discontent, such urban settings served as hubs of revolutionary conspiracy against the government. From here arson attacks on government outposts and monuments were led, the clouds of smoke hanging over the city once inspiring comparisons to the eruption of Vesuvius and the fall of Babylon (Evenson, 1979). The hiding places within this tortuous urban environment, however, also constituted an ideal defensive formation against the police or any advancing intruder. Ostensibly addressing public health problems arising from overcrowding and urban blight, but primarily concerned with popular insurgency and urban warfare threatening the government of Napoleon III, Haussmann, the Prefect of the Seine *département*, had responded by razing much of the medieval centre of Paris. The narrow, tortuous streets throughout much of central Paris were thus replaced by wide boulevards, emulating the redesign of Rome under Sixtus V (Roth, 1993). Haussmann's airy, exposed arterial thoroughfares created a new standard of an emerging metropolitan environment where access to air and sun came in response to current discoveries that traced the propagation of disease to local causes such as dirt, overcrowding, lack of sunlight and deficient air circulation (Sutcliffe, 1971). Calling for spatial accord between plazas, avenues and monuments, Haussmann undoubtedly reinforced an urban design standard that came to be admired by many a planner and architect (Sutcliffe, 1971, pp. 29, 326). At the turn of the century, Haussmann's model came to be followed elsewhere, from Chicago (Wrigley, 1987) to Canberra (Fischer, 1989) and New Delhi (Irving, 1981, pp. 82–87).

However, Haussmann's urban renewal was as much a solution to public health hazard and urban decay as it was a ruthless answer to riots and rife insurrection. To Haussmann's critics, widening of the streets to accommodate cannon fire against the barricades only made sense in viewing the metropolis as a battleground, a place of conflict rather than accord (Cacciari, 1993, p. 22). It was the old, undulating, narrow street or alley, deprived of sun and hygiene, menacing as it was, that formed a hub of propitious surprise where daily life took place. The signature of Haussmann's new design, the destruction of central Paris by the introduction of wide boulevards, now epitomized the ideal of the surprise-free city, geared towards the machine rather than the person, seeking an equilibrium rather than a prospect for challenge in the accidental, and conformity rather than occasion for adventure in the unforeseen.

Disequilibrium as an Inherent Aspect of Contemporary City-form

The mechanized, automated environment of the contemporary city continues to ensure a relatively predictable and purposely surprise-free milieu. Undoubtedly, it thus provides, first and foremost, a relatively safe environment for most urban dwellers. The unexpected outcome of this attempt has been, however, the threat to the dwellers' own humanity. The city, the largest time-regulated, artificial entity, provides protection to most of its residents. It does so by securing physical survival in the city through organization and infrastructure anchored within the image of equilibrium. However, as such it also transforms human individuals into mere components of the metropolis, mechanical parts by necessity. The city thus bends individuals into becoming their own counterfeits. If there is an inherent paradox between human authenticity and survival, then the modern city seems to epitomize it.

One needs only to look at the works of Dostoyevski (*Notes from Underground*), Kafka (*The Trial*), Camus (*The Outsider*), Sartre (*Nausea*) and Beckett (*Waiting for Godot*) to recognize the streak common to them all: dreadful reflections on the dweller of the industrial city. Alienation, the underlying motive of modern existentialism, appears in these authors within contexts of scientific determinism, bureaucracy, achromic behaviour, the industrial bourgeoisie or homelessness. Arguably, urban progress as well as urban decay, the equilibrium *and* the disequilibrium, can be interpreted as aspects of scientific and technological development. However, it is the inherent impossibility of reconciling between the authenticity of the individual and the progress of the city that

leads to the alienation of the city dweller (Akkerman, 1998, pp. 154–170).

Nowhere does the contempt for mechanistic equilibrium in the city register better than in Sartre's *Nausea*. Sartre describes thus his fictitious city of Bouville and its residents, some 80 years after Haussmann's reconstruction of Paris:

They come out of their offices after their day of work, they look at the houses and squares with satisfaction, they think it's *their* city, a good, solid bourgeois city. They aren't afraid, they feel at home. All they have ever seen is trained water running from taps, light which fills bulbs when you turn on the switch, half-breed, bastard trees held up with crutches. They have proof, a hundred times a day, that everything happens mechanically, that the world obeys fixed, unchangeable laws. In a vacuum all bodies fall at the same rate of speed, the public park is closed at 4 p.m. in winter, at 6 p.m. in summer, lead melts at 335 degrees centigrade, the last streetcar leaves Hôtel de Ville at 11.05 p.m. They are peaceful, a little morose, they think about Tomorrow, that is to say, simply, a new today; cities have only one day at their disposal and every morning it comes back exactly the same. (Sartre, 1964, p. 158)

Sartre's likening of the city dwellers to objects, their happiness to a mechanical equilibrium of the city of which they are part, is also a condemnation of fraud imbued by city life precisely due to mechanical adherence to an equilibrium. Indeed, whereas the guiding principle in the design of ideal cities had historically rested on the various notions of the equilibrium, one of the aspects of late modernity has been the cognizance of the urban *disequilibrium*: the authenticity in the ugliness, discordance and insanity of the city.

The conscious experience of the 20th century led to the acknowledgement of the urban ugly, firstly as an attempt at its elimination. In the USA the City Beautiful movement at the turn of the century sprang as a civic programme seeking charm, order and cleanliness in the wealthy flanks of US cities

(Peterson, 1987). Ultimately, however, the late encounter with urban ugliness led not only to its acceptance, but in some quarters of postmodern urban culture also to its celebration, as an acclamation of the disequilibrium itself. Theodor Adorno (1903–1969) explained this as a historical reaction to the notion of classical harmony, as the historical emergence of an antithesis to the beautiful:

> ...the ugly subject matter, it is said, becomes in some higher sense beautiful because it helps produce a dynamic equilibrium. This is in line with one of the motifs of Hegel's aesthetics, where beauty is not the resultant equilibrium *per se* but always the latter together with the tension that produced it. Harmony which tries to disown the tensions that came to rest in it becomes false, disturbing, even dissonant. (Adorno, 1984, p. 68)

Authenticity in the urban ugly, too, rises in an aesthetic meta-equilibrium against attempts at urban mechanistic congruity.

City-form and the Aesthetics of Authenticity

Nowhere else could Adorno's observation be more ample than in postindustrial urban environments. In confirmation, not too long ago, *Newsweek* magazine reported on the transformation of two houses in

> a dilapidated area on Detroit's east side into a kind of living art gallery. Now the painted word *LOVE* stretches across the street. A bathtub in a vacant lot becomes a cornucopia of tires, fenders and road signs, and old bicycles dangle from tree limbs to compose a half-artificial sculpture. (*Newsweek*, 1990, p. 64)

The urban ugly thus epitomizes the disequilibrium but, quaintly, the disequilibrium of the ugly transcends into the only authentic sentiment in a world of coerced consonance.

Urban alienation, as a manifestation of the ugly, itself becomes the only genuine faculty in *The Castle* and *The Trial* of Franz Kafka.

The allusion to the urban context in Kafka's literary work is somewhat less explicit than in Sartre's *Nausea*. Unlike Sartre's novel, *The Trial* and *The Castle* arise from an intense childhood environment, and the display of the inane and the absurd in these two towering works by Kafka does not provide unambiguous condemnation of the modern city. Yet, in order to comprehend Kafka's work one must delve into the built environment of his childhood. Here, again, the tension between the spontaneous and the mechanistic, between mystery and predictability, between the authentic and the fraudulent, emerges unequivocally. Within the context of this tension, ugliness and beauty lose their conventional meaning. The poverty-stricken Josefov district of Prague, near where Kafka grew up, was a hub of phantom-like, petrifying reality:

> Beneath the eaves of these strange medieval houses grouped together under one roof, there were...gloomy little rooms, that reminded the visitor more of an animal's lair than a room for human beings.... There, below, in the smoke-blackened rooms the ears of the visitors would be deafened by the excruciating sounds of the harmonica, or the strings of a badly-tuned harp, plucked by the arthritic fingers of an old, blind harpist. They would awaken profound feelings of melancholy, whilst on the opposite side of the road, behind brightly-lit windows, people would be shouting and dancing to the strains of the piano. Here, among the dreg of the metropolis both easy and hard-earned money, health and youth were squandered away and buried for good. (Frynta, 1960, pp. 57–58)

A continuum of disconcerting bewilderment to many a Prague resident, Josefov met at the turn of the century a fate similar to that of central Paris a few years earlier. In 1893 the Law of Resanitation was decreed, much of Prague's Josefov was demolished and rebuilt, and the main artery now cutting through the formerly dilapidated district was named Paris Boulevard. Here is what Kafka had to say to one of his writer friends after the redesign of Josefov:

The dark corners, the mysterious passages, the boarded-up windows, the dirty yards, the noisy beer-shops and the shuttered inns still live in us. We walk through the broad streets of the newly-built town. Yet our steps and our glance are unsure. Innerly we still shiver as we did in the old streets of misery. Our hearts still know nothing of the resanitation that has been carried out. The sick old Jewish Town is much more real to us than the new hygienic town now surrounding us. (From Kafka's conversation with Gustav Janouch as quoted in Frynta, 1960, pp. 59–60)

The Prague of his youth never left Kafka, precisely for the purity of its absurdity and the authenticity of its disequilibrium. Just as elsewhere, the replanning of Prague's old town was an attempt to introduce convention and public health into the urban form. Yet, by bringing about sanitation it only transformed insanity: the absurd of urban existence had merely moved from Kafka's Josefov into Sartre's Bouville.

Beyond Modernity: Concluding Remarks

The dread of human authenticity within mechanistically imbued fraud, the strain between equilibrium and disequilibrium and the search for meaning were at the heart of urban existence of the 20th century. Recognition of this tension seems to be the wellhead of much of contemporary reflective thought on the city. Harvey (1989) has called on urban designers and planners to recognize the force of self-diversification among city dwellers, and to provide for its expression in what he has labelled "postmodernism in the city". Extreme results of this diversification, such as the centreless urban form of contemporary southern California, have come to be called "postmodern urbanism" (Dear and Flusty, 1998). These unappealing consequences have led Olsen (1986) to conclude that a solution is "neither the starry-eyed propaganda of the town planners and disciples of the [modern] architecture, nor the appalled rejection with which we contemplate what those planners and disciples have done" (Olsen, 1986, p. xi) but in

the recognition of historicity, of the search itself. A contemporary source of postmodernity in urban design, 20th-century ideal urban planning notions such as those of Tony Garnier or Le Corbusier, thus need not be eliminated but, rather, drawn upon as in some of the Art Nouveau of Antoní Gaudí.

Tony Garnier's (1869–1948) mechanistic rationality, which came to define 20th-century urban planning, is best traced to his socialist Ideal City, *Une cité industrielle* (figure 6.12). Here social harmony is exemplified by the non-existence of a police station (much as in Howard's Garden City) or law courts. The adherence to symmetry and visual harmony is substituted by balanced relationships in transportation access to sites, in the distribution of housing and employment and in the cognizance of community needs within the city. As an early spokesman of the International Style in architecture and urbanism, Garnier exerted a primal influence upon urban planning of the early 20th century. Following a meeting with Le Corbusier in 1907, the latter reflected on the profundity of Garnier's ideas as having led to Le Corbusier's own Contemporary City for Three Million People (or *Ville contemporaine* as titled originally).

The 20th century's engrossment in the mechanistic paradigm of traditional science could be no better punctuated than by Le Corbusier's model dwelling, the *Maison Citrohan*; a humorous allusion to the popular French car, the Citroën, pointing to Le Corbusier's profound belief that a house is a "machine for living" (Frampton, 1992, pp. 153–154). As a shelter, the modern metropolis too, in its undertaking for efficacy, is forced to adopt the paradigm of equilibrium in order to streamline human beings residing with its confines. Inadvertently, however, it thus only sharpens their foundational dilemma. To that extent the modern metropolis, ironically, can be credited with the rise of 20th-century existentialism. In its aesthetic expression, existentialism not only coincides with, but also is part and parcel of, the end of the industrial revolution. The brutal manifestations of progress – the overcrowded,

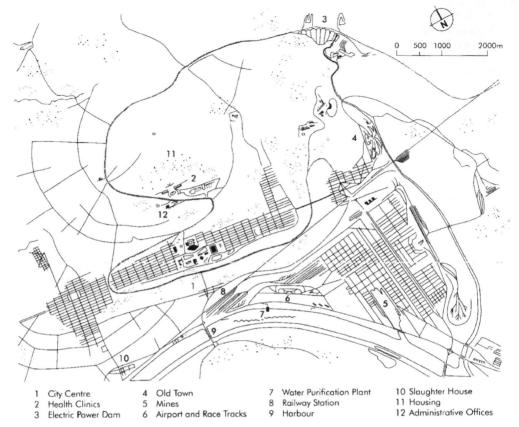

Figure 6.12   Tony Garnier, *Une cité industrielle*, 1917. Estate of Tony Garnier/Musée des Beaux-Arts de Lyon.

1	City Centre	4	Old Town	7	Water Purification Plant
2	Health Clinics	5	Mines	8	Railway Station
3	Electric Power Dam	6	Airport and Race Tracks	9	Harbour

10	Slaughter House
11	Housing
12	Administrative Offices

industrial city and its disequilibria – become the breeding ground of the philosophy of despair. The mechanistic equilibrium of the industrial city, overpowering in its never-ending attempt to consolidate an omnipresent crowd, is perceived by the existentialist writer as humanly fraudulent, only to be discerned on the backdrop of the authenticity of the *dis*equilibrium. The perceived fraud within the mechanistic city thus gives rise to a new brand of dynamic correspondence with the authenticity of the disequilibrium.

Twentieth-century architecture has not remained deaf to the existentialist stance. The architectural quintessence of deliberate disequilibrium is the Sagrada Familia cathedral in Barcelona. Created by Antoní Gaudí (1852–1926) early in the 20th century, the cathedral has been left unfinished, its slender towers competing for attention with huge hoisting cranes that have been purposely left on site. In the true spirit of Barcelona the Sagrada Familia rises over the city as a rebellious pun on the mechanized urbanism surrounding it. Gaudí appears here as an architectural oracle rebutting automatism by embracing it, satirizing the contentment in mechanical eloquence by containing it.

Gaudí too could not have been more prophetic: the gratification of mechanical reasoning itself came to a screeching halt in 1931 when the mathematician Kurt Gödel (1906–1978) showed, on the merits of automatic reasoning in formal logic, that *any* axiomatic system includes true propositions that cannot be proved, i.e. that any axiomatic system is by necessity incomplete (Nagel and Newman, 1993, pp. 45–97). In a figurative sense Gödel echoed the two towering and perpetually incomplete achievements of humans early in the 20th century: the Sagrada Familia and *The Castle*.

However, if automatism in human behaviour is the apparent analogue to the mechanical reasoning of formal logic, should not the imperfection of the city be espoused and incorporated rather than expunged? The last decades of the 20th century witnessed architectural expression very much akin to the notion of designed imperfection and incompleteness, as a celebration of the disequilibrium. In 1984 Bernard Tschumi, in collaboration with Peter Eisenman and the philosopher Jacques Derrida, in their project *Parc de La Villette*, ushered deconstructivism, an aspiration for the unexpected in the way of configurations and uses of conventional objects; in the case of *Parc de La Villette*, follies interspersed at regular intervals leave it to the viewer–user to interpret and even interact with them (Derrida and Eisenman, 1997, pp. 125–160). Frank Gehry's buildings across the USA, in Prague or Bilbao seem to confirm the deconstructivist style by readily rejecting any convention of line, curve and proportion. With its introduction of deliberate peccadillos into common architectural milieux, deconstructivism is as unconventional as it is exhilarating. Could not the urban environment itself be the subject of analogous aesthetic considerations?

Late in the 19th century Camillo Sitte, observing admiringly the medieval *piazze* of Italy, commented: "We, on the other hand, come along afterward, scurrying about with our T-square and compass, presuming to solve with clumsy geometry those fine points that are matters of pure sensitivity" (Sitte, 1880, in Collins and Collins, 1965, pp. 20–21). Twentieth-century urban design did not take serious notice of Sitte's critique. However, the few examples of neighbourhood design for the pedestrian that emerged in the latter part of the century herald perhaps a promise for a new recognition of the individual, rather than of his or her automobile. Kay (1990) suggests that deconstructivism, as a response to postmodernism in architecture, gives hope to the budding new urbanism focusing, precisely, on the pedestrian in streetscape. Such recognition will ultimately have to grow into cognizance of the legitimacy of the imperfect and the incomplete in city form. The prospect of imperfection, as an endearing attribute of the city, may yet provide an impetus in designing our cities, neighbourhoods and streets in a fashion that will, again, inspire the genius of sense and intellect in their inhabitants.

ACKNOWLEDGEMENT

Thanks are due to two anonymous referees of the *Journal of Urban Design* for their valuable comments and constructive criticism on the earlier version of this study. All artwork was prepared by Keith Bigelow, Department of Geography, University of Saskatchewan.

REFERENCES

Adams, J. (1963) *The Republic of Plato*. Cambridge: Cambridge University Press.

Adorno, T. (1984) *Aesthetic Theory*, trans. C. Lenhardt. London: Routledge & Kegan Paul.

Akkerman, A. (1998) *Place and Thought: The Built Environment in Early European Philosophy*. London: Woodridge.

Apostle, H. G. and Gerson, L. P. (1986) *Aristotle's Politics*. Grinnell, IA: Peripatetic Press.

Barker, E. (1962) Introduction. In R. V. G. Tasker (ed.), *Saint Augustine – The City of God*. London: J. M. Dent & Sons.

Beckett, S. (1989 [1953]) *Waiting for Godot*. Cambridge and New York: Cambridge University Press.

Blake, W. (1939) *Elements of Marxian Economic Theory and Its Criticism*. New York: The Cordon Company.

Bennett, J. A. (1972) *The Mathematical Science of Christopher Wren*. Cambridge: Cambridge University Press.

Buck-Morss, S. (1990) *The Dialectics of Seeing: Walter Benjamin and the Arcades Project*. Cambridge, MA: MIT Press.

Burnet, J. (1964) *Early Greek Philosophy*. Cleveland, OH: Meridian Books.

Burroughs, C. (1994) Streets in the Rome of Sixtus V. In Z. Celik, D. Favro and R. Ingersoll (eds), *Streets: Critical Perspectives on Public Space*. Los Angeles: University of California Press, pp. 189–202.

Cacciari, M. (1993) *Architecture and Nihilism*. New Haven, CT: Yale University Press.

Camus, A. (1961 [1942]) *The Outsider*. Harmondsworth: Penguin.

Chartier, R., Chaussinand-Nogaret, G., Neveux, H. and Ladurie, E. L. (1981) *La Ville classique de la Renaissance aux Révolutions*. Paris: Seuil.

Collins, G. R. and Collins, C. C. (1965) *City Planning According to Artistic Principles by Camillo Sitte*. New York: Random House.

Dear, M. and Flusty, S. (1998) Postmodern urbanism. *Annals of the Association of American Geographers*, 88, 50–72.

Derrida, J. and Eisenman, P. (1997) *Chora L Works*. London: Monacelli Press.

Dickinson, R. E. (1963) *The West European City: A Geographical Interpretation*. London: Routledge & Kegan Paul.

Donno, D. (1981) *The City of the Sun: A Poetical Dialogue by Brother Tommaso Campanella*. Berkeley, CA: University of California Press.

Dostoyevsky, F. (1972 [1864]) *Notes from Underground*. Harmondsworth: Penguin.

Evenson, N. (1979) *Paris: A Century of Change, 1878–1978*. New Haven, CT: Yale University Press.

Fischer, K. F. (1989) Canberra: myths and models. *Town Planning Review*, 60, 155–194.

Frampton, K. (1992) *Modern Architecture*. London: Thames & Hudson.

Friedman, D. (1988) *Florentine New Towns: Urban Design in the Late Middle Ages*. Cambridge, MA: MIT Press.

Friedman, Y. (1962) The ten principles of space town planning, lecture, Essen (June 1962). Reprinted in U. Conrads (ed.), *Programs and Manifestoes on 20th-century Architecture*, trans. M. Bullock. Cambridge, MA: MIT Press.

Frynta, E. (1960) *Kafka and Prague*. London: Batchworth Press.

Harvey, D. (1989) *The Condition of Postmodernity*. Oxford: Basil Blackwell.

Haverfield, F. (1913) *Ancient Town Planning*. Oxford: Clarendon Press.

Hawkes, J. H. (1973) *The First Great Civilizations*. London: Hutchinson.

Held, F. E. (1914) *Johann Valentin Andrea's Christianopolis: An Ideal State of the Seventeenth Century*. Chicago: University of Illinois; New York, Oxford University Press.

Irving, R. G. (1981) *Indian Summer: Lutyens, Baker and Imperial Delhi*. New Haven, CT: Yale University Press.

Jameson, M. (1991) Private space and the Greek city. In O. Murray and S. Price (eds), *The Greek City: From Homer to Alexander*. Oxford: Clarendon Press.

Kafka, F. (1964 [1925]) *The Trial*. New York: Modern Library.

Kafka, F. (1992 [1919]) *The Castle*, trans. W. Muir and E. Muir. London: Minerva.

Kay, J. H. (1990) Architecture. *The Nation*, 250, 27–8.

Lang, S. (1952) The ideal city from Plato to Howard. *Architectural Review*, 112, 91–101.

Logan, G. M. and Adams R. M. (1989) *Thomas More: Utopia*. Cambridge: Cambridge University Press.

Nagel, E. and Newman, J. R. (1993) *Gödel's Proof*. London: Routledge.

Newsweek (1990) Come on: art is my house. 6 August, 64.

Olsen, D. J. (1986) *The City as a Work of Art*. New Haven, CT: Yale University Press.

Owens, E. J. (1991) *The City in the Greek and Roman World*. London: Routledge.

Pastor, L. (1899) *The History of the Popes, volume II*. London: Kegan Paul, Trench, Truebner.

Peterson, J. A. (1987) The City Beautiful movement: forgotten origins and lost meanings. In D. A. Krueckeberg (ed.), *Introduction to Planning History in the United States*. New Brunswick, NJ: Rutgers University Center for Urban Policy Research, pp. 40–57.

Placzek, A. K. (ed.) (1965) *Andrea Palladio – The Four Books of Architecture*. A reprint of translation by Isaac Ware (first published 1570; first English translation, London, 1738). New York: Dover.

Rosenau, H. (1983) *The Ideal City: Its Architectural Evolution in Europe*. London: Methuen.

Roth, L. M. (1993) *Understanding Architecture: Its Elements, History and Meaning*. London: Herbert Press.

Rykwert, J. Leach, N. and Tavernor, R. (1988) *Leone Battista Alberti: On the Art of Building in Ten Books (De re aedificatoria 1485)*. Cambridge, MA: MIT Press.

Sartre, J.-P. (1964) *Nausea*, trans. L. Alexander. New York: New Directions.

Saunders, T. J. (1970) *The Laws of Plato*. Harmondsworth: Penguin.

Schofield, M. (1991) *The Stoic Idea of the City*. Cambridge: Cambridge University Press.

Slater, T. R. (1990) English medieval new towns with composite plans: evidence from the Midlands. In T. R. Slater (Ed.) *The Built Form of Western Cities*. Leicester: Leicester University Press.

Spencer, J. R. (1965) *Filarete's Treatise on Architecture [Trattato d'architettura, 1457]*. New Haven, CT: Yale University Press.

Sutcliffe, A. (1971) *The Autumn of Central Paris: The Defeat of Town Planning 1850–1970*. Montreal: McGill–Queen's University Press.

Tasker, R. V. G. (ed.) (1945) *Saint Augustine – The City God*. London: J. M. Dent & Sons.

Von Gerkan, A. (1924) *Griechische Städteanlagen*. Berlin: Walter de Gruyter.

Wilson, W. H. (1983) Moles and skylarks – coming of age: urban American 1914–1945. In D. A. Krueckeberg (ed.), *Introduction to the Planning History in the United States*. New Brunswick, NJ: Rutgers University Center for Urban Policy Research, pp. 82–121.

Wrigley, R. L. (1987) The plan of Chicago. In D. A. Krueckeberg (ed.), *Introduction to Planning History in the United States*. New Brunswick, NJ: Rutgers University Center for Urban Policy Research, pp. 58–72.

Part III
Philosophy

Social Justice, Postmodernism and the City

David Harvey

The title of this essay is a collage of two book titles of mine written nearly 20 years apart, *Social justice and the city* and *The condition of postmodernity*. I here want to consider the relations between them, in part as a way to reflect on the intellectual and political journey many have travelled these last two decades in their attempts to grapple with urban issues, but also to examine how we now might think about urban problems and how by virtue of such thinking we can better position ourselves with respect to solutions. The question of *positionality* is, I shall argue, fundamental to all debates about how to create infrastructures and urban environments for living and working in the twenty-first century.

Justice and the Postmodern Condition

I begin with a report by John Kifner in the *International Herald Tribune* (1 August 1989) concerning the hotly contested space of Tompkins Square Park in New York City – a space which has been repeatedly fought over, often violently, since the "police riot" of August 1988. The neighbourhood mix around the park was the primary focus of Kifner's attention. Not only were there nearly 300 homeless people, but there were also:

Skateboarders, basketball players, mothers with small children, radicals looking like 1960s retreads, spikey-haired punk rockers in torn black, skinheads in heavy working

boots looking to beat up the radicals and punks, dreadlocked Rastafarians, heavy-metal bands, chess players, dog walkers – all occupy their spaces in the park, along with professionals carrying their dry-cleaned suits to the renovated "gentrified" buildings that are changing the character of the neighborhood.

By night, Kifner notes, the contrasts in the park become even more bizarre:

The Newcomers Motorcycle Club was having its annual block party at its clubhouse at 12th Street and Avenue B and the street was lined with chromed Harley Davidsons with raised "ape-hanger" handlebars and beefy men and hefty women in black leather. A block north a rock concert had spilled out of a "squat" – an abandoned city-owned building taken over by outlaw renovators, mostly young artists – and the street was filled with young people whose purple hair stood straight up in spikes. At the World Club just off Houston Street near Avenue C, black youths pulled up in the Jeep-type vehicles favored by cash-heavy teen-age crack moguls, high powered speakers blaring. At the corner of Avenue B and Third, considered one of the worst heroin blocks in New York, another concert was going on at an artists' space called The Garage, set in a former gas station walled off by plastic bottles and other found objects. The wall formed an enclosed garden looking up at burned-out, abandoned buildings: there was an eerie resemblance to Beirut.

The crowd was white and fashionably dressed, and a police sergeant sent to check on the noise shook his head, bemused: "It's all yuppies".

This is, of course, the kind of scene that makes New York such a fascinating place, that makes any great city into a stimulating and exciting maelstrom of cultural conflict and change. It is the kind of scene that many a student of urban subcultures would revel in, even seeing in it, as someone like Iain Chambers (1987) does, the origins of that distinctive perspective we now call "the post-modern":

Postmodernism, whatever form its intellec-tualizing might take, has been fundamen-tally anticipated in the metropolitan cultures of the last twenty years: among the electronic signifiers of cinema, television and video, in recording studios and record players, in fashion and youth styles, in all those sounds, images and diverse histories that are daily mixed, recycled and "scratched" together on that giant screen that is the contemporary city.

Armed with that insight, we could take the whole paraphernalia of postmodern argu-mentation and technique and try to "decon-struct" the seemingly disparate images on that giant screen which is the city. We could dissect and celebrate the fragmentation, the co-presence of multiple discourses – of music, street and body language, dress and technological accoutrements (such as the Harley Davidsons) – and, perhaps, develop sophisticated empathies with the multiple and contradictory codings with which highly differentiated social beings both present themselves to each other and to the world and live out their daily lives. We could affirm or even celebrate the bifurcations in cultural trajectory, the preservation of pre-existing and the creation of entirely new but distinct-ive "othernesses" within an otherwise hom-ogenizing world.

On a good day, we could celebrate the scene within the park as a superb example of urban tolerance for difference, an exem-

plar of what Iris Marion Young calls "open-ness to unassimilated otherness". In a just and civilized society, she argues, the norma-tive ideal of city life:

instantiates social relations of difference without exclusion. Different groups dwell in the city alongside one another, of neces-sity interacting in city spaces. If city politics is to be democratic and not dominated by the point of view of one group, it must be a politics that takes account of and provides voice for the different groups that dwell to-gether in the city without forming a commu-nity. (Young, 1990, p. 227)

To the degree that the freedom of city life "leads to group differentiation, to the forma-tion of affinity groups" (ibid., p. 238) of the sort which Kifner identifies in Tompkins Square, so our conception of social justice "requires not the melting away of differ-ences, but institutions that promote repro-duction of and respect for group differences without oppression" (p. 47). We must reject "the concept of universality as embodied in republican versions of Enlightenment reason" precisely because it sought to "sup-press the popular and linguistic heterogen-eity of the urban public" (p. 108). "In open and accessible public spaces and forums, one should expect to encounter and hear from those who are different, whose social per-spectives, experience and affiliations are dif-ferent." It then follows, Young argues, that a politics of inclusion "must promote the ideal of a heterogeneous public, in which persons stand forth with their differences acknow-ledged and respected, though perhaps not completely understood, by others" (p. 119).

In similar vein, Roberto Unger, the philo-sophical guru of the critical legal studies movement in the United States, might view the park as a manifestation of a new ideal of community understood as a "zone of heightened mutual vulnerability, within which people gain a chance to resolve more fully the conflict between the enabling con-ditions of self-assertion; between their need for attachment and for participation in group life and their fear of subjugation and depersonalization with which such engagement may threaten them" (Unger, 1987, p. 562). Tompkins Square seems a place where the "contrast between structure-preserving routine and structure transforming conflict" softens in such a way as to "free sociability from its script and to make us available to one another more as the originals we know ourselves to be and less as the placeholders in a system of group contrasts". The square might even be interpreted as a site of that "microlevel of cultural-revolutionary defiance and incongruity" which periodically wells upwards into "the macrolevel of institutional innovation" (ibid, p. 564). Unger is acutely aware, however, that the temptation to "treat each aspect of cultural revolution as a pretext for endless self-gratification and self-concern" can lead to a failure to "connect the revolutionary reform of institutional arrangements with the cultural-revolutionary remaking of personal relations".

So what should the urban policy-maker do in the face of these strictures? The best path is to pull out that well-thumbed copy of Jane Jacobs (1961) and insist that we should both respect and provide for "spontaneous self-diversification among urban populations" in the formulation of our policies and plans. In so doing we can avoid the critical wrath she directs at city designers, who "seem neither to recognize this force for self-diversification nor to be attracted by the esthetic problems of expressing it". Such a strategy can help us live up to expectations of the sort which Young and Unger lay down. We should not, in short, aim to obliterate differences within the park, homogenize it according to some conception of, say, bourgeois taste or social order. We should engage, rather, with an aesthetics which embraces or stimulates that "spontaneous self-diversification" of which Jacobs speaks. Yet there is an immediate question mark over that suggestion: in what ways, for example, can homelessness be understood as spontaneous self-diversification, and does this mean that we should respond to that problem with designer-style cardboard boxes to make for more jolly and sightly shelters for the home-

less? While Jane Jacobs has a point, and one which many urbanists have absorbed these last few years, there is, evidently, much more to the problem than her arguments encompass.

That difficulty is highlighted on a bad day in the park. So-called forces of law and order battle to evict the homeless, erect barriers between violently clashing factions. The park then becomes a locus of exploitation and oppression, an open wound from which bleed the five faces of oppression which Young defines as exploitation, marginalization, powerlessness, cultural imperialism and violence. The potentiality for "openness to unassimilated otherness" breaks apart and, in much the same way that the cosmopolitan and eminently civilized Beirut of the 1950s suddenly collapsed into an urban maelstrom of warring factions and violent confrontation, so we find sociality collapsing into violence (see Smith, 1989, 1992). This is not unique to New York City but is a condition of urban life in many of our large metropolitan areas – witness events in the *banlieues* of Paris and Lyons, in Brussels, in Liverpool, London and even Oxford in recent times.

In such circumstances Young's pursuit of a vision of justice that is assertive as to difference without reinforcing the forms of oppression gets torn to tatters and Unger's dreams of micro-revolutions in cultural practices which stimulate progressive rather than repressive institutional innovation become just that – dreams. The very best face that we can put upon the whole scene is to recognize that this is how class, ethnic, racial and gender struggle is, as Lefebvre (1991) would put it, being "inscribed in space". And what should the planner do? Here is how a subsequent article in the New York Times reflected on that dilemma:

There are neighborhood associations clamoring for the city to close the park and others just as insistent that it remain a refuge for the city's downtrodden. The local Assemblyman, Steven Sanders, yesterday called for a curfew that would effectively evict more than a hundred homeless people camped out in the park. Councilwoman Miriam Friedlander instead recommended that Social Services, like healthcare and drug treatment, be brought directly to the people living in the tent city. "We do not find the park is being used appropriately", said Deputy Mayor Barbara J. Fife, "but we recognize there are various interests". There is, they go on to say, only one thing that is a consensus, first that there isn't a consensus over what should be done, except that any new plan is likely to provoke more disturbances, more violence.

On 8 June 1991, the question was resolved by evicting everyone from the park and closing it entirely "for rehabilitation" under a permanent guard of at least 20 police officers. The New York authorities, situated on what Davis (1990, p. 224) calls "the bad edge of postmodernity", militarize rather than liberate its public space. In so doing, power is deployed in support of a middle-class quest for "personal insulation, in residential work, consumption and travel environments, from 'unsavory' groups and individuals, even crowds in general". Genuinely public space is extinguished, militarized or semi-privatized. The heterogeneity of open democracy, the mixing of classes, ethnicities, religions and divergent taste cultures within a common frame of public space is lost along with the capacity to celebrate unity and community in the midst of diversity. The ultimate irony, as Davis points out, is that "as the walls have come down in Eastern Europe, they are being erected all over [our cities]".

And what should the policy-maker and planner do in the face of these conditions? Give up planning and join one of those burgeoning cultural studies programmes which revel in chaotic scenes of the Tompkins Square sort while simultaneously disengaging from any commitment to do something about them? Deploy all the critical powers of deconstruction and semiotics to seek new and engaging interpretations of graffiti which say "Die, Yuppie Scum"? Should we join revolutionary and anarchist groups and fight for the rights of the poor and the culturally marginalized to express their rights and if necessary make a home for themselves in the park? Or should we throw away that dog-eared copy of Jane Jacobs and join with the forces of law and order and help impose some authoritarian solution on the problem?

Decisions of some sort have to be made and actions taken, as about any other facet of urban infrastructure. And while we might all agree that an urban park is a good thing in principle, what are we to make of the fact that the uses turn out to be so conflictual, and that even conceptions as to what the space is for and how it is to be managed diverge radically among competing factions? To hold all the divergent politics of need and desire together within some coherent frame may be a laudable aim, but in practice far too many of the interests are mutually exclusive to allow their mutual accommodation. Even the best shaped compromise (let alone the savagely imposed authoritarian solution) favours one or other factional interest. And that provokes the biggest question of all – what is the *conception* of "the public" incorporated into the construction of public space?

To answer these questions requires some deeper understanding of the forces at work shaping conflict in the park. Kifner identified drugs and real estate – "the two most powerful forces in [New York City] today". Both of them are linked to organized crime and are major pillars of the political economy of contemporary capitalism. We cannot understand events within and around the park or strategize as to its future uses without contextualizing it against a background of the political-economic transformations now occurring in urban life. The problems of Tompkins Square Park have, in short, to be seen in terms of social processes which create homelessness, promote criminal activities of many sorts (from real estate swindles and the crack trade to street muggings), generate hierarchies of power between gentrifiers and the homeless, and facilitate the emergence of deep tensions along the major social fault-lines of class, gender, ethnicity, race and religion, lifestyle and place-bound preferences (see Smith, 1992).

Social Justice and Modernity

I now leave this very contemporary situation and its associated conundrums and turn to an older story. It turned up when I unearthed from my files a yellowing manuscript, written sometime in the early 1970s, shortly after I finished *Social justice and the city*. I there examined the case of a proposal to put a segment of the Interstate Highway System on an east–west trajectory right through the heart of Baltimore – a proposal first set out in the early 1940s and which has still not been fully resolved. I resurrect this case here in part to show that what we would now often depict as a quintessentially modernist problem was even at that time argued about in ways which contained the seeds, if not the essence, of much of what many now view as a distinctively postmodernist form of argumentation.

My interest in the case at that time, having looked at a lot of the discussion, attended hearings and read a lot of documentation, lay initially in the highly differentiated arguments, articulated by all kinds of different groups, concerning the rights and wrongs of the whole project. There were, I found, seven kinds of arguments being put forward:

1   An *efficiency* argument which concentrated on the relief of traffic congestion and facilitating the easier flow of goods and people throughout the region as well as within the city.
2   An *economic growth* argument which looked to a projected increase (or prevention of loss) in investment and employment opportunities in the city consequent upon improvements in the transport system.
3   An *aesthetic and historical heritage* argument which objected to the way sections of the proposed highway would either destroy or diminish urban environments deemed both attractive and of historical value.
4   A *social and moral order* argument which held that prioritizing highway investment and subsidizing car owners

rather than, for example, investing in housing and health care was quite wrong.
5   An *environmentalist/ecological* argument which considered the impacts of the proposed highway on air quality, noise pollution and the destruction of certain valued environments (such as a river valley park).
6   A *distributive justice* argument which dwelt mainly on the benefits to business and predominantly white middle-class suburban commuters to the detriment of low-income and predominantly African-American inner-city residents.
7   A *neighbourhood and communitarian* argument which considered the way in which close-knit but otherwise fragile and vulnerable communities might be destroyed, divided or disrupted by highway construction.

The arguments were not mutually exclusive, of course, and several of them were merged by proponents of the highway into a common thread – for example, the efficiency of the transport system would stimulate growth and reduce pollution from congestion so as to advantage otherwise disadvantaged inner-city residents. It was also possible to break up each argument into quite distinct parts – the distributive impacts on women with children would be very different from those on male workers.

We would, in these heady postmodern times, be prone to describe these separate arguments as "discourses", each with its own logic and imperatives. And we would not have to look too closely to see particular "communities of interest" which articulated a particular discourse as if it was the only one that mattered. The particularistic arguments advanced by such groups proved effective in altering the alignment of the highway but did not stop the highway as a whole. The one group which tried to forge a coalition out of these disparate elements (the *Movement Against Destruction*, otherwise known as *MAD*) and to provide an umbrella for opposition to the highway as a whole turned out to be the least effective in mobilizing people and constituencies even though it was very articulate in its arguments.

The purpose of my own particular enquiry was to see how the arguments (or discourses) for and against the highway worked and if coalitions could be built in principle between seemingly disparate and often highly antagonistic interest groups via the construction of higher order arguments (discourses) which could provide the basis for consensus. The multiplicity of views and forces has to be set against the fact that either the highway is built or it is not, although in Baltimore, with its wonderful way of doing things, we ended up with a portion of the highway that is called a boulevard (to make us understand that this six-lane two-mile segment of a monster cut through the heart of low-income and predominantly African-American West Baltimore is not what it really is) and another route on a completely different alignment, looping around the city core in such a way as to allay some of the worst political fears of influential communities.

Might there be, then, some higher-order discourse to which everyone could appeal in working out whether or not it made sense to build the highway? A dominant theme in the literature of the 1960s was that it was possible to identify some such higher-order arguments. The phrase that was most frequently used to describe it was *social rationality*. The idea of that did not seem implausible, because each of the seven seemingly distinctive arguments advanced a rational position of some sort and not infrequently appealed to some higher-order rationale to bolster its case. Those arguing on efficiency and growth grounds frequently invoked utilitarian arguments, notions of "public good" and the greatest benefit to the greatest number, while recognizing (at their best) that individual sacrifices were inevitable and that it was right and proper to offer appropriate compensation for those who would be displaced. Ecologists or communitarians likewise appealed to higher-order arguments – the former to the values inherent in nature and the latter to some higher sense of communitarian values. For all of these reasons, consideration of higher-order arguments over social rationality did not seem unreasonable.

Dahl and Lindblom's *Politics, economics and welfare*, published in 1953, provides a classic statement along these lines. They argue that not only is socialism dead (a conclusion that many would certainly share these days) but also that capitalism is equally dead. What they signal by this is an intellectual tradition which arose out of the experience of the vast market and capitalistic failure of the Great Depression and the second world war and which concluded that some kind of middle ground had to be found between the extremism of a pure and unfettered market economy and the communist vision of an organized and highly centralized economy. They concentrated their theory on the question of rational social action and argued that this required "processes for both rational *calculation* and effective *control*" (p. 21). Rational calculation and control, as far as they were concerned, depended upon the exercise of rational calculation through price-fixing markets, hierarchy (top-down decision-making), polyarchy (democratic control of leadership) and bargaining (negotiation), and such means should be deployed to achieve the goals of "freedom, rationality, democracy, subjective equality, security, progress, and appropriate inclusion" (p. 28). There is much that is interesting about Dahl and Lindblom's analysis and it is not too hard to imagine that after the recent highly problematic phase of market triumphalism, particularly in Britain and the United States, there will be some sort of search to resurrect the formulations they proposed. But in so doing it is also useful to remind ourselves of the intense criticism that was levelled during the 1960s and 1970s against their search for some universal prospectus on the socially rational society of the future.

Godelier, for example, in his book on *Rationality and irrationality in economics*, savagely attacked the socialist thinking of Oscar Lange for its teleological view of rationality and its presumption that socialism should or could ever be the ultimate achievement of the rational life. Godelier did not attack this notion from the right but from a marxist and historical materialist perspective. His point was that there are different definitions of rationality depending upon the form of social organization and that the rationality embedded in feudalism is different from that of capitalism, which should, presumably, be different again under socialism. Rationality defined from the standpoint of corporate capital is quite different from rationality defined from the standpoint of the working classes. Work of this type helped to fuel the growing radical critique of even the non-teleological and incrementalist thinking of the Dahl and Lindblom sort. This critique suggested that their definition of social rationality was connected to the perpetuation and rational management of a capitalist economic system rather than with the exploration of alternatives. To attack (or deconstruct, as we now would put it) their conception of social rationality was seen by the left at the time as a means to challenge the ideological hegemony of a dominant corporate capitalism. Feminists, those marginalized by racial characteristics, colonized peoples, ethnic and religious minorities echoed that refrain in their work, while adding their own conception of who was the enemy to be challenged and what were the dominant forms of rationality to be contested. The result was to show emphatically that there is no overwhelming and universally acceptable definition of social rationality to which we might appeal, but innumerable different rationalities depending upon social and material circumstances, group identities, and social objectives. Rationality is defined by the nature of the social group and its project rather than the project being dictated by social rationality. The deconstruction of universal claims of social rationality was one of the major achievements and continues to be one of the major legacies of the radical critique of the 1960s and 1970s.

Such a conclusion is, however, more than a little discomforting. It would suggest, to go back to the highway example, that there was no point whatsoever in searching for any higher-order arguments because such arguments simply could not have any purchase upon the political process of decision-making. And it is indeed striking that the one group that tried to build such overall arguments, MAD, was the group that was least successful in actually mobilizing opposition. The fragmented discourses of those who sought to change the alignment of the highway had more effect than the more unified discourse precisely because the former were grounded in the specific and particular local circumstances in which individuals found themselves. Yet the fragmented discourses could never go beyond challenging the alignment of the highway. It did indeed need a more unified discourse, of the sort which MAD sought to articulate, to challenge the concept of the highway in general.

This poses a direct dilemma. If we accept that fragmented discourses are the only authentic discourses and that no unified discourse is possible, then there is no way to challenge the overall qualities of a social system. To mount that more general challenge we need some kind of unified or unifying set of arguments. For this reason, I chose, in this ageing and yellowing manuscript, to take a closer look at the particular question of social justice as a basic ideal that might have more universal appeal.

Social Justice

Social justice is but one of the seven criteria I worked with and I evidently hoped that careful investigation of it might rescue the argument from the abyss of formless relativism and infinitely variable discourses and interest grouping. But here too the enquiry proved frustrating. It revealed that there are as many competing theories of social justice as there are competing ideals of social rationality. Each ideal has its flaws and strengths. Egalitarian views, for example, immediately run into the problem that "there is nothing more unequal than the equal treatment of unequals" (the modification of doctrines of equality of opportunity in the United States by requirements for affirmative action, for example, recognizes what a significant problem that is). By the time I had thoroughly reviewed positive law theories of justice, utilitarian views (the greatest good of the greatest number), social contract views historically attributed to Rousseau and powerfully revived by John Rawls in his *Theory of justice* in the early 1970s, the various intuitionist, relative deprivation and other interpretations of justice, I found myself in a quandary as to precisely *which* theory of justice is the most just. The theories can, to some degree, be arranged in a hierarchy with respect to each other. The positive law view that justice is a matter of law can be challenged by a utilitarian view which allows us to discriminate between good and bad law on the basis of some greater good, while the social contract and natural rights views suggest that no amount of greater good for a greater number can justify the violation of certain inalienable rights. On the other hand, intuitionist and relative deprivation theories exist in an entirely different dimension.

Yet the basic problem remained. To argue for social justice meant the deployment of some initial criteria to define which theory of social justice was appropriate or more just than another. The infinite regress of higher-order criteria immediately looms, as does, in the other direction, the relative ease of total deconstruction of the notion of justice to the point where it means nothing whatsoever, except whatever people at some particular moment decide they want it to mean. Competing discourses about justice could not be dissassociated from competing discourses about positionality in society.

There seemed two ways to go with that argument. The first was to look at how concepts of justice are embedded in language, and that led me to theories of meaning of the sort which Wittgenstein advanced:

How many kinds of sentence are there? . . . There are *countless* kinds: countless different kinds of use to what we call "symbols", "words", "sentences". And this multiplicity is not something fixed, given once for all: but new types of language, new language games, as we may say, come into existence and others become obsolete and get forgotten. . . . Here the term "language-*game*" is meant to bring into prominence the fact that the *speaking* of language is part of an activity, or a form of life. . . . How did we

learn the meaning of this word ("good" for instance)? From what sort of examples? in what language games? Then it will be easier for us to see that the word must have a family of meanings. (Wittgenstein, 1967)

From this perspective the concept of justice has to be understood in the way it is embedded in a particular language game. Each language game attaches to the particular social, experiential and perceptual world of the speaker. Justice has no universal meaning, but a whole "family" of meanings. This finding is completely consistent, of course, with anthropological studies which show that justice among, say, the Nuer, means something completely different from the capitalistic conception of justice. We are back to the point of cultural, linguistic or discourse relativism.

The second path is to admit the relativism of discourses about justice, but to insist that discourses are expressions of social power. In this case the idea of justice has to be set against the formation of certain hegemonic discourses which derive from the power exercised by any ruling class. This is an idea which goes back to Plato, who in the *Republic* has Thrasymachus argue that:

Each ruling class makes laws that are in its own interest, a democracy democratic laws, a tyranny tyrannical ones and so on; and in making these laws they define as "right" for their subjects what is in the interest of themselves, the rulers, and if anyone breaks their laws he is punished as a "wrong-doer". That is what I mean when I say that "right" is the same in all states, namely the interest of the established ruling class. (Plato, 1965)

Consideration of these two paths brought me to accept a position which is most clearly articulated by Engels in the following terms:

The stick used to measure what is right and what is not is the most abstract expression of right itself, namely *justice*. . . . The development of right for the jurists . . . is nothing more than a striving to bring human conditions, so far as they are expressed in legal terms, ever closer to the ideal of justice, *eternal* justice. And always this justice is but the ideologized, glorified expression of the existing economic relations, now from their conservative and now from their revolutionary angle. The justice of the Greeks and Romans held slavery to be just; the justice of the bourgeois of 1789 demanded the abolition of feudalism on the ground it was unjust. The conception of eternal justice, therefore, varies not only with time and place, but also with the persons concerned.... While in everyday life... expressions like right, wrong, justice, and sense of right are accepted without misunderstanding even with reference to social matters, they create... the same hopeless confusion in any scientific investigation of economic relations as would be created, for instance, in modern chemistry if the terminology of the phlogiston theory were to be retained. (Marx and Engels, 1951, pp. 562–4)

It is a short step from this conception to Marx's critique of Proudhon, who, Marx (1967, pp. 88–9) claimed, took his ideal of justice "from the juridical relations that correspond to the production of commodities" and in so doing was able to present commodity production as "a form of production as everlasting as justice". The parallel with Godelier's rebuttal of Lange's (and by extension Dahl and Lindblom's) views on rationality is exact. Taking capitalistic notions of social rationality or of justice, and treating them as universal values to be deployed under socialism, would merely mean the deeper instanciation of capitalist values by way of the socialist project.

The Transition from Modernist to Postmodernist Discourses

There are two general points I wish to draw out of the argument so far. First, the critique of social rationality and of conceptions such as social justice as policy tools was something that was originated and so ruthlessly pursued by the "left" (including marxists) in the 1960s that it began to generate radical doubt throughout civil society as to the veracity of all universal claims. From this it was a short, though as I shall shortly argue, unwarranted, step to conclude, as many postmodernists now do, that all forms of metatheory are either misplaced or illegitimate. Both steps in this process were further reinforced by the emergence of the so-called "new" social movements – the peace and women's movements, the ecologists, the movements against colonization and racism – each of which came to articulate its own definitions of social justice and rationality. There then seemed to be, as Engels had argued, no philosophical, linguistic or logical way to resolve the resulting divergencies in conceptions of rationality and justice, and thereby to find a way to reconcile competing claims or arbitrate between radically different discourses. The effect was to undermine the legitimacy of state policy, attack all conceptions of bureaucratic rationality and at best place social policy formulation in a quandary and at worst render it powerless except to articulate the ideological and value precepts of those in power. Some of those who participated in the revolutionary movements of the 1970s and 1980s considered that rendering transparent the power and class basis of supposedly universal claims was a necessary prelude to mass revolutionary action.

But there is a second and, I think, more subtle point to be made. If Engels is indeed right to insist that the conception of justice "varies not only with time and place, but also with the persons concerned", then it seems important to look at the ways in which a particular society produces such variation in concepts. In so doing it seems important, following writers as diverse as Wittgenstein and Marx, to look at the material basis for the production of difference, in particular at the production of those radically different experiential worlds out of which divergent language games about social rationality and social justice could arise. This entails the application of historical-geographical materialist methods and principles to understand the production of those power differentials which in turn produce different conceptions of justice and embed them in a struggle over ideological hegemony between classes, races, ethnic and political groupings as well as across the gender divide. The philosophical, linguistic and logical critique of universal propositions such as justice and of social rationality can be upheld as perfectly correct without necessarily endangering the ontological or epistemological status of a metatheory which confronts the ideological and material functionings and bases of particular discourses. Only in this way can we begin to understand why it is that concepts such as justice which appear as "hopelessly confused" when examined in abstraction can become such a powerful mobilizing force in everyday life, where, again to quote Engels, "expressions like right, wrong, justice, and sense of right are accepted without misunderstanding even with reference to social matters".

From this standpoint we can clearly see that concepts of justice and of rationality have not disappeared from our social and political world these last few years. But their definition and use has changed. The collapse of class compromise in the struggles of the late 1960s and the emergence of the socialist, communist and radical left movements, coinciding as it did with an acute crisis of overaccumulation of capital, posed a serious threat to the stability of the capitalist political-economic system. At the ideological level, the emergence of alternative definitions of both justice and rationality was part of that attack, and it was to this question that my earlier book, *Social justice and the city*, was addressed. But the recession/depression of 1973–5 signalled not only the savage devaluation of capital stock (through the first wave of deindustrialization visited upon the weaker sectors and regions of a world capitalist economy) but the beginning of an attack upon the power of organized labour via widespread unemployment, austerity programmes, restructuring and, eventually, in some instances (such as Britain) institutional reforms.

It was under such conditions that the left penchant for attacking what was interpreted as a capitalist power basis within the welfare state (with its dominant notions of social rationality and just redistributions) connected to an emerging right-wing agenda to defang the power of welfare state capitalism, to get away from any notion whatsoever of a social contract between capital and labour and to abandon political notions of social rationality in favour of market rationality. The important point about this transition, which was phased in over a number of years, though at a quite different pace from country to country (it is only now seriously occurring in Sweden, for example), was that the state was no longer obliged to define rationality and justice, since it was presumed that the market could best do it for us. The idea that just deserts are best arrived at through market behaviours, that a just distribution is whatever the market dictates and that a just organization of social life, of urban investments and of resource allocations (including those usually referred to as environmental) is best arrived at through the market is, of course, relatively old and well-tried. It implies conceptions of justice and rationality of a certain sort, rather than their total abandonment. Indeed, the idea that the market is the best way to achieve the most just and the most rational forms of social organization has become a powerful feature of the hegemonic discourses these last 20 years in both the United States and Britain. The collapse of centrally planned economies throughout much of the world has further boosted a market triumphalism which presumes that the rough justice administered through the market in the course of this transition is not only socially just but also deeply rational. The advantage of this solution, of course, is that there is no need for explicit theoretical, political and social argument over what is or is not socially rational just because it can be presumed that, provided the market functions properly, the outcome is nearly always just and rational. Universal claims about rationality and justice have in no way diminished. They are just as frequently asserted in justification of privatization and of market action as they ever were in support of welfare state capitalism.

The dilemmas inherent in reliance on the market are well known and no one holds to it without some qualification. Problems of market breakdown, of externality effects, the provision of public goods and infrastructures, the clear need for *some* coordination of disparate investment decisions, all of these require some level of government interventionism. Margaret Thatcher may thus have abolished Greater London government, but the business community wants some kind of replacement (though preferably non-elected), because without it city services are disintegrating and London is losing its competitive edge. But there are many voices that go beyond that minimal requirement since free-market capitalism has produced widespread unemployment, radical restructurings and devaluations of capital, slow growth, environmental degradation and a whole host of financial scandals and competitive difficulties, to say nothing of the widening disparities in income distributions in many countries and the social stresses that attach thereto. It is under such conditions that the never quite stilled voice of state regulation, welfare state capitalism, of state management of industrial development, of state planning of environmental quality, land use, transportation systems and physical and social infrastructures, of state incomes and taxation policies which achieve a modicum of redistribution either in kind (via housing, health care, educational services and the like) or through income transfers, is being reasserted. The political questions of social rationality and of social justice over and above that administered through the market are being taken off the back burner and moved to the forefront of the political agenda in many of the advanced capitalist countries. It was exactly in this mode, of course, that Dahl and Lindblom came in back in 1953.

It is here that we have to face up to what Unger calls the "ideological embarrassment" of the history of politics these last hundred years: its tendency to move merely in repetitive cycles, swinging back and forth between *laissez-faire* and state interventionism without, it seems, finding any way to break out of this binary opposition to turn a spinning wheel of stasis into a spiral of human development. The breakdown of organized communism in eastern Europe and the Soviet Union here provides a major opportunity precisely because of the radical qualities of the break. Yet there are few signs of any similar penchant for ideological and institutional renovation in the advanced capitalist countries, which at best seem to be steering towards another bout of bureaucratic management of capitalism embedded in a general politics of the Dahl and Lindblom sort and at worst to be continuing down the blind ideological track which says that the market always knows best. It is precisely at this political conjuncture that we should remind ourselves of what the radical critique of universal claims of justice and rationality has been all about, without falling into the postmodernist trap of denying the validity of *any* appeal to justice or to rationality as a war cry for political mobilization (even Lyotard, that father figure of postmodern philosophy, hopes for the reassertion of some "pristine and non-consensual conception of justice" as a means to find a new kind of politics).

For my own part, I think Engels had it right. Justice and rationality take on different meanings across space and time and persons, yet the existence of everyday meanings to which people do attach importance and which to them appear unproblematic, gives the terms a political and mobilizing power that can never be neglected. Right and wrong are words that power revolutionary changes and no amount of negative deconstruction of such terms can deny that. So where, then, have the new social movements and the radical left in general got with their own conception, and how does it challenge both market and corporate welfare capitalism?

Young in her *Justice and the politics of difference* (1990) provides one of the best recent statements. She redefines the question of justice away from the purely redistributive mode of welfare state capitalism and focuses on what she calls the "five faces" of oppression, and I think each of them is worth thinking about as we consider the struggle to create liveable cities and workable environments for the twenty-first century.

The first face of oppression conjoins the classic notion of exploitation in the workplace with the more recent focus on exploitation of labour in the living place (primarily, of course, that of women working in the domestic sphere). The classic forms of exploitation which Marx described are still omnipresent, though there have been many mutations such that, for example, control over the length of the working day may have been offset by increasing intensity of labour or exposure to more hazardous health conditions not only in blue-collar but also in white-collar occupations. The mitigation of the worst aspects of exploitation has been, to some degree, absorbed into the logic of welfare state capitalism in part through the sheer exercise of class power and trade union muscle. Yet there are still many terrains upon which chronic exploitation can be identified and which will only be addressed to the degree that active struggle raises issues. The conditions of the unemployed, the homeless, the lack of purchasing power for basic needs and services for substantial portions of the population (immigrants, women, children) absolutely have to be addressed. All of which leads to my first proposition: *that just planning and policy practices must confront directly the problem of creating forms of social and political organization and systems of production and consumption which minimize the exploitation of labour power both in the workplace and the living place.*

The second face of oppression arises out of what Young calls *marginalization.* "Marginals", she writes, "are people the system of labour cannot or will not use." This is most typically the case with individuals marked by race, ethnicity, region, gender, immigration status, age, and the like. The consequence is that "a whole category of people is expelled from useful participation in social life and thus potentially subjected to severe material deprivation and even extermination". The characteristic response of welfare state capitalism has been either to place such marginal groups under tight surveillance or, at best, to induce a condition of dependency in which state support provides a justification to "suspend all basic rights to privacy, respect, and individual choice". The responses among the marginalized have sometimes been both violent and vociferous, in some instances

turning their marginalization into a heroic stand against the state and against any form of inclusion into what has for long only ever offered them oppressive surveillance and demeaning subservience. Marginality is one of the crucial problems facing urban life in the twenty-first century and consideration of it leads to the second principle: *that just planning and policy practices must confront the phenomenon of marginalization in a non-paternalistic mode and find ways to organize and militate within the politics of marginalization in such a way as to liberate captive groups from this distinctive form of oppression.*

Powerlessness is, in certain ways, an even more widespread problem than marginality. We are here talking of the ability to express political power as well as to engage in the particular politics of self-expression which we encountered in Tompkins Square Park. The ability to be listened to with respect is strictly circumscribed within welfare state capitalism and failure on this score has played a key role in the collapse of state communism. Professional groups have advantages in this regard which place them in a different category to most others and the temptation always stands, for even the most politicized of us, to speak for others without listening to them. Political inclusion is, if anything, diminished by the decline of trade unionism, of political parties, and of traditional institutions, yet it is at the same time revived by the organization of new social movements. But the increasing scale of international dependency and interdependency makes it harder and harder to offset powerlessness in general. Like the struggle against the Baltimore expressway, the mobilization of political power among the oppressed in society is increasingly a local affair, unable to address the structural characteristics of either market or welfare state capitalism as a whole. This leads to my third proposition: *just planning and policy practices must empower rather than deprive the oppressed of access to political power and the ability to engage in self-expression.*

What Young calls *cultural imperialism* relates to the ways in which "the dominant meanings of a society render the particular perspective of one's own group invisible at the same time as they stereotype one's group and mark it out as the Other". Arguments of this sort have been most clearly articulated by femïnists and black liberation theorists, but they are also implicit in liberation theology as well as in many domains of cultural theory. This is, in some respects, the most difficult form of oppression to identify clearly, yet there can surely be no doubt that there are many social groups in our societies who find or feel themselves "defined from the outside, positioned, placed, by a network of dominant meanings they experience as arising from elsewhere, from those with whom they do not identify and who do not identify with them". The alienation and social unrest to be found in many western European and North American cities (to say nothing of its re-emergence throughout much of eastern Europe) bears all the marks of a reaction to cultural imperialism, and here too, welfare state capitalism has in the past proved both unsympathetic and unmoved. From this comes a fourth proposition: *that just planning and policy practices must be, particularly sensitive to issues of cultural imperialism and seek, by a variety of means, to eliminate the imperialist attitude both in the design of urban projects and modes of popular consultation.*

Fifth, there is the issue of *violence*. It is hard to consider urban futures and living environments into the twenty-first century without confronting the problem of burgeoning levels of physical violence. The fear of violence against persons and property, though often exaggerated, has a material grounding in the social conditions of market capitalism and calls for some kind of organized response. There is, furthermore, the intricate problem of the violence of organized crime and its interdigitation with capitalist enterprise and state activities. The problem at the first level is, as Davis points out in his consideration of Los Angeles, that the most characteristic response is to search for defensible urban spaces, to militarize urban space and to create living environments which are more rather than less exclusionary.

The difficulty with the second level is that the equivalent of the *mafiosi* in many cities (an emergent problem in the contemporary Soviet Union, for example) has become so powerful in urban governance that it is they, rather than elected officials and state bureaucrats, who hold the true reins of power. No society can function without certain forms of social control and we have to consider what that might be in the face of a Foucauldian insistence that all forms of social control are oppressive, no matter what the level of violence to which they are addressed. Here too there are innumerable dilemmas to be solved, but we surely know enough to advance a fifth proposition: *a just planning and policy practice must seek out non-exclusionary and non-militarized forms of social control to contain the increasing levels of both personal and institutionalized violence without destroying capacities for empowerment and self-expression.*

Finally, I want to add a sixth principle to those which Young advances. This derives from the fact that all social projects are ecological projects and vice versa. While I resist the view that "nature has rights" or that nature can be "oppressed", the justice due to future generations and to other inhabitants of the globe requires intense scrutiny of all social projects for assessment of their ecological consequences. Human beings necessarily appropriate and transform the world around them in the course of making their own history, but they do not have to do so with such reckless abandon as to jeopardize the fate of peoples separated from us in either space or time. The final proposition is, then: *that just planning and policy practices will clearly recognize that the necessary ecological consequences of all social projects have impacts on future generations as well as upon distant peoples and take steps to ensure a reasonable mitigation of negative impacts.*

I do not argue that these six principles can or even should be unified, let alone turned into some convenient and formulaic composite strategy. Indeed, the six dimensions of justice here outlined are frequently in conflict with each other as far as their application to individual persons – the exploited male worker may be a cultural imperialist on matters of race and gender while the thoroughly oppressed person may be the bearer of social injustice as violence. On the other hand, I do not believe the principles can be applied in isolation from each other either. Simply to leave matters at the level of a "non-consensual" conception of justice, as someone like Lyotard (1984) would do, is not to confront some central issues of the social processes which produce such a differentiated conception of justice in the first place. This then suggests that social policy and planning has to work at two levels. The different faces of oppression have to be confronted for what they are and as they are manifest in daily life, but in the longer term and at the same time the underlying sources of the different forms of oppression in the heart of the political economy of capitalism must also be confronted, not as the fount of all evil but in terms of capitalism's revolutionary dynamic which transforms, disrupts, deconstructs and reconstructs ways of living, working, relating to each other and to the environment. From such a standpoint the issue is never about whether or not there shall be change, but what sort of change we can anticipate, plan for, and proactively shape in the years to come.

I would hope that consideration of the varieties of justice as well as of this deeper problematic might set the tone for present deliberations. By appeal to them, we might see ways to break with the political, imaginative and institutional constraints which have for too long inhibited the advanced capitalist societies in their developmental path. The critique of universal notions of justice and

rationality, no matter whether embedded in the market or in state welfare capitalism, still stands. But it is both valuable and potentially liberating to look at alternative conceptions of both justice and rationality as these have emerged within the new social movements these last two decades. And while it will in the end ever be true, as Marx and Plato observed, that "between equal rights force decides", the authoritarian imposition of solutions to many of our urban ills these past few years and the inability to listen to alternative conceptions of both justice and rationality is very much a part of the problem. The conceptions I have outlined speak to many of the marginalized, the oppressed and the exploited in this time and place. For many of us, and for many of them, the formulations may well appear obvious, unproblematic and just plain common sense. And it is precisely because of such widely held conceptions that so much welfare-state paternalism and market rhetoric fails. It is, by the same token, precisely out of such conceptions that a genuinely liberatory and transformative politics can be made. "Seize the time and the place", they would say around Tompkins Square Park, and this does indeed appear an appropriate time and place to do so. If some of the walls are coming down all over eastern Europe, then surely we can set about bringing them down in our own cities as well.

ACKNOWLEDGEMENT

I am much indebted to Neil Smith for information and ideas about the struggles over Tompkins Square Park.

REFERENCES

Chambers, I. (1987) Maps for the metropolis: a possible guide to the present. *Cultural Studies*, 1, 1–22.
Dahl, R. and Lindblom, C. (1953) *Politics, Economics and Welfare*. New York: Harper.
Davis, M. (1990) *City of Quartz: Excavating the Future in Los Angeles*. London: Verso.
Godelier, M. (1972) *Rationality and Irrationality in Economics*. London: New Left Books.
Harvey, D. (1973) *Social Justice and the City*. London: Edward Arnold.
Harvey, D. (1989) *The Condition of Postmodernity*. Oxford: Blackwell.

Jacobs, J. (1961) *The Death and Life of Great American Cities*. New York: Vintage.

Kifney, J. (1989) No miracles in the park: homeless New Yorkers amid drug lords and slumlords. *International Herald Tribune*, 1 August, 6.

Lefebvre, H. (1991) *The Production of Space*. Oxford: Blackwell.

Lyotard, J. (1984) *The Postmodern Condition*. Manchester: Manchester University Press.

Marx, K. (1967) *Capital, volume 1*. New York: International Publishers.

Marx, K. and Engels, F. (1951) *Selected Works, volume 1*. Moscow: Progress Publishers.

Plato (1965) *The Republic*. Harmondsworth: Penguin.

Rawls, J. (1971) *A Theory of Justice*. Cambridge, MA: Harvard University Press.

Smith, N. (1989) Tompkins Square: riots, rents and redskins. *Portable Lower East Side*, 6, 1–36.

Smith, N. (1992) New city, new frontier: the Lower East Side as wild, wild west. In M. Sorkin (ed.), *Variations on a Theme Park: The New American City and the End of Public Space*. New York: Noonday.

Unger, R. (1987) *False Necessity: Anti-necessitarian Social Theory in the Service of Radical Democracy*. Cambridge: Cambridge University Press.

Wittgenstein, I. (1967) *Philosophical Investigations*. Oxford: Blackwell.

Young, I. M. (1990) *Justice and the Politics of Difference*. Princeton, NJ: Princeton University Press.

8

The Phenomenon of Place

Christian Norberg-Schulz

Our everyday life-world consists of concrete "phenomena". It consists of people, of animals, of flowers, trees and forests, of stone, earth, wood and water, of towns, streets and houses, doors, windows and furniture. And it consists of sun, moon and stars, of drifting clouds, of night and day and changing seasons. But it also comprises more intangible phenomena such as feelings. This is what is "given", this is the "content" of our existence. Thus Rilke says: "Are we perhaps *here* to say: house, bridge, fountain, gate, jug, fruit tree, window, – at best: Pillar, tower..." (Rilke, 1972, Elegy XI). Everything else, such as atoms and molecules, numbers and all kinds of "data", are abstractions or tools which are constructed to serve other purposes than those of everyday life. Today it is common to mistake the tools for reality.

The concrete things which constitute our given world are interrelated in complex and perhaps contradictory ways. Some of the phenomena may for instance comprise others. The forest consists of trees, and the town is made up of houses. "Landscape" is such a comprehensive phenomenon. In general we may say that some phenomena form an "environment" to others. A concrete term for environment is *place*. It is common usage to say that acts and occurrences *take place*. In fact it is meaningless to imagine any happening without reference to a locality. Place is evidently an integral part of existence. What, then, do we mean with the word "place"? Obviously we mean something more than abstract location. We mean a totality made up of concrete things having material substance, shape, texture and colour. Together these things determine an "environmental character", which is the essence of place. In general a place is given as such a character or "atmosphere". A place is therefore a qualitative, "total" phenomenon, which we cannot reduce to any of its properties, such as spatial relationships, without losing its concrete nature out of sight.

Everyday experience moreover tells us that different actions need different environments to take place in a satisfactory way. As a consequence, towns and houses consist of a multitude of particular places. This fact is of course taken into consideration by current theory of planning and architecture, but so far the problem has been treated in a too abstract way. "Taking place" is usually understood in a quantitative, "functional" sense, with implications such as spatial distribution and dimensioning. But are not "functions" inter-human and similar everywhere? Evidently not. "Similar" functions, even the most basic ones such as sleeping and eating, take place in very different ways, and demand places with different properties, in accordance with different cultural traditions and different environmental conditions. The functional approach therefore left out the place as a concrete "here" having its particular identity.

Being qualitative totalities of a complex nature, places cannot be described by means of analytic, "scientific" concepts. As a matter of principle science "abstracts" from the given to arrive at neutral, "objective" knowledge. What is lost, however, is the everyday life-world, which ought to be the real concern of man in general and planners and architects in particular.[1] Fortunately a way out of the impasse exists, that is, the method known as *phenomenology*. Phenomenology was conceived as a "return to things", as opposed to abstractions and mental constructions. So far phenomenologists have been mainly concerned with ontology, psychology, ethics and to some extent aesthetics, and have given relatively little attention to the phenomenology of the daily environment. A few pioneer works however exist but they hardly contain any direct reference to architecture.[2] A phenomenology of architecture is therefore urgently needed.

Some of the philosophers who have approached the problem of our life-world, have used language and literature as sources of "information". Poetry in fact is able to concretize those totalities which elude science, and may therefore suggest how we might proceed to obtain the needed understanding. One of the poems used by Heidegger to explain the nature of language, is the splendid *A Winter Evening* by Georg Trakl (Heidegger, 1971). The words of Trakl also serve our purpose very well, as they make present a total life-situation where the aspect of place is strongly felt:

A Winter Evening

> *Window with falling snow is arrayed,*
> *Long tolls the vesper bell,*
> *The house is provided well,*
> *The table is for many laid.*
> *Wandering ones, more than a few,*
> *Come to the door on darksome courses,*
> *Golden blooms the tree of graces*
> *Drawing up the earth's cool dew.*
> *Wanderer quietly steps within;*
> *Pain has turned the threshold to stone.*
> *There lie, in limpid brightness shown,*
> *Upon the table bread and wine.*

We shall not repeat Heidegger's profound analysis of the poem, but rather point out a few properties which illuminate our problem. In general, Trakl uses *concrete* images which we all know from our everyday world. He talks about "snow", "window", "house", "table", "door", "tree", "threshold", "bread

and wine", "darkness" and "light", and he characterizes man as a "wanderer". These images, however, also imply more general structures. First of all the poem distinguishes between an *outside* and an *inside*. The outside is presented in the first two lines of the first stanza, and comprises *natural* as well as *man-made* elements. Natural place is present in the falling snow which implies winter, and by the evening. The very title of the poem "places" everything in this natural context. A winter evening, however, is something more than a point in the calendar. As a concrete presence, it is experienced as a set of particular qualities, or in general as a *Stimmung* or "character", which forms a background to acts and occurrences. In the poem this character is given by the snow falling on the window, cold, soft and soundless, hiding the contours of those objects which are still recognized in the approaching darkness. The word "falling" moreover creates a sense of *space*, or rather: an implied presence of earth and sky. With a minimum of words, Trakl thus brings a total natural environment to life. But the outside also has man-made properties. This is indicated by the vesper bell, which is heard everywhere, and makes the "private" inside become part of a comprehensive, "public" totality. The vesper bell, however, is something more than a practical man-made artifact. It is a symbol, which reminds us of the common values which are at the basis of that totality. In Heidegger's words: "The tolling of the evening bell brings men, as mortals, before the divine" (Heidegger, 1971, p. 199).

The *inside* is presented in the next two verses. It is described as a house, which offers man shelter and security by being enclosed and "well provided". It has, however, a window, an opening which makes us experience the inside as a complement to the outside. As a final focus within the house we find the table, which "is for many laid". At the table men come together, it is the *centre* which more than anything else constitutes the inside. The character of the inside is hardly told, but anyhow present. It is luminous and warm, in contrast to the cold darkness outside, and its silence is pregnant with potential sound. In general the inside is a comprehensible world of *things*, where the life of "many" may take place.

In the next two stanzas the perspective is deepened. Here the *meaning* of places and things comes forth, and man is presented as a wanderer on "darksome courses". Rather than being placed safely within the house he has created for himself, he comes from the outside, from the "path of life", which also represents man's attempt at "orienting" himself in the given unknown environment. But nature also has another side: it offers the grace of growth and blossom. In the image of the "golden" tree, earth and sky are unified and become a *world*. Through man's labour this world is brought inside as bread and wine, whereby the inside is "illuminated", that is, becomes meaningful. Without the "sacred" fruits of sky and earth, the inside would remain "empty". The house and the table receive and gather, and bring the world "close". *To dwell in a house therefore means to inhabit the world.* But this dwelling is not easy; it has to be reached on dark paths, and a threshold separates the outside from the inside. Representing the "rift" between "otherness" and manifest meaning, it embodies suffering and is "turned to stone". In the threshold, thus, the *problem* of dwelling comes to the fore (Heidegger, 1971, p. 204).

Trakl's poem illuminates some essential phenomena of our life-world, and in particular the basic properties of place. First of all it tells us that every situation is local as well as general. The winter evening described is obviously a local, nordic phenomenon, but the implied notions of outside and inside are general, as are the meanings connected with this distinction. The poem hence concretizes basic properties of existence. "Concretize" here means to make the general "visible" as a concrete, local situation. In doing this the poem moves in the opposite direction of scientific thought. Whereas science departs from the "given", poetry brings us back to the concrete things, uncovering the meanings inherent in the life-world (Norberg-Schulz, 1963, chapter on "symbolization").

Furthermore Trakl's poem distinguishes between natural and man-made elements, whereby it suggests a point of departure for an "environmental phenomenology". Natural elements are evidently the primary components of the given, and places are in fact usually defined in geographical terms. We must repeat however, that "place" means something more than location. Various attempts at a description of natural places are offered by current literature on "landscape", but again we find that the usual approach is too abstract, being based on "functional" or perhaps "visual" considerations (see, for instance, Appleton, 1975). Again we must turn to philosophy for help. As a first, fundamental distinction Heidegger introduces the concepts of "earth" and "sky", and says: "Earth is the serving bearer, blossoming and fruiting, spreading out in rock and water, rising up into plant and animal... The sky is the vaulting path of the sun, the course of the changing moon, the glitter of the stars, the year's seasons, the light and dusk of day, the gloom and glow of night, the clemency and inclemency of the weather, the drifting clouds and blue depth of the ether..." (Heidegger, 1971, p. 149). Like many fundamental insights, the distinction between earth and sky might seem trivial. Its importance however comes out when we add Heidegger's definition of "dwelling": "The way in which you are and I am, the way in which we humans *are* on the earth, is dwelling..." But "on the earth" already means "under the sky" (Heidegger, 1971, pp. 147, 149). He also calls what is *between* earth and sky *the world*, and says that "the world is the house where the mortals dwell" (Heidegger, 157, p. 13). In other words, when man is capable of dwelling the world becomes an "inside".

In general, nature forms an extended comprehensive totality, a "place", which according to local circumstances has a particular identity. This identity, or "spirit", may be described by means of the kind of concrete, "qualitative" terms Heidegger uses to characterize earth and sky, and has to take this fundamental distinction as its point of departure. In this way we might arrive at an existentially relevant understanding of *landscape*, which ought to be preserved as the main designation of natural places. Within the landscape, however, there are subordinate places, as well as natural "things" such as Trakl's "tree". In these things the meaning of the natural environment is "condensed".

The man-made parts of the environment are first of all "settlements" of different scale, from houses and farms to villages and towns, and secondly "paths" which connect these settlements, as well as various elements which transform nature into a "cultural landscape". If the settlements are organically related to their environment, it implies that they serve as *foci* where the environmental character is condensed and "explained". Thus Heidegger says: "The single houses, the villages, the towns are works of building which within and around themselves gather the multifarious in-between. The buildings bring the earth as the inhabited landscape close to man, and at the same time place the closeness of neighbourly dwelling under the expanse of the sky" (Heidegger, 1957, p. 13). The basic property of man-made places is therefore concentration and enclosure. They are "insides" in a full sense, which means that they "gather" what is known. To fulfill this function they have openings which relate to the outside. (Only an *inside* can in fact have openings.) Buildings are furthermore related to their environment by resting on the ground and rising towards the sky. Finally the man-made environments comprise artifacts or "things", which may serve as internal foci, and emphasize the gathering function of the settlement. In Heidegger's words: "The thing things world", where "thinging" is used in the original sense of "gathering", and further: "Only what conjoins itself out of world becomes a thing" (Heidegger, 1971, pp. 181–2).

Our introductory remarks give several indications about the *structure* of places. Some of these have already been worked out by phenomenologist philosophers, and offer a good point of departure for a more complete phenomenology. A first step is taken with the distinction of natural and man-made phenomena. A second step is represented by the categories of earth–sky (horizontal–vertical) and outside–inside. These categories have spacial implications, and "space" is hence re-introduced, not primarily as a mathematical concept, but as an existential dimension (Norberg-Schulz, 1971, where the concept "existential space" is used). A final and particularly important step is taken with the concept of "character". Character is determined by *how* things are, and gives our investigation a basis in the concrete phenomena of our everyday life-world. Only in this way we may fully grasp the *genius loci*; the "spirit of place" which the ancients recognized as that "opposite" man has to come to terms with, to be able to dwell.[4] The concept of *genius loci* denotes the essence of place.

The Structure of Place

Our preliminary discussion of the phenomena of place led to the conclusion that the structure of place ought to be described in terms of "landscape" and "settlement", and analyzed by means of the categories "space" and "character". Whereas "space" denotes the three-dimensional organization of the elements which make up a place, "character" denotes the general "atmosphere" which is the most comprehensive property of any place. Instead of making a distinction between space and character, it is of course possible to employ one comprehensive concept, such as "lived space".[5] For our purpose, however, it is practical to distinguish between space and character. Similar spatial organizations may possess very different characters according to the concrete treatment of the space-defining elements (the *boundary*). The history of basic spatial forms have been given ever new characterizing interpretations.[6] On the other hand it has to be pointed out that the spatial organization puts certain limits to characterization, and that the two concepts are interdependent.

"Space" is certainly no new term in architectural theory. But space can mean many things. In current literature we may distinguish between two uses: space as three-dimensional geometry, and space as perceptual field (Norberg-Schulz, 1971, pp. 12ff). None of these however are satisfactory, being abstractions from the intuitive three-dimensional totality of everyday experience, which we may call "concrete space". Concrete human actions in fact do not take place in an homogeneous isotropic space, but in a space distinguished by qualitative differences, such as "up" and "down". In architectural theory several attempts have been made to define space in concrete, qualitative terms. Giedion, thus uses the distinction between "outside" and "inside" as the basis for a grand view of architectural history (Giedion, 1964). Kevin Lynch penetrates deeper into the structure of concrete space, introducing the concepts of "node" ("landmark"), "path", "edge" and "district", to denote those elements which form the basis for man's orientation in space (Lynch, 1960). Paolo Portoghesi finally defines space as a "system of places", implying that the concept of space has its roots in concrete situations, although spaces may be *described* by means of mathematics (Portoghesi, 1975, pp. 88ff). The latter view corresponds to Heidegger's statement that "spaces receive their being from locations and not from 'space'" (Heidegger, 1971, p. 154). The outside–inside relation which is a primary aspect of concrete space, implies that spaces possess a varying degree of *extension* and *enclosure*. Whereas landscapes are distinguished by a varied, but basically continuous extension, settlements are enclosed entities. Settlement and landscape therefore have a *figure-ground* relationship. In general, any enclosure becomes manifest as a "figure" in relation to the extended ground of the landscape. A settlement loses its identity if this relationship is corrupted, just as much as the landscape loses its identity as comprehensive extension. In a wider context any enclosure becomes a *centre*, which may function as a "focus" for its surroundings. From the centre space extends with a varying degree of continuity (rhythm) in different directions. Evidently the main directions are horizontal and vertical, that is, the directions of earth and sky. *Centralization, direction* and *rhythm* are

therefore other important properties of concrete space. Finally it has to be mentioned that natural elements (such as hills) and settlements may be clustered or grouped with a varying degree of *proximity.*

All the spatial properties mentioned are of a "topological" kind, and correspond to the well-known "principles of organization" of Gestalt theory. The primary existential importance of these principles is confirmed by the researches of Piaget on the child's conception of space (Norberg-Schulz, 1971, p. 18). Geometrical modes of organization only develop later in life to serve particular purposes, and may in general be understood as a more "precise" definition of the basic topological structures. The topological enclosure thus becomes a circle, the "free" curve a straight line, and the cluster a grid. In architecture geometry is used to make a general comprehensive system manifest, such as an inferred "cosmic order".

Any enclosure is defined by a boundary: Heidegger says: "A boundary is not that at which something stops but, as the Greeks recognized, the boundary is that, from which something begins its presencing" (Heidegger, 1971, p. 154: Presence is the old word for being). The boundaries of a built space are known as *floor, wall* and *ceiling.* The boundaries of a landscape are structurally similar, and consist of ground, horizon, and sky. This simple structural similarity is of basic importance for the relationship between natural and man-made places. The enclosing properties of a boundary are determined by its *openings*, as was poetically intuited by Trakl when using the images of window, door and threshold. In general the boundary, and in particular the wall, makes the spatial structure visible as continuous and/or discontinuous extension, direction and rhythm.

"Character" is at the same time a more general and a more concrete concept than "space". On the one hand it denotes a general comprehensive atmosphere, and on the other the concrete form and substance of the space-definining elements. Any real *presence* is intimately linked with a character (Bollnow, 1956). A phenomenology of character has to comprise a survey of manifest characters as well as an investigation of their concrete determinants. We have pointed out that different actions demand places with a different character. A dwelling has to be "protective", an office "practical", a ball-room "festive" and a church "solemn". When we visit a foreign city, we are usually struck by its particular character, which becomes an important part of the experience. Landscapes also possess character, some of which is of a particular "natural" kind. Thus we talk about "barren" and "fertile", "smiling" and "threatening" landscapes. In general we have to emphasize that *all places have character*, and that character is the basic mode in which the world is "given". To some extent the character of a place is a function of time; it changes with the seasons, the course of the day and the weather, factors which above all determine different conditions of *light*.

The character is determined by the material and formal constitution of the place. We must therefore ask: *how* is the ground on which we walk, *how* is the sky above our heads, or in general: *how* are the boundaries which define the place. How a boundary is depends upon its formal articulation, which is again related to the way it is "built". Looking at a building from this point of view, we have to consider how it rests on the ground and how it rises towards the sky. Particular attention has to be given to its lateral boundaries, or walls, which also contribute decisively to determine the character of the *urban* environment. We are indebted to Robert Venturi for having recognized this fact, after it had been considered for many years "immoral" to talk about "facades" (Venturi, 1967, p. 88). Usually the character of a "family" of buildings which constitute a place, is "condensed" in characteristic *motifs*, such as particular types of windows, doors and roofs. Such motifs may become "conventional elements", which serve to transpose a character from one place to another. In the boundary, thus, character and space come together, and we may agree with Venturi when he defines architecture as "the wall between the inside and the outside" (Venturi, 1967, p. 89).

Except for the intuitions of Venturi, the problem of character has hardly been considered in current architectural theory. As a result, theory has to a high extent lost contact with the concrete life-world. This is particularly the case with technology, which is today considered a mere means to satisfy practical demand. Character however, depends upon *how things are made*, and is therefore determined by the technical realization ("building"). Heidegger points out that the Greek word *techne* meant a creative "re-vealing" (*Entbergen*) of truth, and belonged to *poiesis*, that is, "making" (Heidegger, 1954, p. 12). A phenomenology of place therefore has to comprise the basic modes of construction and their relationship to formal articulation. Only in this way architectural theory gets a truly concrete basis.

The structure of place becomes manifest as environmental totalities which comprise the aspects of character and space. Such places are known as "countries", "regions", "landscapes", "settlements" and "buildings". Here we return to the concrete "things" of our everyday life-world, which was our point of departure, and remember Rilke's words: "Are we perhaps *here* to say..." When places are classified we should therefore use terms such as "island", "promontory", "bay", "forest", "grove", or "square", "street", "courtyard", and "floor", "wall", "roof", "ceiling", "window" and "door".

Places are hence designated by *nouns*. This implies that they are considered real "things that exist", which is the original meaning of the word "substantive". Space, instead, as a system of relations, is denoted by *prepositions*. In our daily life we hardly talk about "space", but about things that are "over" or "under", "before" or "behind" each other, or we use prepositions such as "at", "in", "within", "on", "upon", "to", "from", "along", "next". All these preparations denote topological relations of the kind mentioned before. Character, finally, is denoted by *adjectives*, as was indicated above. A character is a complex totality, and a single adjective evidently cannot cover more than one aspect of this totality. Often, however, a character is so distinct that one word seems sufficient to grasp its essence. We see, thus, that the very structure of everyday language confirms our analysis of place.

Countries, regions, landscapes, settlements, buildings (and their sub-places) form a series with a gradually diminishing scale. The steps in this series may be called "environmental levels" (Norberg-Schulz, 1971, p. 27). At the "top" of the series we find the more comprehensive natural places which "contain" the man-made places on the "lower" levels. The latter have the "gathering" and "focussing" function mentioned above. In other words, man "receives" the environment and makes it focus in buildings and things. The things thereby "explain" the environment and make its character manifest. Thereby the things themselves become meaningful. That is the basic function of *detail* in our surroundings (Norberg-Schulz, 1971, p. 32). This does not imply, however, that the different levels must have the same structure. Architectural history in fact shows that this is rarely the case. Vernacular settlements usually have a topological organization, although the single houses may be strictly geometrical. In larger cities we often find topologically organized neighbourhoods within a general geometrical structure, etc. We shall return to the particular problems of structural correspondence later, but have to say some words about the main "step" in the scale of environmental levels: the relation between natural and man-made places.

Man-made places are related to nature in three basic ways. Firstly, man wants to make the natural structure more precise. That is, he wants to *visualize* his "understanding" of nature, "expressing" the existential foothold he has gained. To achieve this, he *builds* what he has seen. Where nature suggests a delimited space he builds an enclosure; where nature appears "centralized", he erects a *Mal* (Frey, 1949); where nature indicates a direction, he makes a path. Secondly, man has to *symbolize* his understanding of nature (including himself). Symbolization implies that an experienced meaning is "translated" into another medium. A natural

character is for instance translated into a building whose properties somehow make the character manifest (Norberg-Schulz, 1963). The purpose of symbolization is to free the meaning from the immediate situation, whereby it becomes a "cultural object", which may form part of a more complex situation, or be moved to another place. Finally, man needs to *gather* the experienced meanings to create for himself an *image mundi* or *microcosmos* which concretizes his world. Gathering evidently depends on symbolization, and implies a transposition of meanings to one place, which thereby becomes an existential "centre".

Visualization, symbolization and gathering are aspects of the general processes of settling; and dwelling, in the existential sense of the word, depends on these functions. Heidegger illustrates the problem by means of the *bridge*; a "building" which visualizes, symbolizes and gathers, and makes the environment a unified whole. Thus he says:

> The bridge swings over the stream with ease and power. It does not just connect banks that are already there, the banks emerge as banks only as the bridge crosses the stream. The bridge designely causes them to lie across from each other. One side is set off against the other by the bridge. Nor do the banks stretch along the stream as indifferent border strips of the dry land. With the banks, the bridge brings to the stream the one and the other expanse of the landscape lying behind them. It brings stream and bank and land into each other's neighbourhood. The bridge gathers the earth as landscape around the stream. (Heidegger, 1971, p. 152)

Heidegger also describes *what* the bridge gathers and thereby uncovers its value as a symbol. We cannot here enter into these details, but want to emphasize that the landscape as such gets its value *through* the bridge. Before, the meaning of the landscape was "hidden", and the building of the bridge brings it out into the open.

> The bridge gathers Being into a certain "location" that we may call a "place". This

"place", however, did not exist as an entity before the bridge (although there were always many "sites" along the river-bank where it could arise), but comes-to-presence with and as the bridge. (Richardson, 1974, p. 585).

The existential purpose of building (architecture) is therefore to make a site become a place, that is, to uncover the meanings potentially present in the given environment.

The structure of a place is not a fixed, eternal state. As a rule places change, sometimes rapidly. This does not mean, however, that the *genius loci* necessarily changes or gets lost. Later we shall show that *taking place* presupposes that the places conserve their identity during a certain stretch of time. *Stabilitas loci* is a necessary condition for human life. How then is this stability compatible with the dynamics of change? First of all we may point out that any place ought to have the "capacity" of receiving *different* "contents", naturally within certain limits.[7] A place which is only fitted for one particular purpose would soon become useless. Secondly it is evident that a place may be "interpreted" in different ways. To protect and conserve the genius loci in fact means to concretize its essence in ever new historical contexts. We might also say that the history of a place ought to be its "self-realization". What was there as possibilities at the outset, is uncovered through human action, illuminated and "kept" in works of architecture which are simultaneously "old and new" (Venturi, 1967). A place therefore comprises properties having a varying degree of invariance.

In general we may conclude that *place* is the point of departure as well as the goal of our structural investigation; at the outset place is presented as a given, spontaneously experienced totality, at the end it appears as a structured world, illuminated by the analysis of the aspects of space and character.

The Spirit of Place

Genius loci is a Roman concept. According to ancient Roman belief every "independent" being has its *genius*, its guardian spirit. This spirit gives life to people and places, accompanies them from birth to death, and determines their character or essence. Even the gods had their *genius*, a fact which illustrates the fundamental nature of the concept (Paulys, n.d.). The *genius* thus denotes what a thing *is*, or what it "wants to be", to use a word of Louis Kahn. It is not necessary in our context to go into the history of the concept of *genius* and its relationship to the *daimon* of the Greeks. It suffices to point out that ancient man experienced his environment as consisting of definite characters. In particular he recognized that it is of great existential importance to come to terms with the *genius* of the locality where his life takes place. In the past survival depended on a "good" relationship to the place in a physical as well as a psychic sense. In ancient Egypt, for instance, the country was not only cultivated in accordance with the Nile floods, but the very structure of the landscape served as a model for the lay-out of the "public" buildings which should give a man a sense of security by symbolizing an eternal environmental order (Norberg-Schulz, 1975, pp. 10ff).

During the course of history the *genius loci* has remained a living reality, although it may not have been expressively named as such. Artists and writers have found inspiration in local character and have "explained" the phenomena of everyday life as well as art, referring to landscapes and urban milieu. Thus Goethe says: "It is evident, that the eye is educated by the things it sees from childhood on, and therefore Venetian painters must see everything clearer and with more joy than other people" (Goethe, 1786). Still in 1960 Lawrence Durrell wrote: "As you get to know Europe slowly tasting the wines, cheeses and characters of the different countries you begin to realize that the important determinant of any culture is after all – the spirit of place" (Durrell, 1969, p. 156). Modern tourism proves that the experience of different places is a major human interest, although also this value todays tends to get lost. In fact modern man for a long time believed that science and technology had freed him from a direct dependence on places.[8] This belief has proved an illusion; pollution and environmental chaos have suddenly appeared as a frightening *nemesis*, and as a result the problem of place has regained its true importance.

We have used the word "dwelling" to denote the total man-place relationship. To understand more fully what this word implies, it is useful to return to the distinction between "space" and "character". When man dwells, he is simultaneously located in space and exposed to a certain environmental character. The two psychological functions involved, may be called "orientation" and "identification".[9] To gain an existential foothold man has to be able to *orientate* himself; he has to know where he is. But he also has to *identify* himself with the environment, that is, he has to know *how* he is in a certain place.

The problem of orientation has been given a considerable attention in recent theoretical literature on planning and architecture. Again we may refer to the work of Kevin Lynch, whose concepts of "node", "path" and "district" denote the basic spatial structures which are the object of man's orientation. The perceived interrelationship of these elements constitute an "environmental image", and Lynch asserts: "A good environmental image gives its possessor an important sense of emotional security" (Lynch, 1960, p. 4). Accordingly all cultures have developed "systems of orientation", that is, spatial structures which facilitate the development of a good environmental image. "The world may be organized around a set of focal points, or be broken into named regions, or be linked by remembered routes" (Lynch, 1960, p. 7). Often these systems of orientation are based on or derived from a given natural structure. Where the system is weak, the image-making becomes difficult, and man feels "lost". "The terror of being lost comes from the necessity that a mobile organism be oriented in its surroundings" (Lynch, 1960, p. 125). To be lost is evidently the opposite of the feeling of security which distinguishes dwelling. The environmental quality which protects man against getting lost, Lynch calls "imageability", which

means "that shape, colour or arrangement which facilitates the making of vividly-identified, powerfully-structured, highly useful mental images of the environment" (Lynch, 1960, p. 9). Here Lynch implies that the elements which constitute the spatial structure are concrete "things" with "character" and "meaning". He limits himself, however, to discuss the spatial function of these elements, and thus leaves us with a fragmentary understanding of dwelling.

Nevertheless, the work of Lynch constitutes an essential contribution to the theory of place. Its importance also consists in the fact that his empirical studies of concrete urban structure confirm the general "principles of organization" defined by Gestalt psychology and by the researches into child psychology of Piaget.[10]

Without reducing the importance of orientation, we have to stress that dwelling above all presupposes *indentification* with the environment. Although orientation and identification are aspects of one total relationship, they have a certain independence within the totality. It is evidently possible to orientate oneself well without true identification; one gets along without feeling "at home". And it is possible to feel at home without being well acquainted with the spatial structure of the place, that is, the place is only experienced as a gratifying general character. True belonging however presupposes that both psychological functions are fully developed. In primitive societies we find that even the smallest environmental details are known and meaningful, and that they make up complex spatial structures (Rapoport, 1975). In modern society, however, attention has almost exclusively been concentrated on the "practical" function of orientation, whereas identification has been left to chance. As a result true dwelling, in a psychological sense, has been substituted by alienation. It is therefore urgently needed to arrive at a fuller understanding of the concepts of "identification" and "character".

In our context "identification" means to become "friends" with a particular environment. Nordic man has to be friends with fog, ice and cold winds; he has to enjoy the creaking sound of snow under the feet when he walks around, he has to experience the poetical value of being immersed in fog, as Hermann Hesse did when he wrote the lines: "Strange to walk in fog! Lonely is every bush and stone, no tree sees the other, everything is alone. . . ."[11] The Arab, instead, has to be a friend of the infinitely extended, sandy desert and the burning sun. This does not mean that his settlements should not protect him against the natural "forces"; a desert settlement in fact primarily aims at the exclusion of sand and sun. But it implies that the environment is experienced as *meaningful*. Bollnow says appropriately: "*Fede Stimmung ist Übereinstimmung*", that is, every character consists in a correspondence between outer and inner world, and between body and psyche (Bollnow, 1956, p. 39). For modern urban man the friendship with a natural environment is reduced to fragmentary relations. Instead he has to identify with manmade things, such as streets and houses. The German-born American architect Gerhard Kallmann once told a story which illustrates what this means. Visiting at the end of the Second World War his native Berlin after many years of absence, he wanted to see the house where he had grown up. As must be expected in Berlin, the house had disappeared, and Mr Kallmann felt somewhat lost. Then he suddenly recognized the typical pavement of the sidewalk: the floor on which he had played as a child! And he experienced a strong feeling of having returned home.

The story teaches us that the objects of identification are concrete environmental properties and that man's relationship to these is usually developed during childhood. The child grows up in green, brown or white spaces; it walks or plays on sand, earth, stone or moss, under a cloudy or serene sky; it grasps and lifts hard and soft things; it hears noises, such as the sound of the wind moving the leaves of a particular kind of tree; and it experiences heat and cold. Thus the child gets acquainted with the environment, and develops perceptual *schemata* which determine all future experiences. (Norberg-Schulz, 1963, pp. 41ff). The schemata comprise universal structures which are

inter-human, as well as locally-determined and culturally-conditioned structures. Evidently every human being has to possess schemata of orientation as well as identification.

The *identity* of a person is defined in terms of the schemata developed, because they determine the "world" which is accessible. This fact is confirmed by common linguistic usage. When a person wants to tell who he is, it is in fact usual to say: "I am a New Yorker", or "I am a Roman". This means something much more concrete than to say: "I am an architect", or perhaps: "I am an optimist". We understand that human identity is to a high extent a function of places and things. Thus Heidegger says: "Wir sind die Be-Dingten" (Heidegger, 1971, p. 181).[12] It is therefore not only important that our environment has a spatial structure which facilitates orientation, but that it consists of concrete objects of identification. *Human identity presupposes the identity of place.*

Identification and orientation are primary aspects of man's being-in-the-world. Whereas identification is the basis for man's sense of *belonging*, orientation is the function which enables him to be that *homo viator* which is part of his nature. It is characteristic for modern man that for a long time he gave the role as a wanderer pride of place. He wanted to be "free" and conquer the world. Today we start to realize that true freedom presupposes belonging, and that "dwelling" means belonging to a concrete place.

The word to "dwell" has several connotations which confirm and illuminate our thesis. Firstly it ought to be mentioned that "dwell" is derived from the Old Norse *dvelja*, which meant to linger or remain. Analogously, Heidegger related the German "wohnen" to "bleiben" and "sich aufhalten" (Heidegger, 1971, pp. 146ff). Furthermore he points out that the Gothic *wunian* meant to "be at peace", "to remain in peace". The German word for "peace", *Friede*, means to be free, that is, protected from harm and danger. This protection is achieved by means of an *Umfriedung* or enclosure. *Friede* is also related to *zufrieden* (content), *Freund* (friend) and the Gothic *frijön* (love). Heidegger uses these linguistic relationships to show that *dwelling means to be at peace in a protected place*. We should also mention that the German word for dwelling *Wohnung*, derives from *das Gewohnte*, which means what is known or habitual. "Habit" and "habitat" show an analogous relationship. In other words, man knows what has become accessible to him through dwelling. We here return to the *Übereinstimmung* or correspondence between man and his environment, and arrive at the very root of the problem of "gathering". To gather means that the everyday life-world has become "gewohnt" or "habitual". But gathering is a concrete phenomenon, and thus leads us to the final connotation of "dwelling". Again it is Heidegger who has uncovered a fundamental relationship. Thus he points out that the Old English and High German word for "building", *buan*, meant to dwell, and that it is intimately related to the verb *to be*. "What then does *ich bin* mean? The old word *bauen*, to which the *bin* belongs, answers: *ich bin, du bist*, mean: I dwell, you dwell. The way in which you are and I am, the manner in which we humans *are* on earth, is *buan*, dwelling" (Heidegger, 1971, p. 147). We may conclude that dwelling means to gather the world as a concrete building or "thing", and that the archetypal act of building is the *Umfriedung* or enclosure. Trakl's poetic intuition of the inside–outside relationship thus gets its confirmation, and we understand that our concept of *concretization* denotes the essence of dwelling (Norberg-Schulz, 1963, pp. 61ff, 68).

Man dwells when he is able to concretize the world in buildings and things. As we have mentioned above, "concretization" is the function of the work of art, as opposed to the "abstraction" of science (Norberg-Schulz, 1963, pp. 168ff). Works of art concretize what remains "between" the pure objects of science. Our everyday life-world *consists of* such "intermediary" objects, and we understand that the fundamental function of art is to gather the contradictions and complexities of the life-world. Being an *imago mundi*, the work of art helps

man to dwell. Holderlin was right when he said:

> Full of merit, yet poetically, man
> Dwells on this earth.

This means: man's merits do not count much if he is unable to dwell *poetically*, that is, to dwell in the true sense of the word. Thus Heidegger says: "Poetry does not fly above and surmount the earth in order to escape it and hover over it. Poetry is what first brings man onto the earth, making him belong to it, and thus brings him into dwelling" (Heidegger, 1971, p. 218). Only poetry in all its forms (also as the "art of living") makes human existence meaningful, and *meaning* is the fundamental human need.

Architecture belongs to poetry, and its purpose is to help man to dwell. But architecture is a difficult art. To make practical towns and buildings is not enough. Architecture comes into being when a "total environment is made visable", to quote the definition of Susanne Langer (1953). In general, this means to concretize the *genius loci*. We have seen that this is done by means of buildings which gather the properties of the place and bring them close to man. The basic act of architecture is therefore to understand the "vocation" of the place. In this way we protect the earth and become ourselves part of a comprehensive totality. What is here advocated is not some kind of "environmental determinism". We only recognize the fact that man *is* an integral part of the environment, and that it can only lead to human alienation and environmental disruption if he forgets that. To belong to a place means to have an existential foothold, in a concrete everyday sense. When God said to Adam "You shall be a fugitive and a wanderer on the Earth"[13] he put man in front of his most basic problem: to cross the threshold and regain the lost place.

NOTES

1 The concept "everyday life-world" was introduced by Husserl (1936)

2 Heidegger, "Bauen Wohnen Denken"; Bollnow, "Mensch und Raum"; Merleau-Ponty,
   "Phenomenology of Perception"; Bache-
   lard, "Poetics of Space"; also Krause (1974).
3 Ein Winterabend

   Wenn der Schnee ans Fenster fältt,
   Lang die Abendglocke läuter,
   Vielen ist der Tisch bereitet
   Und das Haus ist wohlbestellt.
     Mancher auf der Wanderschaft
   Kommt ans Tor auf dunklen Pfaden.
   Golden blüht der Baum der Gnaden
   Aus der Erde külem Saft.
     Wanderer tritt still herein;
   Schmerz versteinerte die Schwelle.
   Da erglänzt in reiner Helle
   Auf dem Tische Brot und Wein.

4 Heidegger points out the relationship between the words gegen (against, opposite)
   and Gegend (environment, locality).

5 This has been done by some writers, such
   as K. Graf von Dürckheim, E. Straus and
   O. F. Bollnow.
6 We may compare with Alberti's distinction
   between "beauty" and "ornament".
7 For the concept of "capacity" see Norberg-
   Schulz (1963).
8 See Webber (1963), who talks about "non-
   place urban realm".
9 Cf Norberg-Schulz (1963), where the concepts "cognitive orientation" and "cathe-
   tic orientation" are used.
10 For a detailed discussion, see Norberg-
   Schulz (1971).
11 Seltsam, im Nebel zu wandern! Einsam ist
   jeder Busch und Stein, kein Baum sieht den
   anderen, jeder ist allein.
12 "We are the be-thinged", the conditioned
   ones.
13 Genesis, chapter 4, verse 12.

REFERENCES

Appleton, J. (1975) The Experience of Landscape. London.
Bollnow, O. F. (1956) Das Wesen der Stimmungen. Frankfurt am Main.
Durrell, L. (1969) Spirit of Place. London.
Frey, D. (1949) Grundlegung zu einer vergleichenden Kunstwissenschaft. Vienna and Innsbruck.
Giedion, S. (1964) The Eternal Present: The Beginnings of Architecture. London.
Goethe, J. W. von (1786) Italienische Reise, 8, October.
Heidegger, M. (1954) Die Frage nach der Technik. In Vorträge und Aufsätze. Pfullingen.
Heidegger, M. (1957) Hebel der Hausfreund. Pfullingen.
Heidegger, M. (1971) Poetry, Language, Thought, ed. A. Hofstadter. New York.
Husserl, E. (1936) The Crisis of European Sciences and Transcendental Phenomenology. Evan-
   ston, IL.
Lynch, K. (1960) The Image of the City. Cambridge, MA.
Norberg-Schulz, C. (1963) Intentions in Architecture. Oslo and London.
Norberg-Schulz, C. (1971) Existence, Space and Architecture. London and New York.
Norberg-Schulz, C. (1975) Meaning in Western Architecture. London and New York.
Paulys (n.d.) Realencyclopedie der Klassischen Altertumwissenschaft, VII.
Portoghesi, P. (1975) Le inibizioni dell'architettura moderna. Bari.
Rapoport, A. (1975) Australian Aborigines and the definition of place. In P. Oliver (ed.), Shelter,
   Sign and Symbol. London
Richardson, W. J. (1974) Heidegger: Through Phenomenology to Thought. The Hague.
Rilke, R. M. (1972) The Duino Elegies. New York.
Venturi, A. (1967) Complexity and Contradiction in Architecture. New York.
Webber, M. M. (1963) Explorations into Urban Structure. Philadelphia.

9

Recapturing the Center: A Semiotic Analysis of Shopping Malls

Mark Gottdiener

The phenomenon of the mall in the US can only be understood within the context of the fundamental changes in socio-spatial organization affecting the urban environment there over the past thirty years (Gottdiener, 1983, 1985). These are summed up by the concept of "deconcentration," i.e., the general leveling off of population and activities throughout the metropolitan region after years of being concentrated within large city centers. Without question the most important aspect of deconcentration is the demographic reversal of population movement. Once large cities were powerful magnets for migration, but they have now reversed polarity and have become the least favored residential site for the plurality of the population. Since the 1950s in the US the massive movement of people, especially the middle class, to the urban periphery has been accompanied by the general dispersal of commercial, political, financial, and recreational activities as well. This has altered in a fundamental way the morphology of Late Capitalist settlement space.

According to Barthes (1970–1971), the classic city form was organized around a center which possessed material manifestations corresponding to each of the primary forces of social organization. Thus, the classic city had a kind of semantic unity represented by its center within which the specific social practices of politics, religion, business, and cultural interaction had their material correlates. This historical form of city space included a large town square which facili-tated pedestrain mingling and several adjacent buildings including a church or cathedral; a civic building, possibly also housing a court of law; a bank or brokerage house; and, most importantly, a market. In its purity of integration, the classic city center circumscribed the forces of social organization within a specific geographical environment. Physical remnants of this form of agglomeration can still be found in many of the older towns and cities in the US.

At present the hierarchical mode of social organization characteristic of modern society which is not visible but which underlies urban space as a deep structure of social relations no longer necessitates the convergence of seminal social functions in any single space. The essential socio-spatial change produced by deconcentration during the present stage of Late Capitalism has been this breakup of the functional unity of the central city and the dispersal of urban activities throughout polynucleated areas of the larger metropolitan region. Currently, the metropolitan landscape has been altered to accommodate the increasing functional specialization of many different centers which have been dispersed throughout a sprawling network of polynucleated realms. Political administration, to take one example, occurs through the medium of a network of decentralized units of the State: the chain of local jurisdictions, city halls, county offices of administration, police stations, and so on. These are all linked together by electronic modes of communication and computerized methods of record keeping along with a uniformly acknowledged administrative practice of expertise and knowledge. In another example, the economic structure has been articulated into progressively more specialized, decentralized units which have become increasingly independent in their location considerations from the need for centrality and agglomeration. Thus chain stores, factories, branch banking, and mass cultural outlets have all been dispersed in the wider space of urbanization. In short, while the old city center remains, its function has been altered and restructured toward a progressively more specialized role while other functions have been dispersed in a network of deconcentrated minicenters outside the city.

Within the massive regions of metropolitan life, privatized modes of consumption have prevailed. In this new form of space, often called "suburbia," there are few public places set aside for social communion. Everyday life is structured by the many separations of social living: the separation of home from work; of schools from the local neighborhood; of sociability and leisure activities from the propinquity of community. Within such an environment residents left to spend time during the day lack a common public ground for socialization; something which the old town square or center once supplied. Instead, the place of social communion is now located increasingly within the enclosed, climate controlled shopping areas, known as 'malls'. The first fully enclosed mall was built in a suburb near Minneapolis, Minnesota in 1956. According to one developer,

The idea of having an enclosed Mall doesn't relate to weather alone. People go to spend time there – they're equally as interested in eating and browsing as in shopping. So now we build only enclosed malls. (Kowinski, 1978, p. 35)

The large, fully enclosed mall has become the "main street" for the bulk of the metropolitan population living outside the central cities in the US (cf. Jacobs, 1984). As Kowinski has observed, in the newer areas

of the sunbelt, such as California, Texas, and Florida, "Malls *are* the downtown, right from the start" (1978, p. 46).

The commercial power of the mall is almost irresistible. It has become the most successful form of environmental design in contemporary settlement space. In 1977, malls did one half of all retail business in the US, and their return on gross sales ranges from $100 to $300 per square foot (Stephens, 1978). In many metropolitan regions suburban malls have competed retailers located in the central city out of existence causing, in part, the devaluation of the city center itself and a political struggle over the location of retailing. Recently, the mall form has even been imported back into the city with some success by developers interested in converting the blighted value of central city real estate into cash-producing assets. In some cases, such as Ghirardelli Square in San Francisco and Faneuil Hall in Boston, abandoned industrial sites have been renovated for retailing that utilizes suburban mall concepts. As Petros Martinidis has observed, such developments have thus "converted the workers' tragedy into the retailers' blessing". In short, the mall is a distinct architectural form – an enclosed area of separate shops integrated by design elements structured according to the professional practice of mall construction specialists. This form has currently replaced the city center as the most important site for the transformation of production into consumption and under present day conditions of deconcentration. As the entire settlement space of the metropolitan region has been restructured by deep structural changes associated with Late Capitalism (see Gottdiener, 1985), the mall form has been successful in locating with impunity in all areas including the old central city itself.

A semiotic analysis of any aspect of the built environment begins by taking into account the specific design practices which have articulated with space. In the case of malls, they can be understood best as the intersection sites of two distinct structural principles. On the one hand, the mall is the materialization of the retailers' intention to sell consumer goods at a high volume under present-day relations of production and distribution. Thus, it embodies particular representations comprised of signs which are *instrumentally* designed to promote purchasing. On the other hand, the mall is the physical space within which individuals come to participate in a certain type of urban ambiance which they crave at the very same time that they circulate as consumers for the benefit of retailers. This compels a second mode of design practice which then articulates with the first to produce the mall. In effect, then, the transformation of production into consumption takes place within a space that is structured by the intersection of the ideology of profit taking *and* the ideology of consumption. This articulation consisting of two separate ideologies with that of spatial design produces the sign systems of the mall. The following semiotic analysis of malls is based on site visits to enclosed shopping areas within the Los Angeles–Orange County region of Southern California. Whenever possible published information on malls located elsewhere has also been used to complement these first-hand observations (e.g. Jacobs, 1984). A reading of the sign systems which can be found at the mall is organized by recognizing that signification occurs with reference to two separate orders of meaning – the one paradigmatic and the other syntagmatic. The first is with regard to the design motif of the mall itself, or the associational axis of the mall and the second consists of an analysis of the ways in which the separate elements within the mall have been engineered to fit together in metonymical concordance. I shall consider these separately, provided the observation is made

clear that the latter depends heavily on the former.

Paradigm: The Motif of the Mall

The purpose of a mall is to sell consumer goods. The function of mall design, therefore, is to disguise the exchange relation between producer and consumer, which is always more to the former's benefit in capitalist society, and to present cognitively an integrated facade which facilitates this instrumental purpose by the stimulation of consumer fantasies. Thus the mall, taken as a whole, is a sign in itself, because it connotes something other than its principal function through the use of a motif that is its disguise. The motif of the mall serves as a code which integrates the particular consumer fantasy which designers have chosen as the overarching associational image they hope will hide its true instrumental nature. In this sense the motif of the mall is a sign, but it is a sign of a special type which is characteristic of the advertising form under capitalism. Using Hjelmslevian terminology (see figure 9.1), the component parts of the sign are all determined by the instrumental desire for profit-taking. This is the *pre*-condition for the signifying practice and the exo-semiotic co-textual processes represented by the mall. With regard to the sign itself, then, the "substance of the content" is the ideology of consumerism. This ideology exerts an instrumental control over the other aspects of the sign determining its elements, so that the "substance of the expression" is, above all else, a manifestation of that ideology. In short, the formal elements of design existing throughout the mall at the level of the

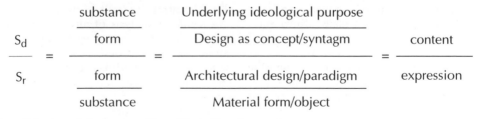

$$\frac{S_d}{S_r} = \frac{\dfrac{\text{substance}}{\text{form}}}{\dfrac{\text{form}}{\text{substance}}} = \frac{\dfrac{\text{Underlying ideological purpose}}{\text{Design as concept/syntagm}}}{\dfrac{\text{Architectural design/paradigm}}{\text{Material form/object}}} = \frac{\text{content}}{\text{expression}}$$

Figure 9.1 A semiotic decomposition of the built environment.

content and also at the level of the expression are all constrained in their respective possibilities by the instrumental function of the mall itself. That is, the over-arching instrumental code of the mall produces a short circuit between the fantasy of consumerism, on the one hand, and its particular materialization in design elements, on the other, at the level of the sign. The code which *unifies* these componential aspects of the sign is the mall's motif.

The motif of the mall is chosen by the designers and architects who apply the knowledge acquired through years of retailing experience. Trade journals, government reports, educational institutions, and the like, all help to produce and distribute the knowledge of mall design. When specific elements achieve particular success in one location, they are often tried elsewhere. Thus, there is a kind of iconic mimesis or "standardization" that mall motifs tend to assume over a period of time. This uniformity of motif choice is the architectural analogue of the marketing research search for canonical forms of appeal to be engineered into consumer products and product logos themselves which have been proven to stimulate consumption. For the case of malls, developers replicate design motifs which have been successful elsewhere in the belief that at other locations the same consumer fantasies will function to attract and hold shoppers.

Recently the motif which Kropkind calls "Ye Olde Kitsch" has become popular. This follows its success in such places as Faneuil Hall in Boston. Orange Country, California has a mall which reproduces this form, called "Olde Towne." As one approaches it a large sign with the logo "Olde Towne" frames its entrance. The mall is neither old nor a town, instead these signifiers float disembodied and detached from their signifieds, a fundamental characteristic of the advertising form, as Baudrillard has observed (1968). The free-floating signifiers are used to denote the code of the mall; its invocation of nostalgia. They serve to prime consumers for the necessary acceptance of further encounters with more disembodied signifiers of the advertising form just inside the entrance from the parking lot. Within this particular mall every store front, including the offices of the security staff, or mall police, mimics the "Hollywood" style imputed to nineteenth-century American towns and as envisioned by architectural practice. Stores are connected by antique streets complete with mock gaslight poles spaced every few yards. The entire ensemble is reminiscent of "Main Street" in Disneyland, a scaled-down version of the type of town which contemporary patterns of development have long since helped to destroy (see Francaviglia, 1974). In fact, malls with unifying motifs, such as Olde Towne, can best be understood in the same manner as the success of Disneyland (Gottdiener, 1982). They thrive on the contextual contrast to the environment around them. The nostalgic yearning for an idealized conception of small town life is generated within a metropolitan milieu where the actual small town and its distinctive social relations have disappeared. The yearning for the intimacy of quaint wood and stucco structures can be understood as produced by an everyday life situated within environments that negate intimacy through the massive sprawling scale of low-density regional development. In short, the success of this particular mall motif and, I contend, of other over-arching design fantasies for malls, depends on its ability to contrast positively with the experience of the everyday environment in the surrounding space. Elements drawing on this contrast are then transformed into material realizations by the professional practice of architects and developers.

This observation can be underscored by the second, equally successful design motif which is also currently popular. It can be called "Hi-Tech Urban," because it recreates the density of the central city by piling up two and three stories around a large, open space which then displays the names of shops in the hi-tech style of steel, plastic, and glass. The prototype of this high-density mall is the Galleria of Milan, Italy. This "Galleria" form as well as the name has been replicated in places such as Houston, White Plains, Sherman Oaks, and Glendale. Less obviously, the

"Hi-Tech Urban" code also characterizes multiple story malls which have been developed with great success in other parts of Southern California, such as Fox Run in LA County, and the Beverly Center in Beverly Hills. "Hi-Tech Urban" is a second form of nostalgia. In places like Los Angeles and the newer cities of the sunbelt, deconcentrated patterns of development have leveled population density to something less than that once possessed by cities in the past. Thus, malls using this second motif recreate the urban space of agglomeration and reproduce in a temporary setting the urban scale of population density as well as the "latent eroticism," to use Barthes' (1970–71) concept, of the city as a ludic center. Within such malls a kind of bird's-eye view is afforded to people at the higher levels who are often seen pausing in their pursuits to watch the pedestrian traffic of shoppers below. The constructed space of the multi-storied, high-density mall transcends for the moment the many separations afflicting life outside it in deconcentrated regions of the metropolis. While such malls fulfill other functions and thereby have an appeal for other reasons, the reliance on nostalgia for the urban environments of the past seems to be a consistent characteristic of currently popular motifs.

In sum, the most important design aspect of a mall is its over-arching motif. The search for a successful one seems to be facilitated by recognition of the contextual relation between the constructed space of the mall itself and a comparison with its surrounding environment. Both "Ye Olde Kitsch" and "Hi-Tech Urban" are variants of nostalgia for the urban socio-spatial experience of the past which contrasts distinctly with the design patterns of present-day deconcentrated metropolitan regions.

Syntagm: The Articulation of Design Elements within the Mall

The second dimension of design involves the engineering of space within the mall itself and the piecing together of appearance alter-

natives for store front facades. The purpose of intra-mall design is solely instrumental – the control of crowds to facilitate consumption. As indicated above, this function must be disguised at the very same instant it is materialized in space. To use Hjelmslev's terminology again, here "the form of the content," which is the over-arching code of the mall, dictates the design elements that will constitute "the form of the expression," so that the disguise which is the mall can be finely tuned in all of its parts. Several distinct techniques are utilized to bring about the harmony of this associational relation. First, malls have ugly, blank walls on their outsides, as all activities are turned inward. In fact, from the parking lot most malls look like concrete bunkers with an occassional logo of a department store serving as the only break in a monolithic pattern of bricks and steel. The purpose of this design is to prevent loitering outside the mall and to quicken the pace with which shoppers leave their cars. According to Stephens (1978) this denial of the street outside can be called "introversion," because the mall design captures the self-enclosed, protectionist atmosphere of the Medieval Castle. Thus, while the world outside may be filled with the vagaries of urban life in a society characterized by conflict and social stratification, the experience within the mall is sheltered within blank fortresslike walls and by the auspices of its feudal-like proprietor, the mall management.

A second feature of mall construction often greets consumers as they enter the main area. Designers have recycled the sign-function of the city as a ludic center within the mall. In a number of cases the entrance is a large open space, like a town square, which includes some form of special attraction not directly related to shopping itself. For example, the Olde Towne Mall (see above) has a full-scale carousel at its center complete with recorded calliope music. For a nominal cost children can ride on it, while parents watch their amused faces. In a second case, just inside the main entrance of the Del Amo Mall in Los Angeles (the largest one in the world) stands a massive, two-story clock tower with a special set of chimes that shoppers can enjoy at regular intervals. At its base instructive signs explain the "unique" features of the clock tower so that shoppers are attracted to its performance as a special event. The tower and its surrounding open space also recycle important elements of the old town square. In this case, the intricate clockworks recall the centers of Renaissance cities in Western Europe with their own ornate town clocks.

Finally, a third example of the mall as ludic center is the use of an open air fountain surrounded by the benches and sidewalk cafes of a Mediterranean-style town square. Such a space can be found, for example, in the Santa Monica Mall, which is centered around a large area filled with light from the skylights three stories above which frames a fountain and seating area for the benefit of weary shoppers. The entire ensemble captures a charged urban ambiance which draws shoppers to pause, to see, and, to be seen. Often this single, ludic center is supplemented by mini-sites offering a variety of foods from fast service to quasi-elegant. In fact, the availability of attractive snacks is an important feature of any mall. As one well-known developer of malls has remarked, "They come to shop, but they stay for the food" (Stephens, 1978).

In any of its manifestations the recapturing of the traditional ludic center creates the illusion of urban civility. Individuals living in environments with few public spaces and low-density demographics can find something which many of them lack and often crave once they enter the mall – a well ordered, open space of social communion. Yet, these areas are but an illusion of public life. They mask the instrumental and highly controlled nature of mall space. In sharp distinction to the heterogeneous mingling and the "illuminating potentiality" (Lefebvre, 1970), of the public city's center, malls are privately owned spaces. The management has the legal power to regulate the kinds of people and activities found there. More specifically, malls can exclude political and union assemblies. This includes the legal right, in the US, to prevent workers from picketing a shop with which they are en-

gaged in some job action. Furthermore, consumers within malls are discouraged from loitering except in places designated for that purpose. For example, it is often not allowed to take snapshots without permission of the management and security guards will quietly inform would-be tourists with cameras of that fact. Thus the recycling of the town square form within the mall by design practice must be recognized as providing only an illusion of civility, as the urban ambiance is harnessed to the profit motives of privately controlled space.

A third feature of the mall is the instrumental sign systems which can be found there. Within these spaces, denotative, even indexical functions of the sign take precedence over connotative functions in order to facilitate the flow of pedestrian traffic. When the connotative function is present, if at all, it exists only to signal a particular status within a stratified society comprised of individuals with variable household budgets. Thus, the logos of stores, for example, are signifiers produced by the highly refined science of marketing. They are meant to signal a certain social status or lifestyle which has been linked to the signifier by the ongoing practice of the advertising industry itself.

Within the mall the appeal of stores is characterized by a general convergence of merchandising around the mimesis of current fashion prescriptions and imperatives. Yet, stores are stratified according to the general range of prices they charge. Consumers pick and choose among this variety by cueing in, through experience, to those establishments which offer merchandising within what are judged as acceptable costs, even though items purchased in separate stores at different prices may look alike because of this convergence of appearance alternatives produced by the ensemble of practices making up the consumption activity of Fashion. The store logo, and signs advertising consumption, such as for sales, denote a type of budgetary envelope wherein consumers can hope to find a variety of items which are constrained within certain expenditure limits. In short, the sign systems of malls are, for the most part, one-dimensional, monosemic indices of consumption. When connotative elements are present, they are merely signals of social status too roughly defined to provide differential information which does anything but complement the narrow fix on the fantasies of consumerism. The sign systems of the mall, therefore, are mere extensions of the content of advertising which appears elsewhere, such as magazines, television, newspapers, and the like, and which are mediated by the logotechniques and interactive processes of Fashion.

There is a second way in which consumption is mediated by mall sign systems. Among the group of stores within any mall there is a hierarchy of identifiability and importance. Malls work principally because of the presence of a few large department stores which pull in customers. Their location defines the overall floor plan, with speciality shops filling up the intervening space between the big draw giants. In fact, malls are classified according to the number of large department stores they can contain. Usually there are at least two, as this number enables designers to "anchor down" the mall and orient its paths on a linear axis. With two stores at opposite ends, customers have to walk from one to the other and thus pass all the lesser known shops in between. The very largest malls contain three or more giant department stores, thus permitting a floor plan with intersecting axes. The largest mall, Del Amo, has nine major department stores. In all of contemporary urban history there has never been a single central city with that many major stores located within one area.

The fourth and final syntagmatic design element involves the engineering of pedestrian flows among the major stores. The business volume of the smaller shops relies primarily on the ease with which the floor plan facilitates browsing and impulse buying. Paths are broken up by obstacles, such as large concrete planters and trash bins, benches, the zig-zagging of store layouts, blank walls which jut out into traffic, and so on. These all function to disorient slightly the ambulation of consumers and force them to take some added time in getting from one place to another. The store fronts of retailers located along these paths must work to entice the impulse buyer to come in. Here the name of the shop and its appearance, while having to preserve the design elements of the mall's central motif, take a secondary role to the display arrangements in the window of the facade itself. The elements of lighting, window dressing, and commodity display assume great importance for such stores. At this level the commodity acts as a sign of itself. Store fronts exploit the advertising signals engineered by manufacturers into the very objects of consumption, such as: clothing designer labels, records and book jacket covers, and motifs of appliance design, as in the "hi-tech" cases of stereo equipment or vacuum cleaners. Such efforts comprise a second way in which the sign systems of the mall function as extensions of mass marketing for the advertising industry in society at large. In fact, the shop in the mall is precisely that venue where the process of production is transformed into consumption through the mediation of advertising practices and the production of consumerist ideology.

Within the mall, however, the activity of consumption and its connection to spectacular forms of consumerist ideology is often stratified according to the differentiation of income levels comprising markets of consumers themselves. The specialization of stores within any single mall enables this constructed space to cater to several different income levels. In some cases malls themselves are distinguished from each other because certain ones cater to the more affluent, thus malls can also be considered stratified according to the income levels they serve. For example, several malls are known for their higher status because they have brought together elite fashion manufacturers and speciality shops which cater to the affluent, up-scale crowd. In such places the name of the retailer indexes status in the same way as the department store logo. At Fashion Island mall, located in Orange County near Los Angeles, one can shop at an Yves St. Laurent showroom, for example, which employs sales people who speak French. In general, therefore, the mall mixes signs of status with commodities that signify their own exchange value. These are signs of a certain type. They are signifiers which connote what is fashionable, what is indicative of a certain socioeconomic status, what belongs to the set of commodities associated with a specific lifestyle, or, finally, and quite simply, what signals to others that the particular consumer has shopped at such and such a mall and not elsewhere. In short, at the level of interaction between mall facade and human behavior, consumerism is fostered by the logotechniques of advertising and fashion. The mall space, therefore, is designed to provide as much free reign as possible, within the confines of its castlelike introverted urban elements, for advertising signals to operate on the pre-conditioned minds of the customers.

Conclusion

The mall represents the consumate device for the conversion of production to consumption because for many metropolitan residents it is the only safe place to meet others in unstructured if nevertheless alienated sociability. People appear at the mall because they are driven to seek a common ground for sociability and by the promise of personal liberation which years of conditioning have firmly established in their minds. As Jacobs (1984) suggests, however, the mall can never satisfy the alienated needs that people seek to fulfill there. In fact, the mall only makes worse the problem of consumer-directed lifestyles. The mall works, therefore, because it harnesses the instrumental control of space to the desires manufactured by modern society.

The significance of this discovery lies with the realization that, in many regions of the metropolis, everyday life and its core of sociability has been usurped by the instrumental space of Late Capitalism and by the pathological consequences of contemporary society, such as high rates of crime, which includes random street violence. The public sphere has evaporated and the space of social interaction necessary to everyday life has been surrendered to the techniques of mass marketing and the commercial control of the mall management. Instrumental spaces, such as malls, can be contrasted with city environments; the latter's public spaces are vestiges of history, it seems, because of the invasion of the city by instrumental space (e.g. Faneuil Hall, in Boston). In the cities of the past associational rights were guaranteed by the constitution, even if they were regulated by the State. Public spaces meant freedom of speech, consociation and assembly. As the availability of such places diminishes or becomes restricted, so too do these fundamental rights.

REFERENCES

Barthes, R. (1970–1) Sémiologie et urbanisme. *L'Architecture d'Aujourd'hui*, 153, 11–13.

Baudrillard, J. (1968) *Système des objets*. Paris: Gallimard.

Francaviglia, R. (1974) Main Street revisited. *Places*, October, 7–11.

Gottdiener, M. (1982) Disneyland: a utopian urban space. *Urban Life*, 11(2), 139–62.

Gottdiener, M. (1983) Understanding metropolitan deconcentration. *Social Science Quarterly*, 64(2), 227–46.

Gottdiener, M. (1985) *The Social Production of Urban Space*. Austin: University of Texas Press.

Jacobs, J. (1984) *The Mall*. Prospect Heights, IL: Waveland Press.

Kowinski, W. (1978) The malling of America. *New Times*, 10(9), 30–56.

Lefebvre, H. (1970) *La révolution urbaine*. Paris: Gallimard.

Stephens, S. (1978) Introversion and the urban context. *Progressive Architecture*, December, 49–53.

Part IV
Politics

10

Why Are the Design and Development of Public Spaces Significant for Cities?

A. Madanipour

[handwritten note: debate more than this ↓]

Much of the recent interest in urban design has focused on the creation and management of public spaces of cities. For years the public spaces of cities have been the subject of debate, from concerns about privatization of space (Loukaitou-Sideris, 1993; Punter, 1990) to the contested nature of public space (Zukin, 1995) and the various ways in which public space can be designed and developed (Carr et al., 1992; Tibbalds, 1992). The city authorities, at the same time, have taken up the task of improving their public spaces, from Barcelona to Birmingham and Berlin among others. But why is there such an interest in urban public spaces? What are the reasons for this focus of attention on public space design and development? Why is it seen to be so significant in urban life? In this paper I set out to find an answer to this question by looking at how designers have approached urban public space, its changing nature and significance through time, and its multiple and contested meanings and roles in the modern urban society.

[handwritten note: Spaces in general, but for what reason?]

Social Construction of Space

The spaces around us everywhere, from the spaces in which we take shelter to those which we cut across and travel through, are part of our everyday social reality. Our spatial behaviour, which is defined by and defines the spaces around us, is an integral part of our social existence. As such we understand space and spatial relations in the same way that we understand the other component parts of our social life. The facts about the world, Searle (1995) argues, can be divided into two categories. The first category is what he calls "institutional facts", facts that exist only by human agreement, because we believe them to exist. Another category is that of brute facts, those that exist independent of human institutions. Most elements of the social world belong to the first category, from money to marriage, property, and government. The fact that a piece of paper has a value of, for example, five pounds is a social fact. Without our institutionalized agreement, it is no more than just a piece of paper. The brute fact about the space of our cities therefore is that it is a collection of objects and people on the surface of the earth. *[handwritten note: They are brute facts]* The social fact about the cities, however, is that these objects and their relationships have been created by human agreement and bear particular significance and meaning for people. The sheer physical presence of roads, schools, and houses does not render them meaningful. It is the collective intentionality, the capacity of humans to assign functions, to symbolize these objects beyond their basic presence that makes them part of the social reality.

The significance of symbolism in the construction of social reality, however, shows how there can be more than one interpretation for the social facts. As one of the most important dimensions of our social world, space finds different interpretations and meanings. As different groups give different meanings to space, it becomes a multi-layered place, reflecting the way places are socially constructed (Knox, 1995).

The various perspectives on space can be classified as those looking from inside, that is the subjective views from the first person's point of view, and those looking from outside, that is the third person's external view. What is a home for one person becomes a mere object for another. What is for one person a refreshing experience of feeling in touch with nature becomes for another party just a person walking past in the park. What is a rich web of emotions and attachments to places of a town for one person becomes a set of statistics on pedestrian behaviour for another. The diversity of views that can be found in the everyday experiences is also traceable in the academic studies of, and professional approaches to, space. The question always is how to approach this multiplicity. Is there a single correct interpretation of space and place? Or does this multiplicity of views mean that we should give in to a kind of relativism, where all interpretations are correct as they each represent a particular, equally valid perspective?

Public Space in the City

In all cities, anywhere in the world and at any time during history, a major characteristic of the social and political organization is the distinction between the public and the private spheres of life. Where individuals can or cannot go in a city is conditioned by the organization and management of space, which determines some of the main patterns of spatial behaviour and social life in general. One of the main ways of organizing space is through defining some places as private and others as public. Some places are protected and set apart from the rest by a complex system of signification: by spatial means such as signs, boundaries, fences, walls, and gates; or by temporal means such as predetermined working hours. This complex

system of codes, expressed through physical objects and social arrangements, signifies private places, where strangers cannot enter without permission or negotiation. Public places, on the other hand, are expected to be accessible to everyone, where strangers and citizens alike can enter with fewer restrictions.

This system of signification and distinction is ultimately embedded in a specific social context and may not be legible for strangers, unfamiliar with the meanings of its codes. Furthermore there are many ambiguous corners around the city, which may or may not be clearly demarcated as public or private. Nevertheless, the bulk of the urban space is carved into a seemingly clear separation of public and private spheres, as best exemplified by thoroughfares which are accessible to everyone, and living places where entry is strictly controlled. Looking at the public–private distinction is therefore one way of decoding and interpreting the social and spatial organization of a city.

Public spaces of a city have always had political significance, symbolizing the power of the state, as exemplified in the parades or the statues of the elite, or where the state is challenged by its opponents, as in demonstrations and revolutions (Madanipour, 1998). Control of public space is therefore essential in the power balance in a particular society. As it was known to the Italian Fascists, whoever controlled the streets controlled the city (Atkinson, 1998).

The dictionary definitions of the public tell us that it is the opposite of the private. The Oxford Dictionary definitions of the public include, "Of or pertaining to the people as a whole; belonging to, affecting, or concerning the community"; "Carried out or made by or on behalf of the community as a whole; authorized by or representing the community; Open or available to, used or shared by, all members of a community; not restricted to private use"; and "provided by local or central government for the community and supported by rates or taxes". On this basis, a public space is provided by the public authorities, concerns the people as a whole, is open or available to them, and is used or shared by all the members of a community.

As with any other definition, this is a generalized statement, each section of which can represent a wide range of possible conditions. Public authorities may or may not legitimately represent or serve a community; availability of space may be based on a diverse and complex set of rules and conditions; all members of a community may or may not be willing or able to use a particular space for functional, symbolic, or any other reasons. In this sense, a generalized definition of this kind becomes an ideal type, with a normative value, rather than necessarily describing the public spaces everywhere. A more accurate definition of public space, however, may be based on the observation that public spaces of cities, almost anywhere and at any time, have been places outside the boundaries of individual or small-group control, mediating between private spaces and used for a variety of often overlapping functional and symbolic purposes. Urban, open public spaces therefore have usually been multipurpose spaces distinguishable from, and mediating between, the demarcated territories of households.

Benn and Gaus (1983) mention the diversity of activities and practices which are categorized as public or private, ranging, for example, from the public availability of books in a library to the public authority possessed by a government. Nevertheless, they identify three broad types which constitute the dimensions of publicness and privateness. These are three dimensions of social organization: access, agency, and interest. Most definitions of public space emphasize the necessity of access, which can include access to the place as well as to the activities within it. Even when a place is owned by private agencies, public access may be secured by law (Vernez Moudon, 1991). Benn and Gaus divide access further into four subdimensions: physical access to *spaces*; access to *activities*; access to *information*; and access to *resources*. Public places and spaces therefore are public because anyone is entitled to be physically present in them. Access to places, however, is

often aimed at access to activities within them. But it is possible to have access to a place but not to the activities going on there, such as access to the meeting of a group of friends in the middle of a public space. Access to information often lies at the heart of debates about privacy, which involves controlling information about ourselves or managing our public appearances. Access to resources allows a degree of influence over public affairs, which is why the issue of agency is a significant one. Where an agent stands, whether acting privately or on behalf of a community, makes a difference to the nature and consequences of their actions. A public agency dealing with a part of urban space has a completely different mode of operation and aims than a private one. In the same way, the dimension of interest plays a major role in determining the public–private distinction. Who are the beneficiaries of a particular action: private individuals or parts of the public as a whole? There are, however, overlaps and ambiguities in these three dimensions, which can be exemplified in the analysis of property with its potentially diverse and complex range of ownership and control. Nevertheless, the three dimensions of access, agency, and interest can be useful in empirical analyses of public spaces. The dimensions of agency and interest clearly direct us towards an appreciation of the multiplicity of perspectives into urban space.

Public Space as Spatial Enclosure

Much that lies outside the private realm of the dwellings may be seen as public space. These spaces may have different functions and shapes, from the dark narrow streets, which encourage the passerby to go through them as quickly as possible, to the wide public squares that invite people to stop and look around. Together, they make up the public spaces of the city. A century ago, Camilo Sitte complained about how the plazas (or public squares) of his day could be empty spaces formed by four streets bordering a piece of land. After studying the spatial organization of a number of old European cities, he formed some clear ideas

Rework in space

Space as enclosure like a room

about how the public spaces of the city should be organized. For him, the main requirement for a public square, as for a room, was its enclosed character, which offered closed vistas from any point within it. The centre of this space was to be kept free and there was a need for a strong relationship between the public space and the buildings around it (Sitte, 1986).

Modernists destroying public space

Modernist design which dominated the 20th century and has shaped many contemporary cities, however, was often against this approach to urban space. Modernism essentially incorporated movement into its view of the world (Giedion, 1967). The functionalism of modernists therefore gave priority to cars and fast movement across urban space, a notion which undermined the close relationship between open spaces and buildings around them. The existing urban enclosures with closed vistas, such as streets and squares, were to be demolished in favour of vast open spaces which provided a setting for a free and flexible location of buildings (Le Corbusier, 1971). Despite their emphasis on the primacy of public interests in the city, as promoted in the Charter of Athens (Sert, 1944), the modernists paid little attention to the historically created public spaces of the city. What they sought was a redefinition of the relationship between public and private space, which would reshape the urban space, creating large quantities of open space for hygienic as well as aesthetic reasons. What resulted was vast expanses of space which could have little or no connection with the other spaces of the city and could be left underused, only to be watched from the top of high-rise buildings or from car windows.

Too open.

For those who remained unconvinced by such an imposition of an abstract notion of space onto the existing urban environment and the everyday life (Lefebvre, 1991), a return to the historic notions of public space seemed inevitable. Once again, creation of spatial enclosure became a main prerequisite in urban design (County Council of Essex, 1973; Cullen, 1971). As nodes and landmarks, public spaces became a means with which to navigate in the city

(Lynch, 1960). Streets and squares became the alphabet with which to read, and design, urban space (Krier, 1979). Creating lively and active edges for these spaces was seen as an important condition of their success. Small, mixed land uses that generate a strong relationship between the public space and the buildings around it were promoted (Bentley et al, 1985). It became absolutely essential for urban design to create "positive urban space", that is, space enclosed by buildings, rather than what is a leftover after the construction of buildings (Alexander et al., 1987). A prime example of these changing and often contradictory interpretations of and approaches to public space is the city centre of Birmingham, which had been dominated by a network of motorways. It was first transformed by dismantling half of the fast road network and then by introducing a number of public spaces, pedestrianized and embellished by public art (Tibbalds/Colbourne/Karski/Williams, 1990).

Urban designers therefore seek to create lively enclosures in urban space, nodes which bring people together for various activities. Through their political and economic significance as well as their aesthetic value, these nodes of human environment are expected to act as an infrastructure for social life. But why has this activity come to the fore as significant for cities?

The new open space

From the Integrated City to Functional Fragmentation

Some spaces have continuously played the role of a distinguished node in the history of a city and the social life of its citizens. As the circumstances of a city have changed, others may have lost their importance and been forgotten or have not found any degree of significance at all. Today, as compared with most historical periods of the past, the importance of public space in the cities has diminished. This has partly been a result of decentralization of cities and despatialization of the public sphere. There is a clear transition from a time when a high degree of sociospatial concentration gave an over-

The loss of importance of public spaces

arching significance to the central public space to a time when places and activities in cities have found a more dispersed spatial pattern. Public space has thus lost many of the functions it once performed in the social life of cities.

The best-known public space of all time was perhaps the ancient Greek agora, the main public square which was the meeting place of the town. It was first and foremost a marketplace, as Aristotle reminds us: "For of necessity in almost every city there must be both buyers and sellers to supply each other's mutual wants; and this is what is most productive of the comforts of life; for the sake of which men seemed to have joined together in one community" (quoted in Glotz, 1929, pp. 21–22). But the agora was more than a marketplace: it was also designed to serve as a place of assembly for the town's people and a setting in which ceremonies and spectacles were performed. The agora therefore was a place which integrated economic, political, and cultural activities. Originally it was just an open space located somewhere near the centre of the town. With specialization of activities and spaces, various public buildings grew around it, such as the meeting place of the city council, the offices of magistrates, temples and altars, fountain houses, law courts, and a covered hall for the use of citizens and merchants. Although with the growth of the city and the need for larger places of assembly some of these activities might eventually be housed elsewhere in the town, the agora remained the heart of the city and its civic activities (Ward-Perkins, 1974). The agora was therefore seen as a necessary condition of city life, both in democracies and in the cities where citizens exercised no political rights at all. Indeed, the Greeks looked down with contempt upon those cultures whose towns did not have such a place of assembly (Glotz, 1929, p. 23).

But we know that the agora and the institutions it housed were not the only vehicles of social integration. The activities which supported the *polis* went beyond the formal democratic institutions of the assembly, the magistrates and the law courts, which clustered in and around the agora and which

have so widely fascinated the scholars. The collective activities of cult associations, groups of friends, age groups, and other types of grouping in the city played an intermediate role in the promotion of social cohesion in the *polis*, providing arenas for socialization, apprenticeship in political life and civic values, and places where the social order could be expressed (Schmitt-Pantel, 1990). In addition to the agora, the communal practices of these groups took place in sanctuaries, gymnasia, and even in the private realm of the house, where a special room catered for the meetings of the head of household (Jameson, 1990). The social cohesion which was being reproduced in these arenas and through these institutions and collective activities was exclusive and hierarchical, where women, slaves, and aliens were kept at bay. Nevertheless, the agora was the main node in a network of public places and collective activities which made up the city-state, even after the political significance of the city-state and its democratic institutions declined with the rise of the Macedonian empire.

The ancient integration of spiritual and temporal did not survive in the Middle Ages, when the distinction between the two found expression in public spaces of cities. In Italian cities, for example, there were two or three principal squares each associated with one set of activities. The cathedral square was separate from the main secular square (Signoria) and from the market square (Mercato) (Sitte, 1986). Despite this specialization of space and functional separation, there was an intensive use of public space for public life. The city squares were decorated with fountains, monuments, statues, and other works of art and were used for public celebrations, state proceedings, and exchange of goods and services. But all this started to change in the modern period, when the public squares of cities started to be used as parking lots and the relationship between them and the public buildings around them almost completely disappeared (Sitte, 1986, pp. 151–154).

In the modern era, the functional integration of the ancient city has almost completely disappeared. The growing size of the city has led to a specialization of space, which has dismantled the symbolic and functional coherence of both public and private spheres. As places of work and living were separated in the industrialization process, life in the private sphere was completely transformed. As new transport technologies have made it possible to live and work outside the city, the central spaces of the city can be avoided by large numbers of citizens. Furthermore, the ability to pass through the urban space at high speeds has undermined the close physical contact between townspeople and their built environment, as had existed throughout history (Sennett, 1994).

Not in contact with our space

The speed of movement has contributed to the despatialization of activities, which is associated with new transport and communication technologies. Following the printed word, networks of communication and transportation have created a despatialized public sphere, severely undermining the political, economic, and cultural significance of the public spaces of the city. The public sphere is formed of a large number of arenas which may never overlap in space or time. As political debates, exchange of goods and services, and participation in rituals and ceremonies can take place in different locations through a variety of means other than face-to-face communication, the functional role of public space, which once could house all these activities, is no longer central in a city. Public spaces of the city have become residual spaces, used for parking cars, or at best associated with particular, limited functions, such as tourism or retail. Many public or semipublic places, from the ancient church to the public libraries and museums of the modern period, have come under pressure from these changes. The modern city has therefore gone through a spatial and temporal dispersion of its functions and a despatialization of some of its activities, which have created multiple nonconverging networks working against the cohesive nodal role of the urban public space.

public space no longer important

Public spaces are residual spaces

Furthermore, many places in cities are open to the public and are seen as public but have particular functional definitions and restrictions. Restaurants, museums, libraries, and theatres are among the public places of a city. These places, however, have a particular functional significance. In the same way that a shopping mall focuses on trade, a restaurant has a definite function and working-hour schedule, which pose its own particular set of restrictions. The open public spaces of the city, which are most accessible and have the most functional overlap and ambiguity, have come under pressure from the specialization and functional disintegration of the modern city.

Reintegration of Sociospatial Fragmentation

The dispersion of cities has had severe social consequences. The rise of the industrial city in the 19th century uprooted large numbers of people from villages and small towns and concentrated them in cities, where the industries were located. But from early on, this led to social and spatial segregation among the middle and working classes. As Engels reported from Manchester in the 1840s, it was possible to live in the city and visit it everyday without coming into contact with the working-class areas (Engels, 1993). From early on, however, this segregation was explosive and caused fear among the political and cultural elite. Sociospatial segregation has remained a feature of the modern city to this day. It is still possible for the citizens to live and work in the suburbs without ever visiting the troubled inner city. While the racial and social segregation of the American city is well known, the European city also suffers from increased threats of social polarization and segregation (Madanipour et al., 1998). Cities that were transformed once through industrialization are being transformed once again through deindustrialization and the transition to a service economy. As before, such transformation has caused fear and anxiety, as some established sociospatial patterns have been destabilized.

Promotion of the public space has been seen as one of the vehicles of confronting this fragmentation and managing this anxiety. Promotion of some form of togetherness

public space a solution

can be seen through various definitions of public space. For example, public space is seen as "the common ground where people carry out the functional and ritual activities that bind a community" (Carr et al., 1992, p. xi), or "space we share with strangers... space for peaceful coexistence and impersonal encounter" (Walzer, 1986, p. 470). By creating areas in which people intermingle, it is hoped that different people can be brought together and a degree of tolerance be promoted. This is especially crucial at a time when the welfare state has come under threat of restructuring, and social fragmentation has intensified.

In this sense, the promotion of public space can be linked to a number of major themes of debate in social and political philosophy. One theme is the relationship between individualism and holism or, as is known in political debates, between libertarians and communitarians: whether the radical autonomy of individuals should be sought or the well-being of a community as a whole. Promoting the public space as a meeting point of the atomized individuals clearly emphasizes the importance of togetherness. Another theme is the separation of the public and the private realms, which is one of the central themes of the liberal political theory and was also promoted by other theorists of the public sphere, such as Arendt (1958) and Habermas (1989). A strong public sphere, where public life is conducted and which is clearly separated from the private realm, is seen to be essential for the health of a society. This line of thinking, however, has been criticized by Marxists, who saw this distinction as rooted in the private ownership of property and therefore leading to alienation, and by feminists, who saw this distinction as associating the private sphere with women and undermining their role in social life. It is also criticized by postmodernists who reject universal tendencies and see the withdrawal from the public sphere as a sign of self-preservation and dynamism of a society by developing new forms of communities.

The separation of the public and private spheres is one of the central themes of liberal political theory. It is therefore not surprising that it is challenged by a number of radical movements, among them Marxist and feminist criticism. The Marxist critique of the public – private dichotomy rests on the concept of alienation. The private control of the means of production and the division of labour result in the alienation of workers from their work, their products, and their fellow human beings. For Marx, the contradiction between the private and public, and in a broader sense between individual and society, belonged to bourgeois society. On the one hand, Marx and his followers did not believe in anything as being private in the sense of standing outside society or as prior to it. On the other hand, they believed that public power of the state would disappear after the establishment of rational self-regulating communities. By the abolition of private property and the division of labour, alienation would be overcome and the public – private distinction would disappear (Kamenka, 1983).

Challenging the dichotomy between the public and private is central to the political struggle of feminism. It is, as Pateman (1983, p. 281) puts it, "ultimately, what the feminist movement is about". Men have been associated with the public realm, and women with the private sphere. The subjection of women to men, it is argued, is obscured by the dichotomy between the public and private and its apparently universal, egalitarian, and individualist order. The problem this poses is that the public world, or civil society, is conceptualized and discussed as being separate from the private domestic sphere, which then becomes forgotten in theoretical discussion. The reality, however, is that these spheres are interrelated and the world of work cannot be understood as separate from the world of domestic life. Indeed, "The sphere of domestic life is at the heart of civil society rather than apart or separate from it" (Pateman, 1983, p. 297).

Some critics of the separation of the public and private spheres go back to the rise of industrial capitalism, which separated the realms of work and home from each other. Before the industrial revolution, the family was the unit of both production and

*Needs to make
spaces attractive*

reproduction, and social life was not split into separate autonomous spheres. The separation of home and work created a male-dominated public sphere of work, as opposed to a private sphere which was identified with women but which also trapped them. Withdrawal from community bonds and splitting of social life into public and private spheres therefore was not a voluntary commitment by many thousands of families that went through this transformation. Dividing the world into public and private spheres, or "privatization", was "an unanticipated consequence of industrialization" and can be one interpretation of the decline of community (Brittan, 1977, pp. 56–58).

*But it
is 70 bad.*
However, others argue that the withdrawal from the public sphere is not necessarily a negative development. It is a sign of dynamism and self-preservation of a society, of fighting against alienation and standing up to ideologies, teachings, and claims to domination or even emancipation (Maffesoli, 1996, p. 46). Rather than lamenting the end of great collective values and the withdrawal into the self, we should view the development of new small groups and existential networks as a positive step forward. It is a new form of organicism in which emotional communities, based on exchange of feeling, are emerging, a new version of Gemeinschaft or a new tribalism (Maffesoli, 1996).

*The
role of
public
space*
Public space mediates between the private spaces that make up the bulk of the city and plays a role in confronting this process of sociospatial fragmentation. Without it, the spatial movement across the city becomes limited and subject to negotiation. As in the medieval factionalism of the Mediterranean city, where neighbourhoods were separated by walls and gates or in the gated neighbourhoods of today, passage across the space (and subsequently communication in social life) of the city is limited and compartmentalized.

Responding to the Demands of a Service Economy

The recent interest in the promotion of urban public spaces can be interpreted as a concern

for the reintegration of fragmented cities. It can also be seen as a means of marketing localities. As localities and regions compete in the world economy to attract increasingly mobile capital, they need to create safe and attractive environments for the investors and their employees (Hall, 1995). The return of aesthetics to city planning is therefore seen as a sign of the return of capital to the city (Boyer, 1990). The new service sector and high-technology industries are far less attached to localities than the heavy industries of the past. The shift of the economic base, from manufacturing industry to the service sector, means that the role of cities is in the process of redefinition. Rather than concentrations of blue-collar workers in industrial cities, the service cities are concentrations of white-collar workers with their very different needs and expectations. This shift has undermined large parts of the workforce, especially the unskilled male workers, and has led to a widening gap in income distribution and a deepening pattern of sociospatial segregation and exclusion. It has also meant the availability of more resources for parts of the cities and the rise of a new interest in the city by high earners, who are reclaiming the city through gentrification and urban regeneration.

In addition to attracting investors and the jobs they create or the employees they bring with them, some local authorities are improving the quality of their environments to attract tourists. Cities that have been known first as industrial and then as run-down places are now promoting themselves as tourist destinations. It is not, however, enough to have a number of impressive buildings and entertainment activities in a city. The public spaces which connect these buildings and activities are also important in the decisions of the tourists. Creation of new public spaces is therefore part of the larger process of creating spectacles in the cities. Waterfront developments, for example, are part of the process of erasing the already fading memory of manufacturing industry. New public spaces of the city are therefore one of the vehicles of changing the image of cities in a very competitive global marketplace and of a reentry of a finite commodity, land, back into the local markets. They are also a vehicle of legitimacy for the local authorities, symbolizing their commitment and effectiveness in urban regeneration. Some also see them as a potential cure for the problems of crime, as the disenchanted youth who are blamed for many ills of the cities can find an arena for socializing and entertainment.

For much of this century, especially after the Soviet revolution and the Great Depression, western societies have witnessed an increased level of intervention by the state in social life. This was a trend which came to its culmination after World War 2, with emphasis on Keynesian economics and the development of the welfare state. As this system started to suffer from a crisis since the mid-1960s, a new agenda emerged, one which questioned the extent of state intervention. The result was a contraction in the role of the state in economic and social affairs. This has been in parallel with the shift out of industrial production. In the transition from the industrial city to the service city, there has been a transformation of the public sector and its role. The large-scale involvement of the private sector has created an imbalance in the development and management of cities, which is manifest in the privatization of space. Promotion of public space seeks to address this imbalance. The pressure to develop leisure facilities in cities is part of the transition to a service economy, where catering for the needs of young professionals with their disposable incomes comes as a priority in economic development. This includes ideas about the 24-hour city, use of cultural industries in urban regeneration, and promoting a European style café culture in British cities. These can be analysed in light of this transition, as necessary elements reclaiming the city from a manufacturing past for a service-based future.

However, there are clear tensions between these various roles of public space. An example of developing public space to confront the sociospatial divide is the city of Berlin, which was divided for more than a generation. Now it is being reintegrated

through a new transport and communication infrastructure and the creation and enhancement of the public spaces and institutions along the lines of division between east and west. By deleting the marks of separation and by creating the possibility of communication and interaction, it is hoped to heal the spatial and ideological divide that shaped the city for most of the second half of the 20th century. The reintegration of the city and its selection as the capital of the united Germany, however, has created new forms of divide. The introduction of a market economy in the east and the end of some special subsidies in the west, as well as new waves of immigration into the city from around the country and around the world have created new challenges and new divisions. The economic and ethnic divisions that are emerging, however, do not seem to be targeted in the creation of new public spaces. The public spaces are therefore not yet addressing the problems of an emerging divide in social groups that marks the city. As the city creates a new hierarchy of social groups, the behaviour of those at the lower levels is carefully watched (and controlled) in the public spaces.

Reintegration of a sociospatially fragmented city may not sit happily with the reimaging of the city as a political focal point or an economic asset. A major form of such tension is now known as the privatization of space.

Privatization of Space

The causes of the privatization of space can be traced back to several changes in urban development processes. Throughout the 20th century, the development companies have been growing in size and complexity. Small, locally based developers working closely with the local elite have given way to large developers whose headquarters are often based outside the locality and who command massive productive capacity. This change, alongside the changes in construction technology, has had major impacts on urban form (Whitehand, 1992). Furthermore, the financing of the development projects and ownership of property have undergone substantial change, as banks and financial institutions are increasingly operating at national and international, rather than local, scale. As development companies are linked with broader capital markets, a growing disjunction can be detected between the development process and localities. If particular developments had some symbolic value for their developers in the past, it is now more the exchange value in the market that determines their interest. As space is stripped of its emotional and cultural value, which is developed only through people's use over time, it is treated as a mere commodity (Madanipour, 1996). What the investors are interested in is a safe return on their investment.

At the same time, the fear of crime has been a major reason for a withdrawal of people from the public sphere (Miethe, 1995). With the decline of the welfare state, the role of the public authorities in the cities has been undermined. The new additions to urban space are often developed and managed by private investors, as the public authorities find themselves unable or unwilling to bear the costs of developing and maintaining public places. A combination of the need for safe investment returns and safe public environments has led to the demand for total management of space, thus undermining its public dimension. From shopping malls to gated neighbourhoods and protected walkways, new urban spaces are increasingly developed and managed by private agencies in the interest of particular sections of the population. It is in response to this privatization trend that development of the public realm is being promoted. Rather than exacerbate sociospatial polarization through the creation of exclusive enclaves and nodes, the development of truly public spaces is expected to promote a degree of tolerance and social cohesion.

The tension between public and private space is by no means new. Perhaps nowhere was this more evident than in the medieval city. The medieval city was a place of trade. The great majority of English towns, for example, were located at the intersection, or the converging points, of major track-

ways. This determined not only the location of the town but also the way its streets and markets were organized (Platt, 1976). One or more marketplaces in the medieval city were devoted to trade, as the main public spaces of the city. However, as Saalman reminds us, "the entire medieval city was a market" (1968, p. 28). This meant that in all parts of the city, in open and closed spaces, whether public or private, trade and production for trade went on. Within this trading space, however, there was a constant struggle between public and private interests, which largely determined the shape of the medieval city. Individuals and households needed space for production, trade, and living. As the availability of space within the walls was limited, there was continuous pressure for claiming space for private use. On the other hand, there was a need for some free movement and interchange of goods and persons and for meeting places, which could also accommodate the trading visitors to the city. All this meant that the city needed public spaces as well. As the public power and its associated public institutions grew, the public spaces and public buildings grew. There was therefore "a fluid balance" between "Infinitely expanding public space and the eternally encroaching buildings" (Saalman, 1968, p. 35). The streets of the medieval city, which appeared to some modern commentators as an anarchic maze, reflecting the behaviour of pack donkeys rather than humans (Le Corbusier, 1971), were indeed formed by constant struggle between public and private interests.

The lines that define the public spaces of the city are often the lines between public and private property. The relationship between public and private space has shaped cities throughout history and has been at the centre of their social organization. However, since the critique of Aristotle against Plato, the role of private property in the city has been the subject of debate. Plato held that, in an ideal city, private property should be shared to promote unity among citizens, especially among a ruling elite, the Guardians (Plato, 1993). Aristotle (1992), on the other hand, argued against seeking excessive unity and emphasized the need for private property and for acknowledging the difference among citizens. He suggested that, "the greater the number of owners, the less respect for common property" (p. 108). As if describing a public housing estate in the second half of the 20th century, Aristotle wrote, "People are much more careful of their personal possessions than those owned communally; . . . the thought that someone else is looking after (common property) for them tends to make them careless of it". He therefore defended the private ownership of property, but held that its use could be communal (p. 113f).

In the modern context, the debate about private property starts with Locke, who argued for a natural right of property ownership, which lies outside social contract and cannot be negotiated. The protection of private property lies at the heart of modern liberal thought as a foundation of individualism which is a hallmark of the Enlightenment era. In their fight against the bourgeoisie, Marx and his followers set up to abolish private ownership of property. Hegel had argued in favour of the institution of private property as an expression of individual self. This was criticized by Marx as causing alienation, rather than realizing the individual self (Scruton, 1996, pp. 434–435).

The social organizations which were established along Marxian lines took up this critique of private property as one of their central doctrines. The socialist cities continued to have public and private spaces, but their ownership, management, and use were radically different from before. After the collapse of the socialist governments, the return of property to private ownership has gone through a troubled route. This change in relationship between public and private ownership has clear parallels in the western economies and has been widely adopted around the world. The privatization of public property has had, and will have, substantial impacts on the shape of cities. In the western context, privatization of space has already transformed the sociospatial organization of cities. As in the medieval cities, the contours of urban space are being carved out of a con-stant tension between public and private relationships. Urban designers can have a significant role in elaborating a public realm which mediates, and promotes a civilized relationship, between private interests and their spatial expressions, private domains.

Conclusion

Cities are threatened by social polarization and segregation, which are expressed in sub-urbanization and inner-city decay. As the state's sphere of control has contracted over the past three decades, as part of a general trend of societal change, the balance of control and production of urban space has favoured private interests. Combined effects of privatization of space and the threat of social fragmentation pose a serious threat for the future of the city. The contribution of urban design to this problem has been the promotion of urban public space as nodes for social integration. This fits well with the change of economic base from the industrial to the service sector, which requires new forms of production and consumption of space.

Throughout history, urban public space has always played a central role in the social life of cities. But they have lost their significance and are no longer the main nodes of all the social networks. Technological change, larger populations, and specialization of activities have led to a fragmentation of functions and a despatialization of public sphere. Treatment of space as a commodity, and stratification of society have led to sociospatial segregation and privatization of space. Treating city design as merely providing an aesthetic experience is in line with marketing the cities and a new attention to cities by capital markets. In this context, public space can once again play an active role in urban life. Urban designers promote spatial enclosures which are positively defined and which accommodate a mixture of people and activities. Creating these inclusive nodes may be a positive step towards reducing the potential conflicts arising from different interpretations and expectations of urban space, and in promoting an urbanism of tolerance and social cohesion.

REFERENCES

Alexander, C., Neis, H., Anninou, A. and King, I. (1987) *A New Theory of Urban Design*. New York: Oxford University Press.

Arendt, H. (1958) *The Human Condition*. Chicago: University of Chicago Press.

Aristotle (1992) *The Politics*. Harmondsworth: Penguin.

Atkinson, D. (1998) Totalitarianism and the street in Fascist Rome. In N. Fyfe (ed.), *Images of the Street*. Sevenoaks: Butterworth.

Benn, S. and Gaus, G. (eds) (1983) *Public and Private in Social Life*. London: Croom Helm.

Bentley, I., Alcock, A., Murrain, P., McGlynn, S. and Smith G. (1985) *Responsive Environments: A Manual*. Sevenoaks: Butterworth.

Boyer, M. (1990) The return of aesthetics to city planning. In D. Crow (ed.), *Philosophical Streets: New Approaches to Urbanism*. Washington, DC: Maisonneuve Press.

Brittan, A. (1977) *The Privatised World*. London: Routledge & Kegan Paul.

Carr, S., Francis, M., Rivlin, L. and Stone, A. (1992) *Public Space*. Cambridge: Cambridge University Press.

County Council of Essex (1973) *A Design Guide for Residential Areas*. Colchester: County Council of Essex.

Cullen, G. (1971) *The Concise Townscape*. Sevenoaks: Butterworth.

Engels, F. (1993) *The Condition of the Working Class in England*, ed. D. McLellan, first published in 1845. Oxford: Oxford University Press.

Giedion, S. (1967) *Space, Time and Architecture: The Growth of a New Tradition*, 5th edn. Cambridge, MA: Harvard University Press.

Glotz, G. (1929) *The Greek City and Its Institutions*. London: Routledge & Kegan Paul.

Habermas, J. (1989) *The Structural Transformation of the Public Sphere*. Cambridge: Polity Press.

Hall, P. (1995) Towards a general urban theory. In J. Brotchie, M. Batty, E. Blakely, P. Hall and P. Newman (eds), *Cities in Competition*. Melbourne: Longman Australia.

Jameson, M. (1990) Private space and the Greek city. In O. Murray and S. Price (eds), *The Greek City: From Homer to Alexander*. Oxford: Clarendon Press.

Kamenka, E. (1983) Public/private in Marxist theory and Marxist practice. In S. I. Benn and G. F. Gaus (eds), *Public and Private in Social Life*. London: Croom Helm.

Knox, P. (1995) *Urban Social Geography: An Introduction*. Harlow: Longman.

Krier, R. (1979) *Urban Space*. London: Academy Editions.

Le Corbusier (1971) *The City of To-morrow, and Its Planning*. London: The Architectural Press.

Lefebvre, H. (1991) *the Production of Space*. Oxford: Blackwell.

Loukaitou-Sideris, A. (1993) Privitization of public open space. *Town Planning Review*, 64(2), 139–67.

Lynch, K. (1960) *The Image of the City*. Cambridge, MA: MIT Press.

Madanipour, A. (1996) *Design of Urban Space*. Chichester: John Wiley.

Madanipour, A. (1998) *Tehran: The Making of a Metropolis*. Chichester: John Wiley.

Madanipour, A., Cars, G. and Allen, J. (1996) *Social Exclusion in European Cities*. London: Jessica Kingsley.

Maffesoli, M. (1996) *The Time of the Tribes: The Decline of Individuality in Mass Society*. London: Sage.

Miethe, T. (1995) Fear and withdrawal from urban life. *Annals of the American Academy of Political and Social Science*, 539, 14–27.

Pateman, C. (1983) Feminist critiques of the public/private dichotomy. In S. E. Benn and G. F. Gaus (eds), *Public and Private in Social Life*. London: Croom Helm, 281–303.

Plato (1976) *Republic*. Oxford: Oxford University Press.

Platt, C. (1976) *The English Medieval Town*. London: Secker and Warburg.

Punter, J. (1990) Privatization of the public realm. *Planning Practice and Research*, 5(3), 9–16.

Saalman, H. (1968) *Medieval Cities*. London: Studio Vista.

Schmitt-Pantel, P. (1990) Collective activities and the political in the Greek city. In O. Murray and S. Price (eds), *The Greek City: From Homer to Alexander*. Oxford: Clarendon Press, pp. 199–213.

Scruton, R. (1996) *Modern Philosophy*. London: Mandarin.

Searle, J. (1995) *The Construction of Social Reality*. London: Penguin.

Sennett, R. (1994) *Flesh and Stone*. London: Faber and Faber.

Sert, J. L. (1944) *Can Our Cities Survive? An ABC of Urban Problems, Their Analysis, Their Solution*. Cambridge, MA: Harvard University Press.

Sitte, C. (1986) City planning according to artistic principles. In G. Collins and C. Collins (eds), *Camillo, Sitte: The Birth of Modern City Planning*. New York: Rizzoli, pp. 129–332.

Tibbalds, F. (1992) *Making People-friendly Towns: Improving the Public Environment in Towns and Cities*. Harlow: Longman.

Tibbalds/Colbourne/Karski/Williams (1990) *City Centre Design Strategy. Birmingham Urban Design Studies, Stage 1*. Birmingham: Birmingham City Council.

Vernez Moudon, A. (ed.) (1991) *Public Streets for Public Use*. New York: Columbia University Press.

Walzer, M. (1986) Pleasures and costs of urbanity. *Dissent*, Fall, 470–5.

Ward-Perkins, J. B. (1974) *Cities of Ancient Greece and Italy: Planning in Classical Antiquity*. New York: George Braziller.

Whitehand, J. W. R. (1992) *The Making of the Urban Landscape*. Oxford: Blackwell.

Zukin, S. (1995) *The Cultures of Cities*. Oxford: Blackwell.

11

Reflections on Berlin: The Meaning of Construction and the Construction of Meaning

Peter Marcuse

"The biggest construction site in Europe" is a self-description of what is happening in Berlin today, but what is being constructed is an image as well as a set of buildings. The big visible pieces include:

- A whole new set of state buildings, in a prominently located government center (the German word is more expressive – "*Regierungsviertel*", a "quarter for ruling") at a cost of billions, for a Germany that sees itself as the dominant country in a united Europe.
- At Potsdamer Platz, the European headquarters of Sony, a major structure for ABB technologies and the central building for Daimler-Benz-Messerschmidt's information products and services, oriented to take advantage of the newly opened eastern market, the whole making virtually a second or third city center.
- Friedrichstraße, before the war a main commercial axis for Berlin, after the war just another street within the anti-market German Democratic Republic, now striving for a role as the luxury shopping street of Germany, the Fifth Avenue of Berlin.
- Huge infrastructure works, a new central railroad station connecting the government center with all Europe, a new auto tunnel under that center, cultural facilities galore, including a new Jewish

Museum, and a host of private speculative office buildings.
- A proposed "Memorial to the Murdered Jews of Europe", often referred to as a Holocaust memorial (the German word is "*Mahnmal*", a "warning monument", rather than simply "memorial", which is "*Denkmal*").

And the fact of so much construction *per se*, the construction cranes and scaffolding everywhere, are now touted as defining the new character of the city (figure 11.1).

The construction of what? Of symbols, of meaning, very consciously. Ostentatiously, the best architects of the advanced world are invited to enter competitions, first conceptually, then for real, for the key sites. Discussions are undertaken in public, with speakers, local and international, invited to comment at public lectures, juries impaneled, special editions of magazines, popular and professional, devoted to the results, and a whole new institution, the City Forum, established by the Senator for City Development, all devoted to elucidating the meaning and implications of the alternatives proposed. The meaning of each building, each style, each facade, the construction materials, the location and its significance in various historical periods – the empire, the first world war, the Weimar Republic, fascism, post-second world war, the divided and the reunited city – are elaborated, with the

Figure 11.1 Berlin – Mahnmal and construction sites. (1) Selected location for Mahnmal; (2) and (3) Alternate locations in Tiergarten; (5) and (6) Alternate locations within Government area; (10) Topography of terror; (A) New auto tunnel; (T) New train tunnel; Dashed lines circumscribe the Government Center and the Potzdamer Platz new construction.

prevailing philosophy of "critical reconstruction" giving major emphasis to pre-1914 history.[1]

Most troublesome perhaps are those constructions dealing with the Holocaust and the Jewish thread in German history; there debate as often leads to apparent paralysis as to decision. Finally, of course, the political leadership asserts itself, the decision is made and is final. The interrelationship of construction decisions with the market (it had collapsed by 1993) and with the national and local budgets is close, and the details of those relationships (to the extent known) are likewise subject to public discussion. Architectural and symbolic analysis, in our best tradition, accompanies all this and extracts its deeper meaning.

But something gets lost in the process. What is being constructed in Berlin can certainly be called meaning; but it can also be called by its short name: *power* (leave aside the Holocaust Mahnmal for the moment). While form, location and symbolism tend to support purpose, the building on a lavish scale of the new Government Center in Berlin, with a paranoiac concern for security,[2] and pomp, and a subservience to every wish for comfort and efficiency and representational fashion by the leaders of the state, is *per se* an expression of the power of that state. In the debates, after the Wall came down, as to whether the government should move from the backwater town of Bonn to the "traditional" capital of Berlin, the image of the arrogance, the imperialism, the mission of world domination that has historically been connected with the German state was a strong undercurrent – feared by the left, implicitly claimed, in the form of an unabashed chauvinism, by the right.

Now the Berlin administration says such issues are "cold coffee", irrelevant, not worthy of further discussion – the decision has been made: the government is building in Berlin. Only the *form* of the construction is open to discussion (and at that only briefly), not its fact. Likewise with what the private market wants to do at Potsdamer Platz or at Friedrichstraße: certainly the private market will be decisive in what will be built, only the

form the buildings will take is open to discussion. But the evil lies more in the construction itself than in its form. Does not history teach the dangers of a strong centralized state intertwined with a strong centralized private economy, certainly, if not only, in Germany? What kind of a priority is it, to build another Government Center (all the facilities of government already exist in Bonn, some even now still being built), a street of luxury shops, a costly and glamorous new office center for prosperous businesses, in a city whose unemployment rate is over 15%,[3] where anti-immigrant agitation is grounded in economic insecurity, with a welfare state being dismantled on all fronts? The meaning of the construction that is going on is not in any doubt. Its meaning lies in the fact of its undertaking. This is indeed the ultimate landscape of power – not because of its form, but because of the very fact of its construction.

Nor are these developments unconscious, the actors hidden, the purposes concealed. Senator Streider, a leader in the city's government, wants to attract affluent people to the center of the city; professional consultants like Dietrich Hoffman-Axthelm justify such policies as following people's tastes and preferences. Which people? Pompous office buildings with 20% luxury housing may be some speculator's (or "market analyst's") view of what is desired, but these are not merely some private real-estate developers putting their private profit ahead of the public good; these are the political leadership's very definition of the public good. They are delighted at the modernization of the older housing stock in the East, but it has led to rent increases of 70% and a classic gentrification-cum-displacement of the existing tenancy.[4]

The Potsdamer Platz development is particularly poignant. That Daimler-Benz-Messerschmidt, a key player in German economic and political power through two world wars, is sold the most visible and most promoted piece of publicly-owned real estate in all Berlin – that fact itself, whatever form the resultant building might take, speaks volumes. These new buildings at Potsdamer Platz *are* the seat of economic power, just as the government center *is* the seat of political power. Their function is to further that power. Their architectural form is one means to that end, but hardly the most important; that they can sit in full comfort at the heart of Berlin, the presumptive new heart of an economically expanded and expansionary Germany, facilitates that function even more. The architectural form might even, arguably, be interpreted as precisely concealing, rather than revealing, function: making a display of glass and its implication of transparency to enclose a building in whose interior manipulations and decisions are made that are anything but transparent to the outside world is more misrepresenting than representing. Further, the lavish use of marble and expensive and exotic materials, the large atriums and huge lobbies, the ostentatious entrances and ornamentation, all suggest that money is no object here, art and impressiveness, not efficiency, are the guiding principle, all coming from concerns whose dedication to the bottom line is at the foundation of their existence. But fact rather than a particular style is the essential point at the Friedrichstraße also – the level of conspicuous display of luxury is what is obscene, its wrapping in high-style architecture only accentuates the underlying evil.

Framing the issues in architectural, or in representational terms, concedes the ball game before it is begun.[5] The issues are power and its uses, wealth and its uses; framing the debate as one about form trivializes the issues, trivializes the history, serves to distract attention (perhaps deliberately?) from the underlying decisions. Postmodernism may, in fact, serve the purposes of power here, but so may other styles; the focus on styles could lead to, but is more likely to distract from, attention to what is really happening. This is, of course, not to say that style is unimportant, or that design decisions do not connect directly with political and social decisions, nor is it to say that decisions such as height limits or contextualism or historic honesty are unimportant. It is only to say that there is a danger that in the

prominence given to such discussions underlying issues are buried. Some cynics even believe that the apparent willingness of some members of the Berlin administration to listen to discussions of architectural form and urban design is the result of a deliberate desire to focus discussion on issues they themselves consider unimportant, to ensure that the really important decisions go unchallenged. Architectural competitions may be held for the government center, but the fact that a "politics-free zone" is to be designated around the key buildings in which demonstrations can be effectively banned, and that the construction program called for underground passageways connecting the offices of members of parliament with the parliament building, "sparing elected officials from direct contact with passersby" (Strom and Mayer, 1997, p. 21), is not a matter left to the architectural jury to influence.

The handling of the built legacy of the German Democratic Republic (GDR) represents an analogous issue of the relationship between form and fact: here the built form is put forward as the fact that requires attention, but the meaning given the form in the official presentation is simply factually wrong, and it is the fact of the existence of the surviving structures, not their form, that leads to state action. The Palace of the Republic was built where the old imperial castle had stood, a castle damaged in the war and torn down with symbolic fervor by the Socialist Unity Party after its consolidation of power in the GDR. Plans for the demolition of the new Palace now are officially grounded in the presence of asbestos in its walls, but expert opinions differ sharply as to how that danger might best be abated, and almost everyone concedes it is hostility to the memory of the GDR that accounts for the likelihood of demolition: its form, so the prevailing belief goes, too vividly and too conspicuously symbolizes the evil that was the East and its Stalinist orientation. In fact the Palace of the Republic is a modernist building, and its construction represented a victory of the more anti-Stalinist factions within the GDR, in the period made more liberal by Kruschev's revelations in the Soviet Union, over the hard-core Stalinists who had wanted to build on that site a high-rise, perhaps in the form of the dominant Moscow-style wedding-cake towers. It contained nine theaters, multiple restaurants and the legislative, but not the executive or party, organs of the state, and was in fact a quite popular and accessible building to the people of East Berlin. Power lay not there, but in the building of the Central Committee of the SED, behind the Palace and located in the prewar headquarters of the National Bank of Germany.

So what the Palace of the Republic in fact symbolized to a large part of Berlin's population was the priority of public space and public life over the private. The idea of combining the seat of the legislature with public theaters and publicly accessible restaurants and entertainment is the exact opposite of what is being developed in the new West Berlin government center, with its fortress-like concept and its careful attention to controlling access and use – not that there were not similar concerns in the GDR, but even so the form of the Palace of the Republic was designed to demonstrate openness rather than control. In this case also, then, to focus attention on the built form, rather than on the facts of the GDR/West German conflict, misses the point. It is the fact of the political leadership's desire to reject and suppress the potentially troublesome legacy of the GDR, not the form of the Palace of the Republic nor the best form for its replacement, that gives meaning to the discussion.

The dispute about the construction of the Holocaust Mahnmal reflects yet another relationship between fact and form, structure and meaning. A monument is, after all, not intended to be a fact in itself, but rather a symbol – in this sense, pure meaning. Here the proposal, endorsed by Chancellor Kohl and funded by the government, is to construct a monument to all the Jewish victims of the Holocaust. Through that act itself, the simple fact of his endorsement of the construction, Kohl expects to be seen as appropriately expressing his rejection of anti-Semitism and the Nazi past, cleansing

himself from this part of German history. But the proposals for the monument vitiate such a purpose. It will be a memorial structure, much like many other war memorials. It will pay tribute to the victims, perhaps by listing names or places, but will say nothing of causes or perpetrators: so victims without villains, a natural catastrophe, not the doing of humans, an event, not an action. And its location will reflect a long-standing pattern in German memorials to the victims of fascism: although geographically it appears centrally located, near where the Berlin wall stood, it will not get in anyone's way; it will simply be one of the many sights of Berlin that its residents or visitors may go to visit if they wish – or leave ignored if they wish. It provides one place where the genocide of the Jews by the German state can be remembered,[6] leaving all other places free of that responsibility.

How different if the monument were to be erected directly in front of the Reichstag, or the Chancellor's imposing office in the new government center! Salomon Korn, for instance, a German Jewish architect now living in Frankfurt and entrusted with representing the Jewish community's views on Jewish memorials, in a brilliant article[7] called attention to early submissions that could really function as a "Mahnmal" in the competition, but were barely touched on by the jury. One of the simplest was for a deep trench directly in front of the main entrance to the Reichstag, whose symbolism might represent the break in German history that the new Reichstag was to represent, but the fact of whose existence would force every German legislator every day of every session to walk around an inescapable reminder of what was once on the other side of that break.[8] Korn rejects the idea of simply demolishing the Brandenburg Gate and strewing its dust over the memorial site as substituting one destruction for another, but suggests instead removing some of its supporting stones and replacing them with temporary wooden ones.[9] Or to put a glass wall in front of the new monument to the "victims of war and violence" – originally to the fallen German soldiers of the first world war – with the names of the concentration camps engraved on it, so everyone wishing to view the first could not by-pass the second and would be made to think about the connection. In any event, to make the monument intrusive to the contemplation and exercise of power. The issue here is not, in the first place, an artistic/aesthetic one, says Korn, but a political/moral one. He's right; the first question at this point is not whether art after Auschwitz is possible, but what Germans today want to say about Germany and the Holocaust.[10] The artistic construction of form must grapple with that issue first, and that requires a pointed, open, and honest discussion that the powers that be do not wish to see occur.

Or, even worse, which they do want to see, but on their terms: encapsulated, at a "high" intellectual level, dominated by "*Sachverständige*", experts (literally "those who understand the thing"), and focusing on the representational/symbolic issues, not the political or moral ones. The jury of Sachverständige (three museum directors, an architect and an American historian) expressed doubt as to whether it was even possible to represent the Holocaust through artistic means.[11] A good question, if hardly ever discussed before. But that should lead the discussion, not to a new focus on a new competition for an "impossible" monument, but rather to what measures a nation might really take to honor the victims of the Holocaust and prevent a continuance of the developments that led to it: discussion of the treatment of minorities and immigrants, for instance, or of the meaning of democracy, or of the role (and perhaps even its physical incorporation) of the new Reichstag, the parliament.

A final example from a smaller scale illustrates the dangers of the current process. In Frankfurt there was a debate about the construction, at the Börneplatz, the site of the former Jewish quarter and adjacent to the old Jewish cemetery, of an office building for the public works administration of the city (including its gas works!). The final solution was the creation of a small museum with the foundations of a few of the old buildings from the old Jewish street preserved under glass and tucked into the corner of the new administration building, and the dedication of a small memorial park behind the building adjacent to the cemetery as a place of "remembrance".[12] Opponents called it, not a memorial park, but a "*Geschichtsentsorgungspark*", a "park for the cleaning of history". The Holocaust memorial in Berlin is likely to become a similar monument to the cleaning, or at least compartmentalizing and historicizing, of history.

If meaning is being constructed in Berlin today, if these various construction projects are to be given meaning, putting them together suggests what that meaning might be. The construction of the Regierungsviertel stands for the power and wealth of the German state, while Potsdamer Platz reflects the power and wealth of German business, and Friedrichstraße, at least in design, reflects the enjoyment of the fruits of that power and wealth in consumption. But the Holocaust memorial, if it is to say anything at all to observers today, must be precisely warning against the consequences of that power and wealth in the hands of an arrogant and asocial state and business community, against the building of the enjoyment of the benefits of wealth and power by some at the expense of the exploitation and domination and ultimately extermination of others. One memorial, on one site, cannot bear the burden of such a message – no matter how it is designed. Power and murder were historically intimately linked in Nazi Germany; one cannot now celebrate the former at the same time as one mourns the latter. No matter how one designs a Holocaust memorial, in the shadow of the new Regierungsviertel, Potsdamer Platz, Friedrichstraße, the meaning of the memorial turns into its opposite, into a final laying to rest rather than a living provocation, as long as power and wealth march on undisturbed all around it.

So the controversies over the meaning of the design of these separate constructions, in the aestheticized focus into which many of them tended to lapse, suppress and conceal deeper issues of responsibility and current policy. The political leadership is quite content to call its commitment to the fact of some memorial, any memorial at all, an adequate response to the need to come to terms with the roots of one of the most terrible actions of modern human history, and to get on with the business of ruling and generating wealth.

Real communication is generally healthy, and certainly there is much to discuss about all this. Difficult political issues and moral judgments are linked to the action of construction of the built environment in Berlin as in few other places on earth. But the controversies around them, to residents and visitors alike, may conceal the issues as well as reveal them. Issues of form can be smokescreens, or they can be the heart of the matter. Telling which is which is an important part of any real understanding of what is to be seen and heard in Berlin today.

NOTES

1   The phrase is that of a major figure in Berlin city government, Hans Stimman; for an excellent discussion, see Huyssens (1997).
2   The ruling Christian Democratic Party supported a "politics-free zone", a *"Bannmeile"*, in which political gatherings and demonstrations can be prohibited, around the area, and 100 million DM are being spent to build underground passages connecting the Bundestag members' offices and parliament building, in part to insulate the members from unwanted contact with the public. See *Der Spiegel* (1996, 8, p. 72–5).
3   The rate is 17.4% in West Berlin as of this writing. The argument that construction provides jobs is of course true, but specious; they are temporary jobs, and would be provided by construction of quite other buildings for quite other uses as well, and target in fact already skilled and well-paid workers or, as seems increasingly the case, foreign workers imported for the purpose to work at lower than the standard wages, thus depressing wage rates generally in the field. Job losses in the manufacturing sector have been 11% between 1991 and 1995, and that loss is expected to continue – 65,000 more by 2010.

4   From a study of modernization in Prenzlauer Berg and Kreuzberg (Winters, 1965, quoted in Strom and Mayer, 1997).
5   The discussion recalls the comments of Ada Louise Huxtable about the Times Square redevelopment debates: "the abuses of zoning and urban design, the default of planning and policy issues, have been subsumed into a ludicrous debate about a 'suitable style', ... leaving all larger planning problems untouched" (Huxtable, 1989).
6   Although it, in fact, has no historic association with the Holocaust. The site was apparently selected because the land was owned by the Federal government, and thus a larger Federal financial contribution could be expected, and because it was empty, so construction could begin quickly without issues of displacement, etc., and further controversy be avoided (letter to the author from Bruno Flierl, 6 January 1998). That it is in a geographically prominent location, near the Brandenburg Gate, although set off from it, spoke for it, but also raised objections to it, some good (too much traffic noise), some bad (too prominent a "thorn in the flesh" (Meier, 1998, p. 23).
7   Korn (1997). In several pieces Korn has stressed the view that such a monument should not only have a real historical link but should also provoke a living dialog with present German life and actions (see, for example, Korn, 1996).
8   Bruno Flierl, East Germany's leading architectural theorist, similarly suggested two appropriate sites at the Place of the Republic in the open space between the two houses of the German Parliament, without going into the type of memorial to be situated there (Flierl, 1997).
9   A comparison with the impact of the handling of churches damaged in the war comes to mind: the Gedächtniskirche in Berlin, carefully preserved and explained in an adjacent modern new building in the center of Berlin, illustrating how the "new Germany" is able seamlessly to incorporate preservation of the past with a downtown of the future, and the Frauenkirche in Dresden, in the GDR, crumbling, trees growing through its open roof, speaking volumes about destruction still felt and not overcome in the present.

10 I have no ideal solution for the monument; indeed, if the jury had been consistent in its reservations, it should simply have resigned. Perhaps a fitting provisional solution would be to leave the site barren and weed-overgrown, with merely a sign: "This is the location at which a monument to the murdered Jews of Europe was to have been erected. Because an understanding of what led those who murdered them to act as they did has not yet been achieved, the site remains barren". A somewhat similar proposal was in fact seriously submitted in the recent competition by Jög Esefeld and his colleagues (called "Scala").

11 In a "Manifesto" published by Werner Hoffman; see *Frankfurter Allgemeine Zeitung*, 18 November 1997, p. 45.

12 The controversy is clearly and insightfully described in a publication of the museum, *Stationen des Vergessens: Der Börneplatz-Konflikt* [Places of forgetting: the conflict about the Börneplatz], Museum Judengasse, Frankfurt am Main, November 1992. See particularly "Damnatio memoriae – Der Börneplatz als Ort kollektiven Vergessens" [The damnation of memories – the Börneplatz as place of collective forgetting], pp. 18–43.

REFERENCES

Flierl, B. (1997) Gedenken durch mehr Denken Wachhalten [Preserving memory through more reflection]. *Neues Deutschland*, 10 April, 14.

Huxtable, A. L. (1989) Times Square renewal (Act II), a farce, 1. *New York Times*, 14 October, A25.

Huyssens, A. (1997) The voids of Berlin. *Critical Inquiry*, 24(1), 57–81.

Korn, S. (1996) Der Tragödie letzter Teil – Das Spiel mit der Zeit. Anmerkungen zum Holocaust-Denkmal in Berlin, bevor das Manhmal für die ermordeten Juden Europas entschieden wird [The last part of the tragedy – the game with time. Comments on the Holocaust Memorial in Berlin, before the memorial for the murdered Jews of Europe is decided]. *Frankfurter Allgemeine Zeitung*, 9 December.

Korn, S. (1997) Durch den Reichstag geht ein Riß [Through the Reichstage runs a split]. *Frankfurter Allgemeine Zeitung*, 17 July, 32.

Meier, C. (1998) Stachel im Fleisch. *Der Tagesspiegel*, 23 January, 23.

Strom, E. and Mayer, M. (1997) The new Berlin. Unpublished typescript.

Winters, T. (1965) Stadterneurung in Prenzlauer Berg. *Die Alte Stadt*, 3, 263.

12

Tilted Arc and the Uses of Democracy

Rosalyn Deutsche

Four years after a public hearing that many critics viewed as a show trial, the United States General Services Administration (GSA) dismantled Richard Serra's *Tilted Arc*, a public sculpture that the agency had installed a decade earlier in New York City's Federal Plaza. The government's action became a cause célèbre in some sectors of the art world, especially among certain left-wing critics who saw it as one episode in a neoconservative campaign to privatize culture, restrict rights, and censor critical art. Briefly, the *Tilted Arc* story unfolded like this:

1979: The GSA commissions Serra to conceive a sculpture for the Federal Plaza site.

1981: Following approval of the artist's concept, *Tilted Arc* is installed.

1985: William Diamond, the GSA's New York regional administrator, names himself chairman of a hearing to decide whether Serra's sculpture should be, as Diamond puts it, "relocated" in order "to increase public use of the plaza." Although the majority of speakers at the hearing testify in favor of retaining *Tilted Arc*, the hearing panel recommends relocation, and Dwight Ink, the GSA's acting administrator in Washington, tries in vain to find alternative sites for the sculpture.

1986 to 1989: Serra pursues several unsuccessful legal actions – based on breach of contract, violation of constitutional rights, and artists' moral rights claims[1] – to prevent *Tilted Arc*'s removal.

1989: *Tilted Arc* is removed.

Then, in 1991, *The Destruction of Tilted Arc: Documents* (Weyergraf-Serra and Buskirk, 1991) appeared, like an act of historic preservation. By that time, of course, the book could do nothing to save the sculpture itself. But it does preserve the record – correspondence, official memos, press releases, hearing testimonies, and legal documents – of a key conflict in the growing controversy about the political functions of contemporary public art. Clara Weyergraf-Serra and Martha Buskirk carefully edited the papers generated in the course of the *Tilted Arc* proceedings, and the publication of this primary material provides a solid foundation for future art-historical and legal scholarship. Some readers will welcome the opportunity to weigh opposing arguments and determine, in retrospect, the merits of an individual public artwork. More importantly, however, *The Destruction of Tilted Arc: Documents* keeps alive – and public – debates about the political issues at stake in the *Tilted Arc* incident. The documents raise timely questions, whose implications extend far beyond arcane art-world matters, about what it means for art and space to be "public." Insofar as the GSA ostensibly dismantled *Tilted Arc* "to increase public use of the plaza," the documents pose related questions about current uses of urban space.

Despite claims to the contrary, the officials presiding over the *Tilted Arc* procedure were far from neutral on these questions. To suggest that the GSA had, in fact, answered them in advance is not to contend, as many

Figure 12.1 Richard Serra's *Tilted Arc*, Federal Office Plaza, New York 1979 (later removed). Reproduced courtesy of the artist. © ARS, New York and DACS, London 2002.

of Serra's supporters did, that the sculpture's fate had been prejudged (though that may also be true). But the GSA *had* adopted prior decisions about the meaning of the terms "use," "public," and "public use" and had built these precedents into the structure of the *Tilted Arc* proceedings from the start. As the editors of *The Destruction of Tilted Arc* point out, official announcements of the hearing contained an implied value judgment, framing the proposed debate as a contest between, on the one hand, *Tilted Arc*'s continued presence in the Federal Plaza and, on the other hand, increased "public use of the plaza" (p. 22). Clearly, it had been predetermined that the sculpture's presence detracted from "public use," but this judgment assumed that definitions of "public" and "use" are self-evident. "The public" was presumed to be a group of aggregated individuals unified by their adherence to fundamental, objective values or by their possession of essential needs and interests or, what amounts to the same thing, divided by equally essential conflicts. "Use" referred to the act of putting space into the service of fundamental pleasures and needs. Objects and practices in space were held to be of "public use" if they are uniformly beneficial, expressing common values or fulfilling universal needs.

Categories like "the public" can, of course, be construed as naturally or fundamentally coherent only by disavowing the conflicts, particularity, heterogeneity, and uncertainty that constitute social life. But when participants in a debate about the uses of public space remove the definitions of public and use to a realm of objectivity located not only outside the *Tilted Arc* debate but outside debate altogether, they threaten to erase public space itself. For what initiates debate about social questions if not the absence of absolute sources of meaning and the concomitant recognition that these questions – including the question of the meaning of public space – are decided only *in* a public space?

That words like "use" and "public" – employed as figures of universal accessibility – suppress conflict will hardly surprise

anyone familiar with prevailing discourses about the built environment. The GSA's verdict, confirming its premise that *Tilted Arc* interfered with the use of a public plaza, was consistent with a host of other opinions handed down throughout the 1980s on the uses of public space and public art. The decision against *Tilted Arc* was not a ruling against public art in general. On the contrary, the verdict coincided and was perfectly consistent with a widespread movement by city governments, real-estate developers, and corporations to *promote* public art, especially something called the "new public art," which was celebrated precisely because of its "usefulness." The new public art was defined as art that takes the form of functional objects placed in urban spaces – plumbing, park benches, picnic tables – or as art that helps design urban spaces themselves. Official efforts to discredit *Tilted Arc* cannot be isolated from attempts to portray other kinds of public art as truly public and useful. Moreover, the promotion of the new public art itself took place within a broader context, accompanying a massive transformation in the uses of urban space – the redevelopment and gentrification of cities engineered throughout the 1980s as the local component of global spatioeconomic restructuring. The *Tilted Arc* proceedings were, then, part of a rhetoric of publicness and usefulness that surrounded the redevelopment of urban space to maximize profit and facilitate state control. *Tilted Arc*, represented by its opponents as elitist, useless, even dangerous to the public, became the standard foil against which conservative critics and city officials routinely measure the accessibility, usefulness, humaneness, and publicness of the new public art.[2]

Although Serra's most astute supporters generally remained detached from urban issues, some countered the accusation that *Tilted Arc* obstructed the use of public space by defending the sculpture precisely because, as Rosalind Krauss argued, it "invests a major portion of its site with a use we must call aesthetic." Because this use is aesthetic, Krauss implied, it is also public: "This aesthetic use is open to every person who enters and leaves the buildings of this complex, and it is open to each and every one of them every day" (p. 81).

Relativizing use, Krauss's strategy challenged determinist notions that space has uses that are simply given and therefore indisputable. But Krauss also mobilized a conception of the aesthetic as a universally accessible sphere – which, coupled with notions of universal publics and uses, is the hallmark of mainstream treatments of public art. Precisely this universalizing vocabulary has made public art so effective as a means of portraying particular uses of space – to fulfill the needs of profit, for one – as advantageous to all. Simply proposing a plurality of equally universal uses of space leaves untouched the depoliticizing language of use that was the most powerful weapon wielded against *Tilted Arc*.

The Destruction of Tilted Arc: Documents invites us, by contrast, to examine the uses of language. Because the volume's title openly supports Serra's contention that "to remove" a work like *Tilted Arc* "is to destroy the work," it promises that the book will not merely report on but will engage in discursive struggles – beginning with the struggle over the meaning of site-specificity. Adopting Serra's terminology, Weyergraf-Serra and Buskirk implicitly defend the materialist approach to aesthetics historically invested in site-specific practices against current efforts to bring site-specificity into conformity with idealist concepts of art. Diamond, the GSA administrator, did not mention destruction. He referred to the sculpture's removal as a "relocation." In fact, Diamond portrayed himself as a virtual urban preservationist who, in keeping with conservative notions of preservation, was seeking to restore a fundamental sociospatial harmony that should have been preserved but was not. Diamond asserted that *Tilted Arc*'s relocation would "restore" and "reinstitute" the Federal Plaza's openness, coherence, and public usefulness.

But calling a site-specific sculpture's removal a relocation obscures a key difference between two aesthetic philosophies: on the one hand, the modernist doctrine that artworks are self-governing objects with stable, independent meanings and can therefore be relocated or moved intact from place to place, and, on the other hand, the idea, which gave rise to site-specific practice, that aesthetic meaning is formed in relation to an artwork's context and therefore changes with the circumstances in which the work is produced and displayed. Seemingly blind to the contradiction between these competing conceptions of art, the officials who opposed *Tilted Arc* did not acknowledge the incompatibility between site-specificity and the "truly public American art" described in the GSA's factsheet about the Art-in-Architecture Program for Federal Buildings. According to the factsheet, the objective of public art is "integration" with a "site," defined in turn as a "total architectural design." Consequently, the factsheet concludes that the Art-in-Architecture Program should sponsor art that "embellishes" federal buildings and "enhance[s]" the building's environment for the occupants and the general public" (p. 23).

But equating site-specific art with art that creates harmonious spatial totalities is so profoundly at odds with the impulse that historically motivated the development of site-specificity that it nearly amounts to a terminological abuse. For the invention of a new kind of artwork that neither diverts attention from nor merely decorates the spaces of its display emerged from the imperative to interrupt, rather than secure, the seeming coherence and closure of those spaces. Site-specific practice has two objectives that emerged in quick succession. Site-specificity sought first to criticize the modernist precept that works of art are autonomous entities and second to reveal how the construction of an apparent autonomy disavows art's social, economic, and political functions. But the politicization of art embodied in this attention to context is offset when artists adopt neutralizing definitions of context. Academic site-specificity, for instance, simply replaces the modernist aestheticization of the artwork with a similar aestheticization of art's architectural, spatial, or urban sites. Other artists and critics neutralize site-specificity by stressing the importance of art's social contexts but then defining society as a determinable object that, unified by a foundation external to art, governs and fixes aesthetic meaning. Both approaches reestablish, at the level of the site, the closure of meaning that site-specificity helped challenge.

Ignoring this challenge, many of *Tilted Arc*'s opponents advocated the sculpture's removal in order to restore the Federal Plaza's coherence. But proponents of a political site-specificity are skeptical about spatial coherence, viewing it not as an a priori condition subsequently disturbed by conflicts *in* space but as a fiction masking the conflicts that *produce* space. Henri Lefebvre, the urban theorist who coined the phrase "the production of space," refers to this homogenizing fiction when he describes late-capitalist space as "simultaneously the birthplace of contradictions, the milieu in which they are worked out and which they tear up, and, finally, the instrument which allows their suppression and *the substitution of an apparent coherence*" (Lefebvre, 1974, p. 420, emphasis added). Against this process, and in striking contrast to the GSA's notion of integration, site-specific works become part of their sites precisely by restructuring them, fostering – we might even say, restoring – the viewer's ability to apprehend the conflicts and indeterminacy repressed in the creation of supposedly coherent spatial totalities.

When Weyergraf-Serra and Buskirk use the term *destruction* to describe *Tilted Arc*'s fate, they take an avowedly partial stand consistent with the abandonment of totalizing perspectives implicit in site-specificity itself. After so many years of cultural critiques of objectivism, it should be unnecessary to point out that admitting partiality is not an abdication of responsibility for factual accuracy or fairness. *The Destruction of Tilted Arc* is scrupulously researched, the documents rigorously footnoted, and the chronology of events and texts painstakingly reconstructed. Far from a license to dissemble, the designation of *Tilted Arc*'s removal as a destruction frankly signals the editors'

desire to support site-specificity as a critical art practice against the current implication that such work can merely affirm its sites. Affirmative site-specific art, endowed with an aura of social responsibility, naturalizes and thus validates the social relations of its sites, legitimating spaces as accessible to all when they may be privately owned or when, tolerating little resistance to corporate or state-approved uses, they exclude entire social groups. The editors' admission of partiality also diverges from the position taken by *Tilted Arc*'s most powerful antagonists who spoke in the name of certainties like "common sense," "reality," and "the people's interest." The appeal to such absolute grounds of meaning sheltered their arguments from political interrogation.

To support the book's argument in favor of *Tilted Arc*, the editors framed the chronologically arranged sections of documents with footnotes and brief introductions that summarize and interpret data, provide supplementary information, or point out inaccuracies and fallacies in opponents' statements. Most candidly declaring the book's partisanship, however, is the inclusion of a general introduction written by Serra himself, a detailed polemic against both the GSA's arguments and subsequent court decisions dismissing the artist's appeals. The frank abandonment of pretensions to documentary impartiality implicit in this choice could have turned the editors' and Serra's introductions into an opportunity not merely to preserve but also to amplify and transform the *Tilted Arc* debate.

But the editors missed this chance. The introductions reiterate the opinions expressed by Serra and his supporters in the documents themselves. As a consequence, the book's intervention in public art discourse stays firmly within the boundaries that shaped – and constrained – discussion in the thick of the *Tilted Arc* controversy. At that time, liberal and left members of the art world who unconditionally supported *Tilted Arc* forged their arguments primarily in opposition to the neoconservative rhetoric mobilized against the sculpture, a reactive position with some serious risks. For if the desire to defeat conservatism exhausts all political contests over the meaning of public art, the problems presented by traditional left ideas of aesthetic politics and of art's public functions will remain uninterrogated. Yet critical thought is hardly united in support of these ideas, nor, for that matter, did the left unanimously defend *Tilted Arc*. To give the impression of a self-evident unity of critical opinion that forms the proper basis for opposing conservatism (a strategy that comes close to mirroring that of *Tilted Arc*'s enemies) is to imply that different critical ideas are divisive forces, giving comfort to the enemy. Because it is important to extend, and reframe, current debates about public art – and not because the book should impart an aura of disinterestedness – the absence of a critical essay by someone other than Serra is regrettable.

This deficiency narrows the book's treatment of several important issues. Consider, for instance, the key issue of site-specificity, which Serra's introduction patiently explains and elaborates. He insists that, because a site-specific work incorporates its context as an essential component of the work, site-specificity denotes permanence. This provides a strategic basis for claiming that *Tilted Arc*'s removal breaches the government contract guaranteeing the sculpture's permanence and, moreover, for disputing Diamond's invention of definitions that make site-specificity compatible with relocation or adjustment. But the relationship between site-specificity and permanence is complex, and the simple equation of the two deviates in significant ways from the principles of contextualist art practice. Given that site-specific projects are based on the idea that meaning is contingent rather than absolute, they actually imply instability and impermanence.

The book's failure to differentiate among different senses of "permanence" repeats a slippage made repeatedly in the Serra camp throughout the hearing when unqualified references to the intrinsic permanence of site-specific works contributed to a blurring of distinctions between the antiessentialist tenets of site-specificity, on the one hand,

and liberal platitudes that "great art" is eternal and possesses "enduring qualities," on the other. In the latter case, permanence is given the property of an essence. But the belief in art's timelessness, in its determination by an aesthetic essence and its independence from historical contingencies, is precisely what contextualist practices challenged in the first place. This is no trivial confusion. Allowing site-specific art to be swept into a realm of transhistorical continuities, it neutralizes – just as Diamond's relocation proposal does – the very shift in contemporary art that decisively opened the artwork to history, politics, and everyday life. This shift wrested art out of an eternal sphere superior to the rest of the social world. Not surprisingly, then, the effort to shore up *Tilted Arc*'s unconditional permanence and therefore its aesthetic privilege coincided with a tendency for *Tilted Arc*'s defenders to evade questions of elitism.

It has been traditional for some leftist voices in the art world to deal inadequately with the problem of elitism, even to dismiss it out of hand. This dismissal parallels a tendency prevalent until recently in broader left discourse, where discussions of democracy often concentrated on exposing the mystifications of formal bourgeois democracy and proposing "concrete" socialist alternatives while ignoring the undemocratic character not only of actually existing socialist regimes but of the left's own theories. Among artists and critics, the failure to take democracy seriously springs in part from the pressure that the left has felt to defend itself against attacks from conservative critics who routinely use anti-intellectual and populist strategies to give democratic legitimacy to authoritarian campaigns against critical art and theory.

These pressures were strong during the *Tilted Arc* hearing. A rhetoric of democracy pervaded the debate, demonstrating the degree to which public art discourse had become a site of struggle over the meaning of democracy. Government officials disparaged critical art under the banner of "anti-elitism," a stance consistent with a general tendency in neoconservative discourse to accuse art of arrogance or inaccessibility in order to champion privatization and justify state censorship in the name of the rights of "the people."

The *Tilted Arc* proceedings exemplified this inversion, combining talk of government's accountability to the public with action by the government in a role resembling that of a private economic actor. From the start, the GSA emphasized its responsibility to protect the people from what it called *Tilted Arc*'s "private" encroachment on public space. Diamond mobilized this protectionist discourse on the day the sculpture was dismantled: "Now," he declared, "the plaza returns rightfully to the people." Later, however, when Serra tried to appeal the decision, the courts protected the government as a property-owning entity. Serra pleaded, first, that he had been denied due process in the form of a fair, impartial hearing and, second, that the GSA's decision violated his First Amendment rights, which prohibit the government from removing a medium of expression on the basis of its content once it has been publicly displayed. The courts dismissed both claims. The judge for the U.S. Court of Appeals for the Second Circuit argued that because the government owned both the sculpture and the Federal Plaza, Serra was never constitutionally entitled to a hearing. Due process in this case was called a "gratuitous benefit," not a right (p. 253). There are parallels between this decision and a conservative legal tendency that, as constitutional scholar Laurence H. Tribe writes, has potentially staggering effects on the exercise of free speech rights. The distinction between "benefit" and "right" recalls the legal distinction between "privilege" and "right," which, says Tribe (1985, p. 189), can be used as a "tool for cutting off the free speech rights of those who rely on the government as an employer, provider of benefits, or property owner." The basis of the distinction is the doctrine that a speaker's First Amendment rights are violated only if she is deprived of something to which she is independently entitled. But no one has the right to enter government property – only the "privilege."

If strictly applied, warns Tribe (1985, pp. 203–4), the right-privilege doctrine could "leave would-be speakers with a right to speak, but nowhere to exercise that right."

Subsequently, Serra claimed, again unsuccessfully, that against the rights of private ownership, he has "moral rights" in the work as an artist. Artists' moral rights are frequently declared in opposition to the privileges of private property, but the GSA implicitly discredited this opposition when it suggested that the government owned the work and the plaza not as a private-property owner, but as "the people": "This space belongs to the government and to the public," said Diamond. "It doesn't belong to the artist.... Not if he sells [his work] to the government.... He doesn't have the right to force his art upon the public forever" (p. 271). Claims of accountability to the public were articulated with action by the government as a property owner, tying the people's interest to the rights of private property in controlling public spaces.

Tilted Arc's proponents spoke for democracy, too. Some testified in favor of the right of free artistic expression or, like Abigail Solomon-Godeau, deplored the denial of due process inherent in Diamond's prejudgment of the case. Benjamin Buchloh stressed the democratic necessity of independent peer review as a guarantee against statism and collective prejudice. Clara Weyergraf-Serra cautioned against the totalitarian dangers of appeals to the people's "healthy instincts." *Tilted Arc*'s advocates thus argued persuasively, and I think justifiably, against a government intervention that could be a textbook example of what Stuart Hall terms "authoritarian populism": the mobilization of democratic discourses to sanction, indeed to pioneer, shifts toward state authoritarianism (Hall, 1988, pp. 123–49). Serra's supporters insistently exposed the manner in which state officials used the language of democracy and such existing democratic procedures as public hearings and petitions to bind popular consent to the coercive pole of state power in so-called public spaces. The importance of this critique can hardly be overestimated. In New York, as in other cities, authoritarian populist measures, coupled with anticrime campaigns – the very strategies rallied against *Tilted Arc* – have authorized the relentless proliferation of pseudo- or private public spaces.

Yet beyond the challenge raised to authoritarian populist notions of public art and to the trivializing reduction of public spaces to harmonious leisure spots or places to eat lunch, and beyond the espousal of formal rights, Serra's supporters made few efforts to articulate democracy, public art, or public space in more radical directions. Insofar as *The Destruction of Tilted Arc: Documents* perpetuates this quiescence, it abandons public art discourse as a site of struggle over the meaning of democracy. Indeed, although Serra alludes briefly to the critical difference between "community" and "public," *The Destruction of Tilted Arc* does not try to define "publicness." The introductions do not, for instance, elaborate the suggestion, broached in Douglas Crimp's and Joel Kovel's hearing testimonies, that a distinction between public space and the state apparatus is essential to democracy. Nor do they amplify the implications for public art discourse of Kovel's crucial point that a democratic public space must be understood as a realm not of unity but of divisions, conflicts, and differences resistant to regulatory power. The *Tilted Arc* controversy is never linked to the efforts currently being made by artists, critics, and curators to recast public art as work that helps create a public space in the sense of a public sphere, an arena of political discourse. And although the word "public" might be applied to Serra's work not so much because *Tilted Arc* occupied a government plaza as because it explored how the viewer, far from a strictly private being, is formed in relation to an outside world, the book never extends this investigation of subjectivity to ask who the subject of a democratic public space is.

Given the neglect of this question, it is hardly accidental that throughout the Serra debate the left's neglect of critical issues about public space and democracy was coupled with a failure to challenge substantially either the myth of great art or its corollary, the myth of the great artist. In fact, *Tilted Arc*'s radical supporters frequently relied, almost by default, on the standard left counterparts of these myths – political-aesthetic vanguardism and the exemplary political artist. Consequently, Serra's proponents offered only a limited and problematic alternative to authoritarian populist conceptions of public art. For vanguardism implies the existence of sovereign subjects whose superior social vision can penetrate illusions and perceive the people's "true" interests, and this idea has itself been charged with authoritarianism – even with the attempt to eliminate public space. According to new theories of radical democracy, public space emerges with the abandonment of the belief in an absolute basis of social unity, a basis that gives "the people" an essential identity or true interest. Public space, in this view, is the uncertain social realm where, in the absence of an absolute foundation, the meaning of the people is simultaneously constituted and put at risk. The vanguard position – the external vantage point on society – is incompatible with a democratic public space.

The Destruction of Tilted Arc vigorously defends public space against neoconservatism, privatization, and state control and helps document the current state of public art discourse. But the book itself reveals that if we want to extend rather than close down public space, it is to questions of democracy that we should turn.

NOTES

1 For a discussion of moral rights, see Buskirk (1991).
2 For an analysis of relationships between discourses of utility and urban redevelopment and a discussion of the "new public art" see "Uneven Development: Public Art in New York City," in R. Deutsche, *Evictions: Art and Spatial Politics*, Cambridge, MA: MIT Press, 1996.

REFERENCES

Buskirk, M. (1991) Moral rights: first step or false start? *Art in America*, 79(7), 37–45.
Hall, S. (1988) Popular-democratic vs authoritarian populism: two ways of "taking democracy seriously." In *The Hard Road to Renewal: Thatcherism and the Crisis of the Left*. London: Verso.
Lefebvre, H. (1974) *La production de l'espace*. Paris: Anthropos.
Tribe, L. (1985) *Constitutional Choices*. Cambridge, MA: Harvard University Press.
Weyergraf-Serra, C. and Buskirk, M. (1991) *The Destruction of Tilted Arc: Documents*. Cambridge, MA: MIT Press.

Part V
Culture

13

Urban Spaces as Cultural Settings

Gwendolyn Wright

The recent rise of interest in urban history among architects and architectural historians signals major shifts in both professions. Architects, absorbing the collapse of an absolutist and ahistorical version of Modernism, are searching for new meanings. They have retrieved history out of the shadows to make it the very basis of contemporary design, providing both a parti for individual buildings and a way of relating buildings to their surroundings. Most architects now seem to draw openly from a range of sources that includes certain admired precedents (whether classical or Modernist – itself now a part of history) which transcend specific locales, as well as more local architectural and urban design traditions. It is almost a commonplace to show how a new building relates to its context – to the city, town, or neighborhood street-scape – and thus pays homage in another way to what came before.

All the same, it is by no means an easy task to embrace the past and the larger urban milieu. Responding to local traditions entails serious appraisal of a complex culture, even for a small place – skills few designers have been taught. And the intellectual challenge of broadening the scope of our architectural canon to include great urban spaces, as well as buildings, requires new approaches. These larger settings cannot always be neatly classified according to specific dates and individual designers. One must consider how they took form and changed over time, acknowledging the cumulative influence of many different groups and persons.

Simultaneous with this shift, the very boundaries of architectural history itself are changing, too. Hitherto the discipline was characterized by a preoccupation with the intentions of the designer and the formal analysis of singular monuments. In recent years the field has suddenly and dramatically expanded. Scholars are examining the relations of architecture: issues of patronage, public authorities and legal codes, site planning, and the socio-political reactions of a community. Buildings are seldom studied in isolation now; in fact, many historians delve into the infrastructure of streets, landscaping, open spaces, and even public services, as they once extended their domain to construction technology. The loosely defined "vernacular" has become a significant field of study, covering everything not designed by architects, ranging from folk traditions to the mass-produced world of speculatively-built housing, amusement parks, and work places. Structures and spaces evoke not just their designers, but all those who bring the built environment into being, those who use or inhabit it, if only by walking through a city street. All of these tendencies have altered the scope and the very enterprise of architectural history. The earlier concerns are still central, of course, but architect and building are now both part of a larger urban setting.

Ideally these two parallel developments can and should benefit one another. Urban historians can teach architects to grasp the complexities of cities – or urban design, incremental changes, and social diversity. Likewise, close associations with architects can remind historians of the formal and conceptual ideals which preoccupy designers, for the methodologies of such scholars must always be able to include a great variety of goals and influences, even those which do not readily fit into a social science model of analysis.

Historians, like architects, often find this larger urban dimension of their work as frustrating as it is compelling. This is even true for the study of cities up through the early modern period, though when "the world... was half a thousand years younger," in the words of Johann Huizinga, "the outlines of all things seemed more clearly marked than to us" (Huysinga, 1924, p. 1). Many diverse forces were at work, in harmony or in conflict, to generate and then continuously modify the urban environment. Unravelling all these influences becomes more than anecdotal background if a historian wants to analyze the placement of Athenian temples, the street and canal pattern of Amsterdam, or the hierarchy of housing in colonial Boston. The scale of earlier cities and the relative clarity of the cultural forces at work do, however, make them easier to take in than most contemporary cities. Historians and architects can more readily perceive the kinds of questions they must ask about cities in any period: What is the effect of a building's location on neighborhood development? What is demolished to make room for a new structure? How does a project affect the local economy and social order?

The interplay of historical forces is even more the case in cities since the early nineteenth century, as the number and diversity of actors has become ever greater, as the scale of cities, their economy, and their cultural complexity has increased almost exponentially. Strangely, for those professional urban historians who focus on the modern era, industrial cities have been the overwhelmingly preferred topic, and statistical analysis the prevailing methodology. In part for this reason, historians concerned with architecture and urban design can open up important new terrains, even if they concentrate on the more traditional building types of their discipline – religious and civic buildings, domestic and commercial architecture, theaters and the like. Cities, after all, often

lure people because of these grand or exciting attractions, as well as their economic potential. And, of course, the two dimensions of urban life are intimately connected. As E. B. White said of America's great metropolis, "No one should come to New York unless he is willing to be lucky" (White, 1949, p. 10).

In this sense, I would argue, those historians concerned with the cultural complexities of life in particular cities, rather than urban historians per se, provide an important model. Carl Schorske's work on Vienna and Basel shows a wide range of cultural and political figures – including architects like Otto Wagner and the amateur architectural historian Jacob Burckhardt – responding to the conditions of their particular cities, even as they experimented within separate professional spheres. (Schorske, 1980, 1989). Richard Goldthwaite's *The Building of Renaissance Florence* (1980) makes us appreciate the great palazzi more fully by explaining their significance in the local economy, their adaptation to changes in aristocratic family life, and their impact on neighborhoods and public space in the city. Jerrold Seigel's (1986) penetrating analysis of Parisian bohemia situates artists and writers within their culture, rather than mythically apart from it, yet never undermines creativity. John Merriman (1985), in turn, brings to life the working-class districts of Limoges, France's first socialist city, stressing the role of neighborhood institutions and the conflicts between tradition and modernity. And Thomas Bender's *New York Intellect* (1987) shows generations of intellectuals responding to the city's commerce and its ethnic diversity, creating new institutions of learning and neighborhoods of cultural vitality.

It is no wonder that cultural history has, in recent years, come to be perhaps the most innovative and exciting specialization in the discipline of history. Yet, while many cultural historians allude to the significance of place and formal symbolism, architecture and urban design still remain tangential to their explorations. This need not be the case.

Even in schools of architecture, urban history can show show major buildings and monuments affected the cities around them: creating distinctive styles and urban spaces, to be sure, and likewise signaling changes in the professional status of artists or the political power of a government or the economic structure of a district. We thereby juxtapose the many constituencies which affected urban design and city life at key moments of the past, even though the primary focus is on designers and their clients. Such an approach can encourage students, most of whom will go on to be architects, planners or preservationists to consider not only their own profession's history, but also how their predecessors' goals differed from their own. It comes quite often as a revelation to see that one's forebears, too, had to respond to the exigencies of the particular cities and societies where they worked. How did earlier architects and planners (an anachronism, of course, by which I mean all those involved in policy decisions) choose their references from the past? How did they respond to the pressures of clients and public groups? How did they affect cities, knowingly and unknowingly? What led them to expand their formal and social horizons to look at problems in new ways? The constraints of modern practice do not seem unduly limiting from such a perspective.

Urban history must, of course, encompass a repertoire of forms and spaces, just as architectural history must cover certain key monuments. But the field should involve techniques for analysis, rather than simply a *Sweet's Catalog* of great spaces one can replicate. Today's design professionals have to see history as more than a canon of precedents or a chronicle of progress. It is a complex and ongoing enterprise, always raising new questions and a multiplicity of alternative images about the past and the present.

All of us concerned with cities in the past and the present should take into account "ordinary" as well as "good" architecture, "boring" as well as grand spaces, "muddled" as well as elegant designs. Unplanned settings, rather than carefully planned urban design, make up most parts of most cities, so we must think how such areas work – whether the goal is understanding their

form in the past or intervening in the present. There is simply no way to do this without taking the cultural domain into account. For example, the significance of the grid varied considerably, as did its proportions and its focus, when it was used by Greek or Roman colonists, by Spanish imperialists, or by American surveyors. The Piazza San Marco and the Washington Mall have evolved over time, in part shaped by aesthetic concerns, in part to function as spaces for political ritual. Less stately settings as well – for example European Jewish ghettos, American commercial strips, or ethnic neighborhoods in any large city – should also be studied as cultural artifacts with both formal and social elements.

No Zeitgeist rule can describe how culture and aesthetics interrelate in all circumstances, not even for one time and place. Yet these two analytical poles are always at work together in urban history. In fact, even a "purely formal" solution, such as Cataneo's ideal towns of the Renaissance or L'Enfant's Washington, DC, suggests the unusual power and abstraction of architect and client in that time and place. And, once the space began to be used, the cultural realm of course further complicates our full understanding of the forms.

The urban historian must, therefore, show how certain kinds of buildings and spaces came to be built and to gain preeminence, while others remained thwarted projects or secret personal visions. This, not incidentally, entails considering which forms gained favor among architects and which – whether the same or different – appealed to more speculative builders and clients. For too long we have studied the history of what architects drew as if it were necessarily the history of how cities looked. We must also consider how the more familiar prototypes relate to less well-known variations or even antithetical images. After all, the influence of a form or style by no means simply filters down through the social structure, nor is it mere backwardness not to copy what is fashionable. Formal choices and cultural priorities were at stake when provincial cities like Boston or Edinburgh introduced variations on the patterns of London. Contemporary regionalism takes on new dimensions.

This approach does not mean that social considerations should usurp the role of formal analysis, but rather that the two must be integrated. Neither society norform is the passive mirror of the other – which should make us suspicious of overly simplistic, static notions of architecture either "reflecting" social forces or "representing" a fixed power relationship to all observers. Both architecture and society are formative, each helping shape the other, and nowhere is this more true than in any kind of urban building. There is no standard formula for connecting the two realms of inquiry; sometimes architecture does respond primarily to the aesthetic concerns of the profession, while society can move in new directions without generating architectural or urbanistic testaments to that change. The shifting influences and responses between these two kinds of reality, the formal and the social, is the very essence of urban history.

This analytic process obviously draws from several disciplines, and even several kinds of history: cultural, social, economic, political and intellectual, as well as architectural. Urban history should ideally juxtapose many perspectives about how cities function and what makes certain places effective, whether in formal, functional, or cultural terms. Only in this way is it possible to take account of the many different "filters" – to use Carlo Ginzburg's (1980) phrase – through which different groups of people see and use the city.

The challenge of doing urban history today lies in being able to conceive of one's work as a synthesis, not just of priorities and even disciplinary techniques, but also of experiences in and visions of a place. To speak of synthesis is not to call for a sweeping portrait of supposedly quintessential elements of urban life or form, but rather to find comprehensible ways to juxtapose the many different approaches to and realities of the city. I stress comprehensible because there is always the risk of simply reeling off facts, stories, and images. This profusion can obviously be overwhelming, and a chaos of

pictures, events, and data – while resonant with one definition of urban life – has little intellectual value.

The urban historian must therefore have a clear goal. In the most general terms, this first entails choosing whether one is seeking to explain the forms more clearly and fully, or to understand the society through this new prism. Michael Baxandall (1985), who provided one of the most compelling examples of cultural history in his work on Renaissance painting, rightly stresses that one must not simplistically attempt to fuse art and society. Yet culture, he continues, does not falsely modulate between the two, so long as it is taken in its classical sense, as the skills, values, knowledge, and means of expression within a society. It is in this sense that urban historians must venture into the cultural domain, seeking the meanings of a variety of forms and form-givers.

The goal of synthesis in urban history is, therefore, that of bringing together the myriad experiences, intentions, and settings of urban places at a given time – without producing a cacophony that is too loud to appreciate. In formal terms, one must consider both monuments and the spaces around them, the ordinary buildings and the pattern of streets and open space, the effect of this composite in the past and changes made over time. One must also distill the distinctive voices of architects and clients, of elite and ordinary citizens. Focusing on the particularities of such groups, and even possible conflicts between them, checks the tendency to subsume real differences under some rubric of a common or universal response to cities and their buildings. No single voice can predominate absolutely. The aesthetic and urbanistic strengths of Daniel Burnham's 1909 Chicago Plan deserve our appreciation, but the historical account must also acknowledge its benefits to the city's industrialists and the critiques of Jane Addams and other reformers who charged that he paid virtually no attention to Chicago's crowded immigrant neighborhoods.

These distinctions are critical for understanding how cities took the form they did and how people experienced them. Even architects and planners, builders and politicians cannot be lumped together as if they viewed the city in the same way because they all have the power to intervene. Most architects see a streetscape in terms of its individual buildings, while builders see it as a unit, based ultimately on the overall development potential, and planners see the same place as a map of legal codes – or social inequities. Other kinds of groups are even more wide-ranging in their reactions to the city. By class, ethnicity, age, and gender people relate quite differently to parks and department stores, for example, or to city halls and civic monuments. Moreover, especially in the modern world, all people experience the city in multiple roles – for example, as residents of a neighborhood, employees in a certain milieu, as members of a political faction or a religious sect. These shifting perspectives, too, affect how they use and relate to cities.

The recognition of such divergences is not merely a populist stance. Indeed, it suggests the necessary, if difficult, responsibility of the historian to explain not only what happened, but also what it meant at the time and what that legacy means to us today – in both our separate identities and our unity as a profession or a nation. It is no longer sufficient to posit a historical narrative that explains urban change – new styles, building types, technologies, and images for cities – by pointing only to the major figures who espoused these innovations. Neither architects nor political leaders can necessarily guarantee that certain innovations will come to be generally accepted, pervading all levels of a city and spreading beyond its boundaries.

For example, the simplification of housing design in the United States at the turn of the last century has by and large been explained as the effect of key architectural innovators, notably Frank Lloyd Wright. By focusing on Chicago, the city where Wright practiced during these years, it is possible to situate him more accurately. It is not that Wright's work did not impress other architects, even builders, carpenters, and the general public.

But they had very different reasons for promoting a turn toward simpler, more standardized dwellings. And the city itself was an embattled arena where each of these groups was trying to seize the right to define what good housing should be. Simply to describe the formal changes would miss the fascinating complexity of attitudes and conflicts which underlay how these architectural forms were seen, where they were built, and how they were used (Wright, 1980, 1988). Understanding what people were trying to do with architecture and urban design at particular moments in the past is one aspect of recovering the meanings of a place. One must take full account of the designer's aesthetic goals and the client's symbolic intentions, no matter what their status; one must bear in mind the constraints of laws, economy, tradition, and fashion, as well as searching for innovations. The various public responses to a design and the changes or compromises they elicit must be taken seriously in their own right, rather than dismissed as philistine efforts to undermine the integrity of the designer. Formal analysis in urban history should not be isolated from such cultural issues, but neither should it be downplayed as incidental. Only in this way can we grasp the full implications of urban places.

Urban history then is both an act of recovery and a creative gesture toward the future, a way to comprehend and build upon places and cultures over time. Architectural design becomes an element in a complex process that creates and transforms place; it is at once memory and vision, problem and resolution, individual and collective expression. The goal, in part, is to be able to orient ourselves – as architects and planners, historians and citizens – to the intricate webs of power and meaning that are thus elaborated, in the past and present, through architectural space. To write urban history is to give narrative form to this process; to design with history in mind is to acknowledge the multiple cultural uses and meanings places can have, in modern society as in the past.

REFERENCES

Baxandall, M. (1985) Art, society, and the Bouguer Principle. *Representations*, 12 (Fall), 32–43.

Bender, T. (1987) *New York Intellect: A History of Intellectual Life in New York City, from 1750 to the Beginnings of Our Own Time.* New York: Alfred A. Knopf.

Ginzburg, C. (1980) *The Cheese and the Worms: The Cosmos of a Sixteenth-century Miller*, trans. J. and A. Tedeschi. Baltimore: Johns Hopkins University Press.

Goldthwaite, R. (1980) *The Building of Renaissance Florence.* Baltimore: Johns Hopkins University Press.

Huizinga, J. (1924) *The Waning of the Middle Ages: A Study of the Forms of Life, Thought and Art in France and the Netherlands in the XIVth and XVth Centuries.* London: Edward Arnold.

Merriman, J. (1985) *The Red City: Limoges and the French Nineteenth Century.* New York: Oxford University Press.

Schorske, C. E. (1980) *Fin-de-siècle Vienna.* New York: Alfred A. Knopf.

Schorske, C. E. (1989) Science as vocation in Burckhardt's Basel. In T. Bender (ed.), *The University and the City from Medieval Origins to the Present.* New York: Oxford University Press.

Seigel, J. (1986) *Bohemian Paris: Culture, Politics, and the Boundaries of Bourgeois Life, 1830–1930.* New York: Viking/Elizabeth Sifton Books.

White, E. B. (1949) *Here Is New York.* New York: Harper & Brothers.

Wright, G. (1980) *Moralism and the Model Home: Domestic Architecture and Cultural Conflict in Chicago, 1873–1913.* Chicago: University of Chicago Press.

Wright, G. (1988) Architectural practice and social vision in Wright's early designs. In V. Scully (ed.), *Nature in the Work of Frank Lloyd Wright.* Chicago: University of Chicago Press.

14

The Urban Landscape

Sharon Zukin

Last night...more than 1,200 guests gathered to celebrate the opening of the Place des Antiquaires, New York's newest antiques center....Cecile Zhilka was the chairwoman of the evening, which benefited the Metropolitan Opera and was marked by the distinct accents of New York and Paris....."I just want to know where I am: in Paris, in New York, or in a new city floating in between them," said Ambassador de Margerie.

New York Times, November 19, 1987

We owe the clearest cultural map of structural change not to novelists or literary critics, but to architects and designers. Their products, their social roles as cultural producers, and the organization of consumption in which they intervene create shifting landscapes in the most material sense. As both objects of desire and structural forms, their work bridges space and time. It also directly mediates economic power by both conforming to and structuring norms of market-driven investment, production, and consumption.

A major result of this cultural mediation is now a blurring of distinctions between many categories of space and time that we experience every day: when the leisure of home life is invaded by well-designed machines, cities appear more alike, and Saturday traffic jams connected with shopping are worse than weekday morning rush hours. In general, spaces that used to stand alone – representing "pure" nature or culture in people's minds – now mix social and commercial functions, sponsors, and symbols. Times that were perceived as distinctive, because the social experience connected with them was either finite or lasted "forever," are now condensed and combined. Although David Harvey has tried to capture these experiences in terms of

a modern "time-space compression" that begins in the Enlightenment, intensifies around the time of World War I, and reaches extreme proportions in the current global economic reorganization, he leaves a lot about these unsettling experiences unsaid. An especially open question is how the visual economy of landscape mediates market culture.[1]

Here Victor Turner's concept of liminality again comes into play. Instead of social groups experiencing moments of liminality, however, the liminal experience of the market is broadened so that new urban spaces are formed, permeated, and defined by liminality. All such spaces stand "betwixt and between" institutions, especially the sacred sphere of culture and the secular world of commerce. Zones where business is transacted and public roles exchanged, liminal spaces institutionalize market culture in the landscape.

Heavily influenced by market norms, liminal spaces no longer offer an opportunity for the kind of creative destruction Turner describes. In the nonmarket and preindustrial situations that he observed, groups were rejuvenated and refreshed by liminality, and social values reaffirmed. Even in the late-nineteenth-century European cities Walter

Benjamin wrote about, urban spaces carried a potential that hesitated between conformity and utopia, a world of commodities or of dreams.[2] Today, urban places respond to market pressures, with public dreams defined by private development projects and public pleasures restricted to private entry. Liminality in the landscape thus resembles the creative destruction that Schumpeter described, reflecting an institutionalized reorientation of cultural patrons, producers, and consumers.

Creative destruction works both for and against architects and designers. They confront conditions in a new market culture quite similar to those that have challenged the autonomy of traditional manufacturers: abstraction of value from material products to images and symbols, global markets, and a shift in the major source of social meaning from production to consumption. Not only do they adapt to these changes, they tailor their products to them; they give visual form to Schumpeter's "perennial gale" of capitalist innovation.

Architects and the Landscape of Power

The two cultural products that most directly map the landscape are architecture and urban form. Because they shape both the city and our perception of it, they are material as well as symbolic. Like the rest of the built environment in a market economy, design and form relate to space in different ways: as a geographical (or topographical) constraint, as a terrain of potential conflict or cohesion, and as a commodity. They tend, therefore, toward constant change and rapid obsolescence. Without neglecting the enormous part played by architecture and urban form in the symbolic attachments of place, we must emphasize how much they are influenced by markets. What buildings and districts look like, who uses them, their diversity or homogeneity, how long they last before being torn down: these qualities reflect the spatial and temporal constraints of a market culture.[3]

While architects today work mainly under corporate patronage, urban planners, real estate developers, and city officials work within a matrix of state institutions and local preferences. Both are neither free nor unfree from market forces and the attachments of place. Although architects most often produce designs for an individual client rather than "on speculation," with the idea of offering them for sale, the business clients who are sources of most commissions impose market criteria by demanding more rentable space in less construction time. Increasingly, these clients are national and international investors (especially Canadian, British, and Japanese). There is thus a practical connection between architecture and urban forms and "multinational capitalism."[4]

New architecture and urban forms are, moreover, produced under nearly the same social conditions as consumer products. They increasingly follow similar patterns of both standardization and market differentiation. Variations are imposed by local real estate markets and the local built environment. Diversity is also encouraged by the incorporation of older urban forms for "sentimental" or aesthetic reasons, in the economic process that David Harvey (1989b) describes as "flexible accumulation" (cf. Logan and Molotch, 1989; Zukin, 1989). Regardless of these precious artifacts, it has become practically impossible to separate the perception of urban form from the effects of internationalized investment, production, and consumption.

After 1945, the process of suburbanization demanded centralized control over finance and construction even while it rapidly decentralized housing and shopping malls, with their anchor stores, controlled environment, and inner streets of shops, and destroyed the commercial viability of many central business districts.[5] From 1973, however, centralized, multinational investment supported both continued decentralization of commercial development and a reconcentration, with enhanced stratification, of urban shopping districts. The same products and ambiance came from multinational corporations in New York, France, Japan, and Italy. Within a few years, both products and ambiance could just as well be found in shops on upper Madison Avenue or Rodeo Drive as on the rue du faubourg St Honoré or the via Montenapoleone. When local merchants were displaced by the higher rents these tenants paid, they correctly blamed the showplace boutiques whose rents were subsidized by their parent multinational corporations. In a subtle recapitulation of earlier transformations, more international investment shifted shopping districts from craft (quiche) to mass (McDonald's or Benetton) production and consumption.[6]

McDonald's and Benetton epitomize the connections between international urban form and internationalized production and consumption. Their shops are ubiquitous in cities around the world, giving strength to the parent firms' strategy of international expansion. An executive at Benetton's US headquarters has even identified the two corporate strategies. "We consider ourselves the fast food in fashion," he says. "We want to be everywhere, like McDonald's" (Belkin, 1986). The companies do differ in the way they run their worldwide operations. While McDonald's sells traditional franchises to local operators, Benetton neither invests in nor collects franchise fees from Benetton stores. Instead, Benetton licenses the right to sell Benetton clothes in individually owned Benetton stores. Further, McDonald's managers buy their food supplies locally. Benetton managers must buy their entire inventory from Benetton.

Both chains maintain uniform standards by other corporate policies. These include rigorous training of store managers; insistence on adherence to company standards for quality and service, and, at Benetton, for decor and window display; and frequent on-site inspections by visitors from company headquarters. Despite the differences in the types of products that they sell, both Benetton and McDonald's owe their growth in part to organizational innovation. Much of their advance centers on production and distribution. McDonald's honed to a fine point the "robotized" operations of fast-food cuisine; Benetton developed cheaper methods for softening wool and dying colored garments,

as well as investing in computerized manufacturing and design and real robots for warehouse operations. In the process, both chains developed a total "look" that merges product, production methods, a specialized consumption experience, and an advertising style. As their "classic" mass-produced sweaters and burgers link consumers around the world, these multinational corporations become more significant players in each domestic economy. McDonald's voracious demand for beef inflicts damage up and down the food chain in cattle-raising countries of Latin America. By contrast, Benetton's new US factory in North Carolina provides (automated) employment to textile workers.[7]

Benetton and McDonald's are landmarks on many local scenes. Yet the social process that supports their production confirms the three structural shifts that we consider important: abstraction, internationalization, and the shift from production to consumption. Significantly, their profits reflect both production of basic goods – clothes and food – and less tangible economic factors of land rent, marketing, and the organization of distribution.

In contrast to the marketing of mass-produced consumer goods, the marketing of architecture has a higher profile. Even though individual buildings have become more standardized, their designers claim to offer their owners more distinction. Professional architects continue to theorize an underlying aesthetic or social program, especially the faux populism that adheres to many postmodern styles. This demotic urge facilitates architects' acceptability to corporate patrons. By means of architectural patronage, corporations gain public acceptance. New "user-friendly" architectural styles for corporate and regional headquarters distinguish the companies that adopt them from those that inhabit the glass boxes commercially adapted from modernism from the 1950s through the 1970s.[8]

Developers who sell office space are less intellectually constrained. "My buildings are a product," a building developer says. "They are products like Scotch Tape is a product, or

Saran Wrap. The packaging of that product is the first thing that people see. I am selling space and renting space and it has to be in a package that is attractive enough to be financially successful." As if to confirm Schumpeter's dour prediction about the decline of entrepreneurs, he adds, "I can't afford to build monuments because I am not an institution" (Drucker, 1987). The architectural critic Ada Louise Huxtable (1987) turns this comment around in her criticism of the monumentally sized, egregiously individualized new skyscrapers that are especially common in New York City. "In the last five years," she says, "a new kind of developer has been remaking the city with something called 'the signature building,' a postmodernist phenomenon that combines marketing and consumerism in a way that would have baffled Bernini but is thoroughly understood by the modern entrepreneur" (see also Forty, 1987).

Signature or "trophy" buildings link the cultural value of architecture with the economic value of land and buildings. This linkage has been propelled, in recent years, by the entry of new property investors, especially foreigners, and inflation in property values. The growth centers are in the bicoastal economy: New York City, Washington, DC, Boston, San Francisco, Los Angeles, which are also major sites of postmodern architecture. Trophy buildings have a dual value to corporate owners. These buildings are identifiable corporate images, and they are salable. As corporations restructure, reducing their work force, they sell their buildings to foreign investors. Thus Citicorp leased space in its slanted-roof headquarters, which cuts the Manhattan skyline, to Japanese investors, and moved a major part of its work force to a new building in Queens.[9]

An emphasis on individualized products that can be identified with individual cultural producers is inseparable from intensified market competition in an age of mass consumption. The "Egyptoid" character of postmodern skyscraper design was paralleled, in the 1920s, by the "Mayan" pyramids of speculative office buildings competing in a real estate boom (Stern et al., 1987). Similar competition among Hollywood film studios for audience loyalty to their products encouraged individual directors to make the "signature film."[10] In architecture, as labor costs have increased and craft skills have atrophied, the burden of social differentiation has passed to the use of expensive materials and the ingenuity of the design itself. And like Hollywood directors, architects assume and even become commercial properties. Philip Johnson is selected as the architect of AT&T's corporate headquarters or Kevin Roche is chosen by the boards of General Foods and the Metropolitan Museum of Art because these architects are already identifiable brand names. As Calvin Tomkins (1977) slyly remarks of Philip Johnson's market savvy, they have the potential to outlive their buildings.

Architects have always been chosen on the basis of both their names and their work. But recently there has been a heightening of both the subjective and objective use of individual architects. Choice of an architect legitimizes a building's sponsor, and offers that sponsor a competitive advantage. By the same token, as architectural design is more broadly diffused, it gains both economic and cultural value. Magazines have joined their coverage of fashion with surveys of new architecture and design; museums have established architecture departments; and architects' drawings have begun to sell at high prices as works of art. Interior design is similarly routinized as an element of both cultural literacy and social distinction. Under these conditions, a larger number of people may be impressed by architects' names than actually know their buildings.[11]

Saying that architects, especially postmodern architects, have adopted the rhetoric of stylistic differentiation because they are aesthetically dissatisfied with modernism tells only part of the story. They also face increasingly stiff competition for corporate commissions. Major architects maintain quasi-corporate offices like those of much larger major law firms. They thus depend on corporate clients to support their practices. There is no automatic correlation between an architectural career path and market differentiation. It has often been noted that Philip Johnson turned to postmodernism during the 1970s after an illustrious 40-year career as a prime exponent of modernism, and now varies his style for each project. After Michael Graves was roundly condemned by architectural colleagues in the early 1980s for turning to postmodernism, he began receiving highly visible corporate and public commissions. By the same token, the visibility of its idiosyncratic late modern building behind the opening credits of the television show "Miami Vice" helped establish the Miami firm Arquitectonica. The speculative real estate boom of the 1920s, like that of the 1980s, suggests that stylistic differentiation among architects supports their commerical expansion. By the 1920s, architects supervised much larger offices and crews than they had before. The costs of land acquisition and construction made them "become as much a part of Big Business as the engineer, the legal counsel and the financier" (Brock, 1931, quoted in Stern et al., 1987, p. 515; see also Kieran, 1987).

Paradoxically, as architecture and design have become more professionalized, with special educational requirements and licensing procedures restricting entry to the profession, their concerns converge with those of their patrons. On the one hand, architects and designers mingle socially with wealthy and famous elites. On the other hand, an emphasis on culture to enhance the commerical values of product and property markets incorporates architects and designers into the landscape of power.

As cities try to lure new capital investment, especially from the high end of business services, they refashion their commercial districts by commissioning new buildings and urban plans. Traditional downtowns were decimated by the flight and decline of industry, and the competition from new shopping centers in the suburbs. Seeking to restore – or create – a vernacular lustre, local interests hire "name" architects, whose reputations should minimize financial risk. Yet these architects work under a dual market constraint: that of their client and that of their firm, both of which demand a distinctive,

salable product. Consequently, architects place their own signature on the landscape, and repeat it wherever they are hired.

Superstar architects create a standardized form that they move from place to place. They also create buildings that look stupendous from a distance – on the city's skyline – but fail to fit in with local "context." This makes an architecture that is less risky for investors but also less evocative of a sense of place.[12] "Suddenly," a Boston architect complains about Fan Pier, a major new project on the waterfront, "the demand for the 'name' architect, often overcommitted elsewhere, has placed these architects and their products side by side." This threatens the historic waterfront with looking like that of any other city.[13] Because of their cultural commodities, superstar architects mediate the leveling of local and regional distinctions by transnational economic investment.

Superstars could be interpreted as a modern version of the Renaissance cult of genius. In the early fifteenth century, Brunelleschi designed palaces and public works for the aristocracies of Florence, Pisa, and Mantua, far surpassing the achievements of local architects. He became "so famous," Vasari (1965, p. 169) writes, "that those who needed to commission important buildings would send for him from great distances to provide his incomparable design and models; people would make use of friends or bring strong influences to bear to secure his services." But the rise of the superstar architect today reflects market competition. It indicates the desire by major corporations in the services to recoup value from long-term, large-scale investments in product development – their buildings. The superstar architect is produced by the same market conditions as the superstar rock group and TV anchor.[14]

From about 1880 to 1930, modern architecture was also spurred by real estate development that demanded constant innovation in the urban landscape. In 1905, when Henry James returned to New York, he deplored the destruction of the city that he knew. He blamed the imminent demise of Trinity Church – sold by its own wardens for real estate development – on "the universal will to move – to move, move, move, as an end in itself, an appetite at any price" (James, 1968, pp. 83–4). In this period, the average longevity of an office building in New York shrank to only twenty years. By the 1920s, production of commercial buildings depended on speculators whose financing got a project underway, architects who could "draw... an imposing picture of a skyscraper; if it is several stories higher than the Woolworth Tower, so much the better," and newspapers that eagerly published "pictures of high buildings, real or imagined, because... readers have a weakness for them" (builder William A. Starrett [1928], quoted in Stern et al., 1987, pp. 19, 513–14).[15]

Commerce and Culture

As in architecture, the visual image that designers create has been integrated into the landscape of power. The growth of a service economy extracts design from the system of material production and makes it a symbol of the power of ideas. Because design can be responsible for a product's success, designers have also become superstars. They are valued for their ability to connect commerce and culture.[16] When the French interior designer Andrée Putman attracted an audience of about a thousand people at the annual meeting of the Los Angeles furniture design industry in 1987, she spoke about the extraordinary recent growth of the design industry. "I don't think 15 years ago it would have been possible to talk to so many people," she said. "There's a kind of fascination and passion internationally for new ideas, and a strange hunger for signatures. Designers are gurus of today, an overly respected animal" (quoted in Giovannini, 1987). They are also public figures and media celebrities. When the French *haute couture* fashion designer Christian Lacroix appeared at a New York clothing store to introduce his first "mass-market" ready-to-wear collection, he was mobbed by shoppers asking for his autograph (Schiro, 1988).

The new cultural value of designers to some degree reflects the general upward reevaluation of the economic significance of high-level services. Historically, however, the role of design in architecture began to overshadow construction as early as the seventeenth century (Zerner, 1977, p. 158). In the early twentieth century, architects from Le Corbusier to Frank Lloyd Wright designed furniture and objects to further their building designs. Only recently, however, has the architect's talent for design been appropriated by a large number of commercial commissions in other fields. Architects are now prominent in marketing small consumer goods, including birdhouses, wrist watches, coffee pots, and dinner plates. The increase in architect-designed furniture, moreover, represents a burgeoning market. The "authentic" reproduction of work by early twentieth-century designers has even benefited Andrée Putman, who manufactures and distributes the work of Eileen Gray.[17]

The most commercially successful architects are the most sought after designers of consumer goods. But this spiral of success constrains architectural designers to meet more market criteria. The risk of mixing bad aesthetic and commercial judgment is suggested by the forced retirement of the fashion designer Halston, who "lost his name" when he lost a franchise to sell fashion to the masses at J. C. Penney. On the other hand, the value of a "name" designer reflects the acumen of his or her business partner at least as much as the quality of design (Anon., 1987; Gross, 1987; Colacello, 1987).[18]

Interior, furniture, and fashion designers have also gained value through department store promotions. Introducing a new product, stores will often identify and commercialize an entire "genre" of design, so that the promotion creates a new linkage between designers, mass consumers, and wealthy patrons of high culture. At the high end, as Debora Silverman (1986) observes so well, a department store like Bloomingdale's conceives a promotion around imported goods that are designed in New York, mass produced overseas in low-wage plants, and exhibited in a central place in the flagship store as though in a museum. In fact, the promotions that Bloomingdale's organized at the beginning of the 1980s, at the time of Ronald Reagan's first presidential election, were scheduled to coordinate with thematic exhibitions at the Costume Institute of the Metropolitan Museum of Art. Bloomingdale's and the Met thus shared an interest in the cultural consumption of antique Chinese robes and current Chinese imports, French *haute couture* as designed by Yves Saint Laurent, and equestrian costume as marketed by Ralph Lauren. Silverman (1986, p. 11) believes that the revaluation of "aristocratic" taste promoted by both department store and museum promoted the wealthy elites that supported conservative president Ronald Reagan, "a consumerist power elite" (see also Ferretti, 1985; McGuigan, 1986). But the mix of patronage to include both the rich and the famous and department store customers, framed by high culture institutions and commercial establishments, indicates a much broader value of design. Design links the mass public and private elites in a visual organization of consumption.

Department stores have always used design to market the products they sell. But since the 1980s, the competitive need for product differentiation has fostered a reliance on design to shape the whole space of consumption. Department stores have undergone multiple reconfigurations into theme or designer boutiques; lavishly orchestrated promotions celebrate a design motif extracted from history, current films, and regions of the world. Once the emphasis shifted from product to design, social patrons of both fashion and the arts found department stores a receptive context for their special events. The department store sponsors charity galas, receptions for nonprofit cultural institutions, and promotions of work for sale by designers – all in one event, for the same people. By lowering the barriers between commerce and culture, and private patronage and mass consumption, the department store creates a liminal urban space.

Beyond a single store's four walls, new waterfront shopping centers expand a zone of liminality downtown based on visual consumption. Usually built on disused piers in older cities with declining ports, they present shopping as a means of enjoying urban culture. This type of project includes the redevelopment of Boston's Faneuil Hall, Baltimore's Inner Harbor, and South Street Seaport in New York City, all of which used historic preservation laws to subsidize commerical construction. From the 1970s to 1987, federal tax laws supported historic preservation by making it financially advantageous for investors to reuse old urban forms for commercial revitalization. Changes in the tax code in 1986 reduced these advantages and made them more relevant to smaller invetors. Aesthetically, however, historic preservation often mobilizes support for the commercial redevelopment of downtown for consumption uses among those groups that previously opposed urban renewal, highway construction, and large-scale demolition. The principled refusal to destroy old urban forms contrasts with the use of modern architecture, in the 1950s and 1960s, to assert the commercial district's viability. In those years, developers and city governments replaced historic low-rent structures with standardized, "internationalized" office buildings. In a changed sentimental climate after 1965, this high-rise construction suggested alienation. Smaller scale, respect for context, and mixed uses of space were proposed as a way of restoring a visual sense of place.

Shopping centers have replaced political meetings and civic gatherings as arenas of public life. Despite private ownership and service to paying customers, they are perceived as a fairly democratic form of development. Moreover, they are believed to "open" the downtown by creating a sense of place. Downtown developers derive a theme from former economic uses – the harbor, the marketplace, the factory – and offer consumers the opportunity to combine shopping with touristic voyeurism into the city's past. The ambiance of authenticity is important to establish the critical mass of shoppers vital to retail competition. In some downtowns, where a high density of business services creates demand, even an artificial sense of place enhances consumption. In other cities, however, the downtown is still too tied to industrial uses to encourage the liminality of a consumption space.

In the process of revitalizing the waterfront, old piers and Main Streets were turned into emporia of mass consumption. Beneath the image of locality these places project, they are really marketplaces for goods that are not locally produced. "Gourmet foods" and croissant shops were at least initially imported, and the chains of retail clothing stores that fill these urban shopping centers sell mainly imported apparel. Tourist items are nearly always made outside the country. Even products like Samuel Adams beer, which is associated with Boston, and Vermont butter are either produced out of state (the beer in Pittsburgh) or with out-of-state materials (milk for the butter from dairies outside Vermont). Projects like Faneuil Hall are, moreover, developed by national firms and financed by New York money center banks. Like the high-class shopping street, these shopping centers unify international investment, production, and consumption.[19]

Private Consumption and Public Space

The museum, department store, and waterfront shopping center create liminality by opening public space to private consumption. A more provocative example of this liminality is the State of Illinois Center, designed in 1986 by the architect Helmut Jahn. In a variety of large buildings that he previously designed for both the private and the public sectors, Jahn eclectically used architectural elements from every period – the so-called historical references of postmodernism. But the new state office building in Chicago merits attention less for style than for the way it uses space. Under its atrium/rotunda, the eighteen-story public building surmounts a three-level shopping center, with public-access spaces interspersed among the stores. This combination of public and private uses has struck critics as *submerging* public place to private markets. It takes to an extreme the liminality between

public and private urban spaces that began in the nineteenth century.

From the 1880s on, the increasing use of new mechanical inventions for transportation and telecommunications forged hybrid public – private cultural forms. Telephones provided men and women with both accessibility and distraction. Newspapers achieved mass circulation as means of both intimacy and information. Railroads bridged the scale of the journey and arrival in the city with the liminal transparent tunnels of great railroad stations built of iron and glass (Kern, 1983; Schievelbusch, 1979). From this time, urban form has increasingly been defined by the public use of private space. In contrast to the decline of public space for civil society, this sense of place has grown together with means of market consumption.

Social life in modern cities often depends on expanding once exclusive means of market consumption to a broader public. From the 1860s on, coffee houses, tea rooms, and restaurants, which sometimes began as a refuge for middle-class teetotalers, became general places for meeting and entertainment. Department stores, which began as shopping havens for unescorted women, expanded into general bazaars. And hotels, striking "the note of the supremely gregarious state" that Henry James (1968, pp. 102–6) found so typical of America, began as marketplaces of sociability for a wealthy upper class (Thorne, 1980; Barth, 1980; Williams, 1982; Benson, 1986).

James's observations on the grand hotel – the milling crowd, the ladies buzzing with tea-time conversation, the shops providing a cornucopia of rare imported goods, the whole unlike anything seen in Europe – foreshadow Fredric Jameson's description of the Los Angeles Bonaventure, one of the atrium-hotels built by the architect-developer John Portman during the 1970s. Like James, Jameson is struck by the coherence and "publicity" of the hotel's interior world. Unlike James, however, Jameson calls it postmodern that "the *Bonaventura* [sic] as pires to being a total space, a complete world, a kind of miniature city, ... [to which, moreover, there] corresponds a new collective practice, the practice of a new and historically original kind of hyper-crowd." For Jameson, Portman's selection of architectural elements marks the creative destruction of modernism's monumental, although readily comprehensible, scale. Ironically, Jameson neglects to compare the naturally lighted, abnormally high interior central space of Portman's hotels to the architecture of late-nineteenth-century department stores like the Bon Marché (1876). In his view, Portman's atrium expands volume beyond human capacity to experience it; the elevators and escalators extend and accelerate, but also confine, human movement beyond "that older promenade we are no longer allowed to conduct on our own" (Jameson, 1984, pp. 81, 82).

Yet Henry James had already sensed in "the universal Waldorf-Astoria" the entrapment of "the great collective, plastic public" by "the great glittering, costly caravansery." No less than Jameson in the atrium, James sees (1968, pp. 440–1) "the whole housed populace move as in mild and consenting suspicion of its captured and governed state, its having to consent in inordinate fusion as the price of what it seemed pleased to regard as inordinate luxury."

There is a direct line of visual consumption from Henry James at the Waldorf Astoria in New York in 1905 to Fredric Jameson at the Los Angeles Bonaventure. But the public use of private space *inside* the hotel only symbolizes change in the surrounding city. Urban form has been especially vulnerable in recent years to an asymmetry of power favoring the private sector. Since the 1970s, because of the withdrawal of federal funding and the aftermath of local "fiscal crisis," city governments have become more dependent on pleasing private investors, including holders of municipal bonds, property developers, and directors of large banks and corporations. In a small number of cities – New York, Cleveland, Yonkers – nonelected committees drawn from the leadership of large financial institutions have exercised veto power over the city budget since 1975. (Cleveland's Financial Planning and Supervisory Commission was eliminated in 1987; New York City's Municipal Assistance Corporation has assumed new responsibilities for financing, and demanded reorganization of, the transportation and education systems.) Even when new mayors come into office with populist bases or the support of ethnic and racial minorities, as in Chicago and Denver, the city administration's public works are coordinated with private developers (See Judd, 1986; Bennett, 1986; Hartman, 1984).

Constrained both institutionally and ideologically, cities face "a shrinking of the realm of the possible and a shrinking of the realm of the public, simultaneously" (Henig, 1986, p. 243). The material landscape created by the joint efforts of speculative developers, elected officials, financial institutions, and architectural designers responds to these conditions by merging public places and private markets, often under the management of a quasi-public urban development corporation. Significant public life moves inside from the streets.

Following Schumpeter, creative destruction in the economy changes the nature of demand and fosters the deployment and differentiation of capital along new lines. Architectural design and urban form suggest that creative destruction in culture is a similarly directed process. The primacy of visual consumption in the twentieth century fosters the social production of image-makers, whose imagination is ruled by the economic value of both public and private display. The social context of cultural patronage, production, and consumption reduces producers' autonomy from both patrons and consumers. It also drives the transformation of previously bounded institutions – department stores, museums, hotels – into disorienting liminal spaces for both market and nonmarket cultural consumption.

For these reasons, it is impossible for the art museum to be "the domain in which to express the moral brake on conspicuous consumption"; the museum truly "becomes the extension of the department store and another display case for the big business of illusion making" (Silverman, 1986, p. 19) – but it does so for its own "cultural" goals.

While these processes enhance the role of culture in social differentiation, they also equalize perceptions of cultural production "for the market" and "for art." This is the conundrum of postmodern culture.

By the same token, the urban landscape gives both material and symbolic form to the opposition between *market* and *place*. The market's constant pressure to reproduce variety contradicts the constant pressure on place to reproduce stability. While most people really want to enjoy the pleasures of fine buildings, good stores, and beautiful urban spaces, the processes that create them make the city more abstract, more dependent on international capital flows, and more responsive to the organization of consumption than the organization of production.

NOTES

1 See Harvey (1989a, pp. 210–307). Harvey's apparent willingness to incorporate culture into Marxist analysis brings to a head the question of *how* to integrate aesthetics and political economy, culture and capital.
2 In Victor Turner's view, liminality does not exist outside of preindustrial, and certainly precapitalist, society, where social categories are stable. Men and women in an advanced market economy may *choose* a sort of political, professional, or artistic liminality, or marginality; this Turner calls a *liminoid* state. On Walter Benjamin, see Buck-Morss (1989).
3 See Clark (1985, chapter 1), Harvey (1985), Gottdiener (1985), and Logan and Molotch (1987). On the other hand, Herbert Gans (e.g. 1984) argues strenuously against economic reductionism in attempts to explain socio-spatial structures.
4 See Jameson (1984); these issues are less schematically rendered in Logan and Moloch (1987).
5 See Kowinski (1985). "Only financial institutions were in a position to understand the implications of suburbanization, even partially, and to coordinate and plan, however imperfectly," write Mintz and Schwartz (1985, p. 43).

6 "According to fashion experts, Italian companies have consolidated their design, textile and production resources in Milan over the past decade, and though each Italian boutique may be relatively small, it is part of a much larger organization operating on a world scale," writes Giovannini (1986); see also Meislin (1987).
7 Benetton recently expanded by diversifying into financial services, building on its network of outlets – but this basis has turned out to be problematic. On Benetton's history, see Lee (1986) and "Why Some Shopkeepers Are Losing Their Shirts," *Business Week*, March 14, 1988; on McDonald's, see "McWorld?" *Business Week*, October 13, 1986, and Skinner (1985).
8 The extreme "populist" statements are Venturi (1977) and Venturi et al. (1977). On the search for corporate distinction by means of architecture, see Kieran (1987).
9 Besides the Japanese, major foreign investors in trophy buildings include British, Dutch and West German pension funds ("Real estate trophy hunt," *New York Times*, August 23, 1987). Citicorp in *Business Week*, April 3, 1989; General Foods building in *New York Times*, August 19, 1987.
10 Just as Ada Louise Huxtable recognizes the developer's role in producing the signature building, so major film producers, and specific studios, are recognized as much as directors for having created signature films of the 1930s and 1940s. In the 1950s and 1960s, the attempt by noncommercial critics to theorize the director's role and/or deemphasize the commercialism of Hollywood production led to writing about the director as the film's *auteur*.
11 See McGill (1987), and any issue from 1988 of such fashion magazines as *Vogue* and *Elle*. Despite the commercial success of such accounts of architectural history as Rybcynski (1986) and Wolfe (1981), however, there may still be an apparent abysmal ignorance about architectural facts ("Cultural blindspot," *Progressive Architecture*, July 1987, p. 7).
12 "What we hadn't foreseen [in redeveloping downtown San Francisco] was that

there would be a tendency to seek out national firms, and not to take any risk with architecture," the city's director of planning says (*New York Times*, December 5, 1987). See also Goldenberg (1989).

13 The architect continues: "The identity of Boston, Back Bay, and Newbury Street does not reside in the overscaled developer-driven buildings by superstars. We are very guarded (very Yankee) in Boston. We are concerned by what superstars have built here . . . by what is being built . . . and the commitments the all-stars have made for parallel design time for projects in other cities and countries. We are wary of additional watered down, trendy, inflated 'Boston' buildings that will never really become Bostonian" (Marsh, 1987). In general, however, city planning agencies in Boston (and San Francisco) have reacted more strongly than in other cities against speculative overbuilding.

14 "They say that at CBS the most prized assets are the highly celebrated, hard-to-replace television personalities responsible for the network's news coverage" (Cowan, 1987). "'The superstar is the giant bonanza,' said Al Teller, the president of CBS Records. 'The big hit is to develop superstar careers. That is the biggest win you can have'" (Fabrikant, 1987). Conversely, as profits have fallen, many Wall Street financial firms have eliminated their superstars, or highest revenue-producers, and restored power to traditional managers ("The decline of the superstar," *Business Week*, 17 August, 90–8.

15 Andrew Saint (1983, p. 84) suggests that the constant cycles of rebuilding initiated in Chicago from the 1870s by business cycles and by fire resulted in an aggressive construction industry and a commercially oriented group of architects who, "a French observer said, 'brazenly accepted the conditions imposed by the speculator'." American-style market competition among architects could be expected to shock a visitor from France, where commissions were mainly sewed up by a civil service–Ecole des Beaux Arts network.

16 The Japanese language, for example, has imported *deezainah* without attempting to translate it, along with such terms as "advertising copywriter" and "project coordinator," which have no indigenous equivalent (*Business Week*, 13 July 1987, p. 51). Industrial designers become more important when competition among manufacturers turns from sheer cost to product quality – a point much appreciated in current US – Japanese competition (*Business Week*, 11 April 1988, pp. 102–17).

17 Compare Ewen (1988). The posthumous transfer from design sketch or prototype to mass market product reaches ludicrous extremes, as reported in Giovannini (1988).

18 At lower levels of the design professions, however, employees may chafe at the limits on their professional autonomy (see Slavin, 1983).

19 Money center banks guaranteed $20 million in long-term loans and $10 million in short-term loans for Faneuil Hall before construction began, but the loans were all made contingent on a $3 million participation by Boston financial institutions (*Fortune*, 10 April 1978, cited in Mintz and Schwartz, 1985, p. 61). For a discussion of historic preservation as both an aesthetic paradigm and a redevelopment strategy, see Zukin (1989, pp. 75–8).

REFERENCES

Barth, G. (1980) *City People: The Rise of Modern Culture in Nineteenth-century America*. New York: Oxford University Press.

Belkin, L. (1986) Benetton's cluster strategy. *New York Times*, January 16.

Bennett, L. (1986) Beyond urban renewal: Chicago's North Loop redevelopment project. *Urban Affairs Quarterly*, 22, 242–60.

Benson, S. P. (1986) *Counter Culture: Saleswomen, Managers and Customers in American Department Stores, 1890–1940*. Urbana: University of Illinois Press.

Brock, H. I. (1931) From flat roofs to towers and slats. *New York Times Magazine*, 19 April, 6–7, 16.

Buck-Morss, S. (1989) *The Dialectics of Seeing: Walter Benjamin and the Arcades Project*. Cambridge, MA: MIT Press.

Clark, T. J. (1985) *The Painting of Modern Life*. New York: Knopf.

Colacello, B. (1987) The power of Pierre. *Vanity Fair*, September.

Cowan, A. L. (1987) Tisch is holding a hot potato. *New York Times*, 14 March.

Drucker, R. (1987) Speaking at a seminar in Boston, Was Postmodernism the Heir to the Preservation Movement? What Will Come Next?, quoted in Preservation and postmodernism: a common cause? (editorial). *Architectural Record*, June, 9.

Ewen, S. (1988) *All Consuming Images: The Politics of Style in Contemporary Culture*. New York: Basic Books.

Fabrikant, G. (1987) A long and winding road: band's quest for stardom. *New York Times*, 31 July.

Ferretti, F. (1985) "The LA spirit" makes a splash in Brooklyn. *New York Times*, 19 April.

Forty, A. (1987) *Objects of Desire: Design and Society from Wedgwood to IBM*. New York: Pantheon Books.

Gans, H. (1984) American urban theory and urban areas. In I. Szelenyi (ed.), *Cities in Recession*. Beverly Hills, CA: Sage, pp. 278–307.

Giovannini, J. (1986) The "new" Madison Avenue: a European street of fashion. *New York Times*, June 26.

Giovannini, J. (1987) Westweek, star-studded Los Angeles design event. *New York Times*, 2 April.

Giovannini, J. (1988) Marketing Frank Lloyd Wright. *New York Times*, 24 March.

Goldberger, P. (1989) Architecture view: a short skyscraper with a tall assignment. *New York Times*, 26 March.

Gottdiener, M. (1985) *The Social Production of Urban Space*. Austin: University of Texas Press.

Gross, M. (1987) In search of the perfect angel. *New York Times*, 30 August.

Hartman, C. (1984) *The Transformation of San Francisco*. Totowa, NJ: Rowman & Allenheld.

Harvey, D. (1985) *Consciousness and the Urban Experience*. Baltimore: Johns Hopkins University Press.

Harvey, D. (1989a) *The Condition of Postmodernity*. Oxford: Blackwell.

Harvey, D. (1989b) Flexible accumulation through urbanization: reflections on "postmodernism" in the American city. In *The Urban Experience*. Oxford: Blackwell.

Henig, J. R. (1986) Collective responses to the urban crisis: ideology and mobilization. In M. Gottdiener (ed.), *Cities in Stress: A New Look at the Urban Crisis, Urban Affairs Annual Reviews*, 30.

Huxtable, A. L. (1987) Creeping gigantism in Manhattan. *New York Times*, 22 March.

James, H. (1968) *The American Scene*. Bloomington: Indiana University Press (first published 1907).

Jameson, F. (1984) Postmodernism, or the cultural logic of late capitalism. *New Left Review*, no. 146, 53–93.

Judd, D. R. (1986) Electoral coalitions, minority mayors, and the contradictions in the municipal policy agenda. In M. Gottdiener (ed.), *Cities in Stress: A New Look at the Urban Crisis, Urban Affairs Annual Reviews*, 30.

Kern, S. (1983) *The Culture of Time and Space, 1880–1918*. Cambridge, MA: Harvard University Press.

Kieran, S. (1987) The architecture of plenty: theory and design in the marketing age. *Harvard Architecture Review*, 6, 103–13.

Kowinski, W. S. (1985) *The Malling of America*. New York: William Morrow.

Lee, A. (1986) Profiles: being everywhere (Luciano Benetton). *New Yorker*, November 10.

Logan, J. R. and Molotch, H. (1987) *Urban Fortunes: The Political Economy of Place*. Berkeley and Los Angeles: University of California Press.

Marsh, G. E. Jr (1987) Letters. *Architectural Review*, May, 4.

McGill, D. C. (1987) Taking a close look at the art of post-modernist architects. *New York Times*, 31 August.
McGuigan, C. (1986) The avant-garde courts corporations. *New York Times Magazine*, 2 November.
Meislin, R. J. (1987) Quiche gets the boot on Columbus Avenue. *New York Times*, July 25.
Mintz, B. and Schwartz, M. (1985) *The Power Structure of American Business*. Chicago: University of Chicago Press.
Rybcynski, W. (1986) *Home: A Short History of an Idea*. New York: Viking.
Saint, A. (1983) *The Image of the Architect*. New Haven, CT: Yale University Press.
Schievelbusch, W. (1979) *The Railway Journey*, trans. A. Hollo. New York: Urizen.
Schiro, A.-M. (1988) Lacroix: meteor or constant star? *New York Times*, 22 April.
Silverman, D. (1986) *Selling Culture: Bloomingdale's, Diana Vreeland, and the New Aristocracy of Taste in Reagan's America*. New York: Pantheon Books.
Skinner, J. K. (1985) Big Mac and the tropical forests. *Monthly Review*, 37(7), 25–32.
Slavin, M. (1983) Interiors business: jobs are not what they used to be. *Interiors*, September, 130–1.
Stern, R. A. M. et al. (1987) *New York 1930: Architecture and Urbanism between the Two World Wars*. New York: Rizzoli.
Thorne, R. (1980) Places of refreshment in the nineteenth-century city. In A. D. King (ed.), *Buildings and Society*. London: Routledge & Kegan Paul, pp. 228–53.
Tomkins, C. (1977) Forms under light. *New Yorker*, 23 May, 43–80.
Vasari, G. (1965) *Lives of the Artists*. London: Penguin (first published 1550, 1568).
Venturi, R. (1977) *Complexity and Contradiction in Architecture*, rev. edn. New York: Museum of Modern Art.
Venturi, R. et al. (1977) *Learning from Las Vegas*, rev. edn. Cambridge, MA: MIT Press.
Williams, R. H. (1982) *Dream Worlds: Mass Consumption in Late Nineteenth-century France*. Berkeley and Los Angeles: University of California Press.
Wolfe, T. (1981) *From Bauhaus to Our House*. New York: Farrar, Straus & Giroux.
Zerner, C. W. (1977) The new professionalism in the Renaissance. In S. Kostof (ed.), *The Architect*. New York: Oxford University Press.
Zukin, S. (1989) Postscript: more market forces. In *Loft Living: Culture and Capital in Urban Change*, 2nd edn. New Brunswick, NJ: Rutgers University Press.

Part VI
Gender

15

Sexuality and Urban Space: A Framework for Analysis

Lawrence Knopp

Cities and sexualities both shape and are shaped by the dynamics of human social life. They reflect the ways in which social life is organised, the ways in which it is represented, perceived and understood, and the ways in which various groups cope with and react to these conditions. The gender-based spatial divisions of labour characteristic of many cities, for example, both shape and are shaped by people's sexual lives (especially in Western[1] industrial societies). For example, heterosexuality is still often promoted as nothing less than the glue holding these spatial divisions of labour (and, indeed, Western society) together. But on the other hand, these divisions of labour create single-sex environments in which homosexuality has the space, potentially, to flourish (Knopp, 1992).

The density and cultural complexity of cities, meanwhile, has led to frequent portrayals of sexual diversity and freedom as peculiarly urban phenomena. As a result, minority sexual subcultures, and the communities and social movements sometimes associated with these, have tended to be more institutionally developed in cities than elsewhere.[2] On the other hand, the concentration of these movements and subcultures in urban space has made it easier to both demonise and control them (and to sanctify majority cultures and spaces). Hence the portrayal of gentrified gay neighbourhoods such as San Francisco's Castro district as centres of hedonism and self-indulgence, of other gay entertainment areas (such as San Fran-

cisco's South-of-Market) as dangerous sadomasochistic underworlds, of red-light districts as threatening to "family values", of "non-white" neighbourhoods as centres of rape,[3] or, alternatively, of suburbs as places of blissful monogamous (and patriarchal) heterosexuality.

These contradictions, and many others, are reflected in the spatial structures and sexual codings of cities, as well as in individual and collective experiences of urban life.... There remains within the discipline of geography a certain "squeamishness" about exploring these connections (see also McNee, 1984). This persists in spite of a relative explosion of work in other disciplines which concerns itself with relationships between sexuality and space, including discussions of urbanism (Wilson, 1991; Grosz, 1992; Bech, 1993; Duyves, 1992), nationalism (Mosse, 1985; Parker et al., 1992), colonialism (Lake, 1994); and architecture/design (Wigley, 1992; Ingram, 1993).

The small amount of work which *has* been done in this area has tended to reflect the particular concerns and social milieux of those doing it. This has meant a focus on urban gay male and lesbian identities and communities (Levine, 1979; Ketteringham, 1979, 1983; McNee, 1984; Castells and Murphy, 1982; Castells, 1983; Lauria and Knopp, 1985; Adler and Brenner, 1992; Valentine, 1993; Rothenberg and Almgren, 1992; Rothenberg, 1995). Much less attention has been paid to heterosexualities, bisexualities, sexualities organised around practices that may be only contingently related to gender (e.g. sadomasochism and certain fetishes), and (particularly problematically) radical, self-consciously fluid sexualities which reject association with such notions as "identity" and "community" altogether (but see Bell, 1995; Binnie, 1992, 1993). Also neglected have been connections between particular sexualities and spaces in small-town and rural environments, those between sexualities, space and other social relations (such as race – but see Rose, 1993, pp. 125–7 and Elder, 1995), and issues surrounding sexuality and the spatial dynamics of particular social systems (e.g. feudalism, patriarchal capitalism, etc. (but see Knopp, 1992)).

This chapter addresses some of these gaps. In particular, I develop and illustrate a framework for examining the relationships between certain sexualities and certain aspects of urbanisation in the contemporary West. In so doing, however, I implicitly treat "sexualities", as well as "the urban" and "the West", as if they were self-evident and unproblematic empirical "facts". This deflects attention from the diversity within these categories, from their often constricting and oppressive effects, and from the complex social processes and power relations which produce them in the first place. However, because people often relate to such categories as if they were self-evident and unproblematic empirical facts, they have a social power which is every bit as significant as that of many more so-called "material" concerns (e.g. jobs, families, pensions, etc.). This recognition of the problematic yet powerful nature of the categories "sexuality" and "urban" guides the analysis which follows.

Urbanism and Sexualities

Traditional approaches to understanding urbanism can usefully be divided into materialist, idealist and humanist (Saunders, 1986). To oversimplify a bit: materialists see the dynamics of the material production and reproduction of human life as shaping cities;

idealists see the interplays between great ideas as doing this (especially the philosophies and decisions of policy-makers); and humanists see cities more as a kind of subjective experience, to which people ascribe meanings. In the 1970s and 1980s, many analysts noticed that in the contemporary world few if any of the material, political or even cultural processes discussed by these three camps are peculiar to definable geographical units that could be called cities (Saunders, 1986; Paris, 1983). On the basis of this some concluded that "the problem of space...can and must be severed from the concern with specific social processes" (Saunders, 1986, p. 278).[4]

But at about the same time more general social theorists were reaffirming geographers' traditional claim that both space and place matter profoundly in human social life (Giddens, 1979; Thrift, 1983; Sayer, 1989; Lefebvre, 1991; Gottdiener, 1985). Their arguments drew particularly strongly on a humanist insistence that the experience of *place* is socially very powerful. Now most urbanists, regardless of their philosophical perspective, tend to acknowledge this. Many materialists (including many Marxists), for example, now see the "image" and "experience" of the city as important material stakes in the urbanisation process (e.g. Harvey, 1989, 1993; Logan and Molotch, 1987; Cox and Mair, 1988). Urban images and experiences are now seen as manipulated, struggled over and reformulated in ways which are every bit as important to the accumulation (or loss) of social power by different groups as more traditionally material concerns (e.g. control of the production process).

The city and the social processes constituting it are most usefully thought of, therefore, as social products in which material forces, the power of ideas and the human desire to ascribe meaning are inseparable. The same holds true for various sub-areas within the city. I will demonstrate how this approach can be applied shortly, in the context of a discussion of the evolution of contemporary Western cities. Firstly, however, I will identify some particular sexualities which tend to be associated with cities, and particular areas within them, in Western societies.

One of the more detailed general descriptions of Western cities' sexuality, developed from a humanist perspective, is Henning Bech's (1993).[5] Drawing on Lofland (1973), he describes the modern Western city as a "world of strangers", a particular "life-space", with "a logic [and sexuality] of its own". The city's sexuality is described as an eroticisation of many of the characteristic experiences of modern urban life: anonymity, voyeurism, exhibitionism, consumption, authority (and challenges to it), tactility, motion, danger, power, navigation and restlessness.[6] This kind of sexuality, Bech argues, is "only possible within the city", because it depends upon the "large, dense and permanent cluster of heterogeneous human beings in circulation" which is the modern city. It is modern medicine and psychoanalysis, meanwhile, that Bech credits with sexualising these particular experiences. For ironically, both have, in the process of trying to make sense of modern sexualities, actually contributed to their constitutions, particularly by sexualising objects and surfaces (especially body parts). This, in turn, has been part of modern science's more general response to the anxieties precipitated by changes in various social relations (especially gender relations) in the nineteenth and twentieth centuries. Thus the city, as a world of strangers in which people relate to each other as objects and surfaces, becomes an archetypal space of modern sexuality.

There are numerous problems with this formulation.[7] But it is nevertheless quite useful, for Bech describes in detail particular ways in which at least some parts of urban areas have been sexualised in modern Western societies. He also offers the beginnings of an explanation for these. His general description, if not his explanation, would appear in many ways to be fair (although it probably applies more to continental European than Anglo-American and other English-speaking cities).[8] There are other descriptions and explanations as well, however. Elizabeth Wilson (1991), for example, sees densely populated urban spaces as potentially liberating and empowering for women. For this reason such spaces are often associated ideologically with women's sexualities, which are in turn constructed ideologically as irrational, uncontrollable and dangerous. Thus the control of "disorder" in the city is seen by Wilson as very much about the control of women, and particularly women's sexualities. My own work, and that of several others, has emphasised the homosexualisation of gentrified areas in cities by both dominant interests and gays (mostly white middle-class men) seeking economic and political power as well as sexual freedom (Lauria and Knopp, 1985; Knopp, 1987, 1990a; Castells and Murphy, 1982; Castells, 1983; Ketteringham, 1979, 1983; Winters, 1979). A few others have discussed the coding of these (and other) spaces as lesbian or heterosexually female (Rose, 1984; Adler and Brenner, 1992; Bondi, 1992; Rothenberg, 1995). Mattias Duyves (1992), Jon Binnie (1992, 1993), David Bell (1995), Peter Keogh (1992) and Garry Wotherspoon (1991), meanwhile, have emphasised the alternative codings of certain public spaces by gay men for specifically sexual purposes (e.g. cottaging, cruising, etc.). And Davis (1991, 1992), Geltmaker (1992), and I (Knopp, 1992) have emphasised the contested nature of predominantly heterosexually coded urban spaces, such as shopping malls, sports bars and suburbs.

The sexual codings of cities, spaces within cities and the populations associated with them, then, are varied and complex. A few generalisations do seem possible, however: (1) Many of contemporary societies' conflicts and contradictions find expression in these codings; (2) these codings emphasise both erotic and more functional conceptions of sexuality, depending upon the particular areas and populations involved; (3) areas and populations which represent failures of or challenges to aspects of the dominant order (e.g. slums; gentrified areas) tend to be coded in both dominant and alternative cultures as erotic (i.e. as both dangerous and potentially liberatory), while those seen as less problematic tend either to be desexualised or to stress more functional approaches to sexuality; (4) these codings are connected to power relations; and (5) they are (in this latter respect) fiercely contested.

Bech's sociological interpretation of the role of psychoanalysis, and Wilson's of urban design and planning, suggest one link between these sexualisations and power relations: changes in gender relations. Bech argues that modern medicine and psychoanalysis responded to anxieties associated with nineteenth- and twentieth-century revolutions in gender relations by projecting them onto infantile cognitive processes and object-relations, including those through which people develop gender and sexual identities. These then became associated with what Bech sees as a very objectified urban experience. People experience the city, he argues, as well as the other people in it, as objects and surfaces in rapid, dense and impersonal circulation, not primarily as people. In a similar vein, Wilson argues that the architects of modern cities projected anxieties about gender relations onto the maps and infrastructures of cities. Certain areas became feminised and demonised, and infrastructures designed, to facilitate the containment and control of women. These are both useful perspectives but they need to be further developed and linked to other changes in social relations (e.g. industrialisation, suburbanisation, racial segregation) going on at the same time.

Harvey's (1992) and my own recent work (Knopp, 1992) suggest what some of these further links may be, but in a more contemporary context. We have both emphasised connections between culture (and in my case, sexuality) and class interests, in the sense that cultural (and sexual) codings may now be important elements of a city's or neighbourhood's image and experience. These have in turn become central to facilitating capital accumulation and the reproduction of class relations. Glen Elder (1995) highlights the importance of race-based power relations, by focusing on the sexual practices and imaginings that are and are not possible under different racialised political and economic regimes in South Africa. And it must also be emphasised that very real

sexual interests are at stake here, in that those who benefit from certain codings are those whose particular sexual practices and preferences are privileged in those codings. But rather than developing each of these separately I wish now to develop and illustrate a more integrated approach which sees the links between these processes as all-important. For I want to stress that the various sexual codings associated with cities are sites of *multiple* struggles and contradictions, and as such are instrumental in producing, reproducing and transforming both social relations of various kinds (including sexual relations), and space itself.

Contradictions and Struggle: The Sexual and Spatial Dynamics of Urbanisation

In contemporary Western cities, power is still quite closely associated with the production and consumption of commodities, and with white, non-working-class, heterosexually identified men. It is appropriated and exercised, however, through mechanisms in which people who are oppressed in one respect (e.g. as working-class or "non-white") may benefit from oppression in other ways (e.g. as men). These complex and contradictory patterns have been produced, reproduced and contested in the spatial structures of Western societies. These include importantly the built environments, spatial consciousness and lived experiences of cities.

To understand this process, it is useful to consider the nineteenth-century industrial context from which most contemporary Western cities evolved. In the nineteenth century, cities were typically rigidly segregated by class, race and ethnicity, characterised by very traditional gender-based spatial divisions of labour, dominantly coded as heterosexual, and imagined and experienced in terms of public and private spheres of existence.[9] The designs of neighbourhoods, homes, workplaces, commercial and leisure spaces all reflected this. They both presumed and reproduced, among other things, a heterosexualised exchange of physical, emotional and material values in the home, and a racial hierarchy in which white families and societies enjoyed most fully the benefits of a social wage paid for, in part, by transfers of value from non-whites (both inside and outside Western societies) to whites.

The contradictions in this arrangement were numerous. One very important one was a tension between the fixed nature of many aspects of the city's spatial structure (including the social and sexual structures of place-based communities) and the tendency of competition among different factions of privileged classes to produce new and more economically productive spatial structures before the investments in the old ones had been fully amortised (Harvey, 1985).[10] Another, closely linked to this, was the tension between a reliance on particular class, race, gender and sexual structures and the tendency of these structures to create new, potentially disruptive collective and personal consciousnesses. Bech's psychoanalytic interpretation of modern sexualities' fetishising of surfaces, anonymity, etc., can be seen as a particular manifestation of this latter contradiction. But the collective anxiety which he attributes specifically to changes in gender relations can be seen as arising more generally from the sharp distinction between public and private experience which characterised the nineteenth- and early twentieth-century industrial city. The growing consciousness of a "private" sphere of existence facilitated the development of a wide range of new subjectivities and rising expectations of both individual and collective fulfilment and growth (Zaretsky, 1976). This meant that people could explore identities and communities based on the possibility of non-conformist and non-commodified roles and practices. But these opportunities at the same time undermined nineteenth- and early twentieth-century cities' gender-based divisions of labour. They also varied according to people's gender, race, class and sexual locations, as wealth and power continued to concentrate in fewer and fewer hands. Significant contradictions were therefore present in the urbanisation process.

The experience of "public" life in the city was no less contradictory. Many previously non-commodified public experiences (much theatre and sport, for example) were produced and consumed in commodity form, especially by men. Ironically this was a means for these people to develop their "personal" identities and "individual" potentials. But, as I have said, the demand for new experiences included many that were potentially disruptive. As sexual experiences in particular became increasingly dissected, categorised and commodified (e.g. in the ways Bech describes), the possibility of new (but socially disruptive) sexual experiences being profitably produced also increased. The proliferation of commodified homosexual experience, for example, led to a homosexual *consciousness* among some people, and this was very threatening to the heterosexualised gender relations underlying the industrial city.

But these various experiences and contradictions also varied depending upon people's social and spatial locations. White middle-class women and men, for example, were in many respects most likely to experience private life as an opportunity for individual fulfilment through the consumption of experiences and commodities within and outside the home. The white, middle-class and (in the case of gay politics and identities) male biases in much twentieth-century feminism and homosexual consciousness almost certainly reflect this. Working-class white women, on the other hand, were more likely to experience private life as an unwaged world of work and consumption with limited autonomy enjoyed at those times of day when men were away working for wages. The alternative sexual possibilities in this circumstance were, therefore, somewhat more constrained (though still present, since such women often found themselves developing co-operative networks with other women). For working-class non-white women, meanwhile, private life was often experienced still differently, as a balancing act between unwaged and waged domestic and non-domestic labour. The alternative sexual possibilities here were in some ways most constrained of all, although in others they might have been quite substantial (e.g. in the spaces they occupied with other non-white women while engaging in waged labour outside the home). For men of all classes and colours, meanwhile, private life tended (though to varying degrees) to be experienced as the exercise of authority and consumption of values in the home, as well as the consumption of commodified experiences outside the home. Consequently the freedom to explore alternative sexualities was perhaps greater for most men, in general, than for most women (although virulently homophobic and heterosexist ideologies emerged in response to this freedom and penetrated the cultures of many male-coded spaces and experiences).

One result of all this was complex race, class and gender-stratified social movements and everyday struggles organised around sexuality. Waves of "homophile" and, later, gay and lesbian activism dot the histories of late nineteenth- and twentieth-century Western societies (Steakley, 1975; Weeks, 1977; Altman, 1982; D'Emilio, 1983; Katz, 1976; Duberman *et al.*, 1989). Most have been particularly well developed in cities. But these were structured by cross-cutting and complex internal struggles as well. The various cultural codings of urban space reflect *all* of these struggles, as do various waves of social and political reform and economic restructuring.

Initially, the interests and social power of capital, white people, men and heterosexuals can be seen as having converged in such a way as to combat these and other social movements and struggles by coding all non-middle-class, non-white, non-male and non-heterosexual spaces and experiences in cities as in some way sexually depraved and uncontrollable (though in different ways). The social problems associated with nineteenth-century working-class communities (poverty, disease, etc.), for example, frequently were (and continue to be) blamed on the alleged sexual irresponsibility of their residents (Kearns and Withers, 1991). Similarly, areas defined as "black" in Western cities have often also been perceived as sexually dangerous (especially to white women), and this is associated with both black men's and black women's alleged uncontrollable sexualities. Women and

women's spaces, meanwhile, have often been presumed by their very existence to be inviting sexual assaults. And homosexual people and spaces have been associated with all manner of depravity and disease, not the least of which, in the contemporary era, is AIDS. In a recent controversy surrounding an alleged "gay conspiracy to pervert justice" in Scotland, for example, gay spaces such as bars were constantly portrayed as depraved and disgusting by the tabloid press (Knopp, 1994).[11]

But even these codings have from the beginning been contested in ways which reflect struggles internal to these various groups, as well as changes in class relations and other political and economic conditions. In the recent Scottish case, some gays may actually have exploited cultural fears surrounding homosexuality to advance their own personal interests or to retaliate against other gays whom they saw as privileged hypocrites (Campbell, 1993a, b). More commonly, relatively privileged sexual non-conformists (e.g. white gay men) have forged networks and institutions which facilitate the practice of their particular sexualities *as well as* the perpetuation of other structures of oppression. The intersection of these networks and institutions with recent industrial and occupational restructurings (the expansion of mid-level managerial, other white-collar and certain service-sector jobs, whose cultural milieux are socially tolerant) have developed into the material bases of the largely urban-based, predominantly white, and male-dominated gay social and political movements (Lauria and Knopp, 1985). These movements have taken their own alternative codings of space "out of the closet" and into the public sphere, but usually within racist, sexist and pro-capitalist discourses (for an example in which these are discussed see Knopp, 1990b[12]). They have influenced a wide range of predominantly heterosexually coded realms such as neighbourhoods, schools, government bureaucracies, courts, private firms, shopping areas, parks and suburbs. Their most obvious impact has been the proliferation of visible (but disproportionately white, male and middle-class) lesbian and gay commercial, residential and leisure spaces. Vibrant gay commercial and entertainment scenes, for example, as well as the "pink economies" of cities such as Amsterdam, London, San Francisco and Sydney, and much gay gentrification, have attracted a great deal of popular media attention over the last decade (see Binnie, 1995). But these scenes have been developed primarily by and for white middle-class male markets, and have been financed by "progressive" (often gay) capital eager to colonise new realms of experience and to undermine potential threats to its power (Knopp, 1990a, b).

Conclusion: Power, Space and Difference

The analysis above illustrates one way in which a conception of urban spaces as social products, in which material forces, the power of ideas and the human desire to ascribe meaning are inseparable, can be applied. Along the way, it highlights the contingency, yet tremendous importance, of the connections between particular forms of race, class, gender and sexual relations in the urbanisation process. As the various contradictions within particular social systems begin to destabilise those systems, the various interests at stake scramble to form new alliances and "new regimes of accumulation" (Harvey, 1985) which enhance their power. The sexual interests of otherwise highly stratified minority sexual subcultures are no exception.

But "power" in this context is an extremely slippery concept. It would seem fundamentally to be about the capacity to produce, reproduce and appropriate human life, and the socially-defined values associated with it, in a way consistent with one's own interests. It would also seem to be about the exercise of control over these processes. Power is realised, therefore, through social relations.

Social relations, meanwhile, would appear always to be organised around some kinds of difference. And while difference is a fundamental feature of human experience, it has no fixed form or essence. What constitutes it,

ultimately, is different *experiences*. To make these mutually intelligible and socially productive (as well as destructive!), we associate our different experiences with particular markers and construct *these* as the essences of our difference. These markers may be practices, they may be objects (such as features of our bodies), or they may be abstract symbols and language. Because human beings exist in space, these differences and the social relations which they constitute (and through which they are also reconstituted) are also inherently spatial. The relations of sexuality are no exception.

But power is a strangely contradictory thing. It seems always to contain the seeds of its own subversion. As difference is constructed (spatially) to facilitate the accumulation of power, that (spatialised) difference is also empowered. This is true in even the most asymmetrical of power relations. It is manifest in the seemingly endless parade of struggles and social movements organised around difference as difference itself proliferates, and in their spatial manifestations as well.

In a world, then, in which spatiality and sexuality are fundamental experiences, and in which sexuality, race, class and gender have been constructed as significant axes of difference, it should come as no surprise that struggles organised around these differences feature prominently in a process like urbanisation. Their contingent interconnections, their resistance to reduction (one to the other) and their spatial dynamism are testaments to the restlessness, contingency and spatial instability of power itself. As long as human beings continue to exist in space, and as long as our bodies and experiences encompass difference as well as sameness, this contradictory situation will continue.

NOTES

1 By "Western" I mean strongly associated, materially and ideologically, with Western economic, social, political, cultural and intellectual conditions and traditions. I acknowledge the extremely problematic nature of this term (its erasure of the roles

of non-Europeans in making "European" traditions, for example), but defend its use here as a way simply of suggesting some of the historical and geographical contingencies of my argument. See my discussion in the second section on "strategic essentialism".

2   This is not always true, however. Lesbian cultures and communities in the US, for example, are sometimes more closely associated with areas not seen as particularly "urban" (Beyer, 1992; Grebinoski, 1993).

3   I do not mean to suggest here that "non-white" cultures constitute sexual subcultures, that rape is a sexuality, or that rape's association with certain "non-white" people (i.e. black men) is anything but ideological. At the same time, I would argue that to its perpetrators rape is a sexualisation of male social dominance, and that white cultures in the West code black men in particular as potential rapists.

4   In almost the same breath, however, he acknowledges that "all social processes occur within a spatial and temporal context" (p. 278).

5   Actually Bech does not explicitly specify his description as "Western". But he does describe it as "modern", which he in turn defines (implicitly) as Western.

6   Against the charge that what he describes is profoundly "masculinist" (meaning male-oriented and oppressive to women), Bech invokes the argument of some feminists, including Elizabeth Wilson (1991), that such an objection desexualises women and denies them power, leaving them in need of (male) protection and control.

7   Among these is the fact that Bech attempts (albeit with appropriate caveats) to bracket off power relations from his analysis (except, interestingly, in his most gender-based sociological interpretation of the role of psychoanalysis in the production of urban sexuality). But in addition, his claim that the city as a life-space has a "logic of its own" is at best an overstatement. Whatever the "logic" of the urban "life-space", it is unlikely that it is completely disconnected from the (non-city-specific) hierarchically organised social relations which constitute it, or other relations of power which

emerge in the context of it. Bech's own acknowledgement that public space is "restricted and perhaps becoming even more restricted by the interventions of commercial or political agents" (p. 6) would seem to bear this out. Along these same lines, the claim that the sexuality he describes is "only possible in the city" is clearly a tautology, since he defines it in terms of the city in the first place. In fact, all of the sexual experiences he describes can and do take place outside cities as well. Admittedly, many of them usually require a good deal more effort to make things happen outside cities (e.g. anonymous encounters), but this does not link them *necessarily* to such environments. Anonymity, voyeurism, tactility, motion, etc. are all human experiences that can be, and arguably have been, sexualised and desexualised in a variety of places and fashions (and for a variety of reasons), throughout history. Thus they bear no *necessary* relationship to the city. The issue is not, therefore, whether or not a particular sexuality (or sexualities) attaches *necessarily* to the city, but rather how and why urban space has been sexualised in the particular ways that it has.

8   In the American case in particular, the process of nation-building through private profit-oriented land-development (and the associated contradictory ideologies of frontier individualism and utopian communitarianism) has led to a sexualisation of the city which is (arguably) less romantic, less erotic and more masculine than in continental Europe.

9   I wish to emphasise that this distinction between public and private is one which is profoundly ideological, but which functions as one of those powerful essentialisms (Fuss, 1989) which has profound material consequences.

10 See Knopp (1992) for a fuller presentation of this aspect of my argument.

11 One headline read "Two Judges Visited Gay Disco – But One Stormed Out in Disgust!" (*Daily Record*, Edinburgh, 1990).

12 Unfortunately, I privileged class enormously in that particular piece.

REFERENCES

Adler, S. and Brenner, J. (1992) Gender and space: lesbians and gay men in the city. *International Journal of Urban and Regional Research*, 16, 24–34.

Altman, D. (1982) *The Homosexualization of America, the Americanization of the Homosexual.* Boston: Beacon Press.

Bech, H. (1993) Citysex: representing lust in public. Paper presented at Geographies of Desire Conference, Netherlands' Universities Institute for Co-ordination of Research in Social Sciences, Amsterdam.

Bech, H. (1995) Pleasure and danger: the paradoxical spaces of sexual citizenship. *Political Geography.*

Bell, D. (1995) Perverse dynamics, sexual citizenship and the transformation of intimacy. In D. Bell and G. Valentine (eds), *Mapping Desire: Geographies of Sexualities.* London and New York: Rouledge.

Beyer, J. (1992) Sexual minorities and geography. Paper presented at 27th International Geographical Congress, Washington, DC.

Binnie, J. (1992) Fucking among the ruins: postmodern sex in postindustrial places. Paper presented at Sexuality and Space Network Conference on Lesbian and Gay Geographies, University College London.

Binnie, J. (1993) Invisible cities/hidden geographies: sexuality and the city. Paper presented at Social Policy and the City Conference, University of Liverpool, July.

Binnie, J. (1995) Trading places: consumption, sexuality and the production of queer space. In D. Bell and G. Valentine (eds), *Mapping Desire: Geographies of Sexualities.* London and New York: Rouledge.

Bondi, L. (1992) Sexing the city. Paper presented at annual meeting of the Association of American Geographers, San Diego.

Campbell, D. (1993a) Gay myths, criminal realities (part 1). *Gay Scotland*, 71, 9–10, 20.

Campbell, D. (1993a) Gay myths, criminal realities (part 2). *Gay Scotland*, 72, 9–10, 12, 25.

Castells, M. (1983) *The City and the Grassroots.* Berkeley: University of California Press.

Castells, M. and Murphy, K. (1982) Cultural identity and urban structure: the spatial organization of San Francisco's gay community. In N. Fainstein and S. Fainstein (eds), *Urban Policy under Capitalism.* Beverly Hills, CA: Sage.

Cox, K. and Mair, A. (1988) Locality and community in the politics of local economic development. *Annals of the Association of American Geographers*, 78, 307–25.

Davis, T. (1991) "Success" and the gay community: reconceptualizations of space and urban social movements. Paper presented at the First Annual Graduate Student Conference on Lesbian and Gay Studies, Milwaukee.

Davis, T. (1992) Where should we go from here? Towards an understanding of gay and lesbian communities. Paper presented at the 27th International Geographical Congress, Washington, DC, August.

D'Emilio, J. (1983) *Sexual Politics, Sexual Communities: The Making of a Homosexual Minority in the United States, 1940–1970.* Chicago: University of Chicago Press.

Duberman, M., Vicinus, M. and Chauncey, G. (1989) *Hidden from History: Reclaiming the Gay and Lesbian Past.* New York: NAL Books.

Duyves, M. (1992) The inner-city of Amsterdam: gay show-place of Europe? Paper presented at Forum on Sexuality Conference, Sexual Cultures in Europe, Amsterdam, June.

Elder, G. (1995) Of moffies, kaffirs and perverts: male homosexuality and the discourse of moral order in the apartheid state. In D. Bell and G. Valentine (eds), *Mapping Desire: Geographies of Sexualities.* London and New York: Rouledge.

Geltmaker, T. (1992) The queer nation acts up: health care, politics, and sexual diversity in the country of Angels. *Environment and Planning D: Society and Space*, 10, 609–50.

Giddens, A. (1979) *Central Problems in Social Theory.* Berkeley: University of California Press.

Gottdiener, M. (1985) *The Social Production of Urban Space*. Austin: University of Texas Press.

Grebinoski, J. (1993) Out north: gays and lesbians in the Duluth, Minnesota–Superior, Wisconsin area. Paper presented at annual meeting of the Association of American Geographers, Atlanta, April.

Grosz, E. (1992) Bodies-cities. In B. Colomina (ed.), *Sexuality and Space*. New York: Princeton Architectural Press.

Harvey, D. (1989) *The Condition of Postmodernity*. Baltimore: Johns Hopkins University Press.

Harvey, D. (1992) Social Justice, postmodernism and the city. *International Journal of Urban and Regional Research*, 16, 588–601.

Harvey, D. (1993) From space to place and back again: reflections on the condition of postmodernity. In J. Bird, B. Curtis, T. Putnam, G. Robertson and L. Tickner (eds), *Mapping the Futures: Local Cultures, Global Change*. London: Routledge.

Ingram, G. (1993) Queers in space: towards a theory of landscape, gender and sexual orientation. Paper presented at Queer Sites Conference, University of Toronto.

Katz, J. (1976) *Gay American History*. New York: Thomas Crowell.

Kearns, G. and Withers, C. (1991) *Urbanising Britain*. Cambridge: Cambridge University Press.

Keogh, P. (1992) Public sex: spaces, acts, identities. Paper presented at Lesbian and Gay Geographies Conference, University College London.

Ketteringham, W. (1979) Gay public space and the urban landscape: a preliminary assessment. Paper presented at annual meeting of the Association of American Geographers.

Knopp, L. (1978) Social theory, social movements and public policy: recent accomplishments of the gay and lesbian movements in Minneapolis, Minnesota. *International Journal of Urban and Regional Research*, 11, 243–61.

Knopp, L. (1990a) Some theoretical implications of gay involvement in an urban land market. *Political Geography Quarterly*, 9, 337–52.

Knopp, L. (1990b) Exploiting the rent-gap: the theoretical significance of using illegal appraisal scemes to encourage gentrification in New Orleans. *Urban Geography*, 11, 48–64.

Knopp, L. (1992) Sexuality and the spatial dynamics of capitalism. *Environment and Planning D: Society and Space*, 10, 651–69.

Knopp, L. (1994) Rings, circles and perverted justice: gay judges and moral panic in contemporary Scotland. Paper presented at annual meeting of the Association of American Geographers, San Francisco, April.

Lake, M. (1994) Between old world "barbarism" and stone age "primitivism": the double difference of the white Australian feminist. In N. Greive and A. Burns (eds), *Feminist Questions for the Nineties*. Oxford: Oxford University Press.

Lauria, M. and Knopp, L. (1985) Toward an analysis of the role of gay communities in the urban renaissance. *Urban Geography*, 6, 152–69.

Lefebvre, H. (1991) *The Production of Space*. Oxford: Blackwell.

Levine, M. (1979) Gay ghetto. *Journal of Homosexuality*, 4, 363–77.

Lofland, L. (1973) *A World of Strangers*. New York: Basic Books.

Logan, J. and Molotch, H. (1987) *Urban Fortunes: The Political Economy of Place*. Berkeley: University of California Press.

McNee, B. (1984) If you are squeamish... *East Lakes Geographer*, 19, 16–27.

Mosse, G. (1985) *Nationalism and Sexuality*. New York: Fertig.

Paris, C. (1983) The myth of urban politics. *Environment and Planning D: Society and Space*, 1, 89–108.

Parker, A., Russo, M., Sommer, D. and Yaeger, P. (eds) (1992) *Nationalisms and Sexualities*. New York: Routledge.

Rose, D. (1984) Rethinking gentrification: beyond the uneven development of Marxist urban theory. *Environment and Planning D: Society and Space*, 1, 47–74.

Rose, G. (1993) *Feminism and Geography: The Limits to Geographical Knowledge*. Cambridge: Polity Press.

Rothenberg, T. (1995) "And she told two friends": lesbians creating urban social space. In D. Bell and G. Valentine (eds), *Mapping Desire: Geographies of Sexualities*. London and New York: Rouledge.

Rothenberg, T. and Almgren, H. (1992) Social politics of space and place in New York City's lesbian and gay communities. Paper presented at 27th International Geographical Congress, Washington, DC.

Saunders, P. (1986) *Social Theory and the Urban Question*. London: Hutchinson.

Sayer, A. (1989) The "new" regional geography and problems of narrative. *Environment and Planning D: Society and Space*, 7, 253–76.

Steakley, J. (1975) *The Homosexual Emancipation Movement in Germany*. New York: Arno.

Thrift, N. (1983) On the determination of social action in space and time. *Environment and Planning D: Society and Space*, 1, 23–57.

Valentine, G. (1993) Deperately seeking Susan: a geography of lesbian friendships. *Area*, 25, 109–16.

Weeks, J. (1977) *Coming Out: Homosexual Politics in Britain from the Nineteenth Century to the Present*. London: Quartet.

Wigley, M. (1992) Untitled: the housing of gender. In B. Colomina (ed.), *Sexuality and Space*. Princeton, NJ: Princeton Architectural Press.

Wilson, E. (1991) *The Sphinx in the City*. London: Virago.

Winters, C. (1979) The social identity of evolving neighborhoods. *Landscape*, 23, 8–14.

Wotherspoon, G. (1991) *City of the Plain*. Sydney: Hale and Iremonger.

Zaretsky, E. (1976) *Capitalism, the Family and Personal Life*. New York: HarperColophon.

16

Gender Symbols and Urban Landscapes

Liz Bondi

Introduction

Cities, towns and many elements within them are persistent features of social organization. So too are gender divisions. Yet both also have considerable fluidity. Urban environments are everchanging and so too, in different ways, are our ideas and experiences of femininity and masculinity. This article is prompted by an apparent interplay between changing gender identities and changing urban landscapes. More specifically, I am interested in whether it is possible to "read" the urban landscape for statements about, and constructions of, femininity and masculinity, and, if so, what versions of femininity and masculinity are being articulated in contemporary forms of urban change. I take gentrification as a key example of such change, both because of its high visibility within many western cities, and because of suggestions that it is, at least in part, an expression of changing gender divisions (Smith, 1987; Rose, 1989; Warde; 1991, Bondi, 1991). In so doing I seek to extend feminist analyses of urban change by considering the material significance of cultural symbols.

I shall return to the issue of "reading" the landscape shortly, but first note that the opposition between femininity and masculinity is one of the most pervasive yet unexamined dualisms in social thinking. As unexamined discourse it entails complex and subtle shifts between different points of reference, especially between sociological categories, which refer to women and men

as socially differentiated groups, and symbolic categories, which refer to cultural representations or codings of Woman and Man (cf. Moore, 1988; Poovey, 1988). Sayer (1989) has counselled against the use of sets of parallel dichotomies, arguing that "reality" rarely conforms to such straightforward oppositions. In a similar manner I want to argue that an adequate analysis of the relationship between gender divisions and urban change must disentangle symbolic and sociological aspects of gender, rather than assume direct correspondence. In addition, I want to explore the links between gender politics and gentrification with reference to both postmodern architectural style and a broader postmodern culture. In this context I suggest that attempts to unharness symbolic and sociological aspects of gender have important, and not necessarily progressive, political implications.

To develop this argument I begin by examining the use of gender categories in appraisals of architectural forms, and show how both professional and lay versions of this symbolic treatment of gender imply and endorse an essentialist, biological interpretation of gender difference that is challenged by feminists. However, moving on to a discussion of feminist interpretations of the built environment, I argue that a preoccupation with the social content of the lives of women and men has sometimes resulted in a reverse move whereby gender symbolism is reduced to the unproblematic expression of patriarchal interests. Finally, I argue that images of femininity and masculinity associated with gentrification should be interpreted as a re-presentation rather than a transformation of hierarchical gender relations.

Gender Codings in the Built Environment

Architectural meanings

While "[m]eaning in the environment is inescapable" (Jencks, 1980, p. 8), the validity of different approaches to interpreting the built environment is disputed. Semiotics has generated considerable interest as a framework of analysis: the notion of sign systems acknowledges both the existence of nonverbal modes of communication (Rapoport, 1982), and the likenesses between language and other sign systems (Preziosi, 1979; Broadbent et al., 1980; Gottdiener and Lagopoulus, 1986). Linguistic analogies are, however, contentious. For some, "linguistic and architectonic formations dovetail, complement and supplement each other" (Preziosi, 1979, p. 89). For others, attempts to apply analytic concepts from structural linguistics to the interpretation of built forms are deeply flawed, because "[a]rchitecture contains no sentences; buildings do not combine their parts to make predicative or relational assertions" (Kolb, 1990, p. 108, referring to Scruton, 1979). But, as Rustin (1985) points out, terms such as "vocabulary" and "language" persist in the writing of critics of linguistic analogies and are symptomatic of an inevitable interconnectedness between modes of communication. And, while formal grammatical rules for combining words into sentences may have no counterpart in architecture, buildings can more reasonably be compared to texts, which depend upon the operation of more flexible and open-ended conventions and practices (Kolb, 1990, pp. 108–9). Viewed as texts, built environments are open to varied interpretations and it is in this context that I am concerned with possible "readings" (cf. Duncan and Duncan, 1988).

Semiotic approaches have also been criticized for a preoccupation with the internal lexicon of architectural design at the expense of the social context within which the production and consumption of architecture takes place (Dickens, 1980; Duncan, 1987; Knox, 1987). Thus, while Preziosi (1979) and Eco (1980a,b), for example, make ample reference to "context", the former resorts to a highly overgeneralized, evolutionary conception of human society, while the latter acknowledges cultural variations in the meaning of built forms but leaves these more as "disturbance terms" than as an integral part of his analysis. In contrast, I am concerned with what Dickens (1980, p. 356) describes as "an examination of largely shared systems of general beliefs which are partially created and sustained by design", and in this section I examine "general beliefs" about gender difference that are associated with the built environment.

Gender codings

Although there may be no "master language" capable of cataloguing all possible architectural forms (Kolb, 1990, pp. 109–12), there remain dominant themes and notable silences in interpretations of the built environment. In academic writing on architecture, gender is rarely mentioned, but when it is the assumptions at work suggest that a notion of "natural" and oppositional difference is prevalent. Jencks's (1978) discussion of architectural styles provides a useful example. He describes and relates major styles in terms of three apparently uncontentious dichotomies, one of which is a gender dichotomy (see Figure 16.1). He suggests that masculinity is recognized in what is large, solid and powerful, and in what is linear and vertical. Baroque architecture provides a good example of the former, and of the Paris Opera Theatre, Jencks (1978, p. 70) comments, "everywhere statues take up operatic poses, flexing their muscles – even the women look intimidating". Conversely, the slender, the delicate and

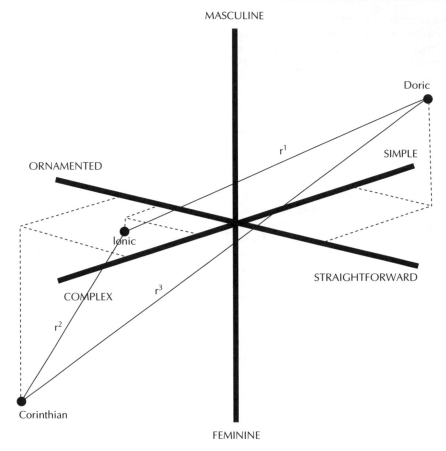

Figure 16.1   Describing architectural styles (Jencks, 1978, p. 73).

above all the curved is coded as feminine, Jencks's (p. 73) description of the domes of the Royal Pavilion, Brighton as "faintly mammarian" illustrating the physical analogy at work. Within this framework, particular styles may be open to more than one interpretation. For example, the Corinthian column is characterized as feminine when the emphasis is on its slenderness, and masculine when the emphasis is on its linearity, especially if also signifying status and power. A single example may be ambiguous: in its combination of slenderness and verticality Toronto's CN tower combines masculine and feminine connotations.

Columns, of course, carry many other connotations (see Eco, 1980b). In some instances these are themselves laden with gender references: for example, as sacred symbols, columns connect heaven and earth, and in this unity are sometimes interpreted as expressing a complementarity between "masculine" and "feminine" principles (Eliade, 1959). But what all these gender references have in common is a reliance upon crude and essentially biological definitions of what is masculine and what is feminine. While appraisals of architectural style may change, the gender codings continue to be set up as opposites, and, in the appeal to supposedly "natural" contrasts between the bodies of women and men, gender difference is presented as unchanging and universal. In this way, these codings reflect and reinforce an ideology in which the social relations of gender are presented as rooted in a socially pristine biological, or "natural" difference (Connell, 1987;

Brittan, 1989). As a consequence of this hierarchical ordering of the social and the biological, these interpretations are insensitive to the interplay between class, status, ethnicity and gender. For example, baroque architecture carries resonances of overblown displays of wealth, of corruption, and of power on the brink of collapse. Masculinity is not a separate, external reference working alongside this but rather a particular version of masculinity is bound up inside it.

Architectural meanings are not confined to the codings used by the professionals, and geographers have increasingly concerned themselves with how urban landscapes express the interests and ideologies of clients, sponsors and consumers (see for example, Harvey, 1987; Ley, 1987; Cosgrove and Daniels, 1988; Mills, 1988; Domosh, 1989). These studies too remain largely silent about gender as a facet of human experience or as a symbolic construct. But popular imagery is replete with gender references. For example, among many other connotations, skyscrapers symbolize power through the use of verticality. While building high is obviously an economic decision prompted by urban land and property markets, the use of verticality to signify power is a very widespread *cultural* choice. Verticality also has religious connotations, as in the "cosmic pillar" reaching from earth towards the heavens, and the appropriation of this association in connection with skyscrapers is suggested by popular references to the "temples" or "shrines" of commerce. But, regardless of the complex historical processes through which links between power and verticality have been created and sustained in a variety of cultures, a popular association with the phallus is also widespread: whether signifying religious or commercial power, verticality operates via a key symbol of masculinity. Although most academic commentators pass this by, almost as if it is too crude to be taken seriously, it is graphically illustrated by the jokes that play on words like "erection". The skyscraper speaks loudly of the masculine character of capital.

A similar combination of anatomical referencing and social association is evident in popular views of suburban residential architecture. Here, feminine coding operates principally through associations with nurturance, domesticity and so on, but again, beliefs about the distinctiveness of women's bodies are at work in the use of curves, and of nooks and crannies. Further, suburbia itself resonates with assumptions about the beneficence of nuclear family living, "complementary" gender roles and heterosexuality. Like the academic architectural lexicon discussed above, these codings interpret gender difference as "natural" and thereby universalize and legitimize a particular version of gender differentiation and a particular form of sexuality.

Symbols in social context

This symbolism illustrates how meanings operate through chains of signifiers: in these examples, buildings operate as symbols of symbolic representations of gender. Neither professional nor lay interpretations explore the relationship between these representations and the lives of women and men inhabiting, working in or moving around these environments, and, in failing to question dominant representations of gender, implicitly endorse and sustain patriarchal gender relations.

The interplay between symbol and social context has become a key theme in recent developments in cultural geography (Cosgrove and Jackson, 1987; Rowntree, 1988; Jackson, 1989). Rejecting attempts to "read off" the social context from cultural products epitomized by the work of the Berkeley school and implicit in the gender references just discussed, the new cultural geography updates Sauer's borrowings from anthropology to argue that no direct correspondence between symbol and social context can be assumed (Jackson, 1989; see also Goss, 1988). Rather, cultural products become symbols the meanings of which are contested and unstable. Interpretations of contemporary urban landscapes as cultural products have drawn on a range of theorizations of the relationship between symbol and social context, encompassing Marxist cultural materialism and postmodern aesthetics (see for example, Jager, 1986; Ley, 1987; Mills, 1988; Caulfield, 1989).

Elsewhere, in a move that in some respects parallels the concern of contemporary cultural geography in the relationship between symbol and social context, feminists have long insisted that what women do, what women are, does not correspond directly to how women are represented in the media, in academia, or in popular culture: much effort has been devoted to challenging sexist stereotypes. Conversely, in her discussion of feminism and anthropology, Henrietta Moore (1988, p. 29) argues that "what 'woman' means culturally cannot be straightforwardly read off from what women do in society". Feminist theory, therefore, provides a useful point of departure in exploring the meaning of urban landscapes.

Feminist Perspectives

Women in the man-made environment

How then have feminist analyses of contemporary urban environments interpreted the interplay between symbol and social context? Early feminist contributions to urban geography were principally concerned with making women's activities and women's lives visible within a discipline preoccupied with men and masculine views of women (Monk and Hanson, 1982). Documentation of women's spatial activities, and of women's experience of urban and suburban living, demonstrated geographical dimensions of unequal gender relations (e.g., Zelinsky et al., 1982; Lewis and Foord, 1984; Pickup, 1984; Tivers, 1985). Attention was drawn to a mismatch between the reality of women's lives, especially the prevalence of a dual role as wage earner and homemaker, and the form of the built environment, especially the spatial separation of functionally differentiated land uses. The built environment was identified as a locus of gender stereo-

types, which gave physical expression to polarized views of women and men by mapping them on to dichotomies between home and work, and between private and public (cf. Siltanen and Stanworth, 1985). The embodiment of these stereotypes in the built environment was interpreted both as a product of patriarchal ideologies, inscribed on the urban landscape through the practices of male-dominated professions, and as a means through which female subordination is enforced, in that the difficulties experienced by women negotiating a built environment based on inaccurate assumptions help to "keep women in their place" (Tivers, 1978; Bowlby et al., 1982; Lewis and Foord, 1984). This notion that the built environment is indeed *man*-made and therefore hostile, or at minimum insensitive, to women's needs is also evident in feminist discussions of architecture (Matrix, 1984; Roberts, 1991).

These accounts have been important in exposing various forms of male bias. First, the lamentably low representation of women in professions including academia, planning and architecture has been highlighted (McDowell, 1979; Matrix, 1984). Secondly, prevalent assumptions guiding the practice of those professions have been shown to embody inaccurate, stereotypical views of women. Thirdly, these biases are not viewed as isolated aberrations but as manifestations of a broader patriarchal order which secures the subordination of women in all aspects of life. However, these interventions are not without flaws. In particular, despite the distinction drawn between stereotypes and social practices, there is a tendency to adopt oversimplified views of both the built environment and femininity.

First, while refuting the view that the built environment reflects gender divisions of labour among its inhabitants, there is a tendency simply to transpose the correspondence to an ideological level: urban planning is interpreted as directly and unproblematically reflecting dominant ideologies. The built environment appears to be immune from the activities and ideas of those who inhabit it, while faithfully representing the ideas and interests of those who plan, design and build it. This interpretation strips the built environment of the meaning it is given by the people who live in it and with the transformations, however modest, that they make. This radical opposition between makers and users, between doers and done to, can be construed as professional (planner or architect) versus ordinary person, but the emphasis on gender-based interests in feminist analyses results in a casting of the agents as professional men, the victims as women, with male inhabitants appearing as beneficiaries and perhaps, via patriarchal ideologies, as indirect agents. Occasionally some reversal of roles is posited, in theory or practice: where women are able to plan and design their own environments, it is assumed that women's needs will be effectively addressed (Hayden, 1982; Wekerle and Novac, 1989).

This reversal highlights the second oversimplification. Although these studies vigorously contest stereotypical views of women, the preoccupation with what women actually do tends to imply that the experiences of women provide the source for accurate representations of femininity, somehow unadulterated by masculine views. This perspective is contested within feminism and I would concur with accounts that argue against the notion of an essential femininity disclosed by women's experiences and that insist instead that no versions of femininity exist outside patriarchal discourse (cf. Weedon, 1987; Alcoff, 1988). We may contest and resist various aspects of the subordination and (mis)representation of women but we inevitably do so from within patriarchy: the identifier "women", upon which feminism draws so strongly, is itself a patriarchal construct. Further, the problem with the built environment is not merely that it embodies misrepresentations of women and men rooted in patriarchal ideologies, but that it is underlain by an assumed unity among women that tends to be endorsed rather than challenged by the femi-

nist critique outlined (cf. Poovey, 1988; McDowell, 1991).

Gender change and urban change

Other feminist work has been more concerned with the construction and dynamism of gender divisions. For example, Mackenzie (1988) interprets the evolution of urban structure in terms of uneasy and short-lived solutions to gender conflict. She argues that the separation between home and work precipitated by large-scale industrialization in the second half of the nineteenth century generated a series of problems, from those of slum housing to the demand for female suffrage, that undermined existing notions of family life among the working and middle classes. She suggests that this crisis over the family was resolved by extending the spatial separation that underlay it, in the form of a reorganization of the urban landscape into a "city of separate spheres" in which new suburban neighbourhoods provided the framework within which both working-class and middle-class family life could be sustained (Mackenzie, 1988, p. 20).

This particular solution was not inevitable, but was the result of complex conflicts and compromises between class and gender interests (Davidoff and Hall, 1987; Phillips, 1987). It both expressed and facilitated the realization of a notion of femininity associated with privacy and homemaking, but equally it enshrined the role of the state – through planning, public education, public housing and so on – in the construction of family life. Its implicit codifications were neither static nor monolithic. For example, although suburbia may be resonant with images of feminine domesticity, it also resonates with images of masculine domesticity: contemporary images of fatherhood have precursors in images of men contributing to the domestic bliss of suburbia by mowing the lawn or "doing-it-themselves" (Segal, 1988; see also Marsh, 1988). And images of suburbia that equate femininity with domesticity have themselves been subject to reinterpretation. For example, discussing the changing gender division of urban space in the UK, McDowell (1983) has drawn attention to the way in which suburban women came to be viewed as an attractive source of labour (nonunionized, cheap and flexible) for many of the industries expanding in the 1960s, which were more sensitive to labour costs and labour relations than to location.

Old solutions have created new problems as the mismatch between urban structure and women's lives demonstrates. Contemporary changes in urban landscapes and in gender divisions may represent responses to these tensions. Several studies suggest that women in well-paid career jobs are important agents of gentrification, whether as partners in dual career households, single women or lone parents (Mills, 1988; Rose, 1989; Warde, 1991). For these women, inner-city neighbourhoods appear to provide a more appropriate environment than suburbia in which to combine professional employment with nontraditional household arrangements and thereby to develop alternative definitions of femininity. And if affluent middle-class women are attempting to transform the urban environment in ways that better accord with these new versions of femininity, it is other women who are particularly vulnerable to the displacement that ensues. These women, including many lone parents (lacking the benefits that go with professional careers) and elderly widows, also experience existing urban patterns as inappropriate to their needs because for reasons of poverty they have always been excluded from the material advantages of suburban residential environments (Winchester and White, 1988; Winchester, 1990; see Madigan et al., 1990).

These accounts attempt to capture both the dynamic interplay between gender and environment, and the contestability of gender identities and gender divisions. However, they remain limited in their treatment of the symbolism of the built environment; they *assume* that architecture and urban design express changing and contested notions of femininity and masculinity rather than exploring how ideas about gender

are inscribed on urban landscapes. Thus, although these studies open up the possibility of examining tensions between representations of gender in the built environment and the social practices of women and men, this possibility is not developed. In the next section I offer some speculative comments on this interplay in the context of gentrification.

Gender, Gentrification and Postmodernism; Beyond Dichotomies?

The symbolism of gentrification

Discussions of the symbolism of gentrification have focused principally on the recodification of class symbols, stressing the tension between what is recuperated and what is obliterated (Jager, 1986; Williams, 1986; see also Goss, 1988). For example, the upgrading of nineteenth century working-class housing is described by Jager (1986) in terms of expunging associations with the lowly class positions of previous inhabitants, while emphasizing associations with the work ethic of their *nouveau riche* landlords and with the cultural élitism of a nineteenth-century aristocracy being usurped by the ascendant industrial capitalist. More generally, the attention paid to both the exterior and the interior of gentrified housing, whether new or old, is laden with class meanings that contribute to a distinctive class identity by transforming local history into heritage (Ley, 1987; Mills, 1988). What is neglected is that the historical resonances of old buildings and the historical allusions of postmodern neovernacular, which together provide the material for gentrification, bear the impress of former ideas about gender identities as well as class identities. Just as with class meanings, the gender connotations of housing and decor are unstable. Thus, it is the *reworking* of gender symbolism (in relation to class symbolism) that also merits attention. While gentrification appears to reject, for example, a Victorian amplification of gender differences, are aspects of former notions of femininity and masculinity, as well as the cultural capital of a former gentry, being selectively recuperated in the painstaking renovation of Victorian housing and interior decor?

Appeals to culture and cultural capital form part of the economics of gentrification, operating as means by which speculators, developers, estate agents, landlords and individual homeowners attempt to increase their assets. But the successful marketing of a "lifestyle" depends upon appeals with which the potential audience are willing to identify. One of the ways gentrification "works" is by signalling a rejection of suburban living, whether or not gentrifiers themselves are exiles from suburbia (Smith, 1987; Mills, 1988). More specifically, gentrification stands in opposition to both the rigid separation between city and suburb, and to the internal homogeneity and monotony of sprawling suburbia. Notwithstanding its economic rationale, this rejection of suburbia is also a rejection of the notion of separate spheres for women and men, gentrification offering less polarized and more diversified images. Likewise, the cultural facilities associated with gentrification typically signal a cosmopolitan social integration of women and men that stands in contrast to a separation evident among other groups. Gentrification is also, at least in some instances, associated with the acceptance of alternatives to heterosexual, nuclear family living (Lauria and Knopp, 1985; Rose, 1989). In a UK context, the interconnections between class, gender and sexuality are nicely illustrated by the contrasting connotations of the wine bar and the pub: the former is metropolitan, middle-class, sexually integrated and more likely to be tolerant of, or at least not openly hostile towards, "alternative" expressions of sexuality; the latter is more likely to be local, working-class, sexually segregated and overtly sexist and heterosexist. In this way, "liberal" representations of gender and sexuality are integral to the class symbolism of gentrification, and to elements of the cultural chauvinism and class-based colonization with which it is associated.

Some observers have interpreted these signs of reduced gender differentiation and sexual tolerance as heralding the erosion of patriarchal power relations (Markusen, 1981; Smith, 1987; Mills, 1988). Gentrification has also been linked to Roland Barthes' notion of the city as an arena of social and erotic possibility, "as the site for our encounter with the other" (Barthes, 1988, p. 199, cited by Caulfield, 1989, p. 625), again suggestive of sexual tolerance and diversity. However, as I go on to show, such interpretations oversimplify the relationship between representations of gender and gender relations.

Postmodern representations

For Caulfield (1989, p. 625) gentrifiers are "people who, not for reasons of exogenous style but of *desire*, find suburbs and modernist spaces unlivable"; gentrification is associated with postmodern cultural and architectural alternatives. The postmodern character of gentrification is important to the argument advanced here for two reasons: first, postmodernism entails a new mode of representation and therefore brings changes in the way symbols acquire meaning(s); and secondly, postmodernism is influenced by philosophical writings in which gender, or more specifically "Woman", figures prominently. These two issues require some elaboration.

Postmodern culture in general and postmodern architecture in particular are clearly responses to the perceived failures of modernism. But beyond this, the meaning and limits of the postmodern are ill-defined. Kolb (1990, pp. 4–5) traces the term to the 1940s, when "it named a breakdown of older unities and the transgression of prohibitions that had been set up by modernism". In architecture, a key prohibition was that of historical referencing and postmodernism is sometimes associated with anything that acknowledges history (which would include virtually all gentrified landscapes). However, modernism also eschews ornamentation, redundancy and ambiguity, leading some commentators to distinguish between a straightforward anti-modern reinstatement of the traditional and vernacular, and post-modern styles that use historical allusions in an intentionally playful, ironic or parodic manner (Jencks, 1978; also see Kolb, 1990). But the latter points up the impossibility of any simple return to former styles: in the contemporary context, revivalism necessarily carries with it opposition to modernism and an implicit evaluation of the styles worthy of revival. The past cannot be re-invented, only re-presented.

Foster's (1985) distinction between a post-modernism of reaction and a postmodernism of resistance is perhaps more pertinent and would certainly appear to have some purchase in relation to landscapes of gentrification, which range in style from unostentatious attempts to resist the dehumanizing effects of modernism and to recover local history and a human scale (Ley, 1987; Caulfield, 1989), to highly profitable ventures concerned with niche marketing and "lifestyles" in a manner committed principally to the commercial opportunities afforded by consumerism (Harvey, 1987; Mills, 1988). However, this diversity notwithstanding, different forms of postmodern architecture have important features in common. In particular, the use of historical styles, whether in an attempt at "authentic" reinstatement or more eclectically, involves a re-use of symbols that inevitably disrupts any simple correspondence between sign and referent: the obvious newness or rehabilitation of, for example, Georgian or Victorian features opens up scope for familiar architectural codes to take on a variety of meanings. This liberation of the sign from constant points of reference is widely recognized in postmodern culture, for example in popular fashion and music where "old" styles, or elements of them, are appropriated and reworked with more or less audacity. Postmodern culture, which is frequently at its most evident in the streets of cities subject to gentrification (see for example, Wilson, 1989), therefore provides a context in which architectural meanings are, more than ever, not merely "given" by architects,

but actively contested and recreated by the users of built environments.

On this interpretation postmodernism is empowering and opens up possibilities for "liberating" existing representations of gender: gender images and stereotypes are less and less tied to particular meanings, and women and men appear to be free to inscribe them with any meanings they choose. Thus, postmodern forms of representation would appear to be conducive to reversals of existing codings and to proliferating versions of femininity and masculinity, so that the rigidities of, say, Victorian gender divisions can be parodied in potentially subversive ways. In so doing, it might also be possible to express differences among women and men more effectively.

Postmodernism also carries some specific gender connotations. As Hutcheon has argued (1989, pp. 20–21) "feminist perspectives have brought about a major shift in our ways of thinking about culture, knowledge, and art ... [and have] meant that representation can no longer be considered a politically neutral and theoretically innocent activity". Feminism therefore has been a key influence in undermining the certainties and authority of modernist forms (Owens, 1985; Huyssen, 1986). Jardine (1985) has tentatively suggested that the prominence of feminism politically and culturally may underlie a tendency in some philosophical writing associated with postmodernism to echo Freud in using "Woman" as a metaphor for the unknown and for suppressed and disruptive elements in dominant forms of knowledge. Certainly, in bringing these elements to the fore, postmodernism has acquired feminine connotations (Bondi, 1990).

How such imagery relates to the social context in which meanings are generated is, however, deeply problematic. In short, despite its promise of empowerment, the postmodern insistence on the liberated sign and on the instability of meaning is more likely to have the reverse effect. To elaborate, in the context of class, while postmodernism is characterized by some commentators in terms of a disruption of the hierarchical separation between high culture and mass culture, it is perhaps better understood as a reworking of cultural distinctions by an urban middle class (many of whom earn their livelihood in the culture industries) consolidating their cultural capital (Dickens, 1989; cf. Bourdieu, 1984). Thus, the apparent cultural "dedifferentiation" associated with postmodernism (Lash, 1988) conceals a "redifferentiation" of class interests. I would advance a parallel argument in relation to gender: rather than signalling a "dedifferentiation" of gender relations, I would suggest that postmodern representations of femininity and masculinity contribute to a "redifferentiation" of gender interests. This arises because of the radical separation between the symbolic and the sociological within postmodernism, a separation that has the effect of denying the importance of power relations in the interpretation of gender imagery. But, in practice, while postmodern forms may "recover" the "feminine" and rework gender stereotypes, they do so on terms that are far from gender neutral. For several feminist commentators the passage from femin*ist* influence to femin*ine* connotations noted above is significant, suggesting that, whatever the emancipatory potentialities of the postmodern unharnessing of the symbolic and the sociological, within a framework of gender inequality and female subordination, androcentric constructions of femininity and masculinity remain dominant (Hartsock, 1987; Moore, 1988; Bondi and Domosh, 1992). So here again, it is inappropriate to assume a straightforward correspondence between representations of femininity and masculinity and the social relations of gender.

Fashioning gender

Against claims that postmodernism dissolves hierarchical gender dichotomies, this account implies that it merely refashions images of femininity and masculinity within a broadly patriarchal culture. Just how this occurs in contemporary urban landscapes still requires detailed elaboration: in this art-icle, I have attempted simply to raise questions concerning the "reading" of such landscapes. In conclusion I hint at some of the possibilities by taking up my metaphorical use of the word "(re)fashion".

While analyses of the gender symbolism of postmodern built forms are lacking, other aspects of contemporary culture have received more attention. In relation to gentrification, the most relevant evidence is provided by feminist interpretations of fashion (see for example, Coward, 1984; Wilson, 1985; Williamson, 1987; McRobbie, 1989). Here, gender codings are dissolved or apparently reversed in unisex clothing and in clothing that appears to conceal conventionally feminine physical attributes. Notwithstanding the real practical freedoms these might offer, within the context of hegemonic heterosexuality it is difficult to resist reading their use in fashion as saying "I can wear something male and ungainly and still look attractive" (Coward, 1984, p. 34). Thus, gender difference is not obliterated but accentuated by the gesture of reversal. Further, supposedly androgynous fashion invariably entails the adoption of men's clothing by women, while the reverse, transvestism, continues to be treated as a perversion. This lack of symmetry is a manifestation of the power inequalities associated with masculinity and femininity. Indeed, images that are claimed to reverse or elide conventional gender oppositions can effectively reinscribe existing hierarchical gender relations if they are detached from any challenge to the power structures that underpin these relations. Discussing images of masculinity associated with the "new man" Rowena Chapman makes this point forcefully:

> Everything changes but stays the same. Men are still the standard of normality. Their acceptance of feminine qualities substantiates their personalities, makes them more rational, more sane, not less. They are valorised by virtue of their gender, affirmed in whatever course of action they choose. Their behaviour changes, but their affirmation remains the same – men still write the rules. (Chapman, 1988, p. 247)

Gentrification generates fashionable urban landscapes peopled by "new men" and "new women". Much of the attention paid to decor and design displays a consciousness of style not dissimilar to that associated with clothing (for some pertinent examples, see Wilson, 1989). Further, fashion and gentrification come together in their use of city streets as a context for the statements about identity being made by their inhabitants. Clothing styles may be more transient than stylish buildings, but as aspects of urban culture they can perhaps be understood as operating on the same continuum. Whether the urban landscape can be read in similar ways to fashion requires examination of both the gender references encoded in particular built environments and the gender practices of their inhabitants. But, as a preliminary interpretation I would suggest that gentrification offers scope for reworking images of femininity and masculinity in ways that encompass diverse and nontraditional forms, but that it does little to disturb existing gender relations.

ACKNOWLEDGEMENTS

An earlier version of this paper was presented at the AAG Annual Conference in Toronto in May 1990. My thanks to Mona Domosh, Peter Jackson, Susan J. Smith and an anonymous referee for their comments on various versions, and to participants at several seminars where I have had the opportunity to discuss my ideas. I have not been able to address anything like all the issues raised, but I hope this article will provide a positive contribution to a continuing debate.

REFERENCES

Alcoff, L. (1988) Cultural feminism versus poststructuralism: the identity crisis in feminist theory. *Signs: Journal of Women in Culture and Society*, 13, 405–36.

Barthes, R. (1988) *The Semiotic Challenge*. New York: Hill and Wang.

Bondi, L. (1990) Feminism, postmodernism and geography: space for women? *Antipode*, 22, 156–67.

Bondi, L. (1991) Gender divisions and gentrification. *Transactions, Institute of British Geographers*, 16, 190–8.

Bondi, L. and Domosh, M. (1992) Other figures in other places: on feminism postmodernism and geography. *Environment and Planning D: Society and Space*.

Bourdieu, P. (1984) *Distinction*. London: Routledge.

Bowlby, S., Foord, J. and McDowlell, L. (1982) Feminism and geography. *Area*, 14, 19–25.

Brittan, A. (1989) *Masculinity and Power*. Oxford: Basil Blackwell.

Broadbent, G., Bunt, R. and Jencks, C. (1980) *Signs, Symbols and Architecture*. Chichester: John Wiley & Sons Ltd.

Caulfield, J. (1989) "Gentrification" and desire. *Canadian Review of Sociology and Anthropology*, 26, 617–32.

Chapman, R. (1988) The great pretender: variations on the new man theme. In R. Chapman and J. Rutherford (eds), *Male Order*. London: Lawrence and Wishart, pp. 225–48.

Connell, R. W. (1987) *Gender and Power*. Cambridge: Polity Press.

Cosgrove, D. E. and Daniels, S. J. (eds) (1988) *The Iconography of Landscape*. Cambridge: Cambridge University Press.

Cosgrove, D. E. and Jackson, P. (1987) New directions in cultural geography. *Area*, 19, 95–101.

Coward, R. (1984) *Female Desire*. London: Granada.

Davidoff, L. and Hall, J. (1987) *Family Fortunes*. London: Hutchinson.

Dickens, P. (1980) Social science and design theory. *Environment and Planning B*, 7, 353–60.

Dickens, P. (1989) Postmodernism, locality and the middle classes. Paper presented at the Seventh Urban Change and Conflict Conference, Bristol, September.

Domosh, M. (1989) A method for interpreting landscape: a case study of the New York World Building. *Area*, 21, 347–53.

Duncan, J. S. (1987) Review of urban imagery: urban semiotics. *Urban Geography*, 8, 473–83.

Duncan, J. and Duncan, N. (1988) (Re)reading the landscape. *Environment and Planning D: Society and Space*, 6, 117–26.

Eco, U. (1980a) Function and sign: the semiotics of architecture. In G. Broadbent, R. Bunt and C. Jencks (eds), *Signs, Symbols and Architecture*. Chichester: John Wiley & Sons Ltd, pp. 11–69.

Eco, U. (1980b) A componential analysis of the architectural sign /column/. In G. Broadbent, R. Bunt and C. Jencks (eds), *Signs, Symbols and Architecture*. Chichester: John Wiley & Sons Ltd, pp. 213–32.

Eliade, M. (1959) *The Sacred and the Profane*. San Diego: Harcourt Brace Jovanovich.

Foster, H. (1985) Postmodernism: a preface. In H. Foster (ed.), *Postmodern Culture*. London: Pluto, pp. ix–xvi.

Goss, J. (1988) The built environment and social theory: towards an architectural geography. *Professional Geographer*, 40, 392–403.

Gottdiener, M. and Lagopoulus, A. Ph. (eds) (1986) *The City and the Sign*. New York: Columbia University Press.

Hartsock, N. (1987) Rethinking modernism: minority vs majority theories. *Cultural Critique*, 7, 187–206.

Harvey, D. (1987) Flexible accumulation through urbanisation: reflections on "post-modernism" in the American city. *Antipode*, 19, 260–86.

Hayden, D. (1982) *The Grand Domestic Revolution*. Cambridge, MA: MIT Press.

Hutcheon, L. (1989) *The Politics of Postmodernism*. London: Routledge.

Huyssen, A. (1986) *After the Great Divide: Modernism, Mass Culture, Postmodernism*. Bloomington: Indiana University Press.

Jackson, P. (1989) *Maps of Meaning*. London: Unwin Hyman.

Jager, M. (1986) Class definition and the esthetics of gentrification: Victoriana in Melbourne. In N. Smith and P. Williams (eds), *Gentrification of the City*. Boston: Allen and Unwin, pp. 78–91.

Jardine, A. (1985) *Gynesis Configurations of Women and Modernity*. Ithaca, NY: Cornell University Press.

Jencks, C. A. (1978) *The Language of Post-modern Architecture*. London: Academy Editions.

Jencks, C. A. (1980) The architectural sign. In G. Broadbent, R. Bunt and C. Jencks (eds), *Signs, Symbols and Architecture*. Chichester: John Wiley & Sons Ltd, pp. 71–118.

Knox, P. (1987) The social production of the built environment: architects, architecture and the postmodern city. *Progress in Human Geography*, 11, 354–78.

Kolb, D. (1990) *Postmodern Sophistications*. Chicago: University of Chicago Press.

Lash, S. (1988) Discourse or figure? Postmodernism as a "regime of signification". *Theory Culture and Society*, 5, 311–36.

Lauria, M. and Knopp, L. (1985) Toward an analysis of the role of gay communities in the urban renaisance. *Urban Geography*, 6, 152–69.

Lewis, J. and Foord, J. (1984) New towns and new gender relations in old industrial regions: women's employment in Peterlee and East Kilbride. *Built Environment*, 10, 42–52.

Ley, D. (1987) Styles of the times: liberal and neo-conservative landscapes in inner Vancouver, 1968–1986. *Journal of Historical Geography*, 13, 40–56.

McDowell, L. (1979) Women in British geography. *Area*, 11, 151–4.

McDowell, L. (1983) Towards an understanding of the gender division of urban space. *Environment and Planning D: Society and Space*, 1, 59–72.

McDowell, L. (1991) The baby and the bathwater: diversity, difference and feminist theory in geography. *Geoforum*, 22, 123–33.

Mackenzie, S. (1988) Building women, building cities: toward gender sensitive theory in the environmental disciplines. In C. Andrew and B. M. Milroy (eds), *Life Spaces*. Vancouver: University of British Columbia Press, pp. 13–30.

McRobbie, A. (1989) Second-hand dresses and the role of the ragmarket. In A. McRobbie (ed.), *Zoot Suits and Second-hand Dresses*. London: Macmillan, pp. 23–49.

Madigan, R., Munro, M. and Smith, S. (1990) Gender and the meaning of the home. *International Journal of Urban and Regional Research*, 14, 625–47.

Markusen, A. (1981) City spatial structure, women's household work, and national urban policy. In C. R. Stimpson, E. Dixler, M. J. Nelson and K. B. Yatrakis (eds), *Women and the American City*. Chicago: University of Chicago Press, pp. 20–41.

Marsh, M. (1988) Suburban men and masculine domesticity 1870–1915. *American Quarterly*, 40, 165–86.

Matrix (1984) *Making Space*. London: Pluto.

Mills, C. (1988) "Life on the upslope": the postmodern landscape of gentrification. *Environment and Planning D: Society and Space*, 6, 169–89.

Monk, J. and Hanson, S. (1982) On not excluding half the human in geography. *Professional Geographer*, 34, 11–23.

Moore, H. (1988) *Feminism and Anthropology*. Cambridge: Polity Press.

Owens, C. (1985) The discourse of others: feminists and postmodernism. In H. Foster (ed.), *Postmodern Culture*. London: Pluto, pp. 57–82.

Phillips, A. (1987) *Divided Loyalties. Dilemmas of Sex and Class*. London: Virago.

Pickup, L. (1984) Women's gender role and its influence on their travel behaviour. *Built Environment*, 10, 61–8.

Poovey, M. (1988) Feminism and deconstruction. *Feminist Studies*, 14, 51–65.

Preziosi, D. (1979) *The Semiotics of the Built Environment*. Bloomington: Indiana University Press.

Rapoport, A. (1982) *The Meaning of the Built Environment*. Beverley Hills, CA: Sage.

Roberts, M. (1991) *Living in a Man-made World*. London: Routledge.

Rose, D. (1989) A feminist perspective on employment restructuring and gentrification: the case of Montreal. In J. Wolch and M. Dear (eds), *The Power of Geography*. Boston: Unwin Hyman, pp. 118–38.

Rowntree, L. B. (1988) Orthodoxy and new directions: cultural/humanistic geography. *Progress in Human Geography*, 12, 575–83.

Rustin, M. (1985) English conservatism and the aesthetics of architecture. *Radical Philosophy*, 40, 20–8.

Sayer, A. (1989) Dualistic thinking and rhetoric in geography. *Area*, 21, 301–5.

Scruton, R. (1979) *The Aesthetics of Architecture*. London: Methuen.

Segal, L. (1988) Look back in anger: men in the 50s. In R. Chapman and J. Rutherford (eds), *Male Order*. London: Lawrence and Wishart, pp. 68–96.

Siltanen, J. and Stanworth, M. (eds) (1985) *Women and the Public Sphere*. London: Hutchinson.

Smith, N. (1987) Of yuppies and housing: gentrification, social restructuring, and the urban dream. *Environment and Planning D: Society and Space*, 5, 151–72.

Tivers, J. (1978) How the other half lives: the geographical study of women. *Area*, 10, 302–6.

Tivers, J. (1985) *Women Attached*. Beckenham: Croom Helm.

Warde, A. (1991) Gentrification as consumption: issues of class and gender. *Environment and Planning D: Society and Space*, 9, 223–32.

Weedon, C. (1987) *Feminist Practice and Poststructuralist Theory*. Oxford: Basil Blackwell.

Wekerle, G. R. and Novac, S. (1989) Developing two women's housing co-operatives. In K. Franck and S. Ahrentzen (eds), *New Households, New Housing*. New York: Van Nostrand Reinhold, pp. 223–42.

Williams, P. (1986) Class constitution through spatial reconstruction? A re-evaluation of gentrification in Australia, Britain and the United States. In N. Smith and P. Williams (eds), *Gentrification of the City*. Boston: Allen and Unwin, pp. 56–77.

Williamson, J. (1987) *Consuming Passions*. London: Marion Boyars.

Wilson, E. (1985) *Adorned in Dreams*. London: Virago.

Wilson, E. (1989) *Hallucinations. Life in the Postmodern City*. London: Radius.

Winchester, H. P. M. (1990) Women and children last: the poverty and marginalization of one-parent families. *Transactions, Institute of British Geographers*, 15, 70–86.

Winchester, H. P. M. and White, P. E. (1988) The location of marginalised groups in the inner city. *Environment and Planning D: Society and Space*, 6, 37–54.

Zelinsky, W., Monk, J. and Hanson, S. (1982) Women and geography: a review and prospectus. *Progress in Human Geography*, 6, 317–66.

17

What Would a Nonsexist City Be Like? Speculations on Housing, Urban Design and Human Work

Dolores Hayden

"A woman's place is in the home" has been one of the most important principles of architectural design and urban planning in the United States for the last century. An implicit rather than explicit principle for the conservative and male-dominated design professions, it will not be found stated in large type in textbooks on land use. It has generated much less debate than the other organizing principles of the contemporary American city in an era of monopoly capitalism, which include the ravaging pressure of private land development, the fetishistic dependence on millions of private automobiles and the wasteful use of energy.[1] However, women have rejected this dogma and entered the paid labor force in larger and larger numbers. Dwellings, neighborhoods and cities designed for homebound women constrain women physically, socially and economically. Acute frustration occurs when women defy these constraints to spend all or part of the work day in the paid labor force. I contend that the only remedy for this situation is to develop a new paradigm of the home, the neighborhood and the city; to begin to describe the physical, social and economic design of a human settlement that would support, rather than restrict, the ac-

The term "sexism" is to be understood in a similar context as racism: a belief that gender is the primary determinant of human traits and capacities, thus establishing a rationale for discrimination in all areas of life on the basis of sex.

tivities of employed women and their families. It is essential to recognize such needs in order to begin both the rehabilitation of the existing housing stock and the construction of new housing to meet the needs of a new and growing majority of Americans – working women and their families.

The Growth of the "Urban Settlement"

When speaking of the American city in the last quarter of the twentieth century, a false distinction between "city" and "suburb" must be avoided. The urban region, organized to separate homes and workplaces, must be seen as a whole. In such urban regions, more than half of the population resides in the sprawling suburban areas, or "bedroom communities." The greatest part of the built environment in the United States consists of "suburban sprawl": single family homes grouped in class-segregated areas, crisscrossed by freeways and served by shopping malls and commercial strip developments. Over 50 million small homes are on the ground. About two thirds of American families "own" their homes on long mortgages; this includes over 77 percent of all AFL-CIO (American Federation of Labor – Congress of Industrial Organizations) members (AFL-CIO, 1975, p. 16).[2] White, male skilled workers are far more likely to be home-owners than members of minority groups and women, long denied equal credit or equal access to housing. Workers commute to jobs either in the center or elsewhere in the suburban ring. In metropolitan areas studied in 1975 and 1976, the journey to work, by public transit or private car, averaged about nine miles each way. Over 100 million privately owned cars filled two- and three-car garages (which would be considered magnificent housing by themselves in many developing countries). The United States, with 13 percent of the world's population, uses 41 percent of the world's passenger cars in support of the housing and transportation patterns described (American Public Transit Association, 1978, p. 29; Motor Vehicle Manufacturers Association, 1977).

Housing and Work

The roots of this American settlement form lie in the environmental and economic policies of the past. In the late nineteenth century, millions of immigrant families lived in the crowded, filthy slums of American industrial cities and despaired of achieving reasonable living conditions. However, many militant strikes and demonstrations between the 1890s and 1920s made some employers reconsider plant locations and housing issues in their search for industrial order.[3] "Good homes make contented workers" was the slogan of the Industrial Housing Associates in 1919. These consultants and many others helped major corporations plan better housing for white male skilled workers and their families, in order to eliminate industrial conflict. "Happy workers invariably mean bigger profits, while unhappy workers are never a good investment," they chirruped (Industrial Housing Associates, 1919; see also Ehrenreich and English, 1975, p. 16). Men were to receive "family wages," and become home "owners" responsible for regular mortgage payments, while their wives became home "managers" taking care of spouse and children. The male worker would return from his day in the factory or office to a private domestic environment, secluded from the tense world of work in an industrial city characterized by environmental pollution, social degradation and personal alienation. He would enter a serene dwelling whose physical and emotional maintenance would be the duty of his wife. Thus the private suburban house was the stage set for the effective sexual division of labor. It was the commodity par excellence, a spur for male paid labor and a container for female unpaid labor. It made gender appear a more important self-definition than class, and consumption more involving than production. In a brilliant discussion of the "patriarch as wage slave," Stuart Ewen has shown how capitalism and antifeminism fused in campaigns for homeownership and mass consumption: the patriarch whose home was his "castle" was to work year in and year out to provide the wages to support this private environment (Ewen, 1976).

Although this strategy was first boosted by corporations interested in a docile labor force, it soon appealed to corporations who wished to move from World War I defense industries into peacetime production of domestic appliances for millions of families. The development of the advertising industry, documented by Ewen, supported this ideal of mass consumption and promoted the private suburban dwelling, which maximized appliance purchases (Walker, 1977). The occupants of the isolated household were suggestible. They bought the house itself, a car, stove, refrigerator, vacuum cleaner, washer, carpets. Christine Frederick, explaining it in 1929 as *Selling Mrs Consumer*, promoted homeownership and easier consumer credit and advised marketing managers on how to manipulate American women (Frederick, 1929). By 1931, the Hoover Commission on Home Ownership and Home Building established the private, single family home as a national goal, but a decade and a half of depression and war postponed its achievement. Architects designed houses for Mr and Mrs Bliss in a competition sponsored by General Electric in 1935; winners accommodated dozens of electrical appliances in their designs with no critique of the energy costs involved.[4] In the late 1940s the single family home was boosted by the Federal Housing Authority (FHA) and Veterans Administration (VA) mortgages and the construction of isolated, overprivatized, energy-consuming dwellings became commonplace. "I'll Buy That Dream" made the postwar hit parade (Filene, 1974, p. 189).

Mrs Consumer moved the economy to new heights in the fifties. Women who stayed at home experienced what Betty Friedan called the "feminine mystique" and Peter Filene renamed the "domestic mystique" (Friedan, 1963, p. 307). While the family occupied its private physical space, the mass media and social science experts invaded its psychological space more effectively than ever before.[5] With the increase in spatial privacy came pressure for conformity in consumption. Consumption was expensive. More and more married women joined the paid labor force, as the suggestible housewife needed to be both a frantic consumer and a paid worker to keep up with the family's bills. Just as the mass of white male workers had achieved the "dream houses" in suburbia where fantasies of patriarchal authority and consumption could be acted out, their spouses entered the world of paid employment. By 1975, the two-worker family accounted for 39 percent of American households. Another 13 percent were single parent families, usually headed by women. Seven out of ten employed women were in the work force because of financial need. Over 50 percent of all children between one and 17 had employed mothers (Baxandall et al., 1976).[6]

The employed woman

How does a conventional home serve the employed woman and her family? Badly. Whether it is in a suburban, exurban or inner city neighborhood, whether it is a split-level ranch house, a modern masterpiece of concrete and glass, or an old brick tenement, the house or apartment is almost invariably organized around the same set of spaces: kitchen, dining room, living room, bedrooms, garage or parking area. These spaces require someone to undertake private cooking, cleaning, child care and usually private transportation if adults and children are to exist within it. Because of residential

zoning practices, the typical dwelling will usually be physically removed from any shared community space – no commercial or communal day care facilities, or laundry facilities, for example, are likely to be part of the dwelling's spatial domain. In many cases these facilities would be illegal if placed across property lines. They could also be illegal if located on residentially zoned sites. In some cases sharing such a private dwelling with other individuals (either relatives or those unrelated by blood) is also against the law.[7]

Within the private spaces of the dwelling, material culture works against the needs of the employed woman as much as zoning does, because the home is a box to be filled with commodities. Appliances are usually single purpose, and often inefficient, energy-consuming machines, lined up in a room where the domestic work is done in isolation from the rest of the family. Rugs and carpets which need vacuuming, curtains which need laundering, and miscellaneous goods which need maintenance fill up the domestic spaces. Employed mothers usually are expected to, and almost invariably do, spend more time in private housework and child care than employed men; often they are expected to, and usually do, spend more time on commuting per mile traveled than men, because of their reliance on public transportation. One study found that 70 percent of adults without access to cars are female (study by D. Foley, cited in Wekerle, 1978). Their residential neighborhoods are not likely to provide much support for their work activities. A "good" neighborhood is usually defined in terms of conventional shopping, schools and perhaps public transit, rather than additional social services for the working parent such as day care or evening clinics.

The need for alternative housing

While two-worker families with both parents energetically cooperating can overcome some of the problems of existing housing patterns, households in crisis, such as subjects of wife and child battering, for example, are particularly vulnerable to its inadequacies. According to Colleen McGrath, every 30 seconds a woman is being battered somewhere in the United States. Most of these batterings occur in kitchens and bedrooms. The relationship between household isolation and battering, or between unpaid domestic labor and battering, can only be guessed, at this time, but there is no doubt that America's houses and households are literally shaking with domestic violence (McGrath, 1979, pp. 12, 23). In addition, millions of angry and upset women are treated with tranquilizers in the private home – one drug company advertises to doctors: "You can't change her environment but you can change her mood" (research by Malcolm MacEwen, cited in *Associate Collegiate Schools of Architecture Newsletter*, March 1973, p. 6).

The woman who does leave the isolated, single family house or apartment finds very few real housing alternatives available to her.[8] The typical divorced or battered woman currently seeks housing, employment and child care simultaneously. She finds that matching her complex family requirements with the various available offerings by landlords, employers and social services is impossible. One environment that unites housing, services and jobs could resolve many difficulties, but the existing system of government services, intended to stabilize households and neighborhoods by ensuring the minimum conditions for a decent home life to all Americans, almost always assumes that the traditional household with a male worker and an unpaid homemaker is the goal to be achieved or simulated. In the face of massive demographic changes, programs such as public housing, Aid for Families with Dependent Children (AFDC), and food stamps still attempt to support an ideal family living in an isolated house or apartment, with a full time homemaker cooking meals and minding children many hours of the day.

By recognizing the need for a different kind of environment, far more efficient use can be made of funds now used for subsidies to individual households. Even for women with greater financial resources the need for better housing and services is obvious. Currently, more affluent women's problems as workers have been considered "private" problems – the lack of good day care, their lack of time. The aids to overcome an environment without child care, public transportation or food service have been "private," commercially profitable solutions: maids and babysitters by the hour; franchise day care or extended television viewing; fast food service; easier credit for purchasing an automobile, a washer or a microwave oven. Not only do these commercial solutions obscure the failure of American housing policies, they also generate bad conditions for other working women. Commercial day-care and fast-food franchises are the source of low paying nonunion jobs without security. In this respect they resemble the use of private household workers who may never be asked how they arrange care for their own children. They also resemble the insidious effects of the use of television in the home as a substitute for development child care in the neighborhood. The logistical problems which all employed women face are not private problems, and they do not succumb to market solutions.

New Approaches

The problem is paradoxical: women cannot improve their status in the home unless their overall economic position in society is altered; women cannot improve their status in the paid labor force unless their domestic responsibilities are altered. Therefore, a program to achieve economic and environmental justice for women requires, by definition, a solution which overcomes the traditional divisions between the household and the market economy, the private dwelling and the workplace. One must transform the economic situation of the traditional homemaker whose skilled labor has been unpaid, but economically and socially necessary to society; one must also transform the domestic situation of the employed woman. If architects and urban designers were to recognize all employed women and their families as a constituency for new approaches to planning and design and were to reject all previous assumptions about "women's place" in the home, what could we do? Is it possible to build nonsexist neighborhoods and design nonsexist cities? What would they be like?

Some countries have begun to develop new approaches to the needs of employed women. The *Cuban* Family Code of 1974 requires men to share housework and child care within the private home. The degree of its enforcement is uncertain, but in principle it aims at men's sharing what was formerly "women's work," which is essential to equality. The Family Code, however, does not remove work from the house, and relies upon private negotiation between husband and wife for its day-to-day enforcement. Men feign incompetence, especially in the area of cooking, and a sexual stereotyping of paid jobs for women outside the home, in day-care centers for example, has not been successfully challenged (Mainardi, 1970).[9]

Another experimental approach involves the development of special housing facilities for employed women and their families. The builder Otto Fick first introduced such a program in Copenhagen in 1903. In later years it was encouraged in *Sweden* by Alva Myrdal and by the architects Sven Ivar Lind and Sven Markelius. Called "service houses" or "collective houses," such projects (figures 17.1 and 17.2) provide child care and cooked

food along with housing for employed women and their families (Muhlestein, 1975). Like a few similar projects in the USSR in the 1920s, they aim at offering services, either on a commercial basis or subsidized by the state, to replace formerly private "women's work" performed in the household. The Scandinavian solution does not sufficiently challenge male exclusion from domestic work, nor does it deal with households' changing needs over the life cycle, but it recognizes that it is important for environmental design to change.

Some additional projects in Europe extend the scope of the service house to include the provision of services for the larger community or society. In the Steilshoop Project, in Hamburg, *Germany*, in the early 1970s, a group of parents and single people designed public housing with supporting services (figure 17.3).[10] The project included a number of former mental patients as residents and therefore served as a halfway house for them, in addition to providing support services for the public housing tenants who organized it. It suggests the extent to which current American residential stereotypes can be broken down – the sick, the aged, the unmarried can be integrated into new types of households and housing complexes, rather than segregated in separate projects.

Another recent project was created in *London* by Nina West Homes, a development group established in 1972, which has

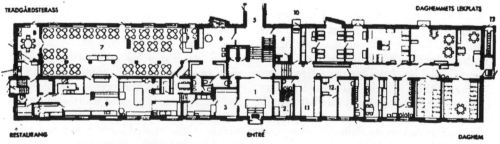

Figure 17.1 Sven Ivar Lind, Marieberg collective house, Stockholm, Sweden, 1944, plan of entrance (*entré*), restaurant (*restaurang*), and day nursery (*daghem*). (1) Entrance hall; (2) doorman's office; (3) restaurant delivery room; (4) real estate office; (5) connecting walkway to Swedberg house; (6) restaurant anteroom; (7) main dining room; (8) small dining room; (9) restaurant kitchen; (10) to day nursery's baby carriage room; (11) day nursery's baby carriage room; (12) office for day nursery's directress; (13) to Wennenberg house's cycle garage.

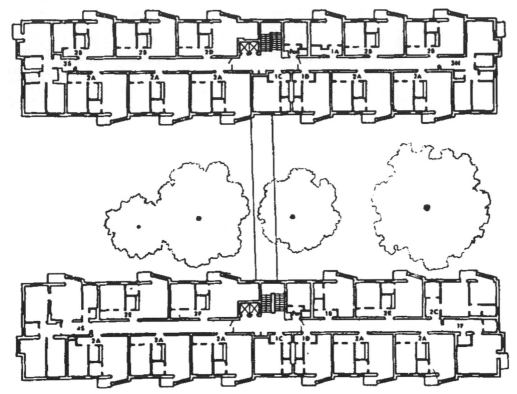

Figure 17.2 Plan of residential floors. Type 2A contains two rooms, bath and kitchenette. Types 1C and 1D are efficiency units with bath and kitchenette. Type 4S includes four rooms with bath and full kitchen.

built or renovated over 63 units of housing on six sites for single parents. Children's play areas or day-care centers are integrated with the dwellings; in their Fiona House project the housing is designed to facilitate shared babysitting, and the day-care center is open to the neighborhood residents for a fee (figure 17.4). Thus the single parents can find jobs as day-care workers and help the neighborhood's working parents as well. (Anon., 1973; Personal interview with Nina West, 1978). What is most exciting here is the hint that home and work can be reunited on one site for some of the residents, and home and child-care services are reunited on one site for all of them.

In the *United States*, we have an even longer history of agitation for housing to reflect women's needs. In the late nineteenth century and early twentieth century there were dozens of projects by feminists, domestic scientists and architects attempting to de-

velop community services for private homes. By the late 1920s, few such experiments were still functioning. (Hayden, 1977 a, b, 1978, 1979, 1979–80, 1980). In general, feminists of that era failed to recognize the problem of exploiting other women workers when providing services for those who could afford them. They also often failed to see men as responsible parents and workers in their attempts to socialize "women's" work. But feminist leaders had a very strong sense of the possibilities of neighborly cooperation among families and of the economic importance of "women's" work.

In addition, the United States has a long tradition of experimental utopian socialist communities building model towns, as well as the example of many communes and collectives established in the 1960s and 1970s which attempted to broaden conventional definitions of household and family.[11] While some communal groups, especially

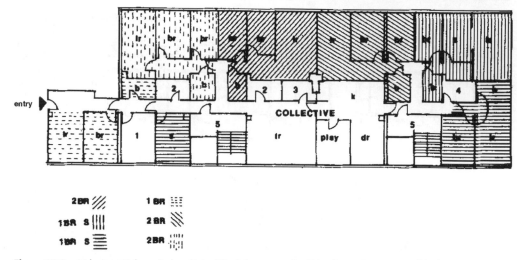

Figure 17.3 *Urbanes Wohnen* (urban living) Steilshoop, north of Hamburg, Germany, public housing for 206 tenants, designed by the tenant association in collaboration with Rolf Spille, 1970 to 1973. Instead of 72 conventional units they built 20 multifamily units and two studios. Twenty-six mental patients were included in the project, of whom 24 recovered. Partial floor plan. Units include private bedrooms (br), living rooms (lr) and some studios (s). They share a collective living room, kitchen, dining room and playroom. Each private apartment can be closed off from the collective space and each is different. (1) Storage room; (2) closets; (3) wine cellar; (4) *buanderie*; (5) fire stair.

religious ones, have often demanded acceptance of a traditional sexual division of labor, others have attempted to make nurturing activities a responsibility of both women and men. It is important to draw on the examples of successful projects of all kinds, in seeking an image of a nonsexist settlement. Most employed women are not interested in taking themselves and their families to live in communal families, nor are they interested in having state bureaucracies run family life. They desire, not an end to private life altogether, but community services to support the private household. They also desire solutions which reinforce their economic independence and maximize their personal choices about child rearing and sociability.

Proposals for Change in the US

Participatory organizations

What, then, would be the outline of a program for change in the United States? The task of reorganizing both home and work can only be accomplished by organizations of homemakers, women and men dedicated

to making changes in the ways that Americans deal with private life and public responsibilities. They must be small, participatory organizations with members who can work together effectively. I propose calling such groups HOMES (Homemakers Organization for a More Egalitarian Society). Existing feminist groups, especially those providing shelters for battered wives and children, may wish to form HOMES to take over existing housing projects and develop services for residents as an extension of those offered by feminist counselors in the shelter. Existing organizations supporting cooperative ownership of housing may wish to form HOMES to extend their housing efforts in a feminist direction. A program broad enough to transform housework, housing and residential neighborhoods must:

- involve both men and women in the unpaid labor associated with housekeeping and child care on an equal basis;
- involve both men and women in the paid labor force on an equal basis;
- eliminate residential segregation by class, race and age;

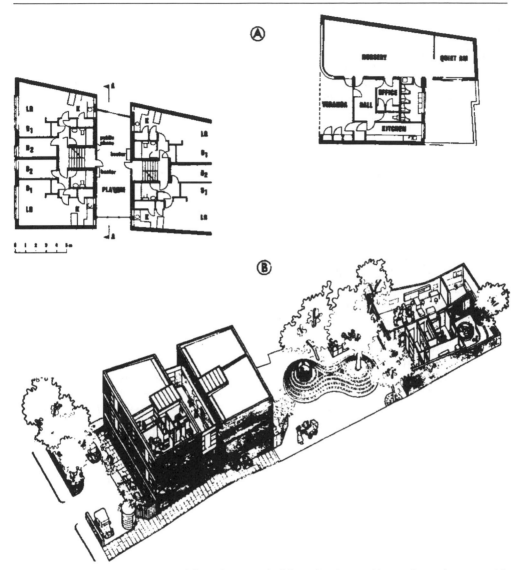

Figure 17.4 *A*, Fiona House, second-floor plan, main building, showing corridor used as a playroom, with kitchen windows opening into it; first-floor plan, rear building, showing nursery school. *B*, Axonometric drawing, Fiona House, Nina West Homes, London, 1972, designed by Sylvester Bone. Twelve two-bedroom units for divorced or separated mothers with additional outdoor play space, and neighborhood nursery school facility. Flats can be linked by intercom system to provide an audio substitute for babysitting.

- eliminate all federal, state and local programs and laws which offer implicit or explicit reinforcement of the unpaid role of the female homemaker;
- minimize unpaid domestic labor and wasteful energy consumption;
- maximize real choices for households concerning recreation and sociability.

While many partial reforms can support these goals, an incremental strategy cannot achieve them. I believe that the establishment of experimental residential centers, which in their architectural design and economic organization transcend traditional definitions of home, neighborhood, city and workplace, will be necessary to make changes on this scale. These centers could be created through renovation of existing neighborhoods or through new construction.

Suppose 40 households in a US metropolitan area formed a HOMES group and that those households, in their composition, represented the social structure of the American population as a whole. Those 40 households would include: seven single parents and their 14 children (15 percent); 16 two-worker couples and their 24 children (40 percent); 13 one-worker couples and their 26 children (35 percent); and four single residents, some of them "displaced homemakers" (10 percent). The residents would include 69 adults and 64 children. There would need to be 40 private dwelling units, ranging in size from efficiency to three bedrooms, all with private fenced outdoor space. In addition to the private housing, the group would provide the following collective spaces and activities:

- a day-care center with landscaped outdoor space, providing day care for 40 children and after-school activities for 64 children;
- a laundromat providing laundry service;
- a kitchen providing lunches for the day-care center, take-out evening meals and "meals-on-wheels" for elderly people in the neighborhood;
- a grocery depot, connected to a local food cooperative;
- a garage with two vans providing dial-a-ride service and meals-on-wheels;
- a garden (or allotments) where some food can be grown;
- a home help office providing helpers for the elderly, the sick and employed parents whose children are sick.

The use of all of these collective services should be voluntary; they would exist in addition to private dwelling units and private gardens.

To provide all of the above services, 37 workers would be necessary: 20 day-care workers; three food service workers; one grocery depot worker; five home helpers; two drivers of service vehicles; two laundry workers; one maintenance worker; one gar-

dener; two administrative staff. Some of these may be part time workers, some full time. Day care, food services and elderly services could be organized as producers' cooperatives, and other workers could be employed by the housing cooperative as discussed below.

Because HOMES is not intended as an experiment in isolated community buildings but as an experiment in meeting employed women's needs in an urban area, its services should be available to the neighborhood in which the experiment is located. This will increase demand for the services and insure that the jobs are real ones. In addition, although residents of HOMES should have priority for the jobs, there will be many who choose outside work. So some local residents may take jobs within the experiment.

In creating and filling these jobs it will be important to avoid traditional sex stereotyping that would result from hiring only men as drivers, for example, or only women as food service workers. Every effort should be made to break down separate categories of paid work for women and men, just as efforts should be made to recruit men who accept an equal share of domestic responsibilities as residents. A version of the Cuban Family Code should become part of the organization's platform.

Similarly, HOMES must not create a two class society with residents outside the project making more money than residents in HOMES jobs that utilize some of their existing domestic skills. The HOMES jobs should be paid according to egalitarian rather than sex-stereotyped attitudes about skills and hours. These jobs must be all classified as skilled work rather than as unskilled or semiskilled at present, and offer full social security and health benefits, including adequate maternity leave, whether workers are part time or full time.

Government programs

Many federal US Housing and Urban Development (HUD) programs support the construction of nonprofit, low and moderate cost housing. In addition, HUD funds are available to provide mortgage insurance for the conversion of existing housing of five or more units to housing cooperatives. Programs from the Department of Health, Education and Welfare (HEW) also fund special facilities such as day-care centers or meals-on-wheels for the elderly. In addition, HUD and HEW offer funds for demonstration projects which meet community needs in new ways.[12] Many trade unions, churches and tenant cooperative organizations are active as nonprofit housing developers. A limited-equity housing cooperative offers the best basis for economic organization and control of both physical design and social policy by the residents.

Other supportive agencies

Many knowledgeable non-profit developers could aid community groups wishing to organize such projects, as could architects experienced in the design of housing cooperatives. What has not been attempted is the reintegration of work activities and collective services into housing cooperatives on a large enough scale to make a real difference to employed women. Feminists in trade unions where a majority of members are women may wish to consider building cooperative housing with services for their members. Other trade unions may wish to consider investing in such projects. Feminists in the co-op movement must make strong, clear demands to get such services from existing housing cooperatives, rather than simply go along with plans for conventional housing organized on a cooperative economic basis. Feminists outside the cooperative movement will find that cooperative organizational forms offer many possibilities for supporting their housing activities and other services to women. In addition, the recently established US Consumer Cooperative Bank has funds to support projects of all kinds which can be tied to cooperative housing.

Rehabilitation

In many areas, the rehabilitation of existing housing may be more desirable than new construction. The suburban housing stock in the United States must be dealt with effectively. A little bit of it is of architectural quality sufficient to deserve preservation; most of it can be esthetically improved by the physical evidence of more intense social activity. To replace empty front lawns without sidewalks, neighbors can create blocks where single units are converted to multiple units; interior land is pooled to create a park-like setting at the center of the block; front and side lawns are fenced to make private outdoor spaces; pedestrian paths and sidewalks are created to link all units with the central open space; and some private porches, garages, tool sheds, utility rooms and family rooms are converted to community facilities such as children's play areas, dial-a-ride garages and laundries.

Figure 17.5A shows a typical bleak suburban block of 13 houses, constructed by speculators at different times, where about two and a half acres are divided into plots of one fourth acre each. Ten driveways are used by 20 cars; ten garden sheds, ten swings, ten lawn mowers, ten outdoor dining tables, begin to suggest the wasteful duplication of existing amenities. Yet despite the available land there are no transitions between public streets and these private homes. Space is either strictly private or strictly public. Figure 17.6A shows a typical one family house of 1,400 square feet on this block. With three bedrooms and den, two-and-a-half baths, laundry room, two porches, and a two-car garage, it was constructed in the 1950s at the height of the "feminine mystique."

To convert this whole block and the housing on it to more efficient and sociable uses, one has to define a zone of greater activity at the heart of the block, taking a total of one and one half to two acres for collective use (figure 17.5B). Essentially, this means turning the block inside out. The Radburn plan, developed by Henry Wright and Clarence Stein in the late 1920s, delineated this principle very clearly as correct land use in "the motor age," with cars segregated from residents' green spaces, especially spaces for children. In Radburn, New Jersey, and in the

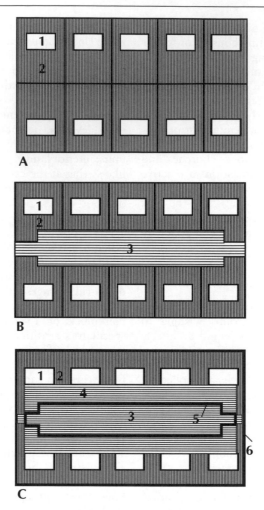

Figure 17.5 Diagram showing some of the possibilities of reorganizing a typical suburban block through rezoning, rebuilding and relandscaping. *A*, Ten single-family houses (1) on ten private lots (2); *B*, the same houses (1) with smaller private lots (2) after a backyard rehabilitation program has created a new village green (3) at the heart of the block; *C*, the same houses (1) and many small private gardens (2) with a new village green (3) surrounded by a zone for new services and accessory apartments (4) connected by a new sidewalk or arcade and surrounded by a new border of street trees (6). In figure *C*, (4) can include space for such activities as day care, elderly care, laundry and food service as well as housing, while (3) can accommodate a children's play area, vegetable or flower gardens and outdoor seating. (5) may be a sidewalk, a vine-covered trellis or a formal arcade. The narrow ends of the block can be emphasized as collective entrances with gates (to which residents have keys), leading to new accessory apartments entered from the arcade or sidewalk. In the densest possible situations, (3) may be alley or parking lot, if existing street parking and public transit are not adequate.

Baldwin Hills district of Los Angeles, California, Wright and Stein achieved remarkably luxurious results (at a density of about seven units to the acre) by this method, since their multiple unit housing always bordered a lush parkland without any automobile traffic. The Baldwin Hills project demonstrates this success most dramatically, but a revitalized suburban block with lots as small as one fourth acre can be reorganized to yield something of this same effect.[13] In this case, social amenities are added to esthetic ones as the interior park is designed to accommodate community day care, a garden for growing

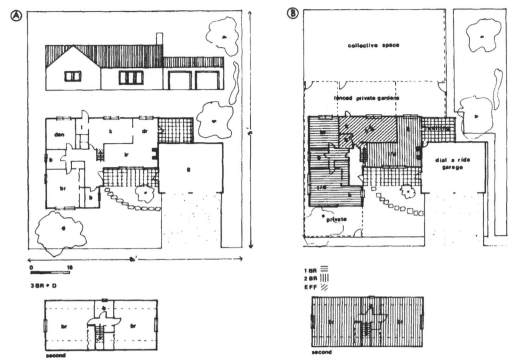

Figure 17.6 *A*, Suburban single-family house, plan, three bedrooms plus den. *B*, Proposed HOMES revitalization, same house converted to three units (two bedroom, one bedroom and efficiency), plus dial-a-ride garage and collective outdoor space.

vegetables, some picnic tables, a playground where swings and slides are grouped, a grocery depot connected to a larger neighborhood food cooperative and a dial-a-ride garage.

Large single family houses can be remodeled quite easily to become duplexes and triplexes, despite the "open plans" of the 1950s and 1960s popularized by many developers. The house in figure 17.6A becomes, in figure 17.6B, a triplex, with a two bedroom unit (linked to a community garage); a one bedroom unit; and an efficiency unit (for a single person or elderly person). All three units are shown with private enclosed gardens. The three units share a front porch and entry hall. There is still enough land to give about two fifths of the original lot to the community. Particularly striking is the way in which existing spaces such as back porches or garages lend themselves to conversion to social areas or community services. Three former private garages out of 13 might be given over to collective uses – one as a central office for the whole block, one as a grocery depot and one as a dial-a-ride garage. Is it possible to have only 20 cars (in ten garages) and two vans for 26 units in a rehabilitated block? Assuming that some residents switch from outside employment to working within the block, and that for all residents, neighborhood shopping trips are cut in half by the presence of day care, groceries, laundry and cooked food on the block, as well as aided by the presence of some new collective transportation, this might be done.

What about neighbors who are not interested in such a scheme? Depending on the configuration of lots, it is possible to begin such a plan with as few as three or four houses. In Berkeley, California, where neighbors on Derby Street joined their backyards and created a cooperative day-care center, one absentee landlord refused to join – his entire property is fenced in and the community space flows around it without difficulty. Of course, present zoning laws must be changed, or variances obtained, for the conversion of single family houses into duplexes and triplexes and the introduction of any sort of commercial activities into a residential block. However, a community group that is able to organize or acquire at least five units could become a HUD housing cooperative, with a nonprofit corporation owning all land and with producers' co-operatives running the small community services. With a coherent plan for an entire block, variances could be obtained much more easily than on a lot-by-lot basis. One can also imagine organizations which run halfway houses – for ex-mental patients, or runaway teenagers, or battered women – integrating their activities into such a block plan, with an entire building for their activities. Such groups often find it difficult to achieve the supportive neighborhood context such a block organization would offer.

Conclusion

Attacking the conventional division between public and private space should become a socialist and feminist priority in the 1980s. Women must transform the sexual division of domestic labor, the privatized economic basis of domestic work, and the spatial separation of homes and workplaces in the built environment if they are to be equal members of society. The experiments proposed are an attempt to unite the best features of past and present reforms in our own society and others, with some of the existing social services available in the United States today. It would be important to begin several demonstration HOMES, some involving new construction following the above program, others involving the rehabilitation of suburban blocks. If the first few experimental projects are successful, homemakers across the United States will want to obtain daycare, food and laundry services at a reasonable price, as well as better wages, more flexible working conditions, and more suitable housing. When all homemakers recognize that they are struggling against both gender stereotypes and wage discrimination, when they see that social, economic and environmental changes are necessary to overcome these conditions, they will no longer tolerate housing and cities, designed around the principles of another era, that proclaim that "a woman's place is in the home."

ACKNOWLEDGEMENT

I would like to thank Catharine Stimpson, Peter Marris, S. M. Miller, Kevin Lynch, Jeremy Brecher and David Thompson for extensive written comments on drafts of this paper.

NOTES

1   There is an extensive Marxist literature on the importance of spatial design to the economic development of the capitalist city, including Lefebvre (1974), Castells, 1977), Harvey (1974) and Gordon (1978). None of this work deals adequately with the situation of women as workers and homemakers, nor with the unique spatial inequalities they experience. Nevertheless, it is important to combine the economic and historical analysis of these scholars with the empirical research of non-Marxist feminist urban critics and sociologists who have examined women's experience of conventional housing, such as Wekerle (1978) and Keller (1978). Only then can one begin to provide a socialist-feminist critique of the spatial design of the American city. It is also essential to develop research on housing similar to Kamerman (1979), which reviews patterns of women's employment, maternity provisions and child-care policies in Hungary, East Germany, West Germany, France, Sweden and the United States. A comparable study of housing and related services for employed women could be the basis for more elaborate proposals for change. Many attempts to refine socialist and feminist economic theory concerning housework are discussed in an excellent article by Ellen Malos (1978). A most significant theroetical piece is Movimento di Lotta Femminile (1972).

2   I am indebted to Allan Heskin for this reference.

3   Gordon (1978, pp. 48–50) discusses suburban relocation of plants and housing.

4   Carol Barkin (1979, pp. 120–4) gives the details of this competition; Ruth Schwartz Cowan, in an unpublished lecture at MIT in 1977, explained GE's choice of an energy-consuming design for its refrigerator in the 1920s because this would increase demand for its generating equipment by municipalities.

5   Eli Zaretsky (1976) develops Friedman's earlier argument in a more systematic way.

6   For more detail, see Kapp Howe (1977).

7   Recent zoning fights on the commune issue have occurred in Santa Monica, California. Wendy Schuman (1977) reports frequent illegal down zoning by two family groups in one family residences in the New York area.

8   See, for example, Brown (1978) and Anderson-Khleif (1979, pp. 3–4).

9   My discussion of the Cuban Family Code is based on a visit to Cuba in 1978; a general review is Bengelsdorf and Hageman (1979). Also see Fox (1973).

10 This project relies on the "support structures" concept of John Habraken to provide flexible interior partitions and fixed mechanical core and structure.

11 Hayden (1976) discusses historical examples and includes a discussion of communes of the 1960s and 1970s, "Edge city, heart city, drop city: communal building today," pp. 320–47.

12 I am indebted to Geraldine Kennedy and Sally Kratz, whose unpublished papers, "Toward financing cooperative housing," and "Social assistance programs whose funds could be redirected to collective services," were prepared for my UCLA graduate seminar in 1979.

13 See also the successful experience of Zurich, described in Wirz (1979).

REFERENCES

AFL-CIO (1975) *Survey of AFL-CIO Members Housing 1975.* Washington, DC: AFL-CIO.

American Public Transit Association (1978) *Transit Fact Book, 1977–8.* Washington, DC: American Public Transit Association.

Anderson-Khleif, S. (1979) Research report for HUD, summarized in Housing for single parents. Research report, MIT–Harvard Joint Center for Urban Studies, April.

Anon. (1972) Bridge over troubles water. *Architects' Journal*, September 27, 680–4.

Barkin, C. (1979) Home, mom, and pie-in-the-sky. MArch thesis, University of California, Los Angeles.

Baxandall, R., Gordon, L. and Reverby, S. (eds) (1976) *America's Working Women: A Documentary History, 1600 to the Present.* New York: Vintage Books.

Bengelsdorf, C. and Hageman, A. (1979) Emerging from underdevelopment: women and work in Cuba. In Z. Eisenstein (ed.), *Capitalist Patriarchy and the Case for Socialist Feminism.* New York: Monthly Review Press.

Brown, C. A. (1978) Spatial inequalities and divorced mothers. Paper delivered at the annual meeting of the American Sociological Association, San Francisco.

Castells, M. (1977) *The Urban Question.* Cambridge, MA: MIT Press.

Ehrenreich, B. and English, D. (1975) The manufacture of housework. *Socialist Revolution*, 5, 16.

Ewen, S. (1976) *Captains of Consciousness: Advertising and the Social Roots of the Consumer Culture.* New York: McGraw-Hill.

Filene, P. (1974) *Him/Her/Self: Sex Roles in Modern America.* New York: Harcourt Brace Jovanovich.

Fox, G. E. (1973) Honor, shame and women's liberation in Cuba: views of working-class émigré men. In A. Pescatello (ed.), *Female and Male in Latin America.* Pittsburgh: University of Pittsburgh Press.

Frederick, C. (1929) *Selling Mrs Consumer.* New York: Business Bourse.

Friedan, B. (1963) *The Feminine Mystique.* New York: W. W. Norton.

Gordon, D. (1978) Capitalist development and the history of American cities. In W. K. Tabb and L. Sawyers (eds), *Marxism and the Metropolis*. New York: Oxford University Press.

Harvey, D. (1973) *Social Justice and the City*. London: Edward Arnold.

Hayden, D. (1976) *Seven American Utopias: The Architecture of Communitarian Socialism, 1790–1975*. Cambridge, MA: MIT Press.

Hayden, D. (1977a) Challenging the American domestic ideal. In S. Torre (ed.), *Women in American Architecture*. New York: Whitney Library of Design, pp. 22–39.

Hayden, D. (1977b) Catharine Beecher and the politics of housework. In S. Torre (ed.), *Women in American Architecture*. New York: Whitney Library of Design, pp. 40–9.

Hayden, D. (1978) Melusina Fay Pierce and cooperative housekeeping. *International Journal of Urban and Regional Research*, 2, 404–20.

Hayden, D. (1979) Two utopian feminists and their campaigns for kitchenless houses. *Signs: Journal of Women in Culture and Society*, 4(2), 274–90.

Hayden, D. (1979–80) Charlotte Perkins Gilman: domestic evolution or domestic revolution. *Radical History Review*, 21 (Winter)

Hayden, D. (1980) *A "Grand Domestic Revolution": Feminism, Socialism and the American Home, 1870–1930*. Cambridge, MA: MIT Press.

Industrial Housing Associates (1919) Good homes make contented workers. Edith Elmer Wood Papers, Avery Library, Columbia University.

Kamerman, S. B. (1979) Work and family in industrialized societies. *Signs: Journal of Women in Culture and Society*, 4(4), 632–50.

Kapp Howe, L. (1977) *Pink Collar Workers: Inside the World of Woman's Work*. New York: Avon Books.

Keller, S. (1978) Women in a planned community. Paper prepared for the Lincoln Institute of Land Policy, Cambridge, MA.

Lefebvre, H. (1991) *The Production of Space*. Oxford: Blackwell.

McGrath, C. (1979) The crisis of domestic order. *Socialist Review*, 9 (Jan./Feb.).

Mainardi, P. (1970) The politics of housework. In R. Morgan (ed.), *Sisterhood Is Powerful*. New York: Vintage Books.

Malos, E. (1978) Housework and the politics of women's liberation. *Socialist Review*, 37 (Jan./Feb.), 41–7.

Motor Vehicle Manufacturers Association (1977) *Motor Vehicle Facts and Figures*. Detroit: Motor Vehicle Manufacturers Association.

Movimento di Lotta Femminile (1972) Programmatic manifesto for the struggle of housewives in the neighborhood. *Socialist Revolution*, 9 (May/June), 85–90.

Muhlestein, E. (1975) Kollektives Wohnen gestern und heute. *Architese*, 14, 3–23.

Schuman, W. (1977) The return of togetherness. *New York Times*, March 20.

Walker, R. (1977) Suburbanization in passage. Unpublished draft paper, Department of Geography, University of California, Berkeley.

Wekerle, G. (1978) A woman's place is in the city. Paper prepared for the Lincoln Institute of Land Policy, Cambridge, MA.

Wirz, H. (1979) Back yard rehab: urban microcosm. *Urban Innovation Abroad*, 3 (July), pp. 2–3.

Zaretsky, E. (1976) *Capitalism, the Family, and Personal Life*. New York: Harper and Row.

Part VII
Environment

18

Sustainability and Cities: Summary and Conclusions

Peter Newman and John Kenworthy

In the Preface to this book we presented a set of questions to guide the book's wide-ranging discussion and exploration of sustainability in cities and its relationship to automobile dependence. Here we would like to summarize the approaches we have made to answering these questions.

The Concept of Sustainability and Its Relationship to Cities

- *What is sustainability?* Sustainability is a concept developed in the global political arena that attempts to achieve, simultaneously, the goals of an improved environment, a better economy, and a more just and participative society, rather than trading off any one of these against the others. While its primary context is global, sustainability is seen to be meaningful and achievable only when it is practiced through local initiatives with global significance.
- *How does sustainability apply to cities?* Sustainability can be applied to cities through extending the metabolism approach to human settlements so that a city can be defined as becoming more sustainable if it is reducing its resource inputs (land, energy, water, and materials) and waste outputs (air, liquid, and solid waste) while simultaneously improving its livability (health, employment, income, housing, leisure activities, accessibility, public spaces, and community).

- *What are sustainability goals and indicators for a city?* Sustainability goals and indicators are ways to incorporate the many overlapping areas of sustainability into a city's consciousness about what it values. They should cover the natural environment, resources, wastes, and human livability, the latter of which embraces the critical economic dimensions of a city. Each city needs a process to define a comprehensive list of important sustainability indicators and, in particular, ones that set it apart from others, such as Seattle's returning salmon, or The Hague's number of breeding storks, or Copenhagen's number of public seats. It then needs to build an awareness of a process that seeks to improve these indicators each year.
- *How does a city make a Sustainability Plan?* Sustainability Plans, or Local Agenda 21 Plans (as required in Agenda 21 and agreed to by all nations), are community-based processes that (1) create a set of objectives that fulfill the sustainability agenda, (2) set out indicators that show how the progress toward sustainability can be measured, (3) assess how the city is performing on these criteria, and (4) provide policy options about how it can do better. The plans are updated annually.
- *How can Sustainability Plans help move a city forward?* A Sustainability Plan enables a city to focus on its global setting (increasingly required for its economic

and social future), to create an integrated, community-centered approach to its future that is not usually possible within traditional professions, and to identify its local constraints and opportunities for innovation. The plan links a city into the global Agenda 21/sustainability networks and thus provides an opportunity to motivate creative, local contributions to a global audience.

- *How does city size relate to sustainability?* There are many ways that larger cities can contribute to sustainability through their economies of scale and density, which help to reduce per capita levels of resources and wastes and improve livability. However, they need to be constantly strengthening these advantages because local capacity limits on air, water, and land are frequently stretched in larger cities. Nevertheless, the idea that small cities are more sustainable than large ones is not supported by the findings in this book; thus it is important that all cities, regardless of size, tackle the sustainability agenda.

The Problem of Automobile Dependence at the End of the Twentieth Century

- *How are cities shaped?* The urban form of cities is shaped primarily by transportation technology, but this works through economic and cultural priorities about infrastructure and where people like to live and work – the urban, suburban, and exurban choices.
- *What is automobile dependence?* Automobile dependence is when a city or area of a city assumes automobile use as the dominant imperative in its decisions on transportation, infrastructure, and land use. Other modes thus become increasingly peripheral, marginal, or nonexistent until there are no real options for passenger travel other than the automobile.
- *How does sustainability relate to automobile dependence?* Automobile dependence is the primary force driving cities to increase their use of land, energy,

water, and other materials; their production of transportation-related air emissions (both greenhouse gases and local smog-related emissions), traffic noise, and stormwater pollution (due to the extent of asphalt in Auto Cities); and their economic problems due to the high capital costs of sprawl-related infrastructure, direct transportation costs, and indirect transportation costs (road accidents, pollution, etc.); along with the transportation-related loss of the public realm, safety, and community. It is not possible to solve sustainability in cities without addressing automobile dependence.

- *How has sustainability been addressed in other eras of city development?* The transition from the Walking City to the Transit City was due to the need to solve the problems of pollution and overcrowding resulting from the Industrial Revolution. It was achieved through a combination of new technology, new urban design and management strategies, and new visions for social change. As the Auto City has reached its zenith and created new problems of sustainability, a similarly creative combination of solutions is required.
- *Can Auto City problems be solved by incremental changes (largely engineering), or do they require more fundamental urban system changes?* Addressing the problems in a short-term technological way is necessary, but if that is all that is done, it will ultimately only exacerbate these problems since automobile use will continue to rise. Therefore, more long-term urban system changes are needed that can also accommodate technological change in a positive way.
- *What are the new economic forces confronting the Auto City?* New studies show that significant economic problems are associated with Auto Cities due to their excessive automobile use (inefficiencies from direct and indirect costs) and the amount of land lost and opportunity costs that result from the diversion of capital into nonproductive suburban infrastructure.

- *Are globalization and information technology leading to greater or less automobile dependence?* The trend in global cities (information-based economies) is toward the need for face-to-face interactions for the creative aspects of economic functions, and these are best nurtured and developed in quality urban environments where the emphasis is on traffic-free space surrounded by a dense mix of different urban activities. Such environments are inherently much lower in automobile dependence. Thus automobile dependence can be reduced under these new economic parameters, which are tending to favor the social qualities of pedestrian-and transit-oriented land use.

- *What are the social views about automobile dependence and the continuing provision of Auto City infrastructure?* Despite the popularity of the automobile, most surveys show that people don't want priorities to emphasize Auto City infrastructure, such as freeways, but want greater development of transit systems, better conditions for walking and cycling, and a reduced need to travel in urban environments, which support the development of human community.

- *What kinds of scenarios face Auto Cities in an era of oil depletion?* It is possible to imagine scenarios in which oil dependence issues lead to fundamentally different choices that can mean Auto Cities either begin the process of reshaping themselves to be more sustainable or else enter a decline phase that is very hard to reverse.

The Pattern of Automobile Dependence and Global Cities

- *What are the patterns of automobile dependence in global cities?* US and Australian cities are the most extensive in their dependence on the automobile, as shown by their transportation patterns, infrastructure, and land use. Canadian cities are less automobile-dependent, with better transit and greater integration of

land use. European cities are three to four times less automobile-dependent than US cities in terms of automobile use, infrastructure, and land use intensity. Wealthy Asian cities (Singapore, Hong Kong, and Tokyo) are eight times less automobile-dependent than US cities. However, the newly industrializing Asian cities (Bangkok, Jakarta, etc.) are showing a marked and rapidly growing automobile orientation in their transportation patterns and infrastructure, and although fringe land uses are developing greater auto orientation, their overall land use patterns are still dense and strongly favor transit and nonmotorized modes. They are therefore classified as automobile-dominated rather than automobile-dependent.

- *How do transportation patterns relate to technology, infrastructure, economics, and urban form?* The fuel efficiency of motor vehicles cannot explain the large variation in gasoline use in the world's cities, but the extra efficiency and "transit leverage" of transit technology can explain it. The infrastructure variations in terms of road supply, parking, transit service, and the relative speed between traffic and transit, are all closely related to the level of gasoline and automobile use. The price of gasoline, incomes, and the level of wealth (GRP) in a city do not relate strongly to automobile use. Land use patterns, on the other hand, are closely correlated with automobile use and the levels of transit use, walking, and cycling, confirming the structural characteristics of automobile dependence and the inevitability of addressing urban form in the sustainability agenda.

- *What are the trends in automobile use, transit, and density?* Automobile use is increasing in all but a few cities (Stockholm and Zurich), but there are large differences in rates of growth. US cities grew the most despite predictions that suburbanization of work would slow down car use. Australian cities grew much less, indicating that the reurbanization process may be influencing travel patterns. Transit use increased in all cities despite predictions of its demise globally. Spectacular increases in Europe continue to set the benchmark. Density patterns indicate an historic reversal is occurring globally, with increases or reversal of declines evident nearly everywhere. This may be related to the information-based economy. Inner city growth is much more evident than in previous periods except in US cities, where density increases are mostly occurring in outer suburban "edge cities" that are heavily auto-dependent.

- *How do the direct and indirect economic costs of transportation vary in cities?* Automobile dependence as we have defined it is a combination of physical planning parameters. The new perspective that has emerged from the economic data presented in this book is that automobile dependence is not good for the economy of cities and that cities that are able to provide a balance of transportation options are more efficient on almost every economic indicator. This includes indicators covering external costs related to environmental and safety factors, but also the direct costs of transportation. The overall effect is that automobile-dependent Australian and US cities use 12 to 13 percent of their city wealth on their passenger transportation systems; Canadian and European cities use 7 to 8 percent; wealthy Asian cities use 5 percent; and more-automobile-oriented, newly industrializing Asian cities use 15 percent of their city wealth on transportation. The implication for sustainability is that reducing automobile dependence is good for the economy of cities.

- *What does this suggest about the future of Auto Cities?* A case is made that there is no technological or economic inevitability underpinning automobile dependence. Indeed, it is suggested that the emerging processes of globalization and information-based employment could be highlighting the importance of face-to-face contact and therefore the need for reducing automobile dependence. The continuation of unsustainable auto-

mobile dependence is more than likely due to cultural factors, all of which can be overcome.

A Vision of Reduced Automobile Dependence

- *What are the myths about the inevitability of the Auto City?* We have identified ten myths concerning the inevitability of automobile dependence due to wealth, climate, the spatial extent of some nations, the age of cities, the need for physical and mental health, the lure of rural living, the power of the road lobby and the land development lobby, and the lack of nonautomobile-based options provided by the traffic engineering and town planning professions. All are potential problems in particular cities, but are open to change through cultural and political processes.

- *How can cities reduce their automobile dependence?* Theoretical approaches and case studies are presented of cities from around the world that have (1) changed their transportation infrastructure priorities to favor new transit or nonmotorized modes and achieved reductions in automobile use, (2) traffic-calmed critical streets (and across broad urban regions), inducing reductions in traffic, as well as significantly improving the quality of the urban environment and hence all elements of urban sustainability, (3) integrated transportation and land use through urban villages that are more transit-oriented and pedestrian-friendly, (4) constrained urban sprawl through effective growth management programs such as green belts, and/or (5) introduced taxes on automobiles, thus better reflecting the true costs of this mode vis-à-vis nonautomodes, and enabling alternative infrastructure to be built.

- *Why is city planning so important to reducing automobile dependence?* Much of the attention of policy makers in the United States and Australia has been directed toward civilizing the automobile rather than reducing automobile dependence. However, greater efficiency can just lead to greater use, and this washes out much of the technological advance, as well as creating more traffic-related problems. Much of the academic literature has stressed the need to control automobile use through congestion pricing, but this has significant political and equity impacts unless it is part of an overall approach to reducing automobile dependence. Economic penalties will work if there are alternatives that are viable. Planning that shifts infrastructure priorities and addresses the underlying land use aspects of automobile dependence is thus seen to be more fundamental, while an isolated tough economic approach to automobiles remains largely in the realms of academic debate.

- *What is a future "Sustainable" City vision with reduced automobile dependence?* The future "Sustainable" City (replacing the Auto City) is envisioned as a multicentered city linked by good-quality transit on radial and orbital lines. Within the centers, walking-oriented characteristics would be favored, and such new nodes would be located to provide work, shops, and local services within bicycling distance or a short, demand-responsive local transit trip of all present suburban areas. Such a city is seen to be consistent with the emerging telecommunication/services city, which is showing evidence everywhere that face-to-face contact is still critical for an urban economy.
- *How can this future "Sustainable" City be achieved in stages?* The stages are considered to be (1) revitalizing the central and inner cities, (2) focusing development on transit-oriented locations that already exist and are underutilized, (3) discouraging urban sprawl by growth management strategies, and (4) extending transit systems, particularly rail systems, and building associated urban villages to provide a subcenter for all suburbs.
- *What cities are already showing reduced automobile dependence?* The best

examples of reducing automobile dependence are to be found in European cities, especially Stockholm, Copenhagen, Zurich, and Freiburg, with continuing success being shown by the wealthy Asian cities Singapore, Hong Kong, and Tokyo, and selected poorer cities, such as Curitiba in Brazil. In Canada, Toronto and Vancouver have shown some good signs, which are reflected in significantly better land use and transportation characteristics than in US or Australian cities. In the United States, Boulder, Portland and Boston are showing that tackling automobile dependence can begin even in the world's most automobile-oriented nation, with a range of positive results, such as more compact housing, a more vital public realm, revitalization of central and inner areas, and better transit systems. However, it will take longer for such changes to be reflected in the overall statistics characterizing these cities. Signs of reversal are also evident in Australian cities, where growth in automobile use has been declining for a number of years in parallel with active reurbanization of inner-city areas and new rail systems as in Perth.

Greening the Automobile-Dependent City

- *How do other aspects of sustainability, such as management of the water cycle, solid waste, urban agriculture, and greening, fit into the future "Sustainable" City concept?* These approaches to sustainability are all necessary to reduce the inflow of resources and outflow of wastes in a city. They are also important in creating a more economically efficient city and a more attractive, quality urban environment, which is essential for a lively community and a vital economy.
- *Why are local, community-scale options proving to be more sustainable?* Water, waste, agriculture, and green space management require knowledge of particular local urban environments and thus require local involvement in management.

The latest technology for making more efficient use of water and providing more complete treatment of waste is developing at a small scale suitable for community management. Renewable energy technology is also better applied at a small scale, and new light rail technologies provide strong focal points for galvanizing community involvement in reshaping urban form and streetscapes.

- *Is there a conflict between greener cities and lower-energy cities?* There is a conflict only if there is no flexibility provided in the planning system for the provision of more compact, higher-density development to foster the creation of a multi-centered, mixed-use urban form. If no increases in density can be allowed, as some commentators (e.g., Troy, Stretton, Gordon, and Richardson) seem to be suggesting, then automobile dependence will continue. It is argued here that this will not only jeopardize low-energy goals, but will also undermine greener-city goals; local urban ecology goals seem to thrive where there is a symbiotic partnership with strong communities oriented to the sustainability agenda, and such communities rarely seem to form in automobile-dependent areas unless perhaps they are deliberate communities set up for that sole purpose.

- *Why is there conflict over density and transit in sustainability discussions and can this be resolved?* "Density" and "transit" seem to be mostly negative concepts in Anglo-Saxon traditions. This comes from industrial era cities where dense slums and transit were associated with poverty and pollution. The British Town and Country Planning Association adage "Nothing is gained by overcrowding" is associated with auto dependence. This approach, which has dominated English town planning for much of the twentieth century, is now being contested, though it is still a powerful part of the urban culture in English-speaking cities. It is a major barrier to city sustainability if allowed to be the dominant driving force in urban design, since it

prevents the successful development of pedestrian-scale urban villages and transit systems. The resolution seems to be occurring with the creation of low-density eco-villages in rural but not urban areas and the simultaneous provision of higher-density urban villages to overcome automobile dependence and density reductions in areas of local ecological servicing (waste recycling, permaculture, etc.).

- *What is local urban ecology, where is it happening and how does it relate to global urban sustainability?* Local urban ecology is the process that tries to bring together all of the aspects of sustainability in a single development, whether it is a house or a group of buildings or an industrial estate. It is an innovative, design-based exercise with few rules or norms. Examples are now appearing everywhere as the need for integrated demonstrations of sustainability becomes more and more a local agenda. The best examples appear to be occurring in Denmark where there are forty-five documented demonstrations in Copenhagen alone. They relate to global sustainability when they fulfill the goals of reducing resources and waste while improving livability. However, there are also examples of an approach that just creates, for instance, a more self-sufficient building, which, while achieving some improvements in urban ecology, actually increases automobile dependence and isolation, thus obliterating any claim to true sustainability. This shows the importance of community-based urban ecology (as in many rich examples of Danish ecological urban renewal).

Promoting Urban Change

- *How has urban professional praxis been shaped by modernism and the Auto City?* The urban professionals who have shaped our cities for the past fifty years have been strongly influenced by modernism, with its "one best way" and its clear separation of disciplines. This has given rise to simplistic transportation models with their self-fulfilling prophecies of congestion, freeway building, more congestion, and more freeway building; to planning systems totally acquiescent to "unavoidable" increases in automobile dependence; to rigid separation of urban functions by zoning; to uniform low-density architecture in suburbs and high-rise towers in CBDs; to streets that serve no other function than the moving of vehicles; to "big pipes in and big pipes out" approaches to water management; and to various expressions of "straightening out" nature in cities.

- *How is urban professional praxis now being challenged by postmodernism and sustainability?* Sustainability is part of the postmodern phenomenon that recognizes that the assumptions of modernism are now inadequate for solving the ecological and human development issues of our age. However, the sustainability agenda goes beyond the deconstruction of our society and begins to reconstruct it around the goals of ecological sensitivity and local, organic processes in communities. Urban professional praxis that fails to respond to these new imperatives will become more and more irrelevant, a passenger on a rudderless, postmodern ship.

- *What is the organic city tradition?* The organic city tradition traces the values and approaches of ecological sensitivity and local organic processes in communities back through a number of nineteenth and twentieth century urban critics who could see the inherent failings of modernism, and links those views to fundamental values concerning community processes, natural processes, heritage, and artistic expression.

- *Can the organic city tradition be a guide for future professional praxis?* This approach does provide a guide for revamping professional praxis in line with sustainability through its (1) recognition of values associated with the environment, social justice, heritage, the public realm, the urban economy, and

community; (2) delight in the diversity of expression of these values at a local level in terms of housing, transportation/urban form options, fuel types, an appropriate balance in infrastructure priorities, and cultural diversity; (3) crossing of boundaries in the physical and natural environment of cities, in disciplines, and in cultures; and (4) facilitation of organic community processes.

- *What are some detailed guidelines for sustainability in urban professional praxis?* Detailed guidelines are provided in such areas as sustainability in new development, the New Urbanism, economic impacts of urban options and better transit–land use integration. Collectively, these guidelines point to a need for a major rewriting of most of the technical planning manuals and regulations used so effectively for so many years to roll out the fabric of the Auto City. A new and diverse urban fabric, responsive to local and global needs for sustainability, will require new processes with the same stamp of authority afforded to their auto-oriented counterparts for more than half a century.

Ethics, Spirituality, and Community in the City

- *What are the ethical foundations for city sustainability from traditions of local ecology, human ecology, and urban ecology?* Three traditions are traced through the life and work of three people: Gilbert White, E. F. Schumacher, and Jane Jacobs, who are shown to be in the organic, communitarian tradition that is sensitive to local ecological and community values. They are seen to have played critical roles in the development of sustainability as it applies to cities.

- *What spiritual tradition do they come from?* These pioneers in the application of organic, ecological values are all from within the Western spiritual tradition, rather than from Eastern views. This strong Western spiritual tradition of care, stewardship, and justice is not often recognized in discussions on environmental ethics. That such influential writers and thinkers come from our own spiritual tradition is seen as important for the West, because although the framework may be consistent with views from other traditions, the ethical base for sustainability in cities is not foreign to Western thinking. This is empowering to communities throughout the Western world that most need to tackle the sustainability agenda, but that may have come to accept a jaundiced view of their own spiritual capacity to be part of constructive change.

- *How can individuals and cities express these traditions today – in particular, how do they relate to the Auto City?* The fundamental value that drives automobile dependence and unsustainability in cities is privatism, or isolationism; this is the same ancient value that was viewed from the very foundations of the Western spiritual tradition as the destroyer of cities. This value discards all community or environmental obligations in the constant drive to find privacy, self-fulfillment, and consumption. Modernist technology makes such a quest easier than ever before. However, the values that can be used as antidotes to isolationism/privatism are also alive and well. It is suggested that these include (1) developing a "sense of place" through a sense of history, a sense of social justice, and a sense of nature in local communities; (2) revealing the true character of automobile dependence in activist fights over infrastructure priorities and other planning issues; (3) being pro-urban rather than trying to escape the city; and (4) practicing hope rather than despair over sustainability issues.

- *What is the role of the community, in groups such as churches and community artists?* The community needs to be a community and to dramatize its values in new and creative ways. Examples are given from the United States, Europe, and Australia of communities that have expressed their organic/ecological values in creative ways to claim some symbolic victories for sustainability in cities.

- *Is there hope for sustainability in our cities?* Yes! The opportunities for cities that are dominated by the automobile to overcome this dependence are always there. They need to be grasped or else unsustainable patterns will become entrenched. However, successful case studies are being shown globally and the ability of civil society to dramatize their visions and link to such successes has never been so good.

19

Conservation as Preservation or as Heritage: Two Paradigms and Two Answers

G. J. Ashworth

Why Generalize?

The conservation of the built environment is, in essence, a practical activity conducted at the local level as an integral part of place management for collective, generally public, goals; guided by detailed legislative frameworks, local policy guidelines and professional working practices. Each building, district, town, as well as the people who use them, is essentially unique. Indeed, much of the intrinsic purpose of conservation, whether made explicit or not, is the discovery and enhancement of distinctiveness in the shaping of local identities for diverse reasons. Generalization would thus seem to be not only impossible, but contrary to the spirit of the exercise; and a search for theoretical notions an irrelevant distraction from the technical business of preservation and the practical issues of the local management of the built environment.

However, as in all planning, the making of choices is unavoidable and choice inevitably implies forgoing other non-selected alternatives. In conservation, these choices are expressed quite simply in the questions of what should be conserved, how should it be selected, where, in what quantity, and for whom? Without answers, the process cannot proceed. From this simple, and perhaps seemingly self-evident point, stem almost all the dilemmas and difficulties inherent in such management. This would cause prob-

lems enough if it were not for the existence of two distinct and usually contradictory prevalent paradigms. These provide two different sets of answers which are not only frequently contradictory, or at least mutually exclusive, but what is worse, they are also mutually unintelligible to those who express them, which renders dialogue, let alone compromise or synthesis, between them all but impossible.

The argument of this paper is to make explicit and thus contrast the premises upon which these two different approaches to the contemporary management of past built environments are based.

The Paradigms

For convenience, I have labelled these "preservation" and "heritage" respectively, in the full knowledge that these, and other such terms, are frequently used elsewhere very loosely – indeed often as synonyms. Each, it will be argued, has essentially different objectives, definition of resources and the criteria for their selection, view of the interpreted product, and strategies of intervention. From these flow differences of instruments, organizational structures and working practices and thus, ultimately, ways of viewing the past and its relevance for the present (figure 19.1).

Preservation, the protection from harm, is easy to define, and to understand as a

PRESERVATION   HERITAGE

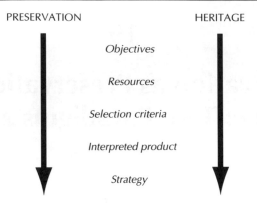

Objectives

Resources

Selection criteria

Interpreted product

Strategy

Figure 19.1   Approaches to the management of the past.

planning activity; although the implications of this are far more complex (as will be argued below). It has had an historic primacy and, for at least a century, a near monopoly of intervention approaches to the management of the past. It has shaped the creation of comprehensive and rigorous legal frameworks and public financial subsidy systems enforced by well-established, and often powerful, state agencies in most countries as well as internationally, supported by influential private organizations and pressure groups.

The term "heritage" is used here with a specific definition that distinguishes it from preservation and not, as is frequently encountered, as a term describing almost anything inherited from the past or destined for the future. The differences and relationships between the past (all that has previously happened), the histories, memories and imaginations of that past, and heritage, the contemporary uses of these, are shown in figure 19.2. Clearly, the understanding of heritage derives specifically from the application of terminology, techniques and philosophies drawn from marketing science to public sector, nonprofit, organizations with collective goals (see Ashworth and Voogd, 1990, 1994).

At this point, it might be objected that there is a third and intermediate, or transitional, approach, namely "conservation" (using the term in its distinctive European meaning and not, as in North America, a synonym for preservation). However, conservation developed out of preservation, as a logical extension of it and largely as a result of the success of the preservation movement. It can be summarized as a series of "not only but also" statements, such as: not only buildings but also ensembles are to be preserved, selected not only by intrinsic but also extrinsic criteria and managing not only forms but also functions. It is thus not an alternative to preservation but a series of compromises about the goals, methods and focus of attention, resulting from the experience of integrating preservational policies into more general local land-use management in the course of the 1960s and 1970s (see the classic definition in Burke, 1976, or the application of conservation in Dutch urban planning practice by NIROV, 1986).

These approaches, as presented here, do reflect a certain chronology in their adoption as working methods, at least in the countries of northwestern Europe. There is, however, no implied progression in the sense of either logical inevitability or desirability. In many countries, all such approaches can be encountered simultaneously, each relying upon its own judicial and even organizational structures, and containing recognizable elements drawn from more than one approach. In practice, historic sites and relict structures are managed in a variety of quite different ways, even within the same national or urban situation, and no single administrative or executive model can be deduced or is being suggested.

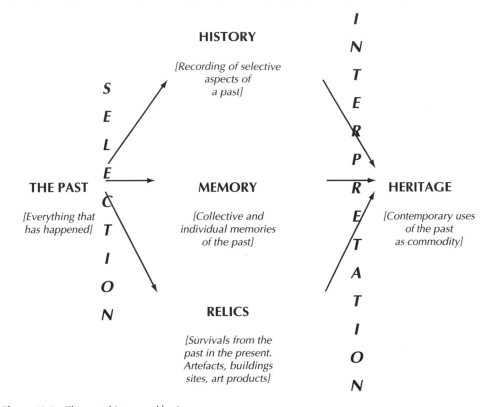

HISTORY

*[Recording of selective
aspects of
a past]*

S
E
L
E
C
T
I
O
N

I
N
T
E
R
P
R
E
T
A
T
I
O
N

THE PAST

*[Everything that
has happened]*

MEMORY

*[Collective and
individual memories
of the past]*

HERITAGE

*[Contemporary uses
of the past
as commodity]*

RELICS

*[Survivals from the
past in the present.
Artefacts, buildings
sites, art products]*

Figure 19.2   The past, history and heritage.

Despite such caveats, the argument here is that the preservation approach has a pre-eminence: historically, being the first to develop; morally, in that its justifying assumptions dominantly pervade the normative discussion; and practically, in that the creators and curators of the critical resources, whether monuments, sites or historic districts and cities, hold almost unanimously the premises of this approach. This dominance of the traditional preservation approach is being challenged and undermined by two imperatives. From the demand side, the past is being consumed in an increasing variety of ways, for the satisfaction of increasingly strongly-felt needs, whether political, social, psychological or economic. In short, more and more people want the past now in more and more different ways that owe nothing to the traditional preservational premises. Secondly, and from the supply side, the providers of historic resources are becoming

increasingly dependent on these consumer demands for their financial, political and ethical support. This dependence may be a consequence, as in most western countries, of previous successes which have resulted in ever-increasing lists of monuments, sites and historic districts. In any event, preservation organizations, management systems and philosophies established in one set of circumstances are now faced, however reluctantly, with quite different external pressures. It is largely, if sometimes unconsciously, in response to these imperatives that the heritage planning approach has evolved and now somewhat uneasily coexists with older, more established, approaches.

My position, to anticipate the conclusion of the argument, is that the most important problem facing the management of these aspects of the past is just that this dominant traditional preservation paradigm is inherently incapable of either accommodating or rejecting these more recent imperatives. From this stems many of the detailed management on-site problems and, more fundamentally, a number of basic policy dilemmas. If left unresolved, these threaten the future management of the past. The argument will now proceed to examine the premises underlying both preservation and heritage approaches in terms of the central elements in the management process.

The Choices

Of Objectives

The overall objective of preservation is, in principle, simple, clear and a moral imperative. The historically aberrant idea that aspects of past built environments should be preserved has been a consensus among dominant intellectual élites in western countries for only about four generations, and a majority view of citizens for probably no more than two (see the historical accounts in Ashworth, 1991 or Larkham, 1996). The preservation movement has exhibited, during its short existence, many of the characteristics of a crusade: with charismatic prophets, moral righteousness unchallenged among believers, simplistic division of good preservationists and evil developers, and a clear unwavering vision of an ultimate goal. It is a rescue operation heroically and unselfishly salvaging some small portion of the architectural riches which were, and still are, being destroyed at an alarming rate. The rescue of almost any structure is thus a self-evident contribution to the betterment of this and future generations. Answers to the question "why?", on the rare occasions when it is posed, are answered by irrefutable general statements usually containing an unargued "should". For example, "Our cities should provide visible clues to where we have been and where we are going" (Ford, 1978) or "The excitement of the future should be anchored in the security of the past" (Lynch, 1960). Further discussion of objectives is unnecessary, untimely given the urgency of the task, and probably *a priori* evidence of a lack of commitment to the

cause. The "why ask why?" question is improper.

The ultimate objective, therefore, is no less than the total preservation of the preservable. The "how much/how many?" question would be inappropriate. If each Notre Dame or Venice makes a unique contribution to human welfare now and in the future, then the question of how many do we want or need to preserve cannot be asked, and the objective of preservation planning must be to preserve, completely, and as the values are not time-bound, for ever, all that is deemed preservable. The consequences of this in Western Europe (Burtenshaw et al., 1991) or North America (Baer, 1995) now endanger the capacity to change.

Once the past is viewed as a heritage resource to be sold to consumers, then such questioning becomes not only possible but essential, and it becomes clear that there are many reasons why elements of the past should be remembered and memorialized. The point is not just that there are many uses of the past, but that these use different products for different markets. Conflict is not inevitable, but the realization that the past is multi-sold is an essential prerequisite for the avoidance of conflict. If there are many objectives, and many pasts, then there are thus many options for development of any particular heritage. Indeed, heritage at all is not only selectable but equally rejectable. There is thus no inevitable or desirable end-state, and the "how much/how many?" question becomes not only askable but answerable. What proportion of the present building stock should be preserved? How many cathedrals or palaces can we afford? How many fossilized historic museum-cities do we need? Such questions cannot be answered in absolute, immutable and indisputable terms, but they can be answered for a particular time, place and society.

Of Resources

If the motive for preservation is clear, so also is the dimension of the task. Historic resources are assumed to be in fixed supply, both in the sense that there is one unique unreproducible Stonehenge or Taj Mahal, and also that there is – in principle – a finite quantity of the preservable. The "listing" procedures begun in most Western European countries in the last quarter of the nineteenth century (Larkham, 1996) and in North America in the middle of the twentieth century (Fitch, 1990) all assumed that this was a once-forever task and that an end-state would be reached, within a single generation, when a complete inventory of the national patrimony would exist. Equally, it was assumed that the financial outlay would consist of a single initial subsidy for restoration followed by a steady-state maintenance expenditure. Neither assumption has so far proved correct, with both monument lists and expenditures inflating alarmingly. This would, at the least, seem to suggest that there is just more than was suspected; and, at worst, cast doubt on the existence of any limit.

Similarly, preservation assumes that any specific place has a fixed endowment of historic resources, whether structures, sites or historic associations. The only management option is to preserve, or not, some proportion of this fixed quantity. The place management authority is, by its resource endowment, locked in to a limited range of options. The more valued the resource, the more complete is this lack of choice, which is most apparent in the smaller European "gem" cities (Ashworth and Tunbridge, 1990), such as Rothenburg, Ribe, Naarden, Aigues Mortes, Eger and the like, whose planning options are almost totally constrained by the existence, welcome or not, of the historic resource which determines the justification, selection, preservation techniques, interpretation, products and markets – leaving little flexibility in the choice of place planning or management goals or strategies.

Heritage products, however, are created by a commodification process through which tradable commodities are produced from historic resources to satisfy various markets by selecting, packaging and interpreting whichever resources from the past

are required. Resources are created both in the sense that previously overlooked past are now used, but also because the past is not just what we care to remember but also what we care to imagine. The pasts of Dickens and Brontë as well as Robin Hood and Ivanhoe have been more recently joined by the cast of every television soap. Resources are thus limited only by the capacity of the human imagination to create them.

Among the many policy consequences of this is that places are therefore not locked into an inescapable resource-bound heritage. The past is a quarry of resource possibilities of which only a very small fraction will ever be commodified. If the interpretation, not the resource, is the product then many different historic place-products can be sold at different times or even at the same time, using the same resources in the same place but as different products to different markets. The opportunities for development strategies are obvious, and there are many success stories in the literature. Economically bankrupt, physically deteriorating and negatively-perceived nineteenth-century heavy industrial cities from Lowell, Massachussetts to Bradford, Yorkshire, can be revitalized using newly-discovered resources of industrial archaeology, social history and Victorian literature. However, the disadvantage of these seemingly advantageous if curious characteristics of the resource stems from the same qualities. Everywhere has a unique, flexible and infinitely commodifiable past; thus heritage is a game anywhere can play and everywhere probably will. Even Jane Austen's Bath, Mozart's Salzburg or Michaelangelo's Florence are just ephemeral development options created by a fickle, fashion-prone demand.

Of the Criteria for Selection

Selection of what is preservable is necessary, and thus criteria must be established. The criteria for such selection are assumed to be intrinsic to the monument, artefact or even site itself (it is old, aesthetically beautiful or historically significant). At least in theory, such criteria are deducible and immutable in all such cases. This premise would seem not to rule out moving buildings, as long as authenticity of context is not invoked. This is, of course, more the rule than the exception: museum collections, "Skansen"-type assemblies of buildings collected from elsewhere, preserved buildings moved *in toto* into museums (e.g. Lincoln's cabin, Ottawa's Rideau Chapel, Louis Sullivan's Chicago Stock Exchange trading floor), museum ships, and the routine shifting of North American preserved buildings out of the path of developments. These could all be justified on the basis of intrinsic criteria.

Such criteria are, in principle, objectively determinable: all who look can see. In practice, however, it is assumed that they can be recognized and assessed only by the artistic taste leaders who declare, using their skills, that a monument or site has self-evident value. These "experts" thus play a critical role in deciding what is worth preserving. Most of the protective legislation and national inventories state what appear to be objective intrinsic criteria for listing or area designation assuming that age, artistic or historic "significance" and substantial "authenticity", are recognizable and incontrovertible qualities.

Authenticity is the ultimate determinant of value, and thus both a criterion and a justification. The most commonly-encountered rationale for preserving surviving buildings and sites is that they represent an accurate record of what has occurred in, and what has been produced by, the historical experience of occupation of a place. Potential additions to the preserved stock must pass the test of authenticity of both the object itself, and of its contribution to the accurate reflection of the historical record as a whole. In addition, authenticity is used as a test of the correctness of technique. The process of preservation and subsequent interpretation will be judged against a standard of authenticity which, if infringed, leads to a condemnation of the process, interpretation or enjoyment as unauthentic and thus of lesser value. The critical role of expert authentification is obvious and reflected in the inclusion of historic monument preservation at the minister-ial level, most usually with museums and arts funding placed in ministries of culture rather than with local government or urban affairs. Such agencies are likely to be staffed by specialists in architecture or art history and contribute to cultural policies, rather than policies for urban development or management (cf. Hewison, 1995).

That authenticity is a "dogma of self-delusion" (Lowenthal, 1992, p. 184) that does not provide identifiable, self-evident criteria creates many practical problems. Any intervention affects the authenticity of the object which ceases to have a natural life-span and thus becomes fossilized in time. It is also extracted, presumably, from its non-preserved spatial context as well as "sacralized" by the act itself that transforms a building into a monument. Survival over time is a result of natural hazards, durability of materials, fortunes of war, pressures for economic development and social conservatism. Thus distortions to the accurate revelation of the past exist even before its preservation has begun. Selection for preservation is further likely to favour the spectacular over the mundane, the large over the small, the beautiful over the ugly and the unusual over the commonplace. Similarly in terms of management, protection from natural or arbitrary human damage is almost never sufficient, but leads inexorably – and with no clear philosophical distinction – to maintenance of what is, replacement of missing or defective parts (York Minster), restoration of what was (the "Polish School of Conservation", Milobedski, 1995), replica reconstruction of what might have been (the Stoa in Athens), to the creation of what was, but somewhere else (Venetian palazzi in Disney World; the Parthenon at Nashville, Tennessee; Anne Hathaway's Cottage in Victoria, Canada) to what could or should have been but never was (Castell Coch, Wales; Dutch town, Nagasaki).

The criteria for heritage selection are sought not in the intrinsic qualities of the forms but in the contemporary uses made of these: they are extrinsic and derived from various political, social or economic benefits assumed to ensue from the process of heritage product creation. It is chosen not because it is valuable but because it has valued effects. Such criteria are not self-evident, objectively determinable nor stable in space and time. What is here or now considered as valuable heritage resources may not be there or then.

Selection is thus determined by the market. The focus of attention is not the object but the user, and especially the nature of the relationship between the modern user and the preserved past. The result is the "sacralization" of a place or object through interpretation, without which it would otherwise be unremarkable, or even physically indistinguishable from others. The value created by this process of "enshrinement" becomes cumulative as the initial marking is reinforced by use as the consumer's interest is legitimated by the presence of other users.

If the idea of the existence of an objective, universal and measurable set of intrinsic criteria can be shown to be unhelpful in practice, then authenticity (in the sense of an accurate revelation, through architecture and urban design, of the past as a fixed truth) must be replaced by a more useful concept. At a simple level, the choice may therefore be not between authentic and unauthentic preservation, but a decision on how much modification of authenticity is acceptable. The argument can be taken further by shifting the focus of attention to the consumer. "Real" and "contrived" (Cohen, 1988) are not recognizable qualities. From the viewpoint of the user, authenticity lies in the nature of the experience not the object. Ultimately, then, authenticity is what and where we experience it, and it is the nature and motives of the "we" in these contexts that are worth investigating.

Of the Interpreted Product

Preservation assumes that the preserved building/site has a single, stable, universal meaning and market. If there is an informed expert consensus on the objective of preservation, on the criteria for its selection and on the manner of its consumption, then it is assumed that it always conveys the same experience to the consumer. In marketing terms, there is not only a single unsegmented market, but the buyer-benefit obtained is always the same. In semiotic terms, the meaning is universal and stable. Interpretation is, therefore, a barely-tolerated intermediary between the "intent of the artist" (or "the message of the past") and the receptive observer. Indeed, the need for any interpretation other than the authentification ("this is a genuine...", "on this very spot...", "...slept here" etc.) will be viewed as distracting ("the work speaks for itself"), or by definition of an appropriate customer, unnecessary ("if you do not know, you should not be here"). Deviations from this will be denigrated as "bowdlerization" if the message is incorrect, "popularization" if it is for an insufficiently-informed market, or "commercialization" if performed for private profit.

Taken further, if interpretation is obvious, minimal and seen as merely descriptive (helping the artefact communicate its intrinsic and immutable worth to the visitor), then the idea that interpretations of the past should play contemporary political or social roles will be denied, or at least distanced as mere propaganda. The preserver, and presenter of the preserved, is only preserving and presenting what was, and is not responsible for extrinsic values that might intrude.

Heritage, however, is invariably multisold and its interpretation is polysemic and unstable through time. First, the interpretation not only enhances or packages the product; it *is* the product. Therefore, different products can be created from the same resources by different interpretations. This not only permits multi-selling if markets can be not only segmented but also separated, but also allows the product-line to be successively developed to satisfy a continuously developing demand. Secondly, the same resource is capable of being used to convey a variety of different messages either successively or simultaneously to different consumers. Thirdly, what is considered to represent the past, and thus be worthy of passing on to a future, is itself an ephemeral judgement of a present that is choosing which past it wishes to represent it at that moment. The physical durability of many heritage products means that they are likely to endure longer than their initial interpretation. This, in turn, determines that much of the effort of heritage planning is, in practice, not the creation of new resources but the reinterpretation of existing heritage products. Cities, their buildings, monuments, memorials and even nomenclature are in a process of almost continuous reinterpretation as the needs of producers and consumers change and, as this reinterpretation process is rarely ever complete, any specific place is generally a cacophony of past and present messages – many of which will be now contradictory, undesirable or just undecodable.

Of Urban Management Strategies

Relating the conservation of the urban built environment to the broader management of cities again produces two contrasting positions.

Preservation assumes an inherent conflict between preservation and development, as stability and change are juxtaposed and preservation is viewed as a brake selectively applied to slow the pace of change. There is a perceived "trade off between the past and the future" (Baer, 1995), at least in the sense that future developments must be stopped, managed, or, at worst, accepted grudgingly. The effects of preservation upon urban functions pose secondary *post-hoc* problems as the act of protection (monument listing or historic city designation) is itself the objective and, once achieved, the process is logically complete. Of course, in practice, the defensive policy of mere preservation from harm almost inevitably leads to active intervention to maintain the monument, site or district in its current state. Almost inevitably, the fact of preservation leads to a series of economic, sociological and political consequences. In local physical planning terms, the preservation of urban forms has a direct and obvious impact upon their current functions. Preservation does not deny the import-

ance of these consequences but regards them as a secondary problem that does not enter into the original preservation decision nor influence the preservation management.

A major practical consequence of this position is that increases in the contemporary use of the preserved product must be met by managing and, if necessary, restricting demand. If conflict occurs between form and function, even if such conflict is occasioned by the preserved form generating increased demands through the very intrinsic values that led to its preservation, then an absolute priority is accorded to preservation over use. The consumer of the preserved artefact is tolerated for so long as the consumption is for the approved motives and in the correct manner; but is accorded no absolute rights to experience what has been preserved. Demand is to be managed and, if necessary, restricted to match the fixed capacity of supply even to the extent of its total permanent exclusion.

Heritage is a function and thus a development option: there is, therefore, no inherent contradiction between heritage and development, as the former is just an option for the latter. There are many urban development strategies which make some use of heritage but, equally, it must be accepted that some developments preclude any role for the commodified past. Heritage does not preclude development, but also is not essential to it. Consequently, heritage planning cannot be isolated from other planning strategies: still less is it a special form of planning applicable only in a special type of city or district.

Logically, the over-use of heritage products is impossible: increases in demand for the product are met by increasing supply. The demand creates the product which activates the resources and, therefore, excessive demand should be met by either increased supply or rising prices. The occasions when this does not occur can be regarded as failures of an inadequately operating market or symptoms of a faulty management of demand; not a limited supply of resources. This creates more options and fewer constraints than are allowed by the premises of preservation planning; but, equally, presents more choices with fewer absolute principles governing their outcome.

Synthesis in Practice?

This discussion of the premises arising from different paradigms for the management of the past might be dismissed as mere theorizing if it were not that they are reflected in almost every aspect of practice. It is generally not that any particular approach is self-consciously adopted in its entirety, rather that aspects of preservation and heritage approaches can be identified at different times. Indeed, in many cases, there is evidence of differences between the users of heritage – who tend towards a heritage approach – and those who preserve and maintain many of the essential resources – who consider use to be subordinate to continued existence. Thus, even within a commodification model, those involved in the resource management agencies are more likely to pursue preservational approaches. Such differences can be as much misunderstandings, or lack of communication resulting from the style of management of the involved agencies, their terminologies, practices and assumptions, as inevitable conflicts of interest.

It can be argued that some degree of synthesis, or at least coexistence, between the approaches is inevitable. Even with preservational planning approaches, where the objectives are determined by public authorities, and the instruments are statutory designations that restrict the operation of private rights over property, there is still a dependence, to a greater or lesser degree, upon the same free market that is being constrained. This paradox is central to the search for economically-viable occupiers of such premises within mixed economies. The point that individual property owners, pursuing their private interests within markets, invest many times more capital and energy into the creation and maintenance of preserved buildings than do all state agencies together, needs constant reiteration.

All management of the past is a partnership of some sort between regulatory planning designed to manage functional change to achieve desirable collective goals and private individuals and companies pursuing their interests as owners, entrepreneurs, or customers. The partnership may be between an active initiating private sector and a public sector reacting (where necessary) to resolve conflict, support or restrain particular functions and encourage the attainment of particular functional mixes. Market planning approaches, however, result in an intrinsically different form of public-private partnership. The distinction is not so much in the nature of the organizations that engage in the process, as in their methods. The philosophy, procedures and terminology of market planning have been translated from private-sector experience, but are largely operated by public-sector organizations with collective goals. The management of the past through market planning is more than just a terminological substitution; it is a way of viewing the "historic product" and the "heritage customer", as well as the assumption of their conjunction within a market. Viewed in that way, the previously important distinctions between public and private-sector organizations and methods no longer apply; and a quite different form of partnership emerges. The elements that contribute to the urban product, for example, may be publicly-owned museums or privately-owned theme parks, which may be marketed through public promotional agencies or private advertising services. Both are "sold" on the same market, often for the same mix of social-educational and commercial entertainment objectives. The distinction in form of ownership has thus in itself little importance to our topic.

Finally, three conclusions can be drawn from either approach. First, it is clear from both sets of arguments above that the past that now exists – whether through preservation or heritage planning – is a phenomenon that has been created and shaped by a series of intervention decisions – whether made consciously with this end in mind or not. It has not evolved as the consequence of a series of abstract, random and uncontrolled processes; rather its existence is the clear result of planning and its maintenance depends upon management, whether such intervention occurs from the public or private sectors, whether in pursuit of collective or individual goals and whether in pursuit of a preservation or a heritage paradigm.

Secondly, there are many instances in the above account where conflict, if not inevitable, is at least predictable. Most obviously, there are potential conflicts between the wide range of motivations that have led to the preservation or creation of historic resources. In most cases, the "what is heritage?" and "whose heritage?" questions receive multiple answers. Heritage cannot be other than selective and, therefore, rejection is inherent in a process that must also disinherit. This raises numerous complex issues which have elsewhere (Tunbridge and Ashworth, 1996) been labelled "heritage dissonance". Here it is merely noted that the past is a contested resource and that the deliberate selection inherent in the creation and management of the past can both cause and resolve such contests.

Thirdly, the very variety of goals and objectives, and diversity of functions, introduces a multiplicity of organizations with an interest in, and responsibility for, the management of the past. Important roles are played by a large number of governmental, psuedo-governmental, commercial and non-commercial private associations and groups, as well as concerned individuals. The balance of responsibility between them varies enormously in different national systems, but the very plurality of such groups, and the fragmentation of effective controls between them, together with their concomitant variety of objectives, underlines the necessity for some coordinating intervention. Such a central role has been assumed in various cases by national or local government agencies, by philanthropic charitable bodies, by associations of commercial businesses, by profit-seeking financial or property investment organizations, or by particular local coalitions of all of these interests.

It must be remembered that, as in most histories, the history of planning for the past is usually an account of the actual or potential "winners"; the successful projects and programmes. The danger of this is that it may appear to exaggerate the seeming ease of the process and its apparent, almost self-evident, importance to so many local interests. Such accounts necessarily neglect the failures, as well as those places which have never seriously considered, or have considered and rejected, what is after all only one, rejectable, option for development. Accounts of success must not lead to an underestimation of the opposition or the costs to heritage developments, nor conceal that real alternatives for most cities exist.

Finally, even the success stories should reveal not the ease of the achievement, but the necessity for continuous sensitive management to mitigate and resolve potential and actual conflicts.

REFERENCES

Ashworth, G. J. (1991) *Heritage Planning*. Groningen: GeoPers.
Ashworth, G. J. and Tunbridge, J. E. (1990) *The Tourist-Historic City*. London: Belhaven.
Ashworth, G. J. and Voogd, H. (1990) *Selling the City*. London: Belhaven.
Ashworth, G. J. and Voogd, H. (1994) Marketing and place promotion. In A. Gold and S. Ward (eds), *Promoting Places*. London: Wiley.
Baer, W. C. (1995) When old buildings ripen for historic preservation: a predictive approach to planning. *Journal of the American Planning Association*, 61, 82–94.
Burke, G. (1976) *Townscapes*. Harmondsworth: Penguin.
Burtenshaw, D., Bateman, M. and Ashworth, G. J. (1991) *The European City: Western Perspectives*. London: Fulton.
Cohen, E. (1988) Authenticity and commoditisation in tourism. *Annals of Tourism Research*, 15, 371–86.
Ford, L. R. (1978) Continuity and change in historic cities. *Geographical Review*, 68, 253–73.

Fitch, J. M. (1990) *Historic Preservation: Curatorial Management of the Built World*. Charlottesville: University Press of Virginia.

Hewison, R. (1995) *Culture and Consensus*. London: Methuen.

Larkham, P. J. (1996) *Conservation and the City*. London: Routledge.

Lowenthal, D. (1992) Authenticity? The dogma of self-delusion. In M. Jones (ed.), *Why Fakes Matter: Essays on Problems of Authenticity*. London: British Museum Press.

Lynch, K. (1960) *The Image of the City*. Cambridge, MA: MIT Press.

Milobedski, A. (1995) *The Polish School of Conservation*. Krakow, International Cultural Centre.

NIROV (1986) *Ruimtelijke Ordening en Monumentenzorg*. The Hague: Staatsuitgevenj.

Tunbridge, J. E. and Ashworth, G. J. (1996) *Dissonant Heritage: the Management of the Past as a Resource in Conflict*. London: Wiley.

20

Zoöpolis

Jennifer Wolch

(W)ithout the recognition that the city is of and within the environment, the wilderness of the wolf and the moose, the nature that most of us think of as natural cannot survive, and our own survival on the planet will come into question.

Botkin, 1990, p. 167

Introduction

Urbanization in the west was based historically on a notion of progress rooted in the conquest and exploitation of nature by culture. The moral compass of city-builders pointed toward the virtues of reason, progress, and profit, leaving wild lands and wild things – as well as people deemed to be wild or "savage" – beyond the scope of their reckoning. Today, the logic of capitalist urbanization still proceeds without regard to nonhuman animal life, except as cash-on-the-hoof headed for slaughter on the "disassembly" line or commodities used to further the cycle of accumulation.[1] Development may be slowed by laws protecting endangered species but you will rarely see the bulldozers stopping to gently place rabbits or reptiles out of harm's way.

Paralleling this disregard for nonhuman life, you will find no mention of animals in contemporary urban theory – whether mainstream or Marxist, neoclassical or feminist. The lexicon of mainstream theory, for example, reveals a deep-seated anthropocentrism. Urbanization transforms "empty" land through a process called "development," to produce "improved land" whose developers are exhorted (at least in neoclassical theory) to dedicate it to the "highest and best use." Such language reflects a peculiar perversion of our thinking: wildlands are not "empty" but teeming with nonhuman life; "development" involves a thorough denaturalization of the environment; "improved land" is invariably impoverished in terms of soil quality, drainage, and vegetation; and judgments of "highest and best use" reflect profit-centered values and interests of humans alone, ignoring not only wild or feral animals but captives such as pets, lab animals, and livestock who live and die in urban space shared with people. Marxian varieties of urban theory are also anthropocentric, setting "the urban" as a human stage for capitalist production, social reproduction of labor, and capital circulation and accumulation. Similarly, feminist urban theory, when grounded primarily in socialist and liberal feminisms (rather than ecofeminism), avoids questions of how patriarchy and gendered social practices shape the fate of animals in the city.[2]

Our theories and practices of urbanization have contributed to disastrous ecological effects. Wildlife habitat is being destroyed at record rates as the urban front advances worldwide, driven in the First World by suburbanization and edge-city development, and in the Second and Third Worlds by pursuit of a "catching-up" development model which produces vast rural to urban migration flows and sprawling squatter landscapes

(Mies and Shiva, 1993). Entire ecosystems and species are threatened, while individual animals crowded out of their homes (or dumped) must risk entry into urban areas in search of food or water, where they encounter people, vehicles and other dangers. The substitution of pets for wild nature in the city has driven an explosion of the urban pet population, polluting urban waterways as well as leading to mass killings of dogs and cats. Isolation of urban people from the domestic animals they eat has distanced them from the horrors and ecological harms of factory farming, and the escalating destruction of rangelands and forests driven by the market's efforts to create/satisfy a lust for meat. For most free creatures, as well as staggering numbers of captives such as pets and livestock, cities imply suffering, death, or extinction.

The aim of this paper is to foreground an urban theory that takes nonhumans seriously. In the first part, I clarify what I mean by "humans" and "animals," and provide a series of arguments suggesting that a *transspecies urban theory* is necessary to the development of an eco-socialist, feminist, anti-racist urban praxis. Then, in the second part, I argue that current considerations of animals and people in the capitalist city (based on US experience) are strictly limited, and suggest that a transspecies urban theory must be grounded in contemporary theoretical debates regarding urbanization, nature and culture, ecology, and urban environmental action.

Why Animals Matter (Even in Cities)

The rationale for considering animals in the context of urban environmentalism is not transparent. Urban environmental issues traditionally center around the pollution of the city conceived as human habitat, not animal habitat. Thus the various wings of the urban progressive environmental movement have avoided thinking about nonhumans, and have left the ethical as well as pragmatic ecological, political and economic questions regarding animals to be dealt with by those involved in the defense of endan-

gered species or animal welfare. Such a division of labor privileges the rare and the tame, and ignores the lives and living spaces of the large number and variety of animals who dwell in cities. In this section, I argue that even common, everyday animals should matter.

The Human–Animal Divide: A Definition

At the outset, it is imperative to clarify what we mean when we talk about "animals" or "nonhumans" on the one hand, and "people" or "humans" on the other. Where does one draw the line between the two, and upon what criteria? This is probably humankind's Ur-question, since the biological, social and psychological construction of what is human depends unequivocally on what is animal. At various times and places particular answers to this Ur-question have gained hegemony. In many parts of the world beliefs in transmogrification or transmigration of souls provide a basis for beliefs in human-animal continuity (or even coincidence). But in the western world animals have for many centuries been defined as fundamentally different and ontologically separate from humans. This is despite the fact that the explicit criteria for establishing the human–animal difference have changed over time (have they souls? can they reason? talk? suffer?). All such criteria have routinely used humans as the standard for judgment. The concern is, can animals do what humans do? rather than can humans do what animals do (breathe in water, simultaneously distinguish 30 different odors, etc.)? Thus judged, animals are inferior beings. Such convictions were widely popularized by Thomas Aquinas and René Descartes among others. And although the Darwinian revolution declared a fundamental continuity among species, humans (or rather white men) still stood firmly astride the apex of the evolutionary chain. Lacking souls or reason, and below humans on the evolutionary scale, animals could still be readily separated from people, objectified and used instrumentally for food, clothes, transportation, company or spare body parts.

Agreement about the human/animal divide has recently collapsed. Critiques of post-Enlightenment science have undermined claims of human-animal discontinuity, and exposed the deeply anthropocentric and androcentric roots of modernist science (e.g. Birke and Hubbard, 1995). Greater understanding of animal thinking and capabilities now reveals the astonishing range and complexity of animal behavior and social life, while studies of human biology and behavior emphasize the similarity of humans to other animals. Claims about human uniqueness have thus been rendered deeply suspicious. Debates about the human–animal divide have also raged as a result of sociobiological discourses about the biological bases for human social organization and behavior, and feminist and anti-racist arguments about the social bases for human differences claimed to be biological. Long held beliefs in the human as social subject and the animal as biological object have thus been destabilized.

My position on the human/animal divide is similar to that of Noske, who like Haraway, Plumwood, and others, argues that "animals do indeed resemble us a great deal" but that their "otherness" must also be recognized by people. (Noske, 1989; Haraway, 1991; Plumwood, 1993; see also work by ethologists such as Griffin, 1984). This otherness is not simply the result of obvious morphological differences as emphasized by the life sciences; such an emphasis essentializes animals by reducing them to their biological traits alone. This is an unforgivable tactic when directed toward specific categories of people (e.g., women) but somehow deemed perfectly acceptable for animals, despite the misleading conclusions that result. Those who minimize human-animal discontinuity also obliterate animal otherness through the denial of difference. Both extremes are anthropocentric, and deny the possibility that animals as well as people socially construct their worlds and influence each other's worlds; the resulting "animal constructs are likely to be markedly different from ours but may be no less real." (Noske, 1989, p. 158)

Animals have their own realities, their own worldviews – in short, they are *subjects* not objects.

This position is rarely reflected in eco-socialist, feminist and anti-racist practices which have conceptualized "the environment" in one of three ways: (1) as set of scientifically defined biological, geophysical and geochemical assemblages or systems, e.g., biosphere, lithosphere, ecosystem, etc.; (2) as a stock of "natural resources," the essential medium for human life and source of economic well-being whose quality must therefore (and only therefore) be protected;[3] or (3) as an active but somehow unitary subject that responds in both predictable and unpredictable (often uncooperative) ways to human interference and exploitation and which must be respected as an independent force with inherent value. The first scientific approach, which denies any subjectivity to nature, is covertly anthropocentric; it predominates in mainstream, managerial environmentalism but also lies at the base of many progressive analyses of urban environmental problems. The second resourcist line of thinking, often embedded in the first approach as a rationale for looking at the urban environment in the first place, is blatantly anthropocentric; it is common not only among reform environmentalists but also in more radical elements of environmentalism including the environmental justice movement. The third approach, often framed in explicitly ecocentric terms, seems an improvement (and in many ways is). But in emphasizing ecological holism it backgrounds interspecific differences among animals (human and nonhuman), as well as the differences between animate and inanimate nature, the latter having subjectivity only in the metaphoric sense or perhaps at the level of atomic particles and other diverse quanta. This view prevails in many strands of green thought offered by deep ecologists (see, for example, Plumwood, 1993), scientific Gaians, and environmental historians (reacting to the perceived postmodern relegation of landscape to socially-constructed text) (Demeritt, 1994). Thus, in most forms of progressive environmentalism, animals have been either objectified and/or back-grounded.

Thinking Like a Bat: The Question of Animal Standpoints

The recovery of animal subjectivity implies an ethical and political obligation to redefine the urban problematic and to consider strategies for urban praxis from the standpoints of animals. Granting animals subjectivity at a conceptual level is a first step. Even this is apt to be hotly contested by human social groups who have been marginalized and devalued by claims that they are "closer to animals" and hence less intelligent, worthy, or evolved than, say, white males. It may also run counter to those who interpret the granting of subjectivity as synonymous with a granting of rights, and object either to rights-type arguments in general or to animal rights specifically. (A recovery of the animal subject does not imply that animals have rights although the rights argument does hinge on the conviction that animals are subjects of a life.)[4] A more difficult step must be taken if the revalorization of animal subjectivity is to be meaningful in terms of day-to-day practice. We not only have to "think like a mountain" but also to "think like a bat" – somehow overcoming Nagel's classic objection that because bat sonar is not similar to any human sense, it is humanly impossible to answer a question such as "what it is like to be a bat?" (Nagel, 1974).

Is it impossible to think like a bat? There is a parallel here with the problems raised by standpoint (or multipositionality) theories of knowledge that assert that a variety of individual human differences (such as race, class or gender) so strongly shape experience and thus interpretations of the world, that any suggestion of a single position marginalizes others. For example, the essentialist category "woman" silences differences of race, and in so doing allows the dominant group to create its own master narrative, define a political agenda, and maintain power. Such polyvocality may lead to a nihilistic relativism and a paralysis of political action. But the response cannot be to return to practices of radical exclusion and denial of difference. Instead, we must recognize that individual humans are embedded in social relations and networks with people similar or different, and upon whom their welfare depends.[5] This realization allows for a recognition of kinship but also of difference, since identities are defined not only through seeing that we are similar to others, but that we are also different from them. Using what Haraway terms a "cyborg vision" that allows "partial, locatable, critical knowledge sustaining the possibility of webs of connection called solidarity," (Haraway, 1991, p. 191), we can embrace kinship as well as difference and encourage the emergence of an ethic of respect and mutuality, caring and friendship.[6]

The webs of kinships and differences that shape individual identity involve both humans and animals. It is easy to accept in the abstract that humans depend upon a rich ecology of animal organisms. But there is also a large volume of archeological, paleo-anthropological, and psychological evidence suggesting that concrete interactions and interdependence with animal others are indispensable to the development of human cognition, identity and consciousness, and to a maturity which accepts ambiguity, difference and lack of control.[7] In short, animals are not only "good to think" (to borrow a phrase from Levi-Strauss) but indispensable to learning how to think in the first place, and how to relate to other people.

Who are the relevant animal others? Unlike Shepard, who maintains that only wild animals play a role in human ontology, I argue that many sorts of animals matter, including domesticated animals. Domestication has profoundly altered the intelligence, senses, and life ways of creatures such as dogs, cows, sheep and horses, so as to drastically diminish their otherness. So denaturalized, they have come to be seen as part of human culture. But wild animals have been appropriated and denaturalized by people too. This is evidenced by the myriad ways wildlife is commercialized and incorporated into human culture. And like domestic animals, wild animals can be profoundly impacted by human actions, often leading to significant behavioral adaptations. Ultimately, the division between wild and domestic must be seen as a permeable social construct; it may be better to conceive of a *matrix* of animals who vary with respect to the extent of physical or behavioral modification due to human intervention, and types of interaction with people. In such a matrix, animals range from those whose bodies and lifeways remain unaffected by humans and who have no contact with people (a dwindling number of species), to those who are "built-to-suit" and sleep with us under the bedclothes at night. In other cells of the matrix are a host of more ambiguous and complex cases – livestock, feral animals, lab animals, the genetically engineered, "pet" lizards, turtles or tarantulas, and trout from the fish farm.

Our ontological dependency on animals seems to have characterized us as a species since the Pleistocene. Human needs for dietary protein, desires for spiritual inspiration and companionship, and the ever-present possibility of ending up as somebody's dinner required thinking like an animal. This role of animals in human development can be used as an (anthropomorphic) argument in defense of wildlife conservation or petkeeping. But my concern is how human dependency on animals was played out in terms of the patterns of human-animal interactions it precipitated. Did ontological dependency on animals create an interspecies ethic of caring and webs of friendship? Without resurrecting a 1990s version of the Noble Savage – an essentialized indigenous person living in spiritual and material harmony with nature – it is clear that for most of (pre)history, people ate wild animals, tamed them, and kept them captive, but also respected them as kin, friends, teachers, spirits, or gods. Their value lay both in their similarities with and differences from humans. Not coincidentally, most wild animal habitats were also sustained.

Re-enchanting the City: An Agenda to Bring the Animals Back In

How can animals play their integral role in human ontology today? How can ethical re-

sponses and political practices engendered by the recognition of human-animal kinship and difference be fostered? How can this develop in urban settings where everyday interaction with so many kinds of animals has been eliminated? In the west, many of us interact with or experience animals only by keeping captives of a restricted variety or eating "food" animals sliced into steak, chop and roast. We get a sense of wild animals only by watching *Wild Kingdom* re-runs or going to Sea World to see the latest in a long string of short-lived "Shamus." In our apparent mastery of urban nature, we are seemingly protected from all nature's dangers but chance losing any sense of wonder and awe for the non-human world. The loss of both humility and the dignity of risk results in a widespread belief in the banality of day-to-day survival.

To allow for the emergence of an ethic, practice and politics of caring for animals and nature, we need to renaturalize cities and invite the animals back in – and in the process re-enchant the city.[8]

I call this renaturalized, re-enchanted city *zoöpolis*. The reintegration of people with animals and nature in zoöpolis can provide urban dwellers with the local, situated everyday knowledge of animal life required to grasp animal standpoints or ways of being in the world, interact with them accordingly in particular contexts, and motivate political action necessary to protect their autonomy as subjects and their life spaces. Such knowledge would stimulate a thorough rethinking of a wide range of urban daily life practices: not only animal regulation and control practices, but landscaping, development rates and design, roadway and transportation decisions, use of energy, industrial toxics and bioengineering – in short, all practices that impact animals and nature in its diverse forms (e.g., climate, plant life, landforms, etc.). And, at the most personal level, we might rethink eating habits, since factory farms are so environmentally destructive *in situ*, and the western meat habit radically increases the rate at which wild habitat is converted to agricultural land worldwide (to say nothing of how one feels about eating cows, pigs, chickens or fishes once they are embraced as kin).

While based in everyday practice like the bioregional paradigm, the zoöpolis model differs in including animals and nature in the metropolis rather than relying on an anti-urban spatial fix like small-scale communalism. It also accepts the reality of global interdependence rather than opting for autarky. Moreover, unlike deep ecological visions epistemically tied to a psychologized individualism and lacking in political-economic critique, urban renaturalization is motivated not only by a conviction that animals are central to human ontology in ways that enable the development of webs of kinship and caring with animal subjects, but that our alienation from animals results from specific political-economic structures, social relations, and institutions operative at several spatial scales. Such structures, relations and institutions will not magically change once individuals recognize animal subjectivity, but will only be altered through political engagement and struggle against oppression based on class, race, gender and species.

Beyond the city, the zoöpolis model serves as a powerful curb on the contradictory and colonizing environmental politics of the west as practiced both in the west itself and as inflicted on other parts of the world. For example, wildlife reserves are vital to prevent species extinction. But because they are "out there," remote from urban life, reserves can do nothing to alter entrenched modes of economic organization and associated consumption practices that hinge on continual growth and make reserves necessary in the first place. The only modes of life that the reserves change are those of subsistence peoples who suddenly find themselves alienated from their traditional economic base and further immiserated. But an interspecific ethic of caring replaces dominionism to create urban regions where animals are neither incarcerated, killed, nor sent off to live in wildlife prisons but instead are valued neighbors and partners in survival. This ethic links urban residents with peoples elsewhere in the world who have evolved ways of both surviving and sustaining the forests,

streams, and diversity of animal lives, and enjoins their struggles. The western myth of a pristine arcadian wilderness, imposed with imperial impunity on those places held hostage to the International Monetary Fund and World Bank in league with powerful international environmental organizations, is trumped by a post-colonial politics and practice that begins at home with animals in the city.

Ways of Thinking Animals in the City

An agenda for renaturalizing the city and bringing animals back in should be developed with an awareness of the impacts of urbanization on animals in the capitalist city, how urban residents think about and behave toward animal life, the ecological adaptations made by animals to urban conditions, and current practices and politics arising around urban animals. The goal is to understand capitalist urbanization in a globalizing economy and what it means for animal life; how and why patterns of human-animal interactions change over time and space; urban animal ecology as science, social discourse, and political economy; and transspecies urban practice shaped by managerial plans and grassroots activism. Figure 20.1 lays out a metatheoretical heuristic device that links together the disparate discourses of the transspecies urban problematic.

Animal town: urbanization, environmental change and animal life chances

The city is built to accommodate humans and their pursuits, yet a subaltern "animal town" inevitably emerges with urban growth. This animal town shapes the practices of urbanization in key ways (for example, by attracting or repelling people/development in certain places, or influencing animal exclusion strategies). Animals are even more profoundly affected by the urbanization process under capitalism, via extensive denaturalization of rural or wild lands, and widespread environmental pollution. The most basic types of urban environmental

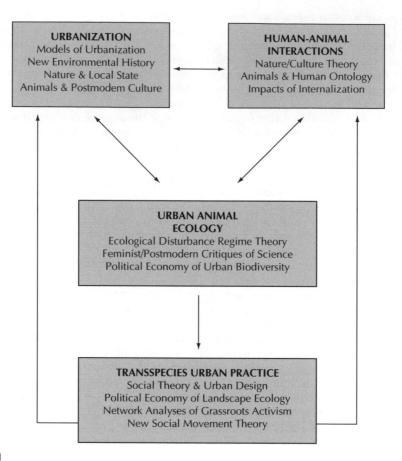

Figure 20.1

change are well-known. (Sprin, 1984; Hough, 1995). Some wild animal species, such as rats, pigeons, and cockroaches, adapt to and may even thrive in cities. Others are unable to find appropriate food or shelter, adapt to urban climate, air quality or hydrological changes, or tolerate contact with people. Captive animals, of course, are mostly restricted to homes, yards, or purpose-built quarters such as feed lots or labs, but even the health of pets, feral animals, and creatures destined for dissecting tray or dinner table can be negatively affected by various forms of urban environmental pollution.

Metropolitan development also creates spatially extensive, patchy landscapes and extreme habitat fragmentation that especially affects wildlife. Some animals can

adapt to such fragmentation and to the human proximity it implies, but more commonly animals die *in situ* or migrate to less fragmented areas. If movement corridors between habitat patches are cut off, species extinction can result as fragmentation intensifies, due to declining habitat patch size (Frankel and Soulé, 1981; Gilpin and Hanski, 1991), deleterious edge effects (Soulé, 1991), distance or isolation effects (which can intensify over time), and related shifts in community ecology (Shaffer, 1981). Where fragmentation leads to the loss of large predators, remaining species may proliferate, degrade the environment and threaten the viability of other forms of wildlife. Weedy, opportunistic and/or exotic species may also invade to similar effect.

Such accounts of urban environmental change and habitat fragmentation are not typically incorporated into theories of urbanization under capitalism. Most explanations of urbanization, for example, do not explicitly address the social or political-economic drivers of urban environmental change, especially habitat fragmentation.[9] Most studies of urban environments restrict themselves to the scientific measurement of environmental quality shifts or describe habitat fragmentation in isolation from the social dynamics that drive it.[10] This suggests that urbanization models need to be reconsidered to account for the environmental as well as political-economic bases of urbanization, the range of institutional forces acting on the urban environment, and the cultural processes that background nature in the city.

Efforts to theoretically link urban and environmental change are at the heart of the new environmental history, which reorients ideas about urbanization by illustrating how environmental exploitation and disturbance underpin the history of cities, and how thinking about nature conceived of as an actor (rather than a passive object-to-be-acted upon) can help us understand the course of urbanization. Cronon's treatise on 19th century Chicago, for example, highlights how building the metropolis (especially its meat trade) involved wholesale environmental transformation of large-scale landscape regions in which Chicago's economy was embedded, a transformation nevertheless shaped by nature-imposed constraints (Cronon, 1991). Contemporary urbanization, linked to global labor, capital and commodity flows, is simultaneously rooted in exploitation of natural "resources" (including wildlife, domestic and other sorts of animals), and actively transforms regional landscapes and the possibilities for animal life – although not always in the manner desired or expected, due to nature's agency. Revisiting neo-marxian theories of the local state as well as neo-Weberian concepts of urban managerialism to analyze relations between nature and the local state could illuminate the structural and institutional contexts of, for example, habitat degrad-

ation. One obvious starting place is growth machine theory, since it focuses on the influence of rentiers on the local state apparatus and local politics (Logan and Molotch, 1987). Another is the critique of urban planning as part of the modernist project of control and domination of others (human as well as nonhuman) through rationalist city building and policing of urban interactions and human/animal proximities in the name of human health and welfare (Wilson, 1991; Boyer, 1983; Philo, 1996). Lastly, urban cultural studies may help us understand how the aesthetics of urban built environments deepen the distanciation between animals and people. Contemporary cities are characterized by Sorkin and others as a series of theme parks, some of which seek to provide inhabitants with a sanitized version of the arcadian, edenic life (Sorkin, 1992). Wilson goes further in demonstrating how urban simulacra such as zoos and wildlife parks have increasingly mediated human experience of animal life (Wilson, 1992). Real live animals can actually come to be seen as less-than-authentic since the terms of authenticity have been so thoroughly redefined; no doubt this is one reason that most environmental movements exclude companion animals and livestock from the "nature" they are trying to defend. The distanciation of wild animals has simultaneously stimulated the elaboration of a romanticized wildness used as a means to peddle consumer goods, sell real estate, and sustain the capital accumulation process – reinforcing urban expansion and environmental degradation (Snyder, 1990).

Reckoning with the beast: human interactions with urban animals

The everyday behavior of urban residents also influences the possibilities for urban animal life. The question of human relations with animals in the city has been tackled by empirical researchers armed with behavioral models, who posit that people make cities more or less attractive to animals through their behavior (for example, human pest management and animal control practices, urban design, provision of food and water for feral animals, wildlife, etc.). These behaviors, in turn, rest on underlying values and attitudes toward animals. In such values-attitudes-behavior frameworks, resident responses are rooted in cultural beliefs about animals, but also in the behavior of animals themselves: their destructiveness, charisma and charm, and less frequently, their ecological benefits. Conventional typologies of animal values focus on economic, social, ecological values (Gray, 1993; Decker and Goff, 1987), and most emphasize positive values relevant to wildlife management and wildlife-focused recreation, or the value of companion animals to human physical and mental health (Gray, 1993; Decker and Goff, 1987; Arkow, 1987). However, people also hold negative values toward animals. In the case of wildlife, the strength and frequency of such values depends on the proximity and density of wild animals, and wildlife agency per se, namely the costs wild animals impose on human well-being and property, such as structural damage to buildings, damage to landscaping, aesthetic insults (noise, odor, dung), and risks of disease or injury.

Attitudes toward animals have been characterized on the basis of survey research and the development of attitudinal typologies. Findings suggest that urbanization increases both distanciation from nature and, paradoxically, concern for animal welfare. Kellert, for example, found that urban residents were significantly less knowledgeable about animals and the natural environment, and had lower naturalistic attitude scores (Kellert, 1984). They were also less apt to hold utilitarian attitudes and more likely to have moralistic and humanistic attitudes, suggesting that they were concerned for the ethical treatment of animals, and were focused on individual animals such as pets and popular wildlife species. Urban residents of large cities were more supportive of protecting endangered species, less in favor of shooting or trapping predators to control damage to livestock, more apt to be opposed to hunting, and supportive of allocating additional public resources for programs to increase wildlife in cities. Domestic and attractive

animals were most preferred, while animals known to cause human property damage or to inflict injury to humans were among the least preferred.

Almost no systematic research has been conducted on urban residents' behavior toward wild or unfamiliar animals they encounter or how behavior is shaped by space or by class, patriarchy, or social constructions of race/ethnicity. Moreover, the behavior of urban institutions involved in urban wildlife management or animal regulation/control has yet to be explored.[12] Conventional wisdom characterizes the responses of urban residents and institutions to local animals in two ways: (1) as "pets" who are implicitly granted agency in affecting the urban environment, given the social or economic costs they impose; or (2) as objectified "pets" who are observed, photographed, and so on. Such animals, including actual pets, farm animals visible in the neighborhood, and charismatic wildlife, provide companionship, an aesthetic amenity to property owners, or recreational opportunities such as birdwatching and feeding wildlife (King et al., 1991; Shaw et al., 1985).

How can we gain a deeper understanding of human interactions with the city's animals? The insights from wider debates in nature/culture theory are most instructive and help put behavioral research in proper context. (Haraway, 1989; Evernden, 1992; Plumwood, 1993). Increasingly, nature/culture theorizing converges on the conviction that western nature/culture dualism, a variant of the more fundamental division between object and subject, is artificial and deeply destructive of the Earth's diverse lifeforms. It validates a theory and practice of human/nature relations that backgrounds human dependency on nature. Hyperseparating nature from culture encourages its colonization and domination. The nature/culture dualism also incorporates nature into culture, denying its subjectivity and giving it solely instrumental value. By homogenizing and disembodying nature, it becomes possible to ignore the consequences of human activity such as urbanization, industrial production, and agro-industrialization, on specific creatures and their terrains (another example of what O'Connor (1988) terms the "second contradiction of capitalism")

The place-specific version of the nature/culture dualism is the city/country divide. Historically emblematic of human culture, the city seeks to exclude all remnants of the country from its midst, especially wild animals. The radical exclusion of most animals from everyday urban life may disrupt development of human consciousness and identity, and prevent the emergence of interspecific webs of friendship and concern. This argument filters through several variants of radical ecophilosophy. In some versions the centrality of "wild" animals is emphasized, while the potential of tamer animals, more common in cities but often genetically colonized, commodified, and/or neotenized, is questioned. In other versions, the wild-tame distinction in fostering human-animal bonds is minimized, but the progressive loss of interspecific contact and thus understanding is mourned.[13] Corporeal identity may also become increasingly destabilized, as understandings of human embodiment traditionally derived through direct experience of live animal bodies/subjects evaporates or is radically transformed. Thus what we now require are theoretical treatments explicating how the deeply ingrained dualism between city (culture) and country (nature), as it is played out ontologically, shapes human–animal interactions in the city.

The ahistorical and placeless values–attitudes–behavior models also miss the role of social and political–economic context on urban values and attitudes toward animals. Yet such values and attitudes are apt to evolve in response to place-specific situations and local contextual shifts resulting from nonlocal dynamics – for example, the rapid internationalization of urban economies. Deepening global competition threatens to stimulate a hardening of attitudes toward animal exploitation and habitat destruction in an international "race to the bottom" regarding environmental/animal protections.

An Urban Bestiary: Animal Ecologies in the City

The recognition that many animals coexist with people in cities has spurred the nascent field of urban animal ecology. Grounded in biological research and heavily management-oriented, studies of urban animal life focus on wildlife species; only a few focus on the ecology of urban companion or feral animals.[14] Most studies tend to be highly species- and place-specific. Only a fraction of urban species have been scrutinized, typically in response to human-perceived problems, risk of species endangerment, or because of their "charismatic" character. The most common mammals studied are large herbivores (primarily white-tailed and mule deer), large predators (including bears, cougars, and coyotes), and smaller mammals such as raccoons, skunks, squirrels, foxes, and javelina. A large variety of avifauna has also been studied, including both native and exotic species such as starlings, house sparrows, and pigeons. Lastly, a few reptile and amphibian species have received attention but only a small number of studies of urban insects or aquatic species have been completed, and even fewer attempts have been made to consider entire urban faunal assemblages. While some of this research indicates wildlife adaptation to urbanization (as with starlings and raccoons) many species poorly tolerate urbanization-generated environmental change, especially habitat fragmentation.

Ecological theory has moved away from notions of holism and equilibrium, toward a recognition that processes of environmental disturbance, uncertainty, and risk cause ecosystems and populations to continually shift over certain ranges varying with site and scale (Pickett and White, 1985; Botkin, 1990).[15] This suggests the utility of reconceptualizing cities as ecological disturbance regimes rather than ecological sacrifice zones whose integrity has been irrevocably violated. In order to fully appreciate the permeability of the city/country divide, the heterogeneity and variable patchiness of urban habitats and the possibilities (rather than impossibilities) for urban animal life must be more fully incorporated into ecological analyses. This in turn could inform decisions concerning prospective land-use changes (such as suburban densification or down-zoning, landscaping schemes, and transportation corridor design) and indicate how they might influence individual animals and faunal assemblages in terms of stress levels, morbidity and mortality, mobility and access to multiple sources of food and shelter, reproductive success, and exposure to predation.

Scientific urban animal ecology is grounded in instrumental rationality and oriented toward environmental control. The effort by Michael Soulé to frame a response to the postmodern reinvention of nature, however, demonstrates the penetration into ecology of feminist and postmodern critiques of modernist science (Souté and Lease, 1995).[16] Hayles (1995), for instance, argues that our understanding of nature is mitigated by the embodied interactivity of observer and observed, and the positionality of the observer. Animals, for example, construct different worlds through their embodied interactions with these worlds (i.e., how their sensory and intellectual capabilities result in their worldviews). And although some models may be more or less adequate interpretations of nature, the question of how positionality determines the models proposed, tested and interpreted must always remain open. At a minimum, such thinking calls for self-reflexivity in ecological research on urban animals, and ecological toolkits augmented by rich ethnographic accounts of animals, personal narratives of nonscientific observers, and folklore.

Lastly, scientific urban animal ecology is not practiced in a vacuum. Rather, like any other scientific pursuit, it is strongly shaped by motives of research sponsors (especially the state), those who use research products (such as planners), and ideologies of researchers themselves. Building on the field of science studies, claims of scientific ecology must thus be interrogated to expose the political economy of urban animal ecology and

biodiversity analysis. How are studies of urban animals framed, and from whose perspective? What motivates them in the first place: developer proposals, hunter lobbies, environmental/animal rights organizations? To illustrate, ecological studies of mountain lions in California, stimulated by rising human–lion interactions in metropolitan areas, range widely in perspective. At one pole are those sponsored by the California Department of Fish and Game (dependent on funds from hunter/angler fees, and part of a larger structure revealingly termed The Resources Agency) which conclude that the lion population is rising dangerously; at the other are studies done on behalf of the pro-cougar Mountain Lion Foundation, suggesting that urban encroachment has placed lions at risk of extinction. Sorting out the conflicting reports requires not only evaluation of their technical merits but also how they are enframed by epistemological and discursive traditions in scientific ecology and embedded in larger social and political-economic contexts.

Redesigning nature's metropolis: from managerialism to grassroots action

A nascent transspecies urban practice has appeared in many US cities. This practice involves numerous actors, including a variety of federal, state and local bureaucracies, planners and managers, and urban grassroots animal/environmental activists. In varying measure, the goals of such practice include altering the nature of interactions between people and animals in the city, creating minimum-impact urban environmental designs, changing everyday practices of the local state (i.e. wildlife managers and urban planners), and more forcefully defending the interests of urban animal life.

Wildlife managers and pest control firms increasingly face local demands for alternatives to extermination-oriented policies. In the wildlife area, approaches were initially driven by local protests against conventional practices such as culling. Now managers are more apt to consider in advance resident reactions to management alternatives and to adopt participatory approaches to decision-making in order to avoid opposition campaigns. Typically, alternative management strategies require education of urban residents to increase knowledge and understanding of, and respect for, wild animal neighbors, and to underscore how domestic animals may harm or be harmed by wildlife. There are limits to educational approaches, however, stimulating some jurisdictions to enact regulatory controls. For example, conventional landscaping produces biologically sterile, resource-intensive environments, leading some cities to pass regulations emphasizing native species to reduce resource dependence and create habitat for wildlife. Other regulatory targets include common residential architectures and approaches to building maintenance, garbage storage, fencing, landscaping and companion-animal keeping that are detrimental to wildlife.

Wild animals were never a focus of urban and regional planning. Nor were other kinds of animals, despite the fact that a large proportion of homes in North America and Europe shelter domestic animals. This is not surprising given the historic location of planning within the development-driven local state apparatus. Since the passage of the US Endangered Species Act (ESA) in 1973, however, planners have been forced to grapple with the impact of human activities on endangered species. To reduce the impact of urbanization on threatened animals, planners have adopted such land use tools as zoning, including urban limit lines and wildlife overlay zones; public land acquisition; transfer of development rights; environmental impact statements; and wildlife impact/habitat conservation linkage fees (Leedy et al., 1978; Nelson et al., 1992). None of these tools is without severe and well-known technical, political, and economic problems, stimulating the development of approaches such as habitat conservation plans (HCPs), regional landscape-scale planning efforts to avoid fragmentation inherent in project-by-project planning and local zoning control. Only a small number of HCPs have been developed or are in progress. Beatley's evaluation suggests that despite some benefits,

there are serious questions concerning whether HCPs can preserve sufficient habitat; create adequate landscape connectivity to maintain genetic viability; secure adequate funds for technical analyses, planning, and compensation required to offset losses to landowners; or protect target species during multi-year HCP planning processes (Beatley, 1994). Several HCPs collapsed before completion (National Research Council, Committee on Scientific Issues in the Endangered Species Act, 1995). In addition, the entire ESA-driven single-species (versus multi-species/ecosystemic) approach of HCPs is hotly contested on ecological grounds (since ecosystem protection can conflict with legal requirements for individual species protection). Politically, the HCP process can provide developers a way around the ESA entirely since it allows some "takings" of endangered wildlife species and thus may reduce threats to the Act's integrity. (Saldana, 1994). More generally HCPs, like other strategies involving decommodification of urban land (such as conservation trusts or easements), play into a resource managerialism strategy beneficial to development capital (Luke, 1995).

Despite the ESA, minimum-impact planning for urban wildlife has not been a priority for either architects or urban planners. Wildlife-oriented residential landscape architecture remains uncommon. Most examples are new developments (as opposed to retrofits), sited at the urban fringe, planned for low densities, and thus oriented for upper-income residents only. Many are merely ploys to enhance real estate profits by providing homebuyers, steeped in an anti-urban ideology of suburban living emphasizing proximity to "the outdoors," with extra "amenity" in the form of proximity to wild animal bodies. Planning practice routinely defines other less attractive locations which host animals (dead or alive), such as slaughterhouses and factory farms, as "noxious" land uses and isolates them from urban residents to protect their sensibilities and the public health.

Wildlife considerations are also largely absent from the US progressive architecture/

planning agenda, as are concerns for captives such as pets or livestock. The 1980s "costs of sprawl" debate made no mention of wildlife habitat, and the adherents to the so-called new urbanism and sustainable cities movements of the 1990s rarely define sustainability in relation to animals. The new urbanism emphasizes sustainability through high density and mixed use urban development, but remains strictly anthropocentric in perspective. Although more explicitly ecocentric, the sustainable cities movement aims to reduce human impacts on the natural environment through environmentally sound systems of solid waste treatment, energy production, transportation, housing, and the development of urban agriculture capable of supporting local residents (Van der Ryn and Calthorpe, 1991; Stren et al., 1992; Platt et al., 1994). While such approaches have long term benefits for all living things, the sustainable cities literature pays little attention to questions of animals per se.[17]

Everyday practices of urban planners, landscape architects and urban designers shape normative expectations and practical possibilities for human-animal interactions. Their practices, however, do not reflect desires to enrich interactions between people and animals through design. Even companion animals are ignored; despite the fact that there are more US households with companion animals than children, such animals remain invisible to architects and planners.[18] What explains this anthropocentrism on the part of urban design and architectural professions? Social theories of urban design and professional practice could be used to better understand the anthropocentric production of urban space and place. Cuff, for example, explains the quotidian behavior of architects as part of a collective, interactive social process conditioned by institutional contexts including the local state and developer clients to favor the growth orientation of contemporary urbanism (Cuff, 1991). Evernden argues that planning and design professionals are constrained by the larger culture's insistence on rationality and order and the radical exclusion of animals from the city (Evernden, 1992). The look of the city as

created by planners and architects, dominated by standardized design forms such as the suburban tract house surrounded by manicured, fenced lawn, reflects the deep-seated need to protect the domain of human control by excluding weeds, dirt and – by extension – nature itself.

Environmental designers drawing on conservation biology and landscape ecology have more actively engaged the question of how to design new metropolitan landscapes for animals and people than have planners or architects. (Foreman and Godron, 1986). At the regional scale, wildlife corridor plans or reserve networks are in vogue (Little, 1990; Smith and Hellmund, 1993). Wildlife networks and corridors are meant to link "mainland" habitats beyond the urban fringe, achieve overall landscape connectivity to protect gene pools, and provide habitat for animals with small home ranges. Neither reserve network models nor wildlife corridors have escaped criticism from within the scientific establishment, mostly due to potentially deleterious edge effects.[19] Can corridors protect and reintegrate animals in the metropolis? Corridor planning is a recent development, and we need case-specific political-economic analyses of corridor plans to answer this question. Preliminary experience suggests that at best large-scale corridors can offer vital protection to gravely threatened keystone species and thus a variety of other animals, while small-scale corridors can be an excellent urban design strategy for allowing common small animals, insects and birds to share urban living space with people. However, grand corridor proposals can degrade into an amenity for urban recreationists (since they often win taxpayers' support only if justified on recreational rather than habitat conservation grounds). At worst, corridors may become a collaborationist strategy that merely smoothes a pathway for urban real estate development into wilderness areas.

A growing number of urban grassroots struggles revolve around the protection of specific wild animals or animal populations, and around the preservation of urban wetlands, forests, and other wildlife habitat due to their importance to wildlife. Also, growing awareness of companion animal wants and desires has stimulated grassroots efforts to create specially-designed spaces for pets in the city such as dog parks (Wolch and Rowe, 1993). Political action around wildlife appears to arise as a result of particular episodes in urban history.[20] Activism around companion animals, for example, is often targeted at local animal shelters selling stray pets to bio-medical research labs, or at cities that ban dogs from parks or prohibit off-leash dog play considered essential to the health and happiness of urban canines.

We have very little systematic information about what stimulates such grassroots transspecies urban practices, or about the connections between such struggles and other forms of local eco/animal activism. It is not clear if grassroots struggles around animals in the city are linked organizationally either to larger-scale environmental activism or green politics, or to traditional national animal welfare organizations. Ephemeral and limited case study information suggests that political action around urban animals can expose deep divisions within environmentalism and the animal welfare establishment. These divisions mirror the broader political splits between mainstream environmentalism and the environmental justice movement, between animal rights organizations and environmentalists, and between groups with animal rights versus animal welfare orientations. For example, many mainstream groups only pay lip service to social justice issues and so many activists of color continue to consider traditional environmental priorities such as wildlands and wildlife – especially in cities – as at best a frivolous obsession of affluent white suburban environmentalists, and at worst reflective of pervasive elitism and racism. Local struggles around wildlife issues can also expose the philosophical split between holistic environmental groups and individualist animal rights activists; for example, such conflicts often arise over proposals to kill feral animals in order to protect native species and ecosystem fragments. Reformist animal welfare organizations such as urban humane

societies, concerned primarily with companion animals and often financially dependent on the local state, may be wary of siding with animal rights/liberation groups critical not only of state policies but also standard practices of humane societies themselves.[21]

The rise of organizations and informal groups acting to preserve animal habitats in the city, change management policies, and protect individual animals indicates a shift in everyday thinking about the positionality of animals. If such a shift is underway, why and why now? One possibility is that ecocentric environmental ethics and especially animal rights thinking, with its parallels in discourses on racism, sexism, and "speciesism," have permeated popular consciousness and stimulated new social movements around urban animals. Other avenues of explanation may open up by theorizing transspecies movements within the broader context of new social movement theory, which points to these movements' consumption-related focus, grass-roots, localist, and anti-state nature, and linkages to the formation of new sociocultural identities necessitated by the postmodern condition and contemporary capitalism. (Touraine, 1988; Melucci, 1989; Scott, 1990). Viewed through the lens of new social movement theory, struggles to resist incursions of capital into urban wildlife habitat or defend the interests of animals in the city could be contextualized within larger social and political-economic dynamics as they after forms of activism and change individual-level priorities for political action. Such an exercise might even reveal that new social movements around animals transcend both production and consumption-related concerns, and instead reflecting a desire to span the human/animal divide by extending networks of caring and friendship to nonhuman others.

Toward Zoöpolis

Zoöpolis presents both challenges and opportunities for those committed to eco-socialist, feminist and anti-racist urban futures. At one level, the challenge is to overcome deep divisions in thinking about nonhumans and their place in the human moral universe. Perhaps more crucial is the challenge of political practice, where purity of theory gives way to a more situated ethics, coalition-building and formation of strategic alliances. Can progressive urban environmentalism build a bridge to those people struggling around questions of urban animals, just as reds have reached out to greens, greens to feminists, feminists to those fighting racism? In specific contexts where real linkages are forged, the range of potential alliances is apt to be great, extending from groups with substantial overlap with progressive environmental thinking, to those whose communalities are more tenuous and whose foci are more parochial. Making common cause on specific efforts to fight toxics, promote recycling, or shape air quality management plans with grassroots groups whose raison d'être is urban wildlife, pets, or farm animal welfare may be difficult. The potential to expand and strengthen the movement is significant, however, and should not be overlooked.

The discourse of zoöpolis creates a space to initiate outreach, conversation and collaboration in these borderlands of environmental action. Zoöpolis invites a critique of contemporary urbanization from the standpoint of animals, but also from the perspective of people who together with animals suffer from urban pollution and habitat degradation, and who are denied the experience of animal kinship and otherness so vital to their well-being. Rejecting alienated theme park models of human interaction with animals in the city, zoöpolis instead asks for a future in which animals and nature would no longer be incarcerated beyond the reach of our everyday lives, leaving us with only cartoons to heal the wounds of their absence. In a city re-enchanted by the animal kindom, the once-solid Enchanted Kingdom might just melt into air.

NOTES

1   Such commodified animals include those providing city dwellers with opportunities for "nature consumption" and a vast array of captive and companion animals sold for profit.

2   For example, only two segments/articles of CNS have been devoted to the animal question ("Symposium: Animal rights and wrongs," CNS, 3(2), 1992, on whether animals have rights; and Barbara Noske's article "Animals and the green movement in the Netherlands," CNS, 5, 1994, on animal movements in Holland), neither of which focused on questions of urbanization. Other contributions to CNS have dealt with endangered animal species but do not engage with the issue of animal subjectivity; rather, species endangerment is seen as the flashpoint for struggle between capital, labor, environmentalists and the state, which is the object of analysis. But see Bunton (1993) and Noske (1989) for insightful treatments of animal rights and social justice, and domestication and its relation to capitalism.

3   Ironically, this may involve protection from "unnatural" animals such as cattle, feral or exotic animals.

4   For the seminal argument concerning animals as "subjects-of-a-life," see Regan (1986).

5   This argument follows those of Plumwood (1993). See also Benjamin (1988) and Grimshaw (1986).

6   This in no way precludes self-defense against animals such as predators, parasites or microorganisms that threaten to harm people.

7   This evidence has been extensively marshalled by Shepard (1978, 1982, 1996).

8   As highlighted in the following section, there are many animals that do, in fact, inhabit urban areas. But most are uninvited, and many are actively expelled or exterminated. Moreover, animals have been largely excluded from our *understanding* of cities and urbanism.

9   See, for example, Dear and Scott (1981).

10 An example is Laurie (1979).

11 See the three-part study by Kellert (1979, 1980a, b).

12 For an exception, see Shaw and Supplee (1987).

13 Shepard (1993) stresses the wild, while others are more inclusive, such as Noske (1989) and Davis (1995).

14 For exceptions, see Beck (1974) and Haspel and Calhoun (1993).

15 In extreme form, the disturbance perspective can be used politically to rationalize anthropogenic destruction of the environment; see Worster (1993) and Trepl (1994). But see also the response to Trepl from Levins and Lewontin (1994).

16 For feminist/postmodern critiques of science, see Harding (1986), Haraway (1989) and Birke (1994).

17 An interesting exception is the green-inspired manifesto for sustainable urban development (Berg et al., 1986), which recommends riparian setback requirements to protect wildlife, review of toxic releases for their impacts on wildlife, habitat restoration, a department of Natural Life to work on behalf of urban wilderness, citizen education, mechanisms to fund habitat maintenance, and the "creation" of "new wild places."

18 Ironically, they are not quite so inconsequential to the marketing folks at Bank of America, whose series of home loan advertisements began with a neotraditional suburban home with a white man out front. The next ad showed a similar home and a white woman, and the next portrayed a person of color, but the most recent shows the face of a friendly golden retriever!

19 Simberloff and Cox (1987) argue that they may help spread diseases and exotics, decrease genetic variation or disrupt local adaptations and co-adapted gene complexes, spread fire or other contagious catastrophes, and increase exposure to hunters, poachers and other predators. However, Noss (1987) maintains that the best argument for corridors is that the original landscape was interconnected.

20 For examples of such conflicts, see McAninch and Parker (n.d.) and LaGanga (1993).

21 Such practices include putting large numbers of companion animals to death on a routine basis, selling impounded animals to bio-medical laboratories, etc.

REFERENCES

Arkow, P. (ed.) (1987) *The Loving Bond: Companion Animals in the Helping Professions.* Saratoga, CA: R & E Publishers.

Beatley, T. (1994) *Habitat Conservation Planning: Endangered Species and Urban Growth.* Austin: University of Texas Press.

Beck, A. M. (1974) *The Ecology of Stray Dogs: A Study of Free-ranging Urban Animals.* Baltimore: York Press.

Benjamin, J. (1988) *The Bonds of Love: Psychoanalysis, Feminism and the Problem of Domination.* London: Virago.

Benton, T. (1993) *Natural Relations: Ecology, Animal Rights and Social Justice.* London: Verso.

Berg, P., Magilavy, B. and Zuckerman, S. (eds) (1986) *A Green City Program for San Francisco Bay Area Cities and Towns.* San Francisco: Planet Drum Books.

Birke, L. (1994) *Feminism, Animals and Science: The Naming of the Shrew.* Buckingham: Open University Press.

Birke, L. and Hubbard, R. (eds) (1995) *Reinventing Biology: Respect for Life and the Creation of Knowledge.* Bloomington: Indiana University Press.

Botkin, D. B. (1990) *Discordant Harmonies: A New Ecology for the Twenty-first Century.* New York: Oxford University Press.

Boyer, C. M. (1983) *Dreaming the Rational City: The Myth of American City Planning.* Cambridge, MA: MIT Press.

Cronon, W. (1991) *Nature's Metropolis: Chicago and the Great West.* New York: Norton.

Cuff, D. (1991) *Architecture: The Story of Practice.* Cambridge, MA: MIT Press.

Davis, K. (1995) Thinking like a chicken: farm animals and the feminine connection. In C. J. Adams and J. Donovan (eds), *Animals and Women: Feminist Theoretical Explorations*. Durham, NC: Duke University Press.

Dear, M. and Scott, A. J. (1981) *Urbanization and Urban Planning in Capitalist Society*. London: Methuen.

Decker, D. J. and Goff, G. R. (eds) (1987) *Valuing Wildlife: Economic and Social Perspectives*. Boulder, CO: Westview Press.

Demeritt, D. (1994) The nature of metaphors in cultural geography and environmental history. *Progress in Human Geography*, 18(2).

Evernden, N. (1992) *The Social Creation of Nature*. Baltimore: Johns Hopkins University Press.

Foreman, R. T. T. and Gordon, M. (1986) *Landscape Ecology*. New York: John Wiley and Sons.

Frankel, O. H. and Soulé, M. E. (1981) *Conservation and Evolution*. Cambridge: Cambridge University Press.

Gilpin, M. E. and Hanski, I. (eds) (1991) *Metapopulation Dynamics: Empirical and Theoretical Investigations*. New York: Academic Press.

Gray, G. G. (1993) *Wildlife and People: The Human Dimensions of Wildlife Ecology*. Urbana: University of Illinois Press.

Griffin, D. (1984) *Animal Thinking*. Cambridge, MA: Harvard University Press.

Grimshaw, J. (1986) *Philosophy and Feminist Thinking*. Minneapolis: University of Minnesota Press.

Haraway, D. (1989) *Primate Visions: Gender, Race, and Nature in the World of Modern Science*. New York: Routledge.

Haraway, D. (1991) *Simians, Cyborgs, and Women: The Reinvention of Nature*. New York: Routledge.

Harding, S. (1986) *The Science Question in Feminism*. Ithaca, NY: Cornell University Press.

Haspel, C. and Calhoun, R. E. (1993) Activity patterns of free-ranging cats in Brooklyn, New York. *Journal of Mammology*, 74.

Hayles, K. N. (1995) Searching for common ground. In M. E. Soulé and G. Lease (eds) *Reinventing Nature? Responses to Postmodern Deconstruction*. Washington, DC: Island Press.

Hough, M. (1995) *City Form and Natural Process*. New York: Routledge.

Kellert, S. R. (1979) *Public Attitudes toward Critical Wildlife and Natural Habitat Issues, Phase I*. Washington, DC: US Department of Interior, Fish and Wildlife Service.

Kellert, S. R. (1980a) *Activities of the American Public Relating to Animals, Phase II*. Washington, DC: US Department of Interior, Fish and Wildlife Service.

Kellert, S. R. (1980b) *Knowledge, Affection and Basic Attitudes toward Animals in American Society, Phase III*. Washington, DC: US Department of Interior, Fish and Wildlife Service.

Kellert, S. R. (1984) Urban Americans' perceptions of animals and the natural environment. *Urban Ecology*, 8.

King, D. A., White, J. L. and Shaw, W. W. (1991) Influence of urban wildlife habitats on the value of residential properties. In L. W. Adams and D. L. Leedy (eds), *Wildlife Conservation in Metropolitan Environments*. Washington, DC: National Institute of Urban Wildlife.

LaGanga, M. L. (1993) Officials to kill Venice ducks to halt virus. *Los Angeles Times*, May 22, A1.

Laurie, I. (ed.) (1979) *Nature in Cities*. New York: Wiley.

Leedy, D. L., Maestro, R. M. and Franklin, T. M. (1978) *Planning for Wildlife in Cities and Suburbs*. Washington, DC: US Government Printing Office.

Levins, R. and Lewontin, R. C. (1994) Holism and reductionism in ecology. *CNS*, 5.

Little, C. E. (1990) *Greenways for America*. Baltimore: Johns Hopkins University Press.

Logan, J. R. and Molotch, H. L. (1987) *Urban Fortunes: The Political Economy of Place*. Berkeley: University of California Press.

Luke, T. W. (1995) The nature conservancy or the nature cemetery? *CNS*, 6(2).

McAninch, J. B. and Parker, J. M. (1993) Urban deer management programs: a facilitated approach. *Transactions of the 56th North American Wildlife and Natural Resources Conference*, 56, 191.

Melucci, A. (1989) *Nomads of the Present: Social Movements and Individual Needs in Contemporary Society.* Philadelphia: Temple University Press.

Mies, M. and Shiva, V. (1993) *Ecofeminism.* London: Zed Books.

Nagel, T. (1974) What is it like to be a bat? *Philosophical Review*, 83.

National Research Council, Committee on Scientific Issues in the Endangered Species Act (1995) *Science and the Endangered Species Act.* Washington, DC: National Academy Press.

Nelson, A. C., Nicholas, J. C. and Marsh, L. L. (1992) New fangled impact fees: both the environment and new development benefit from environmental linkage fees. *Planning*, 58.

Noske, B. (1989) *Humans and Other Animals: Beyond the Boundaries of Anthropology.* London: Pluto Press.

Noss, R. F. (1987) Corridors in real landscapes: a reply to Simberloff and Cox. *Conservation Biology*, 1.

O'Connor, J. (1988) Capitalism, nature, socialism: a theoretical introduction. *CNS*, 1.

Philo, C. (1996) Animals, geography and the city: notes on inclusions and exclusions. *Environment and Planning D: Society and Space.*

Pickett, S. T. A. and White, P. S. (eds) (1985) *The Ecology of Natural Disturbance and Patch Dynamics.* Orlando, FL: Academic Press.

Platt, R. H., Rowntree, R. A. and Muick, P. C. (eds) (1994) *The Ecological City: Preserving and Restoring Urban Biodiversity.* Minneapolis: University of Minnesota Press.

Plumwood, V. (1993) *Feminism and the Mastery of Nature.* London: Routledge.

Regan, T. (1986) *The Case for Animal Rights.* Berkeley: University of California Press.

Saldana, L. (1994) MSCP plans the future of conservation in San Diego. *Earth Times*, Feb./Mar., 4–5.

Scott, A. (199) *Ideology and the New Social Movements.* London: Unwin Hyman.

Shaffer, M. L. (1981) Minimum population sizes for species conservation. *BioScience*, 31.

Shaw, W. W. and Supplee, V. (1987) Wildlife conservation in rapidly expanding metropolitan areas: informational, institutional and economic constraints and solutions. In L. W. Adams and D. L. Leedy (eds), *Integrating Man and Nature in the Metropolitan Environment.* Washington, DC: National Institute of Urban Wildlife.

Shaw, W. W., Mangun, J. and Lyons, R. (1985) Residential enjoyment of wildlife resources by Americans. *Leisure Sciences*, 7.

Shepard, P. (1978) *Thinking Animals: Animals and the Development of Human Intelligence.* New York: Viking Press.

Shepard, P. (1982) *Nature and Madness.* San Francisco: Sierra Club Books.

Shepard, P. (1993) Our animal friends. In S. R. Kellert and E. O. Wilson (eds), *The Biophilia Hypothesis.* Washington, DC: Island Press.

Shepard, P. (1996) *The Others.* Washington, DC: Earth Island Press.

Simberloff, D. and Cox, J. (1987) Consequences and costs of conservation corridors. *Conservation Biology*, 1.

Smith, D. S. and Hellmund, P. C. (1993) *Ecology of Greenways: Design and Function of Linear Conservation Areas.* Minneapolis: University of Minnesota Press.

Snyder, G. (1990) *The Practice of the Wild.* San Francisco: North Point Press.

Sorkin, M. (ed.) (1992) *Variations on a Theme Park.* New York: Noonday Press.

Soulé, M. E. (1991) Land use planning and wildlife maintenance: guidelines for conserving wildlife in an urban landscape. *Journal of the American Planning Association*, 57.

Soulé, M. E. and Lease, G. (eds) (1995) *Reinventing Nature? Responses to Postmodern Deconstruction.* Washington, DC: Island Press.

Sprin, A. W. (1984) *The Granite Garden: Urban Nature and Human Design.* New York: Basic Books.

Stren, R., White, R. and Whitney, J. (1992) *Sustainable Cities: Urbanization and the Environment in International Perspective.* Boulder, CO: Westview Press.

Touraine, A. (1988) *The Return of the Actor: Social Theory in Postindustrial Society.* Minneapolis: University of Minnesota Press.

Trepl, L. (1994) Holism and reductionism in ecology: technical, political and ideological implications. *CNS*, 5.

Van der Ryn, S. and Calthorpe, P. (1991) *Sustainable Cities: A New Design Synthesis for Cities,
Suburbs, and Towns*. San Francisco: Sierra Club Books.

Wilson, A. (1992) *The Culture of Nature: North American Landscapes from Disneyland to the
Exxon Valdez*. Cambridge, MA: Blackwell.

Wilson, E. (1991) *The Sphinx in the City: Urban Life, the Control of Disorder, and Women*.
Berkeley: University of California Press.

Wolch, J. and Rowe, S. (1993) Companions in the park: Laurel Canyon Dog Park, Los Angeles.
Landscape, 31.

Worster, D. (1993) *The Wealth of Nature: Environmental History and the Ecological Imagination*.
New York: Oxford University Press.

Part VIII
Aesthetics

21

Aesthetic Theory

Jon Lang

Interior designers, architects, landscape architects, and urban designers have long been concerned with creating aesthetic experiences for others. One of the normative issues in design today is concerned with the positions to be taken on who these "others" should be. One of the observations frequently made by both professionals (such as Montgomery, 1966) and nonprofessionals (such as Wales, 1984) is that we design in order to receive accolades from our peers. It suffices to say here that one of the concerns of design is with the creation of the beautiful or the delightful. The search for an understanding of what is beautiful in the built and natural environments has been an exasperating one but not one deserving of Ruskin's (1885) caricature of the endeavor:

> It is the province of aesthetics to tell you (if you did not know already) that the taste and colour of a peach are pleasant; and to ascertain (if it is ascertainable, and you have the curiosity to know) why they are so.

This does remain a good definition of the purpose of aesthetic theory, however. Aesthetics is worth pursuing because we know that taste preferences are not absolute. The taste and the color of peaches are not to everybody's liking. There are different tastes concerning peaches as well as buildings. The science of aesthetics is concerned with (1) identifying and understanding the factors that contribute to the perception of an object or a process as a beautiful or, at least, a pleasurable experience, and (2) understanding the nature of the human ability to create

and to enjoy creating displays that are aesthetically pleasing. There are two broad approaches to the study of aesthetics. The first involves the study of the processes of perception, cognition, and attitude-formation, while the second involves the study of aesthetic philosophies and the creative processes. The first is psychological in character, and the second is largely metaphysical and psychoanalytical (see, for instance, Ehrenzweig 1967). The first is concerned with positive theory and the second with the normative theories of designers as artists. The concern here is with the former.

In studying aesthetics, many people, particularly in Western society since the Renaissance, differentiate between those elements in the environment that are considered works of art and those that are not – between architecture and buildings. This is an artificial distinction, and although it is not made here, it does have to be recognized. The study of aesthetic objects deals with the individual as an observer and contemplator, while the study of the experiencing of the environment as a whole considers the individual as a participant in life, of which the built environment is a part. People do indeed stand and stare and analyze the structure of buildings, landscapes, and paintings. This is not a characteristic behavior in all societies, nor was it in earlier times in Western civilization, nor is it characteristic of all people in Western cultures today. These other societies did produce what we call art but their attitudes seem to have been very different from ours today in that they did not consider such artifacts works of art (Berlyne, 1974). The concern in this chapter is with the contribution of the behavioral sciences to the understanding of the aesthetic experiencing of the built world around us as part of our everyday lives.

While the psychological study of aesthetic experience can be said to have started with Gustav Fechner in 1876, there has been a prevailing feeling, as Ruskin suggested, that aesthetic values cannot be subjected to scientific study. This attitude may have been valid in the past because of the narrowness of many investigations of aesthetics. The richness of research during the past century, while by no means providing a complete understanding of the nature of environmental aesthetics, does provide a broad basis for the development of environmental design theory.

The goal of the psychological study of aesthetics has been to proceed from observation to generalization, instead of working downward from deductions. Nevertheless, the branch of philosophy and psychology known as speculative aesthetics is still very much alive for it provides a broad basis for asking what it is about the built environment that should be studied.

Speculative Aesthetics

Speculative aesthetics, like early psychological research, relies heavily on introspective analysis by an individual of his or her own beliefs about what is beautiful and/or pleasurable. There have been several approaches to doing this (see Morawski, 1977). The hermeneutic, phenomenological, existential, and political approaches are all philosophical. These can be contrasted to the scientific or quasi-scientific approaches – the psychoanalytical and the psychological. Hermeneutics relies on the interpretation of the environment as a text. While phenomenology can mean many things, in the study of aesthetics, it focuses on the gleaning of intuitive insights into the cognitive relationship between person and environment. The existential approach has focused primarily on the creative act and the created artifact. The political approach, mainly Marxist, considers art as a product and representation of the class struggle. The psychoanalytical approach has focused also on the artistic endeavor, explaining it largely in terms of a cathartic act. All these approaches shed some light on art and the environment, but they do not tell us much about how people experience the environment. Of particular interest in creating environmental design theory is the work of a group of people who have drawn on psychological theories as well as introspective analysis in order to construct models of the nature of the aesthetic experience. These models not only provide a useful framework for architectural criticism, but they also are open to testing.

Stephen C. Pepper (1949) identified four schools of such endeavor: the *mechanistic*, the *contextualist*, the *organismicist* (also known as the school of "objective idealism"), and the *formist*. The work of George Santayana (1896), John Dewey (1934), Bernard Bosanquet (1931), and Rudolf Arnheim (1949, 1965, 1977) can be regarded as exemplars of each school, respectively (Cole, 1960). The first three drew their ideas from empiricist schools of perception theory, while Arnheim is a Gestalt psychologist. More recent concepts of aesthetics draw heavily on the work of this group.

In the *mechanistic* approach to aesthetic theory, the artifact is considered to stimulate people with sensations or images coming from it or associated with it. Santayana, like many psychologists since his time, was concerned with the pleasurableness of some sensations. To Santayana, a beautiful environment is one that gives pleasure to its beholder. It is "value positive." This value is said to be intrinsic to the object or event – it is part of its structure. Many of Santayana's ideas reflect the state of psychological theory at the turn of the century. Of particular interest to us today, more than the details of Santayana's philosophy, is the overall distinction he made between sensory value, formal values, and expression or associative value (what will be called here "symbolic value"). This distinction is largely in accord with the ecological approach to perception (see Gibson, 1979).

Sensory values are those generated by pleasurable sensations. They are obtained from the touches, smells, tastes, sounds, and sights of the world. Santayana stated that sensory pleasure may be an element of beauty at the same time as the ideas associated with it become elements of objects – an empiricist position. The sensory experience of the lower senses (touch, smell, and taste), however, does not serve the purpose of intelligence in human beings as well as the experience of the higher senses (sight and hearing), thus they are not as important in the aesthetic appreciation of the environment.

Formal values arise from the order of sensory material. This again is in accordance with the empiricist position on perception. Formal values deal with the pleasurableness of the structure, or patterns, of the artifact or process being considered (Santayana was also very interested in the experiencing of music). Of concern is the perception of the system of relationships that exist in the patterns. Some of these have to do with the patterns *per se* – their proportions and ordering principles. One has to do with what Santayana calls "determinate organization." In this case the form is based on its instrumental function. Santayana notes:

> The organization . . . is served by practical demands. Use requires buildings to assume certain forms, the mechanical perception of our materials; exigency of shelter, light accessibility, economy and convenience can dictate the arrangement of our buildings.

Determinate organization is the same concept as that embodied in the slogan "form follows function" of Santayana's contemporary, Louis Sullivan.

Expression or *associational values* are those that Santayana believed arose from the images evoked by sensory values. Santayana saw the associative process as an "immediate activity." This is something that both psychologists and design critics still have difficulty explaining. It is said that the association enters consciousness directly and "produces as simple a sensation as any process in any organ." He suggested that there are three types of expressive or associational value: *aesthetic, practical,* and *negative.* Aesthetic value is the perception that something is beautiful because of its associations for the observer. Practical values arise from the expression of utility of an object – not only does it have to work but it has to look as if it works. Negative values arise from the pleasure of being shocked, from the grotesque, from frightening or other supposedly unpleasant experiences.

Implicitly or explicitly, most speculations on the nature of the aesthetic experience suggest that it consists of sensory, formal, and associational values. Different writers stress different aspects. Some writers dealing with the aesthetics of the built environment (such as Prak, 1968) focus on the formal and symbolic aspects of it. Some writers focus on works of art; others focus on the everyday world.

John Dewey (1934) objected to the consideration of the aesthetic experience as something apart from everyday life. The aesthetic experience, he suggested, arises from the everyday lives of people, although it may be related to specific things and activities. For Dewey, in contrast to Santayana, sensory value is not fundamental, but it provides the input for the appreciation of the forms of the environment. Unity, he believed, is the highest formal value and can be obtained in many ways, for example, through rhythm – the ordered variation of change – or through symmetry. Dewey also stressed the intrinsic meaning of shapes and forms. In this his thinking paralleled that of the Gestalt psychologists (Köhler, 1929; Koffka, 1935; Wertheimer, 1938) who were his contemporaries. Dewey was particularly concerned with the space – time relationship of the environment so he paid special attention to the sequential character of perception. In this way he anticipated the psychological research of James J. Gibson (1950) and the writings on environmental aesthetics by Martienssen (1956), Thiel (1961), Cullen (1962), and Halprin (1965), all of whom stress the role of *movement* in environmental perception and appreciation. Dewey introduced ideas such as the culmination, anticipation, and fulfillment of expectations in explaining what it is about sequential experiences that gives pleasure.

The organismicist philosophers offer less in the way of a structured approach to environmental analysis. Bosanquet (1931) notes that "the point of aesthetic attitude lies in the fusion of a body and soul, where the soul is a feeling and the body its expression without residue on either side." His is a poetic rather than a behavioral science approach to the study of aesthetic. Yet his philosophy echoes Dewey's.

The formist approach to aesthetics, as exemplified by Arnheim (1949, 1965, 1966, 1977) but historically associated with Albers (1963), Kandinsky (1926), and Klee (1925), stresses the role of the expressive value of patterns of form in aesthetic experience. The linkage between Gestalt theory and aesthetic philosophy is clear and often explicit (for instance, Kepes 1944, Arnheim 1977). The perception of form is explained in terms of the Gestalt principles of field forces and the process of isomorphism. Expression is a function of line and plane and form. The sensory object and the form in which it is presented are said to have direct physiognomic properties which stimulate the brain center of vision, setting up corresponding forces that form the basis of expression. In the Modern Movement in architecture, expression was regarded as the *raison d'être* of art.

All these views of aesthetics have been shaped by contemporary understandings of the perceptual processes and attitude-formation. All are weak in explaining individual differences in attitudes toward the environment. The historical development of empirical aesthetics has consisted of a more serious attempt to deal with these. It has focused more on individual experiences in order to establish what might be universal.

Empirical Aesthetics

The behavioral sciences have relied on scientific or quasi-scientific techniques in the analysis of the aesthetic experience. Most studies have relied on correlational analysis, in which the relationship between two or more factors that vary, either naturally or because one is deliberately manipulated, is measured. Most of the current psychological research has focused on the formal, or structural, aspects of objects as the independent variable and people's subjective feelings about them as the dependent variable. Characteristics of the object are correlated with characteristics of the response which are correlated with characteristics (personality, socioeconomic status, cultural background) of the people concerned.

There have been four important theoretical orientations to these studies: *information-theory* approaches (not to be confused with the Gibson's information-based theory of perception), *semantic* approaches, *semiotic* approaches, and *psychobiological approaches* (Berlyne, 1974). Research within each of these orientations is being conducted at present.

The Information-Theory Approach

Information theory deals with the environment as a set of messages that act as stimuli. There are two approaches to the use of information theory in developing aesthetic theory. The first bases its approach on empiricist theories of form, while the second uses information theory as a framework of analysis. Abraham Moles (1966) works within the first approach, while Rudolf Arnheim's work *Entropy and Art* (1971) is representative of the second.

Moles (and others such as Frank, 1959 and Bense, 1969) considers a building or a landscape to be a composition of elements each of which transmits messages. The pleasurableness of the message is related to its degree of structure. The greater the orderliness of the message, Moles believes, the more intelligible and pleasant it is.

The basic propositions of information-based models of aesthetics can be mapped onto Santayana's framework of *sensory value*, *formal value*, and *associational value*. Sensory values constitute one of the components of the aesthetic experience. The individual receives messages from the environment through the visual, oral and other sensory systems. The research has focused mainly on vision and hearing because they provide most individuals with most information. It has attempted to identify the amounts of information that a person can process optimally. Formal values arise from the structuring of the message. The structure of the built environment is said to vary principally in complexity. Moles differentiates between two types of complexity: structural and formal. The first deals with a status description ("the built environment is composed of...") and the second with a process description ("the built environment is made to..."). The degree of structure in both is the major indicator of aesthetic preferences. Structure *per se* is not, however, the only contributor to the pleasurableness of messages; the content is important, too. Messages are said to have semantic, cultural, expressive, and syntactic information, but the analyses of these has not formed a major part of the research agenda of Moles and others working within the framework of information theory.

Arnheim (1971) also deals with formal values. He does not take issue with Moles's observations on the orderliness of messages. He notes:

The information given literally means to give form and form means structure. The rehabilitation of order as a universal principle, however, suggested at the same time that orderliness by itself is not sufficient to account for the nature of organized systems in general and for those created by man in particular. Mere orderliness leads to increased impoverishment and finally to the lowest level of structure no longer clearly distinguishable from chaos which is the absence of order.

The simplest level of order, according to Arnheim, results from the homogeneity of elements. He believes that more complex orders afford greater pleasure. Thus he concludes:

A structure can be more or less orderly at any level of complexity. The level of ordered complexity is the level of order. The aesthetic is derived from the relation between order and complexity.

Thus, in this view of aesthetics, the perception of environmental quality is associated closely with well-ordered, complex messages. It is also associated with ambiguity in the sense that the structure of the environment contains different ordering principles perceivable by the same person or by different people (see also Rapoport and Kantor, 1967). The observation is that the greater the multiplicity of meaning the greater the pleasurableness of the environment, provided a sense of order is maintained.

The Semantic Approach

The semantic approach focuses on the meaning of elements of the environment and not on the patterns of the structure *per se*. The meaning is a learned association between the object and an idea. The approach draws heavily on some basic ideas from linguistics.

[In a written language] the word results from the combination of a particular form with a particular meaning...the form of the word signifies "things" by virtue of the "concept" associated with the form...in the minds of the speakers of the language. (Lyons, 1968)

Meanings of the built environment are considered in a similar fashion in many interpretive studies of buildings. This line of thinking is characteristic of many of the recent writings on the subject (such as Norberg-Schulz, 1965).

The Semiotic Approach

Like the semantic approach, the semiotic approach to environmental aesthetics is derived from linguistics and can be seen as either an extension of the semantic approach or as a contradiction to it (Gandelsonas, 1974). If one believes it to be concerned with both learning and the transfer of meaning, then it is an extension of the semantic approach. If one asserts that learning is different from the formation of associations in context, then it is a contradiction (Berlyne, 1974). The approach is based on the writings of the philosopher Ferdinand de Saussure (1915). De Saussure considered the associational relationship between pattern and meaning to be internal to the sign, but he stressed that the context is important because the same element may mean different things in different places (see also Morris, 1935). Thus, the semiotic approach to environmental aesthetics is concerned with the cultural system of meanings of the natural and built environments. The semantic and semiotic approaches to environmental aesthetics have had a profound influence on recent thinking about architecture (see Broadbent et al., 1980) and provide the theoretical basis for much of the ideology of Post-Modernism in architecture (Jencks, 1969, 1977).

The Psychobiological Approach

The psychobiological approach has antecedents in Gestalt psychology. It explains aesthetic responses to patterns of the built environment in terms of the neurophysiological processes of the brain. Recent research within this approach is characterized by the work of D. E. Berlyne (1974). Berlyne suggests that the arousal level of an individual is correlated with his or her perception of the interestingness of the environment. The arousal level is dependent on the structure of the environment and on the personality and motivational or needs level of the individual. The environmental characteristics may be: (1) of a psychophysical nature (such as color, intensity); (2) of an ecological nature "involving a correlation with events that promote or threaten biological adaptation"; or (3) of a structural or a collative nature (variables such as simplicity or complexity, expectedness or surprisingness, clarity or ambiguity). The basic conclusion is that pleasure arises when adverse conditions are removed or moderate levels of arousal are achieved. Moderate levels of arousal occur when there are moderate levels of deviation

from the norm, or the adaptation level (Helson, 1948, 1964).

Empirical Aesthetics and Environmental Design Theory

The research agenda of empirical aesthetics has been concerned primarily with "the experimental investigation of judgments of preference for simple stimuli." The goal has been "to build up from below those stimuli and combinations which would be used in complete works of art" (Pickford, 1972). This is the goal that Fechner set himself. The assumption is that as stimulation varies so does the perception of the aesthetic quality of the source, be it a painting, a building, or a landscape. Thus, if one could measure the stimulation afforded by different patterns of the physical environment, say, and understand the hedonic responses of different people to these, then one would have an empirical theory of environmental aesthetics. This is not possible, however. At least, it is not yet possible!

There has been much experimental research. There have been many studies of the expressiveness of lines, masses, and volumes, of what makes a form simple or complex, of perceptions of order, of color preferences, and so on. Subjects have included adults, children, and people of different socioeconomic groups and cultural backgrounds. These studies show that there are some agreements and some disagreements. Several correlations have been established and these show that "beauty is largely in the eye of the beholder." Certainly the early goal of showing that some patterns and symbols are perceived universally as beautiful has not been achieved.

No unified theory or generally accepted model of environmental aesthetics has emerged from all this research. The problem simply may be that the theories of perception implicit and explicit in the questions posed by psychologists in the course of empirical research on aesthetics are ill-founded. They are all sensation-based theories. Many are highly empiricist in nature. Yet the correlations between environmental characteristics and subjective feelings about them do exist and cannot simply be dismissed. A reinterpretation of the approaches of speculative aesthetics and empirical aesthetics allows a synthetic model to be offered. This model seems to promise much in understanding environmental aesthetics.

A Tentative Approach to Environmental Aesthetics

The environment, as has been argued earlier, can be considered to consist of a nested set of behavior settings. The basic hypothesis here is that people's responses to a place are to its structure as a behavior setting. Their attitude toward the behavior setting can be explained in terms of their attitudes toward the standing pattern of behavior occurring there and the people involved as well as the milieu. In terms of environmental design theory, however, the concern is largely with the milieu. This narrower concern does introduce a distorting factor in analyzing people's everyday experience.

A broad definition of aesthetic experience would encompass all the goals of design because "pleasure" is derived from the fulfillment of each of them. Thus, people get pleasure from an environment whose structure well affords standing patterns of behavior in a physiologically comfortable way. To achieve this, the structure of the environment has to be related uniquely to the needs and purposes of the people involved in terms of their organismic, personality, social group, and cultural characteristics within a specific geographic context.

Given an environment that well affords a standing pattern of behavior, it is aesthetically pleasing if it provides pleasurable sensory experiences, if it has a pleasing perceptual structure, and if it has pleasurable symbolic associations. This means that the variables of stimulus energy – the intensity of light, color, sound, odor, and touch attended to by a user or observer – are pleasurable. It means that the formal attributes – the patterning of the environment through the structuring of surfaces, textures, illumination, and colors – are pleasurable. It means that the associations

evoked by the patterns are pleasurable. As Santayana suggested, these seem to be the three major dimensions of the aesthetic experiencing of the environment.

There are some major assumptions about the nature of the perceptual processes behind this statement. It assumes that aesthetics is concerned with the experiencing of beauty or pleasurableness. It assumes that inputs to the nervous system can be differentiated from perceptions of the world. There is much evidence that people do seek certain types of sensations (Gibson, 1966) and that we do seek to enjoy the patterns of the environment for their own sake. It assumes that certain patterns of the environment may resonate more pleasantly than others because of the neural structure of the human perceptual system. It assumes that the associational meanings – the symbolism – of the environment is important, consciously or subconsciously, to people.

Little has been said about *sensory aesthetics* in recent years. What has been written is based largely on introspection (such as Rasmussen, 1959; Heschong, 1979) rather than on experimentation, although historically this was the major subject of experimental concern (see Boring, 1942). The reason is that people do not pay much attention to sensations – the self-awareness of the arousal of the sensory systems – that we obtain from the environment. We can do so. We can pay attention to the environment as patches of color, or to the sensation of the wind deforming our skin, or to the tensions in our muscles as we walks across a floor, but we seldom do. We become aware of sensations when they deviate from the norm, when they become pleasant or unpleasant. There are situations when the sensations one receives are very pleasantly arousing. Walking through patches of light and shade, standing on a beach when the wind is blowing in one's face and the air one breathes is rich in ozone, being hot and feeling a cooling breeze that has blown across water – these are all situations in which one becomes aware of the sensory aspect of perception. Sensory aesthetics is an important component of a person's response to the environment. The paucity of research on the subject at a level of concern to environmental designers makes it a topic that is impossible to pursue in this book. It remains an area of potential contribution by the behavioral sciences to environmental design theory.

Formal aesthetics has been of central concern to designers since the inception of a self-conscious concern about design. The focus of this concern has been on the visual structure of the environment. It is so also in this book. This does not deny the role of sonic, tactile, and olfactory experience in a person's appreciation of the environment. The focus of research has been on the visual, except for the study of the acoustic qualities of different patterns of buildings and rooms. This research has been more the subject of physical science research rather than of behavioral science. Thus, the contribution of the behavioral sciences to environmental design theory is largely in the area of visual qualities of the environment. The concern is with its syntactic or geometric qualities. There is some concern as to whether formal aesthetics is something separate from symbolic aesthetics. Perhaps it is just another symbol system that designers have created to communicate with themselves and a few other of the cognoscenti. The concept of expression, in particular, has been the subject of much controversy. It depends on whether one accepts the Gestalt theory of perception as to whether one considers expression to be a topic of formal or symbolic aesthetics. It will be considered in both places here to illustrate the basic issue.

Symbolic aesthetics is concerned with the associational meanings of the environment that give people pleasure. The environment is inevitably a symbol system giving "concrete expression to concepts of values, meanings and the like" (Rapoport, 1977). The symbolism of the environment is thus central to one's liking or disliking of it.

Conclusion – Works of Art

An object or environment can be regarded as a work of art if it communicates a message from one person or group to another. Some objects are purposefully designed to serve this purpose; others acquire this role over time. In the latter case the work may not have been perceived originally as a work of art but it acquires this meaning. Works of art are thus artificial displays. The display may be a formal one – of patterns *per se* – or a symbolic one dealing with associational values. This definition covers works such as paintings, musical compositions, buildings, and landscapes that were created purposefully as works of art as well as objects that were perceived as serving purely utilitarian purposes but came to be regarded as works of art. Thus, a West African sculpture which was perceived to be simply a means to ward off evil spirits may come to be regarded as a work of art even though its creator never thought of it as such.

If one accepts this definition, then a number of observations can be made about buildings, landscapes, and urban designs:

1. Not all their message are regarded as those that can qualify them as works of art. Artificial criteria (norms) have been established to define what is and what is not a work of art. These norms differ for different populations and vary over time. They are established by "tastemakers" (Lynes, 1954). Thus, a mill on the fall line of New England may not have been regarded as a work of art at the time of its construction but it may be now because (a) perceptions of the messages the building communicates have changed, and/or (b) the values regarding its formal patterns or its associated meanings have changed.

2. It is open to debate as to whether:

(a) any of the criteria is biologically based or whether they are all culturally determined;

(b) the distinction between formal and symbolic aesthetics has a basis in human psychology; it is possible that formal displays are simply a subcategory of symbolic ones;

(c) there is a difference between expressive and symbolic messages communicated through built form.

The answers to the second and third of these depend on the answer to the first. There are competing theories of perception, and accepting one over another leads to different answers to the above questions.

3. The built environment can be configured to be a work of art on any dimension of human experience.

REFERENCES

Albers, J. (1963) *Interaction of Color*. New Haven, CT: Yale University Press.

Arnheim, R. (1949) The Gestalt theory of expression. *Psychological Review*, 56, 156–71.

Arnheim, R. (1965) *Art and Visual Perception*. Berkeley and Los Angeles: University of California Press.

Arnheim, R. (1966) *Towards a Psychology of Art*. Berkeley and Los Angeles: University of California Press.

Arnheim, R. (1971) *Entropy and Art: An Essay on Disorder and Order*. Berkeley and Los Angeles: University of California Press.

Arnheim, R. (1977) *The Dynamics of Architectural Form*. Berkeley and Los Angeles: University of California Press.

Bense, M. (1969) *Einführung in die informationstheoretische Aesthetik*. Reinbek: Rohwolt.

Berlyne, D. E. (1960) *Conflict, Arousal and Curiosity*. New York: McGraw-Hill.

Boring, E. G. (1942) *Sensation and Perception in the History of Experimental Psychology*. New York: Appleton-Century.

Bosanquet, B. (1931) *Three Lectures on Aesthetics*. London: Macmillan.

Broadbent, G. (1966) Creativity. In S. A. Gregory (ed.), *The Design Method*. New York: Plenum Press.

Broadbent, G., Bunt, R. and Llorens, T. (eds) (1980) *Meaning and Behavior in the Built Environment*. New York: John Wiley.

Cole, M. v. B. (1960) A comparison of aesthetic systems: background for the identification of values in city design. Mimeograph, University of California at Berkeley.

Cullen, G. (1962) *Townscape*. London: Architectural Press.

de Saussure, F. (1915) *Course in General Linguistics*, trans. W. Barker. New York: McGraw-Hill (1959).

Dewey, J. (1920) *How We Think*. London: Heath.

Dewey, J. (1934) *Art as Experience*. New York: Putnam.

Ehrenzweig, A. (1967) *The Hidden Order of Art: A Study in the Psychology of Artistic Imagination*. Berkeley: University of California Press.

Fechner, G. T. (1876) *Vorschule der Aesthetik*. Leipzig: Gebr. Mann.

Frank, H. (1959) *Grundlagenprobleme der Informationsästhetik und erste Anwending auf die Mime pure*. Quickborn: Verlag Schnelle.

Gandelsonas, M. (1974) Linguistic and semiotic models in architecture. In W. R. Spillers (ed.), *Basic Questions of Design Theory*. New York: American Elsevier, pp. 39–54

Gibson, J. J. (1950) *The Perception of the Visual World*. Boston: Houghton Mifflin.

Gibson, J. J. (1966) *The Senses Considered as Perceptual Systems*. Boston: Houghton Mifflin.

Gibson, J. J. (1979) *An Ecological Approach to Visual Perception*. Boston: Houghton Mifflin.

Halprin, L. (1965) Motation. *Progressive Architecture*, 46(7), 126–33.

Helson, H. (1948) Adaptation level as a basis for a quantitative theory of frames of reference. *Psychological Review*, 55, 297–313.

Helson, H. (1964) *Adaptation-level Theory*. New York: Harper & Row.

Heschong, L. (1979) *Thermal Delight in Architecture*. Cambridge, MA: MIT Press.

Jencks, C. (1969) Semiology and architecture. In C. Jencks and G. Baird (eds), *Meaning in Architecture*. New York: George Braziller, pp. 11–26.

Jencks, C. (1977) *The Language of Post-modern Architecture*. London: Academy.

Kandinsky, W. (1926) *Punkt und Linie zu Flache*. Munich: Langen. Published in English as *Point and Line to Plane*. New York: Guggenheim Museum, *c*.1947.

Kepes, Gyorgy (1944) *Language of Vision*. Cicago: Paul Theobald.

Klee, P. (1925) *Pädagogisches Skizzenbuch*. Munich: Langen. Translated by S. Moholoy-Nagy as *Pedagogical Sketchbook*. New York: Praeger, 1953.

Koffka, K. (1935) *Principles of Gestalt Psychology*. New York: Harcourt Brace.

Köhler, W. (1929) *Gestalt Psychology*. New York: Liveright.

Lyons, J. (1968) *Introduction to Theoretical Linguistics*. New York: McGraw-Hill.

Martienssen, R. D. (1956) *The Idea of Space in Greek Architecture*. Johannesburg: Witwatersrand University Press.

Moles, A. (1966) *Information Theory and Esthetic Perception*. Urbana: University of Illinois Press.

Montgomery, R. (1966) Comment on "Fear and House-as-Haven in the Lower Class." *Journal of the American Institute of Planners*, 32(1), 31–7.

Morawski, S. (1977) Contemporary approaches to aesthetic inquiry: absolute demands and limited possibilities. *Critical Inquiry*, 4 (Autumn), 55–83.

Morris, C. (1938) *Foundations of a Theory of Signs*. Chicago: University of Chicago Press.

Norberg-Schulz, C. (1965) *Intentions in Architecture*. Cambridge, MA: MIT Press.

Pepper, S. C. (1949) *The Basis of Criticism in the Arts*. Cambridge, MA: MIT Press.

Pickford, R. W. (1972) *Psychology and Visual Aesthetics*. London: Hutchinson Educational.

Prak, N. L. (1968) *The Language of Architecture*. The Hague: Mouton.

Rapoport, A. (1967) The personal element in housing: an argument for open-ended design. *Interbuild-Arena*, 14 (October), 44–6.

Rapoport, A. (1977) *Human Aspects of Urban Form*. New York: Pergamon.

Rapoport, A. and Kantor, R. E. (1967) Complexity and ambiguity in environmental design. *Journal of the American Institute of Planners*, 33(4), 210–21.

Rasmussen, S. E. (1959) *Experiencing Architecture*. Cambridge, MA: MIT Press.

Ruskin, J. (1885) *Works*. New York: John Wiley.

Santayana, G. (1896) *The Sense of Beauty*. New York: Dover, 1955.

Thiel, P. (1961) A sequence-experience notation for architectural and urban spaces. *Town Planning Review*, 32, 33–52.

Wales, Prince of (1984) Quoted in the *Times of India*, May 27, v.

Wertheimer, M. (1938) Gestalt theory, The general theoretical situation, and Laws of organization. In W. D. Ellis (ed.), *A Source Book of Gestalt Psychology*. London: Routledge & Kegan Paul, pp. 1–88.

The Urban Artifact as a Work of Art

Aldo Rossi

As soon as we address questions about the individuality and structure of a specific urban artifact, a series of issues is raised which, in its totality, seems to constitute a system that enables us to analyze a work of art. As the present investigation is intended to establish and identify the nature of urban artifacts, we should initially state that there is *something in the nature of urban artifacts that renders them very similar – and not only metaphorically – to a work of art*. They are material constructions, but notwithstanding the material, something different: although they are conditioned, they also condition.

This aspect of "art" in urban artifacts is closely linked to their quality, their uniqueness, and thus also to their analysis and definition. This is an extremely complex subject, for even beyond their psychological aspects, urban artifacts are complex in themselves, and while it may be possible to analyze them, it is difficult to define them. The nature of this problem has always been of particular interest to me, and I am convinced that it directly concerns the architecture of the city.

If one takes any urban artifact – a building, a street, a district – and attempts to describe it, the same difficulties arise which we encountered earlier with respect to the Palazzo della Ragione in Padua. Some of these difficulties derive from the ambiguity of language, and in part these difficulties can be overcome, but there will always be a type of experience recognizable only to those who have walked through the particular building, street, or district.

Thus, the concept that one person has of an urban artifact will always differ from that of someone who "lives" that same artifact. These considerations, however, can delimit our task; it is possible that our task consists principally in defining an urban artifact from the standpoint of its manufacture: in other words, to define and classify a street, a city, a street in a city; then the location of this street, its function, its architecture; then the street systems possible in the city and many other things.

We must therefore concern ourselves with urban geography, urban topography, architecture, and several other disciplines. The problem is far from easy, but not impossible, and in the following paragraphs we will attempt an analysis along these lines. This means that, in a very general way, we can establish a logical geography of any city; this logical geography will be applied essentially to the problems of language, description, and classification. Thus, we can address such fundamental questions as those of typology, which have not yet been the object of serious systematic work in the domain of the urban sciences. At the base of the existing classifications there are too many unverified hypotheses, which necessarily lead to meaningless generalizations.

By using those disciplines to which I have just referred, we are working toward a broader, more concrete, and more complete analysis of urban artifacts. The city is seen as the human achievement *par excellence*; perhaps, too, it has to do with those things that can only be grasped by actually experiencing a given urban artifact. This conception of the city, or better, urban artifacts, as a work of art has, in fact, always appeared in studies of the city; we can also discover it in the form of greatly varying intuitions and descriptions in artists of all eras and in many manifestations of social and religious life. In the latter case it has always been tied to a specific place, event, and form in the city.

The question of the city as a work of art, however, represents itself explicitly and scientifically above all in relation to the conception of the nature of collective artifacts, and I maintain that no urban research can ignore this aspect of the problem. How are collective urban artifacts related to the works of art? All great manifestations of social life have in common with the work of art the fact that they are born in unconscious life. This life is collective in the former, individual in the latter; but this is only a secondary difference because one is a product of the public and the other is for the public: the public provides the common denominator.

Setting forth the problem in this manner, Claude Lévi-Strauss brought the study of the city into a realm rich with unexpected developments. He noted how, more than other works of art, the city achieves a balance between natural and artificial elements; it is an object of nature and a subject of culture. Maurice Halbwachs advanced this analysis further when he postulated that imagination and collective memory are the typical characteristics of urban artifacts.

These studies of the city which embrace its structural complexity have an unexpected and little-known precedent in the work of Carlo Cattaneo. Cattaneo never explicitly considered the question of the artistic nature of urban artifacts, but the close connection in his thinking between art and science as two concrete aspects of the development of the human mind anticipates this approach. Later I will discuss how his concept of the city as the ideal principle of history, the connection between country and city, and other issues that he raised relate to urban artifacts. While at this point I am mostly interested in how he approaches the city, in fact Cattaneo never makes any distinction between city and country since he considers that all inhabited places are the work of man: " ... every region is distinguished from the wilderness in this

respect: that it is an immense repository of labor.... This land is thus not a work of nature; it is the work of our hands, our artificial homeland."

City and region, agricultural land and forest become human works because they are an immense repository of the labor of our hands. But to the extent that they are our "artificial homeland" and objects that have been constructed, they also testify to values; they constitute memory and permanence. The city *is* in its history. Hence, the relationship between place and man and the work of art – which is the ultimate, decisive fact shaping and directing urban evolution according to an aesthetic finality – affords us a complex mode of studying the city.

Naturally we must also take into account how people orient themselves within the city, the evolution and formation of their sense of space. This aspect constitutes, in my opinion, the most important feature of some recent American work, notably that of Kevin Lynch. It relates to the conceptualization of space, and can be based in large measure on anthropological studies and urban characteristics. Observations of this type were also made by Maximilien Sorre using such material, particularly the work of Marcel Mauss on the correspondence between group names and place names among Eskimos. For now, this argument will merely serve as an introduction to our study; it will be more useful to return to it after we have considered several other aspects of the urban artifact – of the city, that is, as a great, comprehensive representation of the human condition.

I will interpret this representation against the background of its most fixed and significant stage: architecture. Sometimes I ask myself why architecture is not analyzed in these terms, that is, in terms of its profound value as a human thing that shapes reality and adapts material according to an aesthetic conception. It is in this sense not only the place of the human condition, but itself a part of that condition, and is represented in the city and its monuments, in districts, dwellings, and all urban artifacts that emerge from inhabited space. It is from this point of view that a few theorists have tried to analyze the urban structure, to sense the fixed points, the true structural junctions of the city, those points from which the activity of reason proceeds.

I will now take up the *hypothesis of the city as a man-made object*, as a work of architecture or engineering that grows over time; this is one of the most substantial hypotheses from which to work.

It seems that useful answers to many ambiguities are still provided by the work of Camillo Sitte, who in his search for laws of the construction of the city that were not limited to purely technical considerations took full account of the "beauty" of the urban scheme, of its form: "We have at our disposal three major methods of city planning, and several subsidiary types. The major ones are the gridiron system, the radial system, and the triangular system. The subtypes are mostly hybrids of these three. Artistically speaking, not one of them is of any interest, for in their veins pulses not a single drop of artistic blood. All three are concerned exclusively with the arrangement of street patterns, and hence their intention is from the start a purely technical one. A network of streets always serves only the purposes of communication, never of art, since it can never be comprehended sensorily, can never be grasped as a whole except in a plan of it. In our discussions so far street networks have not been mentioned for just that reason; neither those of ancient Athens, of Rome, of Nuremberg, or of Venice. They are of no concern artistically, because they are inapprehensible in their entirety. Only that which a spectator can hold in view, what can be seen, is of artistic importance: for instance, the single street or the individual plaza."

Sitte's admonition is important for its empiricism, and it seems to me that this takes us back to certain American experiences which we mentioned above, where artistic quality can be seen as a function of the ability to give concrete form to a symbol. Sitte's lesson beyond question helps to prevent many confusions. It refers us to the technique of urban construction, where there is still the actual moment of designing a square and then a principle which provides for its logical trans-

mission, for the teaching of its design. But the models are always, somehow, the single street, the specific square.

On the other hand, Sitte's lesson also contains a gross misperception in that it reduces the city as a work of art to one artistic episode having more or less legibility rather than to a concrete, overall experience. We believe the reverse to be true, that the whole is more important than the single parts, and that only the urban artifact in its totality, from street system and urban topography down to the things that can be perceived in strolling up and down a street, constitutes this totality. Naturally we must examine this total architecture in terms of its parts.

We must begin with a question that opens the way to the problem of classification – that of the typology of buildings and their relationship to the city. This relationship constitutes a basic hypothesis of this work, and one that I will analyze from various viewpoints, always considering buildings as moments and parts of the whole that is the city. This position was clear to the architectural theorists of the Enlightenment. In his lessons at the Ecole Polytechnique, Durand wrote, "Just as the walls, the columns, &c., are the elements which compose buildings, so buildings are the elements which compose cities."

Typological Questions

The city as above all else a human thing is constituted of its architecture and of all those works that constitute the true means of transforming nature. Bronze Age men adapted the landscape to social needs by constructing artificial islands of brick, by digging wells, drainage canals, and watercourses. The first houses sheltered their inhabitants from the external environment and furnished a climate that man could begin to control; the development of an urban nucleus expanded this type of control to the creation and extension of a microclimate. Neolithic villages already offered the first transformations of the world according to man's needs. The "artificial homeland" is as old as man.

In precisely this sense of transformation the first forms and types of habitation, as well as temples and more complex buildings, were constituted. The *type* developed according to both needs and aspirations to beauty; a particular type was associated with a form and a way of life, although its specific shape varied widely from society to society. The concept of type thus became the basis of architecture, a fact attested to both by practice and by the treatises.

It therefore seems clear that typological questions are important. They have always entered into the history of architecture, and arise naturally whenever urban problems are confronted. Theoreticians such as Francesco Milizia never defined type as such, but statements like the following seem to be anticipatory: "The comfort of any building consists of three principal items: its site, its form, and the organization of its parts." I would define the concept of type as something that is permanent and complex, a logical principle that is prior to form and that constitutes it.

One of the major theoreticians of architecture, Quatremère de Quincy, understood the importance of these problems and gave a masterly definition of type and model:

"The word 'type' represents not so much the image of a thing to be copied or perfectly imitated as the idea of an element that must itself serve as a rule for the model.... The model, understood in terms of the practical execution of art, is an object that must be repeated such as it is; type, on the contrary, is an object according to which one can conceive works that do not resemble one another at all. Everything is precise and given in the model; everything is more or less vague in the type. Thus we see that the imitation of type involves nothing that feelings or spirit cannot recognize...."

"We also see that all inventions, notwithstanding subsequent changes, always retain their elementary principle in a way that is clear and manifest to the senses and to reason. It is similar to a nucleus around which the developments and variations of forms to which the object was susceptible gather and mesh. Therefore a thousand things of every kind have come down to us, and one of the principal tasks of science and philosophy is to seek their origins and primary causes so as to grasp their purposes. Here is what must be called 'type' in architecture, as in every other branch of human inventions and institutions.... We have engaged in this discussion in order to render the value of the word *type* – taken metaphorically in a great number of works – clearly comprehensible, and to show the error of those who either disregard it because it is not a model, or misrepresent it by imposing on it the rigor of a model that would imply the conditions of an identical copy."

In the first part of this passage, the author rejects the possibility of type as something to be imitated or copied because in this case there would be, as he asserts in the second part, no "creation of the model" – that is, there would be no making of architecture. The second part states that in architecture (whether model or form) there is an element that plays its own role, not something to which the architectonic object conforms but something that is nevertheless present in the model. This is the *rule*, the structuring principle of architecture.

In fact, it can be said that this principle is a constant. Such an argument presupposes that the architectural artifact is conceived as a structure and that this structure is revealed and can be recognized in the artifact itself. As a constant, this principle, which we can call the typical element, or simply the type, is to be found in all architectural artifacts. It is also then a cultural element and as such can be investigated in different architectural artifacts; typology becomes in this way the analytical moment of architecture, and it becomes readily identifiable at the level of urban artifacts.

Thus typology presents itself as the study of types that cannot be further reduced, elements of a city as well as of an architecture. The question of monocentric cities or of buildings that are or are not centralized, for example, is specifically typological; no type can be identified with only one form, even if all architectural forms are reducible to types. The process of reduction is a necessary, logical operation, and it is impossible to talk about problems of form without this presupposition. In this sense all architectural theories are also theories of typology, and in an actual design it is difficult to distinguish the two moments.

Type is thus a constant and manifests itself with a character of necessity; but even though it is predetermined, it reacts dialectically with technique, function, and style, as well as with both the collective character and the individual moment of the architectural artifact. It is clear, for example, that the central plan is a fixed and constant type in religious architecture; but even so, each time a central plan is chosen, dialectical themes are put into play with the architecture of the church, with its functions, with its constructional technique, and with the collective that participates in the life of that church. I tend to believe that housing types have not changed from antiquity up to today, but this is not to say that the actual way of living has not changed, nor that new ways of living are not always possible. The house with a loggia is an old scheme; a corridor that gives access to rooms is necessary in plan and present in any number of urban houses. But there are a great many variations on this theme among individual houses at different times.

Ultimately, we can say that type is the very idea of architecture, that which is closest to its essence. In spite of changes, it has always imposed itself on the "feelings and reason" as the principle of architecture and of the city. . . .

Aesthetic Ideology and Urban Design

Barbara Rubin

In the early 1970s, the Atlantic Richfield Oil Company (ARCO) sponsored a series of advertisements which appeared in popular magazines in the United States. Entitled "The Real...The Ideal," the series featured full-color, full-page institutional ads intended to draw attention not to ARCO and its products, but to the American social malaise and especially to its urban manifestations. In one typical ad, "The Real" was depicted as an urban commercial street described generically as "Main Street garish...neon nightmares...graceless buildings...billboards [that] block out the sun" (figure 23.1). By contrast, ARCO's "The Ideal" was represented not by a commercial environment, but by Frank Lloyd Wright's famous "Falling Water," a residence built for a wealthy client in rural Bear Run, Pennsylvania. ARCO's description of "The Ideal" called for "structures designed for beauty and long life as well as for practicality. Man's greatest architectural achievements are those that blend in perfectly with the natural environment, or somehow create an environment of their own. They become as permanent as their natural surroundings."

Implicit in ARCO's juxtaposition of these images of a national "real" and a national "ideal" is the assertion that urban commercial environments are inevitably ugly and probably immoral, and, by contrast, that rural or suburban environments are wholesome and beautiful. Implied also through the medium of advertisement is the notion that we all share a uniform and homogeneous perception of environmental wholesomeness and beauty, and that we are in agreement that "Falling Water" might be an attainable reality for everyone if only we clean up the garish neon nightmares which have become our cities.

An even less sympathetic view of the urban environment was promulgated in advertisements published by Volvo, the Swedish auto maker. In promoting the reliability of its product, Volvo presented its auto as a mobile fortress – "A Civilized Car Built for an Uncivilized World." The "uncivilized world," to Volvo, is the contemporary city symbolically represented in its ad as a wall dense with graffiti (figure 23.2). Graffiti, as we well know, have come to be associated with juvenile gangs, urban poverty, alienation, lawlessness, and racial minorities – the stereotypic components of the "uncivilized world" as viewed by the predominantly white, upper-middle class American to whom Volvo markets its cars.

The diversity of an urban population, or the cosmopolitan range of goods and services exchanged, is rarely taken as an index of urban success by students of urban culture. Instead, urban success is found in a catalogue of a city's noncommercial, nonindustrial institutions: a philharmonic orchestra, art museums, parks, religious and historical shrines, theaters, fine-arts architecture, and unified, monumentalizing plans.

This dichotomy between urban function and urban "culture" reflects a deeper polarization in Western civilization wherein sensitivity to art, music, poetry and other "exalted manifestations of the human spirit" are appreciated essentially and ostensibly for their own intrinsic formal qualities. By placing

The real

A new American art form is emerging:
Main Street Garish.
Some of our cities have become neon nightmares.
Billboards block out the sun.
Graceless buildings flank artless avenues.
Man is separated from nature.

In our haste to build and sell, we have constructed
a nation of impermanence. There is a feeling of built-in
obsolescence in our cities and homes

Figure 23.1 "The Real" as seen by the Atlantic Richfield Oil Company in its advertising campaign of the early 1970s. (Photo: *Time Magazine*, September 3, 1973, p. 26.)

The Volvo 164
A CIVILIZED CAR BUILT FOR AN UNCIVILIZED WORLD.

Figure 23.2 The Uncivilized World according to Volvo: the company's 1973 multimedia promotional theme for radio, television and the press. (Photo: *Time Magazine*, November 12, 1973, p. 42.)

a primary value upon aesthetic behaviors associated with transcendental aspirations, students of culture have been unable to come to terms with the city – the modern city – as a symbolic manifestation of values mediated by forms. As a result, we have not yet been provided with demystified and pragmatic characterizations of urban form and urban function and the ideological relationships between the two. Instead, the modern city is persuasively characterized as an environment of "endless string commercial strips," "thickets of bill-boards," "unsightly mixed usages," "cheap, tawdry honky-tonk store fronts," "a gross commercial carnival," "a Barnum and Bailey world." These are aesthetic responses to urban function which reflect unspoken but deep antipathies

toward a society "committed to the maintenance of efficiency and preservation of individual liberties through free enterprise"
(Berry, 1963, p. 2).

Who Designs the Cities?

In the history of urbanization in the United
States, the few master plans which trans-
cended functional prerequisites can be exemplified by George Washington's late
eighteenth century commission to Pierre
L'Enfant to design the nation's new capital
city. In contrast to the planned design
of Washington, DC, most cities in the United
States evolved as pragmatic mosaics of
individual functions within a geomorpho-
logical framework. By 1890, almost thirty
percent of the entire US population was
living in cities as a result of unprecedented
urban growth during the nineteenth century
(Handlin and Handlin, 1975, p. 143).

In the shift from a rural culture to an increasingly urban one, the centers of social
and economic power in the United States
also shifted. In the nineteenth century,
the inventor-entrepreneur was chiefly responsible not only for the growth of cities
already in existence, but also for the new
towns and cities which developed around
his workshop or factory (Meier, 1963,
p. 76). As an "old money" agrarian aristocracy shifted its base of operation from the
rural estate to the city, it confronted a "new
money" entrepreneur indigenous to the metropolitan environment. This confrontation
engendered conflict. In coming to the city,
the agrarian aristocracy:

wished more than indulgence in a lavish
style of life ... it also wished general acqui-
escence in its position.... The aristocracy –
genuine and putative – wished to bring with
them the commodious features of their
landed estates. They expected the city to
provide them with the elegant squares to
set off their homes, with picturesque monuments, and with parks and boulevards ...
for the gentleman on horseback and for the
lady in her carriage. (Handlin and Handlin,
1975, pp. 21–2)

City-building entrepreneurs were neither
to the manor born nor yet socialized by the
responsibilities and protocols of economic
power. The urbanizing agrarian aristocracy,
unable to compete in numbers or in economic strength with the urban entrepreneur,
nonetheless asserted its birthright claim
to preeminence. Seizing upon the transcendental symbols of high culture, the agrarian
elite:

transformed the theater, the opera and
the museums into institutions, to display
it dominance.... [It] turned music into
classics, art into old masters, literature
into rare books, possessions symbolic of its
status. (Handlin and Handlin, 1975,
pp. 21–2)

Following suit, the inventor-entrepreneur
similarly staged himself according to his own
standards and priorities for measuring
success and accomplishment. He built his
corporate and commercial buildings as
monuments to, and advertisements of, himself. While the culture elite were competing
for Old Master paintings, the emergent titans
of industry were competing for preeminence
on the urban horizon (figure 23.3). A city's
capacity to support museums, operas,
theaters, and art galleries was limited by
civil interest and collective financing; a city's
capacity for monuments to commerce and
industry was constrained only by the limitations of space.

Predictably, the culture elite could find
little comfort in their control of "enculturat-
ing" institutions. By the latter part of the
nineteenth century, they had moved their
theater of operation to aesthetic criticism
of the urban environment. Because they controlled the institutions of "official culture,"
their aesthetic campaigns carried weight and
credibility. They found urban commercial
streets to be "bizarre, blatant, and distracting." Although they understood well the
competitive nature of "free enterprise" with
its base in individual liberty, they objected to
the use of the city as a backdrop for "hideous
advertisements ... [buildings with] striking
colors ... great height [and] sudden littleness

Figure 23.3 An example of commercial competition for skyline dominance: the Bromo-Seltzer Tower Building in Baltimore, Maryland.

in a wilderness of skyscrapers" (Robinson, 1901, p. 132).

The inventor-entrepreneur, on the other hand, despite his anarchic and individualistic approach to economic competition as manifested in his use of urban space in the late nineteenth century, entertained "cultural" aspirations commensurate with his wealth (Lynes, 1955, p. 167). These aspirations became a source of vulnerability. Employing the tyranny of high culture aesthetics – *terra incognita* to the entrepreneur – the culture elite soon joined forces with architects, designers, planners, and social reformers, a highly cosmopolitan corps of professional taste-makers. By this alliance, they attempted to codify and disseminate standards of "good taste" in the latter half of the nineteenth century.[1] The "good taste" industry was relatively new, however, and no hierarchical ranking of "schools of good taste"

or "morally correct" style was available. Merchant kings and entrepreneurs, industrialists and inventors, employed architects or designers whom they believed respectable, only to find photographs of their new corporate headquarters illustrating "Architectural Aberrations," a regular feature in the professional journal, *The Architectural Record* (figure 23.4). Under these circumstances, confusion prevailed.

Confusion Resolved

The promulgation of legislated aesthetics would not occur until the middle of the twentieth century.[2] In the late nineteenth century, persuasion by example alone was to suffice, and a very effective program it became. The

Figure 23.4 An "Architectural Aberration": the Record Building in Philadelphia. (Photo: *Architectural Record*, Vol. 1, No. 3, p. 262.)

medium which was to carry the message was already in place.

A series of international expositions and world's fairs had been held in England, Germany, France, Austria, and in the United States (New York and Philadelphia) during the second half of the nineteenth century. These events were arenas in which nations vied with each other to display cultural and economic superiority; they were showcases in which technological innovation could be disseminated worldwide (Pickett, 1877). An implicit dimension of all these fairs became, eventually, quite explicit: the forms of architectural packaging came to be as important as the didactic displays they contained. The occasion of the 400th anniversary celebration of Columbus's discovery of the New World provided the opportunity for the culture elite, in alliance with professional taste-makers, to create the first world's fair explicitly intended to set a standard for architectural and urban design. The fair was held in Chicago in 1893. According to Daniel Burnham, its supervising architect, the overall plan of the exposition and its individual buildings was intended:

> to inspire a reversion to the pure ideal of the ancients.... The intellectual reflex of the Exposition will be shown in the demand for better architecture, and designers will be obliged to abandon their incoherent originalities and study the ancient masters of building. There is shown so much of fine architecture here that people have seen and appreciated this. It will be unavailing hereafter to say that great classic forms are undesirable. The people have a vision before them here, and words will not efface it. (Anon., 1894, p. 292)

In other words, the prevailing aesthetic confusion of the late nineteenth century called for the imprinting, by example, of appropriate architectural design. A precedent, of a sort, existed. In France, l'Ecole des Beaux Arts increasingly had sought to train architects whose designs would blend artfully with the earlier buildings which crowded most of the major cities of Europe (Hamlin, 1953, pp. 605–9).[3] The Beaux Arts

style received its first major American showing at the Chicago Fair of 1893. For the United States, the imported historicism of Beaux Arts design had not to reconcile new urban construction with sanctified architectural relics; American cities were too new to be so demanding of architects' sensitivity and erudition. Instead, the importation of this eclectic Classic/Renaissance/Baroque idiom was intended to codify, by virtue of its "high culture" associations with Europe and Antiquity, the hierarchical framework by means of which "good taste" in America could be distinguished from "bad taste."

The Economics of the Ideal

The Columbian Exposition at Chicago, or "White City" as it was popularly called, had a phenomenal impact. Its courts, palaces, arches, colonnades, domes, towers, curving walkways, wooded island, ponds, and botanical displays elicited ecstatic responses from visitors to whom the "White City" was little short of a fairyland. Its monumental sculptures and gondola-studded water courses and lagoons (created expressly for the Exposition) were tangible references to the "jewel of Italy" – Venice (figure 23.5). And its ground plan, complex and curvilinear, was the antithesis of the nineteenth century urban grid pattern characteristic of most American cities.

The fair as a three-dimensional architectural pattern book opened – and closed – to mixed reviews. Some found in its historic references to European architecture evidence of America's economic and cultural maturity; to others it was a blatant and calculated exploitation of architectural style as social and cultural propaganda, masking "the monstrous evils and injustices of *fin-de-siècle* America" (Fitch, 1948, p. 127).[4] Arguments over the implications of the fair's imported Beaux Arts style masked a more portentous feature, to wit: that its grand-planning design and monumental architecture derived from a single, unified, imposed aesthetic program, and was possible only under circumstances of centralized, authoritarian control. In addition, the realization of so grand a scheme

Figure 23.5   At the Chicago Exposition of 1893, Daniel Chester French's Statue of the Republic rises from the waters of the Grand Basin in front of the arched peristyle crowned with quadriga. (Photo: *Shepp's World's Fair Photographed*, Globe Bible Publishing Co., Chicago, 1893, p. 23.)

was possible only through decentralized funding, and most of the funding was derived from the public. Public guarantee of debenture bonds purchased by banks and railroads and other corporations, public subscription through stock purchases (unbacked and unguaranteed, and subsequently unredeemed), and public admission fees to the fair itself, made construction of the Exposition possible (Anon., 1893). The Exposition represented no financial burden to the elite taste-makers, their lobbyists, theoreticians, and technicians, or to the city builders and commercial-industrial magnates for whom it was intended as an object-lesson in design. Such were the economics of "The Ideal."

The Economics of the Real

It was intended that the Chicago Exposition of 1893 create an image of an urban ideal

which would be "widely understood and approved (Cawelti, 1968, p. 319)." To accomplish that end, individual liberties and competitive enterprise were suspended for the higher good of unified planning and aesthetic qualities. These ideals, as exemplified by the "White City," seemed to require no visible means of economic support. Nonetheless, the success of the Exposition was definitely measured in economic terms – increased railroad revenues and an estimated $105,000,000 left in Chicago by the 3,000,000 visitors to the fair (Anon., 1893).

By the late nineteenth century, the demographics peculiar to international expositions had given rise to a class of petty entrepreneurs who specialized in exploiting the commercial opportunities the fairs made possible. At the Philadelphia Centennial Exposition of 1876, for example, "shrewd outsiders" developed a "play area" beyond the sacrosanct precincts of the city-owned Exposition grounds, in a section which became known as Shantyvile (McCullough, 1966, pp. 31–4). By 1893, the offerings of these businessmen were for the first time acknowledged as a formal component of an Exposition (ibid.). But because the emerging ideology of urban aesthetics could not admit commerce, and since by definition commerce could not be aesthetic, a separate quarter within the walled precincts of the Chicago Exposition was set aside for these commercial activities – a quarter which became known as the Midway Plaisance or amusement zone.

The Midway Plaisance was a separate strip, arranged in a rigid grid pattern, set perpendicular to the grounds of the Exposition proper. In stark contrast to the sinuous arrangement of parks, ponds, and palaces in the "White City," the Midway was a street one mile long by one city block wide, with a central axis upon which commercial attractions lined up neatly along each side. In its straightforward presentation of commercial functions and in its morphology, the Midway Plaisance anticipated the twentieth century string commercial strip or linear shopping center.

Originally, the Midway had been conceived as "Department Q of the Ethnological Division," established for the purpose of gathering "the peculiar and unknown peoples of the world" for display. (Barry, 1901, p. 8). Because a living museum of mankind did not conform to the aesthetic program of the fair, Department Q was assigned quarters adjacent to, rather than integrated with, the Exposition city, and was left to its own devices for funding. By virtue of the necessity of turning a profit simply to exist, the "living museum" and its attendant support activities (curio stands, food stands, amusement rides and entertainments) quickly became a "hilarious amusement zone . . . synonymous for masked folly" (ibid.).

Environments, more or less authentic, were constructed to display their exotic inhabitants: Dahomean, Dutch, Turkish, and American Indian villages, a Moorish Palace,

Figure 23.6 "The Streets of Cairo," a popular exotic environment of the Midway Plaisance, World's Columbian Exposition, 1893. (Photo: *Shepp's World's Fair Photographed*, Globe Bible Publishing Co., Chicago, 1893, p. 507.)

a Chinese Pagoda, and a street in Cairo (figure 23.6). Cultural merchandising proved effective. The raucous, colorful, competitive commerce of the Midway developed as the antithesis of the noneconomic aesthetic ideal of the Beaux Arts "White City." Although the Midway may have sacrificed some veracity in environmental design in favor of sensational impact, visitors judged its impact to be:

> far better than any dead collection of antiquities. To see the people themselves, alive, moving, acting in their costumes, manners, buildings, businesses, is far more instructive than to look at their remains in art, or their empty armor, or their skeletons. (Snider, 1895, pp. 360–1)

The Midway Plaisance and the "White City" alike were architectural illusions. Each was an ephemeral environment in which structures were built merely of stucco applied over lath (attached to framing). The stucco had been ingeniously worked to create the impression of permanent materials: brick, marble, travertine, granite, and other materials and techniques of construction which suggested a material and structural integrity. Almost all the buildings on both the Midway Plaisance and in the "White City" were dismantled and discarded at the conclusion of the Exposition. It was only the "White City," however, which was intended "to leave a residue in the minds of men and in printer's ink" (Bancroft, 1893, p. 4).

The Exposition's spiritual residue was made manifest in tangible programs and artifacts which appeared outside the walled city. The Chicago fair was credited with stimulating the "City Beautiful" movement which spread nationwide through the organization of local municipal arts societies (Robinson, 1901, p. 275; Kriehn, 1899; Blashfield, 1899). It was a movement concerned solely and exclusively with urban aesthetics and not with the economic realities of urban function or the social realities of poverty and class stratification which made the city "ugly."

Civic beautification programs developed the Exposition's Baroque and Neoclassical architectural vocabulary and planning syntax in new banks, city halls, schools, skyscrapers, fire stations, and urban squares throughout the United States (figure 23.7). Urban furniture, such as Dewey Arch in New York City:

> stirred local pride and national interest, and for a mile up Fifth Avenue to the top of Murray Hill its features are most prominent in the view of that thronged thoroughfare. For the whole distance, in a blaze of color by day and a glare of electric flashlights by night, the sculpture and the lines of the Arch...stand out. (Warner, 1900, p. 276)

Dewey Arch was not alone in commanding this spectacular vista; set against it:

> in the daytime, [is] a thirty foot cucumber, in bright green on an orange background

Figure 23.7 An urban "Ideal" confronts an urban "Real": Dewey Arch vs. Heinz Pickles in Madison Square, NewYork. (Photo: *Municipal Affairs*, Vol. IV, 1900, p. 275.)

> above a field of scarlet, lettered in white.... In the evening the dancing flash-light of the "57 varieties" of beans, pickles, etc. [is] thrown in the faces of all who throng Madison Square. (Ibid.)

The sacred "ideal" of the "White City" as well as the profane "real" of the Midway had escaped the controlled precincts of the Exposition, but in the urban milieu the boundaries separating the "real" from the "ideal" blurred. No form was sacrosanct, and no medium was immune to exploitation (figure 23.5). Even the sculptural centerpiece of the Chicago Exposition – Daniel Chester French's monumental Statue of Columbia – ultimately found its way into billboard advertising, and is, in reproduction, an awesome presence in Hollywood's commercial necropolis, Forest Lawn (figure 23.8).[5]

Figure 23.8 One-third the size of the original Statue of the Republic, Forest Lawn's "Republic" stands opposite a monumental statue of George Washington in the cemetery's Court of Freedom. Also an original, this "Republic" was one of two produced by French after the Chicago Exposition. (Height: 18 feet 2 inches; head and arms of Carrara marble, remainder cast in bronze with draperies overlaid with gold.)

Overwhelming the aesthetic program so clearly delineated by the Chicago Exposition, the "advertising curse" proliferated across urban landscapes of America. Its progress was viewed by taste-makers as "a measure at once of progress of civilization and lack of culture" (ibid., p. 269). Fundamentally different from the outset, "The Real," unlike "The Ideal," had to pay its own way.

Migrations of the Propaganda Machine

Despite the massive initial impact of the "White City," the Exposition's aesthetic propaganda almost immediately began to dissipate over space and time. To capitalize on the energy and momentum begun by the Chicago Exposition, a series of similar fairs throughout the United States quickly followed: in 1897, Nashville; in 1898, Omaha; in 1901, Buffalo; in 1904, St Louis; in 1905, Portland. At each, the separation

of commerce and culture was maintained essentially as had been the case at Chicago. Beaux Arts "White Cities," with minor variations and in a different scale, were reproduced at each new site to reinforce the ideals of architectural and urban design (figure 23.9). Whereas the aesthetic ideal for urban design remained more or less static, the competitive ethic of commerce fueled the continued evolution of Midway merchandising.

Midway concessionaires migrated with the expositions. In continuously adjusting and adapting their entertainments and attractions, they sought the optimum synthesis of art and commerce. It was a dual concern which made the Midway zone a dynamic environment for architectural merchandising (figure 23.10). No environment was too exotic and no experience too alien to escape commercial exploitation on the midway. At the Buffalo Pan-American Exposition of 1901, where Midway visitors were offered a trip to the moon, an enervated critic lamented:

> The prodigal modern Midway is fairly using up the earth. A few more Expositions and we shall have nothing left that is wonderfully wonderful, nothing superlatively strange; and the delicious word "foreign" will have dropped out of the language. Where shall we go to get us a new sensation? Not to the heart of the Dark Continent; Darkest Africa is at the Pan American. Not to the frozen North; we have met the merry little fur-swathed, slant-eyed Eskimos behind their papier-mache glacier at Buffalo. Not to the far islands of the Pacific; Hawaiians, and little brown Filipinos are old friends on the new Midway. Not to Japan; tea-garden geisha girls, and trotting, jin-riksha men have rubbed the bloom off that experience. Not Mexico, not Hindoostan, not Ceylon, not the Arabian Desert, can afford us a thrill of thorough-going surprise.... The airship Luna leaves in three minutes for a Trip to the Moon... not satisfied with exhausting the earth, they have already begun upon the universe. Behold, the world is a sucked orange. (Hartt, 1901, p. 1096)

Figure 23.9 In the Beaux Arts tradition, a "White City" constructed for the Louisiana Purchase Exposition, St Louis, 1904: Festival Hall and the Grand Basin. (Photo: *The Universal Exposition*, Official Publication, St Louis, 1904.)

The exposition impulse had migrated to California by 1915. On the occasion of the opening of the Panama Canal, California was host to not one, but two, international expositions. Grand design for expositions had not been substantially altered in the westward migration of world's fairs. At the San Francisco Exposition of 1915, the Beaux Arts architectural environment was a polychrome version of Chicago's "White City." At the San Diego Exposition, held simultaneously with San Francisco's, the same building technology (stucco applied to lath attached to framing) was used to create an Hispanic/colonial "mission style" architecture which would ultimately make its own distinctive contribution to the architectural history of California.

As an object lesson for urban designers, the San Francisco Beaux Arts landscape was anachronistic even before it opened; it represented the last grand floresence of what had begun with the Chicago Exposition of 1893. The entertainment zone at San Francisco,

however, was to be of some consequence in its impact upon urban design.

The Midway at the San Francisco Exposition was host, for the most part, to attractions and concessions of proven commercial viability. For the first time at an Exposition, the fair's administrators and designers turned their attention to Midway design. Not only were the professional services of Exposition designers offered to Midway concessionaries, but the Exposition management announced the requirement that all concessions were to be self-identifying without the aid of billboards or signs (Todd, 1921, p. 155).

As a result of the sanction against signing, the Midway at the San Francisco Exposition became a zone of out of scale "signature architecture." Each attraction became an advertisement of itself either in its three-dimensional form or by means of visual cues – "facade architecture" – attached to the front of the structure. A gigantic Golden Buddha announced the presence of

Figure 23.10 An extraordinary facade on the Zone: the entrance to Dreamland, "A Midway Mystery at the Pan-American Exposition," Buffalo, 1901. The "mystery" was how to exit after entering. "Dreamland" was a maze. (Photo: *The World's Work Magazine*, August 1901.)

a Japanese concession (figure 23.11). "Tin soldiers," approximately ninety feet tall, housed merchandise booths in their feet (figure 23.12). The Atchison, Topeka and Santa Fe Railway constructed a scale model of the Grand Canyon of Arizona; the Union Pacific Railway reproduced Yellowstone Park (with Old Faithful and the Inn); a large and realistic pueblo was occupied by real Indians, and a scale model of the Panama Canal had an actual working canal with an ocean at each end. Other exhibits included the Blarney Castle, a Samoan Village, and a troupe of Maori tribesmen who also camped on the zone (ibid., pp. 147–58). Amusements and displays, as advertisements of themselves, depended on their architectural merchandising for continued commercial success.

On the opening day of the Exposition, all but twenty-six feet of the entire Midway footage of six-thousand feet had been sold to concessionaires. Along these empty twenty-six feet, the concessions manager ordered that false fronts be erected and painted to make the vacant footage appear to belong to adjacent occupied booths and theaters (ibid., p. 158). In an aesthetic peculiar to commerce, any sign of activity – however illusory – was preferable to a void. Emptiness disrupted economic symmetry and signalled dysfunction and blight.

Leaving the Walled City

Midway design was acknowledged to be of "a necessary garishness," whereas the Exposition proper had been designed for another sort of impact: "to refine and uplift and dignify the emotions" (ibid., pp. 155, 173). Both were architecturally didactic. It is hardly surprising, however, that American entrepreneurs chose to exploit the idiom of the amusement zone for the architecture of commerce: the Midway mode was the end result of two decades of intensive experimentation and refinement of commercial forms, in the hothouse environment of Midway competition.

In California, and especially in southern California, the transition from Midway to urban commercial street was relatively simple. The stucco construction methods employed to produce ephemeral structures for the expositions were particularly suited to southern California's mild climate. The addition of cement to the stucco mixture – a technological breakthrough which occurred in time for the San Diego and San Francisco Expositions and which enabled the stucco to carry pigment – was the essential ingredient for stabilizing this previously unreliable building material.[7]

This new genre of commercial architecture was most apparent in Los Angeles, where the streets seemed choked with windmill bakery shops, giant tamales, Sphinx heads, outdoor pianos, owls, and landlocked ships (figure 23.13).[8] The ultimate origin of these structures was confirmed by a visitor to Los Angeles in the 1920s who noted that here was a city where "one must even buy one's daily bread under the illusion of visiting the

Figure 23.11   The golden Buddha claiming attention for the "Japan Beautiful" exhibit on "The Zone" at the Pan-Pacific Exposition in San Francisco, 1915. (Photo: Special Collections, University Research Library, University of California, Los Angeles.)

Figure 23.12   Ninety-feet tall, these monumental toy Tin Soldiers housed stores in their feet on "The Zone" at the Pan-Pacific Exposition in San Francisco, 1915. (Postcard: Special Collections, University Research Library, University of California, Los Angeles.)

Figure 23.13 a, A windmill bakery in Los Angeles in the 1920s (photo: Los Angeles Public Library); b, a tamale food stand in Los Angeles in the 1930s (photo: Los Angeles Public Library); c, an evangelical ship of good hope, The Haven of Rest Radio Studio, constructed in the mid-1930s, and still in use in North Hollywood; d, The Hoot

Midway Plaisance" (Comstock, 1928). The unreality of this dispersed Midway land-scape was heightened by the presence of the film industry in Hollywood. A Swiss visitor to Los Angeles in 1929 wondered:

Why do they build special Hollywood towns? One hardly knows where the real city stops and the fantasy city begins. Did I not see a church yesterday and believe it belonged to a studio – only to find out it was a real church? What is real here and what is unreal? Do people live in Los Angeles or are they only playing at life? (Moeschlin, 1931, p. 98)

The convergence of urban commercial realities and Hollywood commercial fanta-sies, in addition to the profusion of Midway-style structures in southern California, began to earn for the region its reputation as the home of the hard sell – a region in which "culture" did not vitiate commercial dens-ities, but where commerce became instead the predominant form of culture. Nonethe-less, Midway-style architecture was not unique to southern California. A poultry store on Long Island established itself in The Big Duck; a dairy stand in Boston could be found in a gigantic milk bottle; a Cincinnati snack shop was built into a giant sandwich flanked by monumental salt and pepper shakers; a Texas gas station was built in the shape of an oil derrick, and one in North Carolina was built as a sea shell; in Iowa, a giant coffee pot housed a diner, and in New Orleans a nightclub named Crash Landing was partially constructed from the front end of a Lockheed Constellation (com-plete with wings).[9] These, and countless examples which have escaped documenta-tion, bore witness to the nationwide exploit-ation of Midway "signature architecture" in which form often quite literally followed function.

Architectural idiosyncracy in the Midway genre quickly established itself as a success-ful medium for merchandising. By the late 1920s, suburban business districts (which followed suburban residential subdivision and development) had their share of "signa-ture" structures and façade architecture. The encroachment of commerce upon the subur-ban residential fringes became synonymous, to critics, with social pathology. Displeasing architectural design seemed to represent an environmental threat equivalent to garbage dumps:

In American cities of any considerable size our new outlying business centers frequently are becoming the ugliest, most unsightly and disorderly parts of the entire city.... Build-ings of every color, size, shape and design are being huddled and mixed together in a most unpresentable manner. A mixture of glowing billboards, unsightly rubbish dumps, hideous rears, unkempt alleys, dirty loading docks, unrelated, uncongenial mix-tures of shops of every type and use, with no relation to one another; shacks and shanties mixed up with good buildings; perfectly square, unadorned buildings of poor design, are bringing about disorder, unsightliness and unattractiveness that threaten to mar the beauty and good appearance of the resi-dential regions of American cities. (Glaab and Brown, 1967, pp. 294–5, quoting real estate developer Jesse C. Nichol, 1926)

But the spatial organization of a society ideologically committed to the maintenance of efficiency and preservation of individual liberties through free enterprise permitted and even required the areal repetition of commercial centers and the competitive and economical design of the structures which comprised them.

Franchise Architecture

By the middle of the twentieth century, the rhetoric of economic competition, fundamental to Midway philosophy and

Owl Icecream Shop in Los Angeles in the 1920s (photo: Special Collections, University Research Library, University of California, Los Angeles); e, The Big Red Piano Store, built in Los Angeles in the 1930s and a survivor until the mid-1970s when preservationists attempted to transplant ir (phoro: Seymour Rosen, SPACES, Inc.); f, a real estate office in the head of a sphinx, Los Angeles (undated) (photo: John Pastier).

morphology, had become formula. Signature architecture ultimately served as the cornerstone upon which a massive franchise industry developed in the United States after World War II.

Franchising in the United States has been a method of marketing and distribution of goods and services based upon a clear delineation of territory. The geographic foundations for American franchising can be traced to the system of merchandising devised by the Singer Sewing Machine Company at the end of the Civil War. Later, the auto industry developed a similar system of franchised dealers for achieving a national distribution of cars, and with the proliferation of auto franchises, a national network of franchised service stations was also established. Similarly, at the turn of the century, Coca-Cola and Pepsi Cola launched their soft drink empires based solidly upon the use of franchised distributors. By the 1920s, the well-known names of Howard Johnson and A&W Root Beer had entered the American franchise scene. This franchise method of distribution, however, did not inspire widespread emulation until the 1950s (Anon., 1972, pp. 1–2).

Often mistaken for a giant corporate monolith intent upon smothering the nation with its corporate presence, each unit within a franchise is actually a locally owned business operated by independent entrepreneurs. Owners typically buy the right or privilege to do business in a franchisor's prescribed manner, in a specific geographic region, and for a specific period of time. The purchase of a franchise generally involves the use of the parent company's methods, symbols, trademarks, architectural style, and network of wholesale suppliers (Vaughan, 1974, p. 2). The effort to produce a "packaged appearance" and to maintain a "chain identity" despite independent ownership has made modern franchising successful within the context of multiple competitors for the same market (Rosenberg and Bedell, 1969, p. 44).

The franchise system was almost a century old when it suddenly became a widespread phenomenon in the United States. At the end

of World War II, a growing pool of economically alienated Americans, especially returning veterans and displaced farmers, dreamed the dream of financial and personal independence conferred through private ownership of a business (Vaughan, 1974, p. 2). So successful were some franchise operations that the United States seemed, in the 1950s and 1960s, to be overrun by franchised hamburgers, ice cream, donuts, fried chicken, motels, and rental cars, all engaged in mortal combat for national, regional, and local markets. In almost every case, a franchise was closely identified with its signature architecture. One of the most successful franchises – McDonald's hamburgers – underwent in twenty years an architectural evolution indicative of the manner in which values are mediated by forms.

McDonald's became a franchise operation in 1955. The original McDonald's stand was built in San Bernardino, California, by the brothers McDonald who owned and operated a drive-in, fast-food stand under their name. The transformation of this single stand into an international franchise network was made by Ray Kroc, a travelling salesman impressed by the volume of business generated by this single store.[10] Integral to the transformation was the McDonald's name and the signature structure which was to become synonymous with the product in its initial phase of expansion: a building with red and white stripes, touches of yellow, oversized windows, and a distinctive set of arches which went up through the roof. These "golden arches," when viewed from the proper angle, described the letter "M" (figure 23.14). A generation of Americans has proved that such highly abstract signature architecture can effectively come to signify standardized hamburgers, milk-shakes, and french-fried potatoes.

As the franchise system began to expand, however, the original McDonald's signature structure was found to be inappropriate in temperate climates. The building had been designed for San Bernardino's semidesert location; it had a wide roof overhang, huge windows, no basement, and required only an evaporative cooler on its roof, with no

Figure 23.14 Original McDonald's architecture of the 1950s. (Advertising post card offering one free hamburger for redemption of card.)

space provided for a heating plant (Kroc, 1977, p. 70). Acknowledging the importance of signature architecture to franchise success, the corporation designed a series of adaptations for different climatic conditions which would result in no discernible displacement of signature elements. By the mid-1960s, McDonald's "golden arches" blanketed the nation, each stand keeping score of the number of hamburgers (by then in the billions) which had been sold by McDonald's. At the same time, evidence began to accumulate from California – the hearth region which had generated the original form – that golden-arched hamburger sales were in decline (ibid.). Because Los Angeles had been the cradle of drive-in restaurants, the parent company sent an investigator to the city. He conducted his field research in front of "an invitingly clean" McDonald's which was doing no business, and observed:

the flow of people in bizarre looking cars and the pedestrians walking brightly ribboned dogs, typical Angelinos in their habitat. [He concluded]: "The reason we can't pull people in here is because these golden arches blend right into the landscape. People don't even

see them. We have to do something different to get their attention." (Ibid., p. 127)

The Los Angeles experience highlighted a major limitation of the extreme forms of signature architecture: in a hyper-competitive commercial environment, by some Alice-in-Wonderland inversion, the extraordinary becomes normal and thus invisible; the restrained and understated stand out.

In the mid-1960s, McDonald's initiated a new architectural style for its franchised structures. Agreeing now with critics who had long decried the original flat-roofed, candy striped, golden-arched design as a major contributor to visual blight in America, McDonald's "new" architectural recipe drew upon "elite," conventional forms, materials, and behavioral modes: brick-surfaced buildings with mansard roofs, pseudo-antique furnishings and fixtures, and interior eating areas (ibid, p. 161).[11] Because the franchise logo was heavily invested in the "golden arch" motif, that element, in an abbreviated, scaled-down, detached, two-dimensional version, was preserved as the signature

Figure 23.15   The McDonald's "new look" of the late 1960s: brick walls, mansard roof and interior dining spaces. Constructed in Santa Monica in the 1960s.

feature, completely independent of the structure itself (figure 23.15). The separation of the signature element from the structure made good economic sense because it eased the transition in recycling a building to other commercial uses.

Following the McDonald's example, many franchises in the 1960s eschewed signature architecture in favor of portable statements of franchise identities placed adjacent to the relatively conventional buildings they occupied (figures 23.16 and 23.17). Others, however, elected to accept the risk of investing identity and success in a continuation of Midway merchandising (figure 23.18). Moreover, the earlier stages of franchise architecture seem to have stimulated a renaissance in architectural design based more closely on Midway principles. Entrepreneurs operating businesses unassociated with franchise networks began, in the late 1960s, once again to exploit unusual forms and architectural assemblages intended to arrest, amaze, and delight. Gigantism as exploited in the 1915 San Francisco Expo-

sition, and subsequently in the 1920s and 1930s in regions sustaining urbanization and suburbanization, began to reappear (figure 23.19). Unlike the early stucco structures, these latter twentieth century architectural whimsies represent substantial economic investments: a bulldozer office building for a heavy equipment company; Victoria Station (from whose initial success was cloned a chain and numerous independent imitators) as a restaurant in an assemblage of freight cars and cabooses; and Best Products Company has claimed national attention with its "indeterminate facade" buildings – among others, a showroom in Sacramento which appears to have had a bite taken out of one corner (actually its entryway) (Kinchen, 1977).

Under these circumstances of heightened architectural merchandising, it was inevitable that the architecture of modern urban commerce would be drawn ever more closely to its source. "Theme" shopping centers and malls of the 1970s now provide the illusion of other times and other places. Like

Figure 23.16 Jack in the Box: a rectangular building with changeable facade and freestanding sign, in Los Angeles.

the Midway Plaisance they emulate, they represent walled enclaves wherein are merchandised an international panoply of products, services, and exotic experiences (figure 23.20). The ultimate architectural statement in this regard is, of course, Disneyland, itself a synthesis of the great American world's fairs of the nineteenth and twentieth centuries.[12] There is, in fact, less and less to distinguish between the conventional forms of retail merchandising and the Disney version of wonderland: an architectural review of the opening of a new regional shopping center in Los Angeles was entitled "A New Kind of Amusement Park" (Seidenbaum, 1976).

The Compelling Aesthetic

As the styles and forms of the architecture of urban commerce evolved in the United States, so too did the actors competing for dominance of the social and economic life of the city. The main features of urban morphologies had been, for the most part,

delineated and established by industrialists and entrepreneurs during the late nineteenth and early twentieth centuries. The latter part of the twentieth century might be characterized as a period of the filling-in of urban interstices. Key economic functions – industrial, commercial, and governmental – continue to occupy central places and satellite nodes, and within them, express increasing densities through vertical expansion. Less costly horizontal expanses of the city are still claimed by the petty entrepreneur, however.

The problems of gaining control of urban space – and ultimately of urban life – which engaged the rural agrarian elite in contending for the nineteenth century city – are the same problems which confront the corporate elite today. Not surprisingly, members of the contemporary elite exploit the same institutions through which their predecessors had sought to accomplish the same objective. Centers of culture and their taste-making, trend-setting, culture-validating functions have come to be controlled on a national

Figure 23.17 Colonel Sanders' Kentucky Fried Chicken, with brick detailing, mansard roof and free-standing sign, in Santa Monica.

scale by political, corporate, and elite-family dynasties. Business and genealogy play the same role on regional and local scales. Higher education, in particular, has been acknowledged as probably "the single most powerful factor" in the standardization of taste, and indeed, in the standardization of culture (Burck, 1959).[13] Thus it is also not surprising to find in the latter half of the twentieth century that the corps of professional taste-makers has expanded to include educators whose role it is to disseminate "official culture" as defined by those who increasingly control their institutions. Just as the nineteenth century agrarian elite sought to neutralize and divert the growing economic power of the corporate entrepreneur, the corporate elite, now dominant, seeks to control and manipulate mass culture and the petty entrepreneur.

The exploitation of the American ideology of urban aesthetics is difficult to refute. Its objectives are appealing, and it seems not to conflict with that other American ideology which postulates a society committed to the preservation of individual liberties through free enterprise. In the nineteenth century, the culture elite and professional taste-makers excoriated the corporate monoliths which had begun to dominate the urban skyline. Their twentieth century counterparts devote their critical faculties to condemnation of the myriad small businesses which have filled in the urban interstices and occupy now-valuable urban space. The contemporary urban boulevard is characterized as "a gross carnival of signs and billboards...with no style or unity, little architecture and few aesthetics" (Faris, 1974). Urban commerce is described as a "relentless, oppressive attack on the senses...the beat of the sell is nearly constant, like living under a tin roof in a monsoon" (Chapman, 1977). The small businessman is accused of:

crude architectural huckstering which never helped the economy of a town. It helped kill it. It destroyed not only the integrity of old buildings but also the town's integrity – the image of innocence, wholesomeness and honesty. (von Eckardt, 1977)

The canons of these critics would thus exclude from the marketplace of the city those who are usually the most lively and the most vulnerable – the small businessmen and entrepreneurs whose capital is so limited and whose footholds so tenuous that their survival depends upon maximally effective, portable icons: neon signs, billboards and fiberglass totems (figure 23.21). Not surprisingly, aesthetic campaigns gain momentum when urban commercial space appreciates in value.

Where "crude architectural huckstering" metamorphoses into massive corporate success, however, the contempt of taste-makers is supplanted by respect. When it became evident that the McDonald's formula was working, its architectural aspect soon became:

the object of much serious discussion in architectural classes. James Volney

Figure 23.18 The first successful Taco Bell made its appearance in Los Angeles in 1963 and became a franchise in 1965. By the mid-1970s, 325 franchises had been sold, with the largest concentration of Taco Bells in the Middle West, California, and Texas. This one, photographed in Santa Monica, was constructed in 1966. ("A Promising Manana," *Forbes,* Vol. 120, August 1, 1977.)

Figure 23.19 Office building in a two-story tractor, built by the United Equipment Company near Fresno, California; architect-designed structure was completed in 1977.

Righter, who teaches architecture at Yale, says he believes the [new] style "holds great potential in that it links the energy of the lively American 'pop' forms with functional utility and quality construction." (Kroc, 1977, p. 161)

Ada Louise Huxtable, architecture critic for the *New York Times,* began to find "aesthetic merit and cultural meaning" in these urban vernacular commercial forms (Huxtable, 1978). And with transparent cynicism, Charles Jencks, writer and teacher of architectural history has suggested that:

> Since you can't escape Bad Taste any more, the only thing you can do is apply standards to it and discover when it is really subversive and enjoyable. Today, most man-made things are horribly mediocre, but happily, a few of them are really awful. We have to cultivate principles of banality not just to survive but to keep the lovably ridiculous from slipping into the merely no-account. (Jencks, 1973)

Professional taste-makers are doing precisely that. In 1976, the Society for Commercial Archaeology was founded "to promote the understanding, documentation and preservation of significant structures and symbols of the commercial built environment" (Liebs, 1978). Earlier, Yale architect Robert Venturi paid tribute to a spectacular efflorescence of gambling architecture in his book, *Learning from Las Vegas* (Venturi et al., 1972). In the process of manufacturing

Figure 23.20 Old Town Mall, an enclosed shopping center constructed in the early 1970s in Torrance, California, was designed with Disneyland's Main Street as its architectural model.

academic and professional capital, taste-makers have begun to invest the remnants of an earlier age of architectural refugees from world's fair Midways with the aura of transcendental meaning. Los Angeles's few surviving hotdogs, donuts, and derbies are now being apotheosized as significant Urban Art:

> Of all the landmarks threatened with eventual extinction by bulldozer and high rise, none will be mourned with such mixed feelings as the[se] grandly eccentric monuments. ... Holdovers from a more rococo era, they gave Southern California a colorful and often unwelcome stamp in the 20s and 30s as the home of architectural anarchy. ... In retrospect, the worst of the kookie structures seems less abortive than ill-timed. With the advent of pop art and "camp" movements, they might have found homes in art galleries rather than on street corners. (Anon., 1965)

In the ideology of American aesthetics, it is understood that those who make taste make

money, and those who make money make taste. In the twentieth century, this logic manifests itself primarily in an urban context: it is pivotal in the battle for urban territory and urban markets. No one worries the farmer for his unaesthetic barns. All ideologies have their time and their space.

This Is Not a Conclusion

A fundamental contradiction is evident in examinations of the forms and structures of contemporary American commerce in its urban context. Investigations of function and morphology have revealed the operation of coherent, efficient systems. The inherent instability of the urban economic environment is accepted as a corollary of the "free enterprise" system. Nevertheless, urban economic networks have been abstracted and analyzed quantitatively and cartographically, revealing evidence of logic and order accepted by most scholars and policymakers. In contrast, the material culture of urban commerce, the framework within

Figure 23.21 Lowe's Tire Man, an attention-getter on Lincoln Boulevard, a commercial route in Los Angeles.

which networks of distribution and consumption are operationalized, has been portrayed in diametrically opposite terms. Few students of culture would claim that the architectural forms and the syntax of commercial competition conform to discernible patterns deriving from a coherent system of belief and behavior, parallel to the "free enterprise" logic which provides a rational basis for the analysis of economic behavior. The three-dimensional space occupied by urban commerce – the heritage of World's Fair amusement zones – is invariably characterized as dysfunctional, even pathological. How is this conceptual disjunction, originating in different aspects of one and the same urban space, and within a single framework of objectives, to be explained?

One explanation resides in the fact that the "aesthetic impulse" which filters perception of three-dimensional space has little to do with the formal appreciation of shapes, colors, or combinations thereof. As chron-

icled in this paper, the merchandising of "good taste" in urbanizing America long ago coalesced as an aesthetic ideology which has permeated public policy and public programs. Urban "ugliness" and urban "blight," variously defined, have been employed as rhetorical gambits in propaganda campaigns to control the use of appreciating urban space. Typically, the costs of aesthetic programs, beginning with the "White City" of 1893, have been borne most heavily by those who benefit from them the least. Yet aesthetic ideology continues to mold attitudes toward environmental design and urban development because it is reinforced by academics and policy-makers who operate as powerful allies of "official culture." Aesthetic ideology remains a potent vehicle for the perpetuation of urban, economic, and social inequalities, and serves as reinforcement for another oppressive ideology: that our economy is based upon the maintenance of efficiencies through free enterprise.

It is only a matter of time before academics and policy-makers will be forced to confront the inconsistencies and disjunctions arising from the evidence of their own research. Ultimately they will have to go beyond the quantifiers' and cartographers' two-dimensional discussions of the mechanics of urban economics and the impressionistic value-judgements of critics and historians of architecture. To begin, they will have to examine the manipulations and special pleadings which have operated to distort and impede their understanding of the symbolic, syncretic, and integrated nature of that dauntingly complex nexus which is the modern American city. In that vast no-man's land separating "The Real" from "The Ideal" lie many opportunities for enlightenment.

NOTES

1 Periodicals such as *Cassel's, Harper's New Monthly, Lippencott's, Atlantic Monthly, Scribners*, and others regularly featured treatises on appropriate and inappropriate development or embellishment of urban

space, and appropriate life styles for urban culture.

2 In 1949, Congress passed the Federal Housing Act, making available a number of federal aids to local redevelopment agencies for the rehabilitation of substandard housing. The Housing Act required that displaced families be found housing, but it was not necessary to return them to their original site. As a result, virtually any urban site could be declared blighted by a local authority, and then reclaimed for shopping centers, luxury housing, or other high-yielding projects developed by private companies benefiting from public subsidies. By 1954, urban redevelopment was no longer viewed with alarm as a form of social engineering; rather, its programs were increasingly interpreted as the federal sanctioning of the use of police power to achieve aesthetic ends by seizing urban properties through condemnation in areas judged (by developers, planners and politicians) to be "blighted," and to rebuild these areas in conformity with imposed "master plans" (Scott, 1969, p. 491).

3 Many aspiring American architects received their training at l'Ecole des Beaux Arts in the nineteenth century and returned to the United States to promote a revival of its particular form of architectural historicism. The principal designer of the Chicago Exposition of 1893, Daniel Burnham, had not been trained at l'Ecole, but clearly subscribed to its principles.

4 For a summary of reactions to the Chicago Exposition, see Coles and Reed (1961, pp. 137–211).

5 An illustration of a cut-out Statue of Columbia gracing a billboard in Newark Meadows can be found in Warner (1900, p. 274). For an analysis of the development of Forest Lawn Cemetery, see Rubin (1976).

6 The Hispanic/colonial tradition in California architecture is discussed in Rubin (1977).

7 The Chicago Exposition of 1893 had been called "The White City" because technicians

were unable to introduce pigment successfully into the stucco. The fair's promoters thus made a virtue out of a limitation in bestowing upon the colorless landscape the title "White City" (Anon., 1914, 1915; Denieville, 1915).

8 The structures illustrated, and others, are discussed and illustrated in Mayo (1933), Anon. (1965), Jencks (1973), and Fine (1977).

9 Long Island's Big Duck is illustrated in Blake (1964, p. 101) and discussed in Venturi and Brown (1971) and Wines (1972). The Sankey Milk Bottle and seashell service station are illustrated in *Historic Preservation*, 30(1).

10 Two books chronicle Ray Kroc's machinations in transforming a San Bernadino drive-in hamburger stand into an international franchise.

11 More recent McDonald's construction has superseded the mansard style, with emphasis on conforming to regional architectural flavor. A McDonald's constructed in 1977 in Santa Monica features a red-tiled roof and stucco walls in keeping with southern California's largely fabricated Spanish colonial tradition. In San Francisco, near City Hall, a McDonald's completed in August 1978 exhibits a formal modernism consistent with the most up-to-date construction in civic buildings and avant garde residential construction: greenhouse windows, large expanses of concrete wall meeting at unusual angles, and ornamental graphics.

12 Evidence for the origin of Disneyland is discussed in Rubin (1975).

13 The role of education and its impact upon the "American Way of Life: is cogently discussed in O'Toole (1977). Objections to the use of public cultural institutions and public monies for the dissemination and validation of "official culture" were outlined in an *anti catalog* (The Catalog Committee of Artists Meeting for Cultural Change, New York, 1977).

REFERENCES

Anon. (1893) The World's Fair balance sheet. *Review of Reviews*, 8 (November), 522–3.

Anon. (1894) Last words about the World's Fair. *Architectural Record*, III(3).

Anon. (1914) The color scheme at the Panama-Pacific International Exposition – a new departure. *Scribner's Magazine*, 56(3), 277.

Anon. (1915) The Great Internation Pan-Pacific Exposition. *Scientific American*, 112 (February 27), 194–5.

Anon. (1965) Low camp – a Kook's Tour of southern California's fast-disappearing unreal estate. *Los Angeles Magazine*, 10 (November), 35–6.

Anon. (1972) *Franchised Distribution*. New York: The Conference Board Inc.

Bancroft, H. H. (1893) *The Book of the Fair*. Chicago: The Bancroft Co.

Barry, R. H. (1901) *Snap Shots on the Midway of the Pan-American Exposition*. Buffalo, NY: R. A. Reid.

Berry, B. J. L. (1963) Commercial structure and commercial blight. Research paper no. 85, Department of Geography, University of Chicago.

Blake, P. (1964) *God's Own Junkyard*. New York: Holt, Rinehart and Winston.

Blashfield, E. H. (1899) A word for municipal art. *Municipal Affairs*, 3, 582–93.

Boas, M. and Chain, S. (1977) *Big Mac: The Unauthorized Story of McDonald's*. New York: New American Library.

Burck, G. (1959) How American taste is changing. *Fortune*, 60(1), 196.

Cawelti, J. C. (1968) America on display: the World's Fairs of 1876, 1893, 1933. In F. C. Jahar (ed.), *The Age of Industrialism in America*. New York: Free Press.

Chapman, J. (1977) Los Angeles is just too much. *Los Angeles Times*, June 28, part II, 7.

Coles, W. A. and Reed, H. H. Jr (1961) *Architecture in America: A Battle of Styles*. New York: Appleton-Century-Crofts.

Comstock, S. (1928) The great American mirror: reflections from Los Angeles. *Harper's Monthly*, May, 715–23.

Denieville, P. E. (1915) Texture and color at the Panama-Pacific Exposition. *Architectural Record*, 38(5), 563–70.

Faris, G. (1974) Santa Monica Boulevard: the grotesque and the sublime. *Los Angeles Times*, February 17, part XI, 1

Fine, D. M. (1977) LA architecture as a blueprint for fiction. *Los Angeles Times Calendar*, December 11, 20–1.

Fitch, J. M. (1948) *American Building*. Boston: Houghton Mifflin.

Glaab, C. and Brown, A. T. (1967) *The Emergence of Metropolis: A History of Urban America*. London: Macmillan.

Hamlin, T. (1953) *Architecture through the Ages*. New York: G. P. Putnam's Sons.

Handlin, O. and Handlin, M. F. (1975) *The Wealth of the American People*. New York: McGraw-Hill.

Hartt, M. B. (1901) The play side of the Fair. *The World's Work*, August.

Huxtable, A. L. (1978) Architecture for a fast-food culture. *New York Times Magazine*, February 12, 23.

Jencks, C. (1973) Ersatz in LA. *Architectural Design*, 53(9), 596–601.

Kinchen, D. M. (1977) Indeterminate facade building opens. *Los Angeles Times*, April 17, part VIII, 5.

Kriehn, G. (1899) The city beautiful. *Municipal Affairs*, 3, 597

Kroc, R., with Anderson, R. (1977) *Grinding It Out: The Making of McDonald's*. Chicago: Henry Regnery Co.

Liebs, C. H. (1978) Remeber our not-so-distant past? *Historic Preservation*, 30(1), 35.

Lynes, R. (1955) *The Taste-makers*. New York: Harper and Bros.

McCullough, E. (1966) *World's Fair Midways*. New York: Exposition Press.

Mayo, M. (1933) *Los Angeles*. New York.

Meier, R. L. (1963) The organization of technological innovation in urban environments. In O. Handlin (ed.), *The Historian and the City*. Cambridge, MA: MIT Press.

Moeschlin, F. (1931) *Amerika vom Auto aus*. Zurich: Erlenbach.

O'Toole, J. (1977) *Work, Learning and the American Future*. San Francisco: Jossey-Bass.

Pickett, C. E. (1877) The French Exposition of 1878. *San Francisco Examiner*, October 26.

Robinson, C. M. (1901) *Modern Civic Art*. New York: G. Putnam's Sons.

Rosenberg, R. and Bedell, M. (1969) *Profits from Franchising*. New York: McGraw-Hill.

Rubin, B. (1975) Monuments, magnets and pilgrimage sites: a genetic study in southern California. Unpublished doctoral dissertation, University of California, Los Angeles.

Rubin, B. (1976) The Forest Lawn aesthetic: a reappraisal. *Journal of the Los Angeles Institute of Contemporary Art*, 9, 10–15.

Rubin, B. (1977) A chronology of architecture in Los Angeles. *Annals, Association of American Geographers*, 67, 521–37.

Scott, M. (1969) *American City Planning since 1890*. Berkely: University of California Press.

Seidenbaum, A. (1976) A new kind of amusement park. *Los Angeles Times*, May 9, part VII, 1.

Snider, D. J. (1895) *World's Fair Studies*. Chicago: Sigma Publishing Co.

Todd, F. M. (1921) *The Story of the Exposition*. New York: G. P. Putnam's Sons.

Vaughan, C. L. (1974) *Franchising: Its Nature, Scope, Advantages, and Development*. Lexington, MA: Lexington Books.

Venturi, R. and Brown, D. S. (1971) Ugly and ordinary architecture of the decorated shed. *Architectural Forum*, 135 (November), 64–7.

Venturi, R., Brown, D. S. and Izenour, S. (1972) *Learning from Las Vegas*. Boston: MIT Press.

von Eckardt, W. (1977) The huckster peril on Main Street, USA. *Los Angeles Times*, December 7, part II, 11.

Warner, J. D. (1900) Advertising run mad. *Municipal Affairs*, IV (June).

Wines, J. (1972) Case for the big duck. *Architectural Forum*, 136 (April), 60–1.

Part IX
Typologies

24

The Third Typology

Anthony Vidler

From the middle of the eighteenth century two dominant typologies have served to legitimize the production of architecture: The first, returned architecture to its natural origins – a model of primitive shelter – seen not simply as historical explanation of the derivation of the orders but as a guiding principle, equivalent to that proposed by Newton for the physical universe. The second, emerging as a result of the Industrial Revolution, assimilated architecture to the world of machine production, finding the essential nature of a building to reside in the artifical world of engines. Laugier's primitive hut and Bentham's Panopticon stand at the beginning of the modern era as the paradigms of these two typologies.

Both these typologies were firm in their belief that rational science and later, technological production, embodied the most progressive forms of the age, and that the mission of architecture was to conform to and perhaps even master these forms as the agent of material progress.

With the current re-appraisal of the idea of progress, and with this, the critique of the Modern Movement ideology of productivism, architects have turned to a vision of the primal past of architecture – its constructive and formal bases as evinced in the pre-industrial city. Once again the issue of typology is raised in architecture, not this time with a need to search outside the practice for legitimation in science or technology, but with a sense that within architecture itself resides a unique and particular mode of production and explanation. From Aldo Rossi's transformations of the formal struc-

ture and institutional types of eighteenth century urbanism, to the sketches of Leon Krier that recall the "primitive" types of shelter imagined by the eighteenth century philosophes, rapidly multiplying examples suggest the emergence of a new, third typology.

We might characterize the fundamental attribute of this third typology as an espousal, not of an abstract nature, not of a technological utopia, but rather of the traditional city as the locus of its concern. The city that is, provides the material for classification and the forms of its artifacts over time provide the basis for recomposition. This third typology, like the first two, is clearly based on reason, classification, and a sense of the public in architecture; unlike the first two, however, it proposes no panacaea, no ultimate apotheosis of man in architecture, no positivistic escatology.

I

The small rustic hut is the model upon which all the wonders of architecture have been conceived; in drawing nearer in practice to the simplicities of this first model essential faults are avoided and true perfection is attained. The pieces of wood raised vertically give us the idea of columns. The horizontal pieces that surmount them give us the idea of entablatures. Finally, the inclined pieces that form the roof, give us the idea of pediments. This all the masters of the art have recognized. (M. A. Laugier, 1755)

The first typology, which ultimately saw architecture as imitative of the fundamental order of Nature itself, allied the primitive rusticity of the hut to an ideal of perfect geometry, revealed by Newton as the guiding principle of physics. Thus, Laugier depicted the four trees, types of the first columns, standing in a perfect square; the branches laid across in the form of beams, perfectly horizontal, and the boughs bent over to form the roof as a triangle, the type of pediment. These elements of architecture, derived from the elements of nature, formed an unbreakable chain and were interrelated according to fixed principles: if the tree/column was joined in this way to the bower/hut, then the city itself, agglomeration of huts, was likewise susceptible to the principle of natural origin. Laugier spoke of the city – or rather the existing, unplanned and chaotic reality of Paris – as a forest. The forest/city was to be tamed, brought into rational order by means of the gardener's art; the ideal city of the late eighteenth century was thereby imaged on the garden; the type of the urbanist was Le Nôtre, who would cut and prune an unruly nature according to the geometrical line of its true underlying order.

The idea of the elements of architecture referring in some way to their natural origin was, of course, immediately extensible in the idea of each specific kind of building representing its "species" so to speak, in the same way as each member of the animal kingdom. At first the criteria applied to differentiate building types were bound up with recognition, with individual physiognomy, as in the classification systems of Buffon and Linnaeus. Thus, the external affect of the building was to announce clearly its general species, and its specific sub-species. Later this analogy was transformed by the functional and constitutional classification of the early nineteenth century (Cuvier), whereby the inner-structure of beings, their constitutional form, was seen as the criterion for grouping them in types.

Following this analogy, those whose task it was to design the new types of public and private buildings emerging as needs in the early nineteenth century began to talk of the plan and sectional distribution in the same terms as the constitutional organiza-

tion of species; axes and vertebrae became virtually synonymous. This reflected a basic shift in the metaphor of natural architecture, from a vegetal (tree/hut) to an animal analogy. This shift paralleled the rise of the new schools of medicine and the birth of clinical surgery.

Despite the overt disgust that Durand showed toward Laugier – laughing at the idea of doing without walls – it was Durand, professor at the Polytechnique, who brought together these twin streams of organic typology into a lexicon of architectural practice that enabled the architect, at least, to dispense with analogy altogether and concentrate on the business of construction. The medium of this fusion was the graph paper grid which assembled on the same level the basic elements of construction, according to the inductively derived rules of composition for the taxonomy of different building types resulting in the endless combinations and permutations, monumental and utilitarian. In his *Receuil* he established that the natural history of architecture resides so to speak in its own history, a parallel development to real nature. In his *Lessons* he described how new types might be constructed on the same principles. When this awareness was applied in the next decades to the structural rationalism inherited from Laugier the result was the organic theory of Gothic "skeletal" structure developed by Viollet le Duc. The operation of the romantics on classic theory was simply at one level to substitute the Cathedral for the Temple as the formal and later the social type of all architecture.

II

The French language has provided the useful definition, thanks to the double sense of the word type. A deformation of meaning has led to the equivalence in popular language: a man = a type; and from the point that the type becomes a man, we grasp the possibility of a considerable extension of the type. Because the man-type is a complex form of a unique physical type, to which can be applied a sufficient standardization. According to the same rules one will establish for this physical type an equipment of standard habitation: doors, windows, stairs, the heights of rooms, etc. (Le Corbusier, 1927)

The second typology, which substituted for the classical trinity of commodity, firmness and delight, a dialectic of means and ends joined by the criteria of economy, looked upon architecture as simply a matter of technique. The remarkable new machines subject to the laws of functional precision were thus paradigms of efficiency as they worked in the raw materials of production; architecture, once subjected to similar laws, might well work with similar effectiveness on its unruly contents – the users. The efficient machines of architecture might be sited in the country-side, very much like the early steam engines of Newcomen and Watt, or inserted in the fabric of the city, like the water pumps and later the factory furnaces. Centralized within their own operative realm, hermetically sealed by virtue of their autonomy as complete processes, these engines – the prisons, hospitals, poor houses – needed little in the way of accommodation save a clear space and a high wall. Their impact on the form of the city as a whole was at first minimal.

The second typology of modern architecture emerged toward the end of the nineteenth century, after the take off of the Second Industrial Revolution; it grew out of the need to confront the question of mass-production, and more particularly the mass-production of machines by machines. The effect of this transformation in production was to give the illusion of another nature, the nature of the machine and its artificially reproduced world.

In this second typology, architecture was now equivalent to the range of mass-production objects, subject themselves to a quasi-Darwinian law of the selection of the fittest. The pyramid of production from the smallest tool to the most complex machine was now seen as analgous to the link between the column, the house and the city. Various attempts were made to blend the old typology with the new in order to provide a more satisfactory answer to the question of specifically architectonic form: the primary geometries of the Newtonian generation were now adduced for their evident qualities of economy, modernity and purity. They were, it was thought, appropriate for machine tooling.

Equally, theoreticians with a classical bias, like Hermann Muthesius stressed the equivalence of ancient types – the temple – and the new ones – the object of manufacture – in order to stabilize, or "culturalize" the new machine world. A latent neo-classicism suffused the theories of typology at the beginning of the contemporary epoch, born of the need to justify the new in the face of the old. The classical world once again acted as a "primal past" where in the utopia of the present might find its nostalgic roots.

Not until the aftermath of the first world war was this thrown off, at least in the most advanced theories – articulated with more and more directness by Le Corbusier and Walter Gropius. A vision of Taylorized production, of a world ruled by the iron law of Ford supplanted the spuriously golden dream of new-classicism. Buildings were to be no more and no less than machines themselves, serving and molding the needs of man according to economic criteria. The image of the city at this point changed radically: the forest/park of Laugier was made triumphant in the hygienist utopia of a city completely absorbed by its greenery. The natural analogy of the enlightenment, originally brought forward to control the messy reality of the city, was now extended to refer to the control of entire nature. In the redeeming park the silent building-machines of the new garden of production virtually disappeared behind a sea of verdure. Architecture, in this final apotheosis of mechanical progress, was consumed by the very process it sought to control for its own ends. With it, the city, as artifact and polis dissappeared as well.

In the first two typologies of modern architecture we can identify a common base, resting on the need to legitimize architecture as a "natural" phenomenon and a development of the natural analogy that corresponded very directly to the development of production itself. Both typologies were in some way bound up with the attempts of architecture to endow itself with value by means of an appeal to natural science or production, and instrumental power by means of an assimilation of the forms of these two complementary domains to itself. The "utopia" of architecture as "project" might be progressive in its ends, or nostalgic in its dreams, but at heart it was founded on this premise: that the shape of environment, might, like nature herself, affect and hereby control the individual and collective relations of men.

III

In the first two typologies, architecture, made by man, was being compared and legitimized by another "nature" outside itself. In the third typology, as exemplified in the work of the new Rationalists, however, there is no such attempt at validation. Columns, houses, and urban spaces, while linked in an unbreakable chain of continuity, refer only to their own nature as architectural elements, and their geometries are neither naturalistic nor technical but essentially architectural. It is clear that the nature referred to in these recent designs is no more nor less than the nature of the city itself, emptied of specific social content from any particular time and allowed to speak simply of its own formal condition.

This concept of the city as the site of a new typology is evidently born of a desire to stress the continuity of form and history against the fragmentation produced by the elemental, institutional, and mechanistic typologies of the recent past. The city is considered as a whole, its past and present revealed in its physical structure. It is in itself and of itself a new typology. This typology is not built up out of separate elements, nor assembled out of objects classified according to use, social ideology, or technical characteristics: it stands complete and ready to be decomposed into fragments. These fragments do not reinvent institutional type-forms nor repeat past typological forms: they are selected and reassembled according to criteria derived from three levels of meaning – the first, inherited from the ascribed means of

the past existence of the forms; the second, derived from the specific fragment and its boundaries, and often crossing between previous types; the third, proposed by a recomposition of these fragments in a new context.

Such an "ontology of the city" is in the face of the modernist utopia, indeed radical. It denies all the social utopian and progressively positivist definitions of architecture for the last two hundred years. No longer is architecture a realm that has to relate to a hypothesized "society" in order to be conceived and understood; no longer does "architecture write history" in the sense of particularizing a specific social condition in a specific time or place. The need to speak of nature of function, of social mores – of anything, that is, beyond the nature of architectural form itself – is removed. At this point, as Victor Hugo realized so presciently in the 1830's, communication through the printed work, and lately through the mass media has apparently released architecture from the role of "social book" into its own autonomous and specialized domain.

This does not, of course, necessarily mean that architecture in this sense no longer performs any function, no longer satisfies any need beyond the whim of an "art for art's sake" designer, but simply that the principal conditions for the invention of object and environments do not necessarily have to include a unitary statement of fit between form and use. Here it is that the adoption of the *city* as the site for the identification of the architectural typology has been seen as crucial. In the accumulated experience of the city, its public spaces and institutional forms, a typology can be understood that defies a one-to-one reading of function, but which at the same time ensures a relation at another level to a continuing tradition of city life. The distinguishing characteristic of the new ontology beyond its specifically formal aspect is that the city polis, as opposed to the single column, the hut-house, or the useful machine, is and always has been political in its essence. The fragmentation and recomposition of its spatial and institutional forms thereby can never be separated from their received and newly constituted political implications.

When typical forms are selected from the past of a city, they do not come, however dismembered, deprived of their original political and social meaning. The original sense of the form, the layers of accured implication deposited by time and human experience cannot be lightly brushed away and certainly it is not the intention of the new Rationalists to disinfect their types in this way. Rather, the carried meanings of these types may be used to provide a key to their newly invested meanings. The technique or rather the fundamental compositional method suggested by the Rationalists is the transformation of selected types – partial or whole – into entirely new entities that draw their communicative power and potential criteria from the understanding of this transformation. The City Hall project for Trieste by Aldo Rossi, for example, has been rightly understood to refer, among other evocations in its complex form, to the image of a late eighteenth century prison. In the period of the first formalization of this type, as Piranesi demonstrated, it was possible to see in *prison* a powerfully comprehensive image of the dilemma of society itself, poised between a disintegrating religious faith and a materialist reason. Now, Rossi, in ascribing to the city hall (itself a recognizable type in the nineteenth century) the affect of prison, attains a new level of signification, which evidently is a reference to the ambiguous condition of civic government. In the formulation, the two types are not merged: indeed, city hall has been replaced by open arcade standing in contradiction on prison. The dialectic is clear as a fable: the society that understands the reference to prison will still have need of the reminder, while at the very point that the image finally loses all meaning, the society will either have become entirely prison, or, perhaps, its opposite. The metaphoric opposition deployed in this example can be traced in many of Rossi's schemes and in the work of the Rationalists as a whole, not only in institutional form but also in the spaces of the city.

This new typology is explicitly critical of the Modern Movement; it utilizes the clarity of the eighteenth century city to rebuke the fragmentation, decentralization, and formal disintegration introduced into contemporary urban life by the zoning techniques and technological advances of the twenties. While the Modern Movement found its Hell in the closed, cramped, and insalubrious quarters of the old industrial cities, and its Eden in the uninterruped sea of sunlet space filled with greenery – a city became a garden – the new typology as a critique of modern urbanism raises the continuous fabric, the clear distinction between public and private marked by the walls of street and square, to the level of principle. Its nightmare is the isolated building set in an undifferentiated park. The heroes of this new typology are therefore not among the nostalgic, anticity utopians of the nineteenth century nor even among the critics of industrial and technical progress of the twentieth, but rather among those who, as the professional servants of urban life, have directed their design skills to solving the questions of avenue, arcade, street and square, park and house, institution and equipment in a continuous typology of elements that together coheres with past fabric and present intervention to make one comprehensible experience of the city.

For this typology, there is no clear set of rules for the transformations and their objects, nor any polemically defined set of historical precedents. Nor, perhaps, should there be; the continued vitality of this architectural practice rests in its essential engagement with the precise demands of the present and not in any holistic mythicization of the past. It refuses any "nostalgia" in its evocations of history, except to give its restorations sharper focus; it refuses all unitary descriptions of the social meaning of form, recognizing the specious quality of any single ascription of social order to an architectural order; it finally refuses all eclecticism, resolutely filtering its "quotations" through the lens of a modernist aesthetic. In this sense, it is an entirely modern movement, and one that places its faith in the essentially public nature of all architecture, as against the increasingly private and narcissistic visions of the last decade. In this it is distinguished from those latter-day romanticisms that have also pretended to the throne of post-modernism – "townscape", "strip-city" and "collage-city" – that in reality proposed no more than the endless reduplication of the flowers of bourgeois high culture under the guise of the painterly or the populist. In the work of the new Rationalists, the city and its typology are reasserted as the only possible bases for the restoration of a critical role to public architecture otherwise assassinated by the apparently endless cycle of production and consumption.

25

Typological and Morphological Elements of the Concept of Urban Space

Rob Krier

Introduction

The basic premise underlying this chapter is my conviction that in our modern cities we have lost sight of the traditional understanding of urban space. The cause of this loss is familiar to all city dwellers who are aware of their environment and sensitive enough to compare the town planning achievements of the present and the past and who have the strength of character to pronounce sentence on the way things have gone. This assertion alone is of no great service to town planning research. What has to be clearly defined is what should be understood by the term urban space and what meaning it holds within the urban structure, so that we can go on to examine whether the concept of urban space retains some validity in contemporary town planning and on what grounds. "Space" in this context is a hotly disputed concept. It is not my intention here to generate a new definition but rather to bring its original meaning back into currency.

Definition of the Concept "Urban Space"

If we wish to clarify the concept of urban space without imposing aesthetic criteria we are compelled to designate all types of space between buildings in towns and other localities as urban space.

This space is geometrically bounded by a variety of elevations. It is only the clear legibility of its geometrical characteristics and aesthetic qualities which allows us consciously to perceive external space as urban space.

The polarity of internal–external space is constantly in evidence in this chapter, since both obey very similar laws not only in function but also in form. Internal space, shielded from weather and environment is an effective symbol of privacy; external space is seen as open, unobstructed space for movement in the open air, with public, semi-public and private zones.

The basic concepts underlying the aesthetic characteristics of urban space will be expounded below and systematically classified by type. In the process an attempt will be made to draw a clear distinction between precise aesthetic and confused emotional factors. Every aesthetic analysis runs the risk of foundering on subjective questions of taste. As I have been able to observe from numerous discussions on this topic, visual and sensory habits, which vary from one individual to the next, are augmented by a vast number of socio-political and cultural attitudes, which are taken to represent aesthetic truths. Accepted styles in art history – for example, baroque town plans, revolutionary architecture etc. – are both useful and necessary.

However, my observations indicate that they are almost always identified with the social structure prevailing at the time in question. Certainly it can scarcely be proved that, because of the wishes of the ruling classes and their artists, the stylistic canons of the period in European art history between 1600 and 1730 appeared almost to be determined by fate. Of course for the historian every period of history forms a unit with its own internal logic, which cannot be fragmented and interchanged with elements of other periods at will.

The creative person, such as the artist, may use a completely different method of approach. The decisions he makes in deploying his aesthetic skills are not always based on assumptions which can be unequivocally explained. His artistic "libido" is of enormous importance here. The cultural contribution of an age develops on the basis of a highly complex pattern of related phenomena, which must subsequently be the subject of laborious research on the part of historians. This example throws us right into a complex problem which appears the same in whichever period of history we consider. We must discuss this example exhaustively before we start constructing our rational system. Each period in art history develops gradually out of the assimilated functional and formal elements which precede it. The more conscious a society is of its history, the more effortlessly and thoroughly it handles historical elements of style. This truism is important in as far as it legitimises the artist's relationship with the universally accepted wealth of formal vocabulary of all preceding ages – this is as applicable in the 20th as in the 17th century.

I do not wish to rally support for eclecticism, but simply to warn against an all too naive understanding of history, which has been guilty of such misjudgements as representing urban architecture amongst the Romans as markedly inferior to that of the Greeks, which from an historical point of view is simply not true. The same mistake persists today, as can be seen from attitude to the architecture of the 19th century.

Our age has a remarkably distorted sense of history, which can only be characterised as irrational. Le Corbusier's apparent battle against the "Académie" was not so much a revolt against an exhausted, ageing school as the assumption of a pioneering stand in which he adopted its ideals and imbued them with a new and vigorous content.

This so-called "pioneering act" was a pretended break with history, but in reality was an artistic falsehood. The facts were these: he abandoned the tradition current until then that art supported by the ruling classes enjoyed the stamp of legitimacy and, being at an advanced stage of development, materially shaped the periods which followed. It was a revolt at one remove, so to speak, for the "Académie" lived on, and indeed came itself to share the same confused historical sense as the followers of the revolution.

I am speaking here about the modern age in general, and not about its exponents of genius who tower above the "image of the age". Rather than be indebted to elitist currents in art, the generation around the turn of the century sought new models. They found them in part in the folk art of other ages and continents, which had hitherto attracted little attention.

There began an unprecedented flurry of discovery of anonymous painting, sculpture, architecture, song and music of those peoples who were considered underdeveloped, and their contribution to culture was for the first time properly valued without regard to their stage of civilisation. Other artists sought their creative material in the realm of pure theory and worked with the basic elements of visual form and its potential for transformation (the "abstracts"). Yet others found their material in social criticism and the denunciation of social injustice and carried out their mission using formally simple methods (the "expressionists"). The break with the elitist artistic tradition was identical to the artist's struggle for emancipation from his patron – the ruling class and its cultural dictatorship – which had been brewing even before the French revolution.

The example of the baroque town layout has already been mentioned, and the question raised of the identity of form, content and meaning. We must be more exact in asking:

1 Was the resulting form the free expression of the creative artist?

2 Alternatively, were the artistic wishes of the employing class imposed on the artist, and was he forced to adopt their notions of form?

3 Do contemporaneous periods exist, which on the basis of different cultural traditions in different countries or continents where similar social conditions prevail, produce the same artistic solutions?

4 Alternatively, are there non-contemporaneous periods which led to fundamentally different artistic solutions, each being a stage in the development of the same cultural tradition in the same country under the same conditioning social factors?

In this series of permutations, the following factors are relevant: aesthetics, artist, patron, social environment, leeway given to artistic expression, formal restrictions imposed by the patron, formal restrictions imposed by the social environment, fashion, management, level of development, technology and its potential applications, general cultural conditions, scientific knowledge, enlightenment, nature, landscape, climate etc. We can conclude with a fair degree of certainty that none of these interrelated factors can be considered in isolation.

With this brief outline of the problem, we should just add a word of caution about an over-simplistic undiscriminating outlook. It is certainly worth trying to establish why certain kinds of urban space were created in the 17th century which we now identify with that period. And it would be even more interesting to examine the real reasons why 20th century town planing has been impoverished and reduced to the lowest common denominator.

The following classification does not make any value judgements. It enumerates the basic forms which constitute urban space, with a limited number of possible variations and combinations. The aesthetic quality of each element of urban space is characterised by the structural interrelation of detail. I shall attempt to discern this quality wherever we are dealing with physical features of a spatial nature. The two basic elements are the street and the square. In the category of "interior space" we would be talking about the corridor and the room. The geometrical characteristics of both spatial forms are the same. They are differentiated only by the dimensions of the walls which bound them and by the patterns of function and circulation which characterise them.

The Square

In all probability the square was the first way man discovered of using urban space. It is produced by the grouping of houses around an open space. This arrangement afforded a high degree of control of the inner space, as well as facilitating a ready defence against external aggression by minimising the external surface area liable to attack. This kind of courtyard frequently came to bear a symbolic value and was therefore chosen as the model for the construction of numerous holy places (Agora, Forum, cloister, mosque courtyard). With the invention of houses built around a central courtyard or atrium this spatial pattern became a model for the future. Here rooms were arranged around a central courtyard like single housing units around a square.

Figure 25.1

The Street

The street is a product of the spread of a settlement once houses have been built on all available space around its central square. It provides a framework for the distribution of land and gives access to individual plots. It has a more pronouncedly functional character than the square, which by virtue of its size is a more attractive place to pass the time than the street, in whose confines one is involuntarily caught up in the bustle of traffic. Its architectural backdrop is only perceived in passing. The street layouts which we have inherited in our towns were devised for quite different functional purposes. They were planned to the scale of the human being, the horse and the carriage. The street is unsuitable for the flow of motorised traffic, whilst remaining appropriate to human circulation and activity. It rarely operates as an autonomous isolated space, as for example in the case of villages built along a single street. It is mainly to be perceived as part of a network. Our historic towns have made us familiar with the inexhaustible diversity of spatial relationships produced by such a complex layout.

Figure 25.2

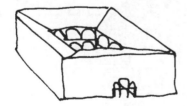

Figure 25.3   House

Typical Functions of Urban Spaces

The activities of a town take place in public and private spheres. The behavioural patterns of people are similar in both. So, the result is that the way in which public space has been organised has in all periods exercised a powerful influence on the design of private houses.

We might almost infer the existence of a kind of social ritual, which produces a perfect match between individual and collective. What concerns us above all here are those activities which take place in the town in the open air: i.e. actions which a person performs outside the familiar territory of his own home and for which he utilises public space, as for example travelling to work, shopping, selling goods, recreation, leisure activities, sporting events, deliveries etc. Although the asphalt carpet which serves as a channel for the movement of cars is still called a "street", it retains no connection with the original significance of the term. Certainly the motorised transportation of people and goods is one of the primary functions of the town, but it requires no scenery in the space around it. It is different in the case of the movement of pedestrians or public transport vehicles which move at a moderate speed, like carriages. Today we have boulevard situations which apparently draw their life from the *défilé* of flashy cars and pavement cafes are visited despite the fact that the air is polluted by exhaust fumes. Looking at planning schemes of the turn of the century one can appreciate that in cosmopolitan cities such as Paris, Rome or Berlin, the air was polluted in a different way: by horse manure, stinking sewage and uncollected refuse. A problem of urban hygiene, as old as the town itself, with the only difference that people can be poisoned by

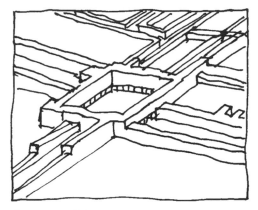

Figure 25.4 Urban structure

carbon monoxide but scarcely by horse manure.

On medical grounds we can no longer indulge in this kind of boulevard romanticism. While the automobile in its present form continues to occupy streets, it excludes all other users.

Let us give a brief outline here of the characteristic functions of the space defined by the square and the street.

The square

This spatial model is admirably suited to residential use. In the private sphere it corresponds to the inner courtyard or atrium. The courtyard house is the oldest type of town house. In spite of its undisputed advantages, the courtyard house has now become discredited. It is all too easily subject to ideological misinterpretation, and people are afraid that this design may imply enforced conformity to a communal lifestyle or a particular philosophy.

A certain unease about one's neighbours has undoubtedly led to the suppression of this building type. Yet in the same way as communal living has gained in popularity for a minority of young people with the disappearance of the extended family, the concept of neighbourhood and its accompanying building types will most certainly be readopted in the near future.

In the public sphere, the square has undergone the same development. Market places,

parade grounds, ceremonial squares, squares in front of churches and townhalls etc., all relics of the Middle Ages, have been robbed of their original functions and their symbolic content and in many places are only kept up through the activities of conservationists.

The loss of symbolism in architecture was described and lamented by Giedion in *Space, Time, Architecture*. The literary torch which he carried for Le Corbusier in the 30s, and for Jorn Utzon in the 60s, expressed his hope that this loss would perhaps be compensated by a powerful impetus towards artistic expression. He hoped for the same thing from new construction techniques. I have already stressed the importance of the poetic content and aesthetic quality of space and buildings. It is not my wish to introduce into this discussion the concept of symbolism, with all its ethical and religious overtones: and I would also like to warn against the arbitrary confusion of aesthetic and symbolic categories. If I maintain that the Louvre, instead of being a museum, might equally well be housing, a castle, an office building etc., let me make it clear that I am speaking of space or building type, not of external detailing or historical and socio-political factors which led to this structural solution. The aesthetic value of the different spatial types is as independent of short-lived functional concerns as it is of symbolic interpretations which may vary from one age to the next.

Another example to clarify this argument:

The multi-storeyed courtyard house, from the Middle Ages up to modern times, was the building type which acted as the starting point for the castle, the renaissance and baroque palace etc. The Berlin tenements of the 19th century are also courtyard houses, but nowhere near being palaces. Anyone familiar with the architecture of Palladio should draw the right conclusion from this. The lavish use of materials certainly does not play the decisive role here. If that were the case, Palladio would long since have fallen into oblivion. So, even in the 20th century, I can

Figure 25.5   The square as intersection of two roads, fixed point of orientation, meeting place.

construct a building with an inner courtyard without remotely aiming to imitate the palace architecture of the 16th century and the social class which produced it. There is no reason why the building types used by extinct dynasties to design their residences and show their material wealth should not serve as a model for housing today.

(I must add here that my critique of the ways of seeing such architectural forms applies mainly to the German cultural scene. By and large a frighteningly vague sense of history predominates in this country.)

The early Christians were not afraid to adopt the building type of Roman judicial and commerical buildings, the basilica, as the prototype of their religious monuments.

Le Corbusier took his rows of "redents" from baroque castles.

No contemporary public squares have been laid out which could be compared with urban squares like the Grande Place in Brussels, the Place Stanislas in Nancy, the Piazza del Campo in Siena, the Place Vendome and the Place des Vosges in Paris, the Plaza Mayor in Madrid, the Plaza Real in Barcelona etc. This can only occur firstly when it can be endowed with meaningful functions, and secondly is planned in the right place with the appropriate approaches within the overall town layout.

What are the functions which are appropriate to the square?

Commercial activities certainly, such as the market, but above all activities of a cultural nature. The establishment of public administrative offices, community halls, youth centres, libraries, theatres and concert halls, cafes, bars etc. Where possible in the case of central squares, these should be functions which generate activity twenty-four hours a day. Residential use should not be excluded in any of these cases.

The street

In purely residential areas streets are universally seen as areas for public circulation and recreation. The distances at which houses are set back from the street, as regulations demand in Germany today, are so excessive that attractive spatial situations can only be achieved by gimmickry. In most cases, there is ample space available for gardens in addition to the emergency access required for public service vehicles. This street space can only function when it is part of a system in which pedestrian access leads off the street. This system can be unsettled by the following planning errors:

1 If some houses and flats cannot be approached directly from the street but only from the rear. In this way the street is deprived of a vital activity. The result is a state of competition between internal and external urban space. This character-

isation of space refers to the degree of public activity which takes place in each of these two areas.

2 If the garages and parking spaces are arranged in such a way that the flow of human traffic between car and house does not impinge upon the street space.

3 If the play spaces are squeezed out into isolated areas with the sole justification of preserving the intimacy of the residential zone. The same neurotic attitude towards neighbours is experienced in flats. The noise of cars outside the home is accepted, yet indoors children are prevented from playing noisily.

4 If no money can be invested in public open spaces, on such items as avenues of trees, paving and other such street furniture, given that the first priority is the visual appeal of space.

5 If the aesthetic quality of adjacent houses is neglected, if the facing frontages are out of harmony, if different sections of the street are inadequately demarcated or if the scale is unbalanced. These factors fulfil a precise cultural role in the functional coherence of the street and square. The need to meet the town's function of "poetry of space" should be as self-evident as the need to meet any technical requirements. In a purely objective sense, it is just as basic.

Can you imagine people no longer making music, painting, making pictures, dancing...? Everybody would answer no to this. The role of architecture on the other hand is not apparently seen as so essential. "Architecture is something tangible, useful, practical" as far as most people are concerned. In any case its role is still considered as the creation of cosiness indoors and of status symbols outdoors. Anything else is classed as icing on the cake, which one can perfectly well do without. I maintain that a stage in history when architecture is not granted its full significance shows a society in cultural crisis, the tragedy of which can scarcely be described in words. Contemporary music expresses it adequately.

Figure 25.6 The street as artery and means of orientation.

The problems of the residential street touched on here apply equally to the commercial street. The separation of pedestrains and traffic carries with it the danger of the isolation of the pedestrian zone. Solutions must be carefully worked out which will keep the irritation of traffic noise and exhaust fumes away from the pedestrian, without completely distancing one zone from the other. This means an overlapping of these functions, to be achieved with considerable investment in the technological sphere, a price which the motorised society must be prepared to pay. This problem will remain much the same even when the well-known technical shortcomings and acknowledged design failings of the individual car have been ironed out. The number of cars, and their speed, remains a source of anxiety. With the way things are going at the moment, there seems little hope of either factor being corrected. On the contrary, nobody today can predict what catastrophic dimensions these problems will assume and what solutions will be needed to overcome them.

It is completely absurd to labour under the misapprehension that one day the growing need to adopt new modes of transport will leave our countryside littered with gigantic and obsolete monuments of civil engineering.

In fact, one is inclined to think that, considering the level of investment in the car and all that goes with it, a fundamental change is no longer feasible in the long term.

All this illustrates the enormous conflict of interests between investments for the demands of machine/car and investments for living creature/man; it also indicates that there is a price to be paid for the restoration of urban space, if our society is to continue to value life in its cities.

Back to the problem of the commercial street which has already been outlined. It must be fashioned differently from the purely residential street. It must be relatively narrow. The passer-by must be able to cast an eye over all the goods on display in the shops opposite without perpetually having to cross from one side of the street to the other. At least, this is what the shopper and certainly the tradesman would like to see. Another spatial configuration of the shopping street is provided by the old town centre of Berne, in which pedestrains can examine the goods on display protected by arcades from the inclemency of the weather. This type of shopping street has retained its charm and also its functional efficiency up to the present day. The pedestrian is relatively untroubled by the road, which lies on a lower level. This street space can serve as an example to us.

The same can be said of the glass-roofed arcades or passages which originated in the 19th century. Strangely enough, they have fallen out of favour today. From the point of view of ventilation it was obviously disadvantageous then to lead the street frontage into a passageway. With today's fully air-conditioned commercial and office buildings, however, this building type could come back into fashion. Protection against the elements is a financially justifiable amenity for shopping streets in our latitudes. The arcaded street, developed by the Romans from the colonnades which surrounded the Greek Agora, has completely died out. The remains of such formal streets can still be found at Palmyra, Perge, Apameia, Sidon, Ephesus, Leptis Magna, Timgad etc.

The appearance of this type of street is a fascinating event in the history of town planning. With the increased prosperity of Roman rule, a need arose for the uniform

Figure 25.7 One type of urban space on three different scales.

and schematic plan of the Greek colonial town to be modified, with emphasis being placed on arterial roads within the homogeneous network of streets, and this was achieved by marking them with particularly splendid architectural features. They certainly had important functional connotations which today can no longer be clearly surmised. Whatever these connotations were, they had an obviously commercial as well as symbolic character, in contrast to the Agora and the Forum, which were reserved primarily for political and religious purposes. Weinbrenner, with his proposed scheme for the improvement of the Kaiserstrasse in Karlsruhe, attempted to revive this idea. The Konigsbau in Stuttgart designed by Leins could be a fragment of the arcaded street of Ephesus. The Romans were astoundingly imaginative in perfecting this type of street space. So, for example, changes in the direction of streets, dictated by existing features of the urban structure, were highlighted as cardinal points by having gateways built across them. In the Galeries St Hubert in Brussels, this problem has been solved on the same principle. By this expedient, the street space is divided up into visually manageable sections, in contrast to the seemingly infinite perspective of the remaining network of streets. It should equally be noted that in rare cases streets broaden out into squares directly without their articulation being marked by buildings. The street and the square were conceived as largely independent and autonomous spaces.

Such devices, used by Roman and Greek town planners to indicate spatial relationships, lapsed into oblivion with the decline of the Roman empire in Europe. Isolated building types such as the forum and the basilica were adopted unchanged in the Middle Ages, for example in monasteries. The forum was no longer employed as a public space. Not so in North Africa and the Near East, and to some extent in Spain, where these ancient types of urban space survived almost unchanged until the turn of the century using traditional construction methods.

Typology of Urban Space

In formulating a typology of urban space, spatial forms and their derivatives may be divided into three main groups, according to the geometrical pattern of their ground plan: these groups derive from the square, the circle or the triangle.

Without doubt the scale of an urban space is also related to its geometrical qualities. Scale can only be mentioned in passing in this typology. I wish to try and deal with the significance of proportions in external space more comprehensively in a later chapter. They do not affect the arrangement of my typology.

Modulation of a Given Spatial Type

The matrix drawn up in figure 25.8 shows, reading from top to bottom: 1, The basic element; 2, The modification of the basic element resulting from the enlargement or reduction of the angles contained within it, where the external dimensions remain constant; 3, The angles remain constant and the length of two sides changes in the same proportion; 4, Angles and external dimensions are altered arbitrarily.

Reading from left to right, the matrix illustrates the following stages of modulation:

1   Angled space. This indicates a space which is a compound of two parts of the basic element with two parallel sides bent.
2   This shows only a segment of the basic element.
3   The basic element is added to.
4   The basic elements overlap or merge.
5   Under the heading "distortion" are included spatial forms which are difficult or impossible to define. This category is intended to cover those shapes which can only with difficulty be traced back to their original geometric model. These shapes may also be described as species born out of chaos. Here the elevation of buildings may be distorted or concealed

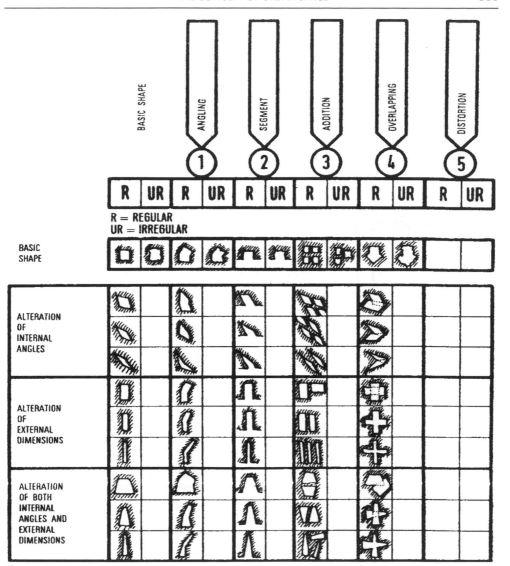

Figure 25.8

to such an extent that they can no longer be distinguished as clear demarcations of space – for example, a facade of mirror glass or one completely obscured by advertisements, so that a cuckoo-clock as big as a house stands next to an outsize ice-cream cone, or an advert for cigarettes or chewing gum stands in place of the usual pierced facade. Even the dimensions of a space can have a distorting influence on its

effect, to such an extent that it ceases to bear any relation to the original. The column headed "distortion" has not been completed in this matrix, as these shapes cannot be diagrammatically expressed.

All these processes of change show regular and irregular configurations.

The basic elements can be modified by a great variety of building sections. I illustrate

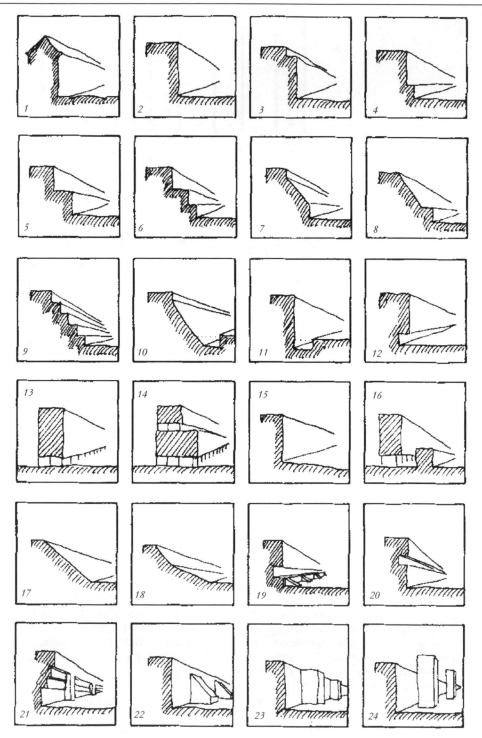

Figure 25.9

here 24 different types which substantially alter the features of urban space. See figure 25.9.

How Building Sections Affect Urban Space

Notes on figure 25.9.

1   Standard traditional section with pitched roof.
2   With flat roof.
3   With top floor set back. This device reduces the height of the building visible to the eye.
4   With a projection on pedestrian level in the form of an arcade or a solid structure. This device "distances" the pedestrian from the real body of the building and creates a pleasing human scale. This type of section was applied with particular virtuosity by John Nash in his Park Crescent, London.
5   Half way up the building the section is reduced by half its depth; this allows for extensive floors on the lower level and flats with access balconies on the upper level.
6   Random terracing.
7   Sloping elevation with vertical lower and upper floors.
8   Sloping elevation with protruding ground floor.
9   Stepped section.
10 Sloping section with moat or free-standing ground floor.
11 Standard section with moat.
12 Building with ground floor arcades.
13 Building on pilotis.
14 Building on pilotis, with an intermediate floor similarly supported.
15 Sloping ground in front of building.
16 A free-standing low building placed in front of a higher one.
17/18 Buildings with a very shallow incline, as for example arenas.
19 Building with arcade above ground level and access to pedestrian level.
20 Building with access balcony.
21 Inverted stepped section.

22 Building with pitched projections.
23 Building with projections.
24 Building with free-standing towers.

Each of these building types can be given a facade appropriate to its function and method of construction.

The sketches reproduced here (figure 25.10) can only give some idea of the inexhaustible design possibilities. Each of these structures influences urban space in a particular way. It is beyond the scope of this work to describe the nature of this influence.

Elevations

Notes on sketches in figure 25.10.

Row 1 left to right. Pierced facade: the lowest level is more generously glazed in each sketch, reducing the solid area to a simple load-bearing structure.

2.   The glazed area within the loadbearing structure can be modified according to taste. The following three pictures show a reverse of the design process portrayed in 1. A solid base forces the glazed area upward.

3.   The window type can be modified horizontally and vertically according to the imagination of the designer.

4.   Faceless modular facade as a theoretical (abstract) way in which the building might be enclosed. The modular facade can be adapted to all variations in the shape of the building. Solid sections of the building can be combined with the grid.

5.   Windowless buildings: windows are placed in niches etc. and the process starts again from the beginning.

6.   Exploration of different geometries. A thematic interpretation of the elevation: lowest level = heavy; middle section = smooth with various perforations; upper part = light, transparent. (One of the sketches of squares shows a variation on this theme on three sides of a square.) Arcades placed in front of houses, different architectural styles juxtaposed.

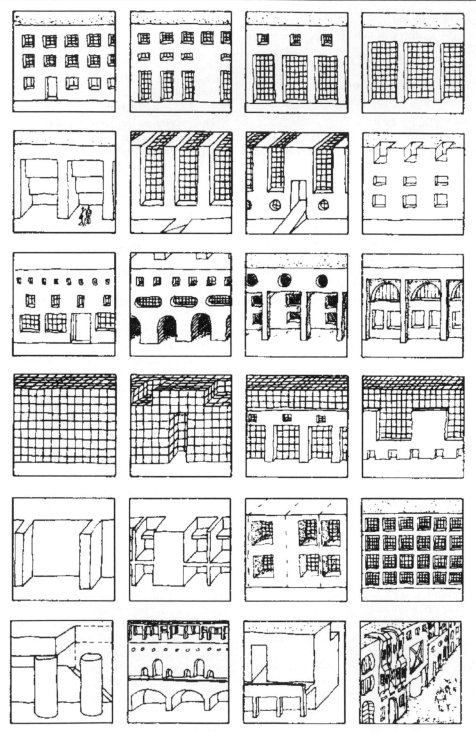

Figure 25.10

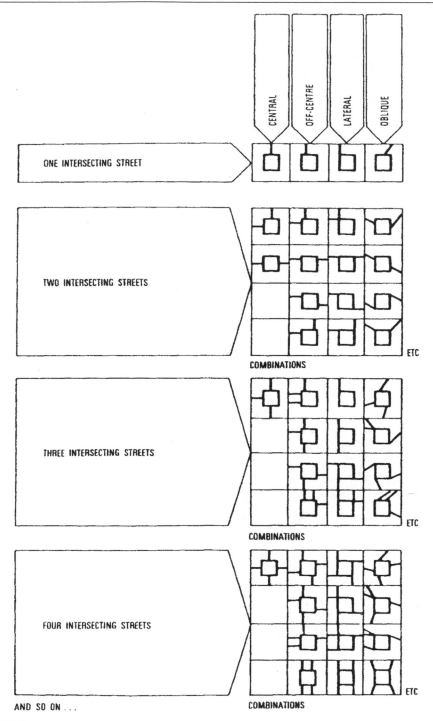

CENTRAL · OFF-CENTRE · LATERAL · OBLIQUE

ONE INTERSECTING STREET

TWO INTERSECTING STREETS

COMBINATIONS   ETC

THREE INTERSECTING STREETS

COMBINATIONS   ETC

FOUR INTERSECTING STREETS

COMBINATIONS   ETC

AND SO ON . . .

Figure 25.11

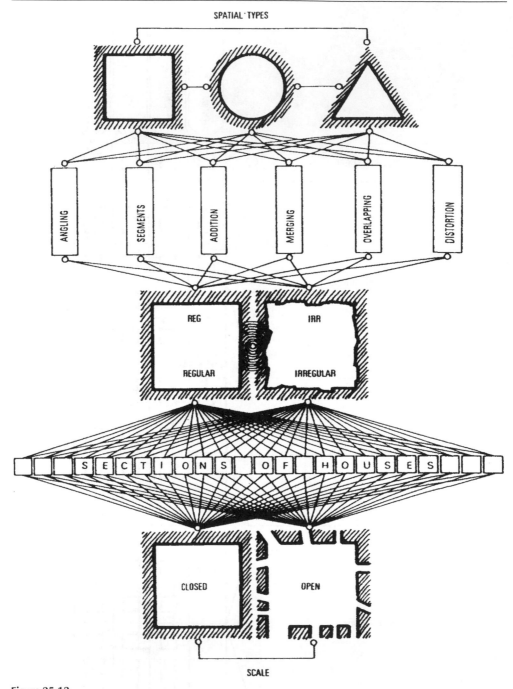

Figure 25.12

Intersections of Street and Square

All spatial types examined up to now can be classified according to the types of street intersection laid out in figure 25.11. As an example here we have a set of permutations for up to four intersections at four possible points of entry. This chart should only be taken as an indication of the almost unlimited range of possible permutations of these spatial forms. To attempt a comprehensive display here wouldconflict with the aim of this typological outline.

The vertical columns of this diagram show the number of streets intersecting with an urban space. Horizontally, it shows four possible ways in which one or more streets may intersect with a square or street:

1 Centrally and at right angles to one side.
2 Off-centre and at right angles to one side.
3 Meeting a corner at right angles.
4 Oblique, at any angle and at any point of entry.

Spatial Types and How They May Be Combined

We may summarise the morphological classification of urban spaces as follows:

The three basic shapes (square, circle and triangle) are affected by the following modulating factors: angling; segmentation; addition; merging, overlapping or amalgamation of elements; and distortion.

These modulating factors can produce geometrically regular or irregular results on all spatial types.

At the same time, the large number of possible building sections influences the quality of the space at all these stages of modulation. All sections are fundamentally applicable to these spatial forms. In the accompanying sketches I have attempted to make clear as realistically as possible the effect of individual spatial types so that this typology can be more easily accessible and of practical use to the planner.

The terms "closed" and "open" may be applied to all spatial forms described up to now: i.e. spaces which are completely or partially surrounded by buildings.

Finally, many compound forms can be created at will from the three spatial types and their modulations. In the case of all spatial forms, the differentiation of scale plays a particularly important role, as does the effect of various architectural styles on the urban space.

Design exercises can be "played" on the "keyboard" I have just described. Apart from this "formal" procedure, other factors also have their effect on space, and this effect is not insignificant. These factors are the rules governing building construction, which make architectural design possible in the first place, and above all else determine the use or function of a building, which is the essential prerequisite for architectural design. The logic of this procedure would therefore demand this sequence: function, construction and finally the resultant design.

26

Heterotopia Deserta: Las Vegas and Other Spaces

Sarah Chaplin

In this chapter I wish to trace the historiography of two separate phenomena: the heterotopia and Las Vegas. Both Michel Foucault's work on the heterotopia and contemporaneous studies of Las Vegas have become imbricated in architectural discourse, each eliciting provocative insights and new critiques since the late 1960s, as different theorists have responded to and developed these ideas. Foucault first referred to the heterotopia in *The Order of Things*, published in 1966, and then developed the notion into a set of principles with spatial and typological examples in a lecture entitled "Of Other Spaces," which he gave to a group of French architecture students in 1967. During the same period of the mid-1960s, Las Vegas was also capturing the attention of a generation of architecture students: in 1965 Tom Wolfe published an enigmatic essay on the subject, a piece which Reyner Banham claims gave rise to *Learning from Las Vegas*, the outcome of a studio at Yale taught by Denise Scott Brown, Steve Izenour and Robert Venturi. By bringing the heterotopia and Las Vegas together in the context of this discussion, I hope to offer a critical intersection from which to consider the issue of *otherness* in relation to space, and its representation and mediation within contemporary culture.

Otherness is regarded by feminist architectural historian Mary McLeod (1996, p. 1) as "one of the primary preoccupations of contemporary architecture theory," but she claims that the nature of this desire for otherness on the part of architects and architectural theorists alike is "largely unexplored in recent architectural debate" (McLeod, 1996, p. 2). She sees this concern with otherness as a superficial form of postmodern avantgardism on the part of certain architectural practitioners, for whom anything that might be deemed "other" is singularly desirable in a culture which prizes newness and celebrates difference. In her view, however, architects seek and identify otherness in the wrong places and for the wrong reasons, and that, like Foucault, their definition of otherness relies on exclusive and elitist categorisations of space. McLeod's primary contention is that until architects and architectural theoreticians engage with a broader notion of what constitutes the other in spatial terms, this quest is flawed.

I will address a broader notion of spatial otherness by extending the debate beyond the production and design of space, which is the emphasis architectural history has traditionally favoured, to consider otherness from the point of view of the consumption of space, that is to say by treating otherness as a factor of consumption, as witnessed in Las Vegas. In particular, I want to show how otherness becomes a constructed spatial condition which undergoes a process of commodification in Western culture, leading ultimately to its desertification as a concept, an outcome which may be seen to have both positive and negative connotations.

Apart from Foucault, McLeod, Wolfe, Venturi/Scott Brown/Izenour et al., I will also draw upon the work of Gianni Vattimo and Arthur Kroker whose theories are of historiographical significance to the present discussion. In addition, I will refer to Banham's (1982) *Scenes in America Deserta* and Jean Baudrillard's (1988) *America* as two key texts on the American desert, and which offer insights where Las Vegas is concerned. In some senses, I am positioning Las Vegas as the "other" with respect to Los Angeles. Quite apart from Banham's (1973) own study of Los Angeles and Mike Davis' (1990) influential account of the city, much of the work by urban geographers on the heterotopia has made LA the dominant urban case study: in particular, Edward Soja (1989), Edward Relph (1991), Derek Gregory (1994), and even architectural historian Charles Jencks (1993) have argued that the heterotopia is a key concept in postmodern geography, important for understanding a post-metropolis such as Los Angeles. This chapter aims to complement, albeit in a very brief way, work on Los Angeles, but in so doing I hope to show that Las Vegas is in fact a more powerful exemplar in discussions concerning other spaces and the heterotopia.

There is one characteristic which, above all, links the historiographies of Las Vegas and the heterotopia, namely ambivalence. Both have been represented as ambivalent phenomena *per se*, so too have their respective theorisations proved ambivalent in their treatment of them as phenomena.

There is clearly a discursive ambivalence in the way the heterotopia is thematised in Foucault's own work – a cause for concern among some theorists who have probed his writings to account for his ever-drifting emphasis. Benjamin Genocchio has critiqued Foucault's writings on the heterotopia for failing to explain how a spatial separation is effected between heterotopias and their surroundings:

> Foucault's argument is reliant upon a means of establishing some invisible but visibly operational difference which, disposed against the background of an elusive spatial continuum, provides a clear conception of spatially discontinuous ground. Crucially, what is lacking from Foucault's argument is exactly this. (Genocchio, 1995, pp. 38–9)

Figure 26.1 Las Vegas as heterotopia (1998).

Figure 26.2   Casino as heterotopia (1998).

However, far from rendering the heterotopia conceptually unstable and hence unreliable, as Genocchio has hinted, it is Foucault's ambivalent arguments that are so important in gaining an understanding of the way in which other spaces are established culturally. In fact, the positioning of heterotopia both semantically and physically cannot be stable and fixed, since its very purpose is to effect contingency and disrupt continuity.

Henri Lefebvre also accused Foucault of ambivalence on another front, namely for failing to distinguish between two kinds of spatiality:

Figure 26.3   Nevada desert (1998).

Figure 26.4 Las Vegas as everyday other (1998).

Foucault never explains what space it is that he is referring to, nor how it bridges the gap between the theoretical (epistemological) realm and the practical one, between mental and social, between the space of philosophers and the space of people who deal with material things. (Lefebvre, 1991, p. 4)

I am, however, working with this conflation, since I believe that Foucault's lack of explanation was intentional: the spatial ambivalence in his work drew attention to the interdependency between spatial theory and spatial practice. Rather than a gap requiring to be bridged, I would argue that this represents a productive fuzzy field in Foucault's references to different kinds of space. Furthermore, the fact that Foucault's ideas are left so open to interpretation makes his glossing of the heterotopia not necessarily definitive: the reworkings of Foucault's ideas in subsequent texts simply take the concept on their own terms and develop it in new ways, discovering new relevance for the heterotopia within other contexts.

So let me give a brief overview of what Foucault (1993, p. 422) in "Of Other Spaces" called "a sort of systematic description or heterotopology," in which he elaborated six principles of the heterotopia, citing particular architectural typologies for each principle:

1 There is no culture in the world which is not made up of heterotopias, and in every human group there will be counter-sites. Foucault identified two main types, heterotopias of crisis and of deviance, spaces such as prisons, sanatoria and boarding schools which are set aside, placed in parentheses, with sharply demarcated boundaries and rules.

2 Heterotopias invariably undergo transformations over time, as in the cemetery's relationship to a city or a mausoleum's relationship to a house, whereby "a society may take an existing heterotopia, which has never vanished, and make it function in a different way" (Foucault, 1993, p. 423).

3 Heterotopias which have the power of juxtaposing in a single real place different spaces and locations that are incompatible with each other. Foucault cited theatres, cinemas and gardens.

4 In heterotopias of juxtaposition there is a perpetual accumulation of items or experiences over time, such as with museums, libraries, holiday camps and travelling fairs, where these spaces

function as "heterochronisms" which can be either permanent or ephemeral.

5 Heterotopias have their own system of opening and closing "that isolates them and makes them penetrable at the same time" (Foucault, 1993, p. 425). Foucault stated that barracks and Turkish baths operate in this way, as well as American motels.

6 The heterotopia exists between the two poles of illusion and compensation. At one extreme lies the brothel, and at the other, the colony. The final manifestation of the heterotopia which Foucault put forward is the ship, which he says is "the heterotopia par excellence" (Foucault, 1993, p. 425). The ship is both illusion and compensation: it transports its passengers to other worlds, depositing them on foreign shores to discover as yet unknown other spaces, and it also recreates in its own architecture of decks and bridges, saloons and cargo holds, cabins and cocktail lounges, an ordered arrangement which parallels lived reality on *terra firma*.

It is but a small step from the illusory yet compensatory quality of the cruise ship to the saloons and cocktail lounges of a Las Vegas casino. At the level of Foucault's symptomatic principles, Las Vegas would seem a yet more perfect example of the heterotopia, combining the attributes of theatre, cinema, garden, museum, holiday camp, honeymoon motel, brothel and colony, as well as that of the ship. In Las Vegas, heterochronism exists in the form of a multitude of themed resorts which borrow from other places and other times and are then juxtaposed along the Strip without any logical historical or geographical ordering. However, there is more to be derived than this superficial interpretation from a historiographical consideration of the heterotopia in relation to Las Vegas, and vice versa.

Beyond Foucault's six principles, there is a strategic similarity between the staging of Las Vegas' historiography and that of the heterotopia, and in the way that they have become absorbed into architectural discourse. First, there is the discovery of an "other" space, one which operates or displays qualities which were previously unknown, unacknowledged, or whose mere existence or whereabouts was unknown. Second, this space is then identified, mapped or marked in some way (the desert). This has the effect initially of calling attention to its otherness, and then of bringing its otherness under control (Las Vegas, the meadows). Gradually any trace of otherness is reduced or making it disappear by rendering its otherness similar to what is already known (Las Vegas, the frontier town). This process happens in the construction of discourse as much as in the construction of the built environment: new concepts are identified, theoretical neologisms coined, which are then gradually tamed by research, to the point where they become accepted and incorporated within discourse. Lastly, to compensate for the inevitable assimilation and disappearance of the otherness of the other, there is an attempt to reproduce or manufacture otherness with reified images or appropriated and recontextualised examples, as a form of textual, visual or spatial gaming which masks reality (Las Vegas, the spectacle). This follows the precept which Wlad Godzich outlines in his foreword to Michel de Certeau's *Heterologies*: "Western thought has always thematised the other as a threat to be reduced, as a potential same-to-be, a yet-not-same" (Godzich, 1986, p. xiii).

The whole historiographical sequence can thus be summarised as a shift down through the gears: name–tame–same–game. It is a colonial progression, which establishes on the one hand the colonisation of the desert/ Wild West as a frontier in the case of Las Vegas, and on the other hand characterises the intellectual colonisation of Michel Foucault's notion of the heterotopia. By using what might seem an overly linear and mechanistic model to structure this chapter, resting lightly on these headings in order to navigate through the parallel historiographies of the heterotopia and Las Vegas, this is also intended to reflect the capacity for architectural discourse to enter its own "game" stage.

Name

In response to Foucault's six principles and their attendant examples, Steve Connor observes that "once a heterotopia has been named, and more especially, once it has been cited and recited, it is no longer the conceptual monstrosity which it once was, for its incommensurability has been in some sense bound, controlled and predictively interpreted, given a centre and illustrative function" (Connor, 1989, p. 9). Naming thus serves to remove power deriving from otherness, an inevitable consequence of claiming the land or theorising an idea or impression: the other is only truly powerful when it remains unnamed, more so if it proves unnameable. For the other space of the desert to be conquered by civilisation, it first had to be named as a spatial condition; likewise the heterotopia had to be named as an idea in order for it to become discursively apparent and available. This Foucault achieved mainly by differentiating the heterotopia from other ideas to which it relates, in particular the utopia.

Foucault states that the heterotopia is

a sort of counter-arrangement, or effectively realised utopia, in which all the real arrangements that can be found within society are at one and the same time represented, challenged and overturned: a sort of place that lies outside all places, and yet is actually localisable. In contrast to the utopias, these places are absolutely *other* with respect to all the arrangements that they reflect. (Foucault, 1993, p. 422)

A common reading of Las Vegas is that of an effectively realised utopia, a bizarre other world which exists in the middle of the desert, distant from "normal" American cities, a place in which traditional American values are inverted, where other rules apply, and where the natural logic of night and day is abandoned, a city which rearranges the normal relationship between consumption and production. Each individual casino attempts to create an ostensibly utopian environment, designed to appeal to a particular sector of society through its theming and decor, and thereby luring people into the warm embrace of gambling. Nowadays, Las Vegas' main preoccupation is how to sustain its mass appeal and maintain the American public's desire to gamble and be entertained.

Jean Baudrillard, in his ruminations on the United States, identifies this scenario with sweeping Eurocentric chauvinism:

The US is utopia achieved. We should not judge their crisis as we judge our own, the crisis of old European countries. Ours is a crisis of historical ideals, facing up to the impossibility of their realisation. Theirs is the crisis of an achieved utopia, confronted with the problem of its duration and permanence. (Baudrillard, 1988, p. 77)

This places a city like Las Vegas in a paradoxical historical situation: as an achieved utopia, it is the ultimate development of civilisation under capitalist society, and at the same time a manifestation of what Baudrillard (1988, p. 7) famously calls "the *only remaining primitive society*" (emphasis in original). By implication, Baudrillard attributes a degree of conceptual ambivalence to Las Vegas while at the same time depicting the perpetuation of a utopian condition as a doomed prospect: "*Utopia has been achieved here and anti-utopia is being achieved*: the anti-utopia of unreason, of deterritorialisation, of the indeterminacy of language and the subject, of the neutralisation of all values, of the death of culture" (Baudrillard, 1988, p. 97, emphasis in original). Baudrillard's assertions show that utopia inevitably gives way to a new state, one which corresponds to Foucault's depictions of the heterotopia, while at the same time heralding the impending desertification of American culture. Baudrillard is typically moralistic in his attitude towards the USA, and clearly regards the inevitable move towards anti-utopia as an apocalyptic slide. This can be detected in his perception of the desert:

American culture is heir to the deserts, but the deserts here are not part of a Nature defined by contrast with the town...the natural deserts teach me what I need to know about the deserts of the sign. They induce in me an exalting vision of the desert-ification of signs and men. They form the mental frontier where the projects of civil-isation run into the ground. (Baudrillard, 1988, p. 63)

In a particular passage in *The Order of Things*, Foucault articulates the utopia/het-erotopia distinction somewhat differently as a form of mental frontier, arguing that:

Utopias afford consolation: although they have no real locality, there is nevertheless a fantastic, untroubled region in which they are able to unfold; they open up cities with vast avenues, superbly planted gardens, countries where life is easy even though the road to them is chimerical. Heterotopias are disturbing, probably because they secretly undermine language, because they make it impossible to name this *and* that, because they shatter or tangle common names, be-cause they destroy "syntax" in advance, and not only the syntax with which we construct sentences, but also that less apparent syntax that causes words and things (next to and also opposite one another) "to hold to-gether." This is why utopias permit fables and discourse: they run with the very grain of language and are part of the fundamental dimension of the *fabula*; heterotopias desic-cate speech, stop words in their tracks, con-test the very possibility of grammar at its source; they dissolve our myths and sterilise the lyricism of our sentences. (Foucault, 1989, p. xviii)

It is clear that Foucault regards the ability to resist naming as a fundamental characteristic of the heterotopia: its evasiveness provides a powerful sense of agency with which to chal-lenge the easy complacency of utopia.

Italian theorist Gianni Vattimo takes up the challenge which the heterotopia repre-sents with respect to utopia, postulating that there has been a paradigm shift from utopia to heterotopia since the 1960s, a change which he regards as "the most radical transformation in the relation between art

and everyday life" Vattimo (1992, p. 62). Vattimo argues that this shift has brought about a change in the dominant aesthetic sensibility, making contemporary Western society more predisposed towards images and sites of imperfection, compromise, hy-bridity and incompletion. His interpretation of heterotopia aligns it neatly with the dis-course of postmodernity which favours inclusivity, and reproduces it as the post-revolutionary other which single-handedly usurped the previous modernist regime. Vat-timo treats the heterotopia as both the im-petus that produces this shift and also as a *zeitgeist* or prevailing hegemony in its own right, responsible for legitimating the col-lapse of any distinction between high and low culture, between elitist and popular taste, and facilitating a denial of the autono-mous function of art. Likewise, *Learning from Las Vegas* also treats the city as a site of incompletion, issuing a challenge to the architectural establishment to abandon modernist rhetoric in favour of a more popu-lar, ordinary aesthetic.

Tame

Vattimo's own historiographic staging of the heterotopia takes an unexpected turn, how-ever, when he predicts that

the wager on heterotopia, so to speak, will escape being merely frivolous, if it can link the transformed aesthetic experience of mass society with Heidegger's call to an experience of being that is (at last) non-metaphysical...only [then] can we find a way amidst the explosion of the ornamental and heterotopian character of today's aes-thetic. (Vattimo, 1992, p. 74)

In his final analysis, the heterotopian para-digm is recast as one of mindless decoration lacking emotional depth and intellectual dir-ection, a manoeuvre which invokes elitist class distinctions that reproduce the hetero-topia not as a post-revolutionary other, but as a lightweight other to the seriousness of lived experience, and to a proper under-standing of meaning. Las Vegas is present indirectly in these statements, not least because of Vattimo's gambling metaphor, but also in linking the heterotopia to an aesthetic which revolves around mass culture, ornamentation and excess. His naming of the current status of contemporary culture as a heterotopia and his subsequent positioning of the heterotopia as no more than an aesthetic has the effect of taming the concept, shifting it from the status of transitive verb to a vaguely derogatory adjective. Like Baudrillard, Vattimo's reaction to mass culture is Eurocentric and hierarchical, in which his own high-brow taste, to use Pierre Bourdieu's (1994) terms, is inescapable.

If the shift from utopia to heterotopia is to do with the bringing together of art and everyday life and a revolution of taste values, then at its heart lies Pop Art. According to Reyner Banham (1975, p. 78), by the end of the 1950s Las Vegas was "a classic Pop artefact...an expendable dream that money could just about buy, designed for immediate point-of-sale impact, outside the canons of Fine Art." At this stage, the image of Las Vegas was untamed by architectural discourse, in that it was largely unmediated by critical commentaries. It was, however, mediated within popular culture: in his book *Viva Las Vegas* Alan Hess (1993) shows the extent of mediation evident even in the prewar period, by highlighting the caption to a 1939 map: "Las Vegas: still a Frontier Town." This indicates that already Las Vegas had been not only named but also tamed, and that it had become necessary to self-consciously invoke its wilder past as a means of self-promotion. The lawlessness of frontier towns had by the 1930s already been romanticised and mythologised, and the image of Las Vegas' legislative ambivalence was perpetuated through a number of cinematic representations during the 1940s and 1950s, such as *Las Vegas Shakedown* and *The Las Vegas Story*. Then in 1965 Tom Wolfe published his influential essay "Las Vegas (What?) Las Vegas (Can't Hear You! Too Noisy) Las Vegas!!!!" in *Esquire* magazine. Banham admits that after reading the Wolfe essay, he was persuaded that Las Vegas was a necessary stop on his desert itinerary

planned for December of that year. By 1966 he claimed that it was on the itinerary of most architectural students (Banham, 1975, p. 79), and these factors combined to legitimise Las Vegas as an official object of study for architecture: the Venturi/Scott Brown/Izenour team arrived on the scene to record their observations of banal Strip-side architecture like good Beaux Arts scholars a year later, but with the intention of upsetting the architectural apple cart, or at the every least redirecting it towards a consideration of consumption.

It was a populist concern with banal everydayness that brought Venturi, Scott Brown and Izenour to Las Vegas, and led their students to call the Strip "The Great Proletarian Cultural Locomotive." Until this pioneering study (for it was here that architecture found its own metaphorical frontier) Hess (1993, p. 18) remarks, "the rapid growth of this commercial roadside landscape had attracted little attention in the professional press. It was not generally considered architecture." In that sense, Las Vegas stood outside the prevailing architectural discourse in the 1960s, and offered a real, ordinary, banal space which functioned as a counter site with respect to "serious" avant-garde architecture of the time. But Las Vegas was not only "other" to the architectural establishment. Paradoxically, it also maintained its position in a populist context as other when compared to the real, banal spaces of American suburbia. This makes Las Vegas evade an absolute classification, an ambivalent space, and also makes the relativism of the heterotopia self evident. For one social group (what Wolfe called the "culturati"), Las Vegas was vulgar and stood apart from their endeavour. For another, much larger social group, the consumers of the neon spectacle of Las Vegas, it represented something extraordinary, beyond their everyday lives. It was thus simultaneously ordinary and extraordinary, real and unreal. In other words, depending on which perspective is chosen, Las Vegas is heterotopian either by virtue of its everyday qualities, or by virtue of its ability to exist outside the everyday. It is tamed simultaneously by two different discourses, emerging with two different cultural identities relative to two different audiences, one academic, the other consumerist.

Same

Guy Debord in *The Society of the Spectacle* observed dryly that

> tourism, human circulation considered as consumption, a by-product of the circulation of commodities, is fundamentally nothing more than the leisure of going to see what has become banal. The economic organisation of visits to different places is already in itself the guarantee of their equivalence. (Debord, 1977, para. 168)

The proliferation of spaces of equivalence or sameness produces a situation which Kroker has called panic culture. In his estimation, "panic culture is where we live on the edge of ecstasy and dread" (Kroker, 1992, p. 159). In the 1990s, panic is both a product of and the producer of the banal, reworking difference and otherness into sameness, so as to provide safe, predictable experiences for consumers, while still generating desire for the thrill of the other. Kroker (1992, p. 159) sees Foucault as key to an understanding of this culture of panic, maintaining that "in Foucault alone there are to be found all the key panic sites at the fin de millennium." This makes Foucault a "sliding signifier" for Kroker, producing "an ironic meditation on the fate of the relational, sidereal, and topographical postmodern scene" (Kroker, 1992, p. 159).

This notion of panic illuminates a moment in the historiography of both heterotopia and Las Vegas. To return to the issue of the spatially discontinuous ground ambivalently implied in Foucault's heterotopology, a significant change may be seen to be operating in Las Vegas, whereby the spatial discreteness of the casinos as counter-sites gives way to the spatial continuity of Las Vegas as a total leisure environment. Previously, casinos modelled themselves as miniature citadels, each promoting voluntary incarceration with a myriad of ploys: externally ad-

vertising competitive deals, rates and odds, and internally operating a ground plan which was designed specifically to make it difficult to find the exit. However, recent ambitious resort developments have begun to reproduce Las Vegas as a collective spectacle or series of spectacles, in which the Strip functions as a flow of spaces between which pedestrians can move from one fantasy to the next at timed intervals: from a Caesar's Forum shopping mall where the sun sets every hour and the statues come to life, to an erupting volcano at The Mirage, then on to a full-scale pirate battle at Treasure Island, before experiencing the computerised extravaganza of Fremont Street.

Arthur Pope in his study *Ladders*, which details the historiography of urban form in the USA, characterises this shift as part of a general urban trend:

> with the post-war decline of the open urban centre, the possibility of a heterotopia or countersite that may once have existed in the exclusive suburban enclave or fated asylum has diminished. In the absence of open cities, closed developments no longer function as countersites which are both a reflection of and a retreat from the greater urban world. Rather they are now themselves obliged to be the greater world that was heretofore represented by the city and the metropolis. (Pope, 1996, p. 179)

Pope presents the problem of incipient urban sameness as a demise of heterotopian space. For Pope, this is a primary site of panic in late twentieth century urbanism, and he argues that it also invalidates the depictions of casinos in *Learning from Las Vegas*, in which "gambling rooms are established as an antithesis to the street" (Pope, 1996, p. 195). In his view, the closed casino developments which Venturi, Scott Brown and Izenour studied now operate as one continuous mass, such that "what was, in 1968, a chaotic poly-nuclear field has been unified around a single armature of corporate development. The recent appearance of atriums, skybridges and the massive 'theme park casinos' make the case apparent" (Pope,

1996, p. 198). Movement along this armature, however, cannot be solely pedestrian,
since the distances are immense. In order to
transport the (mostly elderly) visitors from
one casino event to the next, or from pavement to casino, there are now moving pave-
ments and monorail systems linking them all
together.

Thus at the level of individual casinos, Las
Vegas is no longer a collection of different
counter-sites but a continuous leisure-orien-
tated mono-culture. Similarly, on a larger
scale, Las Vegas no longer functions as a singular urban counter-site with respect to other
western cities, since its *modus operandi* is
now the same as that adopted by every city
in the USA. The virtually pedestrianised Strip
is now not much different from strategies
adopted by, for example, downtown San
Diego or Minneapolis, which have remod-
elled themselves on leisure environments,
and are now intended to be experienced as
malls or theme parks in their own right. This
reflects, in part, the expectations of the average consumer, for whom the produced space
of the theme park represents an ideal environment: safe, clean, predictable yet diverting.

Game

In Pope's analysis of Las Vegas, Banham's
1975 predictions regarding the effect of
Las Vegas in terms of *laissez-faire* urban
planning and aesthetic control would seem
to have been realised. Banham claimed
that architects and planners were concerned
that Las Vegas pointed the way for all architecture in the future, and that it had become
a counter-image representing "the total sur-
render of all social and moral standards
to the false glamour of naked commercial
competition" (Banham, 1975, p. 80). For
a time, Las Vegas wielded a heterotopian-
style agency, with the effect of questioning
the normal syntax of city planning, and
dissolving the certainties on which such principles of planning had depended. The result
is that city centres throughout Europe
and North America have become "urban entertainment centres," much like the Las
Vegas Strip, where consumption is the new
production, and where "culture industries"
replace manufacturing, in a bid to attract
the global tourism market.

Figure 26.5 Caesar's Forum shops, Las Vegas (1998).

Figure 26.6   Travelators make casinos into one continuum (1998).

As such, beyond the literal gaming which takes place in the casinos, Las Vegas has entered its own game stage, capable of prompting a series of reconsiderations of its own aesthetic *raison d'être* along with that of other spaces. Kroker once again sees Foucault as an insightful thinker where the issue of aesthetic impact is concerned, proposing that "Foucault was one who refused history as a game of truth, only to install in its place the game of effective history, a 'history which descends'" (Kroker, 1992, 159). This game of history is present in the way in which Las Vegas manages its own image of otherness today. Since the publication in 1975 of Banham's essay "Mediated Environments or: You Can't Build That Here," Las Vegas has reinvented itself yet again by means of more and more theatrical architectural forms, and its image has been subject to further cinematic representations; in recent years there has been a plethora of films which use Las Vegas as the main location: Martin Scorsese's *Casino* (1995), Mike Figgis' *Leaving Las Vegas* (1995), Adrian Lyne's *Indecent Proposal* (1993) and Andrew Bergman's *Honeymoon in Vegas* (1992), to name but a few, while Will Smith's pop video for *Gettin Jiggy Wi' It* was shot using a succession of the major resort casinos as backdrops.

Recently, as if to compete with Los Angeles' profiteering from Las Vegas as a film location, the city has taken to staging its own mediation, self-consciously marking moments in the city's unfolding history: 31 December 1996 witnessed the televised demolition of the old Hacienda casino to make way for a more lavish resort. Further evidence of a "game of effective history" lies in the famous Boneyard, where old neon signs are stored. This is now being repackaged to form the "Neon Museum" where Las Vegas icons from the past are preserved and re-presented. In this way, Las Vegas has successfully created its own collective memory, one which is deliberately mythologised in the interests of marketing. The game plays with the image of Las Vegas as place of constant change, in which the main agent at work is theming. Theming is employed as a means to get beyond the basic problem of sameness, and to disguise and prolong the gaming among the various casino developers by making an artificial differentiation between adjacent environments which are otherwise identical in purpose: to maximise profits through gambling and other receipts. This is not to say that theming produces a genuine effect of difference or otherness, since it steers a path close to recognisable

Figure 26.7   Boneyard, Las Vegas (1998).

familiarity: Mark Gottdiener (1997, p. 156) argues that "themed environments display a surprisingly limited range of symbolic motifs because they need to appeal to the widest possible consumer markets."

The Las Vegas skyline has changed over recent years not only because the developer stakes have been raised (neon is now seen by many casino owners as passé), and the clientele has changed somewhat, but also because there has been a historiographical shift in the choice of the themes themselves. As mediated environments, casino resorts and other attractions have moved away from referencing the desert, Hispanic, frontier-town otherness of Las Vegas (the Sands, the Dunes, Desert Inn, El Rancho, Barbary Coast, Golden Nugget, the Frontier) or images associates with gambling itself (The Mint, Lady Luck, Horseshoe), towards themes which seek to create the image of otherness for Las Vegas by means of imported and re-presented other places, producing an exotic mix and a masked reality. The new range of referents can be divided into: historical European (Riviera, Monte Carlo, St Tropez, Caesar's, Continental, San Remo and the newest clutch: The Venetian, Paris, Bellagio); those based on other cities in the United States (New York New York, Or-

leans, Bourbon Street); those which conjure up exotic or mythical locations (Mirage, Aladdin, Luxor, Treasure Island, Imperial Palace, Excalibur, Tropicana, Rio); media or music-derived themes (MGM, Debbie Reynolds, Liberace, All Star, Hard Rock); and those which draw on outer space or the future (Stardust, Stratosphere). These are, in many ways, no more than face-lifts, an inevitable consequence of what Baudrillard (1988, p. 118) calls "astral America": "As for American reality, even the face-lifted variety retains its vast scope, its tremendous scale, and, at the same time, an unspoilt rawness. All societies end up wearing masks." Even Baudrillard, however, ultimately admits his own ambivalence towards Las Vegas, when he evokes a seductive and totalising image of "astral America": "The direct star-blast, as against the fevered distance of the cultural gaze ... Starblasted ... transpolitically by the power game, the power museum that America has become for the whole world" (Baudrillard, 1988, p. 27).

Las Vegas can be regarded as perhaps the most prominent example of this power museum, a hyped-up heterotopia of perpetual accumulation, which survives the numbing onset of sameness by constantly adding to its collection of re-presented architectural

Figure 26.8   Theming: New York, New York, Las Vegas (1998).

trophies which it holds in its cultural gaze: New York, Paris and Venice are shrunk down, remixed and repackaged for the consumer of mediated otherness in a space of convenience. Increasingly, what makes the theming of casinos work is not the architectural facades they present to the street, however, but the selective importation of merchandise and cuisine from these other places available inside, such that a visit to the resort becomes a reified sampler. As Gilles Deleuze has remarked, "the real is not impossible; it is simply more and more artificial" (Deleuze and Guattari, 1983, p. 34).

After excessive gaming is there only cultural exhaustion? What can Las Vegas tell us about the meaning of cultural desertification or the future of the heterotopia? Baudrillard (1988, p. 10) asks the question "how far can we go in the extermination of meaning, how far can we go in the non-referential desert form without cracking up and, of course, keep alive the esoteric charm of disappearance?" In *America*, he establishes a link between gambling and the desert, which harks back to the early themes of the casinos:

> there is a mysterious affinity between the sterility of wide open spaces and that of gambling, between the sterility of speed and that of expenditure... it would be wrong-headed to counterpose Death Valley, the sublime natural phenomenon, to Las Vegas, the abject cultural phenomenon. For the one is the hidden face of the other and they mirror each other across the desert. (Baudrillard, 1988, p. 67)

In making Las Vegas synonymous with the desert, Baudrillard assumes that desertification is culturally disastrous. However, it need not be the case. Iain Chambers has suggested:

> If, as Jean Baudrillard is fond of reminding us, the desert is the place of the empty repetition of dead meanings and abandoned signs, it is also the site of infinity: a surplus, as Emmanuel Levinas argues, that permits others to exist apart and irreducible to ourselves. So the occidental metaphor of emptiness and exhaustion – the desert – perhaps also holds the key to the irruption of other possibilities: that continual deferring and ambiguity of sense involved in the travelling of sounds and people who come from elsewhere, but who are now moving across a landscape that we recognise and inhabit. (Chambers, 1994, p. 84)

By implication, this viewpoint allows for a more positive stage in the historiography of Las Vegas, and at the same time salvages the banalised notion of the heterotopia with a new shift, one which takes into account the temporal and social dynamics of an other space. It also points to the hidden side of Las Vegas, its own resident others: as one of the fastest growing cities in the United States, Las Vegas is home to diverse multi-ethnic groups who have migrated from elsewhere, bringing with them their own cultures and spatial practices. In Las Vegas, there are two kinds of constant deferral in operation: one is highly visible and relates to the deterritorialisations and reterritorialisations of the casinos as they are demolished, rebuilt and renamed (such as El Rancho, whose naming changed twice before any work was done to remodel the casino itself: in January 1996 its sign declared it was to reopen as the Starship Orion, then a year later it had changed to announcing "The Future Home of Countryland"); the other deferral relates to the communities in flux which arrive, establish themselves, and move on.

Figure 26.10 El Rancho: "future home of Countryland," Las Vegas (1998).

The notions of infinity and surplus also serve to re-establish some of the primitive, raw energy to Las Vegas, preserving it from the apocalyptic image that Baudrillard associates ultimately with the desert, and hence precluding an absolute desertification of Las Vegas and the heterotopia as productive cultural forces. For while Baudrillard's reading of Las Vegas would deny the reconstitutive power of the heterotopia, and hence also deny the future as a productive next stage, a more Deleuzian reading preserves something of its positive mobilising force: instead of exhaustion, the desert is a smooth space in which desires may be freely exercised, within which identity can be renegotiated.

Heterotopia deserta, far from existing as a space of abandoned signs, like the Boneyard, is more likely to be found in the irruption of other possibilities: Las Vegas might now be conscious of its past, and seek to profit from it, but it is still dealing in the one commodity which in any society remains perpetually other: the future. Levinas (1987, p. 77) conceives of our relationship to the future in

Figure 26.9 El Rancho: "future home of Starship Orion," Las Vegas (1997).

spatial terms: "The exteriority of the future is totally different from spatial exteriority precisely through the fact that the future is absolutely surprising.... The future is what is not grasped, what befalls us and lays hold of us. The other is the future. The very relationship with the other is the relationship with the future."

REFERENCES

Banham, R. (1973) *Los Angeles: Architecture of the Four Ecologies*. London: Pelican.

Banham, R. (1975) Mediated environments or: you can't build that here. In C. W. E. Bigsby (ed.), *Superculture: American Popular Culture in Europe*. London: Paul Elek.

Banham, R. (1982) *Scenes in America Deserta*. London: Thames and Hudson.

Baudrillard, J. (1988) *America*. London: Verso.

Bourdieu, P. (1994) *Distinction: A Social Critique of Judgement*. London: Routledge.

Chambers, I. (1994) *Migrancy, Culture, Identity*. London: Routledge.

Connor, S. (1989) *Postmodern Culture*. Oxford: Blackwell.

Davis, M. (1990) *City of Quartz*. London: Verso.

Debord, G. (1977) *The Society of the Spectacle*. London: Wheaton.

Deleuze, G. and Guattari, F. (1983) *Anti-Oedipus, Capitalism and Schizophrenia*. Minneapolis: University of Minnesota Press.

Foucault, M. (1989) *The Order of Things*. London: Routledge.

Foucault, M. (1993) Of other spaces. In J. Ockman (ed.), *Architecture Culture, 1943–1968*. New York: Rizzoli.

Genocchio, B. (1995) Discourse, discontinuity, difference: the question of other spaces. In S. Watson and K. Gibson (eds), *Postmodern Cities and Spaces*. Oxford: Blackwell.

Godzich, W. (1986) Foreword: the further possibility of knowledge. In M. de Certeau (ed.), *Heterologies*. Minneapolis: University of Minnesota Press.

Gottdiener, M. (1997) *The Theming of America*. Oxford: Westview Press.

Gregory, D. (1994) *Geographical Imaginations*. Oxford: Blackwell.

Hess, A. (1993) *Viva Las Vegas*. New York: Chronicle Books.

Jencks, C. (1993) *Heteropolis*. London: Academy Editions.

Kroker, A. (1992) *The Possessed Individual*. Toronto: Culture Texts.

Lefebvre, H. (1991) *The Production of Space*. Oxford: Blackwell.

Levinas, E. (1987) *Time and the Other*. Pittsburgh, PA: Duquesnesne University Press.

McLeod, M. (1996) Everyday and "other" spaces. In D. Coleman, E. Danze and C Henderson (eds), *Architecture and Feminism*. New York: Princeton Architectural Press.

Pope, A. (1996) *Ladders*. New York: Princeton Architectural Press.

Relph, E. (1991) Postmodern geographies. *Canadian Geographer*, 35, 98–105.

Soja, E. W. (1989) *Postmodern Geographies: The Reassertion of Space in Critical Social Theory*. London: Verso.

Vattimo, G. (1992) *The Transparent Society*. Cambridge: Polity Press.

Part X
Pragmatics

The Design Professions and the Built Environment in a Postmodern Epoch

Paul L. Knox

UD responding

It has been clear for some time that both urban development and the design professions concerned with urban development – architecture, landscape architecture, planning, and urban design – have been responding to a new and distinctive set of social, economic, demographic, cultural and political forces. At the root of this new context for the design professions and the built environment are structural changes that have been developing for several decades as the dynamics of capitalism have entered a "late" or "advanced" stage marked by a steady shift away from manufacturing employment towards service employment, an increasing dominance of big conglomerate corporations, and an internationalization of corporate activity. Meanwhile, these same dynamics have precipitated some important social transformations: the differentiation of the social order into complex class fractions and the creation of a "new" petite bourgeoisie, for example. These social transformations, in turn, are being reproduced in space through property relations which are articulated by the real estate sector, mediated by the design professions, and reflected and conditioned by the built environment (Gottdiener, 1985; Lefebvre, 1974).

As these structural transformations have been gathering momentum, other shifts – in demography, technology, and in cultural and political life – have been taking place. These include the entry of the baby-boom generation into housing and labor markets, the changing structure and composition of private households, the development of advanced telecommunications and high-technology industries, the articulation of liberal/ecological values of the middle-class baby-boomer counterculture, the retrenchment of public expenditure with the rise of the "new right", *and the emergence of distinctive (post-Modern) movements in the arts, literature and design.* These shifts have, collectively, contributed to what Gappert (1979) calls a "post-affluent" condition in North American society. They are also seen by some as part of a broader sweep of change in which post-Modern movements are closely related to the structural transition to advanced capitalism:

The economic periodization of capital into three rather than two stages (that of "late" or multinational capitalism now being added to the more traditional moments of "classical" capitalism and of the "monopoly stage" or "state imperialism") suggests the possibility of a new periodization on the level of culture as well: from this perspective, the moment of "high" modernism, of the International Style, and of the classical modern movement in all the arts ... would "correspond" to that second stage of monopoly and imperialist capitalism that came to an end with the Second World War. Its "critique" therefore coincides with its extinction, its passing into history, as well as the emergence, in the third stage of "consumer capital", of some postmodernist practice of pastiche, of a new free play of styles and historicist allusions now willing to "learn from Las Vegas", a moment of surface rather than depth, of the "death" of the old individual subject or bourgeois ego, and of the schizophrenic celebration of the commodity fetishism of the image. (Jameson, 1985a, p. 75).

Jürgen Habermas had already suggested that post-Modern art might represent an important, built-in channel of resistance to the instrumental rationalism of the state and the marketplace (see Bernstein, 1985); and Lyotard (1984), for all his polemic on Habermas's theory of legitimation crisis, also recognizes a "postmodern" condition in the world's core economies, wherein the economic rationality and cultural agnosticism of industrial capitalism has been widely rejected – though not yet clearly displaced by a new aesthetics, a new economics, or a new politics.

It follows from this perspective that postmodernism is more than an artistic or literary style or an approach to design. As Dear (1986) points out:

> The hysteria surrounding the rhetoric of postmodern...*style* masks a more profound logic: that is, the way in which the spatial form of the built environment reflects, and in turn conditions, social relations over time and space. (p. 375)

Dear helps to clarify the issue by distinguishing between postmodernism as a *style*, as a *method* and as an *epochal transition*.

In terms of style, postmodern art, literature, architecture and planning are characterized by an engagement with subjectivity and by attempts to restore meaning, rootedness, human proportions and decoration, often employing witty or ironic references to historically and/or culturally specific stylistic conventions.

In terms of method, Dear suggests, postmodernism is characterized by:

i) the essentially hermeneutic nature of discourse, and
ii) the importance of the "text" (building style, in the case of architecture, for example).

At the heart of this approach is *deconstruction*: "unpacking" the meaning of a text and its relation to author/designer and reader/viewer/user. According to Foster (1985), the purpose of deconstructing Modernism is to interrogate the "master narratives" of the dominant ideology. This implies a reconstructive agenda, and Foster argues that such an agenda can take two very different forms: a postmodernism of *reaction* and a postmodernism of *resistance*. This distinction, it seems to me, is crucial to an understanding of the roles of the design professions in the social production of the built environment.

A postmodernism of reaction, according to Foster, is essentially an affective, cosmetic or therapeutic response, often involving a retreat to the lost authenticity and enchantments of traditional or vernacular themes and motifs. Most postmodern architecture can be interpreted in this way although, as Dear (1986) points out, it is potentially confusing to partition off "postmodern architecture" or "postmodern planning" as discrete categories. Postmodern style and method is best regarded as an ideal type, in the Weberian sense.

A postmodernism of resistance, in contrast, seeks to deconstruct Modernism in order to challenge or oppose the dominant ideas that it represents. Some of the urban planning that can be classified as "postmodern" (mostly "radical" planning: see below) can be interpreted in this way, though it might be possible to make an equally convincing case for "radical" planning as a reactive phenomenon.

Allusion has already been made to the idea of postmodernism as an epochal transition: a radical break that represents the sociocultural shifts associated with the onset of advanced capitalist commodity production. Or, as Jameson (1985b, p. 113) puts it:

> A periodizing concept whose function is to correlate the emergence of new formal features in culture with the emergence of a new type of social life and a new economic order.

According to Jameson, a key feature of this transition is the replacement of old systems of organization and perception by a post-modern "hyperspace" in which space and time are being stretched to accommodate the multinational global space of advanced capitalism (Jameson, 1984). The built environment, he goes on to suggest, provides a critical "text" with which to decode this hyperspace.

If we can identify a "radical break" in architecture, it is of course the trend away from the uniformity, functionalism and placelessness of the Modern Movement (or, at least, that version of the Modern Movement that had come to be adopted by centralized decisionmakers as the Esperanto of corporate power, respectability, and efficiency) towards the self-conscious and ironic use of historical and vernacular references in scenographic or decorative counterpoint to modern elements (Frampton, 1985; Portoghesi, 1982). What is less clear is whether this break also involves a widespread rejection of the social objectives and determinist claims of Modernism (Jencks, 1983, 1984), or of the symbolism intended by corporate commissioners of architecture; and whether it really amounts, as Broadbent (1980) suggests, to a Kuhnian paradigm shift within the profession as a whole.

If we can identify a "radical break" in urban planning, it might be the shift away from the rationalist, functionalist, paternalist and evangelistic pursuit of segregated land uses and sweeping renewal schemes towards a more participatory and activist-influenced planning aimed not only at halting renewal schemes but also at preserving and enhancing the neighborhood lifeworld. This is the break associated with the "radical critique" of the 1970s, a break that was initiated – and sustained – by the counterculture baby-boomers who grew into the new sociocultural class of the baby-boom generation: the professionals and intellectuals in the arts and humanities, the media, education and the caring professions. As indicated above, it is a moot point as to whether this should be interpreted as a postmodernism of reaction or of resistance.

Thanks, however, to the economic recessions of the 1980s, the consequent withering of the "urban vision" (Gold, 1984) and the emergence of public–private partnerships in the land-development process, liberalism, radicalism and resistance have in any case been largely eclipsed. Contemporary planning has come to be a pastiche of practice and theory in which both traditional elements (utopian concerns as well as rationalistic systems planning, for example) and radical elements are overshadowed by a discourse that is dominated by pragmatism. Castells has interpreted this expedience as part of the struggle to create new models of economic accumulation, social organization and political legitimation in response to the prolonged crisis (1973–1982) that stemmed from the conjunction of slowed economic growth, rising inflation, increased international monetary instability, suddenly increased energy prices, increased international competition, and intensified problems of indebtedness among less developed nations. According to this interpretation, what is happening is that new relationships between capital and labor are being forged, with capital rapidly recapturing the initiative over wages and conditions. New rôles for the public sector are also being forged, not only in reducing levels of government intervention and support but also in shifting the emphasis from collective consumption to capital accumulation and from legitimation to domination.

What is perhaps most significant for planning is that new international, regional and metropolitan divisions of labor are central to these processes: the variable geometry of capital, labor, production, markets and management will be critical in allowing new relationships to be established (Castells, 1985; Carnoy and Castells, 1984). This, after all, may be the "radical break" that defines postmodern planning. "Already", observes Dear (1986, p. 380), "planners are operating special areas where regular zoning restrictions have been suspended; already there are courses in "public–private" enterprise in planning schools." The inference is that the planning that is now developing is being geared to the spatial and social logic of advanced capitalism: to the commodification

UE becomes a commodity

of the built environment, the recapitalization of the public realm, the legitimation of urban restructuring, and the opening up of the hyperspace of multinational capital. If we accept that this really does add up to the "radical break" that will define postmodern planning, it might be necessary to add a third form of reconstruction to Foster's postmodernism of reaction and postmodernism of resistance. This would be a postmodernism of *restructuring*. Given this possibility, it is worth re-examining postmodern architecture for a moment. We can see now that architecture too is being used to recapitalize, to commodify and to legitimize. Take, for example, the decollectivization/recapitalization of housing in Britain. Symes (1985) provides the example of architects who were given the task, under an Urban Development Grant, of eradicating the public-housing image of a local authority estate, so that the apartments could be put up for sale. The result was the addition of a combination of "private" elements (garages, entrance lobbies and driveways) and post-Modern elements (pitched, pantiled roofs, timber handrails and balconies, and landscaping) to the structurally sound but unmarketable Modern concrete-and-steel "boxes".

Restructuring a modern idea

Whatever the preferred definition or interpretation of postmodernism, it is clear enough that the design professions find themselves in a new epoch that raises a number of intriguing questions. To what extent will the new epoch be defined by the values of the baby boom generation? Will the new epoch produce some kind of "integrating myth" to tie urban design to the social and spatial logic of advanced capitalism, or will it continue to be characterized by a pastiche that reflects the economic fragmentation and cultural pluralism of contemporary cities? Are the design professions likely to become more significant as part of the internal survival mechanisms of capitalism? More immediately, how is the interaction of changing cultural meanings, cognitive orientations, and social structures affecting the design professions and their approach to the built environment? What are the implications for education and manpower in the

Questions of postmodern

design professions? And what are the outcomes in terms of professional turf and the relative autonomy of the various agents within the design professions and the building enterprise?

Compared with other related fields, research on such topics is thin and fragmentary. Moreover, there has for a long time been an overwhelming emphasis on deterministic interpretations of people–environment relationships, a preoccupation with micro-scale interactions between the built environment and human behavior, and a tendency to treat both design and the design professions as independent variables. What are needed are approaches that encompass the reciprocal relationships between individuals, the built environment, the design professions, and society at large (Knox, 1984, 1987). For these to emerge, however, it is clear that a much more intensive and purposive dialogue must take place between all those with an interest in the field: anthropologists, geographers, political scientists and sociologists as well as architects and planners.

Need for a new approach

It must be acknowledged at the outset that these contributions do not purport to address systematically the issues attached to the question of a "postmodern" epoch. They do, however, reflect the multi-disciplinary breadth of interest in the changing rôle and condition of the design professions. At the same time they illustrate the variety of issues that are at stake as we enter this transitional epoch: the interaction of social issues with the imperatives of professionalization, the changing relationship between the media and designers of the built environment, the changing geographical distribution of design professionals, the conflicts and paradoxes arising from the changing position of the building and construction industry, and the shifting rôles, strategies and influence of design professionals in day-to-day situations, for example.

Within this variety, and despite a diversity of theoretical underpinnings and methodological approaches, certain themes recur. One of these concerns the imagery and symbolism surrounding the built environment.

Lots of people involved

and the design professions; another concerns the relative autonomy of design professionals as key actors in the social production of the built environment. Above all, however, they demonstrate the benefits of casting a multi-disciplinary net over a topic such as this. Together, they provide a wide variety of insights and issues that will demand consideration in any attempt to theorize the role of the design professions and the built environment in the postmodern epoch.

REFERENCES

Bernstein, R. (ed.) (1985) *Habermas and Modernity*. Cambridge: Polity Press.

Broadbent, G. (1980) Architects and their symbols. *Built Environment*, 6, 15–28.

Carnoy, M. and Castells, M. (1984) After the crisis? *World Policy Journal*, Spring, 495–516.

Castells, M. (1985) High technology, economic restructuring and the urban-regional process in the United States. In M. Castells (ed.), *High Technology, Space and Society*. Beverly Hills, CA: Sage, pp. 11–40.

Dear, M. (1986) Postmodernism and planning. *Environment and Planning D: Society and Space*, 4, 367–84.

Foster, H. (ed.) (1985) *Postmodern Culture*. London: Pluto Press.

Frampton, K. (1985) *Modern Architecture: A Critical History*. London: Thames and Hudson.

Gappert, G. (1979) *Post-affluent America*. New York: New Viewpoints.

Gold, J. R. (1984) The death of the urban vision? *Futures*, 16, 372–81.

Gottdiener, M. (1985) *The Social Production of Urban Space*. Austin: University of Texas Press.

Jameson, F. (1984) Postmodernism, or the cultural logic of capitalism. *New Left Review*, 146, 53–92.

Jameson, F. (1985a) Architecture and the critique of ideology. In J. Ockman (ed.), *Architecture, Criticism, Ideology*. Princeton, NJ: Princeton Architectural Press, pp. 51–87.

Jameson, F. (1985b) Postmodernism and consumer society. In H. Foster (ed.), *Postmodern Culture*. London: Pluto Press, pp. 111–125.

Jencks, C. (1983) Post-modern architecture: the true inheritor of modernism. *RIBA Transactions*, 2, 26–41.

Jencks, C. (1984) *The Language of Post-modern Architecture*. New York: Rizzoli.

Knox, P. L. (1984) Symbolism, styles and settings: the built environment and the imperatives of urbanized capitalism. *Architecture et Comportement*, 2, 107–22.

Knox, P. L. (1987) The social production of the built environment: architects, architecture and the post-modern city. *Progress in Human Geography*, 11.

Lefebvre, H. (1974) *La Production de l'Espace*. Paris: Anthropos.

Lyotard, J. F. (1984) *The Post Modern Condition*. Minneapolis: University of Minnesota Press.

Portoghesi, P. (1982) *After Modern Architecture*. New York: Rizzoli.

Symes, M. (1985) Urban development and the education of designers. *Journal of Architectural and Planning Research*, 2, 23–38.

28

A Catholic Approach to Organizing what Urban Designers Should Know

Anne Vernez Moudon

Urban design is familiar to both architects and urban planners. Although some continue to associate urban design with tall downtowns and large-scale architecture, most recognize it as an interdisciplinary approach to designing our built environment. Urban design seeks not to eliminate the planning and design professions but to integrate them and in so doing, to go beyond each one's charter. It extends the architect's focus on the built project. It makes urban planning policies operational by taking into account their impact on the form and meaning of the environments produced. Recently, landscape architects have also added some of their concerns to urban design. As a young enterprise at the edge of established professions, urban design must endure many punches, pushes, and pulls. But its institutional survival is essential to guarantee even a glimpse of interdisciplinary activity in planning and design.

Urban design emerged sometime in the 1960s – its exact origins have yet to be determined, coveted as they are by many different groups. The field was born out of a search for quality in urban form. This search continues to date, focused on urban environments that have both functional and aesthetic appeal to those who inhabit them. The thrust of the field has lain in practical rather than academic pursuits: urban designers worry about "what should be done" and "what will work."

By and large also, the "theories" guiding practice have remained at a paradigmatic level, based on different exemplary solutions. The history of the field is characterized by many such theories that have come and gone, the victims of the elusive complexities of practice (to mention only a few such theories: functionalism, modernism, participatory design, neo-rationalism, and pattern languages).

This article poses a different question: "what should urban designers know?" It is based on the premise that a mature, successful practice and its concomitant long-lasting theories rest on "knowing." An attempt to pull together the significant body of existing knowledge, this work starts to define an epistemology *for* urban design – to study the nature and grounds of knowledge necessary to practice urban design.

The approach taken is emphatically catholic. In the laic, generic sense of the word, "catholic" means broad in sympathies, tastes, and interests. Being catholic is not to be nonpartisan, but rather nonsectarian, tolerant of and open to different approaches. Hence the body of knowledge surveyed herein comes from various fields and disciplines allied to urban design that, together, lay the groundwork for an epistemology for urban design. Some of the research is informative in nature, seeking to describe or explain certain phenomena. Other research goes one step further into theory building. The differences between these two types of research will not be discussed specifically, however, because the nature and scope of theory in, of, or for urban design is too undefined to deal with within the confines of this article.

The article is divided into two parts. One scans a conceptual framework delineating the basic elements of a catholic approach to building an epistemology for urban design, including a range of areas of inquiry, research strategies, and research methods. The second part discusses specific areas of inquiry that add to such an epistemology. References are drawn primarily, but not exclusively, from literature available in English.

Scanning Fields of Knowledge

What are the basic sources of knowledge available to the urban designer? In this country, the work of the late Kevin Lynch (1960, 1972, 1981) and especially his studies of people's images of cities perhaps come first to mind as a source of important information. Lynch's influence in putting urban design on the intellectual map of city planning is undeniable and astonishingly broad: not only is his work well known in Europe and Japan, but it is readily used in different fields and disciplines such as planning, architecture, and geography. Recently, Christian Norberg-Schulz (1980, 1985) has grown influential as well. His classification of elements and meanings in environments has impressed both students and practitioners. William Whyte's (1980) work on downtown plazas and Appleyard's (1981) studies of livable streets are often referred to in urban design as well. But also, Grady Clay's (1973) explanations of the American city, J. B. Jackson's (1980, 1984) reconstructions of the American landscape, and Amos Rapoport's (1977, 1982, 1990) elaborate explanations of people's interactions with their environment, all come to mind as substantive studies for urban design. Further contributors include Lewis Mumford (1961), Edmund Bacon (1976), Jonathan Barnett (1986) on the *Elusive City*, Jay Appleton (1975, 1980) on a prospect/refuge theory, and more recently, Anne Whiston Spirn (1984) regarding the ecology of the city. Some of these works lean toward architectural design, others are more landscape architecture oriented, yet others are closer to urban planning concerns.

The list of works of importance in urban design can, and does, go on. Influences are numerous and scattered. Even if Lynch emerges as a powerful figure, his legacy is made less clear when coupled with all the other bits and pieces of research available. In truth, all research and theories are *partial*: they address some but never all of the issues faced by the designer. They also stress a particular view or philosophy of what is important in city design – for instance, Lynch's emphasis on how people see and feel about their environment, Rapoport's focus on the use of and meanings in the built environment, Spirn's concerns for the physical health of the city, and so on. Only when considered together do this research and these theories begin to yield a more complete set of information to the designer. They can indeed be complementary, although sometimes they are also contradictory. To build up actual knowledge in urban design, one should not look for the *correct* approach or theory, but should instead compile and assess all the research that adds to what the urban designer must be familiar with.

Thus the task is to map out knowledge readily available, to identify the collection of works pertaining to the central concerns of urban design, and to devise a conceptual framework organizing this collection. To help gather this collection and map its organization, several elements need to be considered and are reviewed below.

The Normative-Prescriptive Versus Substantive-Descriptive Dilemma

It is important to distinguish first between *normative* or *prescriptive* information (emphasizing the "what should be") and *substantive* or critically *descriptive* knowledge (emphasizing the "what is" and perhaps also the "why") (Lang, 1987; Moudon, 1988). Stated more concretely, *understanding* a city or a part of a city and *designing* it are two different things. Logically, one needs to understand what cities are made of, how they come about and function, what they mean to people, and so on, in order to design "good" cities. So far, research most used in urban design not only looks for explanations of the city, but it customarily moves into evaluation and recommendations for future design.[1] This is not surprising: urban design is a normative, prescriptive field, and urban designers are trained to imagine and execute schemes for the future. While research is usually associated with substantive information and with understanding specific phenomena, it is expected that research for urban design will yield information that has normative dimensions and that eventually helps design. Hence while understanding (describing) cities and designing (prescribing) them are *opposite* conceptual poles, they also represent a *continuum*. These distinctions, however, are usually not well articulated in the planning and design fields. For example, the Anglo-Saxon term "urban design" is coveted by Latins who have to contend with *urbanisme* or *urbanismo*, terms that are clearly more reflective, less action-oriented than "urban design." Only in Italy can one find "urban science" and "urbanism" used commonly to define the spectrum of description versus prescription, research versus design.

Closer to home, Kevin Lynch's work is a good case in point illustrating the tensions between the two conceptual poles: Lynch researched people's mental images and constructs of cities and analyzed the history, evolution, and meaning of places in order to seek better ways to design cities. However, while in *The Image of the City* (1960), substantive information is separated from prescriptive or normative advice, in *A Theory of Good City Form* (1981), the two are closely interwoven. Similarly, as Christopher Alexander and his team (Alexander et al., 1977) rampage through existing cities they deem "good," they collect, sort out, and discard bits and pieces that they believe will constitute patterns or elements for *designing new* cities. However, they are essentially not interested in describing critically existing environments per se. On the architectural side of urban design, the brothers Krier (*Rational Architecture*, 1978) have peaked into a prototypical medieval town for identifying the antidote to the ills of modern design theo-

ries. Their American followers, architects and town planners Duany and Plater-Zyberk (Knack, 1989), have found their norms in the late nineteenth-century American small town, which, after some study, they have then modified and spiced up with garden city and city beautiful theories to establish their own theory of design.

The attractiveness of the normative stand is obvious: it provides unmitigated guidance for designers in their everyday endeavors. Yet its limitations are serious: in the light of the wholesomeness and complexity inherent to design, all normative theories eventually run into difficulties and often fail outright. Further, it is disturbing to find that many normative theories use research to justify or substantiate a priori beliefs when, in fact, the reverse should take place, and research results should be interpreted *to develop* theories.

In order to enter the next generation of urban design theory, urban designers will need to pay more attention to the substantive side of research and to refrain from making quick prescriptive inferences from such research. They will need to separate conceptually the art of description from that of prescription and to devise clear and honest ways of evaluating existing or past situations (for opposing views on this matter, see Jarvis, 1980, and Oxman, 1987). This is not to say that description or substantive work is "true"; that is, free of values and interpretation. Description is just as subjective – dependent on who is doing it – as prescription. As the art of seeing, hearing, smelling, feeling, and knowing, description can only reflect the capabilities and sensitivities of the researcher (Relph, 1984). But if descriptive activity is just as morally bounded as prescription, and if it tells what is right or wrong subjectively, it does nonetheless stop short of venturing into what should be done.

For the design and planning professions to mature properly, time must be taken to focus on substantive information. Some scholars have even advocated the need to describe solely without seeking explanation because they see explanation (the "why" attached to the "what") as yet another incentive not to grasp fully the object or phenomenon being described (Relph, 1984). Whatever the case may be, substantive approaches will force designers and planners to engage personally in the information at hand, to interpret it, and to apply it to the specific context of their activities.

The gap between knowledge and action is not an easy one to bridge. It requires careful synthesis. As the perennial example of substantive information, the use of historical studies provides a case in point: today, work in history is fashionable and touched upon by many urban designers, yet the dialectic between practice and historical knowledge remains elusive at best, and so far seemingly capricious and idiosyncratic. Careful assessment must precede jumping to practical conclusions.

For these reasons, this article focuses on substantive research and theories. A companion part to this article remains to be written, which would map the scope and breadth of normative theory in urban design. Some of this work has been done by French urbanist and philosopher Françoise Choay. Choay has framed an epistemology of urban design as a normative, prescriptive field in two seminal books that, although they include Anglo-Saxon literature, are only available in French. One, *Urbanisme, utopies et réalités* (1965), is an anthology of key texts on urban design since the nineteenth century. The second, *La règle et le modèle* (1980), posits two fundamental texts defining an explicit, autonomous conceptual framework "to conceive and produce new spaces": Alberti's *De re aedificatoria* (1988), first published in 1452, which, according to Choay, proposes rules for urban design, and Thomas More's *Utopia* (1989), first published in 1516 as a model for urban design.

Others have started to assemble normative theories of urban design, notably Gosling and Maitland (1984), Jarvis (1980), and recently, Geoffrey Broadbent (1990). Broadbent's latest book paints a broad yet condensed chronological picture of "emerging *concepts* in urban *space* design" (my emphases of Broadbent's book title). It promises to encourage future critical assessment of the significance and effectiveness of normative theories of and paradigms in urban design.

Concentrations of Inquiry

Substantive research and theories can first be classified by their area of concentration, according to specific views and aspects of the city on which they are focusing. Establishing different concentrations of inquiry is to accept that there are several different lenses through which the design and the making of the city can be viewed and that, in consequence, no single approach to design may suffice. As pedestrian as this realization may appear to, for instance, engineers or physicians who are used to studying their problems from many different angles, it is a challenging proposal to the urban designer accustomed to thinking about singular, "correct" approaches. Nine concentrations of inquiry have been identified: urban history studies, picturesque studies, image studies, environment-behavior studies, place studies, material culture studies, typology-morphology studies, space-morphology studies, and nature-ecology studies. The definition and contents of these areas constitutes the second part of this article.

Research Strategies

The specific research strategies that can be used to develop knowledge are, again, several. One quickly discovers that the choice of a research strategy unveils the true philosophical basis of the research itself. The first research strategy is termed the *literary approach*: it emanates from the humanistic fields – literature and history being the most prominent ones – and it relies on literature searches, references and reviews, and archival work of all kinds, as well as personal accounts of given situations. The intent of the literary approach is to relate a story of a given set of events.

Second is the *phenomenological approach*, which projects a holistic view of the world, everything being related to everything, and whose practice depends entirely on the researcher's total experience of an event. It is similar to the artist's approach because it is both learned and intuitive, synthetic and wholesome, or eidetic (signifying that it uses specific examples of behavior, experience, and meaning to render descriptive generalizations about the world and human living: Seamon, 1987, p. 16). Phenomenologists describe events with all their feelings, senses, and knowledge. They usually refuse to explain the "why" of their findings because they see explanation rooted in interpretation and misinterpretation – leading quickly to abuse of information. Phenomenologists therefore oppose the third research strategy, *positivism*, which portrays the value of description in explanation.

Positivism maintains that knowledge is based on natural phenomena to be verified by empirical science. Positivism implies certainty of cause and effect. It is the tool of the sciences, which are based on the reduction of wholes and on systems of interconnected parts.

While most attempts to describe built environments have used literary or positivistic approaches, phenomenological approaches have recently flourished, according to Seamon, because of a practical crisis in the design fields, where nonholistic approaches have led to partially successful environments, and because of a philosophical crisis in the sciences due to the limitations of positivist thinking. Recently also, however, there have been attempts to reconcile positivism and phenomenology and to see them as complementary (Hardie et al., 1989; Seamon, 1987).

Modes of Inquiry

Specific modes of inquiry are identified to distinguish further between the various research strategies used. Two modes seem to prevail. One is the *historical-descriptive* mode, in which the research is based primarily on accounts of historical evidence – whether on site or via historical documents, plans, drawings, painting, archives, or analyses of the topic. The historical-descriptive mode is generally not used for theory-building purposes, but focuses on highlighting

specific events and things. Literary and phenomenological research strategies usually use this mode of inquiry.

The other mode is *empirical-inductive*, where the research is set to observe a given phenomenon or to collect information on it, which is then described via an analysis of the information gathered. Through induction, the explanations of the phenomenon may be generalized upon to develop a theory. ("Empirical" means relying on experience and observation alone, often without due regard for system or theory, or capable of being verified by observation or experiment. "Empiricism" is the theory that all knowledge originates in experience or the practice of relying upon observation and experiment; it is especially used in the natural sciences.) This mode prevails in positivistic research but can be found in phenomenological work as well.

A third mode is *theoretical-deductive*, in which a theory is developed on the basis of past knowledge, which is then tested via research. Used primarily in quantitative research (Carter, 1976), this mode is rarely found in the design fields, because they encompass problems that are either too complex or, as Horst Rittel has termed them, too wicked to be approached quantitatively (Rittel and Webber, 1972). In such cases, this mode seems to lead to truisms (e.g., all grid plans are the result of a planned approach to making cities) or then to problems that have limited significance to the design of whole environments (e.g., economic theories related to real estate taxation, theories of land use allocation, housing choices, and so on).

Research Focus: Object/Subject

A third screen needs to be applied to areas of inquiry, the research focus. Most research in this country focuses on the study of *people* in the environment. This *subject* orientation emerged in the 1960s when research became seen as a necessary addition to the practice of planning and design. The primacy of subject-oriented research can be explained as a reaction to "old guard" designers' earlier focus on the physical components of the environ-

WHAT URBAN DESIGNERS SHOULD KNOW 367

ment. Theirs was an orientation toward the *object* – a second possible research focus – which became increasingly suspicious as theories of good health, safety, and welfare relying on the need for clean, airy environments continued to bring unsatisfactory results. The ultimate blow to the object orientation of physical planners was the failure of urban renewal schemes, which proved that poverty, not environment, was the primary reason for epidemics, crime, and ethically questionable lifestyles. That good environments can do little to alleviate the basic state of poverty was a hard lesson to learn after four decades of work. From then on, research on the object qualities of the environment became unpopular, and a single focus on people in the environment prevailed with, for instance, sociologist Herbert Gans (1969) as its greatest advocate.

Later, some researchers urged concentration on the interaction between people and environments as a specific phenomenon that could explain well the nature of our environments (see Rapoport, 1977; Moore et al., 1985). Today, the field of person-environment relations, or environment-behavior research, is at least present in planning and design. At the same time, it is under heavy inside and outside criticism largely for neglecting the "environment" part of the person-environment couplet. A return to the study of the object has been advocated by many, especially architects influenced by theorists like Rossi (1964, 1982), who has gone so far as to argue the autonomy of architecture as a discipline that is separate from the sciences and the arts. More modest postures favoring a return to object-oriented research, with complementarity rather than primacy over subject research, have been argued as well by, for instance, geographer M. P. Conzen (1978), environmental psychologists D. Canter (1977) and J. Sime (1986), and architect L. Groat (Moudon 1987). This trend corresponds also to a rising interest in the study of vernacular environments as the physical evidence of people's long-standing interactive relationship with their surroundings. Vernacular environments thus offer attractive prospects: many are unusual phys-

ical objects, yet not the objects of a few planners and designers, but those of traditions and customs that are an intrinsic part of culture. Indeed this "culturally ground object" can uncover the deep relationship between people and environments.

Research Ethos: Etic/Emic

Finally, research needs to be screened for its ethos – this term is selected to depict the "heart" of the research. Two categories of ethos come to mind: the *etic* and the *emic* ethos. Borrowed from anthropology, these terms were first popularized in design circles by Amos Rapoport (1977). They come from *phonetic* – related to the written language – and *phonemic* – related to the spoken language. The difference can be further grasped by comparing the two French terms, *la langue* and *la parole*, the first being language as a structured system of sounds or signs to be studied for its internal logic, and the second, a no less structured, yet only practiced system of sounds. Applied to studies of people and cultures, etic and emic relate to the nature of the source of the information gathered – etic in the case of the informant being the researcher, the person who will use the information, and emic in the case of the informant being the person observed.

Environment and behavior studies were the first to seek to bring an emic orientation to the design professions: they unearthed information about the uses of environments directly from the users, without relying on the opinion of design and planning professionals. However, the actual methods used in person-environment studies can be more or less emic. For instance, unstructured interviews, oral histories, and self-study methods of all sorts are straightforwardly emic. But observations of behaviors, although emic in their intent, are, in the true sense of the term, etic because they are done by professionals. Rapoport has called these research approaches "derived" etic and has opposed them to "imposed" etic approaches, which he condemns as mere fabrications of the researcher's mind.

The importance of getting emically signifi-cant information about the environment cannot be understated. Lynch's (1960) stud-ies of people's images of cities popularized the need for an emic ethos in the information necessary to the planning and urban design professions. These studies complemented earlier works in parallel areas of anthropol-ogy and sociology: the Lynds' critical de-scription of people's lives in *Middletown* (1929); W. Lloyd Warner's *Yankee City* (1963); Herbert Gans's controversial *The Levittowners* (1967); E. T. Hall's compil-ation of an environment both limited and enhanced by our physiological beings, in *The Silent Language* ([1959] 1980) and *The Hidden Dimension* (1966); and Robert Som-mer's *Personal Space* (1969). All opened the door to an enormous field of yet untapped information.

Areas of Concentration

The concerns of urban designers and the nature of the decisions they make are neces-sarily wide-ranging. The interdisciplinary nature of urban design is likely to remain, and it is doubtful that the field will ever become a discipline with its own teachings separate from the established architecture, landscape, and planning professions. But if primarily architectural research (in, for in-stance, building science, architectural styles, or programming) and urban planning re-search (in employment, transportation, and housing demand) are only tangentially rele-vant to urban design, general socioeconomic issues relating to the environment always loom near the foreground of urban design concerns. In this sense, all social science re-search pertaining to the environment is of interest. Similarly, all information concern-ing urban space and form will be useful. Yet a search for breadth must nonetheless be con-strained for the sake of practicality. The lit-erature surveyed focuses on the products of urban design or the human relationship with the built environment and related open spaces. The city, and more generally, the landscape as modified by people; its physical form and characteristics; the forces that

shape it; the ways in which it is designed, produced, managed, used, and changed – all are central to a search for work that informs urban design. This essentially hu-manistic view of urban design justifies, at least within the confines of this article, fur-ther exclusions – to wit, literature on devel-opment and real estate finance, marketing, economic theory, and urban political theory that, unfortunately, relate only marginally at this point to the powers of urban designers.

The literature assembled according to these criteria has then been subjected to vari-ous classification exercises in an effort to identify salient areas of relevant inquiry. Thus the classification proposed emphasizes the types of questions posed by the different research, and groups the different works on the basis of the similarity of their quests rather than on the particularities of the methods used. The classification also offers a conceptual framework that is simple enough for both students and practitioners to remember and to work with over time.

Nine areas of concentration are proposed to encompass research useful to urban design. The list of areas should be seen as open-ended. Further, individual researchers can belong to one or more areas of inquiry, depending on the scope of their particular works. Some of these concentrations will be readily accepted as mainstream urban design. But some will raise eyebrows and need further discussion. The following pages review the nature and coverage of each area of concentration. Included is a ten-tative critique of each area's current status with respect to the level of its development and its current place in building an episte-mology for urban design.

Urban History Studies

The study of urban history has expanded remarkably over the past two decades to include now significant information for the practicing urban designer. This area's early dependence on art history and its traditional emphasis on "pedigreed" environments (Kostof, 1986), on their formal and stylistic characteristics, is gone. Studies of places inhabited by ordinary people, explanations of why and how they inhabit them, have become the focus of an increasing number of scholarly works. Women, special needs groups, and the lower economic echelons of our social class structure are now an integral part of urban historical research. The history of the Anglo-Saxon suburb occupies an important place in historical studies today as suburbs constitute a substantial part of contemporary cities. Further, while Western influences continue to prevail, the overreliance on the European experience is waning, especially with Asian, Islamic, and other cultures embarking into internationally recognized scholarly endeavors.

Classical work on the history of urban form has come from design and planning historians, to include S. E. Rasmussen (1967), A. E. J. Morris (1972), and John Reps (1965), and from historical geographers such as Gerald Burke (1971), Frederick Hiorns (1956), Robert Dickinson (1961), Marcel Poëte (1967), and Henri Lavedan (1941). On the architectural side, there are Norma Evenson (1973, 1979), Spiro Kostof (1991), Norman Johnston (1983), Mark Girouard (1985), and Leonardo Benevolo (1980). Lewis Mumford (1961) remains a powerful critic, although his influence is diminishing with the emergence of more detailed research on various aspects of his writings. But the classical understanding of the history of the city is being enriched and also challenged by the growing explorations of ordinary landscapes, as in the works of Sam Bass Warner (1962, 1968), J. B. Jackson (1984), David Lowenthal and Marcus Binney (1981), Reyner Banham (1971), and recently, John Stilgoe (1982), Edward Relph (1987), and Michael Conzen (1980, 1990). James Vance (1977, 1990) emerges as a wide-ranging scholar of the processes shaping the physical construct of the urban environment. Considering the social history of environments also adds reality to historical forms that in the work of Bernard Rudofsky (1969), Alan Artibise and Paul-André Linteau (1984), Roy Lubove (1967), Anthony Sutcliffe (1984), Dolores Hayden (1981), and Gwendolyn Wright (1981), for

instance, come alive in the descriptions of people's everyday struggles to shape their surroundings. How cities have actually been built is another subject of increasing interest – with Joseph Konvitz (1985), David Friedman (1988), and Mark Weiss (1987) standing out as promising contributors.

Work in history continues to be primarily etic and based on literary research (Dyoz 1968). However, derived etic research is beginning to dominate social history. Similarly, phenomenological approaches are increasingly taken – Relph's and J. B. Jackson's work being some of the best received by urban designers. Historians in this category can be object-or subject-oriented, or they can deal with the interaction between people and the physical environment.

The many new publications on increasingly varied subjects related to urban history exercise a growing influence on design and planning professionals. Correspondingly, a few historians are willing to venture into discussing the implications of historical experience for the present – for instance, Joseph Konvitz (1985), Robert Fishman (1977, 1987), Richard Sennett (1969), and Kenneth Jackson (1985; Jackson and Schultz, 1972). Conversely, design-oriented scholars are reaching out into history in an attempt to develop theory – as for instance, Dolores Hayden (1984), Peter Rowe (1991), and Geoffrey Broadbent (1990).

The emerging richness of the field warrants further classification and analysis to help the urban designer to select the appropriate works and to uncover more than can be recognized in this article. Work in historical geography and urban preservation is worth reviewing as it includes critical inventories of urban environments. Similarly, historical guidebooks of cities, as well as contemporary guides emphasizing a city's history (Wurman, 1971, 1972; Lyndon, 1982) yield material that adds to historical knowledge of particular cities. Finally, journalistic criticism is an area that parallels history in its evaluative approach to existing environments and needs to be explored. While such criticism used to be limited to the isolated, yet powerful works of a few

– for example, Jane Jacobs (1961), Hans Blumenfeld (1979), Ada-Louise Huxtable (1970), Robert Venturi and Denise Scott Brown (Venturi et al., 1977), and recently, Joel Garreau (1991) – several publications have emerged that begin to provide a vehicle for systematic and continued critiques of implemented ideas (for instance, *Places*, the *Harvard Architectural Review*, and others).

Picturesque Studies

Picturesque studies of the urban landscape were the foundations and the keystone of urban design until the late 1960s. Today they keep a prominent position in both education and practice, and they offer some of the widely read introductory texts in urban design. These studies are running personal commentaries of the attributes of the physical environment. Authors identify and describe both verbally and graphically what they think are "good" environments. Such good environments are analyzed for their relevance to contemporary urban design problems.

Object-oriented, these works emphasize the visual aspect of the environment, which is seen as a stage set or a prop of human action. Gordon Cullen's *Concise Townscape* (1961) remains one of the most memorable contributions to urban design in the picturesque style. Cullen caught the fancy of both architects and planners disturbed by the technical, barren aspects of modernism. He helped them to formulate the scope of urban design as an interdisciplinary activity requiring both architectural and planning skills.

Precursors of the picturesque genre include Camillo Sitte ([1889] 1980) and Raymond Unwin (1909), both of whom have recently regained popularity in urban design. While the postwar work of Thomas Sharp (1946) on English villages has yet to be rediscovered by urban designers, Paul Spreiregen's *Urban Design: The Architecture of Towns and Cities* (1965) remains a standard introductory urban design text today. Also prominent are the writings of Edmund Bacon (1976) and Lawrence Halprin (1966, 1972).

The term "picturesque" is not widely recognized to encompass the works of Sitte, Cullen, Bacon, or Halprin. It has been used in this capacity by Panerai et al. (1980) in an effort to capture the emphasis on the pictorial component of the environment that characterizes works in this category. Robert Oxman (1987) used Cullen's own words and called the work "townscape analysis."

For all their popularity, however, picturesque studies are unevenly "practiced," and there have not been publications following this research and thinking mode in several years. Developments in the intellectual context of urban design have lessened the forcefulness of the original picturesque argument. First, if these studies are etic and phenomenological in nature – stands that remain in good currency in contemporary planning and design discourse – they do not espouse these philosophical beliefs in a conscious manner. Rather, they appear to assume a naive "good-professional-knows-it-all" posture that has been rightfully questioned since the early 1970s. Simply put, they lack the literary references of more recent phenomenological writings such as Relph's or J. B. Jackson's. And they lack the theoretical and philosophical underpinnings of a Norberg-Schultz. It follows that picturesque studies do not fare well either with social science approaches in planning and design research: their unabashed etic stand is unacceptable on this score, and the idiosyncratic swinging between highly personal descriptions and specific prescriptions puts these works in an old-fashioned league.

Finally, whereas picturesque studies were innovative in their early consideration of vernacular landscapes, they have been superseded recently by the several bona fide historical works of scholars such as Thomas Schlereth (1985b), Dell Upton (Upton and Vlach 1986), John Stilgoe (1982), R. W. Brunskill (1981, 1982), Stefan Muthesius (1982), and others. Thus picturesque studies maintain a high profile for the beginning student of urban design but do not sustain well more rigorous and deep investigation.

Image studies

Image studies include a significant amount of work on how people visualize, conceptualize, and eventually understand the city. This category would not exist without Kevin Lynch's *The Image of the City* (1960), whose influence was paramount in launching subsequent research. In fact, many planners and designers see image studies as the main contribution of urban design to the design fields. The Lynchian approach is sometimes understood as continuing the picturesque tradition because of its focus on how the urban environment is perceived visually. Yet the posture of image studies is reversed from that of picturesque studies: it is the people's image of the environment that is sought out, not the professional observer's. Thus image studies are intrinsically emic and subject oriented. Lynch had been influenced by the works of E. T. Hall ([1959] 1980, 1966), Rudolph Arnheim (1954, 1966), and Gyorgy Kepes (1944, 1965, 1966). As a student, he was part of Kepes's MIT group of environmental thinkers who sought to create and understand environmental art – art in space and art as space, so to speak.

Image studies are witnesses to the growing influence of the social sciences on design since the 1960s. They focus on the physiological, psychological, and social dimensions of environments as they are used and experienced by people, and on how those aspects do or should shape design and design solutions. The importance given in these studies to the lay person's view of the surrounding environment has transformed urban design activity: not only are Lynch's five elements used (and, according to Lynch himself, abused: Lynch in Rodwin and Hollister 1984), but questionnaires, surveys, and group meetings are now standard fare backing up the majority of complex design processes. Among the many studies looking to verify and to expand on Lynch's findings, the ones that brought systematic comparisons (and oppositions) between the professional's and the lay person's views, were his own student's, Donald Appleyard (Appleyard et al., 1964; Appleyard, 1976).

Working closely with psychologist Kenneth H. Craig, Appleyard's group at the University of California at Berkeley trained many students to research people and environments as a sound basis for urban design. Robin Moore (Moore, 1986) and Mark Francis (Francis et al., 1984; Francis and Hester, 1990) are products of Lynch's and Appleyard's programs and are now themselves eminent contributors in this arena. The scientific basis of their work has in effect closed the loop linking image studies and environment-behavior studies, and these researchers are now commonly associated with this latter area of concentration.

Environment-Behavior Studies

The study of relations between people and their surroundings is an interdisciplinary field whose history has yet to be documented fully. Stemming from work done since the turn of the century in environmental psychology and sociology, these studies have grown rapidly since the 1960s, supported by a variety of federally sponsored laws in such areas as community mental health, energy conservation, environmental protection, and programs directed at special needs populations, children, the elderly, the physically impaired, and others.

In the 1960s, the design and planning professions turned to sociology and environmental psychology as sources of valuable information in this new emic realm of research on the environment. Since then, person-environment relations has become a bona fide part of the architectural profession, covering research on how people use, like, or simply behave in given environments. The field also rapidly spread to urban design as Amos Rapoport, Kevin Lynch, and Donald Appleyard began to investigate the human dimension of neighborhoods, urban districts, and cities at large.

Environment-behavior research, as it is increasingly called today, has until recently been almost totally positivistic. Actually, its original influence on design was due to its science-based approach, which was deemed more serious, reliable, and rational than the

then-traditional intuitive, often highly personal, design process. The introduction of
the social sciences to planning and design
was part of a broader trend of interest in
multidisciplinary activity, itself the product
of system-thinking developed by the military
during World War II. In England, the influences of both modernism and the systems
approach divided architectural schools of
the postwar period into two groups: one at
the Bartlett, where Llewelyn Davis was to
assume a multidisciplinary approach to
design, and the other at Cambridge University, with Martin and March, which was to
focus on space, urban form, and land use
(Hillier, 1986).

In the United States in the early 1960s, the
University of California at Berkeley was first
to create a College of Environmental Design,
thus expanding the professions of architecture and planning to the general design of
environments, including industrial design.
In the new curriculum at Berkeley, "user
studies" (meant to collect information on
people expected to use the facilities to be
designed) and "design methods" involving
the coordination of different interests and
expertise (from the user to the investor)
ranked high on the list of important courses
that students were to take.

Although environment-behavior studies
have recently suffered some setback at least
in architecture (their development is perceived to have taken away from design – or
is it Design?), they are in fact well entrenched
in design thinking. People like Amos Rapoport (1977, 1982, 1990), Robert Gutman
(1972), Michael Brill (Villeco and Brill,
1981), Sandra Howell (Moore et al., 1985),
Jon Lang (1987), Karen Franck (Franck and
Ahrentzen, 1989), Clare Cooper Marcus
(1975; Marcus and Sarkissian, 1986), and
Oscar Newman (1972, 1980) remain important figures in education and practice
nationally. The Environmental Design Research Association (EDRA) celebrated its
twentieth year with many of its members
holding appointments in schools of design
around the country (Hardie et al., 1989).
The term "environmental design research"
has been proposed to cover those studies

that relate specifically to design and to eliminate the polarity and actual conflicts that
the couplet environment-behavior engenders
(Villeco and Brill, 1981).

Influential figures contribute to the field: I.
Altman (1986; Altman and Wohlwill, 1976–
85), D. Canter (1977), L. Festinger (1989),
D. Stokols and I. Altman (1987), and J. F.
Wohlwill (1981, 1985), among others. Principal authors directly related to issues of
urban design include: Amos Rapoport
(1977, 1982, 1990) on residential environments, city, and settlement; Donald Appleyard (1976, 1981) on city and streets; W. H.
Whyte (1980) on urban open spaces and city;
Jack Nasar (1988) on environmental aesthetics; Robin Moore (1986) on children and
environments; Mark Francis (Francis et al.,
1984) on urban open space; William Michelson (1970, 1977) on neighborhoods; Clare
Cooper Marcus (1975; Marcus and Sarkissian, 1986) on residential environments;
both Jan Gehl (1987) and Roderick Lawrence (1987) on streets and residential environments; Oscar Newman (1972, 1980)
on residential environments; and S. and
R. Kaplan (1978) on open spaces. Further,
if most of the studies conducted in this area
relate to ordinary environments, some deal
with differences in values and preferences
between professional designers and lay
people (Canter, 1977; Nasar, 1988).

The broad, multidisciplinary nature of the
field makes information retrieval somewhat
difficult. There are many organizations
sponsoring and publishing research (Moore
et al., 1985), and many journals that have yet
to provide comprehensive indexes. However,
the School of Architecture at the University
of Wisconsin, Milwaukee, has published a
handy bibliography for use by their doctoral
students (Moore et al., 1987). Useful surveys
of the field are also being produced (Altman
and Wohlwill, 1976–85; Moore et al., 1985;
Stokols and Altman, 1987; Zube and Moore,
1987). As an interesting aside, Moore et al.
(1987) include J. B. Jackson and other geographers as part of environmental design research. But in our classification, these works
appear to fit best under material culture
studies. If this overlap is of course proof of

some of the issues related to this classification (and to classification in general), it is also evidence of rich relationships among areas of research, of which only some are commonly associated with urban design.

The primarily positivistic stand of environment-behavior studies has become an area of contention and is cause for criticism less from designers and planners, as mentioned earlier, than from the field's own ranks. Questions are raised as to whether people's attitudes, feelings, behaviors, and so on, should be pigeonholed in such categories as perception and cognition. What about the whole of people and environment relationships? What about the intangible, the spiritual? As noted earlier, these and other issues have led some to use phenomenological methods to carry out research. Further, a perceived overemphasis on the subject at the expense of the object qualities of the environment has led to dissatisfaction. In reaction, a group of researchers, scholars, and theoreticians has emerged, who are offshoots of environment-behavior studies in their concerns yet do not care to be formally related to the field. It was decided to put them in a category loosely called "place studies."

Place Studies

Place studies gather many thinkers who have yet to crystallize as a bona fide group (identified but not articulated as such in Moore et al., 1985, pp. xviii, 59–73). Since the late 1970s, several studies have set out to create knowledge and theories of place that are based on the importance of people's relations to their environment and yet do not fit properly within the environment-behavior category. First, they do not employ solely positivistic research strategies. Second, while the concern for both object and subject is central, the emphasis is on the object as an important preoccupation in design. Third, these studies look for the emotional as well as for the perceptual aspects of people-environment relations. Further, and perhaps most important, they bend toward derived etic and outright etic interpretations. These

studies thus appear as the black sheep of environment-behavior studies: abiding by the principles, but bending some of the basic rules.

Place studies include a great variety of research, which, because of its personal bent, is difficult to categorize further. However, one group of scholars consists of design and planning professionals – this may explain in part some of the object and etic emphases in this category. Norberg-Schulz (1980, 1985), Hester (1975, 1984), Allan Jacobs (1985), Violich (1983), Lerup (1977), Hillier and Hanson (1984), Thiel (1986), Greenbie (1981), Lynch (1972, 1981; most of his work following *The Image of the City*), and recently, Charles Moore and his collaborators (Moore et al., 1988), Seamon and Mugerauer (1989), and Francis and Hester (1990) are all representatives of this group. They share a sophisticated knowledge of the design process, the history of urban form, and the value of the cultural landscape. They show particular empathy for cross-cultural research, and they prefer to turn their attention to vernacular places. Although they also belong to this group, Higuchi (1983) and Ashihara (1983) stand out because of their close ties with picturesque and image studies.

A second group is made up of social scientists who have sought to relate closely to the object of design, as, for instance, Tuan (1974, 1977), Perin (1970, 1977), Sime (1986), Relph (1976), Appleton (1975), Jakle (1987), and Walter (1988). Grady Clay (1973) and Tony Hiss (1990), both journalists, and Mark Gottdiener (1985), a sociologist, also belong to this category. The common trait of these works is their highly individualistic character, combined with the primacy given to the socio-psychological dimension of the built environment and the modified landscape. Place studies research is especially well received in urban design circles, presumably because it incorporates many of the complex relationships that must be synthesized during the design process.

The name "place studies" has been selected to cover the range of these eclectic studies and to reflect the emphasis on the physical environment and on its sensual and emotional contents. It should be noted, however, that environment-behavior studies also claim the concept of place as central to their endeavors (as in Canter, 1977; Rapoport, 1982, 1990; Appleyard, 1981; Lawrence, 1987), thus making the line between the two areas sometimes difficult to draw.

Material Culture Studies

Material culture is a branch of anthropology that focuses on the study of objects as reflections and tools of cultures and societies. While the objects of study are wide-ranging, including stamps, kitchen utensils, clothes, and so on, the field has flourished into a rich and popular scholarly endeavor since utilitarian machines of all kinds have become everyday staples. Elements of the cultural landscape are increasingly part of the field. Geographers have contributed to material culture as well (see Lewis, 1975, for instance). And as architects, landscape architects, and urban designers are becoming more reflective and studying systematically the material manifestations of our environment, they too are adding, even if unknowingly so in many cases, to material culture studies (Wolfe, 1965).

Thomas Schlereth (1982, 1985a) has spent considerable effort to explain the scope and evolution of the material culture studies undertaken over the past eighty or ninety years. A skilled observer and critic of the physical environment (Schlereth, 1985b), he has identified three stages in the development of material culture studies. He calls them the age of collecting, the age of description, and the age of analysis (Schlereth, 1982). Schlereth shows how the field has increased in complexity from a simple collector's activity to a critical scholarly endeavor. Hence initial questions regarding the legitimacy of a field that includes match box collectors and car buffs are no longer posed. Further, as the methods used to present and analyze cultural artifacts grow increasingly sophisticated, material culture studies provide knowledge that parallels and indeed competes with art history: the

study of shopping centers, jewelry, or pigsties no longer has to be justified as "high or low art" (or as any kind of art for that matter), thus enhancing the potential for gathering information about the material world. The growth of the field is particularly important since postindustrial societies continue to "encumber" themselves with an increasingly large plethora of objects that may have little significance in and of themselves, but surely do together and collectively.

For now, material culture studies are, for all intents and purposes, part of the field of American studies. In Europe, ethnographers and ethnologists, and to some extent, urban and ethno-archaeologists, are beginning to expand into the study of more recent cultural artifacts. But my own limited investigations have not detected the emergence of material culture studies per se there.

Schlereth includes J. B. Jackson, Grady Clay, and Robert Venturi as contributors to the study of the material environment, but Henry Glassie, a folk culture scholar, emerges as a giant of the field. Little known to environmental designers, Glassie's work includes detailed analyses of folk houses in Virginia (1968, 1975) and the thorough description of an Ulster community (1982). His meticulous research and complex methodology – a mixture of structuralism and phenomenology – serve as a model for good, significant research. Even closer to designers' interests is Upton and Vlach's (1986) work on vernacular places and Groth's (1990) on cultural landscapes. A close watch on this field will be necessary in the future.

Typology-Morphology Studies

This area of concentration is not well known in the United States. Sometimes associated with the Krier brothers' (Rational Architecture, 1978) and Aldo Rossi's (1964, 1982) works, it is often reduced to an architectural design philosophy that borrows from the premodern city (Vidler, 1976; Moneo, 1978). In fact, typology and morphology research encompasses a long tradition of studying cities, their form, and especially the socioeconomic processes that govern their production. The Kriers and Rossi have relied on such studies. They have popularized the notion that the study of architecture leads to an understanding of society that is as valid as the understanding gained from such established disciplines as economics or sociology. However, neither the Kriers nor Rossi have explicitly introduced to the design fields the substantial data on urban form and urban form-making that have been generated by research in typology and morphology (Moudon in progress).

"Typomorphological studies" – a term coined by Italian architect Aymonino (Aymonino et al., 1966) – use building types to describe and explain urban form and the process of shaping the fabric of cities. Geographers working in this area have preferred to talk about urban morphology only to stress their interest in documenting the form of the city. Others, including architects, convinced that buildings and their related open spaces are the essential elements of city form, have focused on classifying them by type to explain the physical characteristics of cities. They prefer to be called typologists.

All typomorphologists approach the study of building types in a special way: they are not so much interested in the form of buildings or in their architectural style as they are in the relationship between buildings and the open spaces surrounding them. Thus they see buildings and complementary open spaces as interconnecting units of space that are usually defined by the boundaries of land ownership. These units of space are made and manipulated by their owners or users. Together, they constitute the urban fabric. Buildings and open spaces are classified by type: types represent different generations pertaining to successive building traditions, or within each generation, types reflect the different socioeconomic strata of the people for whom they were intended.

Because typomorphologists claim to explain the structure and the evolution of the city, their analyses include all building types, both monumental and ordinary. But they necessarily expend most of their efforts in the study of common residential buildings that constitute the greater part of the urban fabric. Hence typomorphological study differs from works emanating from art history, rejecting not only its focus on special building types (usually highly designed and nonutilitarian ones), but especially its typical isolation of individual buildings from the city as a whole and its treatment of buildings as timeless, unchangeable memories of a past.

Typomorphological studies are object oriented. However, the built environment is treated not as a static object but as one constantly changing in the hands of people living in and using it. Indeed the term "morphogenesis" – the study of processes leading to the formation and transformation of the built environment – is preferred over "morphology" – the study of form – to define the nature of research in this area. The approach is thus rooted in history, as traces of the past are strongly and inescapably ingrained in the dynamics of all urban environments. This approach to history relates directly and specifically to the design and planning professions.

In North America, Barton Myers and George Baird's studies of Toronto (Myers and Baird, 1978) and my own of San Francisco (Moudon, 1986) stand as examples of typomorphological studies. Geographer M. R. G. Conzen is an important figure who has used this approach for British medieval cities (Conzen, 1960; Whitehand, 1981). His training dates from the early part of this century in Berlin, where geographers refined a morphological approach applicable to the study of urban settlements. Geographers influenced by M. R. G. Conzen have organized an Urban Morphology Research Group (1987 to the present) at the University of Birmingham. Membership in the group is expanding rapidly in the English-speaking world and in Europe. Accordingly, the group publications include work from many parts of the world and from several disciplines (Slater, 1990). In Italy, architects have debated the value and methodological issues of typomorphological studies for more than three decades. There, Gianfranco Caniggia (1983; Caniggia and Maffei, 1979) stands out with the most expansive work. He was an assistant of Saverio Muratori (1959; Muratori et al., 1963), who carried out two seminal studies of Venice and Rome in the late 1950s. Lately, Paolo Maretto (1986) is emerging as an important historian in this area. In France, a multidisciplinary group of architects, urban designers, geographers, and sociologists have done such studies for some twenty years (Castex et al., 1980; Panerai et al., 1980). They are now consolidated as a research laboratory called LADRHAUS (Laboratoire de Recherche "Histoire Architecturale et Urbaine – Sociétés"), which works closely with groups in Italy, Spain, and Latin America (Moudon, in progress).

Space-Morphology Studies

This area of concentration was formalized after World War II at Cambridge University with Leslie Martin and Lionel March as the founders of the Center for Urban Form and Land Use Studies. The focus of this research group is to uncover the fundamental characteristics of urban geometries. The underlying assumptions behind these studies include the existence of spatial elements that generate urban form – such as rooms, transportation channels, and so on – and the need for quantifying both elements and their relationships.

Christopher Alexander worked with the Cambridge Group in the early 1960s when he was a student of mathematics just beginning to take an interest in design and architecture. His *Notes on the Synthesis of Form* (1964) reflects the concerns and methods used by the group. While Alexander was quick to reject the value of this approach, others have continued in this direction. Martin and March published basic texts in this area (Martin and March, 1972; March, 1977). The work of Philip Steadman covers the area of architectural geometry (Steadman 1983). William Mitchell, one of Martin and March's collaborators, continues to develop computerized approaches to manipulating spatial elements (Mitchell 1990). Lionel March has in fact taken Mitchell's old position as head of the Department of Architecture at UCLA. Clearly this group reflects

architects' long-standing interest in generating and manipulating form in a systematic way – with D'Arcy Thompson's ([1917] 1961) work as a common philosophical basis, and F. L. Wright's and Le Corbusier's Usonian and Citroën houses as reflections of the fascination for interrelated spatial elements.

Perhaps the most broad-ranging effort in this area is being made at the Bartlett by Bill Hillier and his group. Hillier is researching the underlying generative elements of space and looking for a so-called spatial grammar *as it relates* to social systems. He is thus linking concerns in both the social and geometrical dimensions of space. Quite complex and difficult to understand entirely, Hillier's approach is explained in *The Social Logic of Space* (Hillier and Hanson, 1984). This work is of special interest, however, because it demonstrates the need to stress linkages between environmental design research and research in urban morphology. In this sense, it also belongs to place studies.

In the United States, the space-morphology area had a brief hiatus in the 1960s with the publication of *Explorations into Spatial Structures* (Webber, 1964). A joint University of California at Berkeley and University of Pennsylvania effort, the book summarizes interests and research in categorizing the fundamental elements of environmental space. But while the British research is carried out primarily by architects, this American work is the result of thinking by planners. Unfortunately, the US work has seen little follow-up. Instead, following Webber's own contribution, which questioned the importance of physical and material space relative to its socioeconomic dimension, planners have gone on to explore the functional aspects of urban space. Thus, in the United States, the area of urban spatial structures now deals solely with transportation, land use, and locational variables, at a scale that prohibits the consideration of objective material space (see, for instance, Bourne 1971).

Kevin Lynch and Lloyd Rodwin also tackled the analysis of spatial and morphological elements in their early research

(Lynch and Rodwin, 1958). But this common interest quickly forked out into Lynch's focus on image studies and Rodwin's interest in larger socioeconomic urban models.

Thus, in the 1960s, interest in space-morphology showed possible collaboration between architects and planners on the issue of spatial structures. But the end of the decade brought this to an abrupt halt with the now-obvious professional split over the relative importance of socioeconomic space and over the different scales at which issues of planning and design emerge. In the area of spatial structures today, the legacy of Christaller (Berry and Red, 1961) and the Chicago School of Sociology prevails in the planning fields, while spatial grammars and computers dominate in the architectural arena.

There are independent researchers whose work may also fit this category, because it rests on the geometric characteristics of space. Passonneau and Wurman (1966; Wurman, 1974) studied urban geometries and densities. Stanford Anderson's (1977) mapping of public and private uses of space and Philippe Boudon's (1971, 1991) definition of architecturology also come to mind. Anderson's interest in small-scale definition of territories is unfortunately not applied to enough different cases to permit the development of a theoretical framework for design (Anderson, 1986). Boudon's claim that architectural space is not geometrical space because spatial dimensions are what define architectural space – a 10-foot square room is essentially different from a 100-foot square room, even if their geometries are similar – is challenging but little known in the United States. Searching appropriate ways to describe built space, Boudon argues that space can only be qualified as it stimulates sensory responses: objects cannot be described, but the sensations and feelings they generate can (Boudon, 1971, 1991). This recognition suggests that these works could also fit in place studies.

It is worth mentioning at this point that work in spatial semiotics does not appear to fit well in any of the areas of concentrations devised here. The work is laden with controversy (can architecture be considered to pro-duce systems of signs or languages?) and difficult to understand. Undefined intent and complex method make it tenuous to classify (Gottdiener, 1986). But semiotics could belong to the area of space-morphology if it were accepted that its intent is to uncover a spatial logic in built form.

Finally, space-morphology and typology-morphology overlap in the way they seek to identify the generative structure of space. But they differ fundamentally in that typology-morphology grounds analysis and explanation of space on the history and evolution of material space, while the area of space-morphology remains essentially *a-historical*.

Nature-ecology studies

Recent research and theories have shown urban ecology to be a necessary and essential component of urban design. Light, air, and open space have always been part of the discourse of urban design, but planners and architects have tended to limit the consideration of their impact to the health, comfort, and visual qualities of environments. The role of greenery in the city has been a major concern since the latter part of the nineteenth century – as a romantic drive to bring nature into the exploding metropolis and as a necessary outlet for the recreation of growing masses of urbanites. The second half of the twentieth century has brought serious concerns about excessive energy consumption in urban environments, but most of the work done to address these concerns has dealt primarily with transportation functions and the automobile industry in particular. Some architects also responded at that time by focusing on energy-conscious buildings. Since then, however, the larger field of ecology has grown considerably, affecting many disciplines (Odum, 1971). Urban ecology emerged across disciplinarian boundaries, introducing systemic methods of analyzing and planning the city (Detwyler and Marcus, 1972; Douglas, 1983; George and McKinley, 1974; Goudie, 1990; Havlick, 1974). These methods consider geology, topography, climate, air pollution, water, soils, noise, vegetation, and wildlife. Inclusive approaches to understanding the city and its environs as a naturally balanced environment are now being developed (Gordon, 1990; Todd and Todd, 1984; Van der Ryn and Calthorpe, 1986; Yaro et al., 1988).

Landscape architects are making substantial contributions to this field. Ian McHarg's seminal *Design with Nature* (1971) has been followed by Anne Whiston Spirn's *The Granite Garden* (1984). John Lyle's (1985) and Michael Hough's (1984) recent works also provide essential information for integrating natural processes in city design. These publications demonstrate how the movement of water and air affects pollution and health, how air pollution generated by cars can be alleviated by proper design of streets and buildings, how vegetation affects air flows, and so on. They also include elements of flora and fauna as integral inhabitants and hence determinants of cities. The effect of trees in the urban context is treated in increasing detail (Moll and Ebenreck, 1989). Bridging these new concerns with traditional urban design interests, Anne Spirn is now working on the repercussions of ecological design on urban aesthetics.

Although these works have yet to be brought to the center of urban design, they begin to show the relationships that exist between the more commonly considered social and psychological components of the environment and its biological dimension. The city as an inevitable cultural and ecological system is treated by Kenneth Schneider in *On the Nature of Cities* (1979). Links to urban history are made by Hughes in *Ecology in Ancient Civilizations* (1975). Finally, much of the research carried out in the natural sciences remains to be interpreted for the detailed design of the environment.

Conclusion

This first attempt at building an epistemology for urban design emanated from the practical need to introduce students to a large body of literature, to encourage them to focus their readings, and to help them relate these readings to actual issues and problems of the field. At this pedagogical level, the "catholic approach" has been a successful guide to students as they meander through the complexities of this literature. In return, students will probably help keep the "catholic approach" up-to-date, as new areas are likely to emerge from related fields and as influences on urban design are broadened or simply changed.

The relevance of the "catholic approach" to the larger context of research and practice still awaits acceptance. Future discussions of the validity and usefulness of the nine concentrations of inquiry will, if nothing else, broaden the repertoire of references used by most practitioners. It will help them explain their personal preferences and inclinations and to identify areas of unexpected neglect. More important, however, the nine concentrations proposed map out and, hence, highlight specific foci of professional concerns. Urban history studies offer critical assessments of various design processes and explain their resulting forms. Picturesque studies combine different interpretations of the built environment's visual attributes. Image studies explain ordinary people's visual cognition of cities. Environment-behavior studies begin to assemble the complex puzzle of interactions between people and their surroundings. Place studies bring forth the special meanings, symbols, and generally the deep emotional contents of the built environment and related open spaces. Material culture studies concentrate on the object qualities of the modified landscape and its value to society. Typology-morphology studies explain the products and procedures related to the city-building process. Space-morphology studies offer explanations about the functional impacts of space and its geometry. Finally, nature-ecology studies examine the relationships between the city and the natural environment. These nine areas serve to scan what is known about how cities are made, used, and understood and to focus on ways of developing this knowledge.

The future effectiveness of the field depends on its ability to digest this substantive knowledge and to use it to evaluate normative theories and practices. In the end, knowledge of urban design, as practiced and theorized, and knowledge of the city, as perceived, produced, and lived in, must become intimately related.

NOTE

1   According to Lang (1987), there is also research pertaining to the "procedural" aspects of urban design that relates to how urban design should be practiced and that focuses on methods of practicing urban design – for example, Barnett (1974), Jacobs (1978), and Wolfe and Shinn (1970). Procedural research is not included in this epistemological map.

REFERENCES

Alberti, L. B. (1988) *On the Art of Building in Ten Books (De re aedificatoria)*, trans. J. Rykwert, N. Leach, and R. Tavernor. Cambridge, MA: MIT Press (originally published 1452).

Alexander, C. (1964) *Notes on the Synthesis of Form*. Cambridge, MA: Harvard University Press.

Alexander, C., Ishikawa, S. and Silverstein, M. (1977) *A Pattern Language: Towns, Buildings, Construction*. New York: Oxford University Press.

Altman, I. (1986) *Culture and Environment*. Cambridge: Cambridge University Press.

Altman, I. and Wohlwill, J. F. (eds) (1976–85) *Human Behavior and Environment: Advances in Theory and Research, volumes 1–5*. New York: Plenum.

Anderson, S. (ed.) (1977) *On Streets*. Cambridge, MA: MIT Press.

Anderson, S. (1986) Architectural and urban form as factors in the theory and practice of urban design. In F. Choay and P. Merlin (eds), *A propos de la morphologie urbaine. Volume 2, Communications*. Paris: Laboratoire "Téorie des mutations urbaines en pays développés," Université de Paris VIII.

Appleton, J. (1975) *The Experience of Landscape*. New York: Wiley.

Appleton, J. (ed.) (1980) *The Aesthetics of Landscape: Proceedings of Symposium, University of Hull, 17–19 September 1976*. Didcot: Rural Planning Service.

Appleyard, D. (1976) *Planning a Pluralistic City: Conflicting Realities in Ciudad Guayana*. Cambridge, MA: MIT Press.

Appleyard, D. (1981) *Livable Streets*. Berkeley: University of California Press.

Appleyard, D., Lynch, K. and Myer, J. (1964) *The view from the Road*. Cambridge, MA: MIT Press.

Arnheim, R. (1954) *Art and Visual Perception: A Psychology of the Creative Eye*. Berkeley: University of California Press.

Arnheim, R. (1966) *Toward a Psychology of Art: Collected Essays*. Berkeley: University of California Press.

Artibise, A. F. J. and Linteau, P. -A. (1984) The evolution of urban Canada: an analysis of approaches and interpretations. In *Institute of Urban Studies, Report 4*. Winnipeg: Institute of Urban Studies, University of Winnipeg.

Ashihara, Y. (1983) *The Aesthetic Townscape*. Cambridge, MA: MIT Press.

Aymonino, C., Brusatin, M., Fabbri, G., Lena, M., Loverro, P., Lucianetti, S., and Rossi, A. (1966) *La città di Padova, saggio di analisi urbana*. Rome: Officina edizoni.

Bacon, E. (1976) *Design of Cities*. New York: Penguin.

Banham, R. (1971) *Los Angeles: The Architecture of Four Ecologies*. Baltimore: Pelican.

Barnett, J. (1974) *Urban Design as Public Policy: Practical Methods for Improving Cities*. New York: Architectural Record Books.

Barnett, J. (1986) *The Elusive City: Five Centuries of Design, Ambition and Ideas*. New York: Harper & Row.

Benevolo, L. (1980) *The History of the City*. London: Scolar.

Berry, B. J. L. and Red, A. (1961) *Central Place Studies: A Bibliography of Theory and Applications*. Philadelphia: Regional Science Institute.

Blumenfeld, H. (1979) *Metropolis and Beyond: Selected Essays by Hnas Blumenfeld edited by Paul D. Spreiregen*. New York: Wiley.

Boudon, P. (1971) *Sur l'espace architectural: essai d'épistémologie de l'architecture*. Paris: Dunod.

Boudon, P. (1991) *De l'architecture à l'épistémologie de léchelle*. Paris: Presses Universitaires de France.

Bourne, L. (ed.) (1971) *Internal Structure of the City: Readings on Urban Form, Growth and Policy*. New York: Oxford University Press.

Broadbent, G. (1990) *Emerging Concepts in Urban Space Design*. London: Van Nostrand Reinhold International.

Brunskill, R. W. (1981) *Traditional Buildings of Britain: An Introduction to Vernacular Architecture*. London: Victor Gollancz.

Brunskill, R. W. (1982) *Houses*. London: Collins.

Burke, G. (1971) *Towns in the Making*. London: Edward Arnold.

Caniggia, G. (1983) Dialettica tra tipo e tessuto nei rapporti preesistenza–attualità, formazione–mutazione, sincronia–diacronia. Extracts from *Studi e documenti de architettura*, 11 (June).

Caniggia, G. and Maffei, G. L. (1979) *Composizione architettonica e tipologia edilizia, 1. Lettura dell'edilizia di base*. Venice: Marsilio Editori.

Canter, D. (1977) *The Psychology of Place*. London: Architectural Press.

Carter, H. (1976) *The Study of Urban Geography*. New York: Wiley.

Castex, J., Céleste, P. and Panerai, P. (1980) *Lecture d'une ville: Versilles*. Paris: Editions du Moniteur.

Choay, F. (1965) *Urbanisme, utopies et réalités, une anthologie* Paris Editions du Seuil.

Choay, F. (1980) *La règle et le modèle, sur la théorie de l'architecture et de l'urbanisme*. Paris Editions du Seuil.

Clay, G. (1973) *Close-up: How to Read the American City*. New York: Praeger.

Conzen, M. P. (1978) Analytical approaches to the urban landscape. In K. W. Butzer (ed.), *Dimensions of Human Geography*. Research paper 186, Department of Geography, University of Chicago.

Conzen, M. P. (1980) The morphology of nineteenth-century cities in the United States. In W. Borah, J. Hardoy, and G. Stelter (eds), *Urbanization in the Americas: The Background in Comparative Perspective*. Ottawa: National Museum of Man.

Conzen, M. P. (ed.) (1990) *The Making of the American Landscape*. Boston: Unwin Hyman.

Conzen, M. R. G. (1960) *Alnwick, Northumberland: A Study in Town-plan Analysis*. London: Institute of British Geographers.

Cullen, G. (1961) *The Concise Townscape*. New York: Van Nostrand Reinhold.

Detwyler, T. R. and Marcus, M. G. (1972) *Urbanization and Environment: The Physical Geography of the City*. Belmont, CA: Duxbury.

Dickinson, R. E. (1961) *The West European City: A Geographical Interpretation*. London: Routledge & Kegan Paul.

Douglas, I. (1983) *The Urban Environment*. Baltimore: Edward Arnold.

Dyoz, H. J. (ed.) (1968) *The Study of Urban History*. New York: St Martin's Press.

Evenson, N. (1973) *Two Brazilian Capitals: Architecture and Urbanism in Rio de Janeiro and Brasilia*. New Haven, CT: Yale University Press.

Evenson, N. (1979) *Paris: A Century of Change, 1878–1978*. New Haven, CT: Yale University Press.

Festinger, L. (1989) *Extending Psychological Frontiers: Works of Leon Festinger*. New York: Russell Sage Foundation.

Fishman, R. (1977) *Urban Utopias in the Twentieth Century: Ebenezer Howard, Frank Lloyd Wright, and Le Corbusier*. New York: Basic Books.

Fishman, R. (1987) *Bourgeois Utopias: The Rise and Fall of Suburbia*. New York: Basic Books.

Francis, M., Cashdan, L. and Paxson, L. (1984) *Community Open Spaces: Greening Neighborhoods through Community Action and Land Conservation*. Washington, DC: Island Press.

Francis, M. and Hester, R. (eds) (1990) *The Meaning of Gardens: Idea, Place, and Action.* Cambridge, MA: MIT Press.

Franck, K. A. and Ahrentzen, S. (1989) *New Households, New Housing.* New York: Van Nostrand Reinhold.

Friedman, D. (1988) *Florentine New Towns: Urban Design in the Late Middle Ages.* Cambridge, MA: MIT Press.

Gans, H. J. (1967) *The Levittowners: Ways of Life and Politics in a New Suburban Community.* New York: Pantheon.

Gans, H. J. (1969) Planning for people, not buildings. *Environment and Planning*, 1(1), 33–46.

Garreau, J. (1991) *Edge City: Life on the New Frontier.* New York: Doubleday.

Gehl, J. (1987) *Life between Buildings: Using Public Space.* New York: Van Nostrand Reinhold.

George, C. J. and McKinley, D. (1974) *Urban Ecology: In Search of a Asphalt Rose.* New York: McGraw-Hill.

Girouard, M. (1985) *Cities and People: A Social and Architectural History.* New Haven, CT: Yale University Press.

Glassie, H. (1968) *Pattern in the Material Folk Culture of the Eastern United States.* Philadelphia: University of Pennsylvania Press.

Glassie, H. (1975) *Folk Housing in Middle Virginia.* Knoxville: University of Tennessee Press.

Glassie, H. (1982) *Passing the Time in Baleymenone: Culture and History of an Ulster Community.* Philadelphia: University of Pennsylvania Press.

Gordon, D. (ed.) (1990) *Green Cities.* Montreal: Black Rose.

Gosling, D. and Maitland, B. (1984) *Concepts of Urban Design.* London: Academy Editions.

Gottdiener, M. (1985) *The Social Production of Urban Space.* Austin: University of Texas Press.

Gottdiener, M. (1986) *The City and the Sign: An Introduction to Urban Semiotics.* New York: Columbia University Press.

Goudie, A. (1990) *Human Impact on the Natural Environment.* Cambridge, MA: Blackwell.

Greenbie, B. B. (1981) *Spaces: Dimensions of the Human Landscape.* New Haven, CT: Yale University Press.

Groth, P. (ed.) (1990) *Visions, Culture, and Landscape.* Working papers for the Berkeley Symposium on Cultural Landscape Interpretations. Berkeley: Department of Landscape Architecture, University of California.

Gutman, R. (1972) *People and Buildings.* New York: Basic Books.

Hall, E. T. (1966) *The Hidden Dimension.* Garden City, NY: Doubleday.

Hall, E. T. (1980) *The Silent Language.* Westport, CT: Greenwood (first published 1959).

Halprin, L. (1966) *Freeways.* New York: Reinhold.

Halprin, L. (1972) *Cities.* Cambridge, MA: MIT Press.

Hardie, G., Moore, R., and Sanoff, H. (eds) (1989) *Changing Paradigms.* EDRA 20, Proceedings of Annual Conference. School of Design, North Carolina State University.

Havlick, S. W. (1974) *The Urban Organism: The City's Natural Resources from an Environmental Perspective.* New York: Macmillan.

Hayden, D. (1981) *The Grand Domestic Revolution: A History of Feminist Designs for American Homes, Neighborhoods, and Cities.* Cambridge, MA: MIT Press.

Hayden, D. (1984) *Redesigning the American Dream: The Future of Housing, Work, and Family Life.* New York: W. W. Norton.

Hester, R. (1975) *Neighborhood Space.* Stroudsburg, PA: Dowden, Hutchinson & Ross.

Hester, R. (1984) *Planning Neighborhood Space with People.* New York: Van Nostrand Reinhold.

Higuchi, T. (1983) *The Visual and Spatial Structure of Landscapes.* Cambridge, MA: MIT Press.

Hillier, B. (1986) Urban morphology: the UK experience, a personal view. In F. Choay and P. Merlin (eds), *A propos de la morphologie urbaine. Volume 2, Communications.* Paris: Laboratoire "Téorie des mutations urbaines en pays développés," Université de Paris VIII.

Hillier, B. and Hanson, J. (1984) *The Social Logic of Space.* Cambridge: Cambridge University Press.

Hiorns, F. R. (1956) *Town-building in History: An Outline Review of Conditions, Influences, Ideas, and Methods Affecting "Planned" Towns through Five Thousand Years*. London: George G. Harrap.

Hiss, T. (1990) *The Experience of Place*. New York: Knopf.

Hough, M. (1984) *City Form and Natural Process: Towards a New Urban Vernacular*. Beckenham: Croom Helm.

Hughes, J. D. (1975) *Ecology of Ancient Civilization*. Albuquerque: University of New Mexico Press.

Huxtable, A. L. (1970) *Will They Ever Finish Bruckner Boulevard?* New York: Macmillan.

Jackson, J. B. (1980) *The Necessity for Ruins and Other Topics*. Amherst: University of Massachusetts Press.

Jackson, J. B. (1984) *Discovering the Vernacular Landscape*. New Haven, CT: Yale University Press.

Jackson, K. (1985) *Crabgrass Frontier: The Suburbanization of the United States*. New York: Oxford University Press.

Jackson, K. and Schultz, S. (eds) (1972) *Cities in American History*. New York: Knopf.

Jacobs, A. (1978) *Making City Planning Work*. Chicago: American Society of Planning Officials.

Jacobs, A. (1985) *Looking at Cities*. Cambridge, MA: Harvard University Press.

Jacobs, J. (1961) *The Death and Life of Great American Cities*. New York: Random House.

Jakle, J. A. (1987) *The Visual Elements of Landscape*. Amherst: University of Massachusetts Press.

Jarvis, R. K. (1980) Urban environments as visual art or as social settings? *Town Planning Review*, 51(1), 50–65.

Johnston, N. (1983) *Cities in the Round*. Seattle: University of Washington Press.

Kaplan, S. and Kaplan, R. (1978) *Humanscape: Environment for People*. North Scituate, MA: Duxbury.

Kepes, G. (1944) *Language of Vision*. Chicago: P. Theobald.

Kepes, G. (1965) *The Nature and Art of Motion*. New York: G. Braziller.

Kepes, G. (1966) *Sign, Image, Symbol*. New York: G. Braziller.

Knack, R. E. (1989) Repent, ye sinners, repent. *Planning*, 55(8), 4–13.

Konvitz, J. (1985) *The Urban Millennium: The City-building Process from the Early Middle Ages to the Present*. Carbondale: Southern Illinois University Press.

Kostof, S. (1986) Cities and turfs. *Design Book Review*, 10 (Fall), 9–10, 37–9.

Kostof, S. (1991) *The City Shaped: Urban Patterns and Meanings through History*. Boston: Bulfinch Press/Little, Brown.

Lang, J. (1987) *Creating Architectural Theory: The Role of the Behavioral Sciences in Environmental Design*. New York: Van Nostrand Reinhold.

Lavedan, H. (1941) *Histoire de l'urbanisme: Renaissance et temps modernes*. Paris: Laurens.

Lawrence, R. (1987) *Housing, Dwellings and Homes: Design Theory, Research and Practice*. New York: Wiley.

Lerup, L. (1977) *Building the Unfinished: Architecture and Human Action*. Beverly Hills, CA: Sage.

Lewis, P. F. (1975) Common houses, cultural spoor. *Landscape*, 19(2), 1–22.

Lowenthal, D. and Binney, M. (eds) (1981) *Our Past Before Us?* London: Temple Smith.

Lubove, R. (1967) The urbanization process: an approach to historical research. *Journal of the American Institute of Planners*, 33, 33–9.

Lyle, J. T. (1985) *Design for Human Ecosystem: Landscape, Land Use and Natural Resources*. New York: Van Nostrand Reinhold.

Lynch, K. (1960) *The Image of the City*. Cambridge, MA: MIT Press.

Lynch, K. (1972) *What Time Is This Place?* Cambridge, MA: MIT Press.

Lynch, K. (1981) *A theory of Good City Form*. Cambridge, MA: MIT Press.

Lynch, K. and Rodwin, L. (1958) A theory of urban form. *Journal of the American Institute of Planners*, 24, 201–14.

Lynd, R. S. and Lynd, H. M. (1929) *Middletown: A Study in Contemporary American Culture.* London: Constable.

Lyndon, D. (1982) *The City Observed: Boston.* New York: Random House.

McHarg, I. (1971) *Design with Nature.* Garden City, NY: Doubleday.

March, L. (1977) *Architecture of Form.* Cambridge, MA: MIT Press.

Marcus, C. C. (1975) *Easter Hill Village: Some Social Implications of Design.* New York: Free Press.

Marcus, C. C. and Sarkissian, W. (1986) *Housing as if People Mattered: Site Design Guidelines for Medium-density Family Housing.* Berkeley: University of California Press.

Maretto, P. (1986) *La casa veneziana nella storia della città, dalle origini all'ottocento.* Venice: Marsilio Editori.

Martin, L. and March, L. (eds) (1972) *Urban Space and Structures.* Cambridge: Cambridge University Press.

Michelson, W. (1970) *Man and His Environment.* Reading, MA: Addison-Wesley.

Michelson, W. (1977) *Environmental Choice, Human Behavior, and Residential Satisfaction.* New York: Oxford University Press.

Mitchell, W. J. (1990) *The Logic of Architecture, Design, Computation, and Cognition.* Cambridge, MA: MIT Press.

Moll, G. and Ebenreck, S. (eds) (1989) *Shading Our Cities: A Resource Guide for Urban and Community Forests.* Washington, DC: Island Press.

Moneo, R. (1978) On typology. *Oppositions*, 13 (Summer), 23–45.

Moore, C. W., Mitchell, W. J. and Turnbull, W. Jr (1988) *The Poetics of Gardens.* Cambridge, MA: MIT Press.

Moore, G. T. and the Faculty of the PhD Program (1987) *Resources in Environment-behavior Studies.* Milwaukee: School of Architecture and Urban Planning, University of Wisconsin.

Moore, G. T., Tuttle, P. and Howell, S. C. (eds) (1985) *Environmental Design Research Directions, Process and Prospects.* New York: Praeger Special Studies.

Moore, R. (1986) *Childhood Domain: Play and Place in Child Development.* London: Croom Helm.

Moore, Thomas, Sir, St (1989) *Utopia.* New York: Cambridge University Press (first published 1516).

Morris, A. E. J. (1972) *History of Urban Form: Prehistory to Renaissance.* New York: Wiley.

Moudon, A. V. (1986) *Built for Change: Neighborhood Architecture in San Francisco.* Cambridge, MA: MIT Press.

Moudon, A. V. (1987) The research component of typomorphological studies. Paper presented at the AIA/ACSA Research Conference, Boston, November.

Moudon, A. V. (1988) Normative/substantive and etic/emic dilemmas in design education. *Column 5 Journal of Architecture, University of Washington*, Spring, 13–15.

Moudon, A. V. (in progress) *City Building.* Manuscript.

Mumford, L. (1961) *The City in History: Its Origins, Its Transformations, and Its Prospects.* New York: Harcourt, Brace & World.

Muratori, S. (1959) *Studi per una operante storia urbana di Venezia.* Rome: Instituto Poligrafico dello Stato.

Muratori, S., Bollati, R., Bollati, S., and Marinucci, G. (1963) *Studi per una operante storia urbana di Roma.* Rome: Consiglio nazionale delle ricerche.

Muthesius, S. (1982) *The English Terraced House.* New Haven, CT: Yale University Press.

Myers, B. and Baird, G. (1978) Vacant lottery. *Design Quarterly*, 108 (special issue).

Nasar, J. L. (ed.) (1988) *Environmental Aesthetics: Theory, Research, and Applications.* Cambridge: Cambridge University Press.

Newman, O. (1972) *Defensible Space: Crime Prevention through Urban Design.* New York: Macmillan.

Newman, O. (1980) *Community of Interest.* Garden City, NY: Anchor Press/Doubleday.

Norberg-Schulz, C. (1980) *Genius Loci: Toward a Phenomenology of Architecture*. London: Academic Editions.

Norberg-Schulz, C. (1985) *The Concept of Dwelling*. New York: Rizzoli.

Odum, E. P. (1971) *Fundamentals of Ecology*. Philadelphia: W. B. Saunders.

Oxman, R. M. (1987) *Urban Design Theories and Methods: A Study of Contemporary Researches*. Occasional paper. Sydney: Department of Architecture, University of Sydney.

Panerei, P., Depaule, J.-C., Demorgon, M., and Veyrenche, M. (1980) *Eléments d'analyse urbaine*. Brussels: Editions Archives d'Architecture Moderne.

Passonneau, J. R. and Wurman, R. S. (1966) *Urban Atlas: 20 American Cities. A Communication Study Notating Selected Urban Data at a Scale of 1:48,000*. Cambridge, MA: MIT Press.

Perin, C. (1970) *With Man in Mind: An Interdisciplinary Prospectus for Environmental Design*. Cambridge, MA: MIT Press.

Perin, C. (1977) *Everything in Its Place: Social Order and Land Use in America*. Princeton, NJ: Princeton University Press.

Poëte, M. (1967) *Introduction à l'urbanisme*. Paris: Editions Anthropos (first published 1929).

Rapoport, A. (1977) *Human Aspects of Urban Form: Towards a Man–Environment Approach to Form and Design*. Oxford: Pergamon.

Rapoport, A. (1982) *The Meaning of the Built Environment: A Nonverbal Communication Approach*. Beverly Hills, CA: Sage.

Rapoport, A. (1990) *History and Precedents in Environmental Design*. New York: Plenum.

Rasmussen, S. E. (1967) *London: The Unique City*. Cambridge, MA: MIT Press.

Rational Architecture: The Reconstruction of the European City (1978) Brussels: Editions des Archives de l'Architecture Moderne.

Relph, E. (1976) *Place and Placelessness*. London: Pion.

Relph, E. (1984) Seeing, thinking and describing landscape. In T. Saarinen et al. (eds), *Environmental Perception and Behavior: An Inventory and Prospect*. Research paper no. 29. Chicago: Department of Geography, University of Chicago.

Relph, E. (1987) *The Modern Urban Landscape*. Baltimore: Johns Hopkins University Press.

Reps, J. W. (1965) *The Making of Urban America: A History of City Planning in the United States*. Princeton, NJ: Princeton University Press.

Rittel, H. and Webber, M. M. (1972) *Dilemmas in a General Theory of Planning*. Eorking paper 194. Berkeley: Institute of Urban and Regional Development, University of California.

Rodwin, L. and Hollister, R. M. (eds) (1984) *Cities of the Mind*. New York: Plenum.

Rossi, A. (1964) Aspetti della tipologia residenziale a Berlino. *Casabella*, 288 (June), 10–20.

Rossi, A. (1982) *The Architecture of the City*. Cambridge, MA: MIT Press (first Italian edition 1966).

Rowe, P. (1991) *Making a Middle Landscape*. Cambridge, MA: MIT Press.

Rudofsky, B. (1969) *Streets for People: A Primer for Americans*. Garden City, NY: Anchor Press/Doubleday.

Schlereth, T. J. (ed.) (1982) *Material Culture Studies in America*. Nashville, TN: American Association for State and Local History.

Schlereth, T. J. (ed.) (1985a) *Material Culture: A Research Guide*. Lawrence: University of Kansas Press.

Schlereth, T. J. (ed.) (1985b) *US 40: A Roadscape of the American Experience*. Indianapolis: Indiana Historical Society.

Schneider, K. R. (1979) *On the Nature of Cities: Toward Enduring and Creative Human Environments*. San Francisco: Jossey-Bass.

Seamon, D. (1987) Phenomenology and environment/behavior research. In E. H. Zube and G. T. Moore (eds), *Advances in Environment, Behavior, and Design*. New York: Plenum.

Seamon, D. and Mugerauer, R. (1989) *Dwelling, Place, and Environment*. New York: Columbia University Press.

Sennett, R. (ed.) (1969) *Nineteenth-century Cities: Essays in the New Urban History*. New Haven, CT: Yale University Press.

Sharp, T. (1946) *The Anatomy of the Village*. Harmondsworth: Penguin.

Sime, J. D. (1986) Creating places or designing spaces? *Journal of Environmental Psychology*, 6(1), 49–63.

Sitte, C. (1980) *L'art de bâtir les villes: l'urbanisme selon ses fondements artistiques*. Paris: Editions de l'Equerre (first published 1889).

Slater, T. R. (ed.) (1990) *The Built Form of Western Cities*. London: Leicester University Press.

Sommer, R. (1969) *Personal Space: The Behavioral Basis of Design*. Englewood Cliffs, NJ: Prentice Hall.

Spirn, A. W. (1984) *The Granite Garden: Urban Nature and Human Design*. New York: Basic Books.

Spreiregen, P. (1965) *Urban Design: The Architecture of Towns and Cities*. New York: McGraw-Hill.

Steadman, P. (1983) *Architectural Morphology: An Introduction to the Geometry of Building Plans*. London: Pion.

Stilgoe, J. R. (1982) *Common Landscape of America, 1580 to 1845*. New Haven, CT: Yale University Press.

Stokols, D. and Altman, I. (1987) *Handbook of Environmental Psychology*. New York: Wiley.

Sutcliffe, A. (ed.) (1984) *Metropolis 1890–1940*. Chicago: University of Chicago Press.

Thiel, P. (1986) *Notations for an Experimental Envirotecture*. Seattle: College of Architecture and Urban Planning, University of Washington.

Thompson, D'Arcy, W. (1961) *On Growth and Form*. Cambridge: Cambridge University Press (originally published 1917).

Todd, N. J. and Todd, J. (1984) *Bioshelters, Ocean Arks, City Farming*. San Francisco: Sierra Club Books.

Tuan, Y.-F. (1974) *Topophilia: A Study of Environmental Perceptions, Attitudes and Values*. Englewood Cliffs, NJ: Prentice Hall.

Tuan, Y.-F. (1977) *Space and Place: The Perspective of Experience*. Minneapolis, University of Minnesota Press.

Unwin, R. (1909) *Town Planning in Practice: An Introduction to the Art of Designing Cities and Suburbs*. New York: B. Blom.

Upton, D. and Vlach, J. M. (eds) (1986) *Common Places: Readings in American Vernacular Architecture*. Athens: University of Georgia Press.

Urban Morphology Research Group (1987–present) *Urban Morphology Newsletter*. Department of Geography, University of Birmingham.

Van der Ryn, S. and Calthorpe, P. (1986) *Sustainable Communities: A New Design Synthesis for Cities, Suburbs, and Towns*. San Francisco: Sierra Club Books.

Vance, J. E. Jr (1977) *This Scene of Man: The Role and Structure of the City in the Geography of Western Civilization*. New York: Harper's.

Vance, J. E. Jr (1990) *The Continuing City: Urban Morphology in Western Civilization*. Baltimore: Johns Hpkins University Press.

Venturi, R., Brown, D. S., and Izenour, S. (1977) *Learning from Las Vegas: The Forgotten Symbolism of Architectural Form*. Cambridge, MA: MIT Press.

Vidler, A. (1976) The third typology. *Oppositions*, 7, 28–32.

Villeco, M. and Brill, M. (1981) *Environmental Design Research: Concepts, Method and Values*. Washington, DC: National Endowment for the Arts.

Violich, F. (1983) *An Experiment in Revealing the Sense of Place: A Subjective Reading of Six Dalmation Towns*. Berkeley: Center for Environmental Design Research, College of Environmental Design, University of California, Berkeley.

Walter, E. V. (1988) *Placeways: A Theory of the Human Environment*. Chapel Hill: University of North Carolina Press.

Warner, S. B. (1962) *Streetcar Suburbs: The Process of Growth in Boston, 1870–1900*. Cambridge, MA: Harvard University Press.

Warner, S. B. (1968) *The Private City: Philadelphia in Three Periods of Its Growth*. Philadelphia: University of Pennsylvania Press.

Warner, W. L. (1963) *Yankee City*. New Haven, CT: Yale University Press.

Webber, M. W. (ed.) (1964) *Explorations into Urban Structure*. Philadelphia: University of Pennsylvania Press.

Weiss, M. A. (1987) *The Rise of the Community Builders: The American Building Industry and Urban Land Planning*. New York: Columbia University Press.

Whitehand, J. W. R. (ed.) (1981) *The Urban Landscape: Historical Development and Management, papers by M. R. G. Conzen*. Institute of British Geographers special publication no. 13. New York: Academic Press.

Whyte, W. H. (1980) *The Social Life of Small Urban Spaces*. Washington, DC: Conservation Foundation.

Whyte, W. H. (1988) *City: Rediscovering the Center*. New York: Doubleday.

Wohlwill, J. F. (1981) *The Physical Environment and Behavior: An Annotated Bibliography*. New York: Plenum.

Wohlwill, J. F. (1985) *Habitats for Children: The Impacts of Density*. Hillsdale, NJ: Lawrence Erlbaum Associates.

Wolfe, M. R. (1965) A visual supplement to urban social studies. *Journal of the American Institute of Planners*, 31(1), 51–61.

Wolfe, M. R. and Shinn, R. D. (1970) *Urban Design within the Comprehensive Planning Process*. Seattle: University of Washington.

Wright, G. (1981) *Building the Dream: A Social History of Housing in America*. New York: Pantheon.

Wurman, R. S. (1971) *Making the City Observable*. Minneapolis: Walker Art Center.

Wurman, R. S. (1972) *Man-made Philadelphia: A Guide to Its Physical and Cultural Environment*. Cambridge, MA: MIT Press.

Wurman, R. S. (1974) *Cities – Comparison of Form and Scale: Models of 50 Significant Towns*. Philadelphia: Joshua Press.

Yaro, R. D., Arendt, R. G., Dodson, H. L., and Brabec, E. A. (1988) *Dealing with Change in the Connecticut River Valley: A Design Manual for Conservation and Development*. Amherst: Center for Rural Massachusetts, University of Massachusetts.

Zube, E. H. and Moore, G. T. (1987) *Advances in Environment, Behavior, and Design*. New York: Plenum.

Additional Reading by Category

Note: the following references are included for additional reading by category. In order to avoid redundancy, they largely avoid references already mentioned in the introduction.

1 Theory

Alexander, C. (1964) *Notes on the Synthesis of Form*. Cambridge, MA: MIT Press.

Alexander, C. (1965) A city is not a tree. In J. Thackara (ed.), *Design After Modernism: Beyond the Object*. London: Thames and Hudson, pp. 67–84.

Buchanan, P. (1981) Patterns and regeneration. *The Architectural Review*, 170(1018), 330–3.

Choay, F. (1997) *The Rule and the Model*. Cambridge, MA: MIT Press, chapter 6, pp. 254–69, 420–9.

Cooke, P. (1990) Modern urban theory in question. *Transactions, Institute of British Geographers: New Series*, 15(3), 331–43.

Dickens, P. G. (1979) Marxism and architectural theory: a critique of recent work. *Environment and Planning B*, 6, 105–16.

Dickens, P. (1981) The hut and the machine: towards a social theory of architecture. *Architectural Design*, 51(1/2), 18–24.

Ellin, N. (1996) *Postmodern Urbanism*. Oxford: Blackwell.

Gosling, D. (1984) Definitions of urban design. *Architectural Design*, 54(1/2), 16–25.

Gosling, D. and Maitland, B. (1984) *Concepts of Urban Design*. London: Academy Editions, appendix, pp. 156–7.

Jacobs, J. (1990) Urban realities. In G. Broadbent (ed.), *Emerging Concepts in Urban Space Design*. London: Van Nostrand Reinhold, chapter 7, pp. 138–53.

Jameson, F. (1991) Theories of the postmodern. In *Postmodernism, or, the Cultural Logic of Late Capitalism*. London/New York: Verso, chapter 2, pp. 55–66, 421–2.

Jencks, C. (1987) Post-modernism and discontinuity. AD Profile 65. *Architectural Design*, 57(1/2), 5–8.

Lang, J. (1987) Understanding normative theories of environmental design. In *Creating Architectural Theory: The Role of the Behavioral Sciences in Environmental Design*. New York: Van Nostrand Reinhold, chapter 20, pp. 219–232.

Lynch, K. (1981) But is a general normative theory possible? In *A Theory of Good City Form*. Cambridge, MA: MIT Press, chapter 5, pp. 99–108.

Lynch, K. and Rodwin, L. (1958) A theory of urban form. *Journal of the American Institute of Planners*, 24(4), 201–14.

Minca, C. (ed.) (2001) *Postmodern Geography: Theory and Practice*. Oxford, Blackwell.

Minett, J. (1975) If the city is not a tree, nor is it a system. *Resource for Urban Design Information* (http://www2.rudi.net/bookshelf/classics/city/minett), accessed July 25, 2001.

Peponis, J. (1989) Space, culture and urban design in late modernism and after. *Ekistics*, 56(334/335), 93–108.

Punter, J. (1996) Urban design theory in planning practice: the British perspective. *Built Environment*, 22(4), 263–77.

Rabeneck, A. (1979) A pattern language (review). *Architectural Design*, 49(1), 18–20.

Salingaros, N. (2001) Remarks on a city's composition. *Resources for Urban Design Information* (http://www2.rudi.net/bookshelf/

classics/city/remarkscity.html) accessed July 25, 2001.

Saunders, P. (1985) Space, the city and urban sociology. In D. Gregory and J. Urry (eds), *Social Relations and Spatial Structures*. Basingstoke: Macmillan, chapter 5, pp. 67–89.

Schwarzer, M. (2000) The contemporary city in four movements. *Journal of Urban Design*, 5(2), 127–44.

Shane, G. (1976) Contextualism. *Architectural Design*, 46(11), 676–9.

Shane, G. (1976) Theory versus practice. *Architectural Design*, 46(11), 680–4.

Sternberg, E. (2000) An integrative theory of urban design. *Journal of the American Planning Association*, 66(3), 265–78.

Trancik, R. (1986) Three theories of urban spatial design. In *Finding Lost Space: Theories of Urban Design*. New York: Van Nostrand Reinhold, chapter 4, pp. 97–124, 236–7.

Ward, T. (1979) A pattern language (review). *Architectural Design*, 49(1), 14–17.

2 History

Benevolo, L. (1980) *The History of the City*. London: Scolar Press.

Boyer, M. C. (1994) The place of history and memory in the contemporary city. *The City of Collective Memory*. Cambridge, MA: MIT Press, pp. 1–29, 495–8.

Cosgrove, D. (1998) Landscape and social formation: theoretical considerations. In *Social Formation and Symbolic Landscape*. Madison: University of Wisconsin Press, chapter 2, pp. 39–68.

Gosling, D. and Maitland, B. (1984) *Concepts of Urban Design*. London: Academy Editions.

Hanson, J. (1989) Order and structure in urban design: the plans for the rebuilding of london after the great fire of 1666. *Ekistics*, 56(334/335), 22–42.

Ive, G. (1995) Urban classicism and modern ideology. In I. Borden and D. Dunster (eds), *Architecture and the Sites of History: Interpretations of Buildings and Cities*. Oxford: Butterworth Architecture, chapter 3, pp. 38–52.

Miotto, L. and Muret, J. (1980) Urbanity in history. AD Profile 31. *Architectural Design*, 51(11/12), 8–13.

Moholy Nagy, S. (1968) *The Matrix of Man*. London: Pall Mall.

Mumford, L. (1961) Retrospect and prospect. In *The City in History: Its Origins, Its Transformations, and Its Prospects*. New York: Harcourt Brace and World, chapter 18, pp. 568–76.

Rowe, C. and Koetter, F. (1978) *Collage City*. Cambridge, MA: MIT Press.

Relph, E. (1987) Ordinary landscapes of the First Machine Age: 1900–40. In *The Modern Urban Landscape*. London: Croom Helm, chapter 5, pp. 76–97.

Spriergen, P. D. (1965) The roots of our modern concepts. In *Urban Design: The Architecture of Towns and Cities*. New York: McGraw-Hill, chapter 2, pp. 29–48.

3 Philosophy

Abel, C. (2000) Rationality and meaning in design. In *Architecture and Identity: Responses to Cultural and Technological Change*. Oxford: Architectural Press, chapter 6, pp. 71–84.

Barthes, R. (1967) Semiology and urbanism. In J. Ockman (ed.), *Architecture Culture 1943–1968: A Documentary Anthology*. New York: Rizzoli, pp. 413–37.

Broadbent, G. (1996) A plain man's guide to the theory of signs in architecture. In K. Nesbitt (ed.), *Theorizing a New Agenda for Architecture: An Anthology of Architectural Theory, 1965–1995*. New York: Princeton Architectural Press, pp. 122–140.

Cypher, J. and Higgs, E. (1997) Colonizing the imagination: Disney's wilderness lodge. *Capitalism, Nature, Socialism: A Journal of Socialist Ecology*, 8(4), 107–30.

Jameson, F. (1985) Architecture and the critique of ideology. In J. Ockman (ed.), *Architecture, Criticism, Ideology*. Princeton, NJ: Princeton Architectural Press, pp. 51–87.

Knox, P. L. (1982) The social production of the built environment. *Ekistics*, 49(295), 291–7.

Madanipour, A. (1996) Urban design and the dilemmas of space. *Environment and Planning D: Society and Space*, 14, 331–55.

Norberg-Schulz, C. (1971) Existential space. In *Existence Space and Architecture*. London: Studio Vista, chapter 2, pp. 17–36.

Pile, S. (1996) Conclusion to Part II: psycho-analysis and space. In *The Body and the City: Psychoanalysis, Space, and Subjectivity*. London: Routledge, pp. 145–69.

Sayer, A. and Storper, M. (1997) Ethics unbound: for a normative turn in social theory. *Environment and Planning D: Society and Space*, 15(1), 1–17.

Sayer, A. (1985) The difference that space makes. In D. Gregory and J. Urry (eds), *Social Relations and Spatial Structures*. Basingstoke: Macmillan, pp. 49–66.

Swyngedouw, E. (1996) The city as hybrid: on nature, society and cyborg urbanization. *Capitalism, Nature, Socialism: A Journal of Socialist Ecology*, 7(2), 64–81.

Tschumi, B. (1994) Questions of space. *Architecture and Disjunction*. Cambridge, MA: MIT Press, pp. 54–62.

Wilson, E. (1995) The rhetoric of urban space. *New Left Review*, 209, 146–60.

4 Politics

Al-Hindi, K. F. and Staddon, C. (1997) The hidden histories and geographies of neotraditional town planning: the case of Seaside, Florida. *Environment and Planning D: Society and Space*, 15, 349–72.

Boyer, M. C. (1993) The city of illusion: New York's public places. In P. L. Knox (ed.), *The Restless Urban Landscape*. Englewood Cliffs, NJ: Prentice Hall, chapter 5, pp. 111–26.

Bremner, L. (1994) Space and the nation: three texts on Aldo Rossi. *Environment and Planning D: Society and Space*, 12(3), 287–300.

Brenner, N. (2000) The urban question as a scale question: reflections on Henri Lefebvre, urban theory and the politics of scale. *International Journal of Urban and Regional Research*, 24(2), 361–78.

Campbell, S. (1999) Capital reconstruction and capital accumulation in Berlin: a reply to Peter Marcuse. *International Journal of Urban and Regional Research*, 23(1), 173–9.

Cartier, C. (1999) The state, property development and symbolic landscape in high-rise Hong Kong. *Landscape Research*, 24(2), 185–208.

Cox, K. R. (1981) Capitalism and conflict around the communal living space. In M. Dear and A. Scott (eds), *Urbanization*

and Urban Planning in Capitalist Society. London: Methuen, chapter 16, pp. 431–55.

Dutton, T. (1989) Cities, culture and resistance: beyond Leon Krier and the postmodern condition. *Journal of Architectural Education*, 42(2), 3–9.

Hahn, H. (1986) Disability and the urban environment: a perspective on Los Angeles. *Environment and Planning D: Society and Space*, 4(3), 273–88.

Jencks, C. and Valentine, M. (1987) The architecture of democracy: the hidden tradition. *Architectural Design*, 57(9/10), 8–25.

Krueckeberg, D. (1995) The difficult character of property: to whom do things belong? *Journal of the American Planning Association*, 61(3), 301–9.

Miller, K. (2001) The politics of defining public space. Unpublished article.

Sheller, M. and Urry, J. (2000) The city and the car. *International Journal of Urban and Regional Research*, 24(4), 737–57.

Taylor, P. J. and Peet, D. (1992) Classics in human geography revisited: Harvey, D. (1973) social justice and the city. *Progress in Human Geography*, 16(1), 71–4.

Ward, C. (1973) The utopian community. *RIBA Journal*, 80(2), 87–96.

5 Culture

Alexander, C. (1969) Major changes in environmental form required by social and psychological demands. *Ekistics*, 28(165), 78–85.

Alexander, C. (1971) Major changes in environmental form required by social and psychological demands. *Cities Fit to Live in*. New York: Macmillan, chapter 6, pp. 48–58.

Appleyard, D. (1979) The environment as a social symbol: within a theory of environmental action and perception. *Journal of the American Planning Association*, 45(2) 143–53.

Audirac, I. and Shermyen, A. (1994) An evaluation of neotraditional design's social prescription: postmodern placebo or remedy for suburban malaise? *Journal of Planning Education and Research*, 13(3), 161–73.

Castells, M. (1977) Conclusion: exploratory theses on the urban question. In *The Urban Question: A Marxist Approach*. London: Edward Arnold, pp. 429–36.

Castells, M. (1977) The myth of urban culture. In *The Urban Question: A Marxist Approach*. London: Edward Arnold, chapter 5, pp. 75–85.

Chambers, I. (1993) Cities without maps. In J. Bird, B. Curtis, T. Putnam, G. Robertson and L. Tickner (eds), *Mapping the Futures: Local Cultures, Global Change*. London: Routledge, pp. 188–98.

Cuthbert, A. R. (1985) Hong Kong: density, pathology and urban form. In D. Diamond and J. B. McLoughlin (eds), *Architecture, Society and Space: The High-density Question Re-examined*. Oxford: Pergamon Press, chapter 6, pp. 126–37.

Featherstone, M. (1993) Global and local cultures. In J. Bird, B. Curtis, T. Putnam, G. Robertson, and L. Tickner (eds), *Mapping the Futures: Local Cultures, Global Change*. London: Routledge, pp. 169–87.

Frampton, K. (1983) Towards a critical regionalism: six points for an architecture of resistance. In H. Foster (ed.), *Postmodern Culture*. London: Pluto Press, pp. 16–30.

Gould, P. and White, R. (1995) Mental maps. *Progress in Human Geography*, 19(1), 105–10.

Hall, E. (1959) The vocabulary of culture. In *The Silent Language*. Garden City: Doubleday, chapter 3, pp. 57–81, 222–3.

Hester, R. T., Blazej, N. J., and Moore, I. S. (1999) Whose wild? resolving cultural and biological diversity conflicts in urban wilderness. *Landscape Journal*, 18(2), 137–46.

Hillier, B. (1973) In defence of space. *RIBA Journal*, 80(11), 539–44.

Jameson, F. (1988) Cognitive mapping. In C. Nelson and L. Grossenberg (eds), *Marxism and the Interpretation of Culture*. Basingstoke: Macmillan, pp. 347–57.

Kallus, R. (2001) From abstract to concrete: subjective reading of urban space. *Journal of Urban Design*, 6(2), 129–50.

Montgomery, R. (1998) Is there still life in "the death and life"? *Journal of the American Planning Association*, 64(3), 269–74.

Newman, O. (1973) Defensible space as a crime preventive measure. In *Architectural Design for Crime Prevention*. New York: Institute of Planning and Housing, chapter 1, pp. 1–12.

Newman, O. (1995) Defensible space: a new physical planning tool for urban revitalization. *Journal of the American Planning Association*, 61(2), 149–55.

Rappoport, A. (1975) Toward a redefinition of density. *Environment and Behavior*, 7(2), 133–58.

Stretton, H. (1998) Density, efficiency and equality in australian cities. In K. Williams, M. Jenks, and E. Burton (eds), *Achieving Sustainable Urban Form?* London: E and F N Spon, pp. 45–52.

Tonuma, K. (1981) Theory of human scale. *Ekistics*, 48(289), 315–24.

6 Gender

Borden, I. (1995) Gender and the city. In I. Borden and D. Dunster (eds), *Architecture and the Sites of History: Interpretations of Buildings and Cities*. Oxford: Butterworth Architecture, chapter 23, pp. 317–30.

Boys, J. (1998) Beyond maps and metaphors? Re-thinking the relationships between architecture and gender. In R. Ainley (ed.), *New Frontiers of Space, Bodies and Gender*. London: Routledge, pp. 201–36.

Day, K. (1999) Introducing gender to the critique of privatised public space. *Journal of Urban Design*, 4(2), 155–78.

Knopp, L. (1992) Sexuality and the spatial dynamics of capitalism. *Environment and Planning D: Society and Space*, 10, 651–69.

McDowell, L. (1993) Space, place and gender relations: part 1. Feminist empiricism and the geography of social relations. *Progress in Human Geography*, 17(2), 157–79.

Roberts, M. (1998) Urban design, gender and the future of cities. *Journal of Urban Design*, 3(2), 133–5.

Sandercock, L. and Forsyth, A. (1992) A gender agenda: new directions for planning theory. *Journal of the American Planning Association*, 58(1), 49–59.

Walker, L. (1998) Home and away: the feminist remapping of public and private space in Victorian London. In R. Ainley (ed.), *New Frontiers of Space, Bodies and Gender*. London: Routledge, pp. 65–75, 224–6.

7 Environment

Bosselmann, P., Arens, E., Dunker, K., and Wright, R. (1995) Urban form and climate: case study, Toronto. *Journal of the American Planning Association*, 61(2), 226–39.

Breheny, M. J. (1992) The contradictions of the compact city: a review. In M. J. Breheny (ed.), *Sustainable Development and Urban Form*. London: Pion Limited, pp. 138–59.

Burgess, R. (2000) The compact city debate: a global perspective. In M. Jenks and R. Burgess (eds), *Compact Cities: Sustainable Urban Forms for Developing Countries*. London: Spon Press, pp. 9–24.

Frey, H. (1999) Compact, decentralised or what? The sustainable city debate. In *Designing the City: Towards a More Sustainable Urban Form*. London: E and F N Spon, chapter 2, pp. 23–35.

Gaffikin, F. and Morrissey, M. (1999) Sustainable cities. In F. Gaffikin and M. Morrissey (eds), *City Visions: Imagining Place, Enfranchising People*. London: Pluto Press, chapter 5, pp. 90–103.

Hawken, P., Lovins, A., and Lovins, L. (1999) The Next Industrial Revolution. In *Natural Capitalism: The Next Industrial Revolution*. London: Earthscan, chapter 1, pp. 1–21, 323.

Hough, M. (1984) Urban ecology, a basis for design. In *City Form and Natural Process: Towards a New Urban Vernacular*. London: Croom Helm, Chapter 1, pp. 5–27.

Jenks, M. and Burgess, R. (2000) Compact cities in the context of developing countries: introduction. In M. Jenks and R. Burgess (eds), *Compact Cities: Sustainable Urban Forms for Developing Countries*. London: Spon Press, part 1, pp. 7–8.

McLoughlin, B. (1991) Urban consolidation and urban sprawl: a question of density. *Urban Policy and Research*, 9(3), 148–56.

Myers, B. and Dale, J. (1992) Designing in car-oriented cities: an argument for episodic urban congestion. In M. Wachs and M. Crawford (eds), *The Car and the City: The Automobile, The Built Environment, and Daily Urban Life*. Ann Arbor: University of Michigan Press, chapter 18, pp. 254–73, 320–1.

Newman, P. (1994) Urban design, transportation and greenhouse. In R. Samuels and D. K. Prasad (eds), *Global Warming and the Built Environment*. London: E and F N Spon, pp. 69–84.

Ravetz, J. (2000) Urban form and the sustainability of urban systems: theory and practice in a northern conurbation. In K. Williams, E. Burton and M. Jenks (eds), *Achieving Sustainable Urban Form*. London: E and F N Spon, pp. 215–28, 374–5.

Scoffham, E. and Vale, B. (1998) How compact is sustainable – how sustainable is compact? In M. Jenks, E. Burton and K. Williams (eds), *The Compact City: A Sustainable Urban Form?* London: E and F N Spon, pp. 66–73.

Stone, B. and Rodgers, M. (2001) Urban form and thermal efficiency: how the design of cities can influence the urban heat island effect. *Journal of the American Planning Association*, 67(2), 186–274.

Trepl, L. (1996) City and ecology. *Capitalism, Nature, Socialism: A Journal of Socialist Ecology*, 7(2), 85–94.

Wansborough, M. and Mageean, A. (2000) The role of urban design in cultural regeneration. *Journal of Urban Design*, 5(2), 181–97.

Welbank, M. (1998) The search for a sustainable urban form. In M. Jenks, E. Burton, and K. Williams (eds), *The Compact City: A Sustainable Urban Form?* London: E and F N Spon, pp. 74–82.

Yanarella, E. and Levine, R. (1993) The sustainable cities manifesto: pretext, text and post-text. *Built Environment*, 18(4), 301–13.

8 Aesthetics

Crawford, M. (1992) The fifth ecology: fantasy, the automobile, and Los Angeles. In M. Wachs and M. Crawford (eds), *The Car and the City: The Automobile, the Built Environment, and Daily Urban Life*. Ann Arbor: University of Michigan Press, chapter 16, pp. 222–33, 317–18.

Gottdiener, M. (1997) Themes, societal fantasies, and daily life. In *The Theming of America: Dreams, Visions, and Commercial Spaces*. Boulder, CO: Westview Press, chapter 7, pp. 143–59.

Lynch, K. (1991) The form of cities. In T. Banerjee and M. Southworth (eds), *City Sense and City Design: Writings and Projects of Kevin Lynch*. Cambridge, MA: MIT Press, pp. 35–46.

Scruton, R. (1981) Recent aesthetics in England and America. *Architectural Association Quarterly*, 13(1), 51–4.

Taylor, N. (1999) The elements of townscape and the art of urban design. *Journal of Urban Design*, 4(2), 195–209.

9 Typologies

Abel, C. (1988) Analogical models in architecture and urban design. *Middle East Technical University Journal of the Faculty of Architecture*, 8(2), 161–88.

Abel, C. (2000) Asian Urban Futures. In *Architecture and Identity: Responses to Cultural and Technological Change*. Oxford: Architectural Press, chapter 18, pp. 211–34.

Azaryahu, M. (1996) The power of commemorative street names. *Environment and Planning D: Society and Space*, 14(3), 311–30.

Beune, F. and Thus, T. (1990) Fragmentation of urban open space. In M. J. Vroom and J. H. A. Meeus (eds), *Learning from Rotterdam: Investigating the Process of Urban Park Design*. New York: Mansell and Nichols Publishing, pp. 106–21.

Goode, T. (1992) Typological theory in the United States: the consumption of architectural "authenticity." *Journal of Architectural Education*, 46(1), 2–13.

Hillier, B. (1989) The architecture of the urban object. *Ekistics*, 56(334/335), 5–21.

Kostof, S. (1992) *The City Assembled*. New York: Little Brown and Co.

King, A. D. (1984) The social production of building form: theory and research. *Environment and Planning D: Society and Space*, 2(4), 429–46.

Krier, L. (1978) The reconstruction of the city. In *Rational Architecture Rationelle: The Reconstruction of the European City*. Brussels: Editions Archives d'Architecture Moderne, pp. 38–42.

Lang, J. (1996) Implementing urban design in America: project types and methodological implications. *Journal of Urban Design*, 1(1), 7–22.

Lynch, K. (1958) Environmental adaptability. *Journal of the American Institute of Planners*, 24(1), 16–24.

Perez de Arce, R. (1978) Urban transformations and the architecture of additions. *Architectural Design*, 48(4), 237–66.

Vidler, A. (1978) The third typology. In *Rational Architecture Rationelle: The Reconstruction of the European City*. Brussels:

Editions Archives d'Architecture Moderne, pp. 28–32.

Webb, M. (1990) *The City Square*. London. Thames and Hudson.

Weiss, M. (1992) Skyscraper zoning: New York's pioneering role. *Journal of the American Planning Association*, 58(2), 201–12.

10 Pragmatics

Baer, W. C. (1997) Toward design regulations for the built environment. *Environment and Planning B: Planning and Design*, 24(1), 37–57.

Banai, R. (1996) A theoretical assessment of the "neotraditional" settlement form by dimensions of performance. *Environment and Planning B: Planning and Design*, 23(2), 177–90.

Brine, J. (1997) Urban design advisory panels: south Australia looks to Canadian experience. *Australian Planner*, 34(2), 116–20.

Cuthbert, A. (1994) An agenda for planning in the nineties. *Australian Planner*, 31(4), 206–11.

Gunder, M. (2001) Bridging theory and practice in planning education: a story from Auckland. In R. Freestone and S. Thompson (eds), *Bridging Theory and Practice in Planning Education: Proceedings of the 2001 ANZAPS Conference held at the University of New South Wales 21–23 September 2001*. Sydney: University of New South Wales, pp. 21–32.

Heide, H. T. and Wijnbelt, D. (1996) To know and to make: the link between research and urban design. *Journal of Urban Design*, 1(1), 75–90.

Jacobs, A. and Appleyard, D. (1987) Toward an urban design manifesto. *Journal of the American Planning Association*, 53(1), 112–20.

Jacobs, J. M. (1993) The city unbound: qualitative approaches to the city. *Urban Studies*, 30(4/5), 827–48.

Korllos, T. S. (1980) Sociology of architecture: an emerging perspective. *Ekistics*, 47(285), 470–5.

Noble, D. F. (1998) Digital diploma mills: the automation of higher education (http://www.itc.virginia.edu/virginia.edu/fall98/mills/home.html), accessed November 5, 2001.

Rowley, A. and Davies, L. (2001) Training for urban design. *Quarterly Journal of the Urban Design Group*, 78 (http://www2. rudi.net/ej/udq/78/research-udq78.html), accessed July 25, 2001.

Rowley, A. (1998) Private-property decision makers and the quality of urban design. *Journal of Urban Design*, 3(2), 151–73.

Schurch, T. W. (1999) Reconsidering urban design: thoughts about its definition and status as a field or profession. *Journal of Urban Design*, 4(1), 5–28.

The Congress for the New Urbanism (2001) *Charter of the New Urbanism* (http://www.newurbanism.org/page532096.htm), accessed September 19, 2001.

UK Department of the Environment, Transport and the Regions (2000) *Training for Urban Design* (http://www.planning.detr.gov.uk/urbandesign/training/summary.htm), accessed August 9, 2001.

Index

accumulation, flexible   37–9
accumulation, heterotopia   351
Adorno, Theodore   92
aesthetic confusion, late nineteenth century   294
aesthetic experience   277
aesthetic ideology, urban design   290–311
aesthetic impulse   311
aesthetic theory   275–84
  art   275
  mechanistic   276–7
  psychology   276
  science   275
aesthetics
  associational values   277
  commerce   300
  empiricism   278
  formal   282
  formal values   277
  Hollywood   303
  information theory   278
  legislated   293
  psychobiology   278, 280
  semantics   278, 279
  semiotics   279
  sensory   281
  speculative   276
  symbolic   282
agora, Greek   143
Alberti   83, 365
Alexander, Christopher   364
Ancient Greece,
  cosmic harmony   77–81
animals, ontological dependency   258
Aquinas, Thomas   255
arcades   331
architects, superstar   181
architectural merchandising   306
architecture
  branding   182
  built environment   69–70
  eclecticism   324

franchising   304
mechanical progress   319
modernism   31
modernist   32
mystification   32
nature   318
typology   317–22
Arnheim, Rudolph   279
Arrighi, Giovanni   3
art
  politicization   163
  site-specific   163
  urban artifacts   286–9
  works of   282
Atlantic Richfield Company   290
authenticity
  ambience   183
  of the object   248
auto city   236–7

Baldwin Hills Village   228
Banham, Reyner   347
Barthes, Roland   121
Baudrillard, Jean   345, 351
Beaux Arts movement   31, 34, 294
Bech, Henning   195–6
Beckett, Samuel   91
Benetton   179
Benjamin, Walter   178
Benmayer, Riva   72
Bentham, Jeremy   317
Beverly Center, Beverly Hills   132
Borne Platz, Frankfurt   157
Boston   51
Boudon, Philippe   377
Bramante, Donato   85
Brasilia   32
Buffalo Pan Am Expo   298
built environment
  gender divisions   208
  semiotic decomposition   130

structural transformations   357
built form, meaning   155
Burnham, Daniel   174, 294

Camus, Albert   91
capital
    masculine character   207
    money   38
    symbolic   38
capitalism
    design professions   357
    informational   1
    labor   30
    modernity   30
    natural   2
    primitivism   345
capitalist
    development   29
    investment, built environment   29
    mode of production, transformation   59–61
    urbanization, non-human life   254
    mode of production   61, 64
Castells, Manuel   1, 3, 7, 10
Cattaneo, Carlo   286
Chapman, Rowena   213
Chicago, Columbia Exposition   294
Chicago Plan   174
Choay, Francis   365
Christianopolis   88
cities
    conflict   25
    dispersion and social consequence   144
    greening and lower energy   240
    sexual coding   196
city
    agrarian aristocracy   292
    American   41, 219
    animal ecologies   263
    "beauty"   287
    corporate   30
    corporatist   33
    creative destruction   34
    definition of type and model   288
    disequilibrium   91
    greening   239
    ideal   76, 80, 82
    Keynesian   34–7
    man-made object   287
    market consumption   51
    modernist   32
    multiple coding   102
    non-sexist   218
    organic   241
    planning, Baroque   85
    postmodern   37
    recommodification   64

regions   36
    sense of space, orientation   286
    sexual coding   195
    sexuality   195
    size and sustainability   236
    transformations   321
    typological questions   287
    urban ecology   241
City Beautiful movement   91
civic design   6
civil society, market consumption   184
class distinctions, heterotopia   346
coded realms, heterosexual   198
collective space, collective services   223–6
colonized societies   13
commodification, heritage   247
Connor, Steve   345
conservation
    habitat conservation plans   265
    preservation, heritage   243–52
    urban management   250
consumption
    conspicuous   37
    heterotopia   347
    spatial division   36
Contextualist School   276
corporate power, Esperanto of   359
corporation, public art   162
corporatism   3
    neo-corporatism   3
    welfare goods   4
Cosgrove, Dennis   9
Cox, Kevin   15, 363, 371
Cullen, Gordon   370
cultural history   172
cultural production, market competition
    180
cultural symbols, material significance   204
culture
    commerce   182–4
    dissemination of   308
    elite   292
    gaming   352
    heterotopia   347–8
Cuthbert, Alexander   4
cyborg vision   257

Davis, Mike   113
Dear, Michael   11, 358
Debord, Guy   348
deconstruction   358
Del Amo Mall   134
Deleuze, Gilles   352
democracy, uses of   160
department stores   183
De Quincy, Quatremère   288

Descartes, René   255
designer, cultural value   183
design professions   357–61
   human behavior   360
   late capitalism   357
   research   360
   social production   358
development
   ecosystems   255
   uneven   2
Dewey Arch NTC   297
Dewey, John   277
Disneyland   39, 111
Dostoyevski, Fyodor   91
Duany, Andreas   5
Dürer, Albrecht   87

ecological theory   263
economic currency, architectural aesthetics
      28–42
economy
   global criminal   6
   landscape   28
   pink   199
   world   1
Empedocles   79
Endangered Species Act, USA   265
Engels, Friedrich   108, 144
environment
   childhood   125
   conceptions of   256
environmental
   aesthetics   281–2
   design theory, empirical aesthetics   280
   design, life cycle   222
   ethics, ecocentric   267
   history, urbanization   261
environment–behavior research   371–2
environments
   authentic   296
   ephemeral   296–7
   mediated   351
ethic, interspecies   258
Ewen, Stewart   219
expositions   295–300

Faneuil Hall, Boston   39, 183
Fascism   152
femininity, domesticity   209
Filarete, Antonio Averlino   84
Formist School   276
Foster, Hal   212
Foucault, Michel   341, 344
franchise architecture   303
Freudenstadt   86
Friedan, Betty   220

Galleria, Milan   131
Gans, Herbert   69, 70
Garnier, Tony   93
Gaudí, Antoní   93, 94
gender
   codings, architecture   205–7
   commodification   197
   gentrification   211
   history   71
   interests, redifferentiation   213
   projected anxiety   196
   social relations   206
   symbols, urban landscapes   204–14
genius loci   123
Genocchio, Benjamin   341
gentrification, and symbolism   210
Georges, Eugène   90
Ghiradelli Square   129
Giedion, Siegfried   327
global cities, automobile dependence   237
globalization
   American interventionism   2
   postmodernity   1
Gödel, Kurt   94
Godelier, Maurice   106
good taste, industry   293

Habermas, Jürgen,   358
Habitat, conservation plan   265
Harvey, David   8, 14, 29, 36, 38, 178
Haussmann, Baron   40
Hayden, Dolores   26
Heidegger, Martin   117–20
heritage
   definition   244
   development   250
   the market   251
   products   247
   selection criteria   249
heterosexually coded realms   198
heterotopia
   ambivalence   341
   architectural typologies   343
   desire   353
   naming   345
   positioning of   342
   postmodern geography   341
   representation and mediation   340
   themed resorts   344
   utopia   346
Hillier, Bill   376
Hippodamus   79
history
   appropriated   41
   historicizing   157
   mediated environments   350

holocaust   152
housing, work   219
human, animal   255
human culture, wildlife   257
Huxtable, Aida Louise   40, 46, 69, 70, 309
Hyatt Regency, Portland   39

iconic mimesis   131
ideal city
    medieval   82–3
    Renaissance   83–4
ideology
    aesthetics   290–311
    American aesthetics   310
    instrumental control   130
image
    consumption   36–7
    Modernism   30
imperialism, new   3
industrialization and architecture   31
industrial revolution, typology   317–22
institutional forms, new   50
international debt crisis   35
International Monetary Fund   259

Jacobs, Jane   241
Jahn, Helmut   184
James, Henry   51, 52, 184
Jameson, Frederick   37, 40, 45, 46, 385, 389
Jencks, Charles   15
Johnson, Philip   180–1

Kafka, Franz   77, 91, 92–3
Kiffner, John   101, 102
King, Anthony   13
King, Martin Luther   71
King, Ross   11
Krier, Leon   317, 374
Krier, Rob   374

landscape
    cultural mapping   178
    fragmentation   39
    functional specialization   128
    ideology   207
    reading the   204
language, depoliticizing   163
Las Vegas   340
    theming   350
late capitalism, deconcentration   128
Laugier, M.   317
Le Corbusier   142
Le Notre   318
Lévi-Strauss, Claude   286
liminality   178
Locke, John   149

Lovins, Amory   2
Lynch, Kevin   25, 120, 124, 286

McDonald's   304–5, 48–9
McKinnell, Keith   4
Mcloughlin, Brian   8–10
management, of the past   244
March, Lionel   376
Marshall, Nancy   3,4
Martin, Leslie   376
Marx, Karl   109, 112, 145, 149
master plans, functional prerequisites
    292
material culture
    dwelling   220
    employed women   220
materialism, image   194
meaning
    architecture   212
    concealment   157
    construction   152
    of places   61
    power   154
    public use   162
Mechanistic School   276
memory, heritage   245
metropolitan life, modes of consumption
    129
Michelangelo   85
Miletus   79
modernism
    corporate imagery   35
    dominant regime   31
modernity, social justice   105–7
modern movements   321
Mohenjo-Daro   77
Moles, Abraham   278
Moore, Charles   40
More, Thomas   84–5, 365
Myrdal, Alva   222

natural disasters   6
nature–culture debates   262
new urbanism   5
New York   69–70
Nicholas V   85
non-sexist neighborhood design   223

Olympic Games, Sydney   6
Organismicist School   276

Palladio, Andrea   85, 327
Palmanova   85
Paris   90
pedestrian flow, engineering   134
Pepper, Stephen   276

phenomenology
    and architecture   117
    properties of place   118
    structure   119
Philadelphia Centennial Expo   295
Piazza d'Italia   40
place
    authenticity   41
    language   122
    meaning   116, 118
    phenomenology   116
    power   72
    spirit   123–6
    structure   121
planning
    commodification of the built environment   359
    divisions of labor   359
    failure of urban renewal   367
Plater-Zybeck, Elizabeth   5
Plato   80, 108, 144
polis, Greek   143
political legitimation, crisis   359
politics, animals and nature   258
Pope Sixtus   86
Pope, Arthur   348
Popper, Karl   12
post-Enlightenment science, human–animal
        discontinuity   256
postmodernization   47
postmodernism
    authenticity   212
    capitalism   46
    commodity reification   35
    corporate imagery   35
    cultural logic   45
    ideology   42
    mapping   46
    resistance   358
    restructuring of   360
    social process   47
    symbolic capital   35
    text   358
    urban form   45–52
    urban studies   46
Potzdamer Platz   153–4
power, space, and difference   199
preservation
    authenticity   248
    historic resources   247
    objectives of   246
    semiotics   249
Priene   78
privatization of space   147–9
production, architectural   47
professional praxis, urban change   240
public, conception of   104

public art   160
    democracy   167
    elitism   165
    legitimization   164
    private property   166
public and private space, tension between   148
public and private spheres
    feminism   145
    separation of   145
public realm, privatization   40
public space   140
    crime   148
    definition   141
    design and development of   139–49
    exchange value   148
    liminality   184
    modernist design   142
    private good   4
    privatization   147
    property relations   148
    public–private distinction   141
    social and political philosophy   145
    specialization   144
    symbolism   156
public sphere, social interaction   135
public use, definition of   162
Putman, Andrée   182
Pythagoras   78

Radburn Plan   227
Rapoport, Amos   367
rationalism   15
    new   320
regionalism
    critical   5
    new   3
Relph, Edward   369
Renaissance   81
representation
    femininity   209
    postmodernism   211
research
    ethics, urban design   367
    literary approach   365
    phenomenological approach   365
    positivistic approach   366
Roche, Kevin   180
Roman colonies   79
Rossi, Aldo   15, 327
Rousseau, Jean Jacques   90
Rowe, Colin   31, 73
Roweis, Shoukri   11
rural culture, urban   292

San Francisco Expo   299
San Francisco, gay   193

Santa Monica Mall   133
Santayana, George   276
Sartre, Jean-Paul   91, 92, 93
Sayer, Andrew   7
Schlereth, Thomas   374
Schorske, Karl   14, 172
Scott, Allen   11
Seagram Plaza   35
self-reflexivity, ecological research   264
semiological research   25
semiotic analysis   129, 205
   shopping malls   128–35
semiotic decomposition   130
Serra, Richard   160–8
sexual division of labor, suburban house   219–21
sexuality, capital accumulation   196
shopping malls   128
sign systems, instrumental   133–4
signature architecture, logos   305
signature building   49, 180
Sitte, Camillo   14, 95, 172, 287
social context, symbols   207
social justice   107
   criteria   108
   forms of argument   105
   historical–geographical materialism
      methods   109
   market economy   106
   oppression   111–13
   postmodernism   101–14
social rationality   106
socio-spatial patterns, destabilization   144
Soja, Edward   3
Soong, Tay Kheng   5
Sorkin, Michael   261
Soros, George   13
Souté, Michael   264
space
   ambiguous   4
   economic production   33
   heterotopia   340–54
   liminal   49–50
   sexual coding   195
   social construction   140
   society   59–68
   topology   120
spatial form, dominant class   62–5
spatial otherness   340
spatial political economy   10
spatial type, modulation   332–4
spatial types, combinations of   338
squares   325
   appropriate functions   329
   public sphere   326–7
   residential use   327
St Augustine   82

St Louis, Union Station   41
stagflation   36
Steilshoop project   222
Stein, Clarence   227
Stoicism   80
street   326
   planning error   329
   residential and problems of   330–1
streets, Roman   331
suburbanization, USA   48
superstar architecture   50–1
surveillance   4
sustainability
   automobile dependence   236–7
   cities   235–42
   greening   239
   plans   235
sustainable cities, staging   239
Symes, Martin   360
syntagm, articulation of design   132
syntax, commercial competition   311

Tafuri, Manfredo   8
Taylorized production, neo-classicism   319
Tchen, Kuo Wei   72
Thatcher, Margaret   111
theming, difference   350
theory   7
   political economy   8
   social science   7
   system   8
   urban design   7–10
Tompkins Square Park   101
townscape, bourgeois high culture   322
Trakl, George   117
transportation
   economic costs   238
   urban form   237
transspecies urban practice
   in US cities   264
   urban planning   265
transspecies urban theory   255
Turner, Victor   178
typology   317–22
   city   320
   efficiency   319
   meaning   320
   production of architecture   317
typomorphology   375

Unger, Roberto   102, 103
urban aesthetics, class stratification   297
urban artefacts, urban geography   285
urban change, gender change   209
urban class domination   26
urban density, sexuality   195

urban design
  aesthetic ideology   290–311
  aesthetics production   6
  and anthropocentrism   266
  Beaux-Arts tradition   298–9
  capitalist society   11
  city form   76–95
  city image   364
  classical symmetry   86–7
  commercial exploration   298
  definitions of   10–13
  early modern period   89–90
  employed woman   221
  environment–behavior research
      367, 371
  gender symbolism   210
  image studies   371
  knowledge   363–79
  material culture studies   374
  nature-ecology studies   377–8
  orthodoxy   15
  place studies   373
  recovery of meaning   175
  reduced automobile dependence   238
  rehabilitation   227
  skilling   13
  space-morphology studies   376–7
  substantive research   364
  typology-morphology studies   374–6
  urban commerce   307
  valorization   10
  wildlife habitat   266
  wildlife management   262
  world fairs   294
urban design knowledge, areas of
      concentration   368
urban design research
  empirical-inductive mode   366
  historical-descriptive mode   366
  library approach   365
  phenomenological approach   365
  positivistic approach   366
  theoretical-deductive mode   366
urban design theory   363–5
urban ecology, local   240
urban environment, commercialism   290
urban form
  aesthetics of authenticity   92–3
  creative destruction   185
  demystified   291
  disequilibrium   91
  historiography   348
  history of   369
  internationalized production   179
  multinational capitalism   178
  periodizing   50–2

political power   155
  standardization   48
urban functions, urban culture, dichotomy of   290
urban history
  journalism   370
  picturesque studies   370
  studies   368
  urban function   174
urban ideal, economies of   295
urban landscape   177
  cultural products   207
  economy   28
  feminist theory   208
  history, cultural identity   73
  public history   69–74
  refashioning gender   213
  signature buildings   180
urban meaning   23–6
urban planning
  aesthetic control   349
  radical break in   359
urban praxis, animals   257
urban sameness, heterotopian form   348
urban social change   23–6
urban space
  aesthetics, 323
  art   324
  basic forms   325
  building section   335
  cultural coding   198
  culture   171–86
  definition   323
  demonization and control   193
  elevations   335–6
  historical zones   172
  morphological classification   339
  service economy   146
  sexuality   193–9
  social structure   323–4
  typological and morphological elements
      323–39
urban spaces, typical functions   326
urban theory, wildlife   261
urban vernacular forms   309
urbanism, sexualities   194
urbanization
  animal town   259–60
  demand side   36
  fiscal crisis   36
  sexual and spatial dynamics   196
utopia, heterotopia   346
utopian socialist communities   223

Valentine, Maggie   15
Vattimo, Gianni   346
Venturi, Robert   121

vernacular 70, 171
Vienna, Fin de Siècle 10

Wagner, Otto 15, 172
Wallerstein, Emmanuel 1
White City 294
White, Gilbert 241
wildlife management, urban institutions
    262
wildlife, political action 267
Wittgenstein, Ludwig 108
Wolfe, Tom 347

World Bank 259
World Trade Center 6
World's Fairs 294
Wren, Sir Christopher 87
Wright, Frank Lloyd 290
Wright, Henry 227

Yeang, Ken 5

zoöpolis 254
    bioregional paradigm 259
    theme parks 268